Gift of Jerry Morrow

Jewish and Pauline Studies

W. D. DAVIES

First published in Great Britain 1984
SPCK
Holy Trinity Church
Marylebone Road
London NWI 4DU

Printed in the United States of America

ISBN 0 281 04050 8

Cyflwynedig
i
Carrie Davies
Peggie George
a
Mary Llewelyn

Contents

Acknowledgments

"Law in First-Century Judaism" by W. D. Davies from THE INTER-PRETER'S DICTIONARY OF THE BIBLE, VOL. 3. Copyright © 1962 by Abingdon Press. Used by permission.

"Reflections on Tradition: The 'Abot Revisited." Reprinted from *Christian History and Interpretation: Studies Presented to John Knox,* edited by W. R. Farmer, C. F. D. Moule, and R. R. Niebuhr by permission of Cambridge University Press. Copyright © 1967.

"The Territorial Dimension of Judaism" is reprinted with permission from *Intergerini Parietis Septum* (Eph. 2:14). Essays presented to Markus Barth on his sixty-fifth birthday. Edited by Dikran Y. Hadidian. Pittsburgh Theological Monograph 33; Pittsburgh: Pickwick Press, 1981, 61–98.

"Reflections on the Spirit in the Mekilta: A Suggestion" is reprinted from *Proceedings of Sixth World Congress of Jewish Studies* 3 (1977): 159–72, and is used by permission.

"A Note on Josephus, Antiquities 15:136." is reprinted from *Harvard Theological Review* 47 (1954): 135–40. Copyright © 1954 by the President and Fellows of Harvard College. Reprinted by Permission.

Paul and the Law: Reflections on Pitfalls in Interpretation, 29 Hastings L.J. 1459 (1978); reprinted with permission. © Copyright 1978 HAS-TINGS COLLEGE OF THE LAW.

"Paul and the People of Israel" is reprinted from *New Testament Studies* 24 (1978), pp. 4–39 and is used by permission of Cambridge University Press.

"Paul and the Gentiles: A Suggestion Concerning Romans 11:13–24" was originally published as "Romans 11:13–24. A Suggestion" in *Melanges offerts à Marcel Simon. Paganïsme, Judaïsme, Christianïsme.* Reprinted with permission. (Paris: Editions E. de Boccard, 1978), pp. 131–44.

"Paul and Jewish Christianity According to Cardinal Daniélou: A Suggestion" was originally published in _Recherches de Science religeuse_ 60 (Jan.–Mar. 1972), pp. 69–79, and is reprinted with permission from Editions Beauchesne, Paris.

"Galatians: A Commentary on Paul's Letter to the Churches of Galatia." Reprinted, with permission of the Council on the Study of Religion, Wilfred Laurier University, Waterloo, Ontario, from _Religious Studies Review_ 7 (1981), pp. 310–18.

"From Tyranny to Liberation: The Pauline Experience of Alienation and Reconciliation." Reprinted with permission from _From Alienation to At-Oneness, Proceedings of the Theology Institute of Villanova University,_ edited by Francis A. Eigo, O.S.A., Villanova University Press, © 1977, pp. 93–131.

"Law in the New Testament" by W. D. Davies from THE INTERPRETER'S DICTIONARY OF THE BIBLE, VOL. 3. Copyright © 1962 by Abington Press. Used by permission.

"Conscience and Its Use in the New Testament" by W. D. Davies from THE INTERPRETER'S DICTIONARY OF THE BIBLE, VOL. 2. Copyright © 1962 by Abingdon Press. Used by permission.

"From Schweitzer to Scholem: Reflections on Sabbatai Svi." Reprinted with permission from _Journal of Biblical Literature_ 95 (1976), pp. 529–58.

"The Moral Teaching of the Early Church." Reprinted from _The Use of the Old Testament in the New and Other Essays. Studies in Honor of William Franklin Stinespring,_ edited by James M. Efird. Duke University Press, 1972, pp. 310–332. Copyright © 1972, Duke University Press (Durham, N.C.).

"The Relevance of the Moral Teaching of the Early Church." Reprinted from _Neotestimentica et Semitica: Studies in Honour of Matthew Black,_ edited by E. Earle Ellis and Max Wilcox, with permission of T. & T. Clark (Edinburgh: T. & T. Clark, 1969), pp. 30–44.

Prefatory Note

The publication of this collection of essays, gathered at the urging of many of his students, follows upon Professor W. D. Davies' retirement from the George Washington Ivey Chair in Christian Origins at Duke University. It is intended to salute him on his seventieth birthday. Students at Duke will no longer have the privilege of sitting under a great teacher and scholar. But though he has left his customary classroom, we had hoped that he would continue to teach and to write, and we are glad that Duke's loss has now proved to be Texas Christian University's gain.

In expressing our gratitude and good wishes to Professor Davies through the collecting of these essays, we cannot forget her to whom he dedicated his first book.

The essays are here reprinted in substantially their original form, but there are corrections and additions, sometimes considerable, in the text and footnotes. In the preparation for republication Mr. Richard Countie and Ms. Amy-Jill Levine, both of Duke University Graduate School, made useful suggestions, and Ms. Lu Bacus, Mr. Tracy Howard, Mr. Drew James, and Mr. Andrew Harris at Texas Christian University helped with the indexes. Ms. Therese Boyd, editor at Fortress Press, spared no pains in the making of this volume and, finally, we are grateful to the director, Norman Hjelm, for his interest.

Dale C. Allison

Duke University
Durham, North Carolina

Section 1:
Judaica

1

Law in First-Century Judaism[1]

The term *torah* in Judaism,[2] usually (under the influence of the Septuagint [LXX] translation of it as νόμος) rendered as "law," ranges in meaning from "teaching" or "instruction" to "the totality of the divine revelation, written and oral." It is with this last that we are here concerned.

The nature and content of this revelation in first-century Judaism cannot be determined with exact certainty for three reasons: (a) the period was one of fluidity: the Jewish tradition had not been stabilized in the Mishna (redacted *ca*. A.D. 200–220) but was still in lively process; (b) the law was so variously interpreted by different groups—for instance, the Pharisees, the Sadducees, the Essenes, the Samaritans, Christians and others—that no integrated description of it can be given, and a too systematic presentation of the material must be suspect; (c) the rabbinic sources directly dealing with the law (the Mishna, the Midrašim, etc.) are later than the first century, and, by and large, represent only one current in the Judaism of that time, and only the dominant element within this one current (the Pharisaism of Rabbi Johanan ben Zakkai and his collaborators at Jamnia), so that they can be used only with extreme caution. However, by very careful sifting of these sources, which contain traditional material going back to the first century and earlier, and by the critical use of the Apocrypha and the Pseudepigrapha, Philo, Josephus, and the Dead Sea Scrolls, certain positions can safely be suggested as characterizing first-century Judaism.[3]

THE WRITTEN LAW

Judaism in the first century, as always, postulated that God exists and that he has revealed his nature, character, and purpose, and his will as to what persons should be and do. And, as is the case in other revealed religions, Judaism claimed that in the very act of revelation there had been given a law, which was, therefore, of divine origin and authority, to govern humankind in all the details of life. This law, it was believed, was partly enshrined in the documents now called the Hebrew Bible. The notion of inspired scriptures probably arose in connection with prophecy. While first-century Judaism continued to believe in the biblical conviction that God could reveal himself through angels, messengers, visions, dreams, and voices, the act of prophecy, through which God declared his will, had come to be particularly associated with the activity of the Holy Spirit; all the prophets spoke by the Holy Spirit, and with the last of the prophets some held that the Holy Spirit had ceased from Israel (*b. Yoma* 9*b*; *b. Soṭa* 48*b*; *b. Sanhedrin* 11*a*; etc.). The law of the prophet Moses, the books of the prophets themselves, and, by a natural evolution, all the other books now contained in the Hebrew Bible, came to be conceived as written by persons moved by the Holy Spirit. This connection with prophecy, and thereby with the Holy Spirit, gave to them an inspired character. Although much inspired material had not found a way into the writings of the Hebrew Bible, everything within them was inspired.[4]

The names given to the Hebrew Bible varied. For a long time there was no generic title in use. The books of Scripture were referred to as "the Law and the Prophets" (2 Macc 15:9; 4 Macc 18:10; Matt 5:17; 11:13; Luke 16:16); then the phrase "the Law, the Prophets, and the Writings" (*b. Sanh.* 90*b*) was used. Possibly the first terms used to designate the whole of the law were "the book," "the books," "the holy books" ($\beta\iota\beta\lambda\acute{\iota}o\nu$, $\beta\iota\beta\lambda\acute{\iota}\alpha$ ≐ ספך, etc. [1 Macc 12:9; 2 Macc 8:23]; $\dot{\eta}$ $\iota\epsilon\rho\acute{\alpha}$ $\beta\acute{\iota}\beta\lambda os$; $\beta\iota\beta\lambda\acute{\iota}o\nu$; $\beta\acute{\iota}\beta\lambda\acute{\alpha}$ $\iota\epsilon\rho\acute{\alpha}$, etc. [see an index to Philo]). In the New Testament we find "the Scriptures," $\dot{\eta}$ $\gamma\rho\alpha\varphi\acute{\eta}$ (הכתוב); Philo has $\gamma\rho\acute{\alpha}\mu\mu\alpha\tau\alpha$, $\gamma\rho\alpha\varphi\acute{\eta}$[5]; Josephus has $\tau\grave{\alpha}$ $\iota\epsilon\rho\acute{\alpha}$ $\gamma\rho\acute{\alpha}\mu\mu\alpha\tau\alpha$. The precise contents of "the Scripture" we can deduce. After 70 C.E. there was still discussion in Judaism on the authority of certain books. But probably such discussion at Jamnia, in fact, assumed the authority of the so-called dubious documents; it was concerned not so much with their authority as such as with the problems they posed. Without making this distinction it is dangerous to use the term "canon," which has a Christian provenance, in connection with the discussions at Jamnia. Thus the inspiration of Ezekiel can hardly ever have been seriously doubted, but the wisdom of placing it in the hands of all was questioned because it contained contradictions of the Pentateuch; these were subsequently resolved (*b. Šabbat* 13*b*, etc.). But the following books were in dispute: (a) Ecclesiastes, because it contradicted itself and was more the product of Solomon's own wisdom than of the Holy Spirit; according to Jerome's commentary on Eccl 12:13, the closing words of the book alone eventually secured its place in the canon. (The dispute over this book was lively in the days of

Hillel and Shammai [*m. Eduyoth* 5.3; *m. Yadayim* 3.51], and continued till the third century [*t. Yad.* 2.14]). (b) The Song of Songs, Proverbs, and Ecclesiastes were regarded by some as too profane (*'Abot de Rabbi Nathan* 1.5); Proverbs contradicted itself (26:4–5). (c) Esther was in conflict with the fundamental principle that the law was complete (Lev 27:34) and that no new institution was to be introduced by any prophet after Moses. (Esther and Mordecai concerned the introduction of a new festival, the Day of Purim.)

Eventually, at the school at Jamnia, Ecclesiastes and the Song of Songs were accepted as Scripture. At the same time, other documents were excluded from the canon. *t. Yad.* 2.13 reads: "The Gospel [הגלילנים] and the books of the heretics [ספרי המינים] are not sacred Scripture. The books of Ben Sira, and whatever books have been written since his time, are not sacred Scripture." The exact connotation of "the Gospel" and "books of the heretics" cannot here be discussed,[6] but since Ecclesiasticus was rejected because its author lived in comparatively recent times, when the Holy Spirit had departed from Israel, the same would apply to documents similarly dated, including the gospels and other Christian books (though it is surely incredible that the canonicity of these would ever have been even considered by Judaism).

By the end of the first century, we can be sure that the Hebrew Bible, as we know it, was regarded as canonical although discussion of certain of its books continued to a later date. The phrase used to denote the canonical character of a book was that it "defiled the hands." *m. Ed.* 5.3 illustrates the usage: "According to the School of Shammai the book of Ecclesiastes does not render the hands unclean. And the School of Hillel says: It renders the hands unclean" (הידים קהלת אינו מטמא אח הידים כדכרי כיח שמאי וכיח הלל אומדים מטמא אח). Is this to be taken to mean that the distinction between what defiles the hands and does not, as applied to the Scriptures, was opposed by Shammaites? In *m. Yad.* 4.6 the Sadducees ascribe the distinction to the Pharisees. Thus "the Sadducees say, We cry out against you, O ye Pharisees, for ye say, 'The Holy Scriptures render the hands unclean,' [and] 'The writings of Harmiram [either the books of the heretics or those of Homer] do not render the hands unclean.'" The latter passage reveals that it was out of love for the Scriptures that the Pharisees declared them "to defile the hands," and both passages make it clear that they participate in the quality of things consecrated to God.

Perhaps the most convincing interpretation of the phrase "defile the hands" is that documents so described possessed a contagious quality of holiness which had to be washed away so that it might not be conveyed to mundane objects.[7] As a consequence, the rolls on which the Hebrew Bible was written were treated with extraordinary respect. Later, rules concerning their form and the mode of their composition were drawn up for the copying of the text of the Scriptures. How early such rules existed cannot be precisely determined.

It is tempting to see in the concern for the purity of the text the influence of the critics of Alexandria and Pergamum in the second and third centuries B.C. But it may have been indigenous and needed no outside stimulus. These rolls could not be introduced into an impure place; the honor of the law was jealously guarded (*J.W.* 2.12.2). The question of what languages the law could be translated into was discussed: according to Rabban Simeon Gamaliel, it could only be written in Greek, and although targums were permissible in other languages (*m. Megilla* 1.8; *b. Meg.* 3*a*), these were not to be used as lectionaries (cf. *b. Šabb.* 115*a*).[8] The law had become the consolation of Israel (1 Macc 12:9) for which many were prepared to die (1 Maccabees 56—60; *b. ʿAboda Zara* 17*b*); already in the first century it had become an important part of the liturgy of the synagogue and the chief object of study (*m. ʾAbot* 5.22).

Josephus' words are apt: "But for our people, if anybody do but ask any one of them about our laws he will more readily tell them all than he will tell his own name, and this in consequence of our having learned them immediately as soon as ever we became sensible of anything, and of our having them, as it were, engraven on our souls" (*Against Apion* 2.14). Exaggerated this may be, but it is nonetheless indicative.

This last quotation refers us to the laws as such. Were there distinctions made between the different parts of the Hebrew Scriptures?[9] So far we have referred to the whole of the Hebrew Scriptures as Torah; and, while the translation of this term as "law" is not strictly correct, because it merely covers the meaning of Torah as "commandment" (מצוה), nevertheless, the use of "law" for the whole Torah is significant. Because the fundamental section of the Scripture was the Mosaic law contained in the Hebrew Bible, the Decalogue as such was given prominence (*Mekilta* on Exod 15:26; 20:1; *Song of Songs Rabbah* 5.14–15; Philo, *On the Decalogue*); but it was not to be regarded in any exclusive sense as the Torah. The withdrawal of its recitation from the synagogue service, when it was used by Christians as if it were the whole Torah, points to this (*b. Berakot* 12*a*; *y. Ber.* 3*c*). It is, however, difficult not to think of the Pentateuch as a whole as constituting the Mosaic law; it was called Torah, even in its non-legal aspects (see, for example, Gal 4:21ff).

The authority of the Mosaic law—that is, the Pentateuch—was indicated variously and is related to the question of Revelation.[10] The derivation of the law directly from God (*b. Sanh.* 99*a*; on the relation of the Jewish law to God, see especially *Ant.* Preface 3; *Ag.Ap.* 2.18), or by the mediation of angels from God (*Jubilees* 1:27–28; 2:1ff; 6:22; etc.) emphasized this (the notion that such mediation implied inferiority is a Christian development; Gal 3:19; Heb 2:2). (See chapter 5, herein.) On the other hand, this distinguished it from the Prophets, and the other writings of the Hebrew Bible, which, though produced under the inspiration of the Holy Spirit, only derived their authority from the Law—that is, their agreement with the Pentateuch (*b. Sanh.* 30*b*); Moses was the first and greatest prophet; all that was communicated to prophets, who followed him, he had already received. No prophet could contradict him or change or add to what he had proclaimed (Lev 27:34; Deut 4:2; 13:1ff; *b. Šabb.* 104*a*). For example, in the *y. Sanh.* 11.6.20c. we read:

> Rabbi Simeon ben Yohai [130–160 c.e.] said: Deuteronomy arose and bowed before God, saying: Master of the World, you wrote in your law that a will which is partly void becomes totally void (compare *t. Baba Bathra* 73a: evidence partially false is totally invalid), now Solomon wishes to extract an iota from it. God said: Solomon and thousands like him will be void, but no part of you will be void.

The prophets were guardians of the torah of Moses (2 Macc 2:1ff). The writings outside the Pentateuch are designated "tradition," קבלה, and derive their authority from their "exposition" of the Mosaic law—i.e., from their Sinaitic character. The implication of *b. Nedarim* 22*b* is that the prophets and the writings were made necessary by the sin of Israel whereas the Hexateuch was not. While there was no doubt expressed as to the authority of the Law and the Prophets, the authority of certain documents among the Writings, we saw, was questioned. The Writings were not read in public worship, in the synagogue, as were the Law and the Prophets. Thus all writings in the Hebrew Bible outside the Pentateuch were of second rank, although inspired; that proof texts were often quoted in three verses, from the Law, the Prophets, and the Writings, did not mean that these were all on the same level of importance, but that the last two confirmed or reiterated what was in the Law (*b. Megilla* 31*a*).[11] The sequence, Law, Prophets, Writings, is hierarchical.

Before we leave the written Law, it is necessary to point to revelations of God's law made before that on Sinai. The basic laws essential to man, it was claimed, had been given to Adam (*Mek.* on Exod 19:10; *b. Sanh.* 56*b*; *Deuteronomy Rabbah* 2.17; *Jub.* 3:10–14, 30–31). In addition, Noah had been given, according to some, three (the earliest number according to Professor Flusser, orally), and according to others seven laws (*Mek.* on Exod 20:2; *t. ʿAbod. Zar.* 8.4). *b. Sanh.* 56*ab*; *Jub.* 7:20–21 speak of more general laws, and others refer to thirty commandments given to Noah (*Genesis Rabbah* 98:9; *y. ʿAbod. Zar.* 2.1.40*c*). These Noachian commandments were placed on all mankind and may roughly be taken to correspond to the Stoic "law of nature." David Daube considers them to signal the recognition on the part of Judaism of the extreme improbability that all nations would ever come to obey the whole law; it resigned itself to this fact by insisting only on a minimum of decency for Gentiles. It should also be noted that, after the exodus from Egypt, Israel had received some laws before the revelation on Sinai (Exod 15:25), and that the patriarchs, especially Abraham, were thought to have practiced all the laws, either because they had discovered them for themselves or because they had received a revelation of them. In Philo, both Moses and Abraham are not only examples of lives after the law (νόμιμος βίος) but in themselves incarnations of the Law (Moses is νόμος εμψυχός, and Abraham νόμος αὐτος ὤν καὶ ϑεσμὸς ἄγραφος). (See E. E. Urbach, *The Sages,* pp. 289–93).

THE ORAL LAW

Its Rise

The term "torah" had reference not only to Scriptures, but also to an unwritten tradition, partly interpreting and partly supplementing the written one, and usually referred to as the oral law. The phrase "oral law" (תורה שבעל פה) probably goes back to Hillel (*b. Šabb.* 31*a*), or at least to Gamaliel II (Siphre Deut 33.10). But, in the first century, it was little used, the term "tradition," קבלה, being preferred (so in the NT; Josephus uses παραδόσεις, "traditions";[12] in Philo, νόμος ἄγραφος [see an index to Philo] refers to the natural law; again, in the Rabbis, as we saw, "tradition," קבלה, also refers to the non-Pentateuchal books—for example, *m. ʾAbot* 3.13).

The development of such an oral law was natural on several grounds. No written law can be so exhaustive as to cover all the contingencies of life, and so the ritual and ceremonial as well as the civil and criminal law of the Pentateuch implies, or presupposes, a great deal of custom or usage which was law, although it was not written.[13] Thus Deut 16:18 directs the appointment of judges, but gives no details as to the procedures they are to follow. Presumably such procedures were orally transmitted. Similarly, "custom" was followed in matters such as divorce, the payment of taxes to priests, the observance of the sabbath. As to this last, for example, the Hebrew Bible gives no definition of work that was prohibited, but custom gradually established certain patterns of rest. It is also likely that during the Exile written codes or collections of laws were lost which were never replaced but whose contents were orally preserved, at least in substance.[14]

More specifically, it may be said that while the Scriptures themselves recognize the need for the interpretation and adaptation of the law (for example, Deut 17:8—26:19) by the hands of priests and judges, the biggest impetus to this arose probably at three periods:

a) At the time of Ezra, when the returned exiles had to resettle in Israel and made the law the ground of their life. In this connection the description of Ezra in 7:6ff is significant.

b) During the time when Persian rule gave place to Greek rule in Palestine. Under the Persians the scribes had ruled Israel; they constituted an authoritative body of teachers, versed in "the Book" (hence their name, Sopherim, from the Hebrew ספר), and up to the Greek period they faced conditions of continuity that were manageable in terms of the Book and their interpretation of it. The change to Greek rule interrupted the activity of the Sopherim as an authoritative body, and, at the same time, confronted the nation with bewilderingly new conditions. New ideas and customs had to be considered for which the Sopherim and the law, which they had interpreted, were unprepared. Hence there had to be an expansion of interpretation and a new adaptability, and this meant the growth of oral tradition. This change received some regulation with the establishment of the Sanhedrin in 190 B.C.E. This, an authoritative body of priests and laity, taught and interpreted the law and sought to regulate the life of the people. But again under Antiochus IV Epiphanes (175–163 B.C.E.) books were burned, and there had to be a greater reliance on tradition as such; this gave an impetus to the development of the oral law.[15]

c) There can be little doubt that in the Roman period and in the first century, perhaps especially, economic tensions within the nation contributed to the same development. The needs of the expanding artisan and commercial elements in the nation have been claimed to dictate the concern of the Pharisees with the expansion of the oral law, and the interests of the patrician Sadducees in maintaining the economic status quo, to govern their conservatism on the law; for example, according to Deut 15:2, all loans were remitted in the seventh year. The uncertainty which this introduced into commercial transactions is evident: it could lead to fraud and oppression (Deut 15:9), and the advent of the seventh year would tend to paralyze the economy. Hillel accordingly enacted the rule of the Prosbol. This was a declaration made before a court of law by a creditor and signed by witnesses to the effect that the loan in question would not be remitted under the terms of the seventh-year law (*m. Šebiʿt* 10.3). (Was Hillel introducing Babylonian usage?)[16]

Its Authority

Various factors, then, inevitably produced a rich tradition alongside the written law, and the question arose as to the authority of this tradition. Modern study clearly indicates that no simple or all-encompassing solution is to be found. Ultimately, the oral tradition was rooted in long-established custom; the extent to which individual *halachoth* or larger strata within the Mishna either proceeded from the study of the Scriptures, *midraš halachah*, or were later related to them varies considerably. Accordingly, there are extensive sections of the Mishna which betray no *fundamental* relationship with Scripture whatsoever. The concerns which affected their origin and development must be found elsewhere.[17] In contrast, there are sections where each tradition was grounded in the Scriptures by the use of Midrashic methods. There are passages in the Mishna where there is a direct use of Midrash, as at the following in which we have italicized the quotations from the Hebrew Bible:

M. Maʿaśer Šeni 5.10–14; Yebamoth 12.6; Soṭa 8.1–6. They are presented below:
(1) M. Maʿaśer Šeni [Deut 26:13ff.] which reads:
   At the time of the Afternoon Offering on the last Festival-day they used to make the Avowal. How used a man to make the Avowal? [He said], *I have removed the Hallowed Things out of mine house*—that is Second Tithe and the fruits of Fourth-year plantings; *I have given them to the Levite*—that is the Tithe of the levites; *and also [I have given them]*—that is the Heave-offering and the Heave-offering of Tithe; *to the stranger and the fatherless and the widow*—that is the Poorman's Tithe, Gleanings, the Forgotten Sheaf, and *Peah* (although these do not render the Avowal invalid); *from the house*—that is Dough-offering.
   According to all thy commandment which thou hast commanded me—thus if he granted Second Tithe before First Tithe he may not make the Avowal; *I have not transgressed any of thy commandments*—I have not given from one kind instead of from some other kind or from what has been plucked instead of from what is unplucked or from what is unplucked instead of from what is plucked, or from new produce instead of from old, or from old produce instead of from new; *neither have I forgotten*—I have not forgotten to bless thee or to make mention of thy name over it.

I have not eaten thereof in my mourning—thus if he had eaten during mourning he may not make the Avowal; *nor have I removed ought thereof being unclean*—thus if he had set it apart in uncleanness he may not make the Avowal; *nor given thereof for the dead*—I have not used aught thereof for a coffin or wrappings for a corpse nor have I given it to other mourners; *I have hearkened to the voice of the Lord my God*—I have brought it to his chosen Temple; *I have done according to all that thou hast commanded me*—I have rejoiced and made others to rejoice therewith.

Look down from thy holy habitation from heaven—we have done what thou hast decreed concerning us: do thou also what thou has promised to us; *Look down from thy holy habitation from heaven and bless thy people Israel*—with sons and daughters; *and the ground which thou hast given us*—with dew and wine and with the young of cattle; *as thou swarest unto our fathers*, a land flowing with milk and honey—that thou mayest give flavor to the fruits.

From this they have inferred that Israelites and bastards may make the Avowal but not proselytes and freed slaves, who have no share in The Land. R. Meir says: And not priests and Levites, because they have not received a share from The Land. R. Jose says: They have the cities of the outskirts. [Num 35:2ff.]

(2) *m. Yeb.* 12.6 which reads:

This is the prescribed rite of *halitzah* [Deut 25:7–10]: When the man and his deceased brother's wife are come to the court the judges proffer such advice to the man as befits him, for it is written, *Then the elders of the city shall call him and speak unto him*. And she shall say: *My husband's brother refuseth to raise up unto his brother a name in Israel: he will not perform the duty of a husband's brother to me*. And he shall say, *I like not to take her*. And they used to say this in the Holy Language. *Then shall his brother's wife come unto him in the presence of the elders and loose his shoe from off his foot and spit in his face*—such spittle as can be seen by the judges; *and she shall answer and say, So shall it be done unto the man that doth not build up his brother's house*. Thus far used they to rehearse [the prescribed words]. But when R. Hyrcanus under the terebinth in Kefar Etam [2 Chron 11:6] rehearsed it and completed it to the end of the section, the rule was established to complete the section [to include verse 10]. [To say the words] *And his name shall be called in Israel, The house of him that hath his shoe loosed,* was a duty that fell upon the judges and not upon the disciples. But R. Judah says: It was a duty that fell upon all them that stood there to cry out, "The man that hath his shoe loosed! The man that hath his shoe loosed! The man that hath his shoe loosed!"

(3) *Soṭa* 8.1–6 which reads:

When the Anointed for Battle speaks unto the people he speaks in the Holy Language, for it is written [Deut 20:2ff.], *And it shall be when ye draw nigh unto the battle, that the priest shall approach* (this is the priest anointed for the battle) *and shall speak unto the people* (in the Holy Language), *and shall say unto them, Hear, O Israel, ye draw nigh unto battle this day against your enemies*—and not against your brethren, not Judah against Simeon, and not Simeon against Benjamin, for if ye fall into their hands they will have mercy upon you, for it is written, *And the men which have been expressed by name rose up and took the captives and with the spoil clothed all that were naked among them, and arrayed them and shod them and gave them to eat and to drink and anointed them and carried all the feeble of them upon asses and brought them to Jericho, the city of palm trees, unto their brethren: then they returned to Samaria* [2 Chron 28:15]. Against your enemies do ye go, therefore if ye fall into their hands they will not have mercy upon you. *Let not your heart be faint, fear not nor tremble, neither be ye affrighted . . . Let not your heart be faint* at the neighing of the horses and the flashing of the swords; *fear not* at the clashing of shields and the rushing of the tramping shoes; nor tremble at the sound of the trumpets, *neither be ye affrighted* at the sound of the shouting; *for the Lord your God is he that goeth with you*. They come in the strength of flesh and blood, but ye come in the strength of the Almighty. The Philistines came in the strength of Goliath [1 Sam 17:4]. What was his end? In the end he fell by the sword and they fell with him. The children of Ammon came in the strength of Shobach [2 Sam 10:16]. What was his end? In the end he fell by the sword and they fell with him. But not so are ye, *for the Lord your God is he that goeth with you, to fight for you*. . . . This is the Camp of the Ark.

And the officers shall speak unto the people, saying, What man is there that hath built a new house and hath not dedicated it, let him go and return to his house. . . . It is all one whether he builds a house for straw, a house for cattle, a house for wood, or a house for stores; it is all one whether he builds or buys or inherits [a house] or whether it is given him as a gift. *And what man is there that hath planted a vineyard and hath not used the fruit thereof*. . . . It is all one whether he plants a vineyard or plants five fruit-trees, even if they are of five kinds. It is all one whether he plants vines or sinks them into the ground or grafts them; it is all one whether he buys a vineyard or inherits it or whether it is given him as a gift. *And what man is there that hath betrothed a wife*. . . . It is all one whether he betrothes a virgin or a widow, or even one that awaits levirate marriage, or whether he hears that his brother has died in battle—let him return home. These all hearken to the words of the priest concerning the ordinances of battle; and they return home and provide water and food and repair the roads.

And these are they that may not return: he that builds a gate-house or portico or gallery, or plants but four fruit trees, or five trees that do not bear fruit; or he that takes back his divorced wife; or a High Priest that marries a widow, or a common priest that marries a woman that was divorced or that performed *halitzah*, or an Israelite that marries a bastard or a *Nethinah*, or a bastard or a *Nathin* that marries the daughter of an Israelite—these may not return. R. Judah says: He also that rebuilds his house as it was before may not return. R. Eliezer says: He also that builds a house of bricks in Sharon may not return.

And these are they that stir not from their place: he that built a house and dedicated it, he that planted a vineyard and used the fruits thereof, he that married his betrothed wife, or he that consummated his union with his deceased brother's wife, for it is written, *He shall be free for his house one year: for his house*—this applies to his house; *he shall be*—this is [to include also] his vineyard; *and shall cheer his wife*—this applies to his own wife; *whom he hath taken*—this is to include also his deceased brother's wife. These do not provide water and food and do not repair the roads.

And the officers shall speak further unto the people [*and they shall say, What man is there that is fearful and fainthearted?*] R. Akiba says: *Fearful and fainthearted* is meant literally—he cannot endure the armies joined in battle or bear to see a drawn sword. R. Jose the Galilean says: The *fearful and fainthearted* is he that is afraid for the transgressions that he has committed; wherefore the Law has held his punishment in suspense [and included him] together with these others, so that he may return because of his transgressions. R. Jose says: If a widow is married to a High Priest, or a woman that was divorced or that had performed *halitzah* is married to a common priest, or a bastard or a *Nethinah* to an Israelite, or the daughter of an Israelite to a bastard or a *Nathin*—such a one it is that is *fearful and fainthearted*.

And it shall be when the officers have made an end of speaking unto the people that they shall appoint captains of hosts at the head of the people, and at the rearward of the people; they stationed warriors in front of them and others behind them with axes of iron in their hands, and if any sought to turn back the warrior was empowered to break his legs, for with a beginning in flight comes defeat, as it is written, *Israel is fled before the Philistines, and there hath been also a great slaughter among the people* [1 Sam 4:17]. And there again it is written, *And the men of Israel fled from before the Philistines and fell down slain* [1 Sam 31:1]. . . .

With respect to those cases where the generative force of biblical exegesis may be discerned yet no specific scriptural reference appears, it is most likely that the Midrashic presentation of the oral tradition—that is, its presentation in connection with the text of the Scripture—gave place under the pressures, particularly of Hellenism, in the Greek period, when there was a rapid growth in oral laws, to the Mishnaic method—that is, the presentation of traditions independent of the sacred text, as in most of the Mishna. Not that the Mishnaic method of transmitting the oral law ousted the Midrashic, but the former came to coexist with the latter: both methods continued in use, the one culminating in the redaction of the Mishna, the other in the production of the great Midrashim.[18]

The difficulties inherent in tracing the complex pre-Mishnaic history of the oral law as well as the diversity which characterizes the various strata of the final redaction of the Mishna speak against undifferentiated accounts of the origin, development, or transmission of the oral law.[19] While we have referred to the displacement in part of the Midrashic method by

that more characteristic of the Mishna, it would be erroneous to depict
the latter as an innovation designed simply to deal with an increase in
legislation. Most satisfactory is that view which perceives the Midrashic
and Mishnaic forms of producing *halachoth* as coexisting from the beginning, while giving full recognition to the fact that many laws had only
the remotest, if any, connections with the written Law, while others were
so connected. *M. Hagigah* 1.8 makes this clear:

> [The rules about] release from vows hover in the air and have naught to
> support them; the rules about the Sabbath, Festal-offerings, and Sacrilege
> are as mountains hanging by a hair, for [teaching of] Scripture [thereon] is
> scanty and the rules many; the [rules about] cases [concerning property]
> and the [Temple-]service, and the rules about what is clean and unclean
> and the forbidden degrees, *they have that which supports them, and it is*
> *they that are the essentials of the law* (our italics).

Codification

What is clear, however, is that although the oral law came to be presented in isolation from the text of Scripture, it was regarded as of equal
obligation as the written law. Just as the latter was deemed to have been
included in the revelation given at Sinai so was the oral law. *m. Yad.* 3.2
reads: "[The sages] answered [R. Joshua (first century C.E.)], Ye may
infer nothing about the words of the Law from the words of the Scribes
and nothing about the words of the Scribes from the words of the Law,
and nothing about the words of the Scribes from (other) words of the
Scribes." The words of the Scribes are here equal in authority to those
of the Law, that is, the written Law. In some passages the oral law is
given even greater authority than the written Law, as in *m. Sanh.* 11:3:

> 3. Greater stringency applies to [the observance of] the words of the Scribes
> than to [the observance of] the words of the [written] Law. If a man said,
> "There is no obligation to wear phylacteries" so that he transgresses the
> words of the Law, he is not culpable; [but if he said], 'There should be in
> them five partitions, so that he adds to the words of the Scribes, he is
> culpable.

Nevertheless, it was probably the attempt to connect the oral law with
the Mosaic law that led to the development of rabbinic exegesis. Laws
which could not be so connected were, probably at Jamnia, designated
"Mosaic halakah from Sinai" (הלכה למשה מסיני); eventually even the
grammatical and exegetical rule and methods of rabbinic Judaism were
traced back to Sinai. (See Menahoth 29b cited below, p. 22). It is tempting
to take the statements concerning the equal derivation of the oral and

written law from Moses as playful hyperbole, but only of a few oral laws is it explicitly stated that they were revealed to Moses, and this temptation must be resisted.

The first century was alive with the questions here referred to. On the one hand, the Mishnaic method had become so customary that the century saw collections of important laws dealing with the temple and its ritual as early as the period of the Sopherim, but these were probably never written down. The earliest code mentioned in post-biblical times is the Sadducean criminal code in force down to the time of Queen Alexandra (78 B.C.E.). The *Megillat Ta'anit*, the "Scroll of Fasts," a record of days which it is not lawful to keep as fasts, probably dated in part before 70 C.E., can be regarded as the earliest rabbinical code. This is an anti-Pharisaic work, but it is probable that in the time of Jesus, although the Pharisees for various reasons were seeking to hinder the writing of codes for the public (there was, in fact, no interdict against this), many scholars had secret books of *halachah* which they considered important in codified form.[20] In that period the house of Hillel and the house of Shammai were submitting the oral law to intense discussion. They differed so much that there was a danger that Israel should be faced with two laws rather than one (*t. Soṭa* 14.9).[21] The discussions between them could not but have produced grave religious uncertainty. Toward the end of the first century at Jamnia, under the influence probably of Gamaliel II, attempts were made to bring an end to this uncertainty. The decisions of the school of Hillel were adopted as standard, although in practice authority was often given to the school of Shammai (*y. Ber.* 3*b*; *b. ʿErubin* 13*b*). But the work at Jamnia did not dispel the uncertainty, and it was Akiba's work in collecting *halachoth* that laid the fundamental outlines for the Mishna. Immediately before and after 70 C.E., the need for codification among scholars was probably "in the air." Immediately after 70, the pupils of Rabbi Johanan ben Zakkai, and his younger contemporaries, collected the treatises *Yoma*, *Tamid*, and *Middot*. It is certain that material from this period, as from before 70, which had already been codified, was later included in the Mishna.[22]

Exegesis

On the other hand, along with the activity of a Mishnaic or codifying kind went another which, however, is not to be regarded as inconsistent with this—namely, the development of "exegesis" to connect the oral law with the written law. It has been held that the rules of rabbinic exegesis, or hermeneutics, were derived from classical Greek, Aristotelian models, as employed in the schools of Alexandria.[23] Others regard them as more popular and less rationalized than this view demands. What is clear is that, in the time of Jesus, rules of exegesis had been developed, though it must be understood that the aim of this exegesis may not have been so much the elucidation of the text as the convincing imposition of particular laws upon it. The rabbinic tradition preserves certain catalogues of rules. It ascribes the first to Hillel. His catalogue contained seven rules, while that of Rabbi Ishmael (who flourished 120–35 c.e.) had thirteen. Possibly the rules of Hillel are older than he, consisting of the direct methods of earlier scribes. But that the first century saw developments in this field is clear (for Hillel's rules, see *t. Sanh.* 7.11, Zuckermandel's edition p. 427; *ʾAbot R. Nat.* 37.10; for those of Ishmael, Siphra on Leviticus [preface]; there is an allusion to them in *Mek.* on Exod 13:2).[24]

If we now analyze the oral law, as it was in process in the first century, the following components of it emerge: (a) It contained long-established custom. (b) It incorporated regulations or decrees of a prohibitive kind (גדרות) and enactments of a positive kind (תקנות) issued by individuals or bodies, who at different times had authority to do this—for example, the Prosbol of Hillel. Later than the first century this procedure was justified on scriptural grounds; for our period two things are noteworthy: many oral laws could not be connected with the written law—to such laws the appellation "Mosaic rules from Sinai" was given (see section 2 above); and much in the oral law was in direct contradiction to the written law. Authorities, when necessary, did not hesitate to modify and even to suspend the written law, on their own initiative, without any attempt at elaborate casuistry to justify their procedure. The Prosbol of Hillel is the classic example of this; for other instances see *m. Soṭa* 9.9. (c) The oral law grew from the very study of the written law; new laws which did not belong to the former but were found to be implicit in the latter, were then naturally proclaimed as demands which had fallen into disuse. Along with this went the discovery of principles in the written law to meet the new conditions that were continually being faced.

It was over the validity of this growing oral law that the Pharisees and Sadducees were divided. Josephus has expressed the matter thus: "What I would now explain is this, that the Pharisees have delivered to the people a great many observances by succession for their fathers, which are not written in the law of Moses; and for that reason it is that the Sadducees reject them, and say that we are to esteem those observances to be obligatory which are in the written word, but are not to observe what are derived from the tradition of our forefathers; and concerning these things it is that great disputes and differences have arisen among them" *(An-*

tiquities 13.10.6). It was in their attitude toward the law that other sects also differed. And it is over against a background of intense discussion on the relative claims of the written law and the oral, and of the meaning of the latter, that the ministry of Jesus is to be placed.[25] One caveat is to be issued. Under the impact of Josephus, who emphasized the importance of the Pharisees in the first-century scene, and of the New Testament, where they play a prominent role, the influence of the law in that century has probably been overestimated. While Pharisees, Sadducees, Essenes, and other groups would have been occupied with the law, they constituted only a small portion of the total population; the vast majority were not so interested, being what were technically called "people of The Land," ignorant of the law and indifferent to rules of cleanness and uncleanness.[26]

THE LAW AS THE DEMAND OF THE COVENANT[27]

So far, the content, written and oral, of the Torah, has been indicated. Clearly its scope was exceptionally wide, including what we should call canon, civil, criminal, and even international law, all in one, and embracing the whole range of human activity.[28] A third-century rabbi computed that there were 613 commandments placed upon Israel (*b. Makkot* 23*b*). Doubtless many of these had emerged after the first century, while the majority of them dealt with matters which did not impinge directly on the ordinary life or, as for example, in the case of laws on the priesthood and divorce, concerned only a few within the community. Nevertheless, the importance of the law in first-century Judaism is too obvious to need emphasis.

The change of the title for this section is extremely significant (see note 27). Since the Law was given after the redemption from Egypt, it is not the ground but the concomitant of the latter. The agent of salvation is always Yahweh himself, who out of his mercy elected Israel as his people. The following passage is typical:

"I Am the Lord Thy God" [Exod 20:2]. Why were the Ten Commandments not said at the beginning of the Torah? They give a parable. To what may this be compared? To the following: A king who entered a province said to the people: May I be your king? But the people said to him: Have you done anything good for us that you should rule over us [that is, require obedience]? What did he do then? He built the city wall for them, and he fought their battles. Then when he said to them: May I be your king, they said to him: Yes, yes. Likewise God. He brought the Israelites out of Egypt, divided the sea for them, sent down the manna for them, brought up the well for them, brought the quails for them. He fought for them the battle with Amalek. Then he said to them: I am to be your king. And they said to Him: Yes, yes. [*Mek., Baḥodesh*, (Trans. Lauterbach), 5.]

The Law was given after the election and was Yahweh's demand consequent upon the latter. But the covenantal relationship between Yahweh
and Israel, although it demanded obedience to the Law, was not, finally,
dependent upon that obedience. There was much discussion among the
sages as to why Yahweh had chosen Israel: ultimately he had done so
out of his grace, not for any merit on its part. This is clear by implication
in *m. Sanh.* 10:1: "All Israel has a share in the world to come" whether
they have kept the Law or not. In that same passage there is a clear
recognition that certain categories of Jews, who have deliberately thrown
off the yoke of the Covenant, cannot, however, remain within Israel's
orbit. The passage agrees with all this that, except for sins done "with a
high hand," that is, those that arrogantly or deliberately rejected the Covenant (on these see *Paul and Rabbinic Judaism*, new rev. ed. [Philadelphia:
Fortress Press, 1980], pp. 254ff.]) there was a means of atonement in the
sacrificial system. Whether the distinction between sins done "with a high
hand" and others does not virtually bypass the very essence of the problem of sin, that is, radical disobedience, is debatable (see *Paul and Rabbinic Judaism*, ibid.).[29] But with this question Judaism did not, apparently,
concern itself. (On this absence of a radical understanding of sin in Judaism, see *The Gospel and The Land*, pp. 396–98). Those who deliberately
placed themselves outside the covenant were, at least, not the primary
concern of Judaism, but those who were within it. What way they were
to follow was the center of interest, and their sins were provided for within
the sacrificial system. To be righteous was to be within the Covenant
despite one's failures.

Because the law was regarded as the gracious gift of God to man and
woman, the yoke of the law was readily accepted by the pious, and there
was joy in submission to it. No profound theological justification of obedience was offered or necessary; the stark statement that the law was
commanded by God and was, therefore, to be obeyed, sufficed. This did
not prevent much discussion on the "grounds" or "reasons" for certain
laws—the טעמי תורה: the *Doreshe Reshumoth* (דורשי רשמות) were
concerned with these and other difficulties in the law. In one sense the
development of rabbinic exegesis itself is an attempt at the rationalization
of the oral law, under Hellenistic influences. The classic example of this
acceptance is the statement of Rabbi Johanan ben Zakkai, who, on being
questioned as to the meaning of the seemingly pointless rite dealing with
the red heifer, simply asserted: "The Holy One, blessed be He, merely
says: 'I have laid down a statute, I have issued a decree. You are not
allowed to transgress my decree'; as it is written, 'This is the statute of
the Law'" (*Numbers Rabbah* 19.8).[30]

The sages did come to hold, however, that with obedience came understanding (compare John 7: 17). Within the givenness of the Torah Pharisaic Judaism was extremely rational, that is, it developed its law by argumentation. After 70 C.E. especially, supernatural means of reaching decisions were rejected outright in favour of the majority opinion. A passage from *b. Baba Mesīa* 59a–b is illuminating and deserves full quotation:

We learnt elsewhere: If he cut it into separate tiles, placing sand between each tile: R. Eliezer declared it clean, and the Sages declared it unclean; [59b] and this was the oven of 'Aknai. Why [the oven of] 'Aknai?—Said Rab Judah in Samuel's name: [It means] that they encompassed it with arguments as a snake, and proved it unclean. It has been taught: On that day R. Eliezer brought forward every imaginable argument, but they did not accept them. Said he to them: "If the *halachah* agrees with me, let this carob tree prove it!" Thereupon the carob-tree was torn a hundred cubits out of its place—others affirm, four hundred cubits. "No proof can be brought from a carob-tree," they retorted. Again he said to them: "If the *halachah* agrees with me, let the stream of water prove it!" Whereupon the stream of water flowed backwards. "No proof can be brought from a stream of water," they rejoined. Again he urged: "If the *halachah* agrees with me, let the walls of the schoolhouse prove it," whereupon the walls inclined to fall. But R. Joshua rebuked them, saying: "When scholars are engaged in a *halachic* dispute, what have ye to interfere?" Hence they did not fall, in honour of R. Joshua, nor did they resume the upright, in honour of R. Eliezer; and they are still standing thus inclined. Again he said to them: "If the *halachah* agrees with me, let it be proved from Heaven!" Whereupon a Heavenly Voice cried out: "Why do ye dispute with R. Eliezer, seeing that in all matters the *halachah* agrees with him!" But R. Joshua arose and exclaimed: "*It is not in heaven.*" What did he mean by this?— Said R. Jeremiah: That the Torah had already been given at Mount Sinai; we pay no attention to a Heavenly Voice, because Thou hast long since written in the Torah at Mount Sinai, *After the majority must one incline*.

R. Nathan met Elijah and asked him: What did the Holy One, Blessed be He, do in that hour?—He laughed [with joy], he replied, saying, "My sons have defeated Me, My sons have defeated Me." It was said: On that day all objects which R. Eliezer had declared clean were brought and burnt in fire. They then took a vote and excommunicated him. Said they, "Who shall go and inform him?" "I will go," answered R. Akiba, "lest an unsuitable person go and inform him, and thus destroy the whole world." What did R. Akiba do? He donned black garments and wrapped himself in black, and sat at a distance of four cubits from him. "Akiba," said R. Eliezer to him, "what has particularly happened to-day?" "Master," he replied, "it appears to me that thy companions hold aloof from thee." Thereupon he too rent his garments, put off his shoes, removed [his seat] and sat on the earth, whilst tears streamed from his eyes. The world was then smitten: a third of the olive crop, a third of the wheat, and a third of the barley crop. Some say, the dough in women's hands swelled up.

A Tanna taught: Great was the calamity that befell that day, for everything at which R. Eliezer cast his eyes was burned up. R. Gamaliel too was traveling in a ship, when a huge wave arose to drown him. "It appears to me," he reflected, "that this is on account of none other but R. Eliezer b. Hyrcanus." Thereupon he arose and exclaimed, "Sovereign of the Universe! Thou knowest full well that I have not acted for my honour, nor for the honour of my paternal house, but for Thine, so that strife may not multiply in Israel!" At that the raging sea subsided.

It was not that the sages were unaware of irrational, or transrational or even demonic elements in human existence, but they distrusted apocalyptic visions and philosophic flights and preferred by reasoning to arrive at the sober and the practical. This helps to explain the continued distrust of "prophecy" which marks so much in the rabbinic sources, and the tolerance with which they allowed and preserved multiplicity of opinion in recognition of the necessity to avoid the increase of contention in Israel.

b. Temura 16*a* reads as follows:

. . . The [above] text [stated]: "Rab Judah reported in the name of Samuel: Three thousand traditional laws were forgotten during the period of mourning for Moses." They said to Joshua: "Ask"; he replied: *It is not in heaven.* They [the Israelites] said to Samuel: "Ask"; he replied: [Scripture says:] *These are the commandments*, implying [that since the promulgation of these commandments] **no prophet** has now the right to introduce anything new.

Said R. Isaac the Smith: Also the law relating to a sin-offering whose owners have died was forgotten during the period of mourning for Moses. They [the Israelites] said to Phinehas: "Ask"; he replied to them: "*It is not in heaven.*" They said to Eleazar: "Ask." He replied: "*These are the commandments*," implying [that since the promulgation of these commandments] **no prophet** has now the right to introduce anything new. . . .

b. Sanh. 88*b* reads as follows:

It has been taught: R. Jose said: Originally there were not many disputes in Israel, but one Beth din of seventy-one members sat in the Hall of Hewn Stones, and two courts of twenty-three sat, one at the entrance of the Temple Mount and one at the door of the [Temple] Court, and other courts of twenty-three sat in all Jewish cities. If a matter of inquiry arose, the local Beth din was consulted. If they had a tradition [thereon] they stated it; if not, they went to the nearest Beth din. If they had a tradition thereon, they stated it, if not, they went to the Beth din situated at the entrance to the Temple Mount; if they had a tradition, they stated it; if not, they went to the one situated at the entrance of the Court, and he [who differed from his colleagues] declared, "Thus have I expounded, and thus have my colleagues expounded; thus have I taught, and thus have they taught." If they had a tradition thereon, they stated it, and if not, they all proceeded to the

Hall of Hewn Stones, where they [that is, the Great Sanhedrin] sat from the morning *tamid* until the evening *tamid*; on Sabbaths and festivals they sat within the *ḥel*. The question was then put before them: if they had a tradition thereon, they stated it; if nót, they took a vote: if the majority voted "unclean" they declared it so; if "clean" they ruled even so. But when the disciples of Shammai and Hillel, who [sc. the disciples] had insufficiently studied, increased [in number], disputes multiplied in Israel, and the Torah became as two Toroth. From there [the Hall of Hewn Stones] documents were written and sent to all Israel, appointing men of wisdom and humility and who were esteemed by their fellowmen as local judges. From there [sc. the local Beth din] they were promoted to [the Beth din of] the Temple Mount, thence to the Court, and thence to the Hall of Hewn Stones.

Obedience to the law was often claimed to secure merit (זכות) before God. This merit could, moreover, be assessed with some exactitude according to deeds committed, just as guilt (חובה) could be measured by the transgression of the law (עבידה). Every Israelite thus had to give a reckoning (חשבון) before God, and his destiny was determined according to his deeds. As Akiba "used to say: All is given against a pledge, and the net is cast over all living; the shop stands open and the shopkeeper gives credit and the account book lies open, and the hand writes and everyone that wishes to borrow let him come and borrow; but the collectors go their round continually every day and exact payment of men with their consent or without their comment" (*m. ʾAbot* 3.17). Such quotations, however, must not be systematically or literally interpreted. The view that the weighing of deeds of obedience over against those of disobedience was the final criterion for acceptance by God is, finally, inconsistent with the view to which we referred above, that one could be within Israel even though—within certain limits of "high-handedness"—disobedient. (For the view criticized here, see Strack and Billerbeck, *Kommentar*, 4.3ff.) The phrase about assurance in *Gen. Rab.* 76.2 does not mean that the righteous, because of the uncertainty of the number of the deeds of his or her obedience, can have no assurance in this world. Akiba, at least, did not believe that before one could be saved he or she had to have performed in obedience one *mitzwah* more than the total of the *mitzwoth* which he or she had disobeyed. (See *y. Qiddušin* 61*d* [1 : 10]). Str-B 3.28 understood "one mitzwah" here to mean "one mitzwah more than the number of transgressions." But S. Schechter (*Aspects of Rabbinic Theology*, New York, 1901, p. 164) holds the reference to be to the perfect fulfillment of one *mitzwah* as the adequate ground for salvation. In fact, Akiba simply states that obedience to one *mitzwah* (not necessarily perfectly) suffices. (See now E. P. Sanders, *Paul and Palestinian Judaism* [Philadelphia: Fortress Press, 1977], pp. 33–328.)

At first sight such a view implied that a person can fulfill the law and that salvation is his or her own achievement. Moreover, when reward was so closely connected with observance, the temptation to a mechanical obedience unrelated to religious sincerity was a real one. But Judaism was aware of the dangers and difficulties of its attitude toward the Torah.[32] The following passage from *b. Menah.* 29*b* shows how acutely aware were the sages of the disparity between virtue and reward in this life.

> Rab Judah said in the name of Rab, when Moses ascended on high he found the Holy One, blessed be He, engaged in affixing coronets to the letters. Said Moses, "Lord of the Universe, Who stays Thy hand?" He answered, "There will arise a man, at the end of many generations, Akiba b. Joseph by name, who will expound upon each tittle heaps and heaps of laws." "Lord of the Universe," said Moses, "permit me to see him." He replied, "Turn thee round." Moses went and sat down behind eight rows [and listened to the discourses upon the law]. Not being able to follow their arguments he was ill at ease, but when they came to a certain subject and the disciples said to the master, "Whence do you know it?" and the latter replied, "It is a law given unto Moses at Sinai," he was comforted. Thereupon he returned to the Holy One, blessed be He, and said, "Lord of the Universe, Thou hast such a man and Thou givest the Torah by me!" He replied, "Be silent, for such is My decree." Then said Moses, "Lord of the Universe, Thou hast shown me his Torah, show me his reward." "Turn thee round," said He; and Moses turned round and saw them weighing out his flesh at the market-stalls. "Lord of the Universe," cried Moses, "such Torah, and such a reward!" He replied, "Be silent, for such is My decree."

Akiba was killed in the Hadrianic persecutions.

On the ability of man or woman to achieve his or her own destiny, there were differences among Pharisees and Sadducees and others, but it is no accident that among the things enumerated as pre-existing creation was repentance. The rabbis recognized that our nature is so constituted that we cannot escape sin, so that repentance is a condition of our existence. Hence its precosmic creation. Moreover, the law itself ordained the sacrificial system as a means of atonement for sin, though sacrifice without confession of, and compensation for, the wrong done—that is, without true repentance—did not avail. So, too, Judaism recognized the danger of a merely formal obedience to the law by insisting on the necessity for a pure intention behind all obedience (*m. Ber.* 2.1; *Roš Haššana* 3.7), by distinguishing between moral and ceremonial demands, as even in *Num. Rab.* 19.8, by demanding a piety from the heart and not merely a "legal" piety.[33] It is over against these considerations that criticisms of Pharisaism in the Gospels must be assessed. The potency of repentance is such that a single day of it would bring in Israel's redemption (cf. *Pesiqta de Rab Kahana* 163*b*; *b. Yoma* 86*b* and *b. Sanh.* 97*b*).[34] As we saw, the sages were sober rationalists working within a given revelation. Their certainty concerning the revelation in Torah tended to a confidence in the possibility of achieving obedience to the reasonableness of the demands which they found by the application of their own reason. This accounts for the comparative absence of stress on the need for grace which we find in the words of the sages. This is congruous with the comparative absence in their thinking of the miasma of sin.[35] Essentially, repentance for the sages is the frank recognition of the realities of a situation and the consequent will to meet these. They responded to the vicissitudes of life not by indulging in intricate theories of sin and grace or of the meaning of history but by sober arrangements to change them—to face anew the demand of the moment—that is, to repent.

THE LAW AS THE AGENT OF CREATION

We have been concerned with the law mainly as the demand of God. But so profound was the devotion of Judaism to the law that it was given a kind of personal existence. Despite the multiplicity of its demands, the law was conceived of as an entity, which could teach and speak ("The Scripture says, . . . speaks, . . . teaches, etc."; cf. Paul's personification of the law). The personalized unity given to the law is illustrated by the fact that the plural form, "laws" (תורות), occurs usually only when it is necessary to deny the existence of more than one law (*b. Sanh.* 80*b*). The law was a living, unified reality (*b. Šabb.* 31*a*; *t. Soṭa* 14.9).

It was given not only a redemptive but also a cosmic significance. We have seen that the oral law was traced back to Sinai, but the whole law, conceived as revelation, was given still greater antiquity—in fact, a precosmic existence. The way was prepared for this long before the first century through the identification of wisdom with the law. Wisdom in the Hebrew Bible, especially in Proverbs 8, is the agent both of redemption and of creation, its precosmic role being clearly defined. And, as early as Deut 4:6, the law was associated with wisdom, and in Eccl 24:23 the identification of the two was made explicit, so that, by the first century, the precosmic existence of the law and its agency in creation were well established (*Baraita* 3:14—14:1; 4 Macc 1:17; and passim); and, although some of the testimonia adduced below are later than the first century, there can be little doubt that the motifs go back to that period.

The following emphases are noteworthy:

a) The law, like wisdom in Proverbs 8, was regarded as older than the world. Siphre on Deut 11:10 takes Prov 8:22 to mean that the law was created before everything. In *Gen. Rab.* 1 it is made clear that the law not only existed in the mind of God before creation, but that it had actually been created then.

b) The law was connected with the very act of creation. Rabbi Akiba (120–35 C.E.) said: "Beloved are Israel to whom was given a precious instrument wherewith the world was created. It was greater love that it was made known to them that there was given to them a precious instrument whereby the world was created, as it is said, Prov. 4:2" (*m. 'Abot* 3.15; cf Philo, *On the Creation of the World* "[Moses'] exordium [Gen 1:1]. . . consists of an account of the creation of the world implying that the world is in harmony with the Law, and the Law with the world. . .").

c) The Torah was thus one of the pillars of the universe (*m. 'Abot* 1.2 in a saying ascribed to Simon the Just [either 280 or 200 B.C.E.]); later passages speak of the world as having been created for the Law (for example, *Gen. Rab.* 12.2).

d) It followed that in a real sense God himself was bound by and to the law: He had studied it and fulfilled it (*b. 'Abod. Zar.* 3*b*).

e) It was corollary to this that the law was perfect and eternal (1 Enoch 99:2; *Bar.* 4:1; *Ag.Ap.* 4, Philo *Life of Moses* 2.3.14),[36] although later passages have been taken to suggest a distinction between the Pentateuch, at this point, and the rest of Scriptures, the former alone being eternal (*y. Meg.* 1.70). But see the context.

How seriously are we to take these emphases? Are they merely the play of fancy? It may be argued, in the light of the ease with which Judaism ascribed pre-existence[37] to other things than the Law—repentance, Paradise, Gehenna, the throne of glory, the sanctuary, the name of the Messiah (*Pesaḥim* 54*a*; *Gen. Rab.* 1.4, etc.)—that the category of pre-existence in itself was not highly significant. But it was otherwise with the idea of the Law as the instrument of creation. This concept gives expression to one of the most fundamental convictions of Judaism: that the universe conforms to the Law, that nature itself is after the pattern of it. To claim that the law was the instrument of creation was to declare that nature and revelation belonged together; in theological terms, that there was no discontinuity between nature and grace. It was to give cosmic significance to morality, and to cosmic speculation a sobriety it might otherwise have lacked. Nor is the close relationship of God himself to the Law to be lightly treated: for Judaism this meant that religion, revealed in law, was no secondary afterthought but coeval with God himself. Again these emphases raise the possibility that within Judaism there may have been conceptions not far removed from the Platonic doctrine of ideas, albeit expressed far more naively than in Plato. Thus the law had a kind of celestial existence before it came into being on Sinai, and we are reminded of Philo's doctrine of the Word conceived and residing in the mind (λόγος ἐνδιάθετος), the Word expressed (λόγος προφορικός). In any case, the Law was regarded as existing in two places: first, in what Plato would have called the realm of ideas, and, secondly, in time. But this is part of the problem of the relation between symbolism and imagery in Judaism (especially apocalyptic) and Hellenism. It is, however, well to be on our guard against too sharp a distinction between what is Platonic or Hellenistic and what is Hebraic.

This is the best place to ask whether in Hellenistic-Jewish writers such as Josephus and Philo the understanding of the Law was modified under Hellenistic influences. Josephus remained a Jew in his attitude toward the Law, but in three ways he reveals a Hellenistic coloring. His praise of Moses as a pious wise man probably stems from his desire to commend him to the Hellenistic world, as does his interest in supplying reasonable grounds for the Law—he had intended to write a book on this theme. Hellenistic in its appeal is also his understanding of the law in terms of virtue. Hellenistic motifs are still more marked in Philo, although he remained a practicing Jew. He identified the law of Judaism with the law of nature, or the order of the world, because for him God is both creator and revealer. The fathers (Abraham, etc.) were able to live according to the Law, before the Law had actually been given, because reason and revelation are one. This attempt to equate revelation and nature, philosophy and law, led Philo to the use of the allegorical method, but his allegorism never led him to neglect the observance of the Law. Along with his use of allegory went his attempt to find rational grounds for the Law in order to avoid offense to the Hellenistic world.[38]

THE LAW IN THE FUTURE

Finally, we have to ask what role the Law was expected to play in the messianic age or in the age to come. We have seen that it was regarded as perfect and eternal: it was impossible that it should ever be forgotten, no prophet could ever arise who would change it, and no new Moses should ever appear to introduce another law to replace it. Matt 5:18 adequately expresses the dominant first-century doctrine. Note, however, the following:

a) There are a few passages which suggest the cessation in the messianic age of certain enactments concerning sacrifices and the festivals (*Leviticus Rabbah* 9.7; *Yalquṭ* on Prov 9:2); others suggest changes in the laws concerning things clean and unclean (Midrash Tehillim on 146.7; *Lev. Rab.* 13.3). Other passages often claimed to imply changes in the law are of doubtful weight (for example, Siphre on Deut 17:18).

b) Difficulties or incomprehensibilities in the Law would finally be adequately explained. God himself would teach his people in the messianic age (*Num. Rab.* 19.6). The passages which speak of a new law in the messianic age are of a late date, but they may be cogent enough to permit us to assert that the expectation of a new, messianic law was not incompatible with first-century Judaism (see *Tg.* on Isa 12:3). Possibly anti-Christian polemic may have caused the suppression of early evidence for this. In the age to come, beyond the messianic age, commandments were to cease (*b. Ned.* 61*b*). On the whole, however, the picture that emerges is that of a future, when God himself or his Messiah would study the laws, reveal their grounds, return backsliders, and give the law to the Gentiles. Judaism could no more think of the future than of the past and present other than in terms of the eternal law.[40]

2
Reflections on Tradition:
The 'Abot Revisited

As a small token of the honor and friendship in which I hold Professor Knox, I had hoped to present a reexamination of a theme to which he has devoted a great deal of creative thought—that of memory in the New Testament. Unfortunately, circumstances conspired against this. But during the last year I have been compelled to devote myself to another, not wholly unrelated, theme. A recent rereading of the *Pirqe 'Abot* (henceforward *'Abot*) raised again for me the question of the nature of tradition in the Judaism within which Jesus was born and from which the early Christians were largely drawn. I shall here simply set forth certain significant aspects of Jewish tradition as it reveals itself in the *'Abot*. To recognize these, I suggest, is to throw light on some elements at least in the tradition preserved in the NT and to be warned against certain erroneous conclusions that might, at first encounter, be drawn from it.

On first reading the *'Abot* I felt

> . . . like some watcher of the skies
> When a new planet swims into his ken . . .

To read the *'Abot* after being steeped in classical Greek and Hebrew was at once to enter a new and strange world—that of the rabbis. But the *'Abot* is a very singular work: it is utterly unlike the rest of the Mishna. All the other tractates of the Mishna deal with *halakoth*, minute points of law. But the *'Abot* contains no *halakoth*: it is not concerned with the legal disputes and niceties of the rest of the Mishna and is, in some ways, like a miniature Book of Proverbs, designed especially for rabbis and their students. But despite its singularity within the Mishna, the *'Abot* expresses the quintessence of Pharisaism. Indeed, Herford has argued that the *'Abot* was designed as the epilogue to the Mishna. All its contents were gathered together in order to set forth the meaning or spirit of the completed Mishnaic corpus.[1] It is uncertain whether we should follow Herford in this epilogic view of the *'Abot*,[2] but that it expresses the genius of the Mishna and of the Pharisaism which gave it birth, in nonhalakic terms, is clear. The *'Abot* is a document of Pharisaism. Here in the sharp, compact, and

were an indispensable link with the men of the Great Synagogue.[15] In the
ʾAbot de Rabbi Nathan these three prophets are expressly mentioned as
having come up from the exile as they are also in the following:

> Rabban b. Hanah (A.D. 320–75) said in R. Johanan's (A.D. 277–320) name:
> Three prophets went up with them from the Exile: one testified to them
> about (the dimensions of) the altar; another testified to them about the site
> of the altar; and the third testified to them that they could sacrifice even
> though there was no Temple.[16] In a Baraitha it was taught, R. Eleazer b.
> Jacob (A.D. 80–120 or 140–65) said: Three prophets went up with them from
> the Exile: one who testified to them about (the dimensions of) the altar,
> and the site of the altar; another who testified to them that they could
> sacrifice even though there was no Temple; and a third who testified to
> them that the Torah should be written in Assyrian characters. (*b. Zebahim*
> 62*a*.)

It is possible that Malachi should be identified with Ezra, the architect
of postexilic Judaism.

> It has been taught, R. Joshua b. Korha (A.D. 140–65) said: Malachi is the
> same as Ezra, and the Sages say that Malachi was his proper name. R.
> Nahman (A.D. 320–75) said: There is good ground for accepting the view
> that Malachi was the same as Ezra. (The grounds for this view are then
> given.) For it is written in the prophecy of Malachi: *Judah hath dealt treach-*
> *erously and an abomination is committed in Israel and in Jerusalem, for*
> *Judah hath profaned the holiness of the Lord which he loveth and hath*
> *married the daughter of a strange God* (Mal 2:11). And who was it that
> put away the strange women? Ezra, as it is written, *And Shechaniah, the*
> *son of Tehrel, and one of the sons of Elam answered and said unto Ezra:*
> *We have broken faith with our God and have married foreign women* (Ezra
> 10:2). (*b. Megilla* 15*a*.)

In *b. Meg.* 3*a* it is stated that Jonathan ben Uzziel, the author of the
targum, a pupil of Hillel, received the tradition from the three prophets
mentioned. What this means is that Jonathan ben Uzziel's work rested
on an ancient tradition going back to the prophets, so that the interpretation of biblical texts in the School of Hillel may be presumed to have
rested on the work of the prophets. The passage in *b. Meg.* reads:

> R. Jeremiah—or some say R. Ḥiyya b. Abba—also said: The *Targum* of
> the Pentateuch was composed by Onkelos the proselyte under the guidance
> of R. Eleazer and R. Joshua. The *Targum* of the Prophets was composed
> by Jonathan ben Uzziel under the guidance of Haggai, Zechariah and Ma-
> lachi. . . .

The above passages place the prophets in the stream of transmitters of
the tradition. They are placed after the elders. The significance of thus

placing prophets in the chain of tradition must not be overlooked in another dimension.[17] The reference in ʾAbot 1:1 to the elders looks back to Josh 24:31; Judg 2:7. The former passage, which is repeated in Judg 2:7, reads: "And Israel served the Lord all the days of Joshua, and all the days of the elders who outlived Joshua and had known all the work which the Lord did for Israel." But part of this work which the Lord had done for Israel had been the giving of the Spirit to the elders, as is clear from Num 11:16–17:

> And the Lord said to Moses, "Gather for me seventy men of the elders of Israel, whom you know to be the elders of the people and officers over them; and bring them to the tent of meeting, and let them take their stand there with you. And I will come down and talk with you there; and I will take some of the spirit which is upon you and put it upon them; and they shall bear the burden of the people with you, that you may not bear it yourself alone. . . ."

Moses, the mediator of the Torah, is a man of the Spirit, and the Spirit that was given to him was transmitted to the elders who accompanied him to Mount Sinai to receive the Torah. Far from there being any opposition between law and Spirit the opposite seems to have been the case: the transmitters of Torah are bearers of the Spirit.[18] But the Spirit is also *par excellence* the inspiration of prophecy. This assertion is so well attested to that no details need be given in support of it. For Pharisaism, law, Spirit, prophecy belonged together as parts of one complex. And the figure of Joshua—the second link in the Pharisaic chain—is also marked by the Spirit (Num 27:17; Deut 34:9). In Numbers the giving of the Spirit to the elders, which means that they are given the gift of prophecy, precedes the giving of it to Joshua, and in *Midraš Rabbah* much is made of the fact that, although Moses gives of his Spirit to the elders, it remains undiminished and he is still able to endow Joshua with it (see *Numbers Rabbah* on 11:17, Soncino translation, p. 672).[19]

But the prophets are not merely links in a chain of Pharisaic tradition; they themselves are also the source of *halakoth*: they create "tradition." Bacher has collected the references to laws which were instigated by or transmitted through the prophets. The first-century Shammai himself rooted one of his *halakoth* in the prophets, as is clear from *b. Qiddušin* 43a. This contains a comment on *m. Qidd.* 2:1, which reads:

> A man may betroth a woman either by his own act or by that of his agent; and a woman may become betrothed either by her own act or by that of her agent. A man may give his daughter in betrothal while she is still in her girlhood either by his own act or by that of his agent.

The *gemara* to this is concerned with the principle of agency. Shammai bases one of his *halakoth* on the prophet Haggai. The House of Hillel and the House of Shammai differed on the question whether intention is to be taken as deed. Shammai held that intention is as deed. The pertinent words are as follows:

> Now, when it is taught: If he says to his agent, "Go forth and slay a soul," the latter is liable, and his sender is exempt. Shammai the Elder said on the authority of Haggai the prophet: His sender is liable, for it is said, thou hast slain with the sword of the children of Ammon (2 Sam 12:9).[20]

Shammai holds the sender liable to the severest penalty as if he were the actual murderer. Hillel allows a less severe penalty for the sender. (Is he here more removed from Jesus than Shammai? Jesus, like Shammai, emphasizes intention.)

Another example of strictly legal teaching activity being ascribed to the prophets occurs in *b. Roš Haššana* 19*b*. The *m. Roš. Haš.* 1:2 reads as follows:

> Because of six New Moons do messengers go forth (to proclaim the time of their appearing): because of Nisan, to determine the time of Passover, because of Ab, to determine the time of the Fast . . . and because of Adar, to determine the time of Purim (Adar 14th). . . .

The *gemara* on this Mishna in *b. Roš. Haš.* 19*b* reads:

> R. Joshua b. Levi (A.D. 219–79) testified on behalf of the holy community of Jerusalem concerning the two Adars, that they are sanctified on the day of their prolongation [the thirtieth day is known as the day of prolongation as it is the day which is added to make the preceding month full, i.e. contain thirty days]. In the case of the two Adars, the thirtieth day of each is sanctified as the New Moon of the next month [so says the editor of the Soncino translation, p. 81]. This is equivalent to saying that we make them defective, but we do not make them full, and excludes the statement made in a discourse by R. Nahman b. Hisda (A.D. 375–427); (for R. Nahman b. Hisda stated in a discourse): R. Semai (A.D. 200–20) testified in the name of Haggai, Zechariah and Malachi concerning the two Adars that if they [the Beth Din] desired, they could make both of them full, and if they desired they could make one full and the other defective; and such was their custom in the Diaspora. In the name of our teacher [Rab], however, they said: One is always to be full and the next defective, unless you have been informed that the New Moon has been fixed at its proper time [that is, that the Beth Din in Jerusalem fixed the New Moon of Adar II on the thirtieth day of the first Adar, the thirtieth day always being regarded as the "proper time" of New Moon] (Soncino translation, p. 81, n. 3).

It is striking that here Rab goes against a prophetic permission. Typically, on such a matter perhaps, the prophets are more lenient than Rab.

In *b. Sukka* 44*a*, a ceremony connected with the Festival of Tabernacles was regarded by some as instituted by the prophets.

> It was stated, R. Johanan (A.D. 279–320) and R. Joshua b. Levi (A.D. 219–79) differ. One holds that the rite of the willow–branch is an institution of the prophets [that is, according to the editor of the Soncino translation, p. 203, Haggai, Zechariah and Malachi, the prophets of the Second Temple, to whom tradition ascribes many enactments], the other holds that the willow–branch is a usage of the prophets ["sc. they had it only as a custom, and since it did not have the force of a law, no benediction over it is necessary" (Soncino translation, p. 203, n. 6)]. It can be concluded that it was R. Johanan who said, "It is an institution of the prophets," since R. Abbahu stated in the name of R. Johanan, "The rite of the willow-branch is an institution of the prophets." This is conclusive.[21]

Again, in *b. Pesaḥim* 117*a*, the commandment to recite the Hallel Psalms (Pss 113–18) on every important occasion is traced to the prophets:

> The prophets among them [in Israel at the Red Sea] ordained that Israel should recite it [the Hallel Psalms] at every important epoch and at every misfortune—may it not come upon them—and when they are redeemed they recite it [in gratitude] for their redemption.

This is given as what the "Sages taught," that is, it is an old tradition. In the same way the division of the priests into twenty-four classes is traced to the prophets in *m. Ta'anit* 4:1–2, which reads:

> Three times in the year the priests four times lift up their hands during the day (at the Morning Prayer, at the Additional Prayer, at the Afternoon Prayer and at the Closing of the Gates): namely, on the days of fasting, at the *Maamads* and on the Day of Atonement. What are the *Maamads*? In that it is written, Command the children of Israel and say unto them, My oblation, my food for my offerings made by fire, of a sweet savour unto me, shall ye observe to offer unto me in their due season (Num. 28:2)—how can a man's offering be offered while he does not stand by it? Therefore the first prophets (David and Solomon) ordained twenty–four Courses, and for every Course there was a *Maamad* in Jerusalem, made up of priests, and Levites and Israelites. When the time was come for a Course to go up, the priests and Levites thereof went up to Jerusalem, and the Israelites that were of the self-same Course came together unto their own cities to read the story of Creation, and the men of the *Maamad*[22] fasted four days in the week. . . .

In *y. 'Erubin* 21.c.15, the celebration of the New Year festival on two days was traced to the first prophets. Schwab translates as follows: "Les sages reconnaissent, comme R. Juda, que les 2 jours de fête du nouvel an ont été institués par les 1ers prophètes. . . ." (*Talmud Jérusalem* [Paris,

1879], 3:236). From 1 Macc. 9:54 it is clear that the Temple was regarded as having been built according to measurements supplied by the prophets.

> Moreover in the hundred fifty and third year, in the second month, Alcimus commanded that the wall of the inner court of the sanctuary should be pulled down; he pulled down also the works of the prophets (τὰ ἔργα τῶν προφητῶν). . . .

For this Alcimus suffered great torment. Josephus, in the *Antiquities* 12.10.6, makes it explicit that the wall taken down by Alcimus had been there of old and had been built by the prophets.

The view of the prophets which emerges from the above is that of men standing well within the cultic and legal tradition of Pharisaism. It is striking how the cultus and its activity are assumed to have interested the prophets, not in any simple, condemnatory sense, but as part of their living constructive concern. The antitheses of prophet and priest, Spirit and law, which have played so great a part in theological interpretations of Christianity and Judaism, cannot have been so sharp as has been commonly held. Exaggeration must, however, be avoided. The passages showing a connection between the prophecy and the law which Bacher was able to gather within the sea of the rabbinic sources are few. It must also be recognized that the rabbis did consider that the age of prophecy and with it the age of the Spirit had ceased with the last of the prophets,[23] that is, Haggai, Zechariah, and Malachi, although, as we have pointed out elsewhere, there were phenomena in Judaism which pointed to the continued presence of the Spirit after the last of the prophets.

The point to be made here is that rereading the *Abot* has suggested precisely what decades of work by scholars on the OT have revealed, that prophet and priest, law and prophecy, belong together. Attention to rabbinic sources would have spared us many exaggerated notions of the opposition between law and prophecy, priest and prophet. Under the impact of the work of such scholars as Aubrey Johnson,[24] Zimmerli[25] and others, the traditional gulf between these has been gradually lessened. It has been claimed that for a time even Amos worked as a cultic prophet in Bethel.[26] The attempt to prove that the cultic prophets were all false prophets has broken down. Priest and prophet, law and prophecy were not antithetical or mutually exclusive. Prophecy as well as law, prophet as well as priest, are endemic in Judaism. So much the opening of the *Abot* makes clear.[27]

The next antithesis to which a rereading of the *Abot* is pertinent is one which is increasingly being held in truer perspective: it is that between

Semitic, or Palestinian, Judaism and Hellenistic, or Diaspora, Judaism in the first century. This dichotomy has invaded synoptic, Pauline, and Johannine studies. In synoptic studies the detection of Hellenistic elements in the tradition about Jesus was taken to point to a late date and an extra-Palestinian setting. In Pauline studies, it enabled Schweitzer to set a Paul, who he thought was dominated by Palestinian categories, over against John, who was dominated by Hellenistic ones. On the other hand, the same antithesis enabled Montefiore to interpret Paul as a Diaspora Jew who, had he known the superior Judaism of Palestine, would never have embraced the gospel. The dichotomy between Palestinian and Diaspora Judaism made it possible to localize Paul conveniently, according to one's approach, either within or without Palestinian Judaism. In Johannine studies the dichotomy has been evident in works ranging from Dean Inge's famous essay to the latest work by C. H. Dodd, who is aware of the alleged dichotomy, but does not allow it to tyrannize his treatment.

I have elsewhere argued against such a dichotomy, and, as already indicated, it is increasingly being questioned.[28] Here I merely wish to point out how a rereading of the Ăbot has provided many sidelights which make the falsity of the dichotomy still further clear.

First, let us consider the purpose of the chain of tradition with which the Ăbot opens. Here an article by Bickerman is very important. It is entitled "La Chaîne de la Tradition Pharisienne." Bickerman contrasts the lack of historical concern which prevailed in the Hellenistic world between the death of Alexander and the period of Augustus with the prevalence of such a concern from the beginning of the Roman Empire onwards.[29] At that time the Greeks began more and more to look back to classical Greece, its life, art, and literature. And, at the same time, what happened in the Hellenistic world—the return to the past—also happened in Rome[30] and Jerusalem.

Connected with this is a development within the schools of philosophy. Greek philosophers founded "schools" in which the teaching of the founder was transmitted from generation to generation by successive scholars.[31] There were Platonic, Aristotelian, Stoic, Epicurean "schools" in which such transmission took place. For example, Plato's Academy continued to exist during more than eight centuries down to A.D. 529, the date when it was closed by Justinian. Aristotle had followed the example of Plato, and in 322 B.C. had delegated his school to Theophrastus. There emerged lists of the successors who headed these various schools. Already in 200 B.C., Sotion, an Alexandrian who wrote between 200 and 170 B.C., had gathered the lists of successors in these schools; in the

Roman period a literature of succession had arisen. Suidas, for example, held that the Epicurean school lasted from 271 B.C. to 44 B.C., during which period there were fourteen successors.

What was the reason for this concern for establishing the lists of succession in the philosophic schools? Apart from the general concern to return to the ancients, no purely historical factors can be held to account for it. The reason lay elsewhere and deeper. Bickerman points out that ever since the time of Socrates philosophy had not been merely a kind of technical or theoretical knowledge; it had been rather a way of life, discovered and revealed by the founder of the school. The philosopher's way of life was not only to be learned from his books, but from the faithful transmission of his successors who had "lived" his doctrine. In this lay the importance of preserving a "living" succession.

A further point is to be noted. Greek historians were concerned with establishing not only the succession for Greek schools of philosophy but also the succession for pagan, or barbarian, wisdom. In turn, "barbarians" showed the same concern and recorded the successions of their "schools." For example, in the second century A.D. Pomponius Sextus, a distinguished Roman jurist, set forth in his *Enchiridium* the succession of Roman jurists down to his time.[32]

What particularly interests us is that Jews also came to share in this concern with "philosophic" succession. According to Eusebius (*H.E.* 9.30.447a), in the second century B.C. Eupolemos, a Jew, conceived the idea of a succession of prophets from Moses to Joshua. Such a succession is presupposed in ʾ*Abot* 1:1. Josephus is also aware of a prophetic succession, however broken (*Ag. Ap.* 1.8.38 ff.).

It is in the light of all this concern of the Hellenistic world for establishing the succession of philosophic schools, and, as a result, of the concern among Jews also with the idea of succession, that we are to understand the chain of tradition presented at the beginning of the ʾ*Abot*. The Pharisees also—in order to be respectable and respected—wanted to establish their pedigree, or spiritual ancestry. They traced what might be called a professorial succession for their school just as the Platonists did for theirs. True, if we follow Finkelstein, they gave to the succession a peculiar form governed by Hebraic notions of the mystic number fourteen. But the pertinent point here is that, strange as at first sight it might seem, the Pharisaic chain of tradition is, in part at least,[33] an expression of Hellenistic pressures on Judaism. The very manifesto of Pharisaism begins with a Hellenistic convention which sets the ʾ*Abot* in the stream of Hellenistic philosophical interests.

The Hellenistic color of the chain of tradition in Ăbot 1 : 1 ff. is confirmed by a very simple fact. The chain reads as follows:

> Moses received the Law from Sinai and committed it to Joshua, and Joshua to the elders, and the elders to the Prophets; and the Prophets committed it to the men of the Great Synagogue . . . Simeon the Just was of the remnants of the Great Synagogue . . . Antigonus of Soko received [the Law] from Simeon the Just. . . .

There follows upon the above a list of the "pairs" of authorities who transmitted the traditions down to Hillel and Shammai and, with interruptions, beyond to Johannan ben Zakkai.

At first sight the opening list in the Ăbot seems to be thoroughly Jewish, typically Pharisaic or rabbinic. But we have already seen that its inspiration may well have been Hellenistic. And it agrees with this that a striking fact stares the reader in the face. Among the comparatively early transmitters of the tradition there is one who bears a Greek name. This is a more likely view than that "Antigonus" represents some Hebrew name. Antigonus himself, of course, was a Jew, a pre-Tannaitic teacher of the third century B.C. or of the first decades of the second century B.C. It has been suggested that the description of him as "of Soko" implies that he was a considerable figure in his city (see Judg 7 : 14). What is important here is that he bears a Greek name. He lived in a period when Hellenistic influences on Judaism were strong. One might expect such a situation to produce, among leading Jews at least, a reaction against Greek names. In a Pharisaic chain of tradition especially one would expect classical biblical and traditional Jewish names. But here in Ăbot 1 : 3, in the honored chain of tradition, we meet a Greek name. And at once it is to be recognized that this could only be so if Pharisaism were open to Hellenistic influences.[34] The teacher of the first "pair,"[35] who thus occupied a historic position in the development of Pharisaism, bore a Greek name. In all there are eight Greek names among the seventy-two names in the Ăbot and a number of transliterated Greek words.[36]

The saying ascribed to Antigonus of Soko has also pointed to the pressure of Hellenism. It reads as follows:

> Be not like slaves that minister to the master for the sake of receiving a bounty (*peras*), but be like slaves that minister to the master not for the sake of receiving a bounty (*peras*); and let the fear of Heaven be upon you.

Bickerman[37] characterizes the view that *peras* represents the Greek term φόρος as strange, and prefers to expound the verse in terms of the maintenance of slaves in the ancient world. *Peras* stands for rations given to

slaves in the Hellenistic and Roman periods. Antigonus contrasts two
categories of slaves—those who receive *peras* from the owner and those
who do not. The slave is a permanent hireling who is maintained by the
master. There was much discussion as to whether a master was duty
bound to maintain a worthless slave. In such a case, could the master not
refuse the maintenance (*peras*) of the slave? This discussion was found
among the rabbis. Bickerman cites a passage from *m. Giṭṭin* 1:6, which
refers to an ancient tradition. The passage is instructive:[38]

> If a man said, "Deliver this bill of divorce to my wife," or "this writ of
> emancipation to my slave," and he wished in either case to retract, he may
> retract. So R. Meir. But the Sages say: [He may retract] if it was a bill of
> divorce but not if it was a writ of emancipation, since they may act to
> another's advantage in his absence but not to his disadvantage save in his
> presence; for if a man is minded not to provide for his slave, this is his
> right; but if he is minded not to provide for his wife, this is not his right.
> R. Meir said to them: Does he not thereby disqualify his slave from eating
> Heave-offering just as he disqualifies his wife? They answered: [He has the
> right to do so to his slave] because he is his chattel. . . .

Bickerman further points to *b. Baba Qamma* 87*a*, where the view is referred to that a master could wash his hands entirely of any responsibility
for a slave working for him. The view is made explicit in *b. Giṭ. 12a*,
though there was much difference of opinion, which is dealt with in the
passage from *b. Giṭ.* on the question. It is in the light of such ideas that
the saying of Antigonus is to be understood. A man's relation to God is
that of a slave: God can maintain him or not as he chooses. And as Bickerman summarizes Antigonus' saying, it means "there is no compensatory
harmony between man's obedience and divine favor." As in the Book of
Job and in Jesus, "God is boldly compared to the unfair slave-driver
whose conduct violated the unwritten law of the slave system" (See Luke
17:10.).

What is of interest is that Antigonus' saying emerges in the large context
of the problem of theodicy which became acute in Judaism in the Hellenistic age. Bickerman writes as follows:

> [The] optimistic principle of harmony between the obedience to the divine
> Law and prosperity, which for centuries had formed the moral basis of
> Jewish society, began to be challenged seriously in the time of Antigonus.
> One of the recurrent topics in Ecclesiastes written by an earlier contem-
> porary of Antigonus is that of theodicy. Doubters denied that man's success
> or failure correspond to his deserts. Sirach also aimed at vindicating the
> ways of God with men. He advanced the usual arguments: misfortune may
> be a blessing in disguise: God will reward right doing later and so on. A

classicist will remember that at the same time in Athens, Chrysippus laboured to vindicate the dispensation of Providence and was rallied by Epicureans and other unbelievers (*Midr. Qohelot* 9:2).

The saying of Antigonus is part of the failure of nerve of the whole Hellenistic age. Later, the Stoic, Epictetus (*c.* A.D. 50 to *c.* 130), a Phrygian slave, was to meet the same problem in words whose purport is the same as that of those uttered by Antigonus: "I came because it so pleased Him, and I leave, because it so pleases Him, and as long as I live my task is to praise God" (Epictetus, 3.26.29 [Bickerman's translation]).

It might be argued that no direct Hellenistic pressures necessarily called forth Antigonus' saying: might it not have been purely indigenous to Judaism? Is it not such as could normally be expected to emerge wherever, in distinct areas, the problem of theodicy became acute? This possibility must be recognized. But the final words of Antigonus' saying suggest a possible polemic reference: "And let the fear of Heaven be upon you." Is this a direct rejection of the Epicureans, who urged that there were no gods above to be feared, because such as did exist did not interfere with the world? Despite the brute facts of persecution and suffering in the time of Antiochus Epiphanes, when the Epicureans taunted the pious, the fear of heaven, piety, was to remain. Such are the forces that molded the saying of Antigonus: it comes out of the fire of the struggle against Hellenization; it bears a Hellenistic ring and carries a Jewish challenge to the "atheism" that was raising its head so plausibly. In the light of this it is fitting that he should be the teacher of the Pharisaic "pairs." His Greek name is symbolic of the fact that the emergence and nature of Pharisaism is inseparable from the process of Hellenization which engaged Judaism.

An anti-Epicurean motif has been discovered elsewhere in the ʾAbot and has recently been emphasized by Goldin.[39] That the school gathered around R. Johannan b. Zakkai was engaged not only in legal (halakic) discussions and in esoteric doctrine associated with mysticism and with what is now recognized as proto-Gnosticism within Judaism has long been recognized.[40] But Goldin goes further. The School of Rabbi Johannan b. Zakkai, one of the chief links in the chain of Pharisaic tradition as presented by the ʾAbot, was also engaged in discussion of a strictly philosophical kind, and, in particular, in the exploration of ethical problems which were characteristic of the Hellenistic philosophical schools. Goldin refers to the verse in ʾAbot 2:14 which reads: "R. Eleazer (b. Arak), a pupil of Rabbi Johannan b. Zakkai, said: Be alert to study the Law and know how to make answer to an unbeliever; and know before whom thou toilest and who is thy taskmaster who shall pay thee the reward of thy labour.'' The Hebrew word translated ''unbeliever'' here is literally: *Epicurean*. It occurs also in *m. Sanhedrin* 10:1, where we read: ''And these are they that have no share in the world to come: he that says that there is no resurrection of the dead prescribed in the Law, [and he that says] that the Law is not from Heaven, and an Epicurean. . . .'' Under the term ''Epicurean'' Danby understands ''gentiles and Jews opposed to the rabbinical teachings. It is in no way associated with teachings supposed by the Jews to emanate from the philosopher Epicurus. To Jewish ears it conveys the sense of the root *pakar*, 'be free from restraint,' and so licentious and sceptical.'' Is this view of ''epicurean,'' as signifying ''unbeliever'' in a general sense, acceptable? In fact, in the whole of the Mishna, the term ''epicurean'' occurs only in the two places we have mentioned—ʾ*Abot* 2:14 and *m. Sanh.* 10:1.[42] Does it have the strict meaning of an Epicurean? Later the term came to be used very loosely, in a slovenly way; but Goldin insists that both in ʾ*Abot* 2:14 and *m. Sanh.* 10:1 the term is to be understood in its strictly philosophical sense, and there is no reason to disagree.

In this view, the verse in ʾ*Abot* 2:14 is a direct warning against Epicurean philosophy. Eleazer ben Arak has in mind the refutation of Jews who had succumbed to the philosophy of Epicurus. Among other things, that philosophy argued against the conception of God as either creator or providence—at least as popularly held. Against this R. Eleazer ben Arak roundly asserts ''. . . know before whom thou toilest and who is thy taskmaster who shall pay thee the reward of thy labour. . . .'' There *is* a God who watches and rewards. Here R. Eleazer ben Arak joins hands with the traditional opponents of the Epicureans, the Stoics.

And it is not only with the Epicureans that the ʾ*Abot* is concerned: it also looks, so it has been asserted, to the Stoics. The evidence for the interaction of Stoicism and Judaism has yet to be gathered. Here we are concerned only with traces of this interaction in the ʾ*Abot*. According to Goldin the section in ʾ*Abot* 2:9 is patterned after Stoic usage. After listing the virtues of the various scholars who formed Rabbi Johannan b. Zakkai's school, ʾ*Abot* presents the following:

> He [Rabban Johannan b. Zakkai] said to them: Go forth and see which is the good way to which a man should cleave.
> Rabbi Eliezer replied: A liberal eye.
> Rabbi Joshua replied: A good companion.
> Rabbi Jose replied: A good neighbour.
> Rabbi Simeon replied: Foresight.
> Rabbi Eleazer replied: Goodheartedness.

Said Rabban Johannan b. Zakkai to them: I prefer the answer of Eleazer ben 'Arak, for in his word your words are included.

Rabban Johannan said to them: Go forth and see which is the evil way which a man should shun.

Rabbi Eliezer replied: A grudging eye.

Rabbi Joshua replied: An evil companion.

Rabbi Jose replied: An evil neighbour.

Rabbi Simeon replied: Borrowing and not repaying: for he that borrowth from man is as one who borrows from God, blessed be He, as it is said, "The Wicked man borrows and does not repay, but the just man shows mercy and gives" (Ps 36:21, Heb 37:21).

Rabbi Eleazer replied: Meanheartedness.

Said Rabban Johannan to them: I prefer the answer of Eleazer ben 'Arak, for in his words your words are included.

Goldin[43] points out certain characteristics of the above passage which are noteworthy. First, the scholars around Rabban Johannan do not—as we should expect—discuss the Torah, which was for them, as for all Judaism, the central concern. Secondly, the question asked by Rabban Johannan b. Zakkai is of a peculiar import. He asks: ". . . which is the right way to which a man should cleave (*dabaq*)?" The verb *dabaq* connoted a fervor which—in the light of its use in the OT, as in the rabbinic sources—is unmistakable. But the phrase "cleaving to a way" occurs neither in the OT nor in the Dead Sea Scrolls. Rather the fervor implied by the phrase is reminiscent of philosophical questions concerning the good life which were especially typical of the Hellenistic age. τι πράττων ἄριστα βιώσεται, asks Diogenes Laertius. It is this philosophical question that Rabban Johannan b. Zakkai set before his school. Thirdly, the "form" which the discussion of Johannan's question took is Hellenistic. It corresponds to the summary of Stoic teaching drawn up by Diogenes Laertius 7:92 ff. The summary of Stoic ethics there given (see footnote) first presents the matter positively and then negatively.[44] In Stoic circles this was the pattern of discussion. And it is this pattern that emerges in the school of Rabban Johannan ben Zakkai. Goldin suggests that in Abot 2:9 we have the transcript of an actual session in the school of Rabbi Johannan in which the nature of the good life was philosophically discussed in Stoic terms; hence the absence of any reference to the Torah. But, fourthly, in the reply of Simeon ben Nathanel to the second question, "What is the evil way which a man should shun?," Goldin finds an explicit reference to Plato (*Republic* 1:331*d*). Simeon's reply reads: "Borrowing and not repaying. . . ." This recalls, so Goldin holds, the definition of justice in Plato, "truth-telling and paying back what one has received."

It is difficult not to feel that Goldin has here outstripped the evidence. The structure of the passage from Diogenes Laertius seems too elaborate to be profitably compared with that cited from the ʾA̲bot. The concluding words after both sets of answers in the ʾA̲bot, "for in his words are your words included" (*šebiklal de̲baryw di̲breykem*) are perfectly natural in Judaism and they have no parallel in Diogenes Laertius, so that the formal parallelism suggested by Goldin cannot be strong.

But, while the specific Stoic parallel urged by Goldin may not be entirely convincing, it is difficult not to find in ʾA̲bot 3:1 the reflection of Gnostic questions which became familiar to the church, as to Judaism, in the first and subsequent centuries of the Christian era.[45] The words are from Akabya b. Mahalaleel, a pre-Tannaitic rabbi according to some and an early Tanna according to others. Herford prefers to place him in the time of Hillel. The questions with which Gnostics were concerned have been clarified by Festugière.[46] He summarizes the content of salvation in Hellenistic mysticism in the following terms:

> Le contenu de la gnôse peut se résumer en trois points. C'est une connaissance:
>   (1) de Dieu, particulièrement sous son aspect de Sauveur ($\gamma\nu.\ \theta\varepsilon o\tilde{\upsilon}$);
>   (2) de soi, en tant qu'issu de Dieu et susceptible de retourner à Dieu ($\gamma\nu.\ \dot{\varepsilon}\alpha\upsilon\tau o\tilde{\upsilon}$);
>   (3) des moyens de remontrer à Dieu et du mode de cette remontée ($\gamma\nu.\ \dot{o}\delta o\tilde{\upsilon}$).

In a rough way the saying of R. Akabya in ʾA̲bot 3:1 sets forth "a gnosis"—simple, as opposed to the complex artificialities of Gnosticism, but nonetheless providing what the Gnostic looked for in a Pharisaic mold, purified and sobered by biblical realism. The passage reads:

> Akabya b. Mahalaleel said: Consider three things and thou wilt not fall into the hands of transgression. Know whence thou art come and whither thou art going (2 and 3 in Festugière's list) and before whom thou art about to give account and reckoning (1 in Festugière's list). "Whence thou art come"—from a putrid drop; "and whither thou art going"—to the place of dust, worm and maggot; "and before whom thou art about to give account and reckoning"—before the King of kings, the Holy One, blessed is he.

It is difficult not to see in the above a Pharisaic statement set over against Gnosticism—of however incipient a kind. It is not inconsistent with the point of view expressed in *m. Ḥagiga 2:1*:

> Whoever gives his mind to four things, it were better for him if he had not come into the world—what is above? what is beneath? what was beforetime? and what will be hereafter? And whosoever takes no thought for the honour of his Maker, it were better for him if he had not come into the world.

In this passage from Ḥagiga uncontrolled speculation is condemned; in Àbot 3:1 the sober recognition of man's nature, not reflection upon it, is urged. It is also to be noted that Akabya's designation of God as King of kings, the Holy One, blessed be he, may have been evoked by the necessity to assert the utter supremacy of the Holy One over all intermediaries. But this remains a mere conjecture.[47] Moreover, the Gnosticism to which Akabya offers an alternative was not necessarily Hellenistic, but may have been native to Judaism. In Gnostic studies, as in others, the fluidity between Judaism and Hellenism is increasingly recognized but cannot be pursued here (see n. 28).

There is one other minor detail to note. The phrase "and make a fence around the law" has been taken to reflect Hellenistic ideas in which truth is surrounded by a "fence." Clement of Alexandria[48] makes philosophy a φραγμός to the truth, as was pointed out by Taylor long since. Recently the view that the image of a fence around the Torah has been directly derived from Hellenism has been propounded by Professor Stern of London. This view would have increased probability if the term "fence" included exegetical activity, and if, as Daube[49] long since urged, the rabbinic methods of exegesis were based on Aristotelian models. Unfortunately, Professor Stern's lecture is not available to me, but the concept expressed in terms of "a fence" might surely easily arise in different and independent cultures. No specifically Hellenistic origin for it need be postulated. Moreover, if Frankel be right in tracing the whole triadic saying in Àbot 1:1 to the Persian period,[50] then the emergence of the idea of a "fence" in Judaism precedes the Hellenistic period.

To conclude this section at this point, it can be claimed that, although doubts have been expressed on particular points brought forward above, enough has been written to show that a rereading of the Àbot confirms remarkably the emphasis made by Daube, Lieberman, Morton Smith, and others on the falsity of the traditional antithesis placed between Hellenism and Judaism in the first century. Their mutual interaction is attested in this most Pharisaic of documents. The last item referred to in the previous section suggested that Judaism needed a fence to protect itself. Did it need to protect itself against Christianity? This brings us to the last antithesis with which we shall be concerned—that between Judaism and its daughter faith. To judge from the NT we should expect such an antithesis. Paul's epistles reveal the apostle in dialogue with Judaism, and so too does Matthew's Gospel. I have pointed out elsewhere that the prologue of Matthew may even cast a side glance at the succession list or chain of tradition in Àbot 1:1.[51]

But it is difficult to trace any anti-Christian polemic in the Àbot. Certain passages have been urged to point to Christian claims. First, ʾ*Abot* 3:6 which reads:

R. Halafta b. Dosa of Kefar Hanania (A.D. 80–120) said: If ten men sit together and occupy themselves in the Law, the Divine Presence rests among them, for it is written, *God standeth in the congregation of God.* And whence (do we learn this) even of five? Because it is written, *And hath founded his group upon the earth.* And whence even of three? Because it is written, *He judgeth among the judges.* And whence even of two? Because it is written, *Then they that feared the Lord spake with one another: and the Lord hearkened and heard.* And whence even of one? Because it is written, *In every place where I record my name I will come unto thee and I will bless thee.*

R. Halafta b. Dosa (A.D. 80–120, although Danby places him in the latter half of the second century) was a disciple of R. Meir. Was his saying prompted by the parallel one in Matt 18:20? Did he intend to set the "study of the Torah" over against "the gathering in the Name of Jesus" as the place where the Shekinah was present? This is not impossible; R. Halafta was a Galilean as the name of Kefar Hananiah suggests, but the thought expressed by him may be spontaneous; it need not have been evoked by Christianity.

Secondly, an attack on Paul has been detected in ʾ*Abot* 3:11 in the saying by R. Eleazer of Modiim, who lived at the time of the Bar Kokba revolt. It reads:

If a man profanes the Hallowed Things (1) and despises the set feasts (2) and puts his fellow to shame publicly (3) and makes void the covenant of Abraham our father (4), and discloses meanings in the Law which are not according to the Halakah (5), even though a knowledge of the Law and good works are his, he has no share in the world to come (6).

Item 3 above may have reference to Gnostics who made it their practice to put Jews into awkward predicaments.[52] Item 5 is omitted by some manuscripts, but Geiger, who retains it, understands the phrase to refer "to allegorical interpretations of the Torah not in accordance with the Halakah (that is, the authoritative rulings of the law), with special reference to the Christians who taught that it is only the ideas symbolized by the precepts that mattered, but not their actual observance." Others find here a critical reference to Alexandrian allegorists. Item 6 is referred by Israelstam to Jewish Gnostics. It is not impossible to hear echoes in R. Eleazer's words of charges made against Paul in Acts.[54] But that Paul was explicitly in his mind cannot be asserted. In addition, a document which was deliberately anti–Pauline can hardly have included ʾ*Abot* 3:16

without some caution. This reads according to one text: "All is foreseen, but freedom is given; and the world is judged by grace, and not according to works." Danby accepts the following text: ". . . and the word is judged by grace, yet all is according to the excess of works (that be good or evil)." But the change of this text to the more "orthodox" one given in Danby's translation is understandable.[55] The detection of anti-Paulinism, however, must be carried on with the utmost caution: Taylor favors the reading followed by Danby.[56]

But is there not a direct glance at the teaching of Paul in Ăbot 6:2? It reads:

> R. Joshua b. Levi (A.D. 179–219) said: Every day a divine voice goes forth from Mt Horeb, proclaiming and saying, "Woe to mankind for their contempt of the Law!" For he that occupies himself not in the study of the Law is called "reprobate" (NaZuF), as it is written, *As a golden ring in the snout* (Nezem Zahab b'aF) *of a swine, so is a fair woman without discretion.* And it is written, *And the tables were the work of God, and the writing was the writing of God, graven* (haruth) *upon the tables.* Read not *haruth* but *heruth* (freedom), for thou findest no freeman excepting him that occupies himself in the study of the Law; and he that occupies himself in the study of the Law shall be exalted, for it is written, *From Mattanah to Nahaliel, and from Nahaliel to Banroth.*

It is difficult not to see here a rebuttal of a claim that there could be a freedom apart from the law. Was that claim the one made by Paul in Gal 5:1: "For freedom Christ has set us free; stand fast therefore, and do not submit again to a yoke of slavery"? Or is R. Joshua b. Levi too late to be directly concerned with Paul? All the dicta in Ăbot 6, except that of R. Joshua b. Levi, are *baraithas,* that is, dicta of Tannaitic authorship not included in the Mishna. The date of R. Joshua makes it unlikely that he had Paul in mind. Similarly, while the last saying in Ăbot 6:11*b* by Hananiah b. Akashya (A.D. 140–65), which is also found at the end of *m. Makkot* 3:16, it might be used in discussions against Pauline arguments about the law, it is hardly likely to be directed against Paul, but is a natural expression of Pharisaic sentiment (see Isa 42:21). Ăbot 6:11*b* reads:

> R. Hananiah b. Akashya (A.D. 140–65) said: The Holy One, blessed is he, was minded to grant merit to Israel; therefore hath he multiplied for them the Law and commandments, as it is written, *It pleased the Lord for his righteousness' sake to magnify the Law and make it honourable.*

The translation of the last words in Ăbot 2:13—"And be not wicked in thine own sight"—might suggest a dismissal of such thoughts as are expressed, for example, in Rom 7:18. But again, apart from the precise meaning of the words so rendered by Danby, there were others besides Paul who expressed despair.[57]

We are now in a position to assess the degree to which the 'Abot reveals an anti-Christian concern. If anti-Paulinism be present at all in the passages indicated above, it is so by implication only. It is certainly safe to emphasize the absence of any *explicit* anti-Paulinism and anti-Christianity in the 'Abot. Pharisaism was aware of the danger of Christianity to its own life, but in the 'Abot, where Pharisaism reflects upon itself, this awareness does not obviously intrude. Pharisaism had its own life to live, its own inner dialogue and concern that the 'Abot testifies. But, as we have seen, this very concern involved it, if not in explicit anti-Christian polemic, in adaptations to change and especially to Hellenism and the vicissitudes of its own history. And before we turn to the relevance of what has been written above for NT studies, it is well to consider what light the 'Abot throws on the way in which the tradition responded to challenge.

Exigencies of space make it impossible to deal with this at length; the briefest statement must suffice. Two things stand out.

First, the tradition did change to meet challenge. New occasions taught new duties and the most basic of statements were modified to meet new circumstances. The best example of this is supplied by the very first maxim given in 'Abot 1:1: "The men of the Great Synagogue said three things: Be deliberate in judgment, raise up many disciples and make a fence around the Torah." By a comparison of 'Abot de Rabbi Nathan 1 and 2 Finkelstein shows that the original form of the maxim probably was: "Be deliberate in judgment; make a hedge about your words; and *appoint many Sages*." "This was addressed not to a supreme legislative body like the Sanhedrin which in later times claimed authority to add restrictions to those mentioned in Scripture. It is addressed to individual scholars." It is "the directions of the Great Assembly to local scholars and judges." But "Rabbi Judah the Patriarch or one of his predecessors, seeking authority for the claim of the Sanhedrin that it could add new prohibitions as 'hedges' to the Law transformed the original maxim into its current form. It was no longer a command to 'make a hedge about your words'; it became a command to 'make a hedge about the Law.'"[58] This explains both the change in the order of the maxim and of its content.

The above example must suffice here to indicate how flexible was even the most honored maxim: the tradition was pliable.[59]

But second, this pliability must be carefully distinguished from a free creativity. Along with this readiness to change the law as time demanded, there was also a tenacity in holding on to the deposit of the tradition. The scholar who was most praised was the one who held best to the tradition in its exact form.[60] There is no suggestion of an emergent tradition, that is, a newly created tradition which could be foisted onto a rabbi or introduced by a rabbi at will. Rather, words uttered by authorities are very carefully treasured, although they could be modified to suit new conditions. But such modification was always a reinterpretation of a given tradition not the creation of a new tradition. Fixity and pliability are the mark of the tradition in the Àbot.

In the above three antitheses, often assumed, have been found to be absent in the Àbot. This has a bearing on the understanding of tradition—the written memory of the church—in the NT. Our study evokes the following reflections.

First, the antithesis between law and prophet imposed on the OT and Judaism with which we have dealt above was sometimes carried over *mutatis mutandis* into NT studies in several ways. The Spirit-filled communities of the Pauline missions have been contrasted with the more legalistic churches of the Jerusalem wing.[61] Or, again, various ministries in the churches of the NT have been set over against each other. Harnack,[62] for example, distinguished between a charismatic ministry belonging to the whole of the primitive church, consisting of apostles, prophets, teachers, who were of direct divine appointment, and the localized, administrative ministry of bishops and deacons. The tradition in Judaism holds such oppositions—prophecy and law—together in a living tension: it reminds us not to succumb to convenient antitheses which are neat on paper but deny the rich variety of life in the early Christian movement also.

Second, the breakdown of the old rigid antithesis between the Hellenistic and rabbinic has its relevance for NT studies in which the separation of Hellenistic and Semitic elements has often been indulged too freely. The presence of Hellenistic elements in a tradition was almost automatically held to point to a non-Palestinian and late milieu.[63] The Àbot witnesses as does so much else to the Hellenization of Judaism itself and, therefore, to the extreme difficulty if not impossibility of drawing any certain conclusions about the date and provenance of tradition in terms of its Hellenistic features or of the absence of such.

And, third, the combination of a rigid adherence to the deposit of tradition together with readiness to adapt it has an important bearing on our understanding of the tradition preserved in the Gospels. It has been frequently asserted that the early Christian communities had a role not only in the transmission of the tradition but in its formulation and, indeed, its creation. *If it be legitimate to understand the tradition in the gospels at all in the light of that found in the* 'Abot, then greater weight should be given to the preservation of a given deposit of tradition which was adapted and modified by the church as it faced new challenges rather than to a creating of "tradition" *de novo* by the communities. The 'Abot would lead us to expect not that there was a wholesale creation of sayings by the primitive communities which were foisted onto the earthly Jesus but that the church inherited and preserved sayings of Jesus which floated in the tradition, modified them for its own purposes, and, again, ascribed them to Jesus in their new form. The recognition of the original form may not be easy, but it is not always impossible.[64]

The 'Abot, if its evidence be allowed as pertinent, would, then, predispose us to a certain degree of conservatism in the approach to the tradition of the sayings of Jesus. But it also reveals something else. Modern scholars in their approach to the Gospels have been much exercised by the difficulty of treating them as historical documents, so overlaid do they seem to be with interpretation, the "historical" data being subordinated to theological interests. But to a reader coming to the Gospels from the 'Abot the exact opposite is the case. Apart from the chain of tradition in 'Abot 1 and a very brief section dealing with Rabbi Johannan b. Zakkai and his disciples in 2:8, the interest in the 'Abot centers *entirely* on what individual rabbis *said*. There is no biographical or historical interest. The 'Abot concentrates on *sayings*. To turn to the Gospels is at once to recognize their "historical," "biographical" orientation. Here what Jesus *did* counts, not only what he said. The differences between the synoptic Gospels and that of John now appears to lie precisely in their historical dimension. The early Christians not only remembered what Jesus said but what he did: they concentrated on his works as much as on his words. It is this personal, historical reference in the Gospels that a rereading of the 'Abot again unmistakably brings forth. The memory of him—not only of his words—informs the tradition and sets it apart from the rabbinic. The significance of this fact for the understanding of the tradition cannot be pursued here, but it is not to be overlooked.[65]

3
*Reflections on the Territorial Dimension of Judaism**

We shall here attempt to assess the nature and place within Judaism of the doctrine which in various ways asserts there is a special relationship (later to be described) among the God of Israel, the people of Israel, and the Land of Israel. Is that relationship primary or secondary, dispensable or indispensable? Was the territorial doctrine of Judaism one which could be ignored as necessity dictated, simply accidental and peripheral, or an aspect of Judaism without which it would cease to be itself?†

At first encounter the question would seem to be easily open to strict historical investigation and an unequivocal answer. Sources for the understanding of Judaism are abundant: the practice of Jews as it bears upon *Eretz Israel* has been and is open to public and private scrutiny. One would have thought that the proposed question could long ago have been settled. In the course of Jewish history and especially in this century, however, certain unavoidable factors have impinged upon Judaism which have both clouded and clarified the issue and compelled caution.

THE MARKED THEOLOGICAL TRADITION

Let us begin with the doctrine itself. Despite the vicissitudes of Jewish history, the sacred documents on which religious Jews have rested—the Tanak, the Mishna, the Midrashim and the Talmud—the liturgies which they have constantly celebrated, and the observances which they have kept across the centuries all point to The Land as an essential aspect of Judaism. The reader is referred to our work on *The Gospel and The Land;*

---

* My friend Markus Barth has long corresponded and discussed with me this and similar themes. This tribute is offered to him with deep gratitude for his personal stimulus and for his enthusiasm for the continued dialogue between Christians and Jews.
† We use the form "The Land" for *Eretz Israel* because the Sages have always so referred to it. Two Hebrew terms have to be distinguished: *'adamah*, soil, land, earth, and *'eretz* which while not always to be clearly distinguished from *'adamah*, bears also the meaning of a politically defined territory. It is with *'eretz* in this latter sense that we are concerned, that is, with the Land of Israel as territory. The boundaries of the promised land are never precisely defined. As does the Talmud, we use the form the Land for the promised land (*'eretz*) of Israel.

Early Christianity and Jewish Territorial Doctrine (Berkeley: University of California Press, 1974) for a fuller treatment of the evidence.[1] Here we merely summarize the main points of the evidence in defense of the position indicated.

The Evidence of the Classical Sources of Judaism

It would be impossible within the limits of this article to examine the different ways in which the importance of the doctrine of The Land emerges in the Tanak. It finds its fundamental expression in the Pentateuch,[2] but is also abundantly reflected in the other documents of the Tanak. Two elements in the understanding of The Land are central. First, The Land is regarded as promised, or more accurately, as sworn by Yahweh to the people of Israel. The history of the tradition concerning Yahweh's promise, on which there is no widespread critical agreement, is complex. The most probable development seems to be from the recognition of a promise of a territorial patrimony to Abraham, to that of a more extensive territory to the people of Israel, probably under the impact of Davidic imperial ambitions. Alongside the belief in the promise, the conviction prevailed that this promised land belonged especially to Yahweh. Not only did it necessarily belong to him, as did all lands which he had called into being, but it was his peculiar possession to give to his own people: the election of the people was bound up with his promise to give his own land to them.[3] Out of the combination (nay—fusion)[4] of the three elements which were involved in the promise—God, the people, and The Land—there emerged what has to be regarded as an essential belief of religious Jews of the first century and later, that is, of the indissolubility or eternity of the connection between these three realities.

This belief comes to clearest expression in the rabbinic sources, the Mishna, the Midrashim, and the Talmud. This is remarkable and significant because across many centuries the sages, the authors and preservers of those sources, for very good reasons had increasingly suspected any disturbing concentration on hopes for a return to The Land in any messianic context as a delusion and snare likely to distract their people from the essential task of living obedience to the Torah. As we shall later insist, they had accepted the need to acquiesce in the exiled life and to cooperate in foreign lands with foreign rulers. But paradoxically, they continued to shower their praises on The Land, emphatically expressing their concern for it, and recognizing the ultimate indissolubility of Israel's connection with it. The initial stimulus for this concern has been especially connected with the destruction of The Land by the Romans in the war from 66 to

70 c.e. Conditions in Palestine after 70 c.e. were economically very difficult. As a result there developed an increasing tendency for Jews to emigrate from Palestine to neighboring countries, especially Syria. The need to encourage Jews to remain in The Land, and not to depart from areas in it where they were permitted to live, was so urgent that the Pharisaic leaders adopted a policy of extolling the virtues of The Land and encouraging settlement in it.[5] But important as they were, economic factors are not to be regarded as the sole or even main reason for the emergence of the doctrine with which we are concerned. As we have indicated, the roots of the emphasis on The Land are deep in the Tanak. The Tannaitic and other sources build on the Scriptures even though they respond also to economic and political realities. They point to the significance of The Land in the most unambiguous way. There is a kind of "umbilical cord" between Israel and The Land.[6] It is no accident that one-third of the Mishna, the Pharisaic legal code, is connected with The Land. Nine-tenths of the first order of the Mishna, *Zeraim* (Seeds), of the fifth order, *Kodashim* (Hallowed Things), and of the sixth order, *Tohoroth* (Cleannesses), deal with laws concerning The Land, and there is much of the same in the other parts of the Mishna. This is no accident, because the connection between Israel and The Land was not fortuitous, but part of the divine purpose or guidance, as was the Law itself. The choice of Israel and the Temple and of The Land was deliberate, the result of Yahweh's planning. The connection between Yahweh, Israel, The Land, Sinai, the Temple is primordial: it is grounded in a necessity of the divine purpose and is, therefore, inseverable (*Leviticus Rabbah* 13:2). And it is no wonder that the rabbis heaped upon The Land terms of honor and endearment. For them The Land of Israel is called simply *Hâ-âretz*, The Land; all countries outside it are *ḥûtz lâ-âretz*, outside The Land. In *b. Berakot 5a* we read: "It has been taught: R. Simeon b. Yohai says: The Holy One, blessed be He, gave Israel three precious gifts, and all of them were given only through sufferings. These are: The Torah, the Land of Israel, and the World to Come. . . ."

We have seen that behind the glorification of The Land stood passages in the Scriptures. But, in addition to this, two factors could not but increasingly stamp The Land upon the consciousness of Israel. The first is that the Law itself, by which Jews lived, was so tied to The Land that it could not but recall The Land. As we have already stated, one-third of the Mishna deals with The Land and all the agricultural laws in it, as those of Scripture itself do. Consider Lev 19:23, 23:10 and 22, 25:2 and Deut 26:1. These verses make it clear that the agricultural laws are to apply "in The Land." Further, only in Palestine could there be cities of refuge, which were so important in the civil law (Num 35:9f., Deut 4:41f., 19:1f.). True, there are laws not contingent upon The Land; and the distinction between these and their opposite was clearly recognized. But the reward for the observance of the laws was "life in The Land," as is implied in *m. Qidduśin* 1:9–10. The Law itself, therefore, to use current terminology, might be regarded as an effective symbol of The Land: it served as a perpetual call to The Land.

But, secondly, precisely because it was The Land to which the Law most applied, The Land gained in sanctity. In *m. Qidd.* 1:9–10—in the references to The Land, the walled cities of The Land, the wall of Jerusalem, the Temple Mount, the Rampart, the Court of Women, the Court of the Israelites, etc.—it is the connection with an enactment of the Law that determines the degree of its holiness. And, for our purposes especially, it is noteworthy that it is the applicability of the Law to The Land in 1:6 that assures its special holiness. The implication is that Jewish sanctity is only fully possible in The Land: outside The Land only strictly personal laws can be fulfilled, that is, the moral law, sexual law, Sabbath law, circumcision, dietary laws, etc. Of necessity, outside The Land territorial laws have to be neglected. The exiled life is, therefore, an emaciated life, even though, through suffering, it atones. A passage in *b. Soṭa* 14a expresses this point of view in dealing with Moses' failure to enter The Land. Moses, outside The Land, is a suffering servant who atones.

In the light of the above, it is not surprising that both the gift of prophecy—the gift of the Holy Spirit—and the gift of resurrection of the dead were by some connected with The Land. For example, *Mekilta Pisḥa* I reveals both the affirmation of Israel as the only land fit for prophecy and the dwelling of the Shekinah, and efforts made to deal with the difficulties such a position confronted: for example, the fact that Yahweh had appeared outside The Land.

Again, in the view of some rabbis, the resurrection was to take place first in The Land, and the benefits of The Land in death are many (*Genesis Rabbah* 96:5). Some urged that those who died outside The Land would not rise: but even an alien (Canaanitish) slave girl who dwelt in The Land might expect to share in the resurrection. (*b. Ketubot* 111a). At the end of the second century Rabbi Meir, at his death, required that his remains should be cast into the sea off the Palestinian coast, lest he be buried in foreign soil. There is no space or necessity here to enlarge further. The desire to die in The Land, to possess the soil, to make pilgrimages to it, all these manifestations of attachment to The Land history attests. Enough has been written to indicate that the primary documents of Judaism—the

Tanak and Tannaitic Midrashim, and the Talmud—are unequivocal in their recognition that The Land is essential to the true fulfillment of the life to which Israel was called.

The Liturgy and the Observance

The liturgical practice of the Synagogue points to the same witness. Throughout the centuries, beginning with the fall of Jerusalem in 70 C.E., the conscious cultivation of the memory of The Land, concentrated in Jerusalem and the Temple, has continued in Judaism. The rabbis at Jamnia, in demanding that the *Tefillah* or *Shemoneh Esreh* should be said three times a day, morning, afternoon, and evening (*m. Ber.* 4:1ff.), had in mind, among other things, the perpetual remembrances of Jerusalem and The Land. The *Shemoneh Esreh* for the morning and afternoon service corresponded to the morning and afternoon daily whole-offerings in the Temple. There was no time fixed for the evening *Shemoneh Esreh*, but on Sabbaths and Festivals the *Shemoneh Esreh* was to be said four times (there being demanded an additional Tefillah corresponding to the "Addition Offering" presented on those days in the ancient Temple). Three times daily, then, the Jew was required to pray; among other things, he was required to repeat the Fourteenth Benediction (dated by Dugmore in 168–165 B.C.E.), the Sixteenth (possibly pre-Maccabean), and the Eighteenth (40–70 C.E.). These read as follows:

> Be merciful, O Lord our God, in Thy great mercy, towards Israel Thy people, and towards Jerusalem Thy city, and towards Zion the abiding place of Thy glory, and towards Thy temple and Thy habitation, and towards the kingdom of the house of David, the righteous anointed one. Blessed art Thou, O Lord God of David, the builder of Jerusalem. *Benediction* 14.

> Accept [us], O Lord our God, and dwell in Zion; and may Thy servants serve Thee in Jerusalem. Blessed art Thou, O Lord, whom in reverent fear we serve [or, worship]. *Benediction* 16.

> Bestow Thy peace upon Israel Thy people and upon Thy city and upon Thine inheritance, and bless us, all of us together. Blessed art Thou, O Lord, who makest peace. *Benediction* 18.

That there was a deliberate concern with Jerusalem appears from the text in *m. Ber.* 4:1ff., where the rules concerning the *Shemoneh Esreh*, indicated above, are set forth, and where *m. Ber.* 4:5 states that, according to R. Joshua (80–120 C.E.):

> If [a man] was riding on an ass [when the time for the prayer is upon him] he should dismount [to say the Tefillah: Danby]. If he cannot dismount he should turn his face [toward Jerusalem]; and if he cannot turn his face, he should direct his heart toward the Holy of Holies.

The centrality of The Land is clear. The same is also emphasized in *Num. Rab.* 23:7 on Num 34:2. The deliberate recalling of the Temple and, thereby, of Jerusalem and The Land, in the liturgy also appears from *m. Roš Haššana* 4:1–3 and *b. Baba Bathra* 60*b*.

Again other elements in the Jewish liturgy came to be *zêker leḥorebbân*, that is, in memory of the destruction. For three weeks of sorrow, ending on the ninth day of the month of Ab, which is given over entirely for twenty-four hours to fasting, Jews annually recall the destruction of their land. So much has that event become the quintessence of the suffering of Jewry that the ninth of Ab is recognized as a day on which disasters recurred again and again to the Jewish people. Connected with it, significantly, was the decree that the fathers should not enter the promised land. The passage in *b. Taʿanit* 29*a*, which states this, cannot easily be dated. But it is traced to an unknown Rabbi whose words are explained by R. Hama b. Hananiah (279–320 C.E.). The pertinent passage is in *m. Taʿan.* 4:6–7. As a matter of history only the fall of Betar (the Beth Tor of the text), the last stronghold of Bar Kokba, captured by the Romans in 135 C.E., possibly occurred on the ninth of Ab. The first Temple was burned on the seventh of Ab (2 Kgs 25:8–9) or on the tenth of that month (Jer 52:12); the second Temple fell on the tenth (see the dictionaries). The essential feature of the liturgy for the ninth of Ab (which is the only twenty-four-hour fast, apart from the Day of Atonement) was the reading of Lamentations and dirges. Later, on the fast of the ninth of Ab, an addition which concentrates on Jerusalem still further was made to the service. The prayer, as used today, begins with the words:

> O Lord God, comfort the mourners of Zion;
> Comfort those who grieve for Jerusalem.

It ends with:

> Praised are You, who comforts Zion;
> Praised are You, who rebuilds Jerusalem.

So far, in showing how the sentiment for The Land remained powerfully active in Judaism after 70 C.E., we have mostly adduced materials from the Haggadah and the liturgy of Rabbinic Judaism. There was also a more specifically halakic approach to the question of The Land. The ramifications of this development we are unfortunately not competent to trace. We can only refer to two items. In the Jerusalem Talmud, in *Kilʾayim* 7:5 (Krotoshin 31a, line 32) (Venice, line 25), *ʿOrla* 1:2 (ed. Krotoshin 61a, line 11) (Venice, line 9), there is a law which is quoted as giving to Israel, under Jewish law, a legal right to The Land. The law is translated by Lieberman as: "Though soil cannot be stolen, a man can forfeit his right to this soil by giving up hope of ever regaining it." The argument is that "Israel" "never for a moment gave up hope of regaining the soil of Palestine. Never did they renounce their right to Palestine and never have they ceased claiming it in their prayers and in their teachings. It is on this foundation that [Jews] now claim that Eretz Israel belongs to [them]" (S. Lieberman, *Proceedings of the Rabbinical Assembly of America*, Vol. 12, 1949). Not unrelated to this law is that of *ḥᵃzākāh* (prescription) in which the legal right of Israel to The Land was sought. (See *b. Bat.* 28*a*, and notes in the Soncino translation for *ḥᵃzākāh*.) But how early such attempts were and how significant in the discussion of the relationship between Israel and Eretz Israel in the period of our concern we cannot determine. The history of the halakic understanding of that relationship lies beyond the scope of this study, as does the relative place of Haggadah and Halakah in Judaism. (The debate on this question is clarified in J. Neusner, *The Journal of Religion* 59/1 (1979): 71–86, especially 83–84. There Neusner urges that "Halakah is Judaism's primary expression of Theology." Heschel would qualify this.)

Be that as it may be, it is in the Haggadah and the liturgy that the full force of the sentiment for The Land is to be felt. It cannot properly be seen except through Jewish eyes, nor felt except through Jewish words, such as those so powerfully uttered by Abraham Heschel in a book, *Israel: An Echo of Eternity* (New York: Farrar, Straus & Giroux, 1969), which is more a lyrical outburst than a critical study, and in A. Néher's moving essay, "Israël, terre mystique de l'Absolu" in *L'Existence Juive* (Paris, 1962).

So far we have referred to the evidence of the classical sources of Judaism.[7] The same theological conviction that there is an inseverable connection between Israel, The Land and its God continued to be cherished throughout the medieval period and down to the modern. A rough division has been drawn between two periods. The first stretches up to the last revolt of Jews in the Roman Empire in the hope of reestablishing a Jewish state, which followed upon the imposition of harsh anti-Jewish statutes under Justinian (483–565 C.E.), and later the brief three-year reign of Nehemiah, a messianic figure, in Jerusalem from 614 to 617 C.E. It is legitimate to recognize up to that time a living, if intermittent, hope and violent activity directed toward the actual political return of The Land to Israel. From then on, especially after the Arab conquest of The Land in 638 and the building up of the Mosque of Omar on the site of the Temple (in 687–691, a mosque that was to be a center for the Islamic faith), there was, it has been suggested, a change. From then on Jewish devotion to The Land came to express itself for a long period not so much in political activity for the reestablishment of the State of Israel as in voluntary individual pilgrimages and immigrations to The Land.[8] But the division suggested between the two periods indicated must not be made watertight. On the one hand, in the earlier period the Tannaitic and Amoraic sages were wary of political attempts to re-establish the kingdom of Israel in its own land. On the other hand, in the Middle Ages, there was much apocalyptic-messianic speculation and probably much activity aimed at such a reestablishment: the history of this has been largely lost, so that its full strength must remain conjectural even if likely. The extent to which apocalyptic-messianism persisted, to break out finally in Sabbatianism in the seventeenth century, is only now being recognized, under the influence of the work of Gershom Scholem.[9] It fed into the Zionist movement of our times. What we can be certain of is that *Eretz Israel*, as an object of devotion and intense and religious concern continued to exercise the imagination of Jews after the fall of Jerusalem in 70 C.E. and after the Arab conquest: it remained part of the communal consciousness of Jews. In this connection, two facts need to be borne in mind. First, the devotion to The Land, to which we refer, is not to be simply equated with the imaginative notions of other peoples about an ideal land—such as the "Elysium" of Homer, the Afallon of Celtic mythology, the Innisfree of Yeats. Rather it was concentrated on an actual land with a well-known history, a land known to be barren and rugged and to offer no easy life although it was transfused because of its chosenness to be Yahweh's own and Israel's as an inheritance from him. Secondly, the influence of the familiar or customary division of History at the advent of Christ into two periods, B.C. and A.D.,[10] has often tended to create the unconscious assumption among Gentiles that after the first century, Jews *as a people* ceased to have a common history.[11] No less a scholar than Martin Noth saw Israel's history as having come to a ghastly end with the Bar Kokba revolt.[12] But the Jews continued as a people, not simply as a conglomerate of individuals, after that tragic event. The Talmud, the primary document of Judaism in the Middle Ages and afterward to the present time, concerns itself with the way in which the people of Israel should walk. The Talmud has a communal national reference in its application of the Torah to the actualities of the Jews' existence. Its contents, formation, and preservation presuppose the continuance of the self-conscious unity of the people of Israel. It is this that explains the character of the Talmud: it adds

Gemara to Mishna and Rashi (1040–1105 c.e.) to both, to make the tradition of the past relevant to the present. It is realistically involved with the life of the Jewish people over a thousand years of its history.[13]

And in the devotional life of the Jewish community the relationship to The Land remained central.[14] To trace the various expressions of devotion to The Land among Jews across the centuries is beyond our competence. The most noteworthy is that of pilgrimage. The law demanded that every male Israelite should make a pilgrimage to Jerusalem three times a year: at Passover, the Feast of Weeks, and Tabernacles (Exod 23:17; Deut 16:16). During the Second Temple period even Jews of the Diaspora sought to observe this demand. (See, for example, *m. Ta'an* 1:3; J.W. 6:9; *'Abot* 5:4.) After the destruction of the Temple, pilgrimages especially to the Wailing Wall became occasions for mourning: there were pilgrimages throughout the Middle Ages to other holy places.[15] Individual Jews witness to this, a most famous expression coming in the works of the "God-intoxicated" or "God-kissed" Jehudah Halevi, a Spanish physician born in Toledo in 1086. At the age of fifty, he left his beloved Spain on a perilous pilgrimage to Zion. He died, possibly before reaching Jerusalem, but not before expressing his love for The Land and Zion in unforgettable terms such as:

> My heart is in the east, and I in the
> uttermost west—
> How can I find savor in food? How shall
> it be sweet to me?
> How shall I render my vows and my bonds,
> while yet
> Zion lieth beneath the fetter of Edom,
> and I in Arab chains?
> A light thing would it seem to me
> to leave all the good things of Spain—
> Seeing how precious in mine eyes it is
> to behold the dust of the desolate
> sanctuary.[16]

It was not only single, individual pilgrims who sought The Land but groups of communities, as in the case of Rabbi Meir of Rothenburg who in 1286 c.e. sought to lead a great number of Jews from the area of the Rhine to Israel. Later, in 1523, a messianic movement which aimed at a return to The Land was led by David Reuveni and attracted the interest of communities in Egypt, Spain, and Germany. The living Jewish concern to establish an earthly kingdom in Jerusalem may have contributed to the formulation of the seventeenth article of the Confession of Augsburg of

1530.[17] The justification for such a concern was made luminously clear
in the astounding response to the Sabbatian movement from the Yemen
to Western Europe.[18]

These data to which historians point us cannot be ignored. The relative
weight which should be given to the purely *religious* interest in The Land
which led individuals and groups to journey to Israel from a desire to
experience the mystical or spiritual power of The Land, as over against
a political concern to escape and to right the wrongs of exile, we are not
competent to assess. Certainly many pious Jews had no directly political
concern: their sole aim was to recognize that in The Land a relationship
to the eternal was possible as nowhere else. A striking illustration of
spiritual concentration on The Land is provided by Rabbi Naḥman of
Bratzlov (1772–80), who journeyed to Israel. He asserted that what he
had known *before* that journey was insignificant. *Before* there had been
confusion; after "he held the law whole." But all he had desired was
direct contact with The Land. This he achieved by simply stepping ashore
at Haifa. He desired to return immediately. (Under pressure he stayed
and visited Tiberias, but never even went up to Jerusalem.) Again, the
celebrated Maharal of Prague (Rabbi Yehuda Liwa of Loew—Ben Be-
zalel, 1515–1609) understood the nature and role of nations to be ordained
by God, as part of the natural order. Nations were intended to cohere
rather than to be scattered. Nevertheless, he did not urge a political reestablishment of a State of Israel in The Land: that he left to God. Exile
no less than restoration was in His will; the latter *would* come in his good
time, but only then. (The promise of The Land would endure eternally:
return was ultimately assured [Lev 26:44–45].)

It is due to the kind of devotion we have indicated that, despite the
very real geographical and political obstacles, at no time since the first
century has The Land of Israel been wholly without a Jewish presence,
however diminished. The numbers of Jews living in The Land throughout
the centuries have been very variously estimated, but James Parkes
rightly insisted that Jews in Palestine across the centuries were forgotten
by historians. It is certain that in the nineteenth century, first under the
influence of Rabbi Elijah, Ben Solomon Salman of Vilna, known as the
Vilna Gaon (1720–1797), a number of parties of Jews, soon to be joined
by many others, went to Safed in 1808 and 1809. These sought not simply
contact with The Land of which they claimed that "Even in its ruins none
can compare with it,"[19] but permanent settlement. Regarding themselves
as representatives of all Jews, they assumed the right to appeal to other
Jews for aid and reinforcement. Some—as in the case of Rabbi Akiba

Schlessinger of Preissburg (1832–1922)—were driven to go to The Land by the realization of the increasing impossibility of living according to the Torah in Western society, which was becoming increasingly secular. For such The Land became an escape and a refuge from modernism and secularism, a bulwark for the preservation of the religious tradition. After these early settlements to which we have referred, there were other efforts by religious Jews to re-enter The Land whose history cannot be traced here. We must simply note that the Zionist movement, despite its strongly "nationalistic," socialistic, and political character is not to be divorced from this devotion to The Land.[20] We shall deal with this later.

AN INESCAPABLE HISTORICAL DIVERSITY

We have sought in the preceding pages to do justice to the theological role of territory in Judaism. Jewish theology as revealed in its major witnesses points to The Land as of the essence of Judaism. In strictly theological terms, the Jewish faith could be defined as "a fortunate blend" of a people, a land, and their God. But this view has been criticized because in any blend an item may be lost, and in the particular blend referred to, the essential and distinctive significance of The Land, it has been claimed, could be lost. As in discussions of the Trinity the personal identity of each member is carefully preserved and not simply "blended," so in our understanding of Judaism the distinct or separable significance of The Land must be fully recognized. Judaism held to an election of a people and of its election to a particular land: Werblowsky rightly speaks of "une vocation, spirituelle à la géographie."[21]

But Jewish theology has had, like the Christian, to find ways of coming to terms with history. In this section we shall indicate certain actualities of Jewish history which must bear upon any answer to the question of the place of The Land in Judaism.

In the first place, historically the term "Judaism" itself cannot be understood as representing a monolithic faith in which there has been a simplistic uniformity of doctrine either demanded or imposed or recognized about The Land, as about other elements of belief. Certainly this was so at all periods and in all sections of the Jewish community before 70 C.E. And, despite the overwhelming dominance of the Rabbinic form of Judaism, the history of the Jews since that date, although not to the same degree, reveals the same fissiparous, amorphous, and unsystematized doctrinal character. The concept of an adamant, uniform "orthodox" Judaism, which was not stirred by dissident movements and ideas, and by mystical, messianic yearnings which expressed themselves outside of or in opposition to the main, strictly rabbinic, tradition, is no longer tenable.[22] To define the place of *Eretz Israel* in Judaism requires the frank recognition that that place has changed or, more accurately, has received different emphases among various groups and at different times. However persistent some views of and attachment to The Land have been, and however uniform the testimony of the classical sources, there has not been one unchangeable, essential doctrine universally and uniformly recognized by the whole of Judaism. In the Middle Ages a controversy which circled around Maimonides (Rambam) (1135–1204) is illuminating. In his *Dalalat al Harin*, translated into English as the *Guide to the Perplexed*, the Great Eagle never concerned himself directly with "The Land." Although he was so concerned in his commentary on the Mishna, his silence about The Land in the *Guide* caused dismay and dispute among the Rabbis. Naḥmanides (1194–1270) was led to criticize the Great Eagle by insisting that there was a specific *mitzwah* to settle in The Land, a *mitzwah* which Maimonides had ignored: Naḥmanides notes its absence in Maimonides' *Sepher Ha-Mitzwoth*.[23] In modern times Reform Judaism in the United States, anxious to come to terms with Western culture, was careful to avoid any emphasis on any particularistic elements in Judaism which would set Jews apart from their Christian neighbors. Until very recently, when external and internal pressures made themselves felt, the doctrine of The Land tended to be ignored or spiritualized. It was an embarrassment.

The demotion of The Land, along with the messianic idea with its disturbing potentialities, was no less evident in the liberal Judaism of nineteenth century Europe. How far the confused and confusing embarrassment with The Land went there, even among Jewish theologians, appears from Hermann Cohen. In 1880 he claimed that Judaism was already in process of forming a "cultural, historical union with Protestantism."[24] It is not surprising that he could write such paradoxical words as the following: "*The loss of the national state is already conditioned by messianism. But this is the basis of the tragedy of Jewish peoplehood in all its historic depth.* How can a people exist and fulfill its messianic task if it is deprived of the common human protection afforded by a state to its people? And yet, just this is the situation of the Jewish people, *and thus it must needs be the meaning of the history* of the Jews, if indeed this meaning lies in messianism"[25] (our italics). Cohen was concerned with the state and Judaism, but by implication he here not only questioned the messianic destiny of Israel in its own land but, even if he still recognized it as a reality, he so domesticated that destiny in his Western Europe that it bore little resemblance to the dynamism of the messianism expressed in previous Jewish history. Cohen's "messianism" eradicated the Davidic Messiah and the hope of a kingdom of God on earth—and with this any hope for The Land. That the Reform and liberal Judaism in the United States and Europe have recently reintroduced an emphasis on The Land, in response to contemporary events which they could not ignore, cannot obliterate their earlier nonterritorial or antiterritorial attitude. Not unrelated to this discussion in the Reform and liberal Judaism, though not directly connected with those movements, is the insistence by such figures as Aḥad Ha-ʿAm (1856–1927) that Jews first needed to devote themselves to spiritual renewal not to the occupation of a territory. Aḥad Ha-ʿAm founded a select and secret society in 1899 "dedicated to the notion that moral and cultural preparation had to precede the material salvation of the Jews."[26]

Secondly, it is necessary to recognize that the territorial theology with which we are concerned could not but gain increasing attention and therefore emphasis among recent students of Judaism because of the pervasive influence of the Zionist movement. The ascribing of a theological concern with The Land to Jews who entertain no definable Jewish theology or even reject the tradition of their fathers has become insidiously easy because of the Zionist climate within which so much of modern Jewry lives. The temptation to this ascription has understandably been reinforced by understandable sympathy toward the justification of this doctrine which the suffering of Jews in modern Europe so imperatively calls forth.

But sympathy by itself does not necessarily lead to historical truth. At this point it is well to emphasize the complexity and interpenetration of the many forces which combined to initiate the Zionist movement. It held together apparently irreconcilable points of view in a living tension. Any neat dichotomies between religious and political factors in Zionism are falsifications of their rich and mutually accommodating diversity. To read Gershom Scholem's autobiographical pages[27] is to be made aware of the impossibility of presenting clean, clear lines in any picture of the Zionist movement. But this much is certain: the territorial theology of Judaism should not be directly ascribed (the qualifying adverb is important) to the many nonreligious Jews who played a most significant part in Zionist history. The Zionist movement, which has played so prominent a role in our time, can be effectively dated as initiated by the Congress of Basel in 1897. It grew thereafter until, in 1948, after an abeyance of almost twenty centuries, there emerged the State of Israel. But the role of Jewish territorial doctrine and sentiment in the movement has to be carefully assessed: it can easily be exaggerated. At first it was possible for some of the leading Zionists to contemplate the establishment of a state outside The Land altogether—in Uganda, in Argentina, in newly conquered Russian territories in Asia, in Asiatic Turkey, and in North America.[28] The often silent but almost ubiquitous presence of the religious tradition, with its concentration on *Eretz Israel* caused them to change their minds and made the choice of that land as the Jewish homeland inevitable. Herzl, like other Zionist secularists, was compelled to recognize this.

But Zionism remained an expression not only, and probably not even chiefly, of the theological territorial attachment of Judaism, but even more of the nationalist and socialistic spirit of the nineteenth century. In this sense it is a typical product of that century. An examination of the history of Zionism makes its specifically religious motivation less significant than an uncritical emphasis on territorial theology would lead one to expect. Gershom Scholem, in reply to an article by Yeuda Bourla, a novelist who died in 1970, wrote:

> I . . . am opposed, like thousands of other Zionists . . . to mixing up religious and political concepts. *I categorically deny that Zionism is a messianic movement and that it is entitled to use religious terminology to advance its political aims.*
>
> The redemption of the Jewish people, which as a Zionist I desire, is in no way identical with the religious redemption I hope for the future. I am not prepared as a Zionist to satisfy political demands or yearnings that exist in a strictly nonpolitical, religious sphere, in the sphere of End-of-Days apocalyptics. The Zionist ideal is one thing and the messianic ideal is another, and the two do not touch except in pompous phraseology of mass rallies, which often fuse into our youth a spirit of new Sabbatianism that must inevitably fail. The Zionist movement is congenitally alien to the Sabbatian movement, and the attempts to infuse Sabbatian spirit into it has already caused it a great deal of harm.

It seems that Scholem would here largely recognize Zionism as comparable with other nationalistic movements such as those of Italy and many other countries in the nineteenth century. In a summary of forces which led to the triumph of Zionism, Scholem writes with greater fullness as follows:

> If Zionism triumphed—at least on the level of historical decisions in the history of the Jews—it owes its victory preeminently to three factors that left their imprint on its character: it was, all in all, a movement of the young, in which strong romantic elements inevitably played a considerable role; it was a movement of social protest, which drew its inspiration as much from the primordial and still vital call of the prophets of Israel as from the slogans

of European socialism; and it was prepared to identify itself with the fate of the Jews in all—and I mean all—aspects of that fate, the religious and worldly ones in equal measure.[29]

In this admirably balanced assessment (which is as significant for what it does not contain, that is, apocalyptic territorial messianism, as for what it does) Scholem, while recognizing the role of the religious tradition, does not make it the dominant factor. To him Zionism was essentially a socio-political protest.[30] And in the judgment of many Jews the Congress of Basel was important not primarily because it gave expression to a strictly religious hope for The Land, living and creative as that was, but to a concern for the actual economic, political and social distress and often despair of Jews in Europe; it was a response not so much to a crisis in *Judaism* and to an endemic territorial theology as to the plight of the Jewish people.[31] To underestimate the secular character of much of Zionism and to overemphasize its undeniable religious dimensions is to lay oneself open to the temptation of giving to the doctrine of The Land a significance in much of Judaism which would be a distortion.

Again, in the third place, at first sight at least the witness of history could be taken as suggesting that *Eretz Israel* has not been of the essence of Judaism to the extent that the literary sources and liturgies and observances of pious Jews and even the political activity of nonreligious Jews would seem to suggest. Certain aspects of that history are pertinent. We have elsewhere indicated that, although it was assumed, there was a lack of any explicit appeal to the doctrine of The Land in the outbreak of the Maccabean revolt or that against Rome in 66 C.E. This is striking.[32] Even more overlooked have been the expressions in the Maccabean period of protests against and opposition to the Hasmonean rulers who had created an independent state.[33] These protests made the later attitudes of the Pharisaic leaders in coming to terms with Roman rule and in declaring the laws of The Land, wherever Jews dwelt, to be Law, less innovative than has customarily been recognized.[34] And at this point, the nature of the rabbinic attitude across the centuries must be fully recognized. That the doctrine of The Land remained honored among the rabbis cannot be doubted. But despite the facts referred to in the preceding pages, after 70 C.E. until very recent times, it was a doctrine more honored in word than in deed. After 70 C.E. the powerlessness of Jews over against the Roman authorities left the rabbinic leaders no choice other than that of submission and acquiescence to their divorce from "The Land." This submission and acquiescence were to persist and mold the life of the majority of Jews up to the present century and enabled the rabbis to come to terms with the loss of their Temple, City, and Land. As we have seen, protests in various forms against exile did not cease. Lurianic qabbala, for example, was a magnificient attempt to confront the curse of exile, and Sabbatianism in its historical context can be regarded as a desperate lunge at seizing the Kingdom of God which would lead to a return to *Eretz Israel*.[35] But very widely, both in Orthodox Judaism (by which is here meant the main stream of Rabbinic Judaism) and in Reform Judaism in the United States and Western Europe, the question of The Land was eschatologically postponed either as an unacknowledged embarrassment or as a last or ultimate hope. Across the centuries most Jews have lived on the whims of the gentile world: they have not been able to afford the risk of alienating their gentile masters by giving practical expression to their visions of a territorial return to *Eretz Israel*: for most Jews, despite some brilliant exceptions, such visions were a luxury of Sabbath reading, dreams to be indulged in but not actively realized in daily life.[36] Instead the rabbis emphasized that the Torah itself was to become a "portable land" for Jews:[37] it could be obeyed everywhere and could and would constitute the center of Jewish religious identity everywhere. Generally, orthodox Judaism refused to indulge in political speculation and activity which might further a return to The Land, but accepted instead an attitude of quietism. In one of the paradoxes of history, rabbis and apocalyptists were here at one: they both preferred to wait for a divine intervention, usually postponed to an indefinite future, to produce the return.[38] From a different point of view, as we saw, the Reform, in order to accommodate its faith to the nineteenth century and to make it comparable and compatible with Christianity, also preferred to refuse to give to any particular place, "The Land," a special overwhelming significance. In brief, in most rabbinic writers, up to the twentieth century and in some orthodox circles even up to the very present, the significance of The Land, though never denied, has been transferred to the "end of days." Paradoxically, "The Land" retained its geographic character or actuality and was not always transcendentalized, although it was largely *de facto* removed from the realm of history altogether. And in the Reform, "The Land," again in some circles even up to very recent times, was conveniently relegated to a secondary place; its geographic actuality was either sublimated or transformed into a symbol of an ideal society located not necessarily in *Eretz Israel*. Historically then, out of necessity since 70 C.E., the doctrine of The Land as a communal concern (it was often cherished by individual Jews) was largely dormant or suffered a benign neglect in much of Judaism.

What happened is apparent. In their realism the rabbis at Jamnia had triumphed over the Zealots of Masada. They recognized that the power of Rome was invincible: for them Jewish survival lay in sensible, because unavoidable, political submission, and in obedience to the Torah in all aspects of life where this was possible. The law of the country where Jews dwelt became Law. (The principle was *dîna d^e malkwta' dîna'*: see *b. Nedarim* 28a; *b. Giṭṭin* 10b; *b. Baba Qamma* 113a0b; *b. Baba Batra* 54b.) The paradigmatic figure was Joḥanan ben Zakkai, who had only asked of Vespasian permission to found a school where he could teach and establish a house of prayer and perform all the commandments—a spiritual center which accepted political powerlessness. For most of the rabbis after 70 C.E. exile became an accepted condition. For them discretion became the better part of valour. That it is to their discretion that Judaism owes its existence since 70 C.E. can hardly be gainsaid.[39]

In the fourth place, exile itself is the factor which needs emphasis. Vital begins his work *The Origins of Zionism* with the sentence: "The distinguishing characteristic of the Jews has been their Exile." Bickerman writes of the dispersion as follows:

> ". . . the postbiblical period of Jewish history, that is, that following Nehemiah . . . is marked by a unique and rewarding polarity: on the one hand, the Jerusalem center, and on the other, the plurality of centers in the Diaspora. The Dispersion saved Judaism from physical extirpation and spiritual inbreeding. Palestine united the dispersed members of the nation and gave them a sense of oneness. This counterpoise of historical forces is without analogy in antiquity. . . . The Jewish Dispersion continued to consider Jerusalem as the 'metropolis' (Philo), turned to the Holy Land for guidance, and in turn, determined the destinies of its inhabitants."[40]

The fact of exile has been inescapable, and extraordinarily tenacious and creative in the history of Judaism. The *Talmud* itself, like much of the Tanak, was formulated outside The Land. Surprisingly, Judaism did not produce a Theology of Exile on any developed scale until very late. (See now, however, Thomas M. Raitt, *A Theology of Exile: Judgment and Deliverance in Jeremiah and Ezekiel* [Philadelphia: Fortress Press, 1977] who finds this theme developed in the Tanak.) But the presence of large bodies of Jews outside The Land, so that (until the twentieth century) the "exiles" became numerically and otherwise more significant than those who were in "The Land," cannot but have diminished among many Jews the centrality of The Land and influenced their attitudes towards the doctrine concerning it. The conspicuous preeminence of the State of Israel in our time can easily hide the significance of the exile for Judaism[41] throughout most of its history. But the theological preeminence of Jews outside The Land in Jewish history needs no documentation. Apart from all else, their significance in the very survival of Judaism must be recognized. The loss of the Temple and The Land, the centers of Judaism, could be sustained only because there were organized Jewish communities scattered elsewhere.[42] Disaster even at the center did not spell the end of Judaism but could be and was offset and cushioned by its existence elsewhere. From this point of view exile may be regarded as having been the historical condition for the survival of Judaism and Jewry. (That this did not mean a radical decline of the significance of the primary center we shall indicate later.)[43]

The four factors which we have isolated above are to be further connected with what, in a previous study, we called cautionary considerations—the possible place of the "desert" as opposed to The "Land" in Judaism, the secondary role played by Abraham outside the Pentateuch, the transcendentalizing of The Land (pointing to a muted role for it)—which tend to curb the temptation to an excessive emphasis on the territorial dimension of Judaism. We refer the reader to that study. All these factors cannot be ignored.[44]

A CONTRADICTION RESOLVED:
THE JEWS' INTERPRETATION OF
THEIR OWN HISTORY

Our treatment so far has pinpointed what appears to be a contradiction: the theology of Judaism in its main expression points to The Land as of its essence: the history of Judaism seems to offer serious qualifications of this. Can the contradiction between the theology of Judaism and the actualities of its history be resolved? We suggest that the Jews' understanding of their own history comes to terms precisely with this contradiction and resolves it in life, *solvitur ambulando*. What does this mean?

On previous pages we appealed to history in support of the claim that exile as much as, if not more than, life in The Land has significantly marked Jewish history. The force of that appeal, we shall insist, must not be belittled. In isolation, however, it is misleading, because in the Jewish experience—both religious and secular—exile has always coexisted with the hope of a return to The Land. Without that hope the Jewish people would probably have gradually disintegrated and ceased to be. They have endured largely because of the strength of that hope. Here the distinction between exile and simple dispersion is important: the two terms are easily confused. Statistics cannot be supplied, but many Jews throughout the centuries have *chosen* to live outside The Land voluntarily, and many still do. The dispersion of such is not exile. But in most periods most Jews have had no choice and ultimately owe their place in the various countries of the world to the enforced exile of their ancestors. It is with these exiles—not simply with the dispersed—that we are here concerned. This notion of exile must be given its full weight and significance. That Jews outside Palestine conceived of their existence as an exile meant that they were still bound to their home base, to *Eretz Israel*, wherever they were: they were not simply dispersed. G. Cohen has urged that this was the fundamental reason that made possible the continuance of the link between dispersed Jews and *Eretz Israel*. The diaspora had maintained the notion of its existence as a *galuth*, exile. "That is to say, by the time Palestine ceased to be the central Jewish community, its centrality had been so impressed upon the Jewish mind that it could not be uprooted."[45] Many Jews have been sustained largely by the way in which they have traditionally interpreted their own history as revealing a recurring pattern of exile and return. They have understood their existence (in the various countries of their abode) as essentially transient or pilgrim; they have recognized that they have had no abiding country anywhere but have always been "en route" to The Land.

The Scriptures point to the patriarchs in search of The Land; the settlement of The Land is followed by the descent (a necessary "exile") into Egypt, followed by a return thence and the reconquest of The Land. Later there is another exile to Babylon, and again a return in the time of Cyrus. The Hellenistic period saw the rise of a vast dispersion—both voluntary and forced—and the first century revolt against Rome was followed by an exile which continued right down to this century, again only to lead to a return. The pattern of exile and return, loss and restoration, is constant across the sweep of Jewish history. Even the so-called "non-exilic" exile of Jews in Moorish and Christian Spain, where Jews for long enjoyed virtual integration into the societies in which they lived, ended in disaster and a fresh dispersion. Jews have constantly been conditioned by the harsh actualities of their history and their interpretation of them to think of the return. The point is that the pattern of exile and return has been historically so inescapable that it has underlined the belief that there is an inseverable connection between Yahweh, his people and his Land. In Judaism, history has reinforced theology to deepen the consciousness of Jews that The Land was always "there"—whether to be wrestled with in occupation or to return to from exile. As Professor Edmund Jacob has written in a brilliant lecture: "en effet, toute l'histoire d'Israël peut être envisagée comme une lutte pour la terre et avec la terre, comme le combat de Jacob était une lutte avec Dieu et pour Dieu.''[46]

In Jewish tradition the return could be conceived of in two ways. Non-religious Jews in every age could interpret the return to The Land as a political event, that is, as the restoration to Jews of political rights in their own land denied them after the collapse of the Jewish revolt in 70 C.E. (unrealistic as it must have often seemed to non-Jews). Such Jews have often understood exile and return in secular-political-economic terms. Not only secular Jews so thought of the return. In principle, so also did many of the sages. The rabbinical leaders never recognized that the conquest of *Eretz Israel* by any foreign power could be legitimized: the Romans were usurpers, their agents thieves. The Land belonged to Israel because Yahweh had promised it to Israel: its right to it was inalienable. So in the Mishnah it is implicitly regarded as legitimate to evade the Roman taxes (*m. Ned.* 3.4). The ruling powers were to be given obedience, but not cooperation—even in the interest of law and order. To the rabbis the return would involve control of The Land.

But to religious Jews much more was involved than this. To put it simply, to them just as exile was conceived of as the outcome of the wrath of God on a disobedient people, so too the return was to be the manifestation of His gracious purpose for them despite their past disobedience. From this point of view the return was to be a redemption. What to nonreligious Jews was primarily if not always exclusively of political significance, for the religious Jews was of theological significance.

This neat division between the religious and non-religious Jews, like all such divisions, is misleading. Both categories were not watertight; they interacted and were mutually stimulating as well as being very variegated. The concepts of the one permeated those of the other to make for infinite complexity. Although the secular thought in terms of return, and the religious in terms of redemption ultimately, because of the nature of the Tanak, they often dissolved into each other. In the Zionist movement, secular, socialistic Jews constantly found themselves "at home" with the religious elements in the movement, who did not share their political views but provided a common ambience of thought on or sentiment for The Land.

Nevertheless, seeing the return in terms of redemption had certain discernible and definite consequences, as also did seeing it in terms of the restoration of political rights. To the religious Jews, as we have previously indicated, the various exiles the Jewish people have endured were due to the will of God. He had intervened in history to give to the disobedience to the commandments its just punishment in exile. So too, they argued, the return would be an act of divine intervention. The return would be an aspect—a very important one—of the messianic redemption. As such it could not be engineered or inaugurated by political or any other human means: to force the coming of the return would be impious.[47] They best served that coming who waited in obedience for it: men of violence would not avail to bring it in. The rabbinic aloofness to messianic claimants sprang not only from the history of disillusionment with them but from this underlying, deeply engrained attitude. As we saw, it has been claimed that under the rabbis Judaism condemned itself to powerlessness. But if such phraseology be used, it has also to be admitted that that powerlessness was effective in preserving Judaism in a very hostile Christendom and must, therefore, have had its own brand of "power." And there is more. "Orthodoxy" did recognize the dependence of the return upon the divine initiative, but this did not prevent it from always retaining in principle that a certain human obedience could bring that initiative into play. And in Lurianic qabbala, for example, this connection was particularly active.[48]

For the purpose of this essay the significance of the attitude toward their existence in foreign lands and toward the hope of the return which we have ascribed to religious Jews is that despite their apparent quietism in the acceptance of the Torah as a portable land—and this it must be emphasized is only an *Interimsethik*—the hope for the return to *Eretz Israel* never vanished from their consciousness. They remained true "in spirit" to the territorial theology of the Tanak and with the other sources of their faith. Religious Jews generally, especially of the most traditionalist persuasion (except perhaps in modern Germany where they often thought themselves to have been "at home"), have regarded any existing, present condition outside the law as temporary. If not always pilgrims to it in a literal sense, they have always set their face towards The Land. This fidelity has in turn strengthened the continuing belief in the umbilical, eternal connection between the people of Israel and its Land and lent to that Land a "sacred" quality. In the experience of Jews, theology has informed the interpretation of history and history in turn has confirmed the theology.

In reflecting on the answer finally to be given to the question presented to us, in the light of the evidence so inadequately set forth here, an analogy from Christian ecclesiology suggests itself. In Roman Catholicism and high church Anglicanism the distinction has often been drawn, in discussions of the apostolic episcopate, between what is of the *esse* and of the *bene esse* of the Christian Church. Is this distinction applicable to the way in which the main stream of Judaism has conceived of The Land? Judaism has certainly been compelled by the actualities of history to accept "exile" as a permanent and major mark of its existence and as a source of incalculable benefit. Has it implicitly recognized, despite the witness of its classical sources and, indeed, it might be argued, in conformity with much in them, that while life in The Land is of the *bene esse* of all Jewish religious existence, it is not of the *esse*? Moses desired to be in The Land so that he might have the possibility of achieving greater obedience to the Torah: that he did not enter it was a very great deprivation. But it was not fatal to his existence as a Jew. It is the greatest blessing to live in The Land, but this is not absolutely essential. Philo regarded the Diaspora as under the providence of God (*In Flaccum,* 4). A Jew can remain true to his Judaism, however inadequately by the standards set by the sources, as long as he is loyal to the Torah. He can continue in his faith outside The Land, but not outside the Torah. Not The Land but the Torah is of the essence of Judaism; it is, indeed, its relation to the Torah that gives holiness to The Land. From this point of view it could be argued that The Land is of the *bene esse*, not of the *esse* of the Jewish faith.

Yet one is uneasy about this analogy, and that not only because the Torah itself and the Mishna are so overwhelmingly concerned with The Land. The antithesis between *esse* and *bene esse*, conceptually valid as it may seem to be, does not do justice to the place of The Land. We suggest that the way in which the question of The Land was proposed originally, that is, in terms of the essential in Judaism, may in fact itself be misleading and result in a misplacement in our answer. The term "essence" suggests the impersonal and so is as inadequate in dealing with The Land as in dealing with Christianity, as for example was Harnack in using the notion of the "Essence of Christianity."[49] Néher[50] and Lacocque[51] have pointed us to the personification of The Land in Judaism. They seem to us to go too far in ascribing to simile and metaphor and figurative language an actual personalism. But exaggerated as their claims may be, they do guard us against impersonalism in the understanding of the role of The Land. The Land evokes immense and deep emotion among religious Jews: it is "La Terre mystique de l'Absolu." It presents a kind of personal challenge and offers a personal anchorage. The sentiment (a term here used in its strict psychological sense) for The Land is so endemic among religious Jews (we are not here directly concerned with others) and so constantly reinforced by their sacred sources, liturgies, and observances that to set life in The Land over against life outside The Land as *esse* over against *bene esse* is to miss the point. It is better to put the question in another way and ask: does The Land lie at the heart of Judaism? Put in this more personal manner the question answers itself.

In another study we suggested that for Paul as for many in early Christianity, life under the Torah and in The Land was transformed into the life "in Christ," which became the Christian counterpart of the life in The Land of Judaism.[52] Few would not agree that the heart of Christianity (we avoid the term "essence") is Jesus Christ. Similarly, we must acknowledge the heart of Judaism to be the Torah. But to accept Judaism on its own terms is to recognize that near to and indeed within that heart is "The Land." In this sense, just as Christians recognize the scandal of particularity in the Incarnation, in Christ, so there is a scandal of territorial particularity in Judaism. The land is so embedded in the heart of Judaism, the Torah, that—so its sources, worship and theology attest—it is finally inseparable from it. "Il faut . . . ne pas essayer de diviser des choses indivisibles."[53]

The scandal presented by a particular land is no less to be recognized than that provided by a particular person. One may interpret the relation between Israel and The Land as a theological mystery or reject it simply as an unusually bizarre and irritating phenomenon. Many will find the "crass" materiality of the connection between Israel and The Land offensive to their "mystical" or "spiritual" sensitivities: others will find much to satisfy in the emphasis of Judaism on the need to express itself in tangible, material societary or communal form in The Land. Of its historicity in the Jewish consciousness or self identity there can, in any case, be no doubt. To accept it as a fact of historical significance is not of itself to justify it, but it is to begin to understand it, and to respect it as an aspect of Judaism's doctrine of election. "S'il y a un peuple élu, il y a aussi une terre élu."[54] The discussion of The Land drives us to the "mystery" of "Israel," that is, the eschatological purpose of God in his dealings with his people.[55]

4

Reflections on the Spirit
in the Mekilta:
A Suggestion

The *Mekilta* should be recognized as perhaps peculiarly important among Rabbinic sources for the understanding of the New Testament, and I have elsewhere indicated its relevance for this purpose.[1] The *Mekilta of Rabbi Ishmael,* conveniently translated into English by Jacob Z. Lauterbach,[2] is one of the oldest of the Tannaitic Midrashim and covers some of the most significant portions of the Old Testament, Exod 12:1—23:19; 31:12–17; 35:1–3. While it is particularly associated with the school of Rabbi Ishmael, it affords us an insight into the nature and content of the thinking not only of that school, but also of that of Rabbi Ishmael's colleague, Akiba, and other rabbis, who were contemporary with the early Christian movement. Here we shall very briefly point out the way in which the Spirit is dealt with in the *Mekilta.* Two caveats must be issued. First, the *Mekilta* has not been critically examined in terms of textual, form, and redaction criticism, so that the preliminary work necessary for any definitive treatment of any aspect of the *Mekilta* remains to be done. I am fully aware of this important fact and in this paper can only hope to draw attention to, not to exhaust, my theme. And, second, it would be erroneous to look for any systematic treatment of the Spirit in this document. Pharisaic Judaism was not concerned with theological consistency. What we shall find concerning the Spirit is a number of scattered opinions by individual sages, uncoordinated and, apparently, haphazard.

But Heschel[3] has rightly warned against treating the rabbis as untheological even if they were unsystematic, and we shall seek to indicate a theological and historical reason for some of the statements made about the Spirit. Since the *Mekilta* is not arranged in a conceptually progressive manner, but as a series of comments on the biblical text, it will be best to look at each pertinent text as it occurs. We shall concentrate our attention especially on territorial or geographic categories within which the Spirit is discussed and only refer briefly to others. Such a concentration may seem strange to Christian readers. But not so to Jewish ones, who are familiar with a territorial dimension in religious faith which Christians find alien. This dimension is probably more alien than that materialistic connotation which has sometimes been detected in sources dealing with *pneuma* and *rûaḥ* in the first century, which enabled some scholars, for example, to speak of spirit as a *Lichtstoff*.[4] But the distinction between the personal or spiritual and the material was not as emphasized in the first century as now. In the same way the discussion of the Spirit and geography seemed not unnatural to the Tannaitic rabbis.

The first text *Pisḥa* 1 on Exod 12:1 is translated by Lauterbach beginning on page 3, and begins as follows:

> *And the Lord Spoke unto Moses and Aaron in the Land of Egypt Saying*
> . . .
>
> *In the Land of Egypt.* This means outside of the city. You say it means outside of the city; perhaps it means within the city? Since, however, it says: "And Moses said unto him: As soon as I am gone out of the city I will spread forth my hands unto the Lord" (Exod 9:29), should we not apply the argument of *Kal vaḥomer*? If with regard to prayer, the less important, Moses would utter it only outside of the city, it is but a logical inference that with regard to the divine word, the more important, He would speak it to him only outside of the city. And why, indeed, did He not speak with him within the city? Because it was full of abominations and idols.

The very first paragraph introduces a spatial notion which implies that *where* a person prays or God speaks is important. The presence of abominations and idols in the city renders it unclean and unworthy of revelation. Prayer and divine revelation occur more appropriately outside the city. The contamination of the city, it is implied, contaminates the communication between God and man. It is tempting to connect such a thought with a "nomadic ideal" which some have detected—almost certainly unjustifiably—in the Old Testament, but this would be to read too much into the text.[5]

The passage cited continues:

> Before the land of Israel had been especially chosen, all lands were suitable for divine revelations; after the land of Israel had been chosen, all other lands were eliminated. Before Jerusalem had been especially selected, the entire land of Israel was suitable for altars; after Jerusalem had been selected, all the rest of the land of Israel was eliminated. For thus it is said: "Take heed to thyself that thou offer not thy burnt offerings in every place that thou seest, but in the place [Jerusalem] which the Lord shall choose" (Deut 12:13–14). Before the Temple had been especially selected, the whole of Jerusalem was appropriate for the manifestation of the divine presence; after the Temple had been selected, the rest of Jerusalem was eliminated. For thus it is said: "For the Lord hath chosen Zion, He hath desired it for His habitation: This is My resting-place forever" (Ps 132:13–14). Before

Aaron had been especially chosen, all Israelites were qualified for the priesthood; after Aaron had been chosen, all other Israelites were eliminated.
For thus it is said: "It is an everlasting covenant of salt before the Lord,
unto thee and to thy seed with thee" (Num 18:19); and again it says: "And
it shall be unto him, and to his seed after him, the covenant of an everlasting
priesthood" (Num 25:13). Before David had been chosen, all Israelites were
eligible to the kingship; after David had been chosen, all other Israelites
were eliminated. For thus it is said: "Ought ye not to know that the Lord,
the God of Israel, gave the kingdom over Israel to David forever, even to
him and to his sons by a covenant of salt."

The words translated "divine revelations" by Lauterbach are the Hebrew כשרות לדברות, literally, "clean for words or commandments."
To the interpreter, ever since the land of Israel had been chosen, all other
lands became unworthy of divine revelation. Even within the land itself,
in due course, and, finally, even within Jerusalem, the divine presence,
the Shekinah, was confined to the Temple itself. Apparently the choice
of the land refers to the promise to Abraham (Genesis 12, 15, 17) which
came to him outside the land: since that promise, all lands outside Israel
were "unclean."

But such a view created difficulties. God had indubitably spoken to
Moses in Egypt. True, this was outside the contaminated city, but never-
theless it was also outside the land of Israel. And, even more seriously,
God had spoken to prophets outside the land of Israel long after the prom-
ise to Abraham. This difficulty emerges in the next section which we quote
(Lauterbach, p. 5):

> You could say: "I cite the case of those prophets with whom He did speak
> outside of the land of Palestine." True, He did speak with them outside of
> the land, but He did so only because of the merit of the fathers. For thus
> it is said: "A voice is heard in Ramah, lamentation and bitter weeping,
> Rachel weeping for her children; she refuseth to be comforted for her chil-
> dren, because they are not. Refrain thy voice from weeping and thine eyes
> from tears; for thy work shall be rewarded, saith the Lord, and they shall
> come back from the land of the enemy. And there is hope for thy future
> saith the Lord" (Jer 31:15f.). Some say: Even though He did speak with
> them outside of the land, and because of the merit of the fathers, He did
> so only at a pure spot, near water, as it is said: "And I was by the stream
> Ulai" (Dan 8:2). Again it says: "As I was by the side of the great river,
> which is Tigris" (Dan 10:4); "The word of the Lord came expressly unto
> Ezekiel the priest, the son of Buzi, in the land of the Chaldeans by the river
> Chebar" (Ezek 1:3). Some say: He had already spoken with him in the
> land and then He spoke with him outside of the land, for thus it is said:
> "The word of the Lord had come and came to Ezekiel." "Had come" in-

dicates that He had spoken with him in the land; "and came"[6] indicates that He spoke with him outside of the land. R. Eleazar the son of Zadok says: Behold it says: "Arise go forth into the plain" (Ezek 3:22); this declares that the plain was suitable for divine revelation. You can learn from the following that the Shekinah does not reveal itself outside of the land. It is said: "But Jonah rose up to flee unto Tarshish from the presence of the Lord" (Jonah 1:3). Could he have thought of fleeing from the presence of God? Has it not been said: "Whither shall I go from Thy spirit? Or whither shall I flee from Thy presence? If I ascend up into heaven Thou art there; if I make my bed in the netherworld, behold, Thou art there. If I take the wings of the morning, and dwell in the uttermost parts of the sea; even there would Thy hand lead me," etc.? (Ps 139:7ff.). And it is also written: "The eyes of the Lord, that run to and fro through the whole earth" (Zech 4:10); and it is also written: "The eyes of the Lord are in every place, keeping watch upon the evil and the good" (Prov 15:3); "Though they dig into the netherworld . . . though they climb up to heaven . . . though they hide themselves in the top of Carmel . . . though they go into captivity," (Amos 9:2–4); "There is no darkness, nor shadow of death, where the workers of iniquity may hide themselves" (Job 34:22). But Jonah thought: I will go outside of the land, where the Shekinah does not reveal itself. For since the Gentiles are more inclined to repent, I might be causing Israel to be condemned.[7]

In this section the fact of prophecy outside the land is squarely faced and its seriousness as a problem recognized. Two degrees or intensities in the understanding of the Spirit are implied in the rabbinic sources. The spirit could be present in a real, but generalized sense, outside the prophetic experience. For example, R. Gamaliel was governed by the Holy Spirit at one point at least; but it was in the prophets that the Spirit was deemed to be particularly at work. In the intense sense, the Spirit could be claimed to have ceased with the last of the prophets.[8] The activity of prophets—in whom the Spirit was especially at work—outside the land was puzzling. So much must this have been the case that Finkelstein has drawn attention to a passage in *Siphre Deuteronomy* § 175, a comment on Deut 18:15. The latter verse reads in the RSV as follows: "The Lord will raise up for you a prophet like me from among you from your brethren—him you shall heed" (כמני יקים לך יהוה אלהיך אליו תשמעון נביא מקרבך מאחיך). Under the influence of New Testament studies, this passage is usually taken to refer to a single prophet, like Moses, who would emerge at the end of the days. But Finkelstein takes it as a general reference. A prophet, that is, prophets like Moses, would arise from time to time. The singular here denotes an implicit plural. In this Finkelstein follows the understanding of *Siphre*, which interprets the Hebrew מקרבך

in Deut 18:15 (from the midst of thee) to mean: "And not from outside the land of Israel." From this interpretation, Finkelstein concludes that the passage in *Siphre* is drawn from a tradition which had emerged before the Exile when Jeremiah, Ezekiel, and the story of Jonah had arisen. "It is clear," he writes, "that this comment derives from teachers who lived before the fall of Jerusalem in 587 B.C.E. and probably before the exile of Jehoiachin and many Judaites in 597 B.C.E."[9] As we shall see later on, even such a date would not have obviated the difficulty of the presence of the Spirit outside the land because Moses himself was a prophet. And unlike Finkelstein, it was not in terms of chronology that the authorities cited in the *Mekilta* dealt with the problem. In the passage we have quoted they give the following reasons why prophecy broke forth outside the land.

First, because of the merit of the fathers. The reference in the quotation from Jer 31:15f. is to Rachel. She was not strictly one of "the fathers," so that the term "merit of the fathers" refers here in a general sense to pious ancestors, male and female. In *Pesiqta Rabbati* 11b (ed. Friedmann) the passage from Jeremiah "was interpreted to mean that Rachel cried to God for her children who were exiled and God promised her that He would return them to their own land. It was because of Rachel, then, that God communicated with the prophets in the Babylonian Exile to tell them about the return, when and how it was to take place."[10] This notion emerges clearly also in *Exodus Rabbah* 15:4 on 12:1. Israel is redeemed from Egypt on account of its ancestors.

The second reason given for the gift of prophecy outside the land is that the prophets to whom the Spirit came prophesied near water. Water is an agent of cleanliness (see *m.ʿEduyyot* 8:4; J. Neusner, *The Rabbinic Traditions About The Pharisees Before 70,* vol. 1, 1971, pp. 61f.): land that is near water, it is implied, partakes of its purity and becomes clean. It is one of the antinomies of the Hebrew Scriptures that while the sea seems to be symbol of chaos, so that in the ideal future there shall be no more sea (Rev 21:1), water itself is pure and a symbol for the Torah itself. Use is made of this symbolism here in the *Mekilta* to explain why Ezekiel and Daniel prophesied outside the land.

Third, it was claimed, Ezekiel had been able to prophesy outside the land because he had already done so before he had left it. It is an assumption in *Mekilta Pisḥa* 1, in this passage, that the Shekinah, the Divine Presence, normally does not reveal itself outside the land.[11] Related to this is the strong emphasis in a slightly later passage that "prophets prophesy only because of Israel" (*Mekilta Pisḥa* 1, end).

It is instructive to find that, in *Midraš Rabbah* on Exodus the phrase to which the *Mekilta* pays so much attention, that is, "in the land of Egypt," is very little noticed. In fact, it is ignored until well into the discussion of Exod 12:1. When, finally, in *Exod. Rab.* 15:5, the phrase is dealt with, the treatment seems long overdue and is very brief as compared with the almost immediate engagement with it in *Mekilta Pisḥa* 1. Moreover, the whole section is ascribed to one Rabbi, R. Hanina (1st century C.E.), and does not deal with the question of prophecy outside the land at all. The phrase "in the land of Egypt" is simply taken to indicate that God spoke to Moses (Exod 12:1) outside the city, which was full of idol worship, immorality, and uncleanness. In coming to speak to Moses it was necessary for Yahweh himself to avoid the contamination of the city, which is compared to a cemetery, so he remained outside. The whole section, then, bears no resemblance to the treatment in *Mekilta Pisḥa* 1. This suggests that when the *Mekilta* was composed the problem of the land and the Spirit was more acute than when the material in *Midraš Rabbah* was redacted at a later date. We shall suggest a reason for this later.

Another passage in the *Mekilta* seems to denote an emphasis very different from that we noted in *Mekilta Pisḥa* 1 which confined prophecy, the gift of the Spirit, to the land. In *Mekilta Pisḥa* 14 the Shekinah, the presence of God, is declared never to forsake Israel wherever she goes, even into slavery outside the land. The notion is expressed in a comment on Exod 12:41, as follows:

> *Even the Selfsame Day It Came to Pass, that All the Hosts of the Lord Went Out from the Land of Egypt.* The hosts of the Lord are the ministering angels. And so you find that whenever Israel is enslaved the Shekinah, as it were, is enslaved with them, as it is said: "And they saw the God of Israel; and there was under His feet," etc. But after they were redeemed what does it say? "And the like of the very heaven for clearness" (Exod 24:10). And it also says: "In all their affliction He was afflicted" (Isa 63:10). So far I know only that He shares in the affliction of the community. How about the affliction of the individual? Scripture says: "He shall call upon Me, and I will answer him; I will be with him in trouble" (Ps 91:15). It also says: "And Joseph's master took him," etc. (Gen 39:20). And what does it say then? But the Lord was with Joseph" (ibid., 39:21). And thus it says: "From before Thy people, whom Thou didst redeem to Thee out of Egypt, the nation and its God"* (2 Sam 7:23). R. Eliezer says: An idol crossed the sea with Israel, as it is said: "And a rival* passed through the sea" (Zech 10.11). And which idol was it? The idol of Micah.* R. Akiva says: Were it not written in Scripture it would be impossible to

say it. Israel said to God: Thou hadst redeemed Thyself, as though one could conceive such a thing.* Likewise you find that whithersoever Israel was exiled, the Shekinah, as it were, went into exile with them. When they went into exile to Egypt, the Shekinah went into exile with them, as it is said: "I exiled Myself unto the house of thy fathers when they were in Egypt" (1 Sam 2:27). When they were exiled to Babylon, the Shekinah went into exile with them, as it is said: "For your sake I ordered Myself to go to Babylon" (Isa 43:14). When they were exiled to Elam, the Shekinah went into exile with them, as it is said: "I will set My throne in Elam" (Jer 49:38). When they were exiled to Edom, the Shekinah went into exile with them, as it is said: "Who is this that cometh from Edom," etc. (Isa 63:1). And when they return in the future, the Shekinah, as it were, will return with them, as it is said: "That then the Lord thy God will return with thy captivity" (Deut 30:3). Note that it does not say: "The Lord will bring back" (*veheshib*), etc., but it says: "He will return" (*ve-shab*). And it is also said: "With me from Lebanon, my bride" (Cant 4:8). Was she really coming from Lebanon? Was she not rather going up to Lebanon? What then does Scripture mean by saying: "With me from Lebanon?" Merely this: You and I, as it were, were exiled from Lebanon; you and I will go up to Lebanon. [On the difficulties indicated by an asterisk in this translation, see Lauterbach.]

Heschel[12] has gathered together a large number of passages where the same idea occurs. (See, for example, *Exod. Rab.* 23:5 on Exod 15:1). The Shekinah is always and everywhere present with Israel: but the Spirit, according to some, was confined to the land. The relationship between the Spirit and the Shekinah demands separate treatment. In other passages in *Mekilta Pisḥa* the presence of the Spirit at the Exodus—not in the city—is recognized. Consider a passage *Mekilta Beshallaḥ* 3, a comment on Exod 14:13. Moses is rallying the people, who face the Red Sea in terror and murmur against their leader for having brought them out of Egypt at all: they "would rather be slaves to the Egyptians than die here in the wilderness" (Exod 14:12). The *Mekilta* reads as follows:

Stand Still and See the Salvation of the Lord. The Israelites asked him: "When?" Moses said to them: "Today the Holy Spirit rests upon you." For the expression "standing" (*yezibah*) everywhere suggests the presence of the Holy Spirit, as in the passages: "I saw the Lord standing beside the altar" (Amos 9:1). "And the Lord came, and stood, and called as at other times: 'Samuel, Samuel,'" (1 Sam 3:10). And it also says: "Call Joshua and stand in the tent of meeting that I may give him a charge" (Deut 31:14). To what were the Israelites at that moment like? To a dove fleeing from a hawk, and about to enter a cleft in the rock where there is a hissing serpent. If she enters, there is the serpent! If she stays out, there is the hawk! In such a plight were the Israelites at that moment, the sea forming a bar and the enemy pursuing. Immediately they set their mind upon prayer. Of them it is stated in the traditional sacred writings: "O my dove that art in the clefts of the rock," etc. (Cant 2:14). And when it further says: "For sweet is thy voice and thy countenance is comely" (ibid.), it means, for thy voice is sweet in prayer and thy countenance is comely in the study of the Torah. Another interpretation: For thy voice is sweet in prayer and thy countenance is comely in good deeds.

The passages cited indicate that by the Holy Spirit was meant the spirit of supplication or prayer, the spirit of study and good deeds. The salvation could also be understood in terms of "squadrons upon squadrons of ministering angels," the Holy Spirit, apparently being thought of as the spirit of might, as the passage immediately following the one cited above shows:

Another Interpretation: *Stand Still and See,* etc. The Israelites asked Moses: "When?" He answered them: "Tomorrow!" Then the Israelites said to Moses: "Moses, our Master, we have not the strength to endure." At that moment Moses prayed and God caused them to see squadrons upon squadrons of ministering angels standing before them, just as it is said: "And when the servant of the man of God was risen early, and gone forth, behold, a host with horses and chariots was round about the city. And his servant said unto him: 'Alas, my master! how shall we do?' And he answered: 'Fear not: for they that are with us are more than they that are with them.' And Elisha prayed, and said: 'Lord I pray Thee, open his eyes, that he may see.' And the Lord opened the eyes of the young man; and he saw: and, behold, the mountain was full of horses and chariots of fire round about Elisha" (2 Kgs 6:15–17). And so also here Moses prayed at that moment and God caused them to see squadrons upon squadrons of ministering angels standing before them. And thus it says: "At the brightness before Him, there passed through His thick clouds, hailstones and coals of fire" (Ps 18:13)—"His thick clouds," as against their squadrons; "hailstones," as against their catapults; "coals," as against their missiles; "fire," as against their naphtha. "The Lord also thundered in the heavens" (ibid., v. 14)— as against the clasping of their shields and the noise of their trampling shoes. "And the Most High gave forth His voice" (ibid.), as against their whetting the swords. "And He sent out His arrows and scattered them" (ibid., v. 15), as against their arrows. And He shot forth lightnings and discomfited them" (ibid.), as against their shouting. Another Interpretation: *And He Sent Out His Arrows.* The arrows would scatter them, and the lightnings would huddle them together. "*And Discomfited Them.*" He confounded them and brought confusion among them. He took away their signals so that they did not know what they were doing. Another Interpretation. *And Discomfited Them.* Discomfiture here means by pestilence, as in the passage: "And shall discomfit them with a great discomfiture until they be destroyed"[13] (Deut 7:23).

In other passages in *Mekilta Beshallaḥ* 7 (Lauterbach, pp. 252ff.) the gift of the Holy Spirit is accorded to the people of Israel because of their faith. The comment is on Exod 14:31, a remarkable verse which speaks of faith, not only in God, but in Moses his servant. For this faith there is a reward. It prompts the following words in the *Mekilta Beshallaḥ* 7:

> *And They Believed in the Lord and in His Servant Moses.* If you say they believed in Moses, is it not implied by *Kal Vahomer* that they believed in God? But this is to teach you that having faith in the shepherd of Israel is the same as having faith in Him Who spoke and the world came into being. In like manner you must interpret: "And the people spoke against God, and against Moses" (Num 21:5). If you say they spoke against God, is it not implied by *Kal Vahomer* that they spoke against Moses? But this comes to teach you that speaking against the shepherd of Israel is like speaking against Him who spoke and the world came into being.
>
> Great indeed is faith before Him Who spoke and the world came into being. For as a reward for the faith with which Israel believed in God, the Holy Spirit rested upon them and they uttered the song; as it is said: "And they believed in the Lord. . . . Then sang Moses and the children of Israel" (Exod 14:3; 15:1). R. Nehemiah says: Whence can you prove that whosoever accepts even one single commandment with true faith is deserving of having the Holy Spirit rest upon him? We find this to have been the case with our fathers. For as a reward for the faith with which they believed, they were considered worthy of having the Holy Spirit rest upon them, so that they could utter the song, as it is said: "And they believed in the Lord. . . . Then sang Moses and the children of Israel." And so also you find that our father Abraham inherited both this world and the world beyond only as a reward for the faith with which he believed, as it is said: "And he believed in the Lord," etc. (Gen. 15:6). And so also you find that Israel was redeemed from Egypt only as a reward for the faith with which they believed, as it is said: "And the people believed" (Exod 4:31). And thus it says: "The Lord preserveth the faithful" (Ps 31:24)—He keeps in remembrance the faith of the fathers. And it also says: "And Aaron and Hur stayed up his hands," etc. (Exod 17:12).

It is striking that in the *Mid. Rab.* on the passages in Exodus, commented on in the passages in the *Mekilta*, which we have noted, there is again a scarcity, indeed almost a complete absence, of any reference to the Holy Spirit. It is as if there were a deliberate avoidance of connecting the Holy Spirit with the Exodus. It is recognized that Moses is the greatest of the prophets—a familiar thought—but there is only one very brief reference to the Holy Spirit in *Exod. Rab.* 23:2 on Exod 15:1, in the name of Rabbi Abbahu (third century).

As *Mekilta Pisḥa*, so *Mekilta Shirata* on Exod 15:1 again makes a reference to the Holy Spirit. The song of Moses after the parting of the Red Sea greatly attracted the rabbis. The following passage ascribes the song of Moses and of the people to the Holy Spirit. What is noteworthy is that the rabbis connect the Holy Spirit with the celebration of the manifestation of Yahweh's might: the Spirit celebrates a victory in a holy war. The reference by Akiba to the Hallel, a prayer which came to comprise Pss 113—118, and which came to be decreed for New Moon, Passover, Pentecost, and Tabernacles and Hanukkah, is significant: especially at Passover it evoked militant messianic emotions. The Holy Spirit at the Exodus indicated the presence of the kind of zeal out of which Holy War arose.

Later in *Mekilta Shirata* 3 on Exod 15:2 the Holy Spirit is connected with the recognition of Israel as blessed by its deliverance, the gift of the Torah. It is incomparable and glorified. All this the Spirit declares. In *Mekilta Shirata* 7 the Holy Spirit is made to indicate precisely how the Egyptian enemy was overcome. It has an argumentative function.

The Egyptians at the sea were divided into three groups as regards the Israelites. One group proposed: Let us get from them their money and our money without killing them. One proposed: Let us kill them without taking their money. And one proposed: Let us kill them and also take their money. The one that proposed: Let us take their money without killing them, said: "I will divide the spoil." The one that proposed: Let us kill them without taking their money, said: "My lust shall be satisfied upon them." The one that proposed: Let us kill them and also take their money, said: "My hand shall inherit them." Pharaoh, when still in Egypt, defiantly boasted of five things: "The enemy said: 'I will pursue, I will overtake, I will divide the spoil; my lust shall be satisfied upon them; I will draw my sword, my hand shall destroy them'" (Exod 15:9). As against these five boasts, the Holy Spirit answered and said: "Thou didst blow with Thy wind," etc.; "Thy right hand, O Lord, dasheth in pieces the enemy"; "And in the greatness of Thine excellency Thou overthrowest them that rise up against Thee; Thou sendest forth Thy wrath, it consumeth them as stubble"; "Thou stretchest out Thy right hand," etc. To give a parable, to what can this be compared? To the following: A robber standing behind the king's palace, defiantly says: "If I find the prince, I shall seize him, I shall kill him, I shall crucify him. I shall make him die the most cruel death." So also did the wicked Pharaoh boast defiantly in the land of Egypt: "The enemy said: 'I will pursue, I will overtake,'" etc. But the Holy Spirit laughs at him and says: "Thou didst blow with Thy wind." And it also says: "Thou stretchest out Thy right hand." And so it also says: "Why are the nations in an uproar. . . . Let us break their bands asunder. . . . He that sitteth in heaven laugheth" (Ps 2:1–4). And it says: "Behold, they belch out with their mouth" (ibid. 59:8). And what is written following this? "But Thou, O Lord, shalt laugh" (ibid., v. 9). And so also it says: "Sheba and Dedan, and the merchants of Tarshish," etc. (Ezek 38:13). And it says: "And it shall come to pass in that day, when God shall come . . . shall shake at My presence'' (ibid., vv. 18–20). Thus all these thousands and all these myriads sank as lead because of the boast of one.

The connection of the Spirit with exultation over the enemy emerges also in *Shirata* 10 in dealing with the reference to Miriam as a prophetess in Exod 15:20. The ascription of the term "prophetess" to Miriam occasioned difficulty, and the passage which we note here supplies various erudite reasons for this: appeal is made to her prediction in Exod 2:1–4, where the term *yezibah*, "standing," as elsewhere, is taken to refer to the presence of the Holy Spirit; the phrase "afar off" (*merahok*), in the light of Jer 31:2, is taken to refer to the Holy Spirit and "to know." The treatment of Miriam reveals extreme concern to justify the ascription of prophecy to her. That ascription, in turn, only attests that an outburst of song at the mighty—warlike—works of Yahweh is the work of the Holy Spirit.

When the full extent of the *Mekilta* is considered it has to be recognized that taken in isolation, the discussion of the Spirit is limited, but compared with the material dealing with the same scriptural passages in later *Midrašim* the *Mekilta* shows a concern with the Spirit that was lively. We suggest that this was because some of the materials preserved in the *Mekilta* are more directly influenced by the spread of Christianity than those preserved in later *Midrašim*. At one point, in particular, it may be indicated—very tentatively—that the Christian movement is reflected in the *Mekilta*. Early Christianity spread with rapidity outside the land of Israel: its experience of the Spirit was intense, as New Testament and other documents indicate. That Spirit seemed to defy topography, to ignore the territorial limitation of it to the land of Israel which some Jews at least had set. The encounter of early Christianity with Jewish territorial doctrine I have sought to deal with elsewhere. The engagement of some parts of the *Mekilta* with the relation of the Spirit to the land of Israel may reflect this encounter. Early Christianity radically challenged the view that the Spirit was inextricably related to the land of Israel. The pertinent passages in the *Mekilta* may have arisen, in part at least, out of the attempts to meet this challenge. True, there were examples of the Spirit being experienced outside the land; so some rabbis admitted. But these could be explained away. And with this attitude may be connected the emphasis in other passages in the *Mekilta* on the presence of the Spirit at the birth of the people of Israel at the Exodus. Although there are passages where the Spirit seems to indicate a vindictive aspect such as we associate with the Holy War, in the New Testament generally the Spirit is subordinate to Christ, and interpreted above all as that of love, joy and peace. The new exodus wrought by the finger of God avoided vindictiveness, as is clear in Matt 11:2–6, where in the quotation from Isa 35:5–6; 61:1f the words "Behold, your God will come with vengeance, with the recompense of God" are omitted from Isa 35:4, as are the words: "And the day of vengeance of our God" from Isa 61:2. The *Mekilta*, however, although it recognizes the morally exalted forms of the gifts of the Spirit, does unashamedly connect the Spirit with the destruction of the Egyptians. It does this in a very self-conscious way. May it be that the rabbis whose thought it preserves were conscious of an opposite tendency in the Christian movement? We cannot be sure. But it does seem not impossible that Tannaitic rabbis may have been aware of Christian emphases in the understanding of the Spirit—as geographically ubiquitous and nationally indifferent—which they were concerned to oppose. At least in later sources when Judaism and Christianity were more removed from each other, we notice an absence of any comparable concern with the Spirit.[14]

I can only add, in view of the limitations of space, that the brevity and inadequacy of this contribution is in inverse proportion to my debt to and affection for the one to whom it is offered.[15]

5

A Note on Josephus,
Antiquities 15.136

In a monograph entitled *Torah in the Messianic Age and/or the Age to Come*,[1] I sought particularly to examine the question whether Judaism anticipated a new Torah in its ideal future, however conceived. One passage in Josephus, *Ant.* 15.136 has been suggested as relevant to this purpose because it contains the idea that "the Law was given through angels, an ideal which in Acts 7:53, Gal 3:19, Heb 2:2 is associated with the notion that it was to change." (See Morton Smith, *JBL* [September 1953]:192.) Strack-Billerbeck cite the passage in their comment on Gal 3:19 and take it to refer to the mediation of angels,[2] as do also Grundmann in the *TWNT*[3] and Walter Bauer in his *Wörterbuch*.[4] It is the first aim of this note to follow up a suggestion made to me by Dr. Ralph Marcus that the passage may not refer to angels but to prophets.

The whole section, *Ant.* 15.134–137 (the first two lines), is translated by Whiston-Margouliouth[5] as follows:

> "(134) And whereas observation of covenants takes place among the bitterest enemies, but among friends is absolutely necessary, this is not observed among these men, who think gain to be the best of all things, let it be by any means whatsoever, and that injustice is no harm, if they may but get money by it: (135) is it therefore a question with you whether the unjust are to be punished or not? When God himself hath declared his mind that so it ought to be, and hath commanded us that we ever should hate injuries and injustice which is not only just but necessary in wars between several nations; (136) for these Arabians have done what both the Greeks and Barbarians own to be an instance of the grossest wickedness, with regard to our ambassadors, which they have beheaded, while the Greeks declare that such ambassadors are sacred and inviolable. And for ourselves we have learned from God the most excellent of our doctrines, and the most holy part of our law by angels, or ambassadors; for this name brings God to the knowledge of mankind, and is sufficient to reconcile enemies one to another. (137) What wickedness then can be greater than the slaughter of ambassadors, who come to treat about doing what is right? And when such have been their actions, how is it possible they can either live securely in common life, or be successful in war? In my opinion this is impossible."

The pertinent words in Greek are: ἡμῶν δὲ τὰ κάλλιστα τῶν δογμάτων καὶ τὰ ὁσιώτατα τῶν ἐν τοῖς νόμοις δι' ἀγγέλων παρὰ τοῦ θεοῦ μαθόντων. [δι' ἀγγέλλων L: διαγγέλλων W: om. Lat.].

The reading δι'ἀγγέλων is accepted by Whiston who in his translation, however, placed [or ambassadors] thus in brackets after angels. Margouliouth removed the brackets.

Because of the well-attested tradition that the Law was given by angels it is natural to find the idea here in Josephus,[6] but the following factors *may* justify our finding a reference instead to the prophets as ambassadors of God.

1. The context deals with ambassadors (*presbeis, kêrukes*) between armies or conflicting powers, and ambassadors who were such as could be slain (15.136, 137). A reference to angels who, presumably, could not be slain, would be inappropriate here, but to prophets pertinent; they were human ambassadors from God who might suffer violence and death. It will be recalled that the slaying of prophets was regarded as a peculiarly heinous sin in Israel.[7]

2. In the description of the giving of the Law to Moses on Mt. Sinai in *Ant.*, 3.75–187 there is no reference to the mediation of angels although the idea, as we saw, was fully established in Jewish tradition. It is true that we do not have Josephus' full treatment of the Law because he had reserved this for another work (*Ant.* 3.94 and elsewhere), but even so it is significant that there should be no reference to angels in the section cited. F. J. Foakes Jackson[8] does not mention angels in his discussion of the Law in Josephus; he points out that in *Ag.Ap.* 2.164–167 the laws are largely attributed to the wisdom of Moses: they are not, primarily at least, conceived as dictated by God to the legislator;[9] the idea of a divine initiative in the giving of the Law, an idea implied in that of the mediation of angels as God's agents, is in the background.

3. A passage in *Ag. Ap.* 1.35, which refers to prophets, suggests that in *Ant.* 15.136 also the reference may be to them. The whole section is translated by H. S. J. Thackeray as follows:

It therefore naturally, or rather necessarily, follows (seeing that with us it is not open to everybody to write the records, and that there is no discrepancy in what is written; seeing that, on the contrary, the prophets alone had this privilege, obtaining their knowledge of the most remote and ancient history through the inspiration which they owed to God) (ἀλλὰ μόνων τῶν προφητῶν τὰ μὲν ἀνωτάτα καὶ παλαιοτατα κατὰ τὴν ἐπίπνοιαν τὴν ἀπὸ τοῦ θεοῦ μαθόντων) and committing to writing a clear account of the events of their own time just as they occurred)—it follows, I say, that we do not possess myriads of inconsistent books, conflicting with each other. Our books, those which are justly accredited, are but two and twenty and contain the record of all time.[10]

The context makes it clear that Josephus has confused the function of the priesthood in keeping genealogical registers with that of the prophets in producing their works. This is not surprising in view of the fact, of which we are reminded by Thackeray, "that the historical books of the Old Testament after the Pentateuch were included in the second or prophetical writers portion of the Hebrew Canon and attributed to prophetical writers." What is significant for our purpose, however, is that the prophets, whatever their specific function, like the *angeloi* of *Ant.* 15.136 are said to have learned from God what they gave to men. The phrase κατὰ τὴν ἐπίπνοιαν τὴν ἀπὸ. τοῦ θεοῦ μαθόντων is reminiscent of δι-αγγέλων παρὰ τοῦ θεοῦ μαθόντων in 15.136. In itself this parallel, which was pointed out to me by Dr. Ralph Marcus, cannot be regarded as weighty but it does serve to add force to other factors which we are considering.

4. In the rest of his work Josephus shows no speculative interest in angelology and sometimes seems eager to rationalize or interpret the term *angelos* (angel), perhaps in order to make it more acceptable to his Greek readers; for example, in *Ant.* 4.108 he once calls the divine angel who meets Bileam *theion pneuma*. As has been pointed out by Grundmann, Josephus refers to the Essene interest in angelology as if it were a peculiarity of theirs—a fact which is significant for his own interests.[11] Kittel also pointed out that Josephus,[12] under the influence of rationalism, sometimes avoids the use of the term *angelos,* where the Masoretic Text has the corresponding *mal'ak*, and prefers *phantasma*.[13] (See *Ant.* 5.213.) In 5.277 also the *angelos* is referred to as a *phantasma*. In the MT in Judg 6:11 we have *mal'ak Yahweh,* in the LXX, *angelos kuriou*: Josephus writes of *phantasmatos neaniskou*. (Kittel also refers to *Ant.* 1.331, but this is not strictly relevant to our purpose because in the MT in Gen 32:22f. *mal'ak* does not occur, instead it is *'ish* in Gen 32:25, and in the LXX, *anthrôpos*; Josephus gives *phantasma*: so too the *JW* 5.381, to which Kittel also refers, is not directly relevant here. Neither the MT nor the LXX refer to angels in Gen 12:10–20 so that Josephus's reference to phantoms in the night here has no exact reference to angels.)

5. The term *angelos* is used sometimes in the LXX to refer to prophets and priests. Thus Haggai in 1:12 of the book of that name is referred to as *nabi'* and in 1:13 as a *mal'ak*, which is rendered in the LXX by *angelos*. So in Is 44:26 the plural *mal'akaiw* is rendered by *tôn angelôn autou,*

working

where the preceding reference to *pais* makes the reference to prophets certain. In 2 Chr 36:15: "and the Lord, the God of their fathers, sent to them by his messengers (MT *b*ᵉ*iad mal'akaiw*) rising up early and sending; because he had compassion on his people and on his dwelling place: (16) but they mocked the messengers of God (MT *b*ᵉ*mal'akai hâelohîm*), and despised his words, and scoffed at his prophets (*b*ᵉ *n*ᵉ*bi'aiw* . . .)." The LXX renders 36:15 thus: καὶ ἐξαπέστειλεν κύριος ὁ θεὸς τῶν πατέρων αὐτῶν ἐν χειρὶ προφητῶν ὀρθρίζων καί ἀποστέλλων τοὺς ἀγγέλους αὐτοῦ. . . . (The phrase "rising up early and sending" is associated with God's sending of the prophets in Jer 29:19, 35:14 f., 26:5.) These prophets in 2 Chr 36:15 are referred to in the LXX as *angelous*. [B omits *prophêtôn* here. It may well be that B regards the reference to *angelous* as sufficient to indicate prophets.] In Mal 2:1 the term *angelos kuriou* refers to a priest. In the same way in the NT Isaiah 40:3 is applied to John the Baptist (Matt 11:10, Mark 1:2, Luke 7:27): i.e., John is the *angelos* of God! He is interpreted in the NT as the prophet Elijah. Here again the term *angelos* probably means a prophet.[14]

The above five considerations make it reasonable to assert that in *Ant.* 15.136 the reference *may* be to prophets.

But, in the second place, even if we prefer to translate *angeloi* here by "angels," is the idea of any change in the Law then implied in the passage? It is unlikely. Josephus specifically asserts that it is "the most excellent of our doctrines and the most holy part of our law" that came by angels: they are said to "bring God to the knowledge of mankind." The idea of any necessity for changing the Law in the future is entirely alien to the context. As Kittel[15] pointed out, in the Jewish tradition the mediation of angels in the giving of the Law serves to emphasize the importance of the Law. Only in two places in the NT, in Gal 3:19, Heb 2:2, does this mediation imply any inferiority and is therefore associated with the notion that it was to change, and this is a specifically Christian development. Morton Smith takes Acts 7:53 in this sense, but in fact like Acts 7:38 it emphasizes the exact opposite. In the latter, Stephen's meaning is that the Moses with whom even an angel spake at Sinai was rejected by Israel, and in 7:53 that, although Israel had received the Law as it was ordained by angels—a great privilege—it had been nevertheless disobedient.[16] What we have here is the persistence among Christians of what was primarily a Jewish attitude to mediation by angels, an attitude which Paul and Hebrews rejected.

The upshot of all this is, perhaps, what we should expect. Josephus was not given to Messianic speculation for reasons easy to understand,[17] nor was he himself particularly addicted to the observance of the Law, although he could appreciate the frequent nobility and courage of those who were. It is not surprising therefore that his teaching on the Law offers nothing that is noteworthy in any search as to the presence or absence of the expectation of a change or changes in the Law or of a new Torah in the future in Judaism. He shared the view predominant in the Judaism of his day that the Law was eternally valid. It is enough to refer to *Ag.Ap.* 2.277: "robbed though we be of wealth, of cities, of all good things our Law at least remains immortal (*athanatos diamenei*)." Moreover, there is little reason to doubt that in this matter Philo of Alexandria, although of a very different temper, is like Josephus: he too accepts the eternity of the Law; we cannot enlarge further on this here, but for Philo in the Messianic Age "each nation would abandon its peculiar ways and throwing overboard their ancestral customs, turn to honouring our laws alone. For, when the brightness of their shining is accompanied by natural prosperity, it will darken the light of the others as the risen sun darkens the stars."[18] Into the exact *significance* of this for Philo, however, we cannot enter here.[19]

Section 2:
Pauline Studies

6
Paul and the Law: Reflections on Pitfalls in Interpretation

Because of its importance not only in his epistles and in other parts of the New Testament but also in the encounter between Roman Catholicism, Protestantism, and Judaism, the treatment of the Law by Paul has been and is one of the most discussed subjects in Christian theology and particularly in NT studies. But lawyer readers of this chapter brought up on O. W. Holmes's *The Path of the Law* will find it difficult to relate its contents with "law" in the customary meanings of the term. They will, for example, pounce upon the fact that the word "legislation" only occurs once and indeed, if they persist in reading, will probably insist that, in all that we have written we have not pointed to "law" or "laws" in Paul in the strict sense at all but simply to moral teaching and exhortation; similarly Professor Daube recently distinguished between the few sayings in the Old Testament urging upon Israelites the desirability of procreation—passages which he regards as exhortatory—and later laws, into which these exhortations developed to make procreation a legal duty. To this charge we plead guilty, but guilty of necessity. The genius of Paul was not in legislation. The passages where he gives specific rules of conduct are very few. They deal with the financial support of preachers of the gospel (1 Cor 9:3–18), which Paul justifies in terms of "human analogies" of texts from Deuteronomy, and from the practice in the Jewish temple, and they also deal with questions of marriage, slavery, and food consecrated to idols, on which the Apostle refused to follow the legal logic of messianism and "legislated" in very personal terms (1 Cor 7:1–8:13). That there are, comparatively, so few strictly "legal" discussions in Pauline epistles is highly significant. Of necessity our treatment of the law in Paul has had to be only tangentially legal but rather has centered in the apostle's understanding of the nature of the life "in Christ," by which all aspects of life, including the legal are, for him, to be informed. This concentration on the new life "in Christ" is of the essence of Paul's approach to the law, which comes to be not dismissed by him but transposed to a new key. As will appear, the apostle related all law to religion.

That his challenge to relate religion radically to law and law to religion speaks to our present condition would appear to many, as to ourselves, self-evident. The case for this has recently been stated by Professor H. J. Berman.[1] His argument need not be repeated, so persuasive is it. With this introductory warning to lawyers, we proceed with our specific task.

In the context of this paper we mean by "law" the Torah by which religious Jews have sought to live. As Paul understood it, the term *torah* (usually rendered in Greek by *nomos* and in English by "law") consisted of all the documents to which Christians (but, and this needs to be emphasized, not Paul or any other writers of the New Testament)[2] have come to apply the term "the Old Testament." In first-century Judaism these documents were referred to as the written law, *torah shekathub* or *shebikthab*. Within them, the first five, usually referred to as the Pentateuch, were especially distinguished from the prophetic and hagiographic writings (the *nebi'im* and the *kethubim*) and given an unmistakable prominence as *the* law (*ha-torah*).[3] But alongside this written torah there had developed as its application, either in direct dependence upon it (in the form of *midraš*) or independently of its text (in the form of *mishna*), a body of oral law (*torâh she be'al pe*),[4] which was finally codified around the middle of the second century as the Mishna.[5]

The term *torah,* or law, then, for Paul was very comprehensive. At least four aspects of it have to be borne in mind. First, it includes commandments (*mitzwoth*) which are to be obeyed: it is doubtful whether the term *torah* at any time is completely free of the element of demand, either explicitly or implicitly. Second, it encompasses much that is not legal in the sense of commandment: in particular, in chronologically widely spread documents, it includes the history of the people of Israel as variously interpreted at different stages, the messages of the significant prophets of Israel, and an impressive tradition of wisdom.[6] Third, as a result of a development going back possibly as early as Deuteronomy in the sixth century B.C., the Torah in its totality had come to be regarded as the wisdom after the pattern of which and by means of which God created the world (Proverbs 8).[7] Wisdom, or Torah, came to be regarded not merely as the ground plan which God followed in creating the universe but as his architect. (How far it was personified is debated: the term for this wisdom, *hocmâh,* like the term Torah itself, is in the feminine gender.) Wisdom played a part in creation, as we saw, and it is also peculiarly concerned with revealing the way of life and righteousness to humankind. It confers truth, righteousness, knowledge, judgment, and justice. It is therefore the means of expressing the divine activity both in creation and in morality and knowledge, which activity is the creative and the redemptive purpose of God (Prov. 8:35a, 36b). Fourth, in sum, the term the Torah (the Law) connoted for Paul as a Jew the whole of the revealed will of God in the universe, in nature, and in human society. It is not surprising, therefore, that the term as Paul understood it, indicating the special inheritance of Israel and designed to express the will of God in every detail in which he was immersed, in fact could be taken to indicate a whole cultural tradition which governed his life in its totality. To submit to or to reject the law was to accept or reject a particular culture or way of life in all its intricate ramifications. It is essential to grasp that the Torah represented for Paul not solely the moral demands of God on the individual Jew but also his demand on all his people for a way of life governed by obedience to him in all spheres. The question of Paul's relation to the law, then, is the question of his relation to the whole tradition, indeed the very culture, of the Jewish people among whom he had been born.[8]

The neglect of the complexity of the role of the Torah in its all-encompassing and ubiquitous character in Paul's life as a Jew, to which we have referred, has made it easy for interpreters, concentrating on a particular aspect of the Torah to the exclusion of others, to oversimplify his response to it. In this article, by way of a possible corrective, we shall try to indicate certain considerations that should be operative in any adequate discussion of Paul's attitude to the law. We shall do so indirectly, however, by pointing out pitfalls in interpretation which have led to distortion. The pitfalls are indicated in the following subheadings: (1) the interpretation of the law as simply commandment, (2) the isolation of Paul's treatment of the law from his messianic (revolutionary) situation, (3) the failure to recognize variety and change in that treatment, and (4) the neglect of explicit moral demands in the epistles.

INTERPRETATION OF THE LAW AS SIMPLY COMMANDMENT

First, there has been a tendency to treat *torah* as if it simply meant *mitzwah,* commandment. Protestant theologians generally, but especially those in Germany, have often understood *torah* as commandment and interpreted the Jewish tradition as one requiring obedience to the commandments as the ground of salvation. This diminution of the scope of the Torah to that of *mitzwoth,* commandments, and of salvation to that of the reward for obedience to them has had momentous historical consequences. The traditional Protestant interpretation of the Pauline po-

lemic against the law in Judaism and Jewish Christianity will be familiar
and need not be repeated here.[9] Unfortunately, this interpretation has so
colored the minds of Protestants and even Catholics that it has been difficult for them both to give the law its due place in the corpus of revelation.[10] The doctrine of justification by faith alone, with its corollary of
the inadequacy of the law, has been taken within Protestantism as the
clue to Paulinism. The appeal of that doctrine and, to many, its truth is
altogether natural and is to be fully recognized. A gospel of grace, of
justification by faith alone, cannot but have a powerful attraction for all
sorts and conditions of men, because they know the power of sin and the
dread of guilt. But neither the religious appeal of that doctrine to our
broken humanity, nor indeed the acceptance of it as truth, should be
allowed to govern the interpretation of Paul as a historical figure. The
traditional picture of Saul of Tarsus as suffering pangs of conscience under
the law has recently been severely criticized and dismissed. It has been
urged that the pangs of the introspective conscience are a peculiarity of
Western Christendom and therefore alien to Paul and that his agonizing
engagement with the law was concerned not with his personal moral struggle in seeking to obey it but with the relationship between Jews and Gentiles, that is, over the meaning of belonging to the people of God. Such
a view is not to be unqualifiedly accepted.[11] The pangs of the introspective
conscience or of moral scrupulosity are not confined to Western Christians molded by the misunderstanding of Paul in St. Augustine and in
Luther. Those pangs are universally human; they know no geographic
boundaries. Paul too must have known them. Yet to make the personal
moral struggle of Paul the primary source of his criticism of the law,
understood primarily as commandment, is to ignore the evidence of his
own epistles, which does not support the picture of Paul as a Jew tortured
by his failure to obey the law in his pre-Christian or Christian days. Paul
refers to himself as blameless under the law and his own conscience. The
references to the division within the self in Romans 7 probably reflect a
personal experience but cannot be made normative for the understanding
of his life under the law before Paul encountered Christ. In fact, as we
shall see, so far from being an attack on the law, Romans 7 may be even
a defense of it.

But this apart, to confine the meaning of the Torah solely within the
dimension of the commandments demanding obedience is to ignore the
Jewish understanding of the Torah as containing also the history that was
the background of the commandment. For Paul, as for all religious Jews,
the Torah evoked not only the demands of God given on Sinai and the

tradition which had developed to expound and apply them, but the *story* that lay behind Sinai and that continued in the history of the people of God that came into being there. And this story, it must be emphasized, pointed always to a grace of God which preceded his demand. The decalogue, for example, is introduced by the words, "I am the Lord your God *who brought you forth out of the Land of Egypt, out of the house of bondage*" (Exod 20:1–2). The duties of the decalogue arise out of the deliverance, a deliverance of the unworthy. The precedence of grace over law in Israelite religion persisted, despite its frequent neglect, in Judaism. The ground of obedience in Judaism is gratitude, which has been called "the most ethical of all the emotions." The law and the recognition of the need for obedience to it are not the means of salvation for Judaism but the consequences or accompaniment of it. True, the demands of the law often came to be isolated in Judaism and their covenantal ground in the grace of God to be muted, but the relation of the demands to the grace of God in freeing Israel from Egypt was not severed. The very observance of the law inevitably recalled the Exodus, and the gift of the law itself for Jews, because it was not solely commandment, was regarded as an act of grace and a means to grace.

It follows that the opposition of law to grace which has marked so much of Protestantism, grounded as it is in individualism, that is, in the emphasis on the sinner standing alone before the awful demands of God, in terrible isolation, is a distortion of Paul. Here it is well to note that, although a profundity, Paul was not a peculiarity in the early church. He shared the understanding of the Christian experience which was widespread in that church, and that experience was "covenantal" in character. Early Christians believed that they were living "in the end of the days," in the time of fulfillment.[12] This conviction is to be understood, as is made evident in all the NT in the light of the expectations expressed in the OT and Judaism that at some future date God would act for the salvation of his people.[13] The life, death, and resurrection of Jesus of Nazareth were the fulfillment of these expectations. The moral aspirations of the OT and Judaism, the prophets and the law, were not annulled in the Christian dispensation; they were fulfilled.[14] The early church consciously accepted the moral concern of Israel as it was illumined and completed in the light of the life, death, and resurrection of Jesus.

This acceptance emerges clearly in that in much of the NT the experience of the church was understood as parallel to that of the Jewish people. The emergence of the church was, if not the emergence of a New Israel, at least the entrance of Israel onto a new stage of its history.[15] In the creation of the church the Exodus was repeated, as it were. And as a corollary to the experience of a new Exodus, wrought by the life, death, and resurrection of Jesus the Christ, the church understood itself as standing under the new Sinai of a new Moses. This complex of ideas—Exodus, Sinai, Moses[16]—governs, for example, Matthew's presentation of the Sermon on the Mount[17] and Mark's[18] reference to a new teaching, which John in turn presents as a new commandment.[19]

In its vital contents, then, the moral teaching of primitive Christianity must be understood in relation to the law which Judaism traced back to Sinai; this relationship is variously expressed, sometimes in terms of reform, sometimes in terms of antithesis, and sometimes in terms of fulfillment.[20] What is clear is that, in early Christianity, "law" is bound up with the Christian gospel, as it was bound up with the message of the OT and Judaism.[21] To put this in technical terms, the structure of primitive Christianity is, in some aspects at least, modeled upon, or grows out of, the structure of Judaism. This means that law is integral to the gospel of the NT as it was to that of the OT.[22] Paul's understanding of the Law also is to be understood against this background. It was the concepts we have indicated that largely governed his references to the New Covenant. Paul's background in early Christianity, no less than in Judaism, demands that we cease to interpret Paul's reaction to the law solely in individualistic and moralistic terms and recognize that Pauline Christianity is not primarily an antithesis to law. To respond to this demand is difficult for many reasons. Between us and Paul's treatment of the law stands the Protestant Reformation, and Protestant exegetes, as indicated already, have applied in the most massive way Paul's arguments against the Judaic and Judaizing interpretation of the law to the whole structure of the Mosaic faith. Traditional Protestant exegesis often illumines the Scriptures, but it often also serves as a barrier to the true understanding of them.

But more important are other general but fundamental factors that emerged early in the history of the church to lead to a misinterpretation of the apostle. Paul believed that the crucified Jesus was the Messiah. The interpretation of the significance of such a paradoxical Messiah inevitably led to a radical reassessment and criticism of the messianic ideas of the existing religious and political order. The revolutionary possibilities of the movement which began with Jesus of Nazareth cannot be overemphasized. Paul, who, compared with some other Christians, seems to have been soberly conservative even in his radicalism,[23] contrasts the new order in Christ with the old order under the law with a burning vividness. His sharp antitheses are familiar. From his earliest epistle on, Paul lashed out unrestrainedly against certain Jews.

Two factors are pertinent in the consideration of his violent criticism. It fluctuated with the conditions that he faced. We have no letters of Paul to Jews or to Jewish Christians but only to largely Gentile churches. But these Christian communities were probably composed of Jews and of Gentiles who had been attracted to Judaism through the synagogues. The discussions of Judaism and Jews in Paul's letters are intramural. They are criticisms of the faith, law, institutions, and worship of Jews not from without but from within. Although probably more critical of Judaism than those churches founded by other apostles, the Pauline churches also existed on the threshold of the synagogue. Rhetorically, in diatribe, Paul can address Jews directly even in Romans (2:17; 3:1, 9). The Christian communities to which he wrote were differentiated by certain elements— a common meal, apostolic figures, a way of life or discipline, an awareness of unity in Christ and of living in a new aeon, and a confession of Jesus as Lord—as were other such communities. But in the time of Paul this differentiation did not spell separation. The evidence for the coexistence of early Christians with other Jews within a common heritage need not be repeated here. Did Christianity as a distinct, separate religious movement exist at all before 70 A.D.? Up until then was it not a movement within Judaism in competition with other Jewish movements variously interpreting a common tradition? The term "New Israel" does not appear until the second century, and the very idea of a primitive Christianity before 70 A.D. is probably mistaken: it is a historical myth.[24] Even though Paul can refer in Galatians to *Ioudaismos* (1:13f.),[25] his criticisms of the symbols of Judaism no more signify that he had forsaken Judaism than did the bitter attacks of the sectarians at Qumran against the authorities in Jerusalem signify that they had forsaken it.

This reference to Qumran warns against the common failure to appreciate the multiplicity of ways in which Judaism expressed itself in the early pre-Jamnian period. The weight of scholarly tradition still inclines us to think of Judaism in largely monolithic Pharisaic terms. We read the first century in the light of the later dominant rabbinic Judaism. But Pharisaism itself in the first century was very variegated. The hospitable, comprehensive, theological tolerance and fluidity of Judaism before 70 A.D. allowed various groups to remain within its ambience. Among these were early Christians. Scholem's work on the seventeenth century Messiah, Sabbatai Svi, offers a parallel. Rabbinic scholars refused to take Sabbatianism seriously as a Jewish phenomenon because they operated with a monolithic conception of Judaism, which could not contain Sabbatianism. But that movement was an essentially Jewish phenonemon; it arose within Judaism and despite its revolutionary character remained within it, even when it proclaimed the divinity of Sabbatai.[26] The same applies to much Christian understanding of early Christianity. In accepting the Jew, Jesus, as the Messiah, Paul did not think in terms of moving into a new religion but of having found the final expression and intent of the Jewish tradition within which he had been born. For Paul the gospel was according to the Scriptures; it was not an alien importation into Judaism but the true development of Judaism, its highest point, although, in its judgment on the centrality which some Jews had given to a particular interpretation of the law, it showed a radicalism which amounted to a new creation. Although it had its differentia, the Christian life for Paul was not a non-Jewish phenomenon distinct from and annulling another prior phenomenon, Judaism. Like Sabbatai Svi and Nathan of Gaza in the seventeenth century, he would not have conceived of himself as having ceased to be a Jew (Rom 9:3—11:1) or as having inaugurated a new religion. To make him guilty of totally rejecting the Law of Judaism is to fail to place Paul in his true context, that is, within a Judaism which was not monolithic in character but was a cauldron of opposing views.

Why has the recognition of this simple fact been so difficult and tardy? Apart from the weight of scholarly tradition and conservatism, there are two main reasons, one external and Jewish and the other internal to the churches. First, the external Jewish reason will be explored. The attitude of Jews to Christians who arose among them varied. As Daube pointed out, the assessment of the claims of a messianic movement was difficult.[27] Doubtless the tolerance ascribed to Gamaliel in Acts may not have been typical, but as Hare has shown,[28] the evidence for any very early widespread violent reaction issuing in the persecution of Christians by Jews is not impressive. Most Jews would have been puzzled by Jesus but not necessarily antagonized by him any more than were the seventeenth century Jews by Sabbatai Svi. It was the defection of many Christians from the national cause in the revolt of the Jewish revolutionaries against Rome in the sixties, the catastrophic fall of Jerusalem, and the subsequent struggle of the Jews for survival and the preservation of their identity under the sages at Jamnia, where the Pharisaic leaders gathered after the fall of Jerusalem and gradually established what we call rabbinic Judaism that sharpened and hardened the lines between Jews who did not and those who did follow Christ. The sociological and psychological processes that induce opposed, though related, groups to define each other over against each other, so that even a community of love can come to define itself in terms of hate for its opponents, have become clearer to us in recent years. These processes have been insufficiently exploited in the examination of the emergence of Christianity as a distinct movement from within Judaism and over against it. At this point we need to listen far more to Weber and Freud. The processes that led to the radical separation of Christians from Jews cannot be traced here. What is especially noteworthy is that that separation was subsequent to Paul's day and must not be read back into his engagement with the religion of his fathers. It was the desperate necessity for Jamnian Judaism to close its own ranks against dissidents and to elevate the Torah as interpreted by the Pharisees still more to be *the* way of Jewish life and the reaction among Christians and Jews that contributed most to the emergence of what we call Christianity as a distinct religion.[29] But Paul predated Jamnia.

This leads us to the second internal reason for the tardy recognition that Paul remained within the ambience of Judaism. Put simply it is this: Paul's letters were composed in the context of a dialogue within Judaism. They were later read outside and over against that context. Context determines content. The gospel itself, whoever preached it, could easily be misunderstood. Paul's peculiar and complex interpretation of it was often confusing.[30] During his lifetime he had to face this fact. Concentrating on Paul's insistence that it was not Jews after the flesh who constitute the people of God but those "in Christ," and sometimes coming under pressure from Paul's opponents, some Gentiles initially understood him to mean they were now to enjoy the privileges and ways of the Jews, who were no longer the people of God, and that they were called upon to observe the Law even more zealously than Jews. Overconversion was a common phenomenon. Other Gentiles, probably more numerous, like many Jews who heard him and to whom he wrote, took Paul to demand a complete rejection of the Torah of Judaism and to invite messianic license. For these Paul spelled the total rejection of Judaism, and as we shall see, he opposed them.

And then after his day, when his letters came to be read by Gentiles who little understood Judaism, the misinterpretation of Paul became almost inevitable. These Gentiles often approached the epistles as outsiders incapable of appreciating their setting within what we may call a family dispute, which could explain both their extreme bitterness and, at times, their fine sensibilities. The disputes over the true interpretation of their common Jewish tradition between Paul and his kinsmen, both those who accepted and those who rejected the new faith, were expressed with intensity, not to say ferocity. As long as they were seen as being *intra muros*, they remained endurable. But once removed from this setting they took on a radically negative character. They no longer appeared as attempts at the reinterpretation of a shared tradition but as forages in hostility. In time, though the process was not rapid,[31] what was a disruption among Jews came to be spelled out as the denigration and rejection of Judaism and of the people of Israel as a totality. Paul's criticisms of the Law were intrinsically difficult to understand and, when wrenched from their familial context as read by Gentiles largely untouched by Judaism, were ascribed a rigid coldness and a clinical, a surgical, and a unified antithetical purpose.

ISOLATION OF THE LAW FROM
PAUL'S MESSIANIC SITUATION

What has been written has by implication pointed to the second pitfall which must be avoided in the interpretation of Paul's attitude to the Law: that of isolating it not only from the complexity of the concept of *torah* and from the context of the first century but also from the total messianic situation in which Paul believed himself to be standing. It is clear from Acts and the Pauline epistles that the law was the point at which Paul met violent opposition. Because of this it has been easy to regard his criticism of the law as the ultimate ground for the persecution of the apostle. Jews did not stumble at his doctrine of a Messiah, even a crucified one; Jewish-Christians also believed in such a one. Judaism was hospitably tolerant of messianic claimants.[32] But Paul's acceptance of Gentiles as members of the people of God without the observance of the law passed the possible limits of Jewish tolerance; it was scandalous. But to state the matter this unqualifiedly is misleading. Certainly the immediate cause for Jewish opposition to Paul centered on the law. But his controversial understanding of the law was inextricably bound up with the significance which, through his experience on the road to Damascus, he had come to subscribe to Jesus as the Messiah with the challenge that this had issued to all the fundamental symbols of Jewish life—the Temple, the city, the land, and the Sabbath, as well as the law. To isolate the criticism of the law from the total messianic situation, as Paul conceived it, is both to exaggerate and to emasculate it. That criticism is, in fact, derivative; it is a consequence of the ultimate place which Paul ascribed to Jesus as the Messiah in the purpose of God throughout history.

The messiahship of Jesus was crucial for Paul. He most frequently referred to Jesus as the Lord and usually used the term "Christ" in such combinations as Christ Jesus, Jesus Christ, and the Lord Jesus Christ in a personal and not in a titular sense. But he did not therefore empty the term "Christ" of its messianic connotation,[33] as especially in Rom 9:5, probably Rom 1:2–4; possibly 1 Cor 1:23; Rom 15:7; and Gal 3:16, 6:2. That Jesus had come to be for Paul the Messiah had momentous consequences which were not annulled by Paul's use of other terms for him. In interpreting Jesus as the Christ, Paul could draw upon long standing categories of thought expressed in words and vivid symbols which the Jewish masses and many sages, despite the frowns of others, took literally. The content of these symbols gave them immense evocative powers. Their impact on Paul can be traced particularly in several ways. Here we shall be concerned only with their impact on his understanding of the law.

The immorality and antinomianism of many of the enthusiasts in his churches constituted an embarrassment on two fronts. They drew the criticism of outsiders; "Christian" unruliness could easily be confused with civil disobedience. But more important, they antagonized sober, observing Jews and raised the question of the law. It is fundamental to recognize that a messianic movement inevitably had to come to terms with the law. In dealing with it Paul was no novice, but was informed by the apocalyptic-Pharisaic tradition of Judaism. In that tradition, despite the firmly entrenched doctrine that the law was perfect, unchangeable, and eternal, some expected that Elijah would be a messianic forerunner who would explain obscurities in the law, that in the Messianic Age or in the Age to Come difficulties in the law would be explained, that certain enactments would cease to be applicable, and that there would be changes in the commandments concerning things clean and unclean. But more than all this, there are later passages where a new Torah for the Messianic Age is envisaged[34] and others where the law is to be completely abrogated at that time. As before and after, but especially in the first century when Judaism was more varied than at a later time, the content and character of the one perfect law was a matter of intense debate. How was it to be interpreted? The answers were many. The Temple Scroll reveals that some circles were even prepared to add to the law in the name of Yahweh himself.[35] The Dead Sea Sect, awaiting its Messiah, reveals to us a Judaism at boiling point over the question of the law, demanding total obedience to a particular interpretation of it and expecting new commandments. The houses of Hillel and Shammai understood the law so differently that some feared that two laws might emerge in Israel.[36] When Paul, therefore, dealt with the question of the law in relation to Christ, he was not alone but was part of a world in which the interpretation of Torah for the present and the future was a burning issue. Belief in the advent of the Messiah necessarily brought up acutely the question of the law. The discussions of it in Paul are integrally related to his belief that in Jesus, crucified but raised from the dead, the Messianic Age had begun. As indicated, it is in two epistles especially that these discussions occur.

In Galatians, Paul speaks of Jesus Christ as having appeared in the fullness of time (1:4) to effect deliverance from "this present evil age" (1:5). The same crucified Jesus who had appeared risen from the dead to Paul had induced him "to die to the law" (3:18) and wrought deliverance from its curse (3:13). He had introduced the gift of the Spirit associated in Judaism particularly with the time of the End (3:2, 4:6, 5:6, 16). The promises of God to Abraham were fulfilled "in Christ" (3:16). Paul distinguishes three phases in the history of his people: (1) from Abraham to Moses, a period which he counts as 430 years; (2) from Moses, when the law was given, to the coming of the one true seed of Abraham, Jesus Christ (Gal 3:16, 19), in whom the promise to Abraham was fulfilled and faith in whom confers the blessing of being among the sons of God; and (3) a new epoch, introduced by Jesus, of true sonship in liberty (4:3f., 5:13), a new creation (6:5). This treatment of history in Galatians in terms of the distinction between the promise to Abraham and the law given to Moses and the culmination of the former in Jesus Christ is Paul's own. It gives an eschatological significance to Jesus of Nazareth from which Paul interpreted the law. This is the force of the statements in 1 Cor 10:11 ("For upon us the fulfillment of the ages has come") and in 2 Cor 5:17.

In the epistle to the Romans Paul reveals even more directly how he understood Jesus as Messiah within the history of the people of Israel. He adopts an interpretation of that history not altogether unlike that proposed in the *Tanna debe Eliahu,* a compilation of the third century A.D. probably containing materials taken from the first century. The passage reads: "The world is to exist six thousand years. In the first two thousand years there was desolation [anarchy]; two thousand years the Torah flourished; and the next two thousand years is the Messianic era." (*Sanh.* 97 a, b). Compare this with Paul's division in Rom 4:15, 5:13, 10:4. He conceives of: (1) a period from Adam to the giving of the Law; this was lawless in that during that period, men sinned but transgression was not imputed to them (Rom 4:15, 5:13); (2) a period from Moses to Christ during which the Law reigned and men's sins were imputed as transgressions (4:15); and then (3) a new period inaugurated by Christ in which the writ of the law no longer ran. Christ is the "end of the law." This phrase, in Rom 10:4, refers to a false understanding of the law. But, as earlier in Galatians, where Paul was more categorical and extreme in claiming that Christ by taking upon himself the curse of the law had delivered us from it, so in Rom 7:6 he writes: "But now, [in Christ] having died to that which held us bound, we are discharged from the Law, to serve God in a new way, the way of the spirit, in contrast to the old way, the way of a written code."

Paul, a Pharisee convinced that Jesus was the Messiah, because of this astounding fact could not but regard the law in a new light. We cannot connect Paul with any one Jewish doctrine of the place of the law in the Messianic Age, but his understanding of Jesus Christ in terms of the eschatological expectations of Judaism is unmistakable. This demanded a reorientation amounting to a radical criticism of the law which led to his persecution at the hands of the Jews. The proximate cause of that persecution, then, his treatment of the law, points to an ultimate cause, his Christology, which was at its beginning a messianology. The fact is that given his Jewish view of the law as the eternal, immutable, perfect revelation of God's will and his experience of it as an all-encompassing cultural world, it was only a messianic event of revelatory and cosmic significance that could have induced Paul to reassess the law as he did. To ignore this total messianic context and interpret Paul's response to the law apart from it, as is often done, is to misinterpret.

FAILURE TO RECOGNIZE VARIETY AND CHANGE

The third pitfall to be avoided is that of taking Paul's response to the law as monolithic, as if it were invariable. The customary procedure for dealing with his epistles has been to gather together references to the law, to examine them exhaustively but indiscriminately, and finally, to interpret them as a totality, producing what is usually referred to as Paul's attitude to the law. But, despite the intense labors devoted to this, it is an indulgence in a gross oversimplification. To establish the variety and changes in Paul's approach to the law, we shall now look at the way in which he deals with it in various epistles.

Paul and the Galatian Christians

Paul first deals directly with the law from the point of view of one accepting Jesus as the Christ in Galatians, where he confronts Judaizers and, behind them, the Jews. He writes polemically and looks at the law with the cold eyes of an antagonist. To those who demanded the observance of the law, he asserts that to be under the law was to be under a curse (Deut 27:26; Gal 3:10) and that because the law was given later than the promise to Abraham, requiring faith and not works, it was inferior. And it was inferior also because of its origin; it had not come directly from God but had only been mediated by angels and through a human, Moses (Gal 3:10–20). Moreover the law was morally weak, unable to give righteousness (3:21). Later in the epistle Paul goes even further. To obey the law was to submit to the elemental spirits of this evil world of which the law was one (4:3, 9).[37]

True, Paul does allow a temporary, preparatory role for the law. It served as a tutor (custodian) until Christ (3:24). Unless Gal 3:19 ("Why then the law? It was added because of transgressions, till the offspring should come to whom the promise had been made; and it was ordained by angels through an intermediary.") be taken to imply that sin is revealed by the law, Paul does not clarify how exactly the law fulfills this role; he does so later in Romans. He simply states that under the law, until the coming of Christ, the whole world was prisoner to sin (3:22–23). His recognition of any positive function for the law is extremely grudging. In any case, now that Christ has come, it is no longer necessary. Those who are "in Christ," through the spirit of the Son sent into their hearts by God, have achieved a maturity which transcends the tutelage of the law (4:1). The role of the law was at best that of a beggarly, passing phenomenon. With the cross of Christ the writ of the law came to an end (2:21; 3:13, 19; 5:11). Paul is at his coarsest in dismissing those who oppose this view (5:12).

Even though it was clear to him that some Christians in Galatia took his emphasis on freedom from the law as an excuse for license, enthusiasm in the Spirit bringing its own dangers, this did not frighten Paul into a retreat back to the law. Rather he reaffirmed the sufficiency of the Spirit in Christ to bring forth moral fruit without any guidance from the law. The emphasis of Paul on freedom is unrestrained; he does not balk at its risk (5:13). Nevertheless even in Galatians he finds a substitute for the law that he denounced in the law of the Messiah: the bearing of one another's burdens, or *agapē* (6:2).[38] It is where he introduces this notion that his epistle becomes warmest. That the term "law" in the phrase "the law of the Messiah" in Gal 6:2 is not to be radically differentiated from the concept of the command, *mitzwah*, or *Torah* as if it means simply principle or norm rather than a demand[39] appears from the way in which Paul later, in a calmer mood, went on to deal with enthusiasts at Corinth.

Paul and the Corinthian Christians

At Corinth also Paul was opposed by Jewish-Christian opponents[40] who favored the retention of the Law of Moses and by others who were moved by an enthusiasm leading to license which easily accompanies revolutionary Messianism. To counter this, the apostle of liberty was constrained to call for restraint and for a behavior among Christians governed by the example of Paul's own life (1 Cor 4:16, 11:1) and by that of Christ himself (2 Cor 8:9, Phil 2:4–11). In 1 Cor 4:17 Paul refers to his "ways" in Christ, "moral standards expressed to some extent in recognized patterns of behavior . . . which can be taught,"[41] which he urged everywhere in every church. After all his denials of this in Galatians, it emerges that there *is* a Christian "way," a Christian "law" for Paul. This way was to be informed by the universal practice of Christian congregations (1 Cor 4:17, 11:16, 14:34). So too in 1 Corinthians 6 and 8 the liberty of the Christian is to take consideration of external circumstances. Whereas at Antioch (Gal 2::11ff.) Paul had not hesitated to ignore the scruples of Peter and others, thus ignoring the claims of the weaker brethren, in 1 Corinthians he himself urges the opposite, consideration for them. In 1 Cor 6:12 he qualifies the freedom urged in Galatians; in 1 Cor 7:19, while reiterating the principle declared in Gal 5:6 (6:15), he makes, for him, the astounding statement: "[K]eeping the commandments of God is *everything.*"[42] Paul is not thinking here of the Mosaic commandments; his exact reference is not clear. What is clear is that he refuses to give unfettered sway to the notion that, because they were in the new creation effectuated by Christ, Christians were free from commandments. And in 2 Corinthians, where however he may have been facing different opponents from those he deals with in 1 Corinthians, he came to recognize the Christian life as a life in covenant, and a covenant always implies demand or Law (2 Corinthians 3). In 2 Cor 3:17 he reiterates the principle that where the Spirit of the Lord is, there is freedom, but he now defines this freedom not as the end of demands but as liberty to conform to Christ, to substitute new loyalties for old. The Christian is to be under the constraint of the love of Christ (2 Cor 5:14), and this leads him to live no longer for himself. The constraint of Christ's example constitutes also the ground of Paul's appeal to the collection for the "poor" of Jerusalem (2 Cor 8:8). The constraint of the love of Christ is not a commandment, but it *is* a modification of unqualified freedom. Paul would have appeared very differently to Christians in Galatia and in Corinth; doubtless he would have been accused by the former of antinomianism and by the latter of disciplinarianism or, at least, incipient legalism.

Paul and the Roman Christians

It is in Rom 6:15—7:6 that the nature of the life "in Christ" is most directly expressed, and it is in the same epistle that Paul presents his further critique of the Mosaic Law. Here, as not in Galatians, Paul is careful to recognize that the Law is "holy, righteous and good" (Rom 7:12, 16), that it is spiritual (7:14), that its source is in God (7:22, 25; 8:2, 7), that it is designed for life (7:10), that it is authoritative (7:19), and that it is among the privileges accorded to Israel (9:4). Elements of the critique offered in Galatians are repeated, but in Romans Paul approaches the law, not from an external view point as in Galatians, as if it were an object of his dispassionate or clinical theological reflection, but from within, that is, as experienced. From this point of view he finally asserts in 10:4 that Christ is the end of the law, by which he there means that the attempt to obey the law as a means of salvation ends in failure. That attempt was mistaken in its understanding of the intent of the law. But before he reaches that climactic statement, he had earlier given reasons for his conclusions.[43]

Reiterating that the law was powerless to effectuate the life that it demanded and promised (Lev 18:5), Paul adds to Ps 143:2 ("against Thee no man on earth can be right") the words "*by observance of the Law*." Supposed to bring life, the law was unable to do so (Rom 3:23). In fact, it had the opposite result to that which it intended (7:13), bringing the wrath of God (4:15) and death (1 Cor 15:56; Rom 7:9ff.) upon men. And yet, although the law is the *power* of sin (1 Cor 15:56), Paul refuses to equate it with sin (Rom 7:7). Romans 7 may, in fact, be a defense of the law.

He describes what seems to be his understanding of the condition of all men. The exact reference in Romans 7 has been disputed; it probably describes Paul's own experience as that of all men and describes it in the light of Christ. The law usually confronts us as prohibition, expressing simply the negative aspect of God's will. It reveals sin to man; it gives man a profound knowledge of sin (3:20). It does this not simply because it incites man to break its prohibitions and thus becomes an occasion (*aphormē*) of sin (7:5, 8, 11), on the principle that "forbidden fruit is sweetest." Man's encounter with the commandment of God uncovers what lies behind all sin, the desire to reject the rightful claim of God upon him. The rebellious character of man in his desire to be free from God's constraint and from the covenant with him is revealed by the commandment. This is why Paul can say, "Sin indeed was in the world before the law was given, but sin is not imputed where there is no law" (5:13). Only with the coming of the law does man's sin take on the character of open rebellion. "Where there is no law, there is no transgression" (5:14); "apart from the law sin lies dead; I was once alive apart from the Law, but when the commandment came sin revived and I died'' (7:8b–9a). Thus the law, intrinsically good, subserves the ends of sin, which is intrinsically evil but which is, apart from the opportunity provided by the law, impotent. What was in itself good, the law, has become a power for evil. Although sin is in man before he encounters the law, it is the latter that brings sin to life by presenting the possibility of transgression and appealing to man's rebelliousness.

But how is it that what was intrinsically good, the law, has been thus diverted to the service of evil? Earlier in Galatians (4:9f.), Paul had connected the law with ''the elemental spirits of this world,'' but in Romans he does not mention these. Instead, he connects the weakness of the law with ''the flesh.'' It was not the law that was weak but man in his character as made of flesh (*sarkinos*) that is directed against God. Because sin dwells in man, he cannot do what is right, although he wills it. The force of evil which Paul calls *hamartia,* or *sin,* making the flesh its base of operations, makes the demand of the law powerless (Rom 7:13–24) and even claims man.

Paul's treatment of the law in Galatians, then, differs from that in Romans. In Galatians it is almost unrelievedly pejorative. Was this simply because that epistle offers what was Paul's first serious attempt at dealing with the law? Or was it owing to an untempered, polemic reaction to Jewish Christians who had been as extreme as he himself had been? In Galatians Paul's anger is at its white heat against these opponents, who in his view were reimposing a yoke of bondage upon his churches unnecessarily now that the Messiah had come, and against those Jews who were urging them on with threats. Had Paul's violent reaction to them, sometimes coarsely expressed, been to no avail? Had his opponents in Galatia prevailed? In the light of that failure, was he led to contemplate the possibility that a more conciliatory treatment of the law might be more effective in explaining his position to the Romans, whose support he cherished as he faced the journey to Jerusalem where a confrontation with Jewish Christians again awaited him?[24] No certain answers are possible. But, for whatever reason, Paul was not content simply to repeat the passionate words he had written to the Galatians. In Romans he presents a more positive estimate of the Law even while he still strikes against it. A more restrained and subtle Paul emerges. In Galatians he had treated the Law with a clinical, almost impersonal detachment difficult to reconcile with his Pharisaic past. In Romans he is not less critical but more circumspect and sensitive. The subtle variations in his discussion of the Law militate against any simplistic dismissal of his criticisms of it. It will be clear that any single, monolithic interpretation of Paul's response to the Law is unacceptable.

NEGLECT OF EXPLICIT MORAL DEMANDS IN THE EPISTLES

We have recognized that there is no one Pauline attitude to the Law. But certain constants that constitute what could be described as a common pattern are detectable in Paul's varied responses to it. The tendency not to do justice to these is also a pitfall in the way of a true understanding. For the sake of clarity, these constants to which we refer are here divided into two categories, the vertical and the horizontal, which in fact are inseparable.

The Vertical Dimension

We have previously connected Paul with the general early Christian understanding of the communal aspect of the Christian life and shall do so again. Here we are more concerned with the more directly personal aspects of life in Christ as it is related to the Torah.

First, quite simply, Paul places the demands of the Torah in the light of Christ. For him, the way of the Law gives place to the Law or way of Christ. The tradition to be followed he now seems to identify with the Living Lord himself.[45] On grounds which cannot be repeated here, I have elsewhere urged that Paul understood Jesus as having become the Torah, that is, the totality of the revealed will of God. For him the Torah became concentrated in the Person of Jesus Christ; its demands are now informed by the *agapē* and, indeed, the very presence of Christ.

But what precisely does this mean? I think that it has three aspects which are exceedingly difficult to hold in proper balance. First, the moral life of Christians bears constant reference to, or is molded by, the actual life of Jesus of Nazareth—that is, his ministry of forgiveness, judgment, healing, and teaching.[46] Second, the moral teaching has its point of departure not only in the ministry of Jesus but also in his resurrection. The resurrection was the ground for the emergence of the primitive community as a close-knit and self-conscious group. But the resurrection was also the immediate inspiration of its morality. The resurrection was not only a triumph of life over death, it was also a triumph of forgiveness over sin. The resurrection was an expression, perhaps *the* expression of God's grace in Christ, because the risen Christ came back to those who had forsaken him and fled or who had slept during his agony. He forgave their failure. The resurrection as forgiveness emerges clearly in Paul and elsewhere.[47] The resurrection, which reassembled the scattered disciples to form the church, was founded in the grace of Christ and of God in Christ. It was of a piece with the whole ministry of Jesus, and the morality of the community, like that of his ministry, was to be a morality governed by grace—that is, it was the morality of forgiven men who had known the risen Lord as a forgiving Lord and who in gratitude (the most ethical of the emotions) gave themselves to the good life in His name.[48]

Third, the mode of the presence of this risen Lord in the community was that of "the Spirit." There have been attempts to maintain that the Spirit, in the earliest days of the church, had no ethical significance, that it was merely a wonder-working power, mysterious and nonmoral. But these attempts were vain. It was the Spirit that had inspired the greatest teachers of morality, the prophets, who had discerned between the precious and the vile; it was the Spirit that would create a new heart in the new Israel of Ezekiel's vision and inspire the messianic times with counsel, wisdom, and righteousness. And, above all else, the Spirit was the inspirer of the Scriptures. This in itself implied the ethicality of the Spirit, because it was through these that Israel knew the demands made upon it. Through the resurrection, the Spirit was again experienced.

The coming of the Spirit in primitive Christianity should never be separated from the resurrection as grace. Like the resurrection itself, the coming of the Spirit is "an energy of forgiveness." Thus it became the source of morality because gratitude for forgiveness is the ground of Christian being. Love, joy, peace, righteousness, and every victory "in the moral sphere" are the fruit of the Spirit. The enthusiasm of the Spirit, much as it was open to more superficial expressions, found its true fruit in love.[49]

When, therefore, we say that for Paul the Law had been Christified, we recognize that the earthly ministry of Jesus, the Risen Lord, and the Spirit—inextricably bound together as they are, so that often what was uttered in the Spirit could be ascribed to the earthly Jesus himself—these together became the source of the demand under which the early church lived. Christian morality, in short, always has as its point of reference the life, resurrection, and living Spirit of Jesus Christ. And it is this that determines its manifold dimensions.

To put this geometrically, it was their vertical relationship with the risen Lord, the participation of the early Christians in the experience of being forgiven by the risen Lord and the Spirit that lent to them a common grace wherein they stood. They had been grasped by him and their response was primarily, through the promptings of this Spirit, to him. All

Christian fellowship is rooted in a particular event—immediately in the resurrection and behind this in the life and death of Jesus—with which the resurrection, as we have seen, as an expression of grace was wholly congruous. The ethic of the community is linked to the understanding of an event—the life, death, and resurrection of Jesus. In this the church saw the act of God himself in history.

Now especially in Paul, morality is understood in terms of the appropriation of this event, the recapitulation of it in the life of the believer. To put it in other words, the moral life is a life "in Christ"; it is the living out in daily conduct what it means to have died and risen with Christ. For Paul, morality is inseparable from the life, death, and resurrection of Jesus. He divided his own life clearly into two parts: first, his life under the law when he was a Jew, and second, his life in Christ. The two parts were distinctly separated by his experience on the road to Damascus. The act by which a Christian acknowledged his faith and really began to live "in Christ" was baptism. This act symbolized a death to the old life under the Law and a rising to newness of life "in Christ" or "in the Spirit." By baptism[50] the Christian through faith had died, had risen, and had been justified; he was a new creation. And what was now necessary for him was to become what he was. His moral life is rooted in what he *is*—a new creation in Christ. Just as we call on each other to "play the man," so Christians are called upon to "play the Christian," to be what they are. To use theological jargon, the imperative in Paul is rooted in the indicative. There is a vertical dimension to Christian living, an attachment to the fact of Christ, his life, death, and resurrection.[51]

And so, too, in the fourth Gospel the life of the Christian is to re-enact the self-giving of God in sending Christ into the world. The "love" which exists between the Father and the Son is to be reproduced in the relationship of the disciples to one another. Here again there is a vertical relationship between the believer and Christ and God which determines his relationship with others.[52]

But this vertical dimension of morality in the early church has another aspect that is simpler to understand. Not only the imitation of God's act through dying and rising with Christ, but also the imitation of the Jesus of history (if we may so put it) played a real part in the moral development of the early church. Early Christians looked up to Jesus of Nazareth as a modern educationist would put it, as their "identifying figure." Part of the reason for the preservation of stories about the life of Jesus, such as we have in the Gospels, was the desire to imitate Jesus in his acts.[53] During his ministry, Jesus had demanded readiness to enter upon his way of suffering; his followers were literally to take up the Cross (Mark 8:34). In the life of the early church, while persecution (walking the way of the Cross literally) was always a possibility, more often Christians were called upon to imitate their Lord, in the witness of the common way; this was less spectacular perhaps but no less arduous than readiness to die—in love, forbearance, patience, and mercy—in messianic grace. Luke's change of Mark 8:34 (9:23) is significant.[54] The degree to which the imitation of Jesus informed the lives of early Christians has been variously assessed. But it is difficult to deny its presence. Christ is an object of imitation to Paul as Paul expects to be such an object to his own followers (1 Cor 11:1). The apostle holds up certain qualities of the historic Jesus that were to be imitated; he points to Jesus who pleased not himself (Rom 15:3) and to his meekness and gentleness (2 Cor 10:1), and he commends liberality through a reminder of him who was rich and became poor (2 Cor 8:8–9).[55] The description of love in 1 Corinthians 13, which is probably based upon the life of Jesus, is, in short, a character sketch of him. There can be little question that for Paul every Christian is pledged to an attempted moral conformity to Christ. This is also true of the fourth Gospel (John 13) and 1 Pet 2:2.[56] The life of Jesus is a paradigm of the Christian life.

So far we have noted two aspects of the vertical dimensions of Christian morality in the early church: the Christian is raised up with Christ to newness of life and is to live out his resurrection daily, and he looks to Jesus as an object of imitation. There is another aspect to this vertical dimension. The Christian is taken up into the purpose of God in Christ. To be a believer was to be directed to and by Jesus of Nazareth as the Messiah. That is, there is always an eschatological reference to Christian living: the Christian shares in the purpose of God in the salvation revealed in Jesus. This comes out most clearly in Paul's understanding of his call to be an apostle. This meant for him that he was taken up by God's grace to share in the redemptive activity of God now at work through Christ in the church. True, the apostolic consciousness of Paul was more intense than that of most Christians and his calling as the apostle to the Gentiles, perhaps, unique. But the whole community also was called, that is, caught up into the large counsel of God. Christians were delivered from futility; they shared in the work of salvation, including their own, which was inaugurated by Jesus and which was to be completed in the future. In the light of the redemptive purpose revealed in Christ, they made their decisions, they discerned the things that further and that hinder this purpose, and they became fellow workers with God.[57] The life of early Christians

was a life born of the grace of God in the resurrection and sustained by
the hope of the end; Christian morality is rooted in a "lively hope,"[58]
even as it is informed by the earthly Jesus. It is governed by a memory
and an anticipation.

The Horizontal Dimension

So far, in describing the moral life of Paul and early Christianity, we
have emphasized what we have called its vertical dimension: attachment
to the risen Christ who was one with the Jesus of history, contemplation
of him in imitation, and participation in the divine purpose in him. But
like the early Christians, Paul was not exclusively oriented to these individual vertical realities, and early Christian morality contains an horizontal or human, societal dimension; it is the morality of a community
born of the grace of the resurrection. The NT knows nothing of solitary
religion, and it knows nothing of an individual morality. It points to a
community with a life to live. This community was not to luxuriate in
grace, absorbed in irrelevant, vertical privileges. As a community of
grace, it took practical steps to give expression to grace in its life. How
was this achieved? We may summarize the answer to this question under
two main headings.

The emphasis on the Christian community. First, there was a constant
concern in Paul as among other early Christians for the quality of their
common life. This it was that led to the experiment usually referred to
as the "communism" of the early chapters of Acts.[59] This experiment of
having all things common was the natural, spontaneous expression of life
in the Spirit with which the neglect of the poor was incompatible. This
appears from the naïveté of the experiment. Owners sold their property
and handed over the proceeds to the apostles, who administered a common fund from which the needs of the poor were met, presumably in the
form of common meals. The contributions to the common pool were voluntary (Acts 5:1–11). The experiment failed, not to be repeated in this
form, but it witnessed to the societal or communal morality of the primitive community in its realism and its impracticability. That experiment
took place in the light of an absolute demand for love informed by the
intensity of the church's experience of forgiveness and, therefore, of
grace.

The emphasis on the communal nature of the Christian way persists
throughout the New Testament. It is rooted in a communal emphasis
found in the ministry of Jesus who gathered the Twelve as the representatives of the new community of Israel to follow him.[60] It is probably

from this that there developed Paul's "Christ-Mysticism" which issued not in "a flight of the alone to the Alone" but in the building up of the church, the new community.[61] Along with rationality[62] and the recognition of personal integrity,[63] Paul sets forth the building up of the church as the criterion of Christian action.[64] Similarly, in the Johannine literature one finds the love of the brethren as the mark of the church: "If you love not your brother whom you have seen how can you love God whom you have not seen?"[65]

But the same impulse which led to the experiment in communism, the awareness of the horizontal significance of the life in grace, in part at least, led to other developments, which are especially clear in Paul.

The emphasis on specific moral teaching. The Pauline letters appeal to the words of Jesus as authoritative. These words were at least one source of Paul's moral teaching. The extent to which the Pauline letters are reminiscent of the tradition as represented in the synoptics has been insufficiently recognized. The matter has been the subject of acute debate and continues to be so.

Two factors emerge clearly. First, Paul interweaves words of Jesus almost "unconsciously," as it were, into his exhortations, which suggests that these words were "bone of his bone." The following parallels are clear:

Rom 12:14 Bless those who persecute you; bless and do not curse them.	Matt 5:43 You have heard that it was said, "You shall love your neighbor and hate your enemy."
Rom 12:17 Repay no one evil for evil, but take thought for what is noble in the sight of all.	Matt 5:39 ff. But I say to you, Do not resist one who is evil. But if anyone strikes you on the right cheek, turn to him the other also.
Rom 13:7 Pay all of them their dues, taxes to whom taxes are due, revenue to whom revenue is due, respect to whom respect is due, honor to whom honor is due.	Matt 22:15–22 Render therefore to Caesar the things that are Caesar's, and to God the things that are God's. (22:21b)
Rom 14:13 Then let us no more pass judgment on one another, but rather decide never to put a stumbling block or hindrance in the way of a brother.	Matt 18:7 Woe to the world for temptations to sin! For it is necessary that temptations come, but woe to the man by whom the temptation comes!

Rom 14:14
I know and am persuaded in the
Lord Jesus that nothing is
unclean in itself; but it is unclean
for any one who thinks it
unclean.

Matt 15:11
Not what goes into the mouth
defiles a man, but what comes
out of the mouth, this defiles a
man.

1 Thess 5:2
For you yourselves know well
that the day of the Lord will
come like a thief in the night.

Matt 24:43-44
But know this, that if the
householder had known in what
part of the night the thief was
coming, he would have watched
and would not have let his house
be broken into. Therefore you
also must be ready; for the Son
of man is coming at an hour you
do not expect.

1 Thess 5:13
And to esteem them very highly
because of their work. Be at
peace among yourselves.

Mark 9:50
Salt is good; but if the salt has
lost its saltness, how will you
season it? Have salt in
yourselves, and be at peace with
one another.

1 Thess 5:15
See that none of you repays evil
for evil, but always seek to do
good to one another and to all.

Matt 5:39-47
But I say to you, Love your
enemies and pray for those who
persecute you. . . . (5:44)[66]

In addition to these clear parallels there are many other possible or probable ones.[67]

Second, there is also clear evidence that there was a collection of sayings of the Lord to which Paul appealed (Acts 20:35; 1 Cor 7:10, 9:14, 11:23, 14:37; 1 Thess 4:15–16, and especially 1 Cor 7:25).[68] Not only in matters of a legislative character[69] does Paul find guidance in the words of Jesus, but also in more personal matters (Romans 7), where possibly his discovery of the supreme importance of intention goes back to Jesus. In 1 Cor 7:25 he refers to a word of Christ as a commandment; in two places, once explicitly and once implicitly, he uses the very words "the law of Christ"[70] where the reference is, in part at least, to the teaching of Jesus. This is no declension on Paul's part to a primitive legalism but the recognition of the fact that his exalted Lord was never, in his mind, divorced from Jesus, the teacher, that the Spirit is never divorced from the historic teaching of Jesus.

Nevertheless, there is a difference of emphasis in Matthew and Paul as over against the Johannine literature. The words of Jesus appear in both the former over their wide range. But like John they also sum them up in one word, *agapē*. Thus, the climax of the Sermon on the Mount at Matt 7:12 is the Golden Rule. And Paul, like John and the synoptics, emphasizes the centrality of "love" (Rom 13:8–10; 1 Cor 8:1, 13; Col 3:14; *cf.* John 13:34–35; 1 John 3:1, 2:7–10, 4:7–16). The meaning of the word "love" has again to be noted carefully. Partaking more of active goodwill than of emotion, it can be commanded, as emotions cannot. In 1 John it is used in a down-to-earth manner, involving willingness to share one's goods (1 John 3:17). For Paul it is the fulfillment of the Law and the principle of cohesion in the Christian community. The expression of love is multiple (1 Corinthians 13), but its essential nature is revealed in Christ's dying for men. It is this kind of act that is demanded of those who love.[71]

The necessity which led to the application of the absolutes of Jesus to life led the church to take over for its own use codal material whether from Hellenism or from Judaism or from both. Most of the letters, Paul's and others' in the New Testament, reveal a twofold structure. A first part, dealing with "doctrine," is followed by a second, dealing with "ethics." Romans is typical. Chapters 1 through 11 deal with doctrine, 12:1 and following deal with ethics, and are causally connected with chapters 1 to 11. The ethical sections of the various letters reveal a common tradition of catechesis, which may have been used in the instruction of converts, especially at baptism (*cf.* Rom 12:1; Col 3:8—4:12; Eph 4:20—6:19; Heb 12:1–2; Jas 1:1—4:10; 1 Pet 1:1—5:14).[72] This common tradition must not be regarded as having a fixed pattern, but the similarity in the order and contents of the material in the above sections is too marked to be accidental. The presence in them of the imperative participle (Rom 2:9–19), a form found but not common in Hellenistic Greek but familiar in Hebrew legal documents, suggests that Paul and other Christian writers drew upon codal material, such as is found in the Dead Sea Scrolls, *Mishna Demai* and *Derek Ereṣ Rabba* and *Zoṭa*.[73] There are also parallels to the tradition in the Hellenistic sources. Paul and others in the church probably took over much pagan moral convention from the Jewish Diaspora. Whatever the exact source of the materials, the church found it necessary to borrow from non-Christian sources. It not only domesticated the absolutes of Jesus but also took over domestic virtues from the world.[74]

This brings us to the last aspect of the NT's moral teaching with which we shall deal here. That Paul was able to draw upon moral teaching from

Judaism and Hellenism means that there was for him a continuity between the moral awareness of Christians and of the non-Christian world. Wherein did this continuity lie? It lay probably in the doctrine of creation which the early church held. It cannot be overemphasized that creation and redemption are congenial in the New Testament, as indeed in Judaism. The messianic age had cosmic dimension for Judaism. So too in the New Testament the creator and the redeemer are one. Paul can find in Christ the wisdom—the creative agent—of God, and John and Hebrews can find in him the Word by which all things were made. For Paul the good life is the truly natural life. Morality is rooted in creation.[75]

CONCLUSION

By looking at the historical meaning of the Torah, the historical messianic context, and the theological framework within which Paul worked, we have sought to call on history to readjust the balance of traditional interpretations of his response to the Torah. Such a historical approach, we have recently been reminded, is neither natural nor congenial to lawyers.[76] They tend to be mainly concerned not with the setting, meaning, or intent of laws in the past but with their import for the present. We are not competent to engage in any depth in a discussion of how far history can be a corrective to the interpretation of law in the present, nor is it necessary to do so here. But in this context a biblical student who is wholly unsophisticated in the niceties of the study of law but who has found himself made aware of this lack by the demands of his own discipline may perhaps be allowed to express in a very hesitant manner and at the risk of the charge of naïveté, some reflections on the significance of Paul for the approach to law today.

First, there is the inescapably religious dimension of law in Paul. David Daube began a famous and seminal work by issuing a caution against the too-calm acceptance of the traditional view propounded by H. S. Maine in *Ancient Law* that "law was not always distinguished from religion; and that, originally, all precepts were deemed to be of a religious character."[77] Certainly for Paul the Torah was from God and, to use Daube's phrases, he would have valued every action "according as it may please or displease God." The religious ground and character of the demands under which he conceived himself to be called to live both as a Pharisee and as a Christian were for him axiomatic. To move from Torah in the sense in which a Jew, Paul, understood it, both before and after he came to believe in Jesus as the Messiah, to law as it usually governs and is understood in modern Western societies, requires a leap of imagination.[78] The direct transference of Pauline categories to modern legal systems is inadmissible. Both before and after his call, usually incorrectly called his "conversion,"[79] Paul lived within a religious community. Both Judaism and early Christianity, which before 70 A.D. must not be regarded as a non-Jewish phenomenon,[80] sought to pursue a life governed not by the laws of the Roman state, although these also were honored,[81] but by their own understanding of the traditional Torah. To both religions the notion of a "legal system" resting its authority on grounds other than the divine will revealed, respectively, in the Torah at Sinai and in Christ, would have been alien. For both, "the Law" is a consequence or accompaniment of a preceding religious covenantal commitment. To recognize this is not to ignore the way in which even biblical laws, as Daube again has pointed out, even in what might be regarded as their most crucial aspects have drawn upon and, indeed, been formed under the influence of extrareligious categories and events.[82] Nevertheless, the history of the emergence and development of Law both in Judaism and Christianity has been overcome by religious doctrine and given a religious cast. For Paul especially, although he made use of pagan catechetical commandments, albeit subtly Christianized, the center of his understanding of the way to be followed lay in his religious convictions and affirmations.

The reason for enlarging on this undeniable religious character of all law as Paul understood it is to point to the challenge he presents to all concepts of Law that rest their authority outside the divine will. And Paul raises acutely the question of the interrelation between law and religion. Even the laws of the pagan Roman state for him were ordained by God;[83] they were divinely sanctioned laws necessary to prevent men from devouring one another. Like the laws of the written Torah, they were to be obeyed. Paul challenges any legal system that is grounded only in secular, rational, utilitarian considerations or is understood simply as a way of getting things done. Such a system would, indeed, probably be inconceivable to him. It is self-evident that a challenge to relate radically religion to law and law to religions as Paul did speaks to our present condition. The case for this has recently been stated by Professor H. J. Berman. His argument need not be repeated, so persuasive is it.[84] Rather than pursue this general theme here, important as it is, we merely note the challenge and pass on to more specific ways Paul confronts us in the realm of law which, as Berman made clear,[85] are indeed central aspects of the general theme to which we have referred.

Second, the antithesis between Law and grace which governs much Christian and especially Protestant thinking would have been alien to

Paul. There is little doubt that for him the Torah was an expression of divine grace.[86] Despite the violent criticisms of the Torah that Paul reiterates in his polemic epistles, always there remained in his gospel a demand. This demand, that of *agapē*, could be interpreted as even more austere than that of the multitudinous *mitzwôth*, or commandments, of the Torah. "In Christ" Paul stood under a new Sinai requiring of him a universal *agapē* such as that called for in the Sermon on the Mount and elsewhere in the New Testament, the infinite demand of "the Law of Christ." But this did not mean that he was indifferent to those actualities and intricacies of existence that called for careful legal discrimination, refinement, and casuistry. Daube[87] has shown how in dealing with such human problems as marriage Paul stopped short of following the legal logic of his messianic absolutism but squarely faced the social realities of his day. No less than were the pharisaic sages who had taught him, he too was prepared to make concessions to the complexities of the order of society in which he found himself and to human weakness and sinfulness.[88] He was no fanatic unprepared to bend. Under the constraint of the very Christ whom he had called "the end of the Law," he was ready to be "all things to all men."[89] This required, as we have seen, sensitivity in moral direction. Nor again, convinced as he was of standing in the final messianic period of history and, indeed, of participating in the very inauguration of the "end of the days," the ultimate stage of history, was Paul indifferent to the tradition of his people, moral and otherwise. He was no antinomian; for him the Christian dispensation was the fulfillment and not an annulment of that tradition. Distrust of all law, such as is frequently expressed in our time in the counter culture and elsewhere, and which Protestantism, especially in its Lutheran form, has often fostered, finds no support in Paul.

Notwithstanding the recognition of all of this, to read his epistles is to be radically and inescapably challenged with two questions. The first is what weight should be given to specific rules and laws (*mitzwôth*) such as Paul declared had not been effective for him in the moral, social, and religious life? Paul placed a question mark, if not against these, at least at their side. It is certain that he retained rules and commandments, but they did not play an important, and certainly not an independent, part in his thinking. They indicated for him the direction and quality of life to be aimed at, and as such were necessary, but the dynamic for achieving that quality springs outside them in a recreated life. Into the philosophic and legal discussion raised by this question I am not competent to enter. I merely note that in recent studies by G. C. Christie[90] it is again argued that, if treated as absolutes, all rules and norms and, by implication at least, even specific laws never achieve what they set out to do but tend to become rigid, mechanical, and ossified.

This leads to the more important second question. What is the relation of Law, here used in a more restricted sense than Torah for rules of conduct, to tradition? To put this more clearly: how and to what degree should any legal system be influenced, not to say governed, by the accretions of the past? To what extent are our judges only bound by a preexisting body of law which is consistent, determinate, and explicit, and is therefore deemed to deliver them from prejudice? To what extent should inherited precedents, often described as the creative ark of precedent, the accumulated wisdom of the ages, or what Holmes called "the scattered prophecies of the past" or "the oracles of the law," become normative or directive? Continuity with the past is a necessity for the life of any society; it is the ground of any social predictability and the depository of experience. But continuity alone is not enough. It can throttle. Because laws, no less than other aspects of culture, are subject to corruption and manipulation, the precedents of the ancients reflect not only their principles but also their prejudices. Precedent, like age, is no guarantee of equity or efficacy. Although the phrase "law and order" intends implicitly to indicate respect for personal rights, it can become a last refuge of scoundrels.[91] The early Marxist critique of legal systems is pertinent. Marx and other socialist theorists regarded the traditional Russian legal system, like all existing legal systems, as a cloak for class interest, a device which reflected the claims of the bourgeoisie over the propertyless masses. "The economic structure of society," wrote Engels, "always forms the real basis from which, in the last analysis, is to be explained the whole superstructure of legal and political institutions as well as the religious, philosophical and other conceptions of each historical period." And again he wrote, "The jurist imagines that he is operating with *a priori* principles, whereas they are really only economic reflexes."[92] The element of truth in these statements, exaggerated as they might be judged to be, is self-evident. Like Engels and Marx, *mutatis mutandis*, Paul would assert that, like the mind, the law was subject to corruption. But he did not draw the same conclusions from this as did the socialist theorists. They concluded that in the ideal future the law, like the state, should vanish. In the new classless society, in which the proletariat would play a messianic role, property relations would cease to exist, and thus the law and state which were designed to serve these would not be necessary. There would be "a glorious transition to a new order of equality and freedom without law.''[93] As we have seen, Paul did not succumb to such romantic legal nihilism. He never contemplated an ''exodus from the Law.''[94]

On the other hand, by bringing the legal tradition of his fathers before the judgment seat of the *agapē* of Christ, the apostle did achieve an immense and penetrating simplification of it. To suggest that such a simplification and radicalization as we find in Paul, who was living in the fervor of a messianic situation in which the end of all things was deemed to be almost immediately at hand,[95] can be applied directly to the vast corpus of laws by which modern societies are governed would be quixotic. Daube taught us almost forty years ago that the point of comparison between Christianity and Judaism and any legal system lies not in the absolute demands that characterized the early Christian movement in its first fine careless rapture, but in the later legal developments within Christendom that culminated in canon law. But granted this, one must ask whether in inherited legal systems, including our own, much has inevitably, but no less unfortunately and sometimes tragically, become ossified, depersonalized, encrusted, and corrupted by the interests of those who held power in the past and by their successors in the present.[96] To insist, and rightly so, that the messianic absolutes do not directly apply to nonmessianic conditions is not a valid reason for conveniently relegating them to a benign neglect or to oblivion. Simply because they are *there*, as Sir John Hunt expressed it of Mt. Everest, must not these absolutes be allowed to keep the legal system of any Christian society in a state of constant reexamination? Must not the Law itself, in this sense, be in a state of permanent revolution? Is it not constantly necessary to subject ''Law'' to the burning, penetrating, simplifying light that Paul brought to the Torah of his world?[97]

In the incomplete list of evils to which, we suggested, established and inherited legal systems tend to fall victim, we included depersonalization. By implication Paul particularly addresses this point. Because behind the radical simplification, which is at the same time from another point of view an intensification, to which Paul points, stands what can only be called a personalizing of the approach to law. Paul confronts the life under the Torah in a Spirit rooted in and indeed identified with a Person, so that he related each situation he confronted to the control of that Person, who as we stated earlier had become the Torah and tradition for him.[98] Here again it has to be emphasized that it would be quixotic to dissolve all legal considerations within an anomie of the Spirit. With typical sober common sense Paul refused to contemplate this. But it is fatally easy within a traditional legal system to descend into a game of rules, to don masks, and to impose masks, so that the personal dimension of those involved in the law are ignored. Paul not only called for a simplification of the rules of law but also for their subordination to the *agapē* of Christ. There is more to law than code; there is attitude. The Epistle to Philemon perhaps best reveals this. There Paul, while recognizing that the runaway slave had to be returned to his owner, urged that he should be treated as a dear brother and not be subjected to severe punishment. Certainly this was not exactly a condemnation of a monstrous legal system. And yet by introducing a purely personal consideration in Christ into the case of Onesimus, Paul had set in motion a concern that, taken with due seriousness, could have eroded slavery. We have already referred to his sensitivity in the question of marriage. Paul was no antinomian, but he demands that the Law, even messianic Law, be interpreted in the interests of persons. The words of John Noonan echo the convoluted epistles of the Apostle Paul because he too would bring even the Law captive to the obedience to Christ which is *agapē*:

> The central problem, I think, of the legal enterprise is the relation of love to power. We can often apply force to those we do not see, but we cannot, I think, love them. Only in the response of person to person can Augustine's sublime fusion be achieved, in which justice is defined as "love serving only the loved."[99]

There is one further challenge from Paul. Related to this is an apparently paradoxical condition in which society, perhaps all societies universally, but certainly those in the West, finds itself. On the one hand, under the impact of the amazing developments of modern scientific technology, there is an acute awareness than "new occasions teach new duties" and that "time [often] makes ancient good uncouth." Society is now faced with perplexities and opportunities that are, apparently, new. For these there seems to be no direct guidance from the past. But this awareness of new demands and new possibilities coexists with the sense, born this time of psychological and sociological sophistication and of the brute facts of history, that there are entrenched historical traditions and backgrounds and age-old developments in law, as in other spheres, which hold a dead staying hand over all things. There is a fatalism in law, as part of a wider fatalism, which tends to paralyze the belief in the possibility of radical change: "Plus ça change; plus c'est la même chose." In such a situation Paul is particularly challenging. "Paul's capacity to recognize change," writes Michael Grant in closing his biography of the apostle, "was

uniquely strong." With the need radically to simplify Law, further words
of Grant's deserve quotation. He continues:

> The historian's characteristic view that everything which happens has
> evolved from existing historical tendencies and trends would have seemed
> to him to be disproved by what, in fact, had happened: the redemptive
> death of Jesus Christ. Whether one agrees with him or not—Jews, for ex-
> ample, do not—that Christ's death was this total reversal of everything that
> had taken place hitherto, at all events Paul's general attitude, insisting that
> such totally world-changing occurrences *can* take place, seems plausible,
> defensible and right in our own day; the years which lie immediately ahead
> of us are likely to confirm the cogency of Paul's viewpoint even more in-
> sistently.[100]

Paul assumed that the entrenched and oppressive religious, social, political, and legal structures of his day, what he refers to perhaps as *ta stoicheia tou kosmou*, the elements of this world, can be decisively challenged and transformed. Certain continuities he honored, including
continuity in Law, but he did not allow these to strangle the emerging
new creation which he had embraced in Christ. Perhaps it is his daring
belief in the possibility of a new beginning—in Law, as in other things—
a beginning for him inseparable from Christ, which is Paul's most challenging legacy to mankind.[101]

7

Paul and the People
of Israel*

To understand the Apostle Paul's attitude to his own people, it is necessary to place it in the perspective of his interpretation of the gospel as
a whole. Two main approaches to this have been taken. There are those
who see Paul's point of departure in his conviction that Jesus of Nazareth
was the Messiah and in the transformation of the understanding of the
messianic condition which this demanded.[1] Others point out that in his
epistles Paul seems to be most concerned, not with the messiahship of
Jesus, but with the cricitism of the law, that Paul's call (misnamed a
"conversion") arose from a new insight into the meaning, function and
weakness of the law (and with this, the insight into the nature of the self),
not from a new concept of messiahship. They claim that Judaism, always
tolerant of diversity of belief even in messianic claimants, could absorb
Paul's paradoxical doctrine of a crucified Messiah but could not overlook
Paul's acceptance of Gentiles, sinners who did not observe the law, as
members of the people of God. This passed the limits of Jewish tolerance
and brought down upon the Apostle the wrath of his own people.[2] The
two positions indicated are too polarized. The immediate cause of the
Jewish opposition to Paul centered in the law. But his understanding of
the law was inextricably bound up with the significance which he had
come to ascribe to Jesus of Nazareth as the Messiah and with the challenge
that this issued to all the fundamental symbols of Jewish life. To isolate
the criticism of the law from the total messianic situation as Paul conceived it is both to exaggerate and to trivialize it. That criticism was a
derivative of the place which Paul ascribed to Jesus as the Messiah. True,
he most frequently referred to Jesus as the Lord, and usually used the
term "Christ" (in such combinations as Jesus Christ, Christ Jesus, the
Lord Jesus Christ) in a personal, not titular sense. But he did not thereby
empty the term "Christ" of its messianic connotation, as especially in
Rom. 9:5, probably Rom 1:24, and possibly 1 Cor 2:23, Rom 15:7, Gal

* Presidential Address read at the meeting of *Studiorum Novi Testamenti Societas* at Duke
University, Durham, N.C., August 1976.

3:16, 6:2.[3] That Jesus was for Paul the Messiah had momentous consequences which were not annulled by his use of other terms for him. In interpreting Jesus as the Christ, Paul placed him within the framework, indeed at the high point, of salvation history, which in varying degrees was the concern not simply of circles given to apocalpytic speculation but of all significant currents in Judaism.

We concentrate here on one aspect of the messianic condition which Paul faced. In any messianic movement the figure of the Messiah becomes central, because he is the necessary catalyst for it. Faith in the Messiah, rather than the observance of the traditional norms or the law, becomes the essential mark of belonging to the people of God, the *sine qua non* of the movement. Scholem has made this clear in Sabbatianism (a phenomenon insufficiently explored for the understanding of the New Testament).[4] It is the same in early Christianity.[5] The advent of the Messiah, therefore, raised acutely the question of the constitution of the people of God: is it made up of those who have faith in the Messiah or of those who observe the tradition? Paul redefined the law and Israel in terms of Jesus the Messiah. The messiahship of Jesus is the point of departure for Paulinism, and its inevitable accompaniment, the criticism of the law, its method. But its concern, outcome, and end became—it might well be argued from the beginning[6]—the redefinition of the true nature of the people of God. We here ask what happens to the Jews as an ethnic entity in this redefinition. Since those who believe in Jesus as the Messiah or those who are "in Christ" now constitute "Israel," the people of God, what was the relationship between them and the Jews, Israel after the flesh, in their continuity and discontinuity?

Paul discusses this question especially in four epistles, 1 Thessalonians,[7] Galatians, 2 Corinthians and Romans. We shall not deal with epistles whose Pauline authorship has been seriously questioned nor, for obvious reasons, with Acts.

'ISRAEL' IN I THESSALONIANS

In his earliest epistle, Paul presents the bitterest indictment of the Jews. In 1 Thess 2:14–16 we read:

> For you, brethren, became imitators of the churches of God in Christ Jesus which are in Judea; for you suffered the same things from your own countrymen as they did from the Jews, who killed both the Lord Jesus and the prophets, and drove us out, and displease God and oppose all men by hindering us from speaking to the Gentiles that they may be saved—so as always to fill up the measure of their sins. But God's wrath has come upon them at last!

To judge from Acts, on Paul's first visit to Thessalonica, although some had accepted the gospel, the majority of the Jews there had strongly resented his success. The Thessalonian Christians had nobly endured much suffering at their hands (1 Thess 1:6, 2:14 f.). Paul is grateful. In expressing thanks to them, he refers to their Jewish opponents. In doing so, he combines traditional Christian (both Jewish and Gentile) criticism of Jews, for having crucified Christ and persecuted the prophets (compare Matt 5:12, 23:29–39; Luke 11:47–51), with typical Gentile polemic against the Jews as displeasing to God and enemies of the human race: θεῷ μὴ ἀρεσκόντων καὶ πᾶσιν ἀνθρώποις ἐναντίων. As a result of their conduct the wrath of God has fallen upon them, either "fully" or "at the end." The New English Bible proposes two renderings for the Greek of 1 Thess 2:16c: ἔφθασεν δὲ ἐπ' αὐτοὺς ἡ ὀργὴ εἰς τέλος: either "and now retribution has overtaken them for good and all" or, "now at last retribution has overtaken them" (the latter seconding the RSV.) Here, apparently, no hope is extended to the Jews. They have failed to accept the final challenge of history presented to them in the gospel.[8]

Many have regarded the whole passage, 1 Thess 2:13–16, as a later non-Pauline addition.[9] Elsewhere Paul never accuses the Jews of having crucified Jesus (1 Cor 3:8); specific passages usually cited from Matthew and Acts as Christian parallels to the notion that Jews have slain the prophets are later than Paul and date from after 70 c.e. The use by Paul of the typical Gentile slanders against Jews is unthinkable; and structurally the whole epistle, it is asserted, would be better without 1 Thess 2:13–16, 2:12 being more naturally followed by 2:17 than by 2:13. But, attractive as is this dismissal of the passage as non-Pauline, there is no textual evidence for the omission of 1 Thess 2:13–16, and the structural argument is not certain. The claims that Jews had crucified Jesus and murdered the prophets cannot be neatly postponed to a date after the fall of Jerusalem. As for the severity of the criticism, Jews have often been their own most severe critics. Apart from the prophets, the chronicler, for example, can regard the wrath of God as having fallen upon all his people without the possibility of appeasement (2 Chron 36:15 ff.).

Although the accusation on Paul's lips that it was Jews who crucified Christ in the light of 1 Corinthians and Romans *is* difficult, and although this unqualified attack on the Jews runs counter to Paul's later practice, all this warns against a too ready dismissal of 1 Thess. 2:13–16. On the whole, it is more justifiable to regard it as Pauline than otherwise.[10] Here the apostle castigates the opponents of his mission in the context of a Gentile church suffering persecution directly or indirectly from Jews. In expressing his bitter disappointment,[11] he used traditionally formulated materials. A comparison of Mark 12:1b–5, 7, 8, 9 with 1 Thess 2:15, 16 reveals a common sequence of thought.[12] Both passages draw upon tradition formulated in the Hellenistic churches.[13] This means that it is not necessary to explain the notion that "the wrath has fallen upon the Jews finally or fully" in terms of any extraordinary contemporary event.[14] Mark 12:9 can be used to illuminate 1 Thess 2:16. It reads: "What will the owner of the vineyard do? He will come and put the tenants to death and give the vineyard to others." Here the end has come fully or finally: the Jews, as such, are no longer entrusted with the vineyard of the Lord.

But Mark 12:9 must not be taken to dictate the interpretation of Paul's thought as implying that now the Jews have no hope. They can still hear and respond to the gospel, if they so choose. That the apostle regards their destiny as still an open one appears later from Romans 9–11. Moreover, there is one striking difference between Mark 12 and 1 Thess 2:15–16. In the latter the motif of the hindering of the gospel is given explicit attention; it is implied in Mark 12:7, but not expressed. The determinative words in 1 Thess 2:13–16 are those that refer in 16a to hindering the preaching of the gospel to Gentiles: this indicates heedlessness of God's will and animosity to men. This is Paul's own indictment and is not simply traditional. The anticipation of the inclusion of the Gentiles in the people of God in "the end of the days" was well marked in the eschatological thinking of Judaism: Paul shared in it. To hinder the preaching to the Gentiles was to hinder the very purpose of God. For Paul those Jews who were guilty of this had added the last drop to the cup of their evil deeds: they now had to drink it. The wrath of God has expressed itself finally for this reason. The refusal by Jews to receive the gospel constitutes apostasy (2 Thess 2:3): it is a rejection of God's will and is the work of Satan (2:9).[15] But are we to conclude that *all* Israel has been denied the election and the promise because of this? Paul is not thinking of all Jews, or of Israel as a totality, from whom the election and the promise have been taken away. The term he uses is "Jews" ('Ιουδαῖοι), not "Israelites" ('Ισραηλεῖται), or "Hebrews" ('Εβραῖοι)[16]. The general Jewish failure did not include all Israel, and does not imply that the church has taken over the function of Israel. Paul is thinking not of the Jewish people as a whole but of unbelieving Jews who have violently hindered the gospel. Certainly he does not distinguish between Jewish and Gentile Christians, so that he cannot be thinking of a Gentile church taking over the prerogatives and responsibilities of Jews as a people. It is to go too far, then, to make Mark 12 determinative for the interpretation of 1 Thess

2:15–16. When he wrote to the Thessalonians, Paul had not made up his mind on the final destiny of Israel, and his later epistles reveal his further wrestling with this question. That the failure of the mission to the Jews within an eschatological movement constituted a very serious check to the divine purpose he did not doubt.[17] Paul did not cease to ponder this, but in his very first epistle he deals with the Jewish hindrance to the gospel in largely traditional terms. This first response of his to Jewish opposition in 1 Thess 2:14–16 was unsophisticated, perhaps the unreflecting (and impetuous?) reaction of an early Paul, not to the Jewish people as a whole but to Jews who were violently opposing the preaching of the gospel to Gentiles and thus hindering the divine purpose. Clearly Jews at Thessalonica were alarmed that some of their members and God-fearers in their synagogues were being attracted by the Christian movement. There is no direct indication in the Thessalonian correspondence that they attacked either Paul or the churches over the question of the law. In Thessalonica, perhaps, Paul had not yet begun to welcome Gentiles into the church without demanding circumcision and the law. Possibly he had simply appealed to Jews and God-fearers[18] to believe in the messiahship of Jesus, and in their enthusiasm they had become unruly and antinomian. As we indicated, it is in Galatians and Romans that the question of Jewry, the meaning of "Israel," is more deliberately dealt with.

"ISRAEL" IN GALATIANS

In Galatians, after having stated the principle of justification by faith and not by works (2:15–21), Paul assumes the Jewish conviction that Abraham is the father of Israel, and turns to define Abraham's sons, who constitute "Israel." He is in debate, among others, with Gentile Christians who could not claim physical descent from Abraham. The opponents of Paul, themselves threatened possibly by nationalistic Jews, urged these Gentile Christians to give up Paul's advice and, in order to ensure that they partook in the heritage promised to Abraham, to observe the law and circumcision (sonship to Abraham being possible only in terms of circumcision and the law). Paul, on the other hand, claimed that just as Abraham himself had been justified on account of his faith, so those who were to be his sons were to be similarly justified, while those under the law were under a curse. Moreover, the promise to Abraham concerned not simply Jews but all peoples (*ethnê*, 3:8). In a way which Paul does not explain, Christ by his cross had opened the promise to Abraham to the Gentiles (3:14). In fact, the only true seed of Abraham was Christ himself and those baptized into him (3:16 ff.). "In Christ" the distinction between Jew and Gentile is annulled: it is necessarily annulled if salvation is to be achieved by all because all—Jews and Gentiles—have been unable to fulfill the law. This is implied in Galatians 3; the theme is taken up at more length later in Romans.

Paul demands that the people of God, belonging to Abraham, be defined in a new way. The meaning of "descent" from Abraham has to be radically reconsidered: it no longer has a "physical" connotation. Christian believers are the sons and daughters of God; they can now cry "Abba" and are the heirs of the promise to Abraham. They do not need to observe the law in order to be sons and daughters of God (4:1–12). Paul, possibly using the terms of his opponents, appeals to the law itself to point out that Abraham had two sons—the one born, according to the promise, of Sarah, and the other born, by physical descent, to the slave woman Hagar. These two entities persist in the heavenly Jerusalem and the earthly Jerusalem, respectively. The heavenly Jerusalem (the sons of Sarah) is constituted in part of living Christians so that it already has, so to speak, a bridgehead in this world. Who exactly are the sons of Hagar? Are they Jews or are they Jewish Christians? If Jews, then Gal 4:30, quoting Gen 21:10, 12, implies that Paul is here separating Jews as a totality, that is, the people of Israel, from believers in Christ. But does the context of Gal 4:21–31 point to Jewish Christian Judaizers as the children of the slave woman from whom the believers are to be separated (so that Gal 4:30 is comparable with 1:9 earlier in the epistle)? The attempt to make a distinction between Jews and Jewish Christians here is to split hairs: the latter would encompass the former. The point is that in Galatians Paul is uncompromising, radically insisting on a parting of the ways: as in his discussion of the law, so in his treatment of "Israel." Even when he most forcefully presents the doctrine of justification by faith, Paul, then, is essentially concerned with establishing who constitute the true people of God. Here that doctrine is ultimately part of an attempt to define "Israel": it is part of Paul's uncompromising statement of the case why, now that the Messiah had come and Jews and Gentiles were to be in a new relationship, the latter should not be asked to observe nor indeed should they observe circumcision or the law. In the light of justification by faith alone, Galatians demands a clean repudiation of the dominant traditional understanding of "Israel." Stendahl has put it another way: "Paul's doctrine of justification by faith without the works of the law was primarily a scriptural argument according to the exegetical principles of Judaism in defense of his mission to the Gentiles."[19] And yet there is even in the uncompromising epistle to the Galatians an insinuating ambiguity. Nowhere in it does Paul refer to a new Israel. In Gal 6:15 circumcision is nothing—true; but neither is uncircumcision: what matters is a new creation. This is the shadow of things to come. And is there also another foreshadowing in the same verse? This verse, written in Paul's own hand and probably summing up his position (and recalling the *Shemoneh Esreh*), ends with a prayer for and a declaration of peace and mercy on the Israel of God—which may refer to the Jewish people as a whole.[20]

"ISRAEL" IN 2 CORINTHIANS

In his correspondence with the Corinthian churches, Paul reveals deep concern with the meaning of the Christian community but does not directly deal with the people of Israel as such. One section, 2 Corinthians 3, concerns us because it has been taken to set the Christian dispensation so radically over against Judaism. For our purposes we only deal with it briefly. The opponents of Paul in 2 Corinthians included Jewish Christians.[21] It is important to recognize that in 2 Corinthians 3 Paul is concerned essentially with the contrast between two ministries, not with that between two covenants on which two distinct religions were founded. Paul declares himself the minister of a new covenant, not of the letter but of the spirit. He contrasts the ministry of the covenant of death or of the letter, drawn on stone with Israel at Sinai, which fails, with the ministry of the new covenant which through the Spirit is internal, just, permanent and life-giving (2 Cor 3:6–11). The ministry of the old covenant, and by implication the old covenant itself, had its glory (2 Cor 3:7). Moreover, just as the new covenant conceived by Jeremiah, Jubilees and the sectarians at Qumran did not unambiguously envisage a radical break with the Sinaitic covenant but a reinterpretation, so Paul's new covenant. Thus Jer 31:33 does not look forward to a new law but to "my law," God's sure law, being given and comprehended in a new way. And the adjective *ḥᵃdasah* in Jer 31:33, translated καινῄ by Paul, can be applied to the new moon, which is simply the old moon in a new light. The new covenant of Paul, as of Jeremiah, finally offers reinterpretation of the old. This is not immediately clear because Paul has expressed himself so obscurely. Especially at 3:14, he does refer to the "old covenant," but his meaning has to be carefully disentangled.[22] In 2 Corinthians he has still not resolved his attitude to his own people as the people of the covenant and his confusion has invaded his text. The best interpretation of that section is that the children of the old covenant, the Jews, when they read the *narrative* of the covenant at Sinai, carry a veil which blinds them to the true meaning of what they read. But those who turn to the Lord, the Spirit or Christ (these being virtually identified and at the same time differentiated) find that the veil is removed. They discover the true meaning of the covenant, a new light has been thrown upon it: it is in this sense it has become new. The terms τὸ καταργούμενον and τοῦ καταργουμένου in 2 Cor 3:11, 13 do not refer to the passing away of a "whole religious system based on the law"[23] but to the ministry of Moses and to the glory on Moses' face respectively. The stark antitheses of the early part of the chapter, which can be so easily misunderstood, are illumined by the discussion of the veil. Its outcome is to indicate that Paul as minister of the new covenant was not founding a new religion or a new people, and not dismissing the old covenant but revealing a new meaning and character in it. Through Christ, Paul does not oppose Sinai, but a particular understanding of it. Other passages in Paul indicate what that new meaning in Christ was: it was the revelation of the purpose of God to include all, both Jews and Gentiles, in his promise. What was fundamental was not that the new covenant was wholly other than the old, but that through Christ, the Spirit, Christians penetrated more deeply into the meaning of the latter by universalizing it. 2 Corinthians seems to stand halfway between Galatians and Romans. In the latter condemnation and contrasts do not occupy Paul so much as the need for reconciliation.[24]

"ISRAEL" IN ROMANS

The outcome of Paul's appeals to the Galatians is not known.[25] One thing points to failure there. When later Paul wrote or compiled Romans, although he does not depart from the fundamental understanding of the gospel revealed in Galatians, an almost conciliatory note has entered into his writing. He faces the ordeal of taking the collection to Jerusalem. He was probably aware that the opposition to him in Galatia was succeeding, and that his Jewish opponents in Jerusalem, who were particularly antagonistic, would certainly be encouraged in their hostility by his failure in Galatia. It was, therefore, a matter of anxious urgency for him to gain the understanding support of the Roman Christian community—Jewish and Gentile—for his position as he went up to the Holy City. Although the reasons proposed for the writing of Romans have been multiple, the most likely occasion for it is the one indicated: it was the necessity to sum up for the Roman church his understanding of the gospel as he faced the opposition of Jewish Christians in Jerusalem, the failure of the mission to the Jewish people,[26] and the encroachment of the Parousia.[27] Each of these factors impinged upon his writing, and it is the failure to recognize this by the overexaggeration of one over against the others that has led to inadequate interpretations of Romans as a totality. Paul presents the quintessence of his gospel at the very beginning of his epistle in Rom 1:16–17: it is the power of God unto salvation for everyone—Jew and Greek—who should believe. In it the righteousness of God is revealed from faith to faith. The rest of Romans is an exposition of what this means: Paul understands the gospel as for the world, and immediately sets forth its universal dimension in terms of God's wrath against sin among Greeks and, no less, among Jews (1:18—3:20). There follows the assertion of God's relation to humankind—the revelation of his "righteousness" in response to this human plight, and the response of faith which this demands (3:21—4:25) and the freedom that God's grace ensures (5:1—8:39), that is, freedom from sin (6:1–23), and from the law (7:1–25) and in the spirit (8:1–39). The cosmic and universal scope of the gospel is unmistakable: it is a gospel for the world.[28]

But the very validity or efficacy of the gospel which he preached was poignantly, even agonizingly, challenged for Paul by the refusal of his own people to accept it. Their rejection of Jesus as the Christ called into question for Paul and for his readers what must have sounded like exaggerated claims for the power of God unto salvation through Christ. This was particularly and immediately present to Paul's mind as he wrote Romans. If God who had made the promise to the Jewish people had failed to bring his salvation in Christ to them, what guarantee was there that he would complete the work of the believers' salvation? The failure of the mission to the Jews raised acutely the question of the faithfulness or the reliability of the very God who, Paul had claimed, justified even the ungodly. And so Paul devotes Romans 9–11 to this question. On this view those chapters can be regarded as Paul's justification of God. But it is also important to recognize in the understanding of Romans 9–11 the more immediately historical situation with which Paul was faced. The logic of Paul's argument in 1–8, as it would be understood by Jews, would be that justification before God for all mankind was only possible by faith in Christ. Jews were no less sinners than Gentiles: there was no distinction between them. It was impossible for all to render obedience to the law which was the sign of election in Judaism. By faith "in Christ" alone was it possible to belong to the people of God. And from this angle, the question was inevitable: what then of those who still retained the law? What is the nature of the discontinuity and continuity between the Jewish people and those "in Christ"? To this question also, which was inextricably bound up for him with that of the justification of God himself, Paul turns in 9–11.[29]

As in Galatians, so in Romans Paul, while he also exploits Hellenistic forms and literary genres,[30] takes seriously the scriptures of his people and seeks to deal with the problem in their terms—employing rabbinical and other methods to do justice both to this new emergence, the Christian community, and its matrix, the Jewish people. For him the gospel provides a particular way of understanding and interpreting their tradition.

After stating in Rom 9:1–3 his intense concern for Jews and recognizing their many and great advantages, Paul urges that they have a continued place in the purpose of God. It is incredible that God's declared purpose for them should become a dead letter (9:6). Is the Jewish people replaced as the people of God? In answering this question Paul has recourse to two concepts: that of the remnant, and that of God's sovereignty, which he assumes and refuses to impugn (9:14–29). Throughout history a principle of selection has been at work. This has issued in an ever-emerging remnant. God has "chosen" some, such as Isaac (9:7) and Jacob (9:13), and "hated" or rejected others such as Esau (9:13). In the time of Elijah, 7,000 did not bow the knee to Baal (11:1ff.). So too in the time of fulfillment there are those among the Jews who hear and accept the gospel and those who do not (9:24, 11:17, 25). In Rom 10:1ff. (compare 11:30–31) Paul recognizes that it is the Gentiles who are now ready to accept the gospel and are being incorporated into "Israel," while the Jewish people itself is being disobedient. He implies that the mission to the Jews has failed: they have "heard" the gospel, but they have rejected it (10:16–21).[31] But it cannot be said that the Jewish people as a totality has been disobedient and has, therefore, been replaced as the people of God by a Gentile community, the Church. A remnant has believed, and it remains true that the nucleus of the people of God, the Church, is still Jewish—as Jewish as Paul himself! God has not rejected his people (10:1): he has been, is, and will be faithful to his promise.[32]

Moreover, the Jews who have refused the gospel may change. Under a divine necessity Paul regards his own work as directed especially to the Gentiles. But indirectly, not by any frontal attack, it would also be a means—if Cullmann and Munck are right,[33] *the* means—of bringing about that change. Possibly, although this is not explicitly stated, its results among the Gentiles would show his fellow countrymen what they were missing by rejecting the gospel and spur them to emulation and to the acceptance of Christ, although this last is left unsaid (11:11 ff.). The precise nature of these results, which were to inspire this emulation, Paul does not indicate: did they include the superior moral and spiritual fruits to be revealed by the Gentile Christian community? If so, Paul does not say so. What is explicitly stated is that when the fullness of the Gentiles had come to believe, then Paul looked forward to a time when all Israel would be saved. The Greek is καὶ οὕτως πᾶς 'Ισραὴλ σωθήσεται.[34]

The Jews' rejection of the gospel for Paul, then, was a Pyrrhic rejection: it was temporary. Through their very rejection, they themselves would ultimately be reconciled and thereby bring to completion the reconciliation of the world. That event—the reconciliation of the unbelieving Jews to "Israel," the Church, and *ipso facto* of the world to God—would be "the resurrection of the dead." This enigmatic phrase must not be diluted to mean merely the greatest moral and spiritual blessings in a general way: it denotes rather the inauguration of the end (11:15).[35] This recognition of this role for the Jewish people—it must be emphasized—is in the context of an almost immediate expectation of the end. Paul was not thinking in terms of centuries or even probably of decades during which he contemplated the independent persistence of the Jewish people into an indefinite future, as in fact has historically happened (Rom 13:11–14). But this must not minimize the significance of the recognition of that separate existence as continuing until the very threshold of the end which Paul did not feel called upon to resist. Related to this is that in Rom 15:1–12 he insists that even Jewish Christians who observe various demands of the law "have a place in the church and can stand before God and be accepted by him."[36] Within and without the church the practicing Jew has his place.

All this Paul can believe because for him the whole process of history, past, present, and future, is under the mysterious and sovereign control of God, who is reliable. This does not mean that the apostle is committed to determinism, because the challenge of God's word is always near (10:8) and can win response (11:29). God has consigned all men (including the Jews) to disobedience, that he may have mercy on all (including the Jews, 11:32). Thus Paul holds that within God's purpose the Jewish people always remain the chosen people: their rejection of the gospel has affected only part of Israel and is temporary. The apostle seems to leave their reconciliation to the infinite wisdom of God and no longer regards it as a direct task laid upon him to confront them with the necessity to accept Jesus as the Christ. But that acceptance is finally assured and will prove to be the prelude to the age to come when God's supreme and infinite mercy will be shown to all, Jews and Gentiles. The salvation of the whole Gentile world is to precede but is not to be apart from that of Israel. In the meantime, it is implied, the continued existence of the Jewish people as an ethnic or "national" entity is affirmed within the context, finally, of a cosmic hope.

But this direct presentation of what Romans 9–11 seems obviously to state is too clear. It cloaks many complexities (predestination, election, and above all, the eschatological judgment which sifts all at the end), one of which we must face here. It is this. Has Paul in Romans 11 reintroduced an ethnic dimension into the Christian dispensation which earlier he had seemed to dismiss outright? To this question two totally incompatible answers have been given.

The first answer proposed is startling, indeed in my judgment far more catastrophic for Christian truth than its proponents seem to realize. Recently the charge has been made that Paul was an anti-Semite. Outside Romans 11, anti-Semitism emerges implicitly, it is urged, in his broad interpretation of the Christian life as involving a radical break with Judaism, which it has to leave behind. Inside Romans 11 it emerges explicitly. There Paul's program for the future and for Israel's role in it, which leads to the ultimate desired disappearance of Jews in the church or their absorption by the church, unmasks his anti-Semitism.[37]

What shall we say to this view? Although we cannot substantiate this here, the use of the term anti-Semitism, strictly defined for attitudes and conduct in the early Church is anachronistic. As for Paul, Galatians 5 and Romans 4 make it clear that Abraham, while the supreme exemplar and paradigm of faith and, therefore, of the Christian believer, was also the physical progenitor of Israel the elect people, meaning the people in the flesh. The simple fact of the physical descent of Jews from their father Abraham—called before he was circumcised, that is, when he was a Gentile (4 : 9–12)—(even though the birth of Isaac was indeed a miracle, 4 : 18–22) would have made such racial or genetic anti-Semitism as that of our time impossible for Paul, as also would the mere existence of proselytism. It would serve the interests of accuracy if we dispensed with the use of the nineteenth-century term anti-Semitism, which has a genetic or racial reference, and used rather only "anti-Judaism" in dealing with the New Testament, while fully recognizing that all fanatical intolerance is evil and almost always cruel, whether religiously or racially founded.[38]

More important is another general but fundamental consideration. Paul believed that the crucified Jesus was the Messiah. The interpretation of the significance of such a paradoxical Messiah inevitably led to radical reassessment and criticism of the messianic ideas of the existing religious and political order. The revolutionary possibilities of the movement which began with Jesus of Nazareth cannot be overemphasized. Paul, who, compared with some other Christians, seems to have been soberly conservative even in his radicalism,[39] contrasts the new order "in Christ" with the old order under the law with a burning vividness. His sharp antitheses will be familiar. As we saw from his earliest epistle on, Paul lashed out unrestrainedly against certain Jews.

Two factors are pertinent in the consideration of this violent criticism of Judaism and the Jews. Paul's criticism of the chief symbol of Judaism, the law, was not uniformly negative. It fluctuated with the conditions which he faced. For example, in Romans he abandoned the unqualified dismissal of the law expressed in Galatians.[40] His attachment to the Temple and Jerusalem and to the land remained, emotionally at least, to the end.[41] But far more to be emphasized is another simple fact. We have no letters of Paul to Jews or to Jewish Christians but only to largely Gentile churches. But these Christian communities were probably composed of Jews and of Gentiles who had been attracted to Judaism through the synagogues. The discussions of Judaism and Jews in Paul's letters are intramural. They are criticisms of the faith, institutions, and the worship of Jews not from without but from within. Although probably more critical of Judaism than those founded by other apostles, the Pauline churches also existed on the threshold of the synagogue. Rhetorically, in diatribe, Paul can address Jews directly even in Romans (2:17; 3:1, 9). The Christian communities to which he wrote *were* differentiated by certain elements—a common meal, apostolic figures, a way of life or discipline, an awareness of unity "in Christ," of living in a new aeon, and a confession of Jesus as Lord—as were other such communities. But in the time of Paul this differentiation did not spell separation. The evidence for the coexistence of early Christians with other Jews within a common heritage need not be repeated here. Did "Christianity" as a distinct, separate religious movement exist at all before 70 C.E.? Up till then was it not a movement within Judaism in competition with other "Jewish" movements variously interpreting a common tradition? Let us recall Peter Richardson's insistence[42] that the term "new Israel" does not appear until the second century, and Trocmé's attack on the very idea of a primitive Christianity before 70 C.E. as a historical myth.[43] Even though Paul can refer in Galatians to Ἰουδαϊσμός (1:13f.),[44] his criticisms of the symbols of Judaism no more signify that he had forsaken Judaism than did the bitter attacks of the sectarians at Qumran against the authorities in Jerusalem signify that they had forsaken it.

This reference to Qumran warns against the common failure to appreciate the multiplicity of ways in which Judaism expressed itself in the early pre-Jamnian period. The weight of scholarly tradition still inclines us to think of Judaism in largely monolithic Pharisaic terms. We read the first century in the light of the later dominant rabbinic Judaism. But Pharisaism itself in the first century was very variegated. The hospitable, comprehensive, theological tolerance and fluidity of Judaism before 70 C.E. allowed various groups to remain within its ambience. Among these were early Christians. Scholem's work on the seventeenth-century Messiah, Sabbatai Svi, offers a parallel. Rabbinic scholars refused to take Sabbatianism seriously as a Jewish phenomenon because they operated with a monolithic conception of Judaism, which could not contain Sabbatianism. But that movement was an essentially Jewish phenomenon: it arose within Judaism and despite its revolutionary character remained within it even when it proclaimed the divinity of Sabbatai.[45] The same applies to much Christian understanding of early Christianity. In accepting the Jew, Jesus, as the Messiah, Paul did not think in terms of moving into a new religion but of having found the final expression and intent of the Jewish tradition within which he himself had been born. For him the gospel was according to the Scriptures: it was not an alien importation into Judaism but the true development of it, its highest point, although in its judgment on the centrality which some Jews had given to a particular interpretation of the law it showed a radicalism which amounted to a new creation. Although it had its differentia, the Christian life for Paul was not a non-Jewish phenomenon distinct from and annulling another prior phenomenon "Judaism." Like Sabbatai Svi and Nathan of Gaza in the seventeenth century, he would not have conceived of himself as having ceased to be a Jew (Rom 9:3—11:1) or as having inaugurated a new religion. To make him guilty of anti-Judaism, not to speak of anti-Semitism, is to ascribe to the doctrine and life of first-century Judaism a monolithic character which they did not possess and which Paul himself would not have countenanced, a fact which is quite essential for the true appreciation of his position.

Why has the recognition of this simple fact been so difficult and tardy? Apart from the weight of scholarly tradition and conservatism to which we have referred, there are two main reasons, one external and Jewish and the other internal to the churches. First, the external Jewish reason: The attitude of Jews to Christians who arose among them varied. As Daube pointed out, the assessment of the claims of a messianic movement—to read the signs of the times—was difficult.[46] Doubtless the tolerance ascribed to Gamaliel in Acts may not have been typical but, as Hare has shown,[47] the evidence for any very early widespread violent reaction issuing in the persecution of Christians by Jews is not impressive. Most Jews would have been puzzled by Jesus but not necessarily antagonized by him any more than were the seventeenth-century Jews by Sabbatai Svi. It was the defection of many Christians from the national cause in the revolt against Rome in the sixties, the catastrophic fall of Jerusalem, and the subsequent struggle of the Jews for survival and the preservation of their identity under the sages at Jamnia that sharpened and hardened the lines between Jews who did not and those who did follow Christ. The sociological and psychological processes which induced opposed, though related, groups to define each other over against each other, so that even a community of love can come to define itself in terms of hate for its opponents, have become clearer to us in recent years. They have been insufficiently exploited in the examination of the emergence of Christianity as a distinct movement from within Judaism and over against it. At this point we need to listen far more to Weber and Freud. The processes which led to the radical separation of Christians from Jews we cannot trace here.The separation of Christians from Jews was a "forced withdrawal" in which both were responsible. What is especially noteworthy is that the separation was subsequent to Paul's day and must not be read back into his engagement with the religion of his fathers. It was the desperate necessity for Jamnian Judaism to close its own ranks against dissidents, to elevate the Torah as interpreted by the Pharisees still more to be *the* way of Jewish life, and the reaction to this among Christians and Jews that contributed most to the emergence of what we call Christianity as a distinct religion.[48] But Paul predated Jamnia.

This leads us to the second internal reason for the tardy recognition that Paul remained within the ambience of Judaism. Put simply it is this: Paul's letters were composed in the context of a dialogue within Judaism. They were later read outside and over against that context. Context determines content. The gospel itself, whoever preached it, could easily be misunderstood. Paul's peculiar and complex interpretation of it was often confusing.[49] During his lifetime he had to face this fact. Some Gentiles, concentrating on his insistence that it was not Jews after the flesh who constitute the people of God, but those "in Christ" and sometimes under pressure from Paul's opponents, initially understood him to mean that they were now to enjoy the privileges and ways of the Jews, who were no longer the people of God, and that they were called upon to observe the law even more zealously than Jews. Overconversion was a common phenomenon.[50] Other Gentiles, probably more numerous, like many Jews who heard him and to whom he wrote, took Paul to demand a complete rejection of the ways of Judaism and to invite messianic license. For these Paul spelled the total rejection of Judaism and, as we shall see, he opposed them.

And then after his day, when his letters came to be read by Gentiles who little understood Judaism, the misinterpretation of Paul became almost inevitable. These Gentiles often approached the epistles as outsiders incapable of appreciating their setting within what we may call a family dispute, which could explain both their extreme bitterness and, at times, their fine sensibilities. The disputes between Paul and his kinsmen, both those who accepted and those who rejected the new faith, over the true interpretation of their common Jewish tradition were expressed with intensity, not to say ferocity. As long as they were seen as being *intra muros,* they remained endurable. But once removed from this setting they took on a radically negative character. They no longer appeared as attempts at the reinterpretation of a shared tradition but as forages in hostility. In time, though the process was not rapid,[51] what was a disruption among Jews came to be spelled out as the denigration and rejection of Judaism and of the people of Israel as a totality. Intrinsically difficult to understand, then wrenched from their familial context—read by Gentiles largely untouched by Judaism—Paul's criticisms were ascribed a rigid coldness and a clinical, a surgical and a unified antithetical purpose. Even in the apostle's own lifetime, the tendency to which we refer had already emerged and he regarded it with apprehension.[52] Romans 9–11, and possibly the whole of Romans, may be regarded as the outcome of this apprehension. As we shall see, so far from revealing anti-Judaism, these chapters reveal a Paul conscious of an emerging anti-Judaism among Gentile Christians that could draw on the endemic hostilities of the Greco-Roman pagan world to help it. He is determined to combat this.

But these general considerations do not meet the specific charge that Paul's view of the future and of Israel's role in it in Romans 11 makes explicit that he was anti-Semitic. There in 11:25–32 Paul reveals a mystery about the future. It is this: when the full strength or number of the Gentiles has accepted the gospel, or in another interpretation, when the gospel has been preached to all the Gentiles, then also the "whole of Israel will be saved." But what precisely, it is asked, is this "salvation" in the mind of Paul? It is the absorption of all Jews in the Christian community, that is, the cessation of the distinct existence of Israel as a people. True, Paul allows to Jews a role up to the end, which was to come soon, but they are finally to lose their identity in the life of the Church. It has been claimed that this is explicit if subtle anti-Semitism. Paul anticipated and desired, it is claimed, the end of Judaism and the Jewish people, a μετάβασις εἰς ἀλλὸ γένος. This approach to Rom 11:25ff., crude as it seems, is still very often the unconscious and unexpressed assumption of many. Now that the gospel has come, is there any *raison d'être* for the continued existence of Judaism and Jews?

This specific understanding of Rom 11:25–26 must be squarely faced. To assess it, the following considerations are pertinent. There is the anachronistic use of the term anti-Semitism already noted: the failure to recognize that the salvation to which Paul refers is according to the very scriptures of Judaism and not in antithesis to them (11:26). There is also, above all, the failure to distinguish between history and the age to come. In history, according to Paul, the call of Israel is irrevocable, and the Israelites always remain God's friends for the sake of the patriarchs (11:28). Pre-Christian Jewish eschatology itself had anticipated the final incoming of the Gentiles into the worship of the true God. But this was not regarded as a subtle means of annihilating the ethnic diversity of Gentile life. Over against the Stoics, for example, who contemplated the disappearance of ethnic differences as desirable, Philo and the Palestinian sages anticipated that ethnic and linguistic distinctions would continue into the messianic age—a position rooted in the Old Testament.[53] We might expect Paul to have shared this view. His insistence that "in Christ" there is neither Jew nor Greek (Gal 3:28, Col 3:11) would seem at first sight to exclude it. However, it is clear that unity "in Christ" did not undo ethnic differences. In Christ Jews remain Jews and Greeks remain Greeks. Ethnic peculiarities are honoured (1 Cor 9:22, 10:32). If in Rom 11:32 we accept the reading of 𝔓[46] τὰ παντά rather than τοὺς πάντας, which is usually followed, then Paul makes explicit that in the final reconciliation ethnic distinctions remain.[54] Can we not then simply assert that Jews will remain Jews, as a people, when they are saved, as Paul had himself continued to be an Israelite (11:1)?[55] The apostle thought of the salvation of all Israel at the limit of history not as involving the destruction of its ethnic identity but as its enhancement. What, then, precisely is the salvation of all Israel to which Paul refers?

Two approaches to this question are possible. Rom 11:25–7 can be taken in isolation, as a construction of Paul's peculiar thinking about the end,[56] a special mystery here proclaimed by Paul (11:25) which we should not expect to find either in his own previous writings, or it can be taken as part of a tradition of Jewish and early Christian eschatology on which he drew even though he contributed his own emphasis. The first approach comes to concentrate on the theology of Paul, the second more on his Christology. Let us now pursue these two approaches, setting forth each in as much detail and with as much sympathy as possible.

We examine the former first. Does the term σώζω used absolutely, as in Rom 11:26, imply "conversion," that is, the passage from one religious faith to another? Except in confrontations between paganism and Judaism, such religious conversion was largely unknown in the Greco-Roman world.[57] Moreover, the most customary verbs used to describe them were μεταβάλλειν, ἐπιστρέφειν, στρέφειν,[58] which Paul does not here employ. Does σώζω, which he does use, imply the abandonment of their faith by Jews? The same verb occurs in 1 Cor 9:22 in a context dealing with the "saving" or "gaining" of Greeks and Jews. There it is clear, at least, that Paul is not thinking of salvation in terms of the abandonment of ethnic differences: to the Jew he became as a Jew. In 1 Cor 1:24, "the called" contain Jews and Greeks; the sensitivities of both are honoured (1 Cor 10:32). There are both Jews and Greeks in the one body of the Church (1 Cor 12:13).

But does the saving of the Jew mean the same kind of radical break with his *religion* that the saving of a Gentile implied? There is a difference. In Rom 11:25 Paul considers the condition of Jews to be one of a hardening which caused them to reject the gospel (10:19). For this—allowed by God as it is—they are themselves responsible (10:19: ἀλλὰ λέγω μὴ Ἰσραὴλ οὐκ ἔγνω;).[59] Their salvation therefore will be a deliverance from this condition.[60] Paul does not explicitly claim that all Israel will ultimately believe in Jesus as the Christ,[61] but simply that they will be "saved." The passive form of the verb is to be emphasized. Paul is not thinking of any action inaugurated by Israel: his experience of her obduracy made such an expectation unrealistic (10:18–21). Rather, he thinks of an activity of God whereby he will bring his covenant with them to fruition (11:27).

Does this reference to God's own exclusive activity at the end, and Paul's apparent silence about Christ himself in this context, find support elsewhere in the passage? Rom 11:26 could be taken to support a special activity of God towards Israel at the end. The salvation of all Israel is associated with the coming of "the redeemer" in Isa 59:20:

καὶ ἥξει ἕνεκεν Σιὼν ὁ ῥυόμενος
καὶ ἀποστρέψει ἀσεβείας ἀπο Ἰακώβ.
καὶ αὕτη αὐτοῖς ἡ παρ' ἐμοῦ διαθήκη,
εἶπεν ὁ κύριος. (LXX).

Paul's text is like that of the LXX except that he has ἐκ Σιὼν rather than ἕνεκεν Σιὼν. Like the LXX, he has ὁ ῥυόμενος whereas the MT (which also reveals other differences) simply reads גֹּואֵל. There is nothing in the text of Paul itself to indicate that ὁ ῥυόμενος stands for Christ; it is possible to understand it of God himself.[62] The reference in Rom 11:27 to καὶ αὕτη αὐτοῖς ἡ παρ' ἐμοῦ διαθήκη (Isa 59:21) would then be to the eternal covenant between Yahweh and Israel, exclusively, referred to in Isa 59:21, not to any future covenant as the translation in the NEB implies.[63] This is to be achieved on God's side, through the forgiveness of sin offered to Israel at the end: the covenant in Rom 11:27 seems to be distinct from the new covenant referred to in 1 Cor 11:25 and 2 Cor 3:6, which fulfilled the hope of Jer 31:33 and which embraces both Jews and Gentiles in the church. Against this, it is often asserted that the words ὅταν ἀφέλωμαι τὰς ἁμαρτίας αὐτῶν recall the Jeremianic passage.[64] But the alleged parallel sentence to it at Jer 38:34 (LXX; MT 31:33) reads: ὅτι ἵλεως ἔσομαι ταῖς ἀδικίαις αὐτῶν καὶ των ἁμαρτιῶν αὐτῶν οὐ μὴ μνησθῶ ἔτι.[65] These words are not evoked by Rom 11:27. The latter more directly points to Isa 27:9. It is not to be ruled out, then, that Paul is thinking in Rom 11:27 of the separate covenant which God already has with Israel (the future is read into 11:27a; it is not in the text). He will honor that covenant by forgiving her, because he will not go back on his acts of grace and his calling of Israel (11:27a, 29). On this view the whole process of Israel's salvation at the limit of history will be the work of God. Israel will be brought to conform to his purpose for it from the beginning through the forgiveness of its sins.[66] And this view of the future does not bring Israel into connection with the Christ of the new covenant for Gentiles at all. For Paul, Israel is to retain not only its ethnic identity but its religious peculiarities right to the end of history, when there would be what has been referred to as a divine *coup d'état* to save Israel.[67] By implication Paul has recognized the final failure of his mission to his own people. It has dawned on him "that the Jesus movement is to be a Gentile movement—God being allowed to establish Israel in his own time and way. . . . "[68]

Such an understanding of Rom 11:25-7, however, ignores certain probabilities which the second approach to which we referred takes seriously. Much of the thought of the passage is rooted in traditional materials: it has affinities with Jewish and Christian sources and elsewhere in Paul. He has drawn upon such materials and given his own version of the future in the context of upholding the significance of Israel after the flesh over against Gentile Christians who tended to deny it. Those materials must be consulted in the understanding of his thought.[69] Thus although in Rom 11:26 ὁ ῥυόμενος could refer to Yahweh, it is more likely to refer to Christ, as in 1 Thess 1:10. Moreover, that Paul writes of the redeemer coming out of Zion as we have pointed out elsewhere,[70] probably points to the heavenly Jerusalem, the Church, in heaven and on earth, whence Christ is to appear. (That Christ himself is the agent of their salvation might be further suggested by Paul's omission of εἶπεν ὁ κύριος, which refers to God, from the quotation from Isa 59:21 in Rom 11:21, although since Paul used κύριος of Christ, this is unlikely.) The point is that at the Parousia—at the very limit of history—the Jewish people are forgiven for their culpable hardness, accept Jesus as their Messiah, and thus share in his forgiveness in his covenant, which on this interpretation is best understood in terms of Jer 31:33. *Such a consummation, it cannot be sufficiently emphasized, would be for Paul the consummation of Judaism itself, despite the dislocation involved by the entry of the Gentiles into salvation before the Jews.* Paul was not thinking in terms of what we normally call conversion from one religion to another but of the recognition by Jews of the final or true form of their own religion.

Certainty about the meaning of Rom 11:25–27 is impossible. This is particularly so since the passage contains OT citations, and that in a disputable form. But two facts stand out clearly. First the reference to the salvation of Israel after that of the fullness of the Gentiles in 10:25–27 is set forth as a mystery. The words οὐ γὰρ θέλω ὑμᾶς ἀγνοεῖν ἀδελφοί, in 11:25, in Paul frequently introduce something of importance (Rom 1:13; 1 Cor 10:1; 12:1; 2 Cor 1:8; 1 Thess 5:13; ἀδελφοί appears in 1 Cor 15:1 as Paul introduces the very substance of his preaching). There can be no question but that 11:25–27 is extraordinarily special for Paul. The mystery he there reveals is of the same order as the mystery he reveals in 1 Cor 15:51 concerning the resurrection of the dead (ἰδοὺ μυστήριον ὑμῖν λέγω . . .): it is a new revelation of the divine purpose given especially to him. However, as Sanday and Headlam point out, the γὰρ in 11:25 connects this particular mystery (τὸ μυστήριον τοῦτο) not merely with the preceding discussion about Jewish and Gentile Christians, but with the whole argument about the divine purpose in history from 9:1 up to this point, and, indeed, from 1:1 on.[71] The mystery of the divine purpose as Paul understands it is not revealed in only one dimension. Certainly it concerned the reconciliation of all the Gentiles—of humankind—to God, and it is natural to regard this as the aspect of the divine purpose which was the heart of the mystery revealed to Paul (Rom 16:25; compare Col 1:26; Eph 3:3, 4). But the reconciliation of the Gentiles, as we saw, inevitably raised the question of the reconciliation of the Jews, the theme of 11:25–27. Here Paul claims his thought to be new— a mystery. If this is so, the claim that the interpretation of it must largely be governed by the Jewish eschatological expectations with which Paul was familiar, and should not stray away too much from these falls to the ground. Those expectations had envisaged that the Jews first and then the Gentiles would welcome the Messiah. This expectation Paul certainly discarded.

But on the basis of 11:25–27 can we take a further step and claim that Paul had come to recognize that the Christian movement was to be a Gentile movement[72] and that there were two different kinds of salvation, as it were, one achieved by the direct activity of God for Jews and another through Christ?[73] The attempt to establish this is provocative and stimulating. But it rests too much on silence, on the too rigid isolation of 11:25–27, and on some improbable interpretations of details. Rom 11:11 and 14 are especially difficult to understand in terms of this twofold path. Above all, it does not do justice to a central fact: the mystery about which Paul speaks, staggering as it might seem in content, was throughout in terms of the life, death, and resurrection of Christ and the emergence of the Church. It is this that in the end makes it difficult to be convinced that for Paul the salvation of all Israel would and could finally be outside those terms.

But, secondly, if we hesitate to take the extra step indicated, another fact is indisputable. For Paul the Jewish people continue as God's chosen people despite their rejection of the gospel, which is explained as overruled by God to enable Gentiles to receive it: for him the mission to the Jews had been pursued and had failed. He does not urge that it should be continued because this very failure is part of God's purpose for the inclusion of the Gentiles. Only at the end of history does he anticipate the Jews' acceptance of the gospel (through the forgiveness of sin), which, in view of his statements elsewhere, it is difficult not to recognize as part of his ultimate hope.[74] As for the age to come, the end to be inaugurated at the ultimate inclusion of all Israel in the Christian community, it was to introduce "What eye hath not seen, nor ear heard nor hath entered into the heart of man," when all distinctions known to history, not simply that between Jew and Gentile, are to be transcended and God is to be all in all (compare 1 Cor 15:28).

To sum all this up, in Rom 11:25ff. Paul is concerned to respect two things: the eschatological hope of the gospel and the historical role of the Jewish people in the past and the preservation of that role in the future, within the larger context of the epistle. Both of these are tied up with the faithfulness of God to his promise. This is far removed from anything that can be called anti-Judaism, not to speak of anti-Semitism.[75]

This leads to the second, exactly opposite answer to the question whether Paul in Romans 11 has introduced an ethnic, nationalistic element into a theology otherwise free from this. Has he given to the Jewish people as such a preferential role and treatment in the Christian dispensation? Is there in Paul's Christianity a "favored nation clause" for Jews? We have already suggested that in Romans 9–11 Paul faced an emerging hostile attitude among Gentile Christians towards Jewish Christians and Jews, that is, he faced anti-Judaism.[76] This attitude he rejected. The allegory of the two olives in Rom 11:16–24, the cultivated and the wild olive, best reveals his position. Through their acceptance of the gospel, the Gentiles have been engrafted into the people of God, the olive tree.[77] And this olive tree is continuous with the root of Abraham, so that through incorporation "in Christ" the Gentiles share in the root which is Abraham, as 11:18 indicates.

But Paul is anxious to insist that always the priority lies with Abraham and the Jewish people. Now that they were counted among the people of God, Gentile Christians were tempted to regard themselves as superior not only to the Jews who had been lopped off, but also even to Jewish Christians, whom they already outnumbered (11:18). Some Gentile Christians arrogantly went so far as to claim that the Jews had been lopped off by God with the very purpose of incorporating Gentiles (11:19), the implication being that God had preferred them to the Jews.[78]

Paul, however, refers deliberately to the Gentile Christians as a wild olive. The condition of the Gentiles is that of wildness: they are not "cultivated." As over against Israel, even the Israel after the flesh, they have not undergone an equal divine discipline. In 9:4 (compare 3:1f.) Paul enumerates the benefits of being a Jew by natural descent. In his mind the advantages of the Jews had been the means of producing the cultivated olive which could bear fruit. On the contrary, Gentiles constitute a "wild olive" which by nature, as Dalman noted,[79] never produces useful oil. The Gentiles, in being engrafted into the root, contribute nothing. The necessity of bringing this out forcefully perhaps explains Paul's use of the symbol of the olive rather than that of the more customary one of the vine. The wild vine does produce wild grapes: the wild olive produces nothing useful. Paul's symbolism is doubly deliberate: it suggests his high estimate of Jews and his low estimate of the spiritual attainments of Gentiles. With a side glance at the Roman contempt for Orientals perhaps, Paul emphasizes here that the saving, cultivating element in culture is not the Greco-Roman but the Jewish—a view, of course, which later infuriated the Enlightenment.[80]

Through Christ the Gentiles have now been made partakers of the people of God and share in the benefits that spring from its root, but this does not eliminate the priority of the Jews in that root. Paul tells the Gentiles: "It is not you who bear the root, but the root who bears you" (11:18: οὐ σὺ τὴν ῥίζαν βαστάζεις ἀλλὰ ἡ ῥίζα σέ). As Professor Edmund Jacob puts it, "Le peuple de Dieu n'est desormais plus limité à Israel mais il est porté par Israel."[81] The Jewish root is a necessity to Gentile Christians: they cannot live without it. All Gentile boasting over Jews is ruled out. The Gentiles had been grafted onto the olive, not because of any superior virtue on their part—they were wild and fruitless; the sole reason for their engrafting was their belief (9:19–20). Just as the Jews who had not believed were lopped off, so Gentiles who were now engrafted through their belief could also be lopped off through disbelief. Gentile Christians, therefore, have no ground for claiming any superiority over Jews whether believing or unbelieving. Gentile Christians no less than Jews cannot count on any privilege: God deals with Gentile and Jew alike. In fact, since Jews are by nature related to the root, while Gentiles were not, the probability that those Jews who had been "lopped off" could be reengrafted into the olive was more likely than that Gentiles should ever have been grafted into it in the first place. The advantages of Jews for Paul are real advantages (11:24).

The symbols of the cultivated and the wild olive are used by Paul, then, in his efforts to acknowledge the place of the Jewish people in the Christian dispensation. To be of the root of Abraham physically was an advantage because it was to be within the sphere of certain benefits. The Jewish people were, in this regard, more fortunate than Gentiles: Paul insists on their spiritual advantages. Does all this mean that Paul has reintroduced an ethnic dimension into his understanding of the gospel?

We are now led back to the second answer with which we are concerned. Harnack—the progenitor of many, and therefore I choose him—answered the last question very forcefully. According to him, in Romans 11 Paul has introduced an ethnic element into his theology which he had rejected in Romans 9 and 10. To Harnack, not anti-Judaism and anti-Semitism mark Romans 11, but an affirmation of the people of Israel after the flesh as necessary for the Christian community.[82] Dodd assumed the same position and dealt with it very critically step by step.[83] But obvious as this position seems to be, it is too simplistic. Miles Bourke pointed out in his illuminating monograph[84] that Romans 11 must be placed alongside the previous discussions of the question of Israel in Galatians and in the rest of Romans. If it be agreed that the olive in Romans 11 stands for the community of those who believe "in Christ" and the "root" for Abraham, the man of faith *par excellence* who was called when he was a Gentile, then there is no ethnic ground, limitation or preference for membership in the remnant—the people of God, or "Israel"—as Paul understood it, and the contradiction which Harnack found between Romans 9–10 and Romans 11 disappears. For Paul the sole ground for membership in the people of God is always faith: Käsemann's insistence on this in the interpretation of Romans 9–11 is to be affirmed.[85]

And yet Harnack is not to be wholly dismissed. He and those like him who find a reintroduction of nationalism or ethnicity in Romans 11 fail at one point, it seems to me. They do not sufficiently distinguish the strictly historical from the ethnic and the national. Paul does not allow to Jews any superiority on the ground of race, ethnicity, or nationality, but in the scheme of salvation he does allow them a historical or chronological priority (both in the grace and in the judgment of God, Rom 2:9–10), grounded in the faithfulness of God (see pp. 13f., 34). This, although historically it confers advantages, must not be understood as a preference or as a privilege. (I hope I am not playing with words when I make a distinction between advantage and privilege.)[86] As a matter of history a Gentile, Abraham, became the exemplar of "faith"; as a matter of history, this Abraham, the man of faith, became the "root" of Jews. The religious and the historical are strangely intertwined. It was to Jews that Jesus came first, and historically Jews were the first "in Christ." The words in 1:16, "For it is the power of God unto salvation unto everyone that believeth, to the Jew first and then to the Greek," are very deliberate ('Ιουδαίῳ τε πρῶτον καὶ "Ελληνι.) The introduction of "first" is highly noticeable, and awkward, particularly since Paul's precise intent is to indicate that the gospel is for Gentiles also. He cannot escape the historical priority of the Jews and does not attempt to do so. He takes seriously the history of salvation. Here I think that Käsemann's comment on 1:16 is fundamentally right.[87] The root of the church, Jewish and Gentile, was a Jewish patriarch. Paul insisted that the Jewish people are related to that root and, however partially, have both perpetuated it and been borne by it. Historically, it was they who had provided the immediate human context for, or had been the carriers of, salvation history; they who had borne the dread burden, the terrible, almost unbearable burden of monotheism, of belief in and response to the true God, and of his hope for mankind.[88] The people of Israel have had a peculiar role in the past: Paul projects them for a peculiar role in the future also. The faith which was the root of the church was the faith of Abraham. This makes the Jewish connection to the gospel inescapable. In Romans 11, therefore, it is not so much that Paul retains an ethnic fundament for the gospel. Rather, he realistically recognizes the significance of the history of the Jewish people as such. He wrestles with and insists on preserving the peculiarity of the people of Abraham in history. In Romans 9–11 he reveals anxiety lest Gentile Christians, in the legitimate desire to free themselves of ethnic categories, prompted to this perhaps initially by the apostolic decree of Acts 15,[89] had fallen into anti-Judaism. From this Paul, safeguarding the Jewish chrysalis of the gospel, shrinks with horror.

The question that faced him was extremely delicate. It was not always easy to keep clear the distinction between the people of Abraham as a community of faith and history and as a community in the flesh, that is, as simply an ethnic or "national" group. Harnack and Dodd, I think, failed to preserve this distinction in interpreting Paul. Their confusion is understandable, because the same confusion pressed with awful intensity on Paul himself. Is it possible to separate the historical role of a people from its physical or ethnic actuality without falling into unrealism and fantasy and emptying its historicity of any real significance because its bearers have become strangely disincarnate? The treatment of Jews as pawns in a scheme of salvation history has often led and still leads some Christians and even Christian theologians to dehumanize them.[90] Paul's identification with his kin after the flesh saved him from this dehumani-zation. But always the historical interweaving of the Israel of faith with the Israel after the flesh makes for immense complexity. Judaism refused to separate these. Paul, a Jew-Christian, found it difficult to do so, al-though his Christology and ecclesiology were driving him to the sepa-ration. Paul's quandary was precisely this: how to do justice to the his-torical role of his own people without thereby, *ipso facto*, elevating their ethnic character to a position of special privilege.

This is why the tortuous discussion in Romans 9–11 (where Paul is far more sensitive, mellow and aware than in 1 Thessalonians and Galatians and even 2 Corinthians)[91] ends in a paradox: in Christ there is neither Jew nor Greek and yet a continued place for the Jewish people as such. This paradox has its basis in the stubborn stuff of history itself. As a matter of simple fact, a remnant of the Jewish people was in the church—supplying a solid continuity between those "in Christ" and the Jewish past, rooting the gospel in Judaism, despite its transcendence of the ethnic limitations of the latter, and thus preserving it from the perils attendant upon its too rapid expansion into the Greco-Roman world. Paul's insist-ence on the continued significance of the Jewish people was historically grounded and historically necessary. He refused to follow what his christological ecclesiology seemed logically to demand, that is, a concentration on the body of Christ, *sôma Christou,* with its possibility of exclusivity.[92] Instead he retained the eschatological hope for the Jewish people contained in the promise to Abraham. In true rabbinic fashion he was content to rest in a paradox—a paradox which was of the same order and related to (if not specifically referred to as) the paradox of the justification by faith, that is, the paradox of the justification of the ungodly. But Paul himself was aware of the tensions and ambiguities of this paradox: the complexities of Romans 9–11 testify to this. And he grounded this paradox finally, in 11:28–32, not only in history, but in the unfathomable grace of God, whose wisdom is past finding out, but which forbids God to cast off his ancient people or to revoke his covenant with them—ἀμετα-μέλητα γὰρ τὰ χαρίσματα καὶ ἡ κλῆσις τοῦ θεοῦ. In this way he ties the historical priority and significance of Israel inextricably to his understanding of the faithfulness of God. It is that faithfulness, indeed, that had finally secured the historical significance of Israel. And the divine grace which Paul saw saved Gentiles in Christ will also save all Jews. Hence the conclusion of Romans 11 in a grand doxology, which recalls Deutero-Isaiah and Job and the Psalms, is inevitable. And although Paul's christology cannot be rigidly set against his theology ὅτι ὁ θεὸς ἦν ἐν χριστῷ it is not an accident that this doxology, uniquely in Paul, is not christological but strictly theological (Rom 11:33–36). Paul's very experience in Christ interpreted in the light of the Scriptures of his people leads him to rest in an overarching monotheism of grace which can embrace the differences that now separate Jews and Christians and hold them together. The question forces itself upon us: is not the outcome of Paul's position in Romans 11 that the God of Abraham now revealed in Christ, the God of grace in whom both Jews and Christians share an immemorial faith, encompasses them in a unity which their present nonnegotiable differences over the significance of Jesus as the Messiah must not be allowed to destroy, even though they will not be resolved before the end of history? Whatever the answer to that question, it is not surprising that to characterize the place of Jews in the Christian dispensation Paul, as we emphasized above, employed the term *mustērion.* The NEB very inadequately renders this term as "a very deep truth." Behind Paul's *mustērion* stands the Aramaic *râz,* borrowed from the Persia that spurned Jewish eschatology. Paul recognizes that the role of the Jewish people in the future, as in the past, is not comprehensible apart from the mysterious purpose of God, which is full of grace. For him the existence and continuance of Israel up to the limit of the historical process is grounded in the mysterious divine purpose and is, as such, a source of ultimate blessing. For him, there is no "solution" to the Jewish question until we are at the very limit of history and at the threshold of the age to come, when God will be all in all and the distinctions of this world even between Jew and Gentile transcended and even Christ himself made subordinate to the Father.[93] Till that end comes, even when taken up into the life in Christ, Israel remains identifiably Israel. With his customary clarity C. H. Dodd[94] in particular rightly urged that all this involved the apostle in theological inconsistencies which cannot from a strictly logical perspective be ignored. But may we ask: can grace, can the justification of the ungodly, Jews and Gentiles, ever be logically expressed? Dinkler has urged that to discuss the question of Israel and call it a "mystery" as Paul does is ultimately to say nothing about it and to cloak ignorance in an appeal to an inscrutable divine wisdom.[95] But this is not so. Paul at least provides a basis for the mutual respect and mutual recognition of Christians and Jews as they coexist in history.

Paul was, in fact, a transitional figure, a man of torn consciousness. He was aware that the life in Christ brought to their utmost meaning and limits the categories and symbols of his ancestral faith and constituted a new creation. At the same time his loyalty to and rootedness in that ancestral faith in the living God and in its eschatology made it painfully difficult for him in the actualities of his moment to draw out the logical consequences of that new creation. These were so revolutionary that even the great apostle of liberty drew back. Daube has pointed out an example of a similar withdrawal from the logic of his position in Paul's treatment of marriage. Logically his doctrine of the new creation demanded the abandonment of old ties even within marriage. Because there was a new creation, *everything* would be new! But as 1 Corinthians shows, Paul's dedicated common sense—no, it would be better to say his human sensitivities rooted in Christ—refused to allow him to follow that logic.[96] So was it in his treatment of Israel.

Paul's approach to his own people was governed by a past promise and an eschatology informed by the grace of Christ. To dismiss the eschatological speculation of Paul as an unimportant apocalyptic remnant of his outgrown past and to reinterpret it in terms of anthropology or, again, of some fairly simple, comprehensible interpretation of a contemporary crisis is not enough.[97] Paul took seriously the Old Testament and Judaism. He challenged Marcion before Marcion. For him the particularity of Christ is bound up with the particularity of Abraham and the chosenness of his descendants, because it was the same God who was active in them all.

J. S. Whale,[98] *quem honoris causa nomino,* in commenting on the mysterious faith which goes back to Abraham, asked this question:

> What if so thoroughgoing and absolute a belief in God and his covenantal purpose, the *Sh^{e}ma'* . . . should mean that here in Abraham Ideology really becomes Theology? What if the obsessive, subjective "cognition" expressed in the *Sh^{e}ma'* should point to objective Reality . . . What if the Hexateuch should be right and Marcion wrong?

Paul had no doubt about the affirmative answer to that question. One fundamental challenge of Paul is that we give the same affirmative answer. Can we do so? Or must we agree with the English deist and with so many in the Enlightenment, whose children we also are, that "This doctrine [about the special role of the Jews] surely is false though taught by that great apostle St. Paul"?[99] Must we abandon the eschatological framework of Paul and the place of Israel in it? This question we cannot discuss here.

But standing in the succession of the first president of our society, who urged that our studies reflect and reflect upon the living issues of our times, certain concluding reflections may be permitted.

Paul's treatment of the Jewish question was in response to an actual situation which he faced. Romans 9–11, whatever its precise literary form and origin, deals with a present crisis in the apostle's ministry: the "now" of Rom 11:5 and 11:30 is emphatic. For him the failure of the preaching of the gospel to gain the majority of Jews constituted a serious challenge to an eschatological gospel. The eschatological crisis constituted by the gospel occurred for Paul within Judaism: the Jamnian wall of separation between two religions had not yet been set up. Paul refused a Marcionite solution to the crisis. Instead, as we saw, he warned Gentile Christians against the danger of moral and spiritual superiority and urged them to respect their Jewish root—even when its representatives were rejecting the gospel—and he endured the rejection of Jesus as the Messiah by his own people by resting on the unfathomable faithfulness and grace of their God and his.

The crisis of our confrontation with Judaism in our time has made it possible for us to enter with a deeper sensitivity perhaps into Paul's intent in Romans 9–11, and we may find guidance in it. The incipient anti-Judaism which Paul detected and feared in Gentile Christians bore fruit. It contributed to a climate which made possible the suffering of Jews within Christendom across the centuries, and this has culminated in the anti-Semitism of our time. Any claims that Gentile Christians could ever have made to moral or spiritual superiority have been shattered. And there is

more. It is very precarious to refer to contemporary events.[100] "He who
is wedded to the present will soon be widowed." But Paul wrote before
certain events to which the early church gave theological significance had
happened—the fall of Jerusalem and the dispersion of Jewry following it.
It is legitimate to urge that the modern counterparts of these events must
also be allowed to modify that significance. Like all states, the state of
Israel in its emergence and development is clothed in ambiguity. But that
mere emergence after nineteen centuries of diaspora has put a sharp question mark against much New Testament and early Christian interpretation
of the fall of Jerusalem, and of the wandering of the Jews, as a punishment
for their rejection of the gospel. In that interpretation Paul did not share,
because he had died before the catastrophes referred to had transpired.
To judge from his attitude to antisocial, revolutionary tendencies among
Christians, he would have opposed the war against Rome. For him the
"punishment" of Israel for its failure to accept Jesus as the Messiah was
its self-inflicted exclusion from the true olive. In the presence of that
failure Paul could only rest on the ultimate grace of God. As already
indicated, his warning against a Gentile Christian superiority complex is
now more pertinent than ever, as is our need to recapture his eschatological certainty. Today, freed from the possibility of recognizing the fall
of Jerusalem and the dispersion as divine punishments and yet facing a
Jewry still further confirmed, through suffering, in its rejection of the
gospel, we are in a situation comparable with Paul's before 70 C.E.: our
understanding of the NT has revealed that the primordial relationship
between the followers of Jesus and other Jews was a familial one, except
that their sufferings in modern times have made that connection, for Jews,
save in a purely remote historical sense, incredible. We are in a tragically
paradoxical situation. The study of first-century Judaism is compelling
NT scholars into a post-Jamnian period, that is, into a period which recognizes that the Christian movement began as a movement within Judaism or as a form of Judaism. It is this that in part at least made the
attitude expressed in Vatican II possible. But at the same time the Jewish
experience within Christendom has further increased the gulf between
Jews and Christians. We can comprehend in a new way Paul's agony over
Christians and Jews, both belonging to the same family and yet ever more
alienated. This last we are more aware of perhaps than was even Paul.
But from this pre-Jamnian figure we can learn how to face even that bitter
awareness through the overarching mercy of God revealed in Christ. The
two historical developments to which we have referred, the Holocaust
and the rise of the State of Israel, create within us also a torn conscious-

ness—torn between the abstract theoretical claims of our traditional theologies and eschatologies and the harsh, humbling, and amazing actualities
of history. These actualities demand that we sit again at the feet of Paul,
whose mind is a clue to the pre-Jamnian period, to learn afresh that the
debate between Jews and Christians, separated as they now are, is a
familial one, and that we ourselves must come to recognize that, in the
sense indicated above, we are post-Jamnian.

Before the exclusive rigidities of Jamnia had set in, Paul wrestled with
and, in terms of the eschatological mystery, provided ground in his day
for mutual tolerance and respect between Jew and Gentile Christian. It
is part of the bitter irony of history that this colossus of a man, who had
he been heeded might have created a climate of mutual respect and even
affection between Jews and Christians, was misinterpreted by both and
his theology often used as part of the very scheme of salvation to justify
the infliction of suffering on Jews, so that until very recently Paul has
been regarded as unspeakable among his own people. *Sunt lacrymae
rerum et mentem mortalia tangunt.*[101]

8
Paul and the Gentiles:
A Suggestion Concerning
Romans 11:13–24

In his Epistle to the Romans, chapter 11, Paul presents the allegory of
two olive trees, the cultivated and the wild.[1] It follows upon the apostle's
recognition that most of Israel, his own people, had rejected Jesus of
Nazareth as their long-expected Messiah, and upon Paul's claim that this
very rejection, by a strange twist, had brought salvation to the Gentiles
(11:11). This would come about when Jews would recognize the fruits of
redemption exhibited by Gentile believers and, *mirabile dictu*, be led
through envy and emulation to the acceptance of Jesus as the Messiah.
The whole passage reads as follows in The New English Bible:

> But I have something to say to you Gentiles. I am a missionary to the
> Gentiles, and as such I give all honor to that ministry when I try to stir
> emulation in the men of my own race, and so to save some of them. For
> if their rejection has meant the reconciliation of the world, what will their
> acceptance [*proslèmpsis*] mean? Nothing less than life from the dead! If
> the first portion of dough is consecrated, so is the whole lump. If the root
> is consecrated, so are the branches. But if some [*tines*] of the branches have
> been lopped off, and you, a wild olive [*agrielaios*], have been grafted in
> among them, and have come to share the same root and sap as the olive
> [*elaia*], do not make yourself superior to the branches. If you do so, re-
> member that it is not you who sustain the root: the root sustains you.
>   You will say, "Branches were lopped off so that I might be grafted in."
> Very well: they were lopped off for lack of faith, and by faith you hold your
> place. Put away your pride, and be on your guard; for if God did not spare
> the native branches, no more will he spare you. Observe the kindness and
> the severity of God—severity to those who fell away, divine kindness to
> you, if only you remain within its scope; otherwise you too will be cut off,
> whereas they, if they do not continue faithless, will be grafted in; for it is
> in God's power to graft them in again. For if you were cut from your native
> wild olive and against all nature grafted into the cultivated olive, how much
> more readily will they, the natural olive-branches, be grafted into their na-
> tive stock!

The symbol which concerns us is the olive—the cultivated and the wild
olive. But before introducing these, Paul refers to the root and the

branches. (The symbols of the first fruits, of the dough and the lump in
11:16 we pass by: they serve the same purpose as that of the root and
the branches.) Drawing upon ancient Semitic concepts of solidarity,[2] Paul
indicates that the character of the root of a plant or body carries over
into the plant or body itself (the branches). A living organism such as a
tree cannot be divided into root and branches, as if these were distinct
entities: the quality of the root determines the quality of the tree and its
branches. In 11:1–15, Paul has urged that the ultimate acceptance of Jews
into those "in Christ" would have an inexpressible, beneficial result: he
describes this anticipated result of the "acceptance of Jews" (the term
proslèmpsis is exceedingly difficult to render exactly) as "life from the
dead." This phrase must not be watered down to mean simply untold
spiritual blessings: it denotes the act inaugurating the end.[3] The final act
of all history rests upon the Jews. How could an act of such decisive
significance rest upon the Jews as such? Because, Paul implies in 11:16,
the Jews as a people partake of the character of their root. The root here
doubtless symbolizes Abraham. The characteristics of Abraham, their
father, belong also to Jews: they are "in Abraham" and Abraham "in
them." It follows that Jews, when they should join those "in Christ,"
would bring untold blessing; indeed, as we noted, they would initiate the
coming of the end. Paul's positive evaluation of his own people is clear.

The symbol of the root and the branches provides the apostle with a
fitting introduction to another symbol, that of the olive (*elaia*) in 11:17.
The context demands that this olive be a cultivated one, as over against
a wild olive (*agrielaios*) mentioned in 11:17. Certain (*tines*) of the
branches of the tree of the people of Israel have been lopped off (11:17).
The use of the term "certain" is noteworthy. Whereas the translation
"certain" suggests a minority, Paul here intends that the majority in Israel
(there is a parallel in 3:3) be understood as unbelieving and that most or
a considerable number of the branches have been cut off. The use of
"certain" (*tines*) points to Paul's sensitivity in referring to the unbelief
of his people and of their having been as a result cut off. He avoids doing
so too blatantly.[4]

From what have the unbelieving Jews been cut off? It cannot be that
they have been cut off from the Jewish people considered as an ethnic
entity: they are still Jews. The branches broken off (the use of the passive
verb, in *exeklasthêsan*, as elsewhere in the New Testament, indicates the
action of God himself), then, are those Jews, and they are the majority,
who have refused to be part of the true Israel, the remnant that has believed in Christ. The olive in 11:17 stands for the community of Christian

believers, the Church, at first composed of Jewish Christians of the root of Abraham. In cutting themselves off from these, or in refusing to believe, the Jews were cutting themselves off from the life of the root as Paul understood it, although they still remained Jews after the flesh.[5] Paul expresses himself laconically and clumsily. As the text stands, the Gentiles (the wild olive) who believe are grafted by God into or among, not instead of, the branches lopped off (*en autois*, 11:17)[6] so that they share in the cultivated olive: the horticultural process is unthinkable, and Paul himself admits that it is unnatural (11:24). But the apostle's intent is clear: through their acceptance of the gospel the Gentiles have been engrafted into the people of God, the olive tree. And this olive tree—by the very principle of solidarity to which Paul had appealed in 11:16—is continuous with the root of Abraham, so that through incorporation "in Christ" the Gentiles share in the root which is Abraham, as 11:18 indicates.

But Paul is anxious to insist that always the priority lies with Abraham and the Jewish people. Now that they were in the people of God, Gentile Christians were tempted to regard themselves as superior not only to the Jews, who had been lopped off, but also even to Jewish Christians, whom they already outnumbered (11:18). Some Gentile Christians went so far as to claim that the Jews had been lopped off by God with the very purpose of incorporating the Gentiles (11:19). The implication of this was that God had preferred them to the Jews. Paul confronts this emerging Gentile arrogance head on.

He refers deliberately to the Gentile Christians as a wild olive. The condition of the Gentiles is that of wildness: they are, for Paul, not "cultured" or, more precisely, not "cultivated." As over against Israel, even the Israel after the flesh in the apostle's mind, they have not undergone an equal divine discipline. In 9:4 Paul enumerates the benefits of being a Jew: in his mind the advantages of the Jews had been the means of producing the cultivated olive which could bear fruit. On the contrary, Gentiles constitute a "wild olive" which by nature, be it noted, never produces oil. The Gentiles in being engrafted into the root contribute nothing. Perhaps it is the necessity of bringing this out forcefully that explains Paul's use of the symbol of the olive rather than the more customary one of the vine. The wild vine does produce wild grapes: the wild olive produces nothing useful. Paul's symbolism is doubly deliberate: it suggests not only his high estimate of Israel but also his low estimate of the spiritual attainments of the Gentiles.[7] We return to this later.

The Gentiles through Christ have now, indeed, been made partakers of the people of God and share in the benefits that spring from its root,

Abraham, but this does not eliminate the priority of the Jews in that root. Paul tells the Gentiles: "It is not you who bear the root, but the root bears you" (11:18). The Jewish root is a necessity to Gentile Christians: they cannot live without it. All Gentile boasting over Jews is ruled out.

In 11:19 Paul meets still another Gentile misconception. As we saw, some Gentile Christians had even conceived the idea that the branches which had been broken off, that is, the unbelieving Jews, had suffered this fate by divine purpose in order that the Gentiles might be engrafted into Israel. As we indicated earlier, the implication of this is that God had, in fact, "favored" Gentiles over Jews, who could be and were thereby regarded as inferior. The apostle insists over against this that the responsibility for the unbelief of the Jews rests squarely on themselves, not on the divine preference for Gentiles. It was not that God had grown weary of the Jews, whom he had chosen, and that he had therefore rejected them. Rather the Jews themselves had chosen not to believe. The Gentiles had been grafted onto the olive, not because of any superior virtue on their part; in fact, they had not—so we are to understand—produced spiritual fruits. They were a wild, fruitless olive. The sole reason for their engrafting was their belief (11:19–20). So too, just as with the Jews who had not believed and were lopped off, those Gentiles who were not engrafted through their belief could also lose that status through disbelief. Gentile Christians, therefore, have no ground for claiming any superiority over Jews whether believing or unbelieving. Fear and trembling lest they also should fall into disbelief alone befitted them. Gentile Christians no less than Jews cannot count on any privilege: God deals with Gentile and Jew alike. In fact, since Jews are by nature attached to the root, while Gentiles are not, that is, since Jews in becoming Christian did not have to be grafted on to a wholly alien root, as had the Gentiles who came from paganism (11:23–24), the probability that those Jews who had been "lopped off" could be reengrafted into the olive was more likely than that Gentiles should have been grafted into it at all in the first place. The advantages of Jews are real ones.

Outside the confines of the symbols of the olive and the wild olive, but not unrelated to them, Paul announces a mystery which should rein in the arrogance of Gentiles. The unbelief that has befallen Israel—though only partially—is temporary. When what Paul calls "the fullness of the Gentiles" has been brought into "Israel," as he understood it, then all Israel, that is, the totality of the Jewish people, will be saved. To justify this position Paul appeals to God's irrevocable election of the Jews and to the merit of their fathers ($z^e q\hat{u}th$ $\ni ab\hat{o}t$). In the end, both Gentiles and Jews are included in God's mercy which is as wide as the world.

The symbols of the cultivated and wild olives are used by Paul, then, in his efforts to formulate a philosophy of history, if we may so put it, which would acknowledge the place of the Jewish people in the Christian dispensation. At the very least we may claim that—altogether apart from Christ—Paul regards Jews as spiritually "cultivated" and the Gentiles as "underprivileged." To be of the root of Abraham was an advantage. The Jewish people were, in this regard, superior to Gentiles: Paul insists on their spiritual advantages. In 9:1–5 he expresses both his yearning for the salvation of his own people and his awareness of those advantages. The verses read:

> I am speaking the truth as a Christian, and my own conscience, enlightened by the Holy Spirit, assures me it is no lie; in my heart there is great grief and unceasing sorrow. For I could even pray to be outcast from Christ myself for the sake of my brothers, my natural kinsfolk. They are Israelites: they were made God's sons; theirs is the splendor of the divine presence, theirs the covenants, the law, the temple worship, and the promises. Theirs are the patriarchs, and from them, in natural descent, sprang the Messiah. May God, supreme above all, be blessed for ever! Amen.

The question of the relative importance of Gentiles and Jews in civilization (which so much later occupied Voltaire and others in the Enlightenment) Paul did not directly discuss. But here a suggestion interjects itself. In discussing the "Jewish question" as it emerged in the churches, did Paul cast a deliberate sidelong glance at the anti-Judaism of the Greco-Roman world? Romans 1 and 2 indicate that in the epistle he had the whole world in his purview (1:5, 13 ff., 18 ff.; 2:1; 3:19; compare 1 Cor 15:24–28) as well as the Jews as such (2:17 ff.; 3:1 ff.; 9—11). This attitude toward Jews on the part of Gentiles would be familiar to him. The earliest contacts between Greeks and Jews had led to an idealization of Jews as admirable philosophers. The Maccabean revolt and subsequent events shattered this image and provoked anti-Judaism. Despite their indulgent tolerance of Judaism, the Romans were not immune to this changed attitude.[8] Possibly racism,[9] but other factors also, fostered suspicion and hostility. To the Romans the Jews were part of an Oriental world which was a constant menace militarily (especially in the shape of Parthia), morally, and religiously. The many cults of Oriental and Semitic origin that spread to Rome were resented as corrupting influences.[10] To Romans who might possibly be aware of them, the claims of Jews who indulged in apocalyptic visions of the future when Jerusalem would be the center of the world, drawing the allegiance of all nations, must have seemed as ridiculous as they did later to Voltaire: Paul's "philosophy of history" outlined in Rom 9:11 would have seemed to them equally bizarre.[11] It was not only Jews who claimed to be "peculiar" or "chosen." Although the Romans did not use such language, they too were conscious of a "manifest destiny." Polybius' recognition of a "Fate" or "*Tuchē*" ruling over the development of Rome makes it clear that not only Jews could regard themselves as unique. And it was surely more reasonable to believe in a divine destiny for Romans than for Jews.[12]

The attitude of Gentile Christians toward Jewish Christians in Rome and elsewhere should not be separated from this larger Greco-Roman anti-Judaism. Although many of them had doubtless been proselytes and God-fearers, the Roman Christians to whom Paul wrote, conscious of belonging to no mean city, would find it easy to carry over into the Church the contempt that their neighbors felt for Jews. "The Jewish question" was not an isolated peculiarity of the emerging Christian churches but a phenomenon of the first century Greco-Roman world: one should expect Gentile Christian attitudes toward Jews to reflect those of the surrounding society in general.

Over against this background insufficient attention has been paid to certain facts. In Rom 11:13 ff. Paul addresses the Gentile Christians specifically. The way in which he insists, "But I have something to say to you Gentiles" is striking and points to a special emphasis. And it is significant that he here reverts to an allegory. He seldom used allegories— a mark of Hellenistic literature—and usually preferred either typology or Midrashic or homiletic exposition. Perhaps his very use of allegory here suggests a sensitivity to Gentile forms in addressing Gentiles. He turns to allegory not simply because the immediately preceding metaphors which he had employed in 11:16 made it natural for him to do this but because allegory was especially appropriate to his addressees.

And insufficient attention has been paid to the significance of the symbol of the wild olive ($\dot{\alpha}\gamma\rho\iota\acute{\epsilon}\lambda\alpha\iota o\varsigma$) set against the cultivated olive ($\dot{\epsilon}\lambda\alpha\acute{\iota}\alpha$) in Rom. 11:17–24. Two sources for these symbols have been suggested, the Old Testament (Hos 14:6 and Jer 11:16) and the presence of what was called a $\sigma\upsilon\nu\alpha\gamma\omega\gamma\grave{\eta}$ Ἐλαίας (or Ἐλέας) (a Synagogue of the Olive) in Rome.[13] It has been suggested that some Jewish group in that city had appropriated this name from the Old Testament verses referred to, and that the name of their synagogue provoked Paul's references in Rom. 11:17–24, the first Christian community at Rome having perhaps derived from this synagogue. On this view the apostle's reference to the olive would be particularly telling.[14]

But both suggestions are precarious. In all the Old Testament, the olive is only used of Israel in the two passages indicated. In Hos 14:6 it is not strictly a metaphor for Israel but is only used in a simile: certainly there is no emphasis on or development of the figure. In Jer 11:16–17 the olive becomes an object of the divine judgment—a motif alien to Paul's purpose in Rom 11:17. It is unlikely that these two passages would have inspired Paul's use of the olive in the latter passage, over against the far more customary use of the vine as a symbol for Israel.

As for the "Synagogue of the Olive" there is much dispute. Frey's capitalization of Ἐλαίας indicates his emphatic view that the meaning is Synagogue of Elaia(s), the latter being the name of a place. Although the capitalization is imposed on the text, many have insisted on seeing in Ἐλαίας and Ἐλέας the name of some city from which the members of the synagogue had migrated.[15] Frey insisted that the name *had* to derive from some city or district and, following Reinach, preferred to think of it as pointing to a city of Mysea in Asia Minor, which had served as a port for Perganium. Another suggestion, for obvious reasons—philological and other—unlikely, is that the synagogue was named after Elijah. Most have accepted Schürer's view that the synagogue is named after the olive, as was a synagogue in Sepphoris after the vine. Leon asks why a Roman congregation "should have taken the olive for its symbol." In the light of all this, it is precarious to connect Paul's use of the allegory of the olives in Rom 11:17–24 specifically with a possible Synagogue of the Olive in Rome.[16]

Nevertheless, Leon may be too cautious and may have overlooked one strong reason why Jews in Rome might have been attracted to the symbol of the olive. The broader Greco-Roman context within which Paul was writing may help us here. We have pointed to the unfavorable attitude of the Romans toward the Jewish world. The Roman attitude toward the Greeks was the very opposite. In the first century, as before and after, the influence and repute of Athens in particular remained real. It became the premier seat of learning of the Roman Empire.[17] Schools of philosophy for example, in the first century (a period marked by a reverence for the antiquity of any teaching and anxious to establish links with a glorious past) were concerned with tracing their pedigrees as far back as possible, and especially to illustrious Greek founders.[18] Romans sent their sons for higher training and learning to Athens. We can be sure that the Gentile Christians in Rome, who could appreciate the strong argumentation of Paul in his epistle, would have been aware of the significance of the Greek cultural tradition which was honored in their city as surely as his readers at Corinth were cognizant of the Greek games to which he referred in writing to them (1 Cor 9:24–27).

But there is one tree that is especially connected with Athens. According to legend Athena the gray-eyed goddess, founder of the city of Athens, had planted an olive tree on the very spot where the city now stands on the Acropolis this being considered the most useful of gifts for mortals.[19] Those descended from Athens were called μοιρίαι, "cuttings,"[20] of the olive that had been planted. The Academy of Plato in Athens was set in a garden, probably of olives.[21] The leaves of the wild olive were used for crowns in the Olympic games, as was the oil of the olive.[22] In Paul's writing to Gentiles, the olive could serve as a symbol as powerful as was the vine among Jews: it would naturally evoke Athens and Greek culture. The apostle makes no direct reference to the association of the olive with Athens, the cultural center of the Greco-Roman world. But his readers would be aware of that association. We suggest that the use of the olive—which occurs so very infrequently in a symbolic sense in the Old Testament—to symbolize the Christian community rooted in Abraham in Rom 11:17-24 was not simply the natural development of the preceding metaphors of the dough and the root in 11:16, but the deliberate introduction of a figure which evoked the cultured pagan world.

The force of the symbol depends on the contrast which Paul draws between the cultivated olive ἐλαία and the wild olive ἀγριέλαιος. As we noted, the leaves of the wild olive were used for wreaths for the victors in the Olympic games. This might be taken to suggest that there was no pejorative significance attached to the wild olive. Its leaves could be used to denote the highest honors, equally with the oil from the sacred olive groves of Athens. Nor can we infer that wild olive wood was regarded as inferior from the fact that the timber from the wild olive was used in the construction of the Temple of Jerusalem. The cherubim themselves were made of the same timber (overlaid with gold).[23] The wood of the olive, cultivated or wild, could be polished to a great beauty.[24] Are we, then, to conclude that there was no sharp distinction drawn between the cultivated and the wild olive? This is not so. While the cultivated olive was a mainstay of life—possibly *the* mainstay—[25] the wild olive was notoriously unproductive. As a rule it is but a shrub, with small leaves and a prickly stem. It produces little or no oil. The point is that the wild olive is almost profitless. This is noted by botanists who have written on this theme.[26]

This sharp contrast between the wild and the cultivated olive is important. That Paul represents the Gentiles as a wild olive is a most forceful indictment of their lives. In addressing Gentile Christians, who were prone to look down on their Jewish associates—Christian and other—in terms of the fruitless, inferior wild olive tree, was he deliberately turning the tables on them? The world of pagan culture should surely be symbolized by the cultivated olive which evoked Athens. Instead, Paul points to it in the form of a wild olive. The Gentile Christians came from a wild olive; they had nothing to contribute. To be fruitful they had to be grafted on to the cultivated olive which had Abraham, the father of Israel, as its root. Two things suggest that Paul here, in discussing the Jewish question with Gentile Christians, has in mind also—by implication at least—the larger question of the role and relative importance of Gentiles and Jews in the civilized life or, as we should now put it, in the evolutionary process.

First, we note that despite his violent criticism of his own people, Paul makes a very positive evaluation of their role in history and in the purpose of God. Rom 9—11 makes this clear: the very incidence of the end in a certain sense depends upon or is to accompany the acceptance by Jewish people of Jesus as the Christ. Does this imply a negative approach to the Greco-Roman world? Unlike the sectarians at Qumran and the extreme nationalists of Galilee and Judaea, Paul did not oppose Hellenistic culture in all its forms. Some of these he adopted. A master of the Greek language, he could be Greek to the Greeks.[27] He recognized the distinction between Greek and barbarian.[28] At the beginning of Romans, he castigates Jewish even more than Greek conduct. For missionary purposes especially, he did not shun the ethical, conceptual, linguistic, and literary usages of the Hellenistic world.[29] The use of the symbol of the wild olive for that world, therefore, must be regarded as doubly deliberate—as implying the superiority of the Jewish tradition and the inferiority of the Hellenistic. Apart altogether from Christ, Paul regards Jews as spiritually "cultivated" and Gentiles as "underprivileged." To be of the root of Abraham *was* an advantage. The Jewish people were, in this regard, more fortunate than the Gentiles. Paul insists on their spiritual advantages, as in Rom 9:1–5. The polemic context of Phil 3:6 must not be allowed to obviate their positive implications. When Paul claims that he was a Hebrew of the Hebrews, although he was not speaking antithetically to criticize or reject Hellenism, he was pointing to a tradition (not to a race over against another race), of whose superiority he was convinced. He was doing the same thing in comparing the Gentiles to the wild olive in Rom 11:17–24.

Second, there is the evidence of the Church fathers. The Pauline allegory finds echoes in Cyril of Jerusalem, *Catechesis* 1.4, where the transplanting into the spiritual olive is a change "from sin to righteousness, from corruption to purity."[30] In Gregory of Nazianzen's eulogy "On his

brother St. Caesarius,"[31] his father's change from paganism to the faith
is described in terms of "engrafting from wild olive into the cultivated
olive" (1.3). He contrasts his father with his mother, who "from the
beginning and by virtue of descent . . . was truly a holy lump from the
holy first fruits of the dough" (1.4). Cyril of Alexandria finds the purpose
of God in sending his apostles to be to enlighten those who are ignorant
so as to change them from being wild olives to cultivated ones. (ἵνα τὴν
ἀγριέλαιον εἰς καλλιέλαιον τῇ τοῦ πνεύματος μεταβάλλωσι,
τεχνῇ ἵνα τοὺς κρυπτομένους τῷ βυθῷ τῆς ἀσεβείας, τῷ τῆς
διδασκαλίας ἁλιεύσωσι λόγῳ).[32] In all these fathers cited above the
implication is clear. Gentile life is that of the wild olive: it has to be
transformed. The same emerges more forcefully in Clement of Alexandria.

He interprets "after the rudiments of the world and not after Christ"
of Col 2:8 to mean that "the Hellenic teaching is elementary and [that]
of Christ perfect." He then proceeds to refer to the allegory of the two
olives. The botanical details are as obscure in Clement as in Paul and
need not here be disentangled. For our purpose the point of interest is
that he compares the philosopher with the wild olive. The pertinent words
are:

> "Now the wild olive is inserted into the fatness of the olive," (Rom.
> 11:17) and is indeed of the same species as the cultivated olives. For the
> graft uses as soil the tree in which it is engrafted. Now all the plants sprouted
> forth simultaneously in consequence of the divine order. Wherefore, also,
> though the wild olive be wild, it crowns the Olympic victors. And the elm
> teaches the vine to be fruitful, by leading it up to a height. Now we see
> that wild trees attract more nutriment, because they cannot ripen. The wild
> trees, therefore, have less power of secretion than those that are cultivated.
> And the cause of their wildness is the want of the power of secretion. The
> engrafted olive accordingly receives more nutriment from its growing in the
> wild one; and it gets accustomed, as it were, to secrete the nutriment, be-
> coming thus assimilated to the fatness of the cultivated tree.[33]

In the passage following this Clement, revealing again his negative attitude
to "philosophy," deals with "Different Modes" of engrafting illustrative
of different kinds of conversion. Among these is that "when the wood is
cleft, and there is inserted in it the cultivated branch. And this applies to
the case of those who have studied philosophy (ὁ συμβαίνει ἐπὶ τῶν
Φιλοσοφησάντων): for on cutting through their dogmas, the acknowl-
edgement of the truth is produced in them." Here the philosopher is again
by implication the "wild olive." Clement sees a need to cut through "the
dogmas" of the philosophers, in order to prepare for the insertion of the

cultivated branch, the truth (διατμηθέντων γὰρ αὐτοῖς τῶν δόγματων ἡ ἐπίγνωσις τῆς ἀληθείας ἐγγίνεται)[34].

It is noteworthy that Hellenistic teaching is called both elementary and dogmatic and is, by implication, equated with the wild olive. The wild olive cannot ripen; but can become assimilated to the fatness of the cultivated tree. In his allegory of the cultivated and wild olive, Clement understood Paul to be concerned with Hellenistic culture. All this lends support to the suggestion that in that allegory, Rom 11:17–24, Paul was engaged not only with the Gentile Christians but also with the Gentile world and with its anti-Judaism. By casting Gentiles in the role of the wild olive and reserving the cultivated olive for a community rooted in Abraham, was he not in a way subtle to a modern reader but probably clear to the Christian Gentiles in Rome (who one must assume to have achieved a degree of sophistication to be able to follow the epistle to the Romans at all) opposing the anti-Judaism of the Greco-Roman world and striking a blow for his own kin after the flesh, not only within the context of the Church, but within that of the larger world?

This little suggestion cannot be proved or disproved. Few will be able to assess it with as much judiciousness and comprehensive knowledge, and, I am comforted, with as much of the necessary indulgence, as the honoree of this volume.

9
Paul and Jewish Christianity
According to Cardinal Daniélou:
A Suggestion

As a token of my gratitude for all that I have learned from the one to whom this essay is dedicated, and in recognition of his kindness, I had hoped to write an extensive examination of his work on Jewish Christianity. Circumstances, unfortunately, made this impossible, and I have to limit myself to a very brief statement of one important and extremely interesting possibility which, it seems to me, the results of that work raise. It is the possibility that it demands a reassessment of one aspect of the role of Paul in primitive Christianity.

SIGNIFICANCE AND SPREAD OF
JEWISH CHRISTIANITY

Daniélou distinguishes three possible ways in which the term Jewish-Christianity can be used: first, as designating those *"Jews who acknowledge Christ as a prophet or a Messiah, but not as the Son of God* and thus form a separate class, half-way between Jews and Christians."[1] The Ebionites are the best known of this group. The second possible reference for the term Jewish Christianity is to the Christian community at Jerusalem under the leadership of James and those who were influenced by him.[2] This community dominated the Church, so many have held, until after 70 C.E. And, third, Jewish Christianity can stand for "a type of Christian thought expressing itself in terms borrowed from Judaism."[3]

Daniélou favors the adoption of this third connotation. This connotation not only includes the other two possibilities mentioned, but much else. Indeed, it can connote "men who had broken completely with the Jewish world but who continued to think in its terms."[4] "Thus," writes Daniélou, "the Apostle Paul, though by no means a Jewish Christian in the second of the three senses (mentioned above), was certainly one in this third sense."[5] Moreover, not only converts to Christianity from Judaism are indicated by the term Jewish Christianity in this third sense, but also Gentiles, proselytes, and many formerly loosely associated with the Synagogue, even though they had not taken the final step of circumcision, who had joined the Church. Such would be familiar with the thought forms of Judaism. One is reminded of Munck's[6] insistence that among Gentile converts to Christianity there was a kind of enthusiasm for the forms of thought and practice of Israel which was sometimes extreme.[7] Overconversion is a familiar phenomenon.[8] This made it possible for Munck to regard even the Judaizers, who shadow Paul and dog his footsteps throughout his career, as Gentile converts.

The third definition enables Daniélou to ascribe to Jewish Christianity an extraordinary influence in primitive Christianity. We summarize his conclusions very roughly.[9] First, Jewish Christians, understood in these broad terms, were very widely scattered. There were Jews throughout the Greco-Roman world. Thus Paul discovered Jewish Christians wherever he went. They opposed him bitterly in Galatia, Corinth, Colossae, Rome. Two Roman historians, Suetonius and Tacitus, took Christians at Rome to be a Jewish sect. Papias, Bishop of Hierapolis in Asia Minor (60–130 C.E.), testifies that there were Jewish Christians in Phrygia, and it has been argued that it was such Christians who spread the faith to Alexandria in Egypt.

Even more important, Jewish Christianity spread through the Aramaic-speaking areas in the East. Peoples in such areas would naturally draw the Hebrews of Jerusalem, who understood and spoke their language. It has been customary to claim that Jewish Christians at Pella, isolated from Judaism and from the main stream of the Christian movement in the West, gradually petrified and faded into insignificance. But they produced an apologist for the faith in the second century—Aristo, and they may have been joined by other Jewish Christian refugees after the year 140 C.E. They developed into the sect of the Nazarenes who observed the Sabbath and practiced circumcision. They brought forth their own gospel in Hebrew. Fragments of this have come down to us in the works of St. Jerome, and it was current throughout the area of the Jewish Christian mission.

There were other groups of Jewish Christians in Transjordan and Syria. Irenaeus, Bishop of Lyons, mentions the Ebionites, strict Jewish Christians who took daily baths for purification, and used unleavened bread and water for the Eucharist. They believed, among other things, that Christ was a prophet helped by an archangel. There were other forms of Jewish Christianity in the East, and in the northeast, near Edessa, there flourished certain ascetic Jewish-Christian communities.

What shall we conclude from all this? Although the New Testament does not directly tell us much about the significance and spread of Jewish Christianity, it must have been a very strong, widespread element in the earliest days of the Church.

Everywhere, especially in the east of the Roman Empire, there would be Jewish Christians whose outward way of life would not be markedly different from that of Jews. They took for granted that the gospel was continuous with Judaism; for them the new covenant, which Jesus had set up at the Last Supper with his disciples and sealed by his death, did not mean that the covenant made between God and Israel was no longer in force. They still observed the feasts of Passover, Pentecost, and Tabernacles; they also continued to be circumcised, to keep the weekly Sabbath and the Mosaic regulations concerning food. According to some scholars, they must have been so strong that right up to the fall of Jerusalem in 70 C.E. they were the dominant element in the Christian movement.

But there is another aspect to Jewish Christianity. It was not only geographically widespread but profoundly influential in the realm of thought. We must recognize how much of the literature of the early Christian movement bears the marks of Jewish thinking. First, much of the orthodox literature, that is, literature which came to be received by the main stream of Christianity—the great Church that triumphed over heresies of all kinds in later Christian history—is so marked. We name here only certain texts like the *Didache*, the *Odes of Solomon*, the *Epistle of Barnabas*, the *Shepherd of Hermas*, all of which show affinities with the ideas found in the Qumran Scrolls. Compare, for example, *Did.* 1:1 with 1QS:3. The way of thinking of the Christian document is based upon the twofold way of the document from Qumran. But, secondly, in addition, the various Jewish Christian sects, outside what became the main stream of Christianity, interpreted the gospel in many writings. We have already referred to an apologist called Aristo in Pella and to the *Gospel of the Nazarenes*. The Ebionites also had their own form of a gospel, and the recently discovered *Gospel of Thomas, The Song of the Pearl* contained in the *Acts of Thomas* have been traced back to Jewish Christians in Edessa at the end of the first century. Much of the literature discovered in Nag Hammadi, Egypt, can be similarly connected with Jewish Christian influences. It is difficult to think of any early literature in the Church which does not reveal a Jewish world of thought.

JEWISH WORLD OF THOUGHT

Can we enter into that world? As we saw, long habit has made us think of Jewish Christians as rather simple people who understood Jesus as a prophet or a Messiah but often, as in the case of the Ebionites, not as the Son of God. We regarded their interpretation of the gospel as a superficial one which had failed to cast off naive Jewish ways of thought. This habit of thinking about Jewish Christianity we must now discard.

There never was a "simple" gospel. Jewish Christians were, in fact, rooted in a long apocalyptic tradition of thinking and writing. Ever since the second century B.C.E. at least, there had been groups in Judaism who concerned themselves with the secrets of the universe, who claimed through revelations and visions to have knowledge of the places where unseen forces—angels, and demons, and the souls of men—dwelled, who had unutterable experiences of the unseen world. They claimed also to know the secrets of history, the course of events in the future which had been prepared by God beforehand.

We may illustrate from visions described in 1 Enoch, which we may now take to be pre-Christian.

> And in those days a whirlwind carried me off from the earth
> And set me down at the end of the heavens.
> And there I saw another vision, the dwelling places of the holy,
> And the resting places of the righteous.
> Here mine eyes saw their dwellings with his righteous angels,
> And their resting places with the holy . . .
> And in that place mine eyes saw the Elect One of righteousness . . .
> And I saw his dwelling place under the wings of the Lord of Spirits. And
>   here my eyes saw all those who sleep not: they stand before him and
>   bless him . . .
> and my face was changed;
> for I could no longer behold . . .
> And after that I saw the secrets of the heavens,
> and how the kingdom is divided,
> and how the actions of men are weighed in the balance.
> And there I saw mansions of the elect . . .
> and mine eyes saw there all the sinners being driven from hence which deny
>   the Name of the Lord of Spirits, and being dragged off.

Fantasy and insight, imaginative horror and felicity are all found in this apocalyptic as well as stern, relentless logic, as in passages in the *Serek hayyaḥad* from Qumran, which give a philosophy or interpretaton of history which we summarize in the following tabular form:

The God of Knowledge
(Source of all that is or will be)

1. *The designs of all things*
   (These and all things cannot be changed)

2. *Man created to have dominion over all.*

The Spirit of Truth	*The Spirit of Error*
(comes from the abode of Light = the Prince of Lights = the Angel of Truth)	(comes from the source of darkness = Angel of Darkness)

Both Spirits are in the heart of man

Counsels of Spirit of Truth	*Counsels of Spirit of Error*
(Humility, compassion, etc.)	(Greed, pride, falsehood, etc.)
Rewards for the Sons of Truth	*Punishments for Sons of Error*
(Healing, peace, joy, glory)	(Afflictions, eternal)

3. *The war of the two Spirits in Man*

But

4. *A Period of Ruin for Error is set by God*
   The truth of the world will emerge
   Man will be purified of evil spirit:
   Man will be sprinkled with the Spirit of Truth
   Man will have wisdom, knowledge from God and
   the Sons of Heaven.

5. THE NEW WILL COME.

For the apocalyptists history is a struggle between the good and the bad forces allowed to exist by God. They took an exceedingly gloomy view of the present world and rested their hope in a terrible and a glorious future when God himself would rule. One characteristic of the future, as these seers and visionaries thought, was that it would be like the beginning of the universe: the end would be as the beginning—this was a kind of slogan of their thinking. For example, the author of 4 Ezra, an apocalyptic work written just after 70 C.E. wrote of the end as follows: "And the world shall return to its first silence seven days, as it was at the beginning so that no man is left."

Jewish Christians shared in this way of thinking not only through their reading of the Old Testament, but through such groups as the sectarians at Qumran, the Essenes. And they understood the gospel in these terms. What was the significance of Jesus? For Jewish Christians it was that he alone had entered into the secrets of God and opened them up to men who bore his name, and would lead them into that paradise which was at the beginning and would be at the end: he was Alpha and Omega, the beginning and the end. For them saving faith was the knowledge that there was in all things a wisdom from God, a purpose which controlled all the universe and all history within it, and that this wisdom was in Christ, who was not only the Lord of the individual soul but of all things in heaven and on earth and under the earth. This is a far cry from the extreme simplicity which was once ascribed to Jewish Christianity.

And in two other spheres the influence of Jewish Christianity was deep. First in the sphere of moral teaching. Alongside such theological concepts as we have indicated above, which included all mankind and all the universe in their scope, Jewish Christianity also insisted on a pattern of moral instruction, on two ways—a good and a bad—which men could choose, on the two great commandments of love to God and to the neighbor, on the Angel of Light and the Prince of Darkness, on the spirits of virtues and the demons of vices, on the need for steadfastness and commitment.

And there is a second practical sphere where Jewish Christians left their mark. All readers of the history of the Church and of the New Testament must have asked one very obvious question. How did the later Catholic Church organized under bishops, in a hierarchical system, develop from what seems to have been in the early days a simple society of believers? Broadly speaking there have been two classic answers to this question. Protestants have tended to think of the earliest Christian community as a loosely knit fellowship of the Spirit, a kind of glorified company of enthusiasts, which was filled with ardor but had little sense of order. From this early purity and freedom and spirituality it fell into the rigid, legalistic "clerical" Church of the second century. The community became an organization instead of remaining a living organism. On the other hand, Catholics, Roman and other, have always maintained that order as well as ardor coexisted from the very beginning, that the Church was "organized" from the start. Perhaps Jewish Christianity, which was much influenced by the Essenes, may help us at this point. For example, was it from Jewish Christianity, with its Essene affinities, that the figure of the bishop comes? Or, again, is celibacy to be traced back to the same source? And are the white vestments used by catechumens in later Catholicism a mark of its borrowing from Jewish Christian practice which rested on Essene practice? These questions cannot certainly be answered. But it is very probable that the growth of the institutional aspects of Christianity, like its theology and moral teaching, owes much to Jewish Christianity and through it to the apocalyptic sects of Judaism.

FIRST PHASE OF CHRISTIAN THEOLOGY

The above, then, was the earliest form of Christianity. It was expressed in terms and forms rooted in the apocalyptic Essene and synagogal tradition of Judaism. It lay behind most if not all interpreters of the gospel in the early Church. It was not confined simply to Jewish Christians in the strict sense but even informed the minds and ways of men who had no direct connection with Jewish apocalyptic groups.

Such, then, is Daniélou's emphasis on the Jewish Christianity, which for him formed the substructure of Christian thought and, indeed, con-

stituted the first phase of Christian theology, which was expressed in Jew-
ish-Semitic terms. It was Jewish Christianity in this sense which informed
the mind of Paul, however much it be emphasized that he was born into
the Hellenistic wing of the Church.[10]

The use of the phrase "in the Hellenistic wing of the Church" recalls
us to more traditional ways of thinking of primitive Christianity. It serves
to raise the question whether Daniélou's definition of Jewish Christianity
is so wide that, at the very least, it ignores distinctions in emphasis in
primitive Christianity, which makes the violence of the conflicts within it
extremely difficult to understand.[11] Munck, indeed, partly under the impact of his concern to regard Judaizers as Gentile converts, was led to
deny that there were any deep conflicts and different parties revealed in
the Pauline epistles.[12] Doubtless, it may plausibly be argued that Daniélou
has not sufficiently recognized and emphasized the peculiarities of different groups in early Christianity.

But even if this be admitted and his definition of Jewish Christianity
be regarded as so wide as to become a catch-all, Daniélou has drawn
attention in a signal manner to the depth and dispersion of the ideas which
he perhaps too loosely lumps together as Jewish Christian. At first sight,
he might seem to be open to the criticism levelled against Bultmann for
his isolation of what he called "Pre-Pauline Hellenistic Christianity,"
which he was only able to construct by drawing upon sources widely
separated from Paul in time.[13] But there is a difference. Although Daniélou, like Bultmann, casts his net very widely chronologically and geographically, the content of the ideas to which he appeals are indubitably
pre-Christian, well established in pre-Christian Judaism in the apocalyptic
tradition. Schweitzer and, more recently, Käsemann have long taught us
to regard that apocalyptic as the matrix of early Christian theology. But
it is Daniélou's contribution that has made us far more aware of the fe-
cundity or richness of that apocalyptic, as we have already indicated.
Whether the term Jewish Christianity can be as widely used as by Daniélou or not, he has pointed directly to widespread currents or a vastly
complex world of ideas in apocalyptic which formed the stock in trade
of the Christians with whom Paul had to deal, whether they were Hellenistic or Jewish.

But to recognize this must influence the way in which we think of Paul.
The Apostle has variously been approached in modern scholarship along
certain well-marked avenues—those of the Old Testament, Hellenism,
Hellenistic Judaism, Rabbinic Judaism and Apocalyptic. Each of these
avenues has been fruitful and has illumined, in varying degrees, our understanding of the significance of Paul. Of particular interest to us was

the way in which, formerly, emphasis on the Hellenistic influences upon Paul governed our understanding of him. Older scholars used to picture a Paul who confronted the vast complexity of the Greco-Roman world with its many religious and philosophic currents with a comparatively simple Palestinian gospel. This simple Palestinian gospel he had to reinterpret to the Hellenistic world, and thereby he complicated it. From Dean Inge to Bultmann, Paul, the Hellenizer, has been pictured as the one who changed the simple into the complex.

This understanding of Paul has long been suspect. Schweitzer and Käsemann, as we mentioned, found the complexity of apocalyptic behind Paul. But it is Daniélou who has driven this fact home to us through his reexamination of Jewish Christianity. The result of his work is to raise the question: Was Paul not so much the sophisticated Hellenistic Christian who reinterpreted a Palestinian simplicity to transform it into a subtle theology as the sober and, we would add, rabbinic Christian who, standing within a lush, complicated, esoteric apocalyptic tradition, controlled it and simplified it? To put the matter in other words: did he restrain the apocalyptic subtleties and secrets of the earliest Christians in the direction of sobriety? Daniélou's revelation of the richness of the Semitic element in primitive Christian thought implies, in short, that we must no longer think primarily of Paul as having been an agent of theological subtlety and complication in the early Church; rather, he was the filter through which much apocalyptic speculation was diluted, simplified and purified in the interests of sober common sense. Paul did not so much spur theological developments as control them: he did not so much complicate the early faith as simplify it. To examine this suggestion here is not possible. But I trust that to point to it may, however inadequately, serve to indicate how provocative and stimulating has been Cardinal Daniélou's work. In the light of it the question must now be raised how far Paul was a "reductionist?" Certainly a case could be made for this in his treatment of eschatology. May his treatment of the end be understood not only, and perhaps not primarily, as an exercise in the Hellenization[14] of the simple eschatology of Palestinian Christians, but in its gradual denuding?[15] Nor do Paul's references to the organization of the churches reveal any less reductionist an attitude when, for example, we contrast the organization of his churches with that of the sectarians at Qumran. And in moral teaching also, though perhaps (surprisingly?) not to the same degree, the same attitude may be detected. Was Paul, in Cardinal Daniélou's perspective, not at least as much the end of Semitic complexity as the beginning of Hellenistic complexity in Christianity?[16]

10

Galatians: A Commentary on Paul's Letter to the Churches in Galatia*

The learning, devotion, and critical acumen which have given us this commentary on an epistle whose importance can hardly be exaggerated (the approach to it having so often colored the interpretation of Pauline theology as a whole) are beyond praise. In particular the presentation of the Epistle to the Galatians as a self-apologetic letter standing in a long Hellenistic tradition stemming from the platonic treatment of Socrates brings into full play the vast knowledge of Hellenistic literary and epistolary usage which has established Professor H. D. Betz (henceforth H. D. B.) as the New Testament scholar who has probably most illuminated this field. He recognizes that at certain points his division of the epistle— Epistolary prescript (1:1–5); *Exordium* (1:6–11); *Narratio* (1:12—2:14); *Propositio* (2:15–21); *Probatio* (3:1—4:31); *Exhortatio* (5:1—6:10); Epistolary postscript (*Conclusio*) (6:11–18)—is not without difficulties, particularly in the *Exhortatio,* and also in the fifth argument of the *Probatio* (4:12–20). (See pp. 220–21; 253–55.) But, whether he be followed at every point or not, H. D. B. has clarified the literary structure of Galatians in a new and very enriching manner which often carries conviction and certainly must challenge reexamination.[1] And there are other virtues. The comments on each section and verse are so clearly offered and so informed by knowledge of the classical sources and of the pertinent secondary literature, especially on the Hellenistic side, as to be always immensely instructive. The bibliographical data accompanying them are in themselves an education. Equally important is that the author, despite his awareness of the multiplicity of the trees and their tangled character, never loses sight of the wood. He offers a forceful interpretation of the epistle as a whole in a section on "The Theological Argument in Galatians" (pp. 28–33), which helps to guide the reader throughout. H. D. B. refers to English as his Achilles heel, but he seldom limps. He is to be unreservedly congratulated on his achievement. In the following pages we offer reflections, critical and other.

* Hermeneia—A Critical and Historical Commentary on the Bible (Philadelphia: Fortress Press, 1979).

The author deals rather summarily with questions of place and date, that is, with the precise situation addressed in Galatians. Untouched by the recent tendency exemplified by M. Hengel to reestablish the historical value of Acts (1980), he is uneasy about the data provided by that document and finds it difficult to decide between the South and North Galatian theories of the location of the Galatian churches. He finally favors the latter, placing them in Anatolia in the North rather than in the Roman province proper. Again, because of the unreliability of Acts and the absence of data provided by the epistle itself, he regards all attempts at determining when the epistle was written and where as highly conjectural. Only in relation to one epistle does he explicitly find an acceptable chronological sequence, Galatians having been written before Romans. Although implicitly in some of his comments he seems to us to place it also before 1 Corinthians, the chronological relationship of Galatians to all the other Pauline epistles is for H. D. B. strictly unascertainable. Finally, however, he does hazard that a date somewhere between A.D. 50 and 55 is to be preferred. Galatians for him is an "early rather than late Pauline document" (12). The adjective "early" is not defined except that "the letter seems to belong to the beginning of his difficulties with his opponents, rather than to an advanced stage" (ibid.).

The same uncertainty invades the sociological examination of the Anatolian Galatians. There are places where H. D. B. seems, by implication, to think of them (to use his own ugly term) as "hicks" "from a rough and ungovernable area" (29), and as "common people" who would interpret Paul's illness as "demon possession" (225); but in his main emphases he regards them otherwise, and gives a most illuminating summary of the significant studies of the Galatian people. As to the social and cultural status of the members of the Galatian churches, in view of the highly sophisticated and refined literary manner in which Paul addresses them in his self-apologetic letter, H. D. B. necessarily finds them to have been highly cultured, Hellenized Galatians, prosperous city dwellers, sophisticated, and, insofar as they were originally Celts, assimilated. The allusions to classical Greek and Latin authors which H. D. B. finds it necessary to make in interpreting the epistle certainly seem to require a high degree of sophistication in those to whom it was addressed.

The importance of the way in which H. D. B. deals with the questions of the general sociological milieu and of place and date, that is, of the actual situation addressed, must not be underestimated.

Let us look at the sociological aspect first. The mixed character—Greek, Oriental, Jewish—of the communities and synagogues in the Roman prov-

ince of Galatia—at Lystra, Derbe, Iconium, and elsewhere—was often
taken to lend probability to the South Galatian theory. It was urged that
Paul seems to have found it easier to make an effective impact in areas
where Jews, Gentiles, and Orientals were more intermingled than in
"purer" ethnic communities, either Jewish or Hellenistic.[2] But H. D. B.
makes it clear that even if the Galatian churches were situated in Anatolia
they too were a mixture of Celtic peoples who had become Hellenized
and Romanized. He writes:

> The name Gallograeci which some writers use, expresses this tendency
> towards Hellenization. Celtic names were dropped in favor of Greek names.
> On the other hand some of the customs and institutional structures were
> perpetuated for a long time, and the Celtic language was spoken in rural
> areas as late as the time of Jerome (2).

The South Galatian theory, then, has no edge on the Northern on the
score of a greater ethnic admixture.

But there is an aspect of this question which we must emphasize as a
qualification of H. D. B.'s work. While he recognizes that the Galatian
churches were a mixture (whether originally Celtic or Greek cannot certainly be determined), he insists that the epistle does not presuppose Jews
as resident members of them. For him the churches addressed were ethn-
ically Gentiles. He does refer to recent archeological discoveries which
have turned up Jewish inscriptions in the inner parts of Anatolia. These
might be taken to make probable the existence of synagogues there and
the possible presence of Jews among the Galatian Christians. But H. D.
B. draws no such conclusion. He finds that the argument that Jews must
have been present in the Galatian churches is "well known but un-
founded" (5 n. 21). For him the wholly Gentile character of those churches
is a given: the archeological evidence is too late.

We suggest that this almost unqualified insistence enables H. D. B.
both to overemphasize certain factors and to underestimate others. First,
since according to him, the Galatian churches were made up of highly
cultured, Hellenized-Romanized, assimilated Celts, it is perfectly natural
to consider that they could appreciate the highly sophisticated literary
form which Paul's self-apologetic letter followed, as well possibly as the
literary allusions to which H. D. B. draws our attention. We may surmise
that within such a sophisticated literary convention, they would even
allow themselves to be addressed as "foolish," and even be flattered by
that! (To judge from modern Britain, the assimilated generally seem to
have a penchant for subtlety in literature—a subtlety which perhaps re-

flects the tortuousness of assimilation itself. Among the Welsh, the subtle obscurity of Dylan Thomas comes to mind and he was not alone.) But, second, this sophisticated, Hellenized character of the Galatian churches enabled them to understand what H. D. B. calls "the age-old human dream of freedom," the notion of *eleutheria*, a keynote in the epistle. According to H. D. B., under the impact of Paul's preaching, they had achieved this freedom:

> The concept which best sums up the Galatians' basic self-understanding is the concept of "freedom" (*eleutheria*) [2:4–5; 4:22–31; 5:1, 13]. To them the Christian faith meant that the age-old dream of human freedom had become a reality. For them "freedom" was not a merely theological notion, but they regarded themselves as free from "this evil world" with its repressive social, religious, and cultural laws and conventions. . . . They were the *avant garde*, "a new creation" (καινὴ κτίσις) (29).

Two questions arise. To begin, what is the origin of this "dream"? H. D. B. does not directly deal with the question: he calls it "age-old" and "human." On his understanding of the constitution of the Galatian churches, it was apparently derived from the Hellenistic world. This is made clear indirectly on p. 190, where, in a very rich treatment, H. D. B. draws upon Zeno's *Politeia* (see n. 71); and we do know that the Greco-Roman world had its vision of and hope for a universal humanity. But this leads to a second question. How could the Galatian churches have connected *that* hope with Paul's preaching? What was the link between them? These Galligreci went further; they enthusiastically espoused a society where there would be neither Jew nor Greek, bond nor free, male nor female. They actually had, according to H. D. B., plunged into and accepted a radically revolutionary situation. However dynamic the message of Paul, was the generalized (somewhat vague?) Hellenistic hope for *eleutheria* sufficiently powerful to lead them to this? The assimilated are usually not drawn to enthusiastic revolution.

In response to these questions, we suggest that H. D. B. might qualify his insistence on the Gentile character of the Galatian churches by recognizing that they were largely made up of proselytes and God-fearers living on the fringe of the synagogue. If we do not misjudge his work, H. D. B. has a tendency to ignore or at least minimize a fundamental fact of early Christian, including Pauline, expansion and to move too directly from the Greco-Roman world to the interpretation of Galatians. We refer to the truism that it was the Hellenized Jewish communities of the Greco-Roman world and their *pro-Jewish* peripheries of God-fearing semi-proselytes and proselytes who harbored the earliest Christian cells and served as bases of operation for Paul and other Christian missionaries. Paul was first an apostle to the Greek *Jewish* communities. We assume that in Galatia (whether in Anatolia or in the Roman province—a question not closed) as elsewhere, the apostle was dealing with proselytes and near-proselytes already on the threshold of the synagogue, attracted to Judaism and knowing the activity, the concerns, and the hopes of the synagogue. (We think too easily of Jews as *Palestinian*; they were even more a *Mediterranean* people.)

The recognition of this probability helps to make the condition of the Galatian churches, the character of the epistle, and, indeed, H. D. B.'s own understanding of it—in certain of its aspects—more comprehensible. His analyses of the form of Galatians we have already praised: he has revealed much in the significance of the detailed planning and sequence in it. In the light of a recent emphasis on the interpenetration of Judaism and Hellenism by the first century, that even a Pharisee such as Paul should have been familiar with and used such a form need not surprise one. To his great credit, H. D. B. never forces the evidence in the interests of his own theories. He recognizes that to make the form determinate of the content of what Paul wished to convey to the Galatians would be to contravene the apostle's own attitude toward oratory and worldly wisdom (see pp. 24–25). That form did not dictate content he admits, as we saw in 5:1—6:10 and in 3:1–5. Much, therefore, as we owe to H. D. B. in matters of form, it would be a disservice to the apostle to confuse the medium with the message and to concentrate so on form as not to give priority in interpretation to the substance of the letter. (St. Augustine, as Ms. J. Everts pointed out to me, has words on this. See his *On Christian Doctrine* 4.7. And Professor David Daube long ago taught me that form, unlike substance, tends to be fastened on by instinct rather than deliberation.) The substance of Galatians, if the Galatian churches were Gentile and not very deeply touched by Judaism, is strange indeed. We note the following:

1. The references to and interpretations of the Tanak and the exegetical methods employed point to readers not only highly sophisticated but familiar with the Greek translation of the Jewish scriptures and with the niceties, on a simple level at least, of synagogal biblical study. There is an allegory in Galatians (although some take it to be an example of typology) in 4:21–31, and allegories are more characteristic of Hellenistic than of Jewish literary usage. But it is impossible not to recognize that Galatians is very Judaic (Pharisaic?) in matter and scriptural method. We are justified in assuming that its readers were most likely Gentiles within

the ambit of Judaism. That they were also culturally highly Hellenized is clear from the innumerable parallels between so much in the epistle and the classical Greek and Latin authors to which H. D. B. appeals with such telling force. But a caveat is necessary. The interpenetration to which we have previously referred must be given full weight. By the first century, especially in the Diaspora, Judaism had come to share much of the classical Greek and Hellenistic heritage, and the parallels must not be pressed to suggest ethnic provenance and differences between Jews and Gentiles too directly. It is a pity that H. D. B. includes in his bibliography neither W. L. Knox's *St. Paul and the Church of the Gentiles* (1939) nor Knox's *Some Hellenistic Elements in Primitive Christianity* (1944), nor again G. Klein's *Der älteste christliche Katechismus* (1909). One could have wished for more frequent references to the Greek translation of the Jewish scriptures and to the Tannaitic sources. The classical allusions in Paul are not conscious, but traditional and commonplace, and the Greek translation of the Jewish scriptures and the Masoretic text of the Hebrew Bible (we cannot share H. D. B.'s view [p. 152, n. 135] that Paul may not have known Hebrew) meant more to him than extracanonical materials. It is, perhaps, understandable that the term *synagogē* does not occur in H. D. B.'s Greek index (which we find incomplete for our purposes in other respects) because it does not occur in the text of the epistle, and to judge by an index is unfair. But it is significant that he nowhere finds it necessary to discuss at length the scriptural activity of the synagogue. When he does refer to Pharisaic exegesis it is to discuss the point raised in Schoeps[3] on 3:13 (152, n. 135), and to respond to those who refer to the "rabbinic" methodology of the epistle (14, n. 103). But the exegesis and activity of the synagogue were the matrices within which much of the kind of material we find in Galatians 3 and 4 especially (but also, as we shall suggest, in 5), becomes intelligible. To Gentile readers not deeply influenced by the synagogue, that material would have been remote and puzzling. The substance of Galatians in its form demands an audience of former proselytes, God-fearers, and Jews.

2. The theological content of the epistle points in the same direction. At the risk of simplification and falsification, that theology can be grouped around the gospel that Paul preached and the outcome of that preaching in the coming of the Spirit and the problems all this created. Summarily, though not exclusively, the content of the gospel was Christ crucified. We learn elsewhere that this was to Greeks pure foolishness. It had meaning, however, for those Gentiles who were familiar with Judaism and its messianic hopes. We suggest that these, rather than the more generalized

hopes of the Hellenistic world, were the clue to the vision of a reunited humanity and of the *eleutheria* about which Paul writes and which, in H. D. B.'s judgment, had already been realized in the Galatian churches. It was because they had been proselytes and God-fearers, would-be Jews as it were, that the Galatians addressed by Paul were able to grasp the revolutionary (because it was messianic) character of his message.

The neglect of the Jewish connections of the Galatians perhaps accounts for certain aspects of H. D. B.'s interpretation. In his discussion of the name *Christos Iēsous* in 1:1ff., he does not ask at any point what force the term *Christos* has for Paul. He refers to secondary authorities that *Christos* was a designation of the Messiah as such, and that in Galatians also, for Paul, the term might possibly retain this force. So in his discussion of 2:16 (117), he comments on the title Messiah for Jesus in the phrase: *pistis Iēsou Christou* as follows: "This abbreviation seems to be old and *retains* the character of Christos as a messianic title" (our italics). The implication is that it no longer retains (significantly at least) this character for Paul. And the implication works itself out in the way in which H. D. B. understands Christ's relation to the Christian in inner, spiritual, personal, and not specifically messianic terms. (See for example p. 63, where he understands *en emoi* in 1:16a as meaning "in Paul," not "through Paul," as the context seems to demand, and also p. 71, although his meaning is not always clear.) It is indicative that H. D. B. nowhere, even in referring to the mystical understanding of 1:16, refers to Albert Schweitzer's *The Mysticism of Paul the Apostle* (1931), which he also ignores in discussion of 2:19–20 and 3:26–29, where the eschatological "mysticism" of Schweitzer is certainly to be considered. It seems natural for him—but perhaps misguided of him so exclusively to do so—to connect such astounding passages as Gal. 3:26–29 with Hellenistic hopes rather than with the eschatological tradition of Judaism taken up by Hellenistic Judaism. All this is not to deny the difficulty of understanding such passages as 2:19–20 and 3:26–29, and H. D. B. has undoubtedly rightly evoked a Hellenistic milieu in expounding them. Marcel Simon[4] has recently reinforced the legitimacy of this approach. But it should not be made the dominant approach. It is difficult to escape the impression that H. D. B. has a strong tendency to underestimate the essentially messianic situation within which Paul was writing. How otherwise can he begin with such a sentence as, *"If Paul has connections with apocalyptic terminology* [our italics] . . . ," in commenting on the expression *ho aiōn mellōn* ("the age to come"), which is clearly the Greek equivalent to Hebrew *ha 'ôlâm ha-bâ*? So too for H. D. B. *apokalupsai ton huion auton* in 1:16 is not to be interpreted in terms of Jewish apocalyptic (see p. 70 n. 143). We cannot here enter the terminological debate over "apocalyptic" and "eschatology"; we have elsewhere urged that Paul was a reductionist in apocalyptic.[5] H. D. B. is fully justified in claiming that Paul has modified the apocalyptic terminology (see p. 42 n. 60). In places also he does recognize the apocalyptic dimensions in Paul, in his pessimism (175) and in his occasional references to Romans 9–11 (see especially p. 70). And he admits the apocalyptic character of *ho aiōn ho enestōs ponēros* in Gal 1:4 (see p. 42 n. 58). But his prevailing emphasis is illustrated by his comment on the phrase *to plerōma tou chronou* in Gal 4:4: "The phrase 'the fullness of time' is found only here in Paul but belongs to the Jewish and Christian eschatological language which Paul shared" (206). This is tepid, because that phrase defines the context of Paul's understanding of his own ministry and of the Christian movement. It is probably a technical term for "the end of the days," either the Hebrew *'aḥêrîth ha iâmîm* or *qêṣ hâ îamîm*. Not to recognize and emphasize the high importance of this messianic term for the interpretation of Paul and early Christianity is to read *Hamlet* without the Prince of Denmark. Perhaps his immersion in the classical and Hellenistic and Roman worlds tends to hide this from H. D. B. This is probably why—and very understandably—he does not turn naturally and primarily, as we suggest the situation demands, to messianism as the ultimate and dominantly governing matrix of Paul's epistle to the Galatians.

To substantiate this claim would require the examination of many passages. We illustrate from H. D. B.'s approach to the phrase *ho nomos tou Christou* ("the law of Christ") and to the Spirit. Recognizing the difficulty of fitting the paranetic section in which it occurs into his epistolary framework, he finds the problem of *ho nomos tou Christou* in Gal 6:2 "one of most crucial problems in the whole letter" (299). This admission and the whole discussion illustrate the wholly admirable thoroughness and "honesty" of H. D. B.'s work. But he creates a problem because he is not sufficiently attuned to the messianic world within which early Christianity moved: he fails to recognize a technical messianic phrase. The twofold article—"the Law of the Messiah," not simply "the Law of Christ"—points to a specific concept which Paul, like his opponents, would not have found unnatural or alien: he did not need to borrow it either from an earlier tradition or from his opponents. It was part of his messianic stock in trade.

Again H. D. B. very rightly underlines the central place of the Spirit in the epistle. It was the initial experience of the Spirit that gave birth to the Galatian churches; and it is to that experience that Paul appeals in his theological argumentation with them. Here the epistolary literary details supplied by H. D. B. are telling. Equally convincing is his view that that same enthusiastic experience of the Spirit as it confronted the continuing actualities of human existence created a crisis which helped to produce a favorable reception for Paul's opponents and doubts about "Paul's version of Christianity" (see pp. 28–29). Enthusiasm in the Spirit is certainly not confined to messianic movements. The parallels in Gnostic oracles to which H. D. B. refers are impressive. One could only wish that he had more explicitly recognized that the experience of the Spirit was very markedly connected with the messianic hopes of Judaism, and that together these constituted the point of departure for Paul and for his readers; the latter came from what we suggest were Greek Jewish synagogues in which those hopes were alive.

3. It is not otherwise that we are to approach the *parainēsis* in 5:1–6:10, that is, it is to be related to the tradition of the Hellenistic Jewish synagogue more directly than H. D. B. has done. The many parallels to which he appeals are forceful. One wonders, however, whether the *parainēsis* is to be so immediately related to the Greek and Latin authors and traditions as to the catechetical and homiletical tradition of the Hellenistic synagogues. Between the classics and the synagogue stood figures such as Posidonius, who had mediated and minted the treasures to a more diluted and accessible form. The works of W. L. Knox (1939) and Philip Carrington (1940) could have been consulted in this connection. They would perhaps have tempered H. D. B.'s eagerness to go so directly to classical models. We do not emphasize this, however, because the richness of the materials presented by H. D. B. and their pertinence are unmistakable.

4. So far we have noted specific points where in our judgment a greater attention to the "Jewish connection" would have enriched the work of H. D. B. There is also a more general, but nonetheless crucial, concomitant, if not consequence, of the neglect of such attention. According to H. D. B., in Galatians Paul thinks of two opposed religions: Judaism and Christianity. He regards the epistle as addressed to "the whole of Christianity: Jewish and Gentile Christians, Paulinists and anti-Paulinists" (24). He is aware that the separation of Christianity from Judaism, that is, the establishment of the Christian movement as a distinct and self-conscious new religion, was "gradual and painful" (28). But for him Paul, in Galatians, was thinking in terms of an antithesis to Judaism. H. D. B. refers to "the validity, legitimacy and viability of Paul's *version of Christianity*" (29; our italics), not of his Christian version of Judaism; as a Christian

Paul is an outsider to Judaism (30). On the question of Paul's "conversion," H. D. B. is ambiguous. He both speaks of Paul's "conversion to the Christian faith" (30) and yet holds that "One should not simply take it for granted that Paul had a conversion experience in the sense that he was converted from Judaism to Christianity . . ." (69). But at one point he asserts that for Paul the gift of the Spirit destroys the Torah (31).

In our judgment this understanding of Paul's faith as the expression of a new religion, Christianity, is related to H. D. B.'s emphasis on the predominantly Gentile character of the Galatian Christians without the sufficient recognition that they lived on the fringe of the synagogue and, like Paul himself, were operating in terms of the interpretation of Judaism. There were many "Judaisms" in the first century, and it is arguable that even in Galatians the Christian movement was not for Paul an antithesis to the religion of his fathers but a particular interpretation of it in the light of Christ crucified. We shall return to this later.

Before we close this section it is necessary to recognize that we may have insisted on what H. D. B., in fact, tacitly assumes, namely, that the Galatian Christians were proselytes and God-fearers, although he thinks of them mainly as Gentiles. If so, we wish that he had made this assumption and its implications more clear. He does on occasion refer to Hellenistic Jewish literature (for example, on p. 143) and to Hellenistic Judaism (71, n. 74; 166; 214f.), but a glance at his indexes shows where his literary emphasis lies.

There are passages where it might be argued that the Galatians were wholly non-Jews. Throughout the epistle the readers are under pressure to be circumcised (Gal 2:3; 5:2–12; 6:12–15). But this is not incompatible with their being proselytes and God-fearers. That they can even have contemplated circumcision points to this. So, too, 3:1–15 does not necessarily imply that the Galatians had been altogether outside the Law when they received the Spirit. But does not the description of their condition in Gal 4:8–11 before their acceptance of the gospel require that they were Gentiles untouched by the Law? At first sight the answer would seem to have to be in the affirmative. But there is another possibility. Proselytes and God-fearers who had become Christians could have backslid either to paganism or to a more observant form of Judaism than Paul demanded. And this was probably the twofold possibility that Paul faced in Gal 4:8–11.

My reference to the pressure for the circumcision of the Galatians leads to the second major point where we could have hoped for a more thorough treatment by H. D. B. He does not concern himself unduly with the exact

date of the epistle, proposing vaguely A.D. 50–55. But for H. D. B. especially this is a serious matter because of his methodological concentration on the epistle itself in comparative isolation from the other epistles
and on Paul's opponents. In his fascinating preface, he writes:

> In this commentary Paul's Galatians always stands in the center of inter-
> est. . . . The attempt to harmonize Galatians with other Pauline letters has
> been resisted and so has the attempt to interpret Galatians by interpreting
> "Paul's theology" into it. Special attention is given to the other side of
> Galatians, the theology of the anti-Pauline opposition. To be sure, this other
> side is extremely difficult to reconstruct because of the scarcity of the
> sources. The sources, however, which do exist should be used (15–16).

A primary, though we must add not rigidly exclusive, concentration on
Galatians itself is certainly right, and with reference to the sources he
uses, H. D. B. is to be very highly endorsed and commended. He has
taken seriously sources too long neglected in the interpretation of Paul,
the *Kerygmata Petrou* and Justin Martyr's work particularly. We agree
with him that Schoeps's contributions on Jewish Christianity are far more
significant than has been generally recognized.[6] H. D. B.'s commentary
is likely to have the beneficial effect of turning more and more attention
to these.

But this apart, we must emphasize that the implication of H. D. B.'s
methodology is that as precise a determination as possible of the actual
situation which provoked the epistle should be aimed at if we are to understand the opposition Paul faced. It may be that this is impossible, as
H. D. B. holds, but we should have appreciated a more adequate can-
vassing of the issue, because "context defines content." We have already
suggested that H. D. B.'s underestimation of the Jewishness of the Galatian churches has had significant consequences. May it not be that his
abandonment of the quest for a more precise setting (he allows only four
brief half-pages to the historical situation of the epistle and three very
brief half-pages to its dating) also has such consequences? A more precise
understanding of the historical situation seems especially to be demanded
by H. D. B.'s own understanding of the postscript, 6:11–18, where there
is a possible clue to the actual situations that the Galatians faced. They
were being compelled to be circumcised so that Paul's Jewish opponents
might not be persecuted (6:12). H. D. B. calls the postscript *conclusio*
or *peroratio*. In connection with this, he writes: "Seen as a rhetorical
feature, *the peroratio becomes most important for the interpretation of
Galatians. It contains the interpretative clues to the understanding of
Paul's major concerns in the letter as a whole and should be employed
as the hermeneutical key to the intention of the Apostle*" (313; our italics).

If so, what are we to make of those who compel the Galatian Christians to be circumcised and have thus initiated the crisis in their relations with Paul? Do they provide a clue to the historical setting? H. D. B. finds the passage, 6:11–18, polemical and to that extent "a mixture of objective facts and subjective judgments" (314). With typical caution, he finds it difficult to pinpoint the historical: "The compulsion was probably achieved by putting the pressure on persuasion and conviction of the Galatians (cf. 2:5, 12–13; 3:1a; 5:8). The goal of the adversaries was to get the Gentile Galatians ready to accept circumcision voluntarily" (315).

In an excellent treatment, fully aware of the difficulties of moving from polemics to history (see p. 317), H. D. B. acknowledges that "Paul's flat statement that the circumcised [*hoi peritemnomenoi*: used of those who themselves want to compel circumcision on the Galatians] do not themselves keep the Torah [6:13] is strange." Referring to the works of Morton Smith, W. Lütgert, W. Schmithals, J. Eckert, J. Munck, and R. Meyer, H. D. B. finally admits that he has no solution as to whom the phrase referred. He notes that Gal 2:3, 5:2–12 as well as 6:12, 15 point to the compulsion to be circumcised that the Galatians faced: it was very real. The parallels he offers (316) in the case of Peter in Gal 2:11–14 and 2:3–5 and of Trypho in Justin, *Dialogue* 46, do not seem to us quite adequate, although A. Suhl also finds a basic similarity between the situation faced in Galatians and that in Gal 2:1–14.[7] Does not Galatians point to a more specific, immediately acute situation than is indicated by Galatians 2? R. Jewett has taken this question very seriously and identified the opponents with extreme nationalists[8] ("Zealots": a term which needs careful definition). H. D. B. rejects Jewett's view because the latter builds his case mainly on Acts and because Zealots are not mentioned in the passages he refers to (6 n. 31). The absence of the party name Zealots is understandable: there was no "party" of that name before A.D. 66 probably, although there were "zealots." H. D. B. himself, in any case, is at pains to point out that Paul—in conformity with epistolary usage—deliberately avoids naming opponents (see 49 n. 65, 107, and the reference to C. F. D. Moule.[9] Compare the use of *tines* in Rom 11:17).[10] And does Acts deserve more weight than H. D. B. allows? The question is not closed. We have not been able to examine Jewett's case in detail; it is not generalized as is the response of H. D. B. Two things in Jewett's work appeal to us: its specificity in meeting what seems to us to have been an unusually pointed crisis in the Galatian churches and its sensitivity to the fiery nationalist aspects of the period with which Christian messianism had to come to terms. How far does polemic always obscure the historical? If we deal conservatively with this question, there is much to be said for regarding Galatians as a very specific response to a very specific situation—possibly such as Jewett urges—within the more generalized confrontation of "Christianity" and "Judaism" as H. D. B. understands it (see his appendix on "The Apostolic Conference" and especially p. 82). Some extraordinarily bitter circumstances must have occasioned the severe, at times crudely intemperate, response of the apostle. That the response in Galatians was unmeasured appears from the changes in Paul. H. D. B. looks with reserve at the notion of development in Paul, but, despite his intent to examine the epistle in comparative isolation from the other epistles, he does in fact point to changes between it and Romans (see, e.g., pp. 122; 123; 124; 140f; 148 n. 95; 149 n. 106; 174 n. 109; 176 n. 128, 187, 193, 195 n. 200). Moreover, he notes that even within Galatians itself Paul introduces correctives of his own extremes. Gal 3 : 19–25 he calls a "digression" (*digressio*) designed—after the Hellenistic epistolary usage (an excellent example of how that is useful for the study of Galatians)—"to prevent a wrong conclusion [virtual dismissal of the Torah] the readers might reach on the basis of the preceding" (163). And it is possible, we suggest, that the reference to the "Israel of God" in 6 : 16 may also be such a corrective. In short, Galatians presents the kind of advance and retreat, extreme position and modification thereof, in the presentation of a case which are typical of very acute crises. This may account for what H. D. B. frequently notes, that is, the use of "political" and "military" terms in Galatians.[11]

If H. D. B. is right in his interpretation of 3 : 26–29—as we are inclined to think he is, at least in part—the atmosphere in the epistle is strangely "political"; it is even possibly "military" if Jewett is right. The latter's case deserves serious consideration.

We are driven back to that messianic-nationalist ferment within which the epistle emerged, as we were previously in our discussion of the sociological milieu, and to some particularly fierce expression of it. (It is no accident that one of the key words of Galatians, *eleutheria*, was to appear in its Hebrew form *ḥêrûth* on the coins minted by the Jews in the war against Rome. The definition of *ḥêrûth* was also one of Paul's concerns.) It may be that the precise situation cannot be discovered and H. D. B.'s caution is commendable. We suggest only that a more conscious recognition of a specific, acute crisis of great urgency is required. What, for example, was the impact of the collection on non-Christian Jews, and how did it affect their relations with Christians?

Owing to limitations of space, we must now turn from considerations of sociology and setting to the theological arguments of Galatians as H. D.

B. presents it. We have previously indicated both explicitly and by implication the richness of his treatment. Part of the great strength of this commentary is that it succeeds very effectively, if not entirely so in our judgment, in setting forth the meaning of Galatians. The emphasis placed on freedom and the Spirit is admirable, even though we find their primary background elsewhere than does H. D. B. It is particularly noteworthy that, full of admiration for Martin Luther as he is, H. D. B. presents the doctrine of justification by faith, which is so often given an exaggerated significance, with disciplined balance. His treatment of it on pp. 30–31 excellently assigns to it a due but not inordinate place. And his examination of the Law in Galatians is sensitive, even though we should connect Paul's treatment more closely with messianic speculation.

There are, however, points which cause reserve. We can here concentrate on only a few. Let us begin with the concept of a special Pauline gospel which H. D. B. refers to as "the gospel of the uncircumcision" to be set over against "the gospel of the circumcision." We are not quite convinced, for two main reasons. First, Paul seldom speaks of "my gospel." Where he does once, in Rom 2:16, the content of that gospel turns out to be an apocalyptic commonplace. Did Paul conceive of having a wholly different gospel from the early community? There is much to indicate that he did not. Was the phrase "the gospel of the uncircumcision" more a designation of geographic or ethnic concern or concentration than of content? Was there not only one gospel interpreted with different emphases for uncircumcised and circumcised? For example, on p. 72, in commenting on 1:16, *hina euangelizōmai en tois ethnesin*, H. D. B. writes: "Paul's commission to preach is clearly limited to Gentiles. The formulation 'among the Gentiles' suggests that Paul's mission includes the entire world population apart from the Jews." But is not this to go too far? Is the total limitation to Gentiles justified by the text? Are the Jews excluded? In contradiction to this, it emerges from H. D. B.'s comments on other passages that he does not think Paul excluded Jews from his missionary activity, certainly not at first. The implication of 3:2 (see p. 132) is that when Paul first preached to the Galatians, the question of the Law was certainly not central, if it was dealt with at all; similarly with H. D. B.'s description (28) of the first Pauline preaching. There H. D. B. does not need to refer to the Law at all. And 1:22–24 implies that the earliest preaching of Paul was not of a gospel demanding freedom from the Law and was not exclusively to Gentiles. "Paul does not say that at that early time he preached the gospel free from the Law. If he had done this, the Judean Christians would hardly have approved of it" (80 n. 231). And on p. 80, n. 232, we read: "Perhaps these churches turned against

Paul, when he *began* preaching his gospel with the Torah" (our italics). Further, p. 85: "Clearly the concept of a gospel free from Torah and circumcision must have been a secondary development. Only when this concept was developing could opposition to it have developed." Does not all this put in question H. D. B.'s comment on 1:16 to which we referred? We would go futher than H. D. B's words on p. 85. Not the doctrine or concept of a gospel without Law led to opposition. Rather the simple fact that Paul preached a gospel without dealing with Torah led to an opposition which evoked or created a doctrine of justification by faith. H. D. B. recognizes that doctrine as a polemic and a matter of self-definition both for Paul and for Jewish Christians (we shall return to this). He makes evident that the doctrine was Jewish Christian and pre-Pauline (2:15–16): its secondary character seems clear. If we understand H. D. B. aright, "justification by faith," important as it was, was not the heart of Paul's gospel but a response to criticisms of it.

The comment on 1:16 in which H. D. B. expresses a sharp distinction between the gospel for the Gentiles and for the Jews points again to his tendency to polarize what was Jewish and what was Gentile. The relation between Paul and Judaism and Hellenism is immensely complex, especially in Galatians. Not even H. D. B. can be expected to have an equal awareness of the Jewish and Hellenistic milieus: who, indeed, would be sufficient for this? It is not surprising that at times he slips in his presentation of Judaism or neglects to take relevant aspects of it into consideration. Minor details come to mind. There is his too easy dismissal of the concept of "corporate personality" (143). In his discussion of the term *apostolos,* which in Paul he traces "probably" to Syriac Gnosticism, he never once deals with the term *shaliach.*[12] And his treatment of the role of Gentiles in Judaism provokes uneasiness. Is it true that for Judaism "outside the Torah covenant there is no salvation" (15; see also p. 115 nn. 25, 27)? H. D. B. ignores the doctrine of the Noachian commandments. The interpretation of 4:5 suffers from this lack (208 n. 62); we prefer to follow Burton (1921). The Gentiles are under the laws of the covenant of Noah. A reverse overemphasis on Gentiles in Paul appears in H. D. B.'s comment on 3:14. Does the phrase, *hina eis ta ethnē hē eulogia tou Abraham genētai en Iēsou Christou* mean that only Gentiles are Abraham's heirs? Are Jewish Christians, for example, excluded? Has not H. D. B. dug a chasm here between Jew and Gentile not in Paul's intent?

More important, although he does not always think of Judaism in monolithic terms, H. D. B. apparently assumes the customary dominant understanding of it in terms of justification by works. He refers to "the orthodox Jewish (Pharisaic) doctrine of salvation. This doctrine states that ἄνθρωπος ('a [=any] human being') is in need of δικαιοῦσθαι ('being justified') at the eschatological judgment of God and that this 'justification' can be obtained by doing and thus fulfilling the ordinances of the Torah" (116; see also pp. 162 n. 12, "the normative view"; 168). Over against this is set "faith" in Christ Jesus—a "theological conviction." But it is erroneous to speak of an "orthodox Jewish (Pharisaic) doctrine." The very bracketing of "Pharisaic" after "Jewish" suggests H. D. B.'s own uneasiness with this formulation. There were many "Judaisms" and even many "Pharisaisms" (or at least Pharisees with different views and emphases) in the first century. The concept of a Jewish "orthodoxy" only emerged in the late eighteenth and early nineteenth centuries in response to the Enlightenment and the emancipation of Jews. We assume that, unfortunately, the works of J. A. Sanders[13] and E. P. Sanders[14] were not available to H. D. B. when he wrote. The positions they urge need not be repeated here. That of the latter particularly poses a question mark following the words quoted from p. 116 and will have to be faced in future treatments of Galatians: the works of J. A. Sanders, E. P. Sanders, and D. Patte[15] deserve serious attention on such questions as H. D. B. deals with. To note only one, did Paul think of the coming of Christ as the end of the Torah? In what sense (see esp. p. 178)? H. D. B. seems to rely much on Schoeps's treatment of the Torah (see p. 165).[16] We have elsewhere criticized this in a review of Schoeps reprinted as an appendix to *Paul and Rabbinic Judaism* (1980).

Finally, this provocative commentary compels a central question. If justification by faith is a secondary development, as H. D. B. allows (to use "secondary" here is not to suggest unimportance), where is the heart of the matter in the Galatian struggle? Before Paul, according to H. D. B. (and one of the marks of his commentary is the confidence—perhaps too great confidence—with which it isolates pre-Pauline materials), Jewish Christians had come to see the importance of justification by faith to identify themselves. For them that doctrine was a means of self-identification within Israel. Similarly, the Galatian Christians faced a crisis of self-identity. In dealing with 4:1–7, and especially 1:6, H. D. B. writes: "Paul bases his argument with the Galatian readers upon the fact that they too have experienced the Spirit (3:2–5); what they are in doubt about is whether or not they are 'sons of God' already now, although they are not part of the Sinai Covenant" (210). The comment on 3:26–28 makes this even more clear: "The section 3:26–28 stands apart and seems to

form the center of the *probatio* section (3:1–4:31). Following the discussion of the situation of Jewish Christians which is concluded in 3:25,
3:26–28 turns to Gentile Christians and defines their status before God.
This is the goal toward which Paul has been driving all along" (181; our
italics).

Although we do not agree that this process is "intentionally anti-Jewish" (142), H. D. B. here touches on the heart of the matter. The question
that Paul had to face was the definition or identification of the "People
of God" or of "Israel." Who are in that people of God and who are not?
A reading of Stendahl's recent work[17] would have helped H. D. B. to
clarify the significance of his comments. Even more we note that in thus
pointing to the problem of self-identity for Gentiles and Jews in Galatians,
H. D. B. lends support to the contention of E. P. Sanders in his great
work *Paul and Palestinian Judaism* (1977) that Judaism was concerned,
as were early Christians, with who stands within and remains within the
covenant. In his statement of "The Theological Argument" (28–33), H.
D. B. does not give sufficient prominence to this fundamental aspect of
Galatians. Is it an accident that the apostle comes to the end with the
words, "For neither circumcision nor uncircumcision [might we para-
phrase, neither works nor faith?] is anything but a new creation," and
then adds the tantalizing words, "As for those who will follow this rule—
Peace be upon them, and mercy upon the Israel of God" (H. D. B.'s
punctuation)? What is the meaning of the "Israel of God"? That is ultimately the problem faced throughout the tortuous argumentation of Galatians. This H. D. B. has pointed to but not sufficiently developed and
emphasized.

Space forbids more reflections. Like that of the Catholic scholar Franz
Mussner, this is an indispensable commentary, worthy of Hermeneia. Our
aim here has not been to pit one approach over against another, but to
complement the one with the other. The truth of Galatians is many-headed
and many-splendored and commands many approaches.[18]

11

From Tyranny to Liberation: The Pauline Experience of Alienation and Reconciliation

Among all the subjects dealt with in this conference,* only that for the present lecture is tied down to a particular historical figure. My subject has a simple concreteness for which I am grateful because, while I do not have the competence to enter the abstract realms of metaphysics and theology which the other subjects demand, I can try to deal historically with Paul, with whom I have been living for a long time. But the simplicity to which I refer can be misleading. No historical figure can be easily comprehended; how much less a figure such as Paul who, despite the directness of some of his epistles, is complex and elusive. In addition, he is separated from us by the gulf of centuries and by a language which was itself the outcome of the fusion of more than one culture. To share in the thought of such a figure so as to capture for ourselves without falsification something of his experience and to give to it a body out of the stuff of our own thought in our own time cannot be easy; even a historical treatment of Paul has its own difficulties.

With this warning I turn to the subject. It divides itself naturally into three parts: Paul's understanding, first, of what tyrannizes humanity; second, of the means by which humanity achieves liberation from this and the character of that reconciling liberation; and third, of the possible appropriation of this liberating reconciliation by humanity. To discuss these elements may serve to recall us to the touchstone of our biblical base and, indirectly, to illumine the theme of our conference as a whole.

WHAT TYRANNIZES HUMANITY:
OF HUMAN BONDAGE

The Pauline doctrine of humanity has to be distinguished from others of the first century which, modified and disguised in various ways, have had their counterparts across the centuries and exercised a profound influence.[1] There is first the *Platonic*. This dualism distinguished between

---

* Villanova University Summer Conference, 1975, on Alienation and Reconciliation

the outward, physical and mortal body or flesh of a person, and the invisible, immortal part of him or her, which cannot be destroyed—that is, the essential humanity which is itself a spark of the eternal light, generated out of the being of God and destined to be reunited with him. This doctrine has left traces in Paul (2 Cor 4:16ff. perhaps), but did not govern his understanding. For Paul, man on earth is not a mortal God and God in heaven is not an immortal man after the Platonic model.

Second, there is the *Stoic* view, according to which humanity is simply a part or member (*melos*) of nature; therefore, the good life for humanity is that which is "according to nature" (*kata phusin*). This view also did not influence Paul to any considerable degree, although he does occasionally use Stoic terms (1 Cor 11:14; Rom 1:26). For Paul, humanity was not simply a microcosm of the macrocosm.[2]

But, third, what of the popular undeveloped *Hellenistic* ideas with which Paul came into contact? These conceived of the fusion of a human with God, or the assimilation of a human to God or his absorption in God as not only possible but comparatively commonplace. Claims to divinity were taken calmly; divine men (*theioi anthrôpoi*) were a dime a dozen. Not only emperors could be deified—a phenomenon not altogether incomprehensible, and known not only then but in the twentieth century—but even ordinary mortals. The failure to appreciate the difference between the human and the divine made deification a comparative commonplace. Paul would know of this failure, but it would be utterly remote from his comprehension as a Jew.[3] All this means that the alienation as incarnation in the flesh and conversely as failure to be natural, involved in Platonism and Stoicism respectively, played no significant part in Paul's thought. His understanding of alienation lies elsewhere.

Two things can be claimed of those views which we have noted. First, they reduce the gulf between the nature of humanity and of God: they ignore the Kierkegaardian principle of the qualitative difference between the human mind and the Divine. And, second, because they either became the "essential man" from the physical person or from humanity with nature, they tend to minimize a person's moral responsibility and culpability. This second point holds although in both Platonism and Stoicism there is much moral sensitivity. In Platonism it is the dual nature of a person that is the ground of his or her difficulties; in Stoicism, his or her involvement with nature, which can produce fatalism and the related depression, as par excellence in Marcus Aurelius.[4] It is at the two points indicated that we can probably most conveniently isolate the emphases in Paul's understanding of humanity, an understanding that was rooted in Judaism.

Paul's two emphases are these: he insists (a) on the gulf that separates humanity and God and (b) on the responsibility of humanity before God. And since the God in whom Paul believed was the living, personal God of Abraham, Isaac, and Jacob, Sarah, Rebekah, and Rachel, the alienation of which he speaks—although he does not use that specific term—is a personal one grounded not in the constitution of humanity or of nature but in a person's own responsibility before the living God, his or her addressability by God.

We begin, then, with Paul's understanding of a "gulf" separating humanity from God. A person is a creature (*ktisma*) of God qualitatively different from his or her creator (see Rom 1:18ff.; 2 Cor 4:6; 1 Cor 11:8–12). Especially in Rom 9:19ff. the supposition is that God is the wholly other, and a person in his hands like clay in the hands of a potter. Although this is not an adequate representation of the relationship between them, a human is pliable to God's intent. The peculiarity of humanity for Paul, one might claim, lies in his relationship to God; he rarely sets man as a species over against the animals or angels (1 Cor 15:39; 4:9; 13:1), but rather underlines his creatureliness over against God (1 Cor 1:25; Rom 9:20; 3:4), before whom all human distinctions of nation or race are without significance (Rom 3:28f.; 1 Cor 7:23; 1 Cor 3:21). It is no accident that in Phil 2:7, to become a person is to become "empty" of reputation. As creature, a person does not in himself or herself possess any divinity (Rom 3:5; 1 Cor 3:3; 9:8; Gal 3:15).[5]

It is, then, on humanity's relationship to God, the Creator, not on any intrinsic quality, that Paul's thought rests. This means that, although we shall later refer to it, Pauline anthropology—that is, his understanding of man's flesh (*sarx*), "soul" (*psyche*), spirit (*pneuma*), conscience (*suneidēsis*), mind (*nous*)—for the purpose of this paper is secondary.[6] Rather, to understand Paul's understanding of alienation, we must begin with the relationship of a human to God, which is rooted in the purpose of God in creation.

Paul shared in the understanding of creation of his Jewish contemporaries. We can subtract from his epistles the clear understanding of humanity as having been created by God in his image and subject to him, able to see his glory and enjoy it (Rom 1:21, 23). The meaning of the term "image" (Masoretic Text (MT), *tzelem:* Septuagint (LXX), *eikôn*) in Genesis is much simpler than that often read into it later by Judaism and Christianity: in Paul it certainly conveys the sense of the authentic and adequate expression or the stamp of the original. Humanity as created, while not *as* God, is "after his likeness." This partly means that at creation humanity shared in the glory (MT, *kâbôd*; LXX, *doxa*) of God:

its members were able to see God's glory and participate in it (Rom 1:23). The term "glory" has a range of meanings in the Old Testament which we cannot pursue here.[7] Let it merely be stated that to share in God's glory was to be aware of and to enter into his self-revelatory activity. Humanity, at the beginning, bore God's image and recognized his glory in the sense that its members responded to the self-revelatory activity and demand of God, and as a result—I refer to the biblical myth—were at one with God, with themselves, with each other, and with the beasts around them, and with the natural world. The mark of human life at the beginning was unity: the world, the creation of the one God, reflected the oneness of God. The cosmos as a totality, humanity included, "obeyed" God and thus fulfilled God's purpose for it. Paul understands the purpose of God always in these terms. It is that of bringing into being a humanity bearing his image and his glory. At the beginning this purpose was achieved. The clue to Paul's understanding of "alienation" is in humanity's departure from that purpose. How and why?

The unity intended for and enjoyed by humanity was broken by sin. The biblical myth of the fall, which is assumed by Paul, is the prelude to the disunity we experience. This disunity is expressed as enmity between person and person, even in the family as between Cain and Abel, within the nation between rich and poor, then even more tragically between Jew and Gentile, and particularly and fundamentally, between humanity and creator.[8] Paul lived between two poles. On the one hand, there was his awareness of the original purpose of the creator for his creatures—that is, a life in joyous reverence and obedience and unity; on the other hand, there was his awareness of the actual rejection of that life and the consequent disruption in the world of nature and of humanity, which are inseparable.

Basic to Paul's understanding of the human condition, therefore, is his recognition of a disobedience on the part of humanity. Humankind itself was originally responsible for the disunity of a fallen condition and not because humanity was subject to the limitations of finitude. And yet, this is not the only dimension to its story. Granted that humanity was responsible for the first disobedience, can we explain the whole of its plight simply in terms of that disobedient will? Paul is aware of factors from outside as well as from within humans which impinge on them and lead to their disobedience, so that, while he never excuses humanity, he does recognize forces that are against it.

First, Paul recognizes that humanity is part of a "cosmos," of a created order in which there are three spheres: the human, the world of humanity; the subhuman, that of material things, including the heavenly bodies; and the superhuman, which sometimes includes the stars, more often classified in the subhuman sphere, and requires more definition. Humankind is subject to unseen, superhuman or supernatural forces or powers which are opposed to God and hold individuals and peoples under their sway. Several terms are used to describe these unseen cosmic powers. First, there are angels (*angeloi*). These are celestial beings whose function elsewhere in the New Testament can be positive, but is usually in Paul inferior or negative: in 2 Cor 12:7 they are heavenly forces who have revolted against God and entered the service of the devil. Then there are principalities (*archai*), authorities (*exousiai*), and powers (*dunameis*), dominions (*kuriotētai*), thrones (*thronoi*). All these terms denote apparently the same demonic power. There are, moreover, many lords and gods and spiritual forces of wickedness in heavenly places. Especially important, because of their cosmic significance, are the elements of this world (*ta stoicheia tou kosmou*). The supreme demonic being is the ruler of this world (*ho archôn tou aiônos toutou*), Satan, or Belial; beneath him are the governors of this world.

The precise interpretation of these powers and rulers is difficult. It is often urged that here Paul reveals the influence of Hellenistic, Gnostic astral religious beliefs. But astral beliefs of a similar kind had found root in Israel also. See, for example, Deut 4:19. In *Jubilees* 15:31f. each nation has its own special star-angel assigned to it, the illegitimate worship of which constitutes idolatry. Moreover, apart from currents from the Old Testament, Judaism in Paul's day, as it had been for centuries, was open to Hellenistic influences on all sides. We must assume that Paul was familiar with the "failure of nerve" (*heimarmenē*) before chance (*tuchē*) and fate (*heimarmenē*), classically described by Gilbert Murray,[9] when astrology became the scientific theology of waning heathenism, so that religious men became absorbed in nothing quite so much as in devising means of escape from the prison house of the stars. Hence the popularity of mystery cults and magic.

Paul, then, is familiar with the astrological superstition of his day and freely uses its terminology. He admits that the unseen powers to which such superstition appealed exist. But he does not admit their divinity. Rather, they are weak and beggarly. Nevertheless, through them the whole universe of humanity and nature is in bondage to decay. It is these powers in 1 Cor 2:7-8, not the Romans or the Jews, whom he holds responsible for the crucifixion of Jesus. This raises an acute question. Are the powers, the "disincarnate spirits" about which Thomas Hardy speaks in *The Dynasts,* at the same time unseen, supernatural, cosmic forces and also the actual human instruments or executives which effect their work? The question has been raised whether the governing rulers of this world (*hoi archontes tou aiônos toutou*) are, in fact, symbols of demonic political realities. Although nowhere outside Paul does the term *archontes* (rulers) mean demons, are these powers beings who in some way stand behind what occurs in the world?

That the powers represent unregenerate political and social structures must be considered a real possibility, but that such a political and social dimension exhausts their significance for Paul is unlikely. The principalities, angels, powers, and so forth, of which Paul writes have a cosmic reality of a supernatural order which transcends the purely political and social. The human sphere stands under the constant enmity of supernatural evil powers. Human responsibility for evil lies within a context of a struggle against unseen forces of evil. To that extent the responsibility of humanity is modified, though not denied. Moreover, the cosmic-demonic context of human existence has the corollary for Paul that redemption, to be effective, has to be cosmic or universal in its scope. What we are to make of all this language about unseen forces of evil in Paul we cannot consider at this point. But it is important to recognize its ubiquity and significance for the apostle. Bishop Aulén found in this language one of the dominant motifs of all Christian theology.[10]

So far we have pointed to unseen forces tyrannizing over man. Paul, however, finds the sources of tyranny not only *outside* man, as it were, but *within* him. In this connection four elements in his understanding of the human plight, that is, of humanity's alienation from God, have to be noted: the legacy from Adam, the corruption consequent upon false worship, the evil impulse and weakness of the flesh, and sin itself. In none of the four elements can it be said that Paul is original; he draws upon well-defined elements from Judaism.[11]

1. He relates the sin of every person, that is, the misdirection of his or her life away from the glory of God, or toward disobedience to him, to that of the first man, Adam. While at no point does he remove human responsibility for sin entirely, he does seem in the famous passage Rom 5:12–14 to find a causal relation between our sin and that of Adam. But these verses are notoriously difficult to translate. The passage reads:

> Therefore as sin came into the world through one man and death through sin, and so death spread to all men because all men sinned—sin indeed was in the world before the law was given, but sin is not counted where there is no law. Yet death reigned from Adam to Moses, even over those whose sins were not like the transgression of Adam, who was a type of the one who was to come.

The relation between Adam's sin and those of his successors indicated by these words has been understood in three ways. First, in terms of social influence: as a result of Adam's sin, we are all born willy-nilly into a society that has already experienced sin and thereby been corrupted. This corruption "causes" our corruption.

Second, in terms of biological participation (going back to Augustine's mistranslation of *eph' hō* by *en qui*—in whom). According to this, because a person is "in Adam" by biological descent, Adam's transgression injected a kind of virus into his or her system which made it inevitable that he or she should sin. This theory, usually understood as that of original sin, has had a profound and pernicious effect across the centuries. (But it rests on an impossible translation of *eph' hō*, which cannot mean "in whom.")

Third, and more probably correctly, in terms of the concept of solidarity: not heredity, but incorporation in, or representation by, Adam is the connection between the first man and his descendants. Just as in the OT every individual member of a tribe in himself represented the tribe—as in the story of Achan in Joshua 7:18ff.—so Adam is the representative head of the whole of humankind. His act *is* the act of the race and as such has racial consequences or corporate results. I like to use a simple illustration for this societal unity of men. I was once in the American zone in Bavaria after World War II. There was a report in the local newspapers of a brutal murder of a German woman by American soldiers. One of these at this trial, on being asked who President Harry Truman was, asserted that he had never heard of him. He was no typical American. But his deed was referred to as "American," and all America fell in his fall. Our common humanity involves us in a common guilt. Unjust? Yes. A fact? Yes.[12]

2. Another traditional way in which Paul accounts for man's misdirection is made clear in Romans 1. Here the malaise of humanity's existence springs from its refusal to entertain the aboriginal knowledge of God that was given to it. This leads people to turn away deliberately from the worship of God, the Creator, to that of creatures. But to worship the creatures is to come under the sway of the elements of this world—*ta stoicheia tou kosmou* (Gal 4:8–10). Moreover, the consequence of this idolatry is moral evil expressed in the corruption of people's minds (Rom 1:21–24, 28), sexual perversion (Rom 1:24, 26ff.), and social evils of all sorts (1:29ff.). Paul in Rom 1:18ff. seems to claim two things as natural to people:

(a) A knowledge of God mediated through the phenomena of creation—that is, a knowledge of his invisible being, his power and divinity (1:20). But this knowledge can be "held down," and the consequences of this are impiety (*asebeia*) and unrighteousness (*adikia*). If God be wrongly conceived, he is wrongly worshipped; and to worship him wrongly is to fall into moral depravity.

(b)   An innate knowledge of God's laws (1:32). This applies to Jews and Gentiles alike (2:14). This does not mean that every person possesses the itemized knowledge prescribed by the Jewish Law, but rather what might be called the sum total of that Law, which can be summarized in the so-called Noachian commandments.[13] As a created being, by nature, every person possesses certain universally valid norms which, in Paul's view, are part of God's revelation in creation. And yet humans—both Jew and Gentile—of their own choice have turned the knowledge thus revealed into ignorance. What led him to such a choice Paul does not directly discuss in Romans 1.

3.   Elsewhere Paul seems to fall back on another traditional Jewish doctrine which might help us to understand humankind's fall, the doctrine of the two impulses: the good impulse (*ha-yetzer hâ-tôb*) and the evil impulse (*ha-yetzer hâ-râ'*) in humanity. It is at least possible that Paul makes use of this doctrine in Romans 7. But one thing is very striking. Whereas the rabbis do not seem to have connected the evil impulse with the *sarx* (flesh), it is clear that Paul connects sin with the flesh very closely. Our reference to the doctrine of the evil impulse drives us on to consider Paul's understanding of the "flesh." "*Sarx*," as he uses it, cannot be simply described. At the risk of grave distortion, we may summarize as follows.

The uses of the term can be divided into two main groups: the group in which "flesh" bears a physical connotation, and that in which it has a moral one. In the former group, the "flesh" is not used of animal flesh (*kreas*) but only of the animated flesh of a person in its active, sensual manifestations as it is perceptible to the senses. It is, however, not simply material substance (*hulê*). It is material substance formulated in the human body. So it can sometimes stand for the "self" or "person." Moreover, its meaning can spill over to include the very environment within which a person has to live and becomes synonymous with "the world" (*kosmos*).

More important are those passages in the second group, where a spiritual and moral dimension is manifest in the use of the term "flesh." In many passages in the OT, it represents mere humanity in contrast with God, and hence in its weakness, mortality, impotence and infirmity. Humanity as "flesh" is related to God in this way, not as individuals, but as part of the whole world-order. Humans, over against God, are creatures bound up in the bundle of created existence, but that existence is one that has fallen under the power of sin. So to be in the flesh is to be part of a fallen order, subject to the unseen principalities and powers that control and corrupt it. Consequently, a person's life in the flesh has an inherent tension. It is of God's will that we are in the flesh, but, at the same time, life in the flesh is antagonism to God. The mind of the flesh is enmity towards God.[14]

Yet, it must be insisted that the flesh as physical is not evil for Paul. The term takes into itself, however, a relational dimension. Humanity simply living in the world is in the flesh in a neutral sense; in itself, it is neither good nor evil to be in the flesh in this sense. But when a person, *in* the world, lives *for* the world, he or she is then in the flesh in an evil sense. The setting of the mind on the things of the earth is idolatry, and to be in the flesh then has a pejorative sense. The life in the flesh in this sense stands primarily for a denial of humanity's dependence on God and for a trust in what is of human origin and effort.[15]

Can we, then, say that the flesh tyrannizes humanity and incites it to sin? Not directly. The flesh in Paul is not a mythological concept—that is, it is not conceived of as a demonic being. Nor is it again a purely physiological concept, as if it referred merely to sensuality. Although the flesh in a physical, sensual sense does for Paul provide the base of operation for sin, in this sense being weak, it is not identified with sin: the flesh may be the accomplice to our wickedness but is not the criminal. Paul was too much a Jew to degrade the flesh in itself to the corrupt; but in a strange way he does seem to recognize in this "physical" aspect of humanity the Achilles' heel—necessary to him and yet the point of his vulnerability.[16]

4. But what or who is it, in the last resort, that takes advantage of this vulnerability? The forces working against a person—the unseen powers, the legacy from Adam, the perversion born of false worship, the evil impulse and the weakness of the flesh—are all the instruments of what Paul calls sin. The Greek term he uses for Sin (I use the capital advisedly: for sins Paul also uses transgression, *parabasis,* and for trespass, *paraptôma*) is *hamartia,* the fundamental meaning of which, in accordance with the Hebrew *hâtâ'* which underlies it, is falling short of participation in the divine glory. This condition of

being in sin characterizes not simply a person individually, in all his or her being, including will and mind, but mankind as a corporal entity. The power which causes this condition—sin itself—is not a negative dimension—that is, not the absence of the power to aim at the glory of God. Rather it is a positive personal power with a will of its own to rule. It *came* into the world (Rom 5:12); it reigns there (Rom 5:21); everything is subjected to it (Gal 3:22); men serve it as slaves (Rom 6:6; 7:14; 11:20). It is dead and yet revives (7:8, 9), and pays wages (5:12; 6:23). It dwells in a person (7:17; 8:3), and arouses desire in him or her (7:8). Sin is not simply an absence of the good but an active force toward evil. This force, because it is irrational, is as inexplicable to Paul as to all who have tried to explain it. Of its reality he did not doubt. The expression of it he found in those agents to which we have referred above.[17]

The results of the disobedience and consequent misdirection into which humankind has fallen under the tyranny of sin in all its agents have already been touched upon. But in addition to those moral perversions and divisions, personal, social, and communal or national to which we have referred, two results of the tyranny of sin particularly emerge in Paul.

First, through its fall humankind has fallen under the wrath of God (*hê orgē tou theou*). The idea that God can be angry is familiar in the Old Testament. The same terms are used in that document of human and divine anger. God can be angry with individuals, with a country and its inhabitants, and with the nations. Though slow to abate, the divine anger can be appeased, but it is operative from generation to generation. God can even destroy humankind in his anger. In popular Greek religion also the anger of the gods was not infrequent and certainly easily provoked by amatory and other trivia, so that the notion of an angry God has been regarded as an inferior Hellenistic intrusion in Paul. But every novice in Greek philosophy knew that God was without passion (*apathês*). Philo rejected all anger in God—the divine anger, he thought, was simply a useful fiction to frighten sinners. And recent New Testament scholars, especially those nurtured primarily in the classics, have sought to explain away the wrath of God in Paul as simply a phrase used to express the principle of cause and effect in a moral universe, not a personal divine response to evil. But despite the learning and penetration with which the wrath of God has been "moralized" so that it ceases to be anger, it is still best to understand Paul as thinking in terms of the divine pathos and passion. In Paul, God's wrath is his personal, emotional reaction against sins, though this is never malicious.[18]

The second fact which Paul accepts as a consequence of sin is death (Rom 5:12–16). Across the centuries there have been martyrs and others who have accepted the notion that death can be a good to be accepted and even pursued. Especially in recent times suicide has been sympathetically reexamined, even by Christians; and among non-Christians, to note one example, we recall that Hemingway flirted with suicide and finally executed it. An American poet, Adrienne Rich, has triumphantly conceived of life as a "moving toward death," not as a necessary evil but as a desired good. Most moderns would not go so far; to most of us, is it not true that death is an altogether natural phenomenon, an inevitable accompaniment of our decaying physical powers?

> The woods decay, the woods decay and fall
> And after many summers dies the swan.

Yes. But even to us death has a sting. For Paul it certainly had and for his world. True, in Greek philosophy *soma sêma,* and death is a release. But in the Hellenistic Age the fear of death was ubiquitous: It was much more powerful and widely diffused than among people of recent times. The need for assurance of a life beyond death was real.[19] The author of the Epistle to the Hebrews refers to people as "being through death all their lifetime subject to fear" (2:15). It is the devil who has the power of death (Acts 2:14). For Paul the last tyranny over the natural man is death: the last victory over him, the grave.[20]

LIBERATION: ON BEING "IN CHRIST"

The tyrannies, all the expression of the one overarching tyranny which Paul calls sin, to which people voluntarily and involuntarily submit, have the combined effect of corrupting and misdirecting them. Even more, they create an enmity on the part of humanity toward God (Rom 5:10). But at no point does Paul assert that God hates humanity; he was at one with the author of the Fourth Gospel, in John 3:16: "God so loved the world . . . " (*houtôs gar egapēsen ho theos ton kosmon . . .*), where the tense of the verb "loved" (*egapēsen*) is timeless. God always has, always does, always will love the world, that is, this broken, sinful, dark and misdirected world. Never does the human condition, full of despair as it is, cause Paul to despair of the *love* of God, that is, of his pure, unmerited, persistent, overflowing and redemptive goodwill toward humanity. (The notion of the "death of God" would be incomprehensible to Paul, because it involves a contradiction in terms: people may be dead to God but not

God to people. It is only because humans are diseased that the question whether God exists can seriously occur. The very question denotes a warping of our perceptions, a derangement of our lives.) Ultimately it is the reality of the love of God that constitutes the ground of humanity's liberation from tyranny. It is time to turn to this, the second part of our theme.

The Agency of Liberation: Jesus Christ

To grasp the meaning of liberation, not simply as the negation of the tyrannies to which we referred, but as a positive good, not simply as "freedom from" tyranny but "freedom for" life, it is important in our approach to it to start from the right place. And our starting place for the understanding of liberation in Paul must not be with Paul himself, and not with what tyrannized him. He himself points away from himself and concentrates on the liberator rather than on the liberated—to Jesus Christ, crucified (1 Cor 2:2), in whom he sees the power and the wisdom of God and sanctification and redemption (1 Cor 1:30f.).

It is fundamental that Paul came to see in Jesus of Nazareth, crucified and raised from the dead, the Messiah intended for the people of Israel and for the world (because the Messianic Age in Judaism had worldwide overtones). The way in which he came to this conviction—the date and significance of his so-called conversion, which is more rightly understood as his "call"—is not directly our concern. Nor can we here justify the claim that it was precisely this conviction, rather than a new understanding of the Torah, that was fundamental for Paul.[21] Suffice it to say that Jesus of Nazareth was for him the Messiah. This meant that through him there was a new beginning in the history of humanity.[21] Like all the evangelists, and, indeed, all the writers of the New Testament, Paul was convinced that the age to come, of Jewish expectation, had dawned.

He uses certain contrasts. He refers to an old man and a new man "in Christ" (Rom 6:6; Col 3:10); there is a new life, with new works in the Spirit set over against the works of the flesh (Gal 5:13ff.; 5:24ff.); the fullness of time has come (Gal 3:23); and, above all, the old things have passed away and become new; there is a "new creation." All this is "in Christ" (2 Cor 5:17ff.: *ei tis en Christô, kainē ktisis. ta archaia parêlthen, idou gegonen kaina*). Just as at creation chaos gave place to order, darkness to light, so Paul is conscious of having passed from an evil age of darkness to that of light (2 Cor 4:16). Paul's epistles thrill with the sense of living in a new order. It was bliss for him, "in that dawn to be alive," and "to be young was very heaven." Three aspects of this new order, which spells "liberation," are fundamental:

(1) "It was God who was 'in Christ' reconciling the world to Himself" (2 Cor 4:6; 5:18; Gal 4:4). The act of Christ is the act of God. The gospel is the gospel of God (Rom 1:1, 16, 17; 3:21). Paul's liberation rests on his Christology which, in turn, rests on his theology.

(2) Christ is the person to which the activity of God in Israel's history pointed, and from which the new order begins. The messiahship of Jesus of Nazareth is the starting point of Paulinism.

(3) The new order is the fulfillment of that which the prophets had foretold. The coming of Christ was no arbitrary, sudden intervention of God in history; it was rather the climax of a long process in which God had been at work from the beginning; it was the fruition or fulfillment of God's purpose, not its inauguration (Rom 1:2; Gal 4:4; 1 Cor 15:3).

These three fundamental convictions govern the place which Paul assigns to Jesus Christ in his understanding of history. He interprets that place both in terms of Pharisaic speculation about the various periods into which history can be divided as in Gal 1:4f.; 3:16, 19; 4:4f.; 5:13; 6:5; 2 Cor 5:17; 10:11; Rom 4:15; 5:13ff., and especially in Romans 9—11. In the last he confronts the problem of why so many Jews had rejected the Messiah, and in dealing with it he reveals the nature of the change that Jesus Christ has wrought in history. We indicated previously that the aim of God, as Paul understood it, was to renew humanity according to God's own image. But Paul makes clear that the image of God is Jesus Christ himself. The purpose of God, then, is the transformation or the remaking of humanity into the image of Jesus Christ. And this remaking is possible through Christ himself, who had already given a new direction to humanity.

This simple statement is to be understood in the light of Paul's philosophy or understanding of history. This he derives from the Old Testament and from Judaism interpreted in the light of Christ. Roughly, we may state this "philosophy" as follows:

God's purpose was at work in the very creation of the universe. The universe is not the outcome of chance, but of God's will. The creation, humanity included, was created for harmony between person and person, person and nature, person and God. But, through the sin of Adam, God's purpose was thwarted. God made a new beginning with humanity, however, in a covenant with Abraham; the promise was given that in him all the nations of the earth would be blessed. Abraham responded to the call of God, and through him there came into being a people of God, a people chosen by an act of God's free will and grace. But God's purpose was not automatically secured through the single act of the choice and response of Abraham. Those who were physically descended from Abraham were not all responsive to God's call as their father Abraham had been, so that not all who were physically connected with Abraham were really his children. Thus, of Abraham's two sons only Isaac, who was the child of God's promise, was recognized as a true "son"; Ishmael, the natural son of Abraham by Hagar, was rejected. Similarly, Jacob, the son of Isaac, is the object of God's love, but Esau, his brother, of God's hatred. Merely physical membership in Israel is not enough; by itself, physical descent means little. Thus, as Paul puts it, not all Israel is Israel; that is, not all Jews have responded in obedience to God's demand. Indeed, the majority of those physically descended from Abraham have been disobedient and are, consequently, not considered his true children. In the time of Elijah, there were still seven thousand who did not bow the knee to Baal. A remnant did remain. But this remnant became increasingly smaller; in the day of Isaiah, it was very small. And, as Paul came to see the history of his people, it became increasingly small, until, as we are told in Gal 3:16, there is only one person who can be said to be the true descendant of Abraham, and this person is Jesus. In him alone is the promise to Abraham fulfilled. Paul makes use of the difference between a singular and plural noun to make this point:

> Now the promises were pronounced to Abraham and to his "issue." It does not say "issues" in the plural, but in the singular, "and to your issue"; and the "issue" intended is Christ (Gal 3:16).

Jesus alone represents the people of God's promise. He is the apex of a triangle—a "triangle" within which progressively the "people of God," the true descendants of Abraham, have become increasingly fewer and from which his "false" descendants have been increasingly excluded. A process of exclusion comes to its culmination in Jesus.

The process of exclusion in the history of Israel, which is a record of God's failure to create a people for himself in the world, is the counterpart of that misdirection which Paul discovered in the Gentile world. Both Israelites and non-Israelites were involved in the same fundamental misdirection, although the *symptoms* of this were not always the same. But, in Jesus of Nazareth the misdirection was checked. By the obedience of his life, which issued in death on the cross, the process of exclusion was reversed. Jesus inaugurated a countermovement of inclusion; some among his own people recognized in Jesus the true seed of Abraham and joined in allegiance to him. They constituted a "new" remnant, the beginning of a new Israel. This new Israel was made up of those who had seen and responded to the grace of Jesus, the Christ. They were not only Jews by descent. They soon included Gentiles, and they are destined to include not only all Gentiles but also all Jews who, at present, reject the claims that Jesus is the final figure. In this way, in the emergence of a new Israel, which is to bring all to the recognition of Jesus as the final One and of God as all in all, Paul claims that the whole historic process has been given a new, decisive turn. And not only human history. Jesus has set in motion in history a Spirit that will in the end bring all things—human, superhuman (the angels, the principalities and powers) and subhuman—into the blessing of God. The misdirected universe will be redirected and restored to him who made it. And the purpose of all this, as we have seen, is that humanity may regain the image of God that it had lost through the fall of Adam; and, since Christ *is* the image of God, to be like Christ, to grow into his maturity, is the purpose of God for humanity. And for the universe? That all powers in heaven and earth, all things, may share in the glory of God. Consider 1 Cor 15–20 and Col 1:15–20. For Paul, then, Christianity is not a small matter, but a sweeping understanding of history which is clear, dynamic, and, granting Paul's assumption about Jesus, inspiring.

But, some have objected to speaking of Paul's "philosophy" in this way and presenting his thought in a "linear" fashion. Some interpreters of Paul entirely ignore Romans 9—11, and others minimize their importance.[22] These certainly do injustice to Paul's texts and distort his intent;[23] but, at the same time they recall us to what was central for Paul—his concentration on the significance of Jesus Christ, not as the pivot of a "philosophical" interpretation of history, but as the living Lord to whom Christians are bound in the present and in and through whom the redirecting redemptive process is being realized.

The Marks of Liberation[24]

When Paul gave to Christ this central role in the purpose of God in history, how did the apostle conceive of the actual impact or influence of Christ on people or the liberation he brought, which justified ascribing this role to him? To put the matter otherwise: what happened to those who believed in Christ, who had been taken up into the redemptive purpose of God? We can tap the results of the preaching of Paul to the Gentiles at their earliest in 1 Thess 1:9–10:

> For they themselves spread the news of our visit to you and its effect: how you turned from idols, to be servants of the living and true God, and to wait expectantly for the appearance from heaven of his Son Jesus, whom he raised from the dead, Jesus our deliverer from the terrors of judgment to come.

In the light of this passage, we shall first mention two elementary assumptions that Paul makes about the liberation in Christ—freedom from idolatry and commitment to the "good life"—before we concentrate on the main characteristic of liberation, namely, life in Christ.

(1) Idolatry abandoned. Here there is implied an attack on idolatry, and the proclamation of the one living God of Israel, and this in a context of an eschatological hope. In the light of Paul's emphasis on the catastrophic results of false worship, liberation from idolatry is fundamental to his preaching. He did not need to emphasize this in preaching to the Jews, but in the mission to Gentiles this emphasis was essential—indeed, the presupposition of every other liberation.

(2) Morality embraced. The liberation from false worship was inextricably bound up, however, with the proclamation of Jesus as the eschatological figure raised from the dead, the acceptance of whom carried with it the claim to liberation from immorality. The Thessalonians are called to a "work of faith and labor of love" (1 Thess 1:3) and to walk worthy of God (2:12) and "to abound in love one toward another and toward all" (3:12). Particularly in 1 Thess 4:1ff., Paul emerges as the transmitter to Gentiles of a moral tradition which forbade sexual license and unjust behavior. Whatever else the liberation wrought "in Christ," it was never antinomian. This is as clear from Paul's later epistles as from his first. I quote only one passage, 1 Cor 6:9–10:

> Surely you know that the unjust will never come into possession of the kingdom of God. Make no mistake: no fornicator or idolater, none who are guilty either of adultery or of homosexual perversion, no thieves or grabbers or drunkards or slanderers or swindlers, will possess the kingdom of God.

The struggle of Paul over the Law, which did not engage him in 1 Thessalonians, has always made it easy for scholars to minimize the moral emphasis in his writing. But that he was opposed to "legalism," by which we mean the belief in and the reliance upon one's own achievements as ground of salvation (a concept which is often used to caricature Judaism), must not hide the fact that he was the sworn foe of all antinomianism. Liberation for Paul was never license.[25]

But we can gain further insight into the elements in Paul's understanding of liberation from 1 Thessalonians, in fact, into the essential element in it. (3) The convert clearly recognized in Jesus the Son of God from heaven, the Lord, attested as such by God, who had raised Him from the dead. Paul became related to Christ; and already in his very first epistle we encounter the phrase which is one of the main clues to the understanding of him—the phrase "in Christ." The church of the Thessalonians is "in God the Father and the Lord Jesus Christ" (*en thêo patri kai kuriô Jêsou Christô*). Here the phrase is in embryo. But, in 1 Thess. 2:14, Christians in Judea constitute churches of God which are in Christ Jesus (*en Christô Jêsou*). (Later there are those who are dead "In Christ" [*en Christô*], but they are not without hope—1 Thess 4:13ff.) Certainly, for Paul liberation was a life "in Christ."

Let us begin by asking the meaning of that term "Christ" for Paul. In his epistles he preferred to use the term "the Lord" of Jesus. But, as we saw, this must not be taken to mean that he did not give the messianic significance of Jesus full weight. We have already emphasized this for his understanding of history. At this juncture, in order to express the formative significance of Christ in the actual life of the believer, other factors must be noted. The term "Christ" refers in Paul to two realities.

First, to the actual Jesus who had walked in Galilee. That Paul was uninterested in that historical figure, as had often been alleged, cannot be substantiated. The whole of Paul's theology demanded that he think of the one who redirected history as having had real contact with history. To redirect the world, Jesus had to grapple with it, soil his hands with the dirt of it, and share its blood, toil, sweat, and tears. Jesus, in short, had to encounter sin, although he "knew it not" (2 Cor 5:21). Jesus is a man among men, a concrete tangible figure in history, flesh of our flesh and bone of our bone. For the evidence for Paul's awareness of the actual Jesus, we refer to our work elsewhere.[26]

But, second, equally necessary for Paul's understanding of Jesus' work was that he "*came into*" history from outside it, and was "rooted" outside it. The one who redirects the world has to find his *point d'appui* outside it. Consequently, Jesus for Paul was not simply a historical person: at all points in his activity Paul saw the activity of God himself. Just as the writers of the synoptic Gospels saw the active will of God revealed in the ministry of Jesus—in the healing of the sick, the raising of the dead, the forgiveness of sin, the words of grace and authority—so too Paul was convinced that in Jesus God was at work to deliver the world from Sin and death (2 Cor 5:19; Rom 8:39). Although he never calls Jesus God, he leaves no doubt that Jesus is the channel of the divine purpose and gives him a peculiar status.

He did this especially by ascribing to Jesus certain titles, in particular two. First, while Jesus is distinguished from God the Father, he is given the title "Lord" (Phil 2:6–11; Rom 14:8ff.). In both passages the event which makes Jesus "Lord" is the resurrection, when Jesus, even though he had undergone death, became known to his followers as living in their midst. The title "Lord" would easily be understood by people in the Roman Empire where many lords—Isis, Adonis, and others—were worshipped. It would suggest to them that Jesus was a being to be worshipped. But it would not imply any uniqueness on his part because he was one of many "lords" and "gods" who were worshipped. Certainly, however, the title "Lord" had a deeper significance for Paul. The term "Lord" (*Kurios*) was used in the LXX to translate "Yahweh"—the God who had revealed himself at Mount Sinai (Exod 3:13ff.). The name "Yahweh" became ineffable. The exact pronunciation of it was, in time, forgotten, and Jews, in their failure and refusal to utter it, substituted for it another term, *'Adonai,* usually meaning Lord. It is this "Yahweh" which is really translated by the LXX as "Lord." It refers especially to God as the One revealed to Israel. When Paul used the title "Lord" of Jesus, it is probable that he was thinking of him as *Yahweh* (*'Adonai*), now present among Christians in Jesus Christ, the Lord of the church. Jesus as Lord signifies the presence of the divine among his people.

Second, Paul equates Jesus with the wisdom of God (1 Cor 1:24, 30) and applies to him accordingly a role in the creation and structure of the universe and in the moral life of humanity, after the pattern of that Wisdom which is described in Prov 8:22–34, and which, by the first century, had been equated with the Law of God itself. To call Jesus wisdom was to apply to him the name of the ultimate authority in Judaism, the Law, obedience to which was the ultimate concern of every religious Jew. In Christ, as the wisdom of God, Paul found the ultimate authority over all people, and to obedience to Him humans were to devote their ultimate concern. How a man, Jesus of Nazareth, could be the Lord and the wisdom of God remained a mystery for Paul, as it does for us. Into this, the strictly christological question, we do not need to enter. Suffice it to say that Christ, as the wisdom of God for Paul, had a universal, cosmic, and moral significance.[27]

But, to understand the central phrase "in Christ" with which we are concerned, we must point to still another dimension of Paul's understanding of Jesus Christ. As we saw already, this name—personal as it was and pointing to the individual Jesus of Nazareth in his concrete individuality—had also a messianic and, therefore, a communal dimension. Paul was not given to thinking of people, even Jesus, in isolation, as mere individuals, and the notion of Messiah was bound up with that of a community.[28] This emerges in two ways. Christ is very closely identified with the messianic people which he had called into being, the church. So close was the relationship between the community created by Jesus and himself that Paul refers to it as the body of Christ (*to sōma tou Christou*). Especially in 1 Cor 12:12–13, Jesus seems to be actually identified with the church. Moreover, Jesus is also related to the whole of humanity for Paul; he has become, in fact, the founder of a new humanity. This is the implication of Paul's doctrine of Jesus Christ as "the last Adam" (1 Cor 15:20–49; Rom. 5:12–14). Jesus for Paul is the last, the eschatological Adam whose obedience has canceled out the disobedience of the first and introduced a new humanity, freed from the tyranny of sin and death. As last Adam, Jesus is, or represents, all people as they are obedient to God. In him, representatively, the broken unity of mankind is objectively restored.

In the light of all this, to be "in Christ" comes to mean to be incorporated in a new community, which constitutes a new humanity and, since this is the community of the end, it is marked through Christ by the presence of the Holy Spirit of God, who is very closely related, if not identified, with Christ himself and is the mode of his presence in the community of the end. Christians are, according to Paul, united with one another and with Christ; they share with one another and with Christ in one corporeity. This comes to clearest expression in Paul's treatment of the Last Supper in 1 Cor 11:29. There is a new corporate personality created "in Christ." In a quite physical sense for Paul, Christians are all one "in Christ." It is this unity that he calls the body of Christ. The New Testament knows nothing of individual, solitary religion; it knows rather of an intensely "personal" life, in which Christians are bound together into one reality through their participation "in Christ."[29]

At the beginning of this lecture we recognized that the purpose of God was the creation of a humanity in his image, whose unity was to reflect his own, and that disunity and death were the marks of sin. The doctrine of the Church as the body of Christ, the last Adam, is to be directly related to that disunity. Behind the concept of Christ as the last Adam lies that

of the first Adam. In Paul's world that first Adam had certain characteristics. To grasp these, a glance at Jewish teaching about Adam is necessary: in particular, in his development of the idea of the Church as the
body of Christ, Paul is largely influenced by rabbinic ideas about Adam.

Rabbinic speculation about the creation of the physical body of Adam
was very varied and often even grotesque. But it seems that two dominant
interests were served—the need for emphasizing the unity of all mankind
and the duty of love—though of course, much of the haggadic material
on Adam is playful fantasy and not serious theology. First, then, the fact
that all people are derived from one ancestor, Adam, means that in him
all people are one. There is a real unity of all humanity in him; all belong
to each and each belongs to all. Thus, in *m. Sanh.* 4:5 we read: "Therefore
but a single man was created in the world to teach that if any man has
caused a single soul to perish from Israel, Scripture imputes it to him as
though he had caused a whole world to perish, and if any man saves alive
a single soul from Israel, Scripture imputes it to him as though he had
saved a whole world." It was in order to emphasize that in Adam all
people were one that such strange stories were circulated as to the formation of Adam's body. According to a tradition going back to R. Meir
(c. 150 C.E.), God made Adam out of dust gathered from all over the earth.
"It has been taught: R. Meir used to say: 'The dust of the first man was
gathered from all parts of the earth,' for it is written, 'Thine eyes did see
mine unformed substance' (Ps 139:16), and further it is written, 'The eyes
of the Lord run to and from through the whole earth' (Zech 4:10)." (Epstein comments: "This is perhaps another way of teaching the equality
of man, all men having been formed from one and the same common
clay.")

Later speculation claimed that Adam's head was formed from the earth
of the Holy Land, the trunk of his body from Babylonian soil and his
various members from the soil of different countries. "R. Oshaiah said
in Rab's name: 'Adam's trunk came from Babylon (38b), his head from
Eretz Israel, his limbs from other lands, and his private parts according
to R. Aha from Akra di Agma.'" Epstein, in the page referred to above,
explains that Adam's head, the most exalted part of his body, comes from
Eretz Israel, the most exalted of lands, while Akra di Agma was a place
notorious on account of its immorality. Because of this cosmopolitan
physical structure of Adam, it followed that a person from the East and
one from the West were of the same material formation, and therefore
one. In the deepest sense "there was neither Jew nor Greek." Thus, in

Pirqe Rabbi Eleizer we read:

> The Holy One, blessed be He, spake to the Torah: "Let us make man in
> our image after our likeness" (Gen 1:26). (The Torah) spake before Him:
> Sovereign of all the worlds! The man whom Thou wouldst create will be
> limited in days and full of anger; and he will come unto the power of sin.
> Unless Thou wilt be long-suffering with him, it would be well for him not
> to have come into the world. The Holy One, blessed be He, rejoined: And
> is it for nought that I am called "slow to anger" and "abounding in love"?
> He began to collect the dust of the first man from the four corners of the
> world; red, black, white and "pale green" (which) refers to the body.

Why did he gather man's dust from the four corners of the world?

> Thus spake the Holy One, blessed be He: If a man should come from the
> east to the west or from the west to the east, and his time to depart from
> the world comes, then the earth shall not say, the dust of thy body is not
> mine, return to the place whence thou was created. But (this circumstance)
> teaches thee that in every place where a man goes or comes, and his end
> approaches when he must depart from the world, thence is the dust of his
> body, and there it returns to the dust, as it is said, "For dust thou art and
> unto dust thou shalt return." (Gen 3:19)

In addition to all this, of course, Adam was bisexual, so that in him
there was neither male nor female. The phrase, "This is the book of the
generations of Adam" (Gen 5:1), was interpreted to mean that God revealed to Adam all the generations to come; this really means that all
subsequent generations were in him, as it were. How naively physical
was all this speculation is seen from the fact that different individuals
were conceived as being derived from or attached to different parts of
Adam's body; one might belong to his hair, another to his ear, another
to his nose; they literally formed different members of his body. There
was speculation also on the meaning of Adam's name; the latter was found
to suggest universality or the unity of all mankind in him. We read in 2
Enoch 30:13: "And I appointed him a name from the four component
parts, from East, West, South, and from North." A stood for the East
(*Anatolê*), D for the West (*Dusis*), A for North (*Arktos*), and M for South
(*Mesêmbria*). The same idea meets us in the Sibylline Oracles where we
read: "Yea it is God Himself who fashioned four lettered Adam, the first
man fashioned who completes in his name morn and dusk, antiartic and
artic."

Adam, then, stands for the real unity of humankind in virtue of his
creation. There is also another factor. The nature of Adam's creation is

made the basis of the duty of love, equality, and peace among people.
To quote again *m. Sanh.* 4:5: "Again but a single man was created for
the sake of peace among mankind that none should say to his fellow, My
Father was greater than thy Father . . . " Furthermore, R. Simeon b.
Azzai (120–40 C.E.) deduced the principle of love from Gen 5:1, which
reads, "This is the book of the generations of Adam . . . ":

> Thou shalt love thy neighbor as thyself (Lev 19:18). R. Akiba said: "That
> is the greatest principle in the Law." Ben Azzai said: "The sentence 'this
> is the book of the generations of man' (Gen 5:1) is even greater than the
> other."

Gen 5:1 teaches that all people are the offspring of him who was made
in the image of God.

The relevance of all this to an understanding of Paul's doctrine of the
body of Christ is evident. Christians are, according to Paul, united with
one another and with Christ; they share with one another and with Christ
in one corporeity. This comes out clearly in Paul's treatment of the Last
Supper. In 1 Cor 11:29, he writes: "For he that eateth and drinketh
damnation to himself, not discerning the Lord's body." He here refers
to those who in their conduct at the Holy Communion forgot their unity
with their fellow Christians and with Christ, who failed to recognize that
to partake in the Lord's Supper was not merely to participate in Christ
but also in their fellow Christians, who are one with Christ. Irregularities
at the table of the Lord, such as prevailed at Corinth, denied the solidarity
of all Christians with each other and with their Lord. As Dodd puts it,
"there is a sort of mystical unity of redeemed humanity in Christ," "a
new corporate personality is created in Christ." In a quite physical sense,
Christians are all one in Christ. This unity Paul calls the body of Christ.
He goes on to develop this concept: the body is animated by the Spirit—
a kind of life force that manifests itself in different ways, so that there
are many members in the one body, unity in diversity.

But there is one further note that Paul strikes in this context. The sin
of Adam had not only produced disunity but something even deeper. The
apostle enters into the very spirit of the story of the Fall. One of the
elements in that story was the hatred that emerged—hatred toward God
on the part of Adam and hatred toward humankind, his own brother
Abel—on the part of Cain. True, it is not explicitly stated in Genesis that
Adam hated God, but he did rebel against him and break his commandment. For Paul, as a result of that first transgression, a principle of rebellion, revolt, and independence from God had entered into human ex-

istence. To this condition we may ascribe the description "hatred toward God." Paul came to regard humanity's relationship to God as one of alienation. Humankind needs to be reconciled to God, to make peace with him (see Rom 5:10–11; Col 1:20). Paul recognizes that humanity and nature were at enmity with God but that the death of Jesus has removed this enmity. For Paul, the whole ministry of Jesus was designed to achieve this end: it was a ministry of reconciliation, as in 2 Cor 5:17–21, which we have quoted already. One of the great gifts of Christ was "peace."

In this connection one thing needs to be clearly understood. Paul never asserts that God hates humankind; it is humankind who hates God. Just as he avoids claiming that God is angry with humanity, so Paul avoids ascribing hatred to God. On the contrary, God is concerned with the work of reconciliation. It was God who was "in Christ" reconciling the world to himself. He took the initiative in removing the barrier placed by humanity against him. The attitude of God toward people always is and has been and will be one of love. This is part of Paul's gospel. The gospel does not imply any change in God's attitude toward humanity, but does, where it is appropriated, work a change in humanity's attitude toward God.

The result of this change is that the Gospel introduces what Paul calls "peace." In five passages, Paul refers to God as the God of peace.

> The God of peace be with you all (Rom 15:33).

> The God of peace will soon crush Satan beneath your feet (Rom 16:20).

> And now, my friends, farewell. Mend your ways; take our appeal to heart; agree with one another; live in peace; and the God of love and peace will be with you (2 Cor 13:11).

> The lessons I taught you, the tradition I have passed on, all that you heard me say or saw me do, put into practice; and the God of peace will be with you (Phil 4:9).

> May God himself, the God of peace, make you holy in every part (1 Thess 5:23).

As the third item cited makes especially clear, the term "peace" in Paul certainly retains the sense of concord or agreement or pleasant relationships between person and person. But, it means more. It again recalls for Paul the scene described in Genesis 1. Primordially, humanity was at peace in a world at peace. Everything that God had made was good; order and peace had been called out of chaos. But this peace was disturbed by the fact of sin, which introduced misdirection, created a world at dispeace or at "poor peace," as a modern poet has put it. We are all too familiar with this fact in a world which "puts its peace in impossible things." But, for Paul, as we have reiterated, "in Christ" the condition of misdirection has been reversed. There is peace instead of dispeace. Just as God, at the creation, had called out order and peace from chaos, so in the new creation "in Christ." Humankind is now in a new situation in which its enmity toward God has been removed; it is at peace because newly directed. Within people's lives there is still struggle, but no frustration; there is still discomfort, but no despair, because "in Christ" God is with them. Peace in this sense becomes essentially trust in life itself as lying in the hands of God and directed "in Christ." No one is likely to call Paul a peaceful man. He knew little "peace of mind" in his labors; yet, this "stormy petrel," this turbulent man, knew "a peace that passeth understanding" because he was convinced that life was redirected by his Lord.

The new humanity recreated in Christ, then, is the negation of the divisions introduced by sin: in sex, in social inequality, in international divisiveness, and in the hatred of humanity for God. The liberation with which Paul was concerned was universal in its scope and, in principle, penetrated every realm of human concern: it involved a new creation. Many of the metaphors which Paul uses to expound this liberation—redemption (*apolutōsis,* Rom 3:24, 1 Cor 1:30), adoption (*huiothesia,* Gal 4:1–7), and liberty (*eleutheria,* Gal 5:1, 13)—derive from the Exodus, the new life "in Christ" being the result of a new Exodus into a new Canaan "in him." And because the Exodus from Egypt is most easily understood as a delivery from the economic and inhuman bondage of slavery, it is tempting to understand the Exodus "in Christ" in similar terms, that is, in the categories of political and economic deliverance. That such deliverance is implied in Paul we cannot doubt; but it is not possible to find it directly sketched in the epistles. On the contrary, revolutionary as his doctrine is in theory, there is not a little of the quietist in Paul. We shall return to this later.

The Centrality of the Cross

This brings us to a central aspect of Paul's thought. The Christ he preached as the agent of God's redirection of the world and of its liberation was a crucified figure, who had taken upon himself the sin of the world and, through his costly obedience unto death, wrought man's redirection (2 Cor 5:17–21). The death of Christ—that is, his willingness to take upon himself the consequences of the sins of humankind to the bitter end—is the supreme paradigm of the medium of the Christian liberation. In Rom 3:21–26, Paul equates Jesus with the "mercy seat" (*hilastêrion*) in the

Temple. Once a year, on the Day of Atonement, the high priest of the Jewish people, after elaborate self-purification, entered the Holy of Holies in the Temple at Jerusalem and sprinkled the blood of a sacrificial victim on the mercy seat (*kappôreth; hilastērion*), thereby removing the sin of all the people. Paul declares in Romans 3 that Jesus *is* the place where this act of removing sin is *really* completed: Jesus who died publicly is the effective means of cleansing the stain of sin from mankind.[30] Wherever he is, *there* is the *hilastērion*. The land of Israel, Jerusalem, the Temple itself—all supports to or necessary for the good life in Judaism—are replaced by him.[31] There is a liberating displacement in the gospel of Paul and that on all fronts, geographic and cultic. And this is wrought through the Messiah's obedient death.

This emphasis on the cross of Christ in Paul draws us back to earth, because that cross was not simply a symbol but an actual death. The liberation about which Paul speaks is not cheap, because the love of God in Christ is a costly love: it is love expressed in death. So, too, the liberation of the Christian is costly: it demands a participation in that death. He or she is called upon to die with Christ and to rise with him—language which Paul uses with power. The death of Christ in Paul is "for us," a sacrifice freely offered on our behalf. It has been urged that Paul does not call upon Christians to follow Christ in his cross: that not only is such a following impossible for others than he, but that even in Phil 2:6ff., Paul does not make the connection between the cross and any moral demand.[32] Such a position is untenable. To die with Christ is to share in his obedience: to rise with him is to share in his forgiving love because, whatever else the resurrection meant, it did mark the return of the Lord to those who had betrayed him. It was the supreme expression of his forgiving grace, and in such grace Christians are to participate and thus be liberated. Believers participate "in Christ," enter upon the new humanity, through a death to the self and a birth to forgiveness, received and extended to others. Here is demanded not mystical absorption in a risen Lord, ecstatic or visionary. Paul knew about such absorption but discounted it (2 Cor 12:1–4). There may be room for such experience: there is no reason to condemn it out of hand, provided it be not confused with the essential meaning of being "in Christ." So, too, although to be "in Christ" calls for the imitation of him as the identifying figure of Christians, it is not to a literal copying of a first-century figure that Paul calls the believers. (In all imitation there is a danger of a mechanical reproduction which is irrelevant.) Nor, although Paul regards himself and believers as standing under a new Sinai of the words of Jesus, does his emphasis lie there. Rather, he points to a Lord who was crucified and raised from the dead.[33]

This may be illustrated best from Phil 2:6ff., where Paul probably quotes a very early Christian hymn. The hymn moves on two levels. Paul urges his congregation to be like Christ, who was obedient unto death, and not like the disobedient Adam. He calls them to be generous, self-forgetful, ready to give up privilege and status, as was Christ. Mutual respect in humble service is essential to the Christian moral life.

But, Paul is not content with a simple exhortation to morality. He uses the myth (a word used here in the technical sense of a story about the gods told as if they were human) of a descending and ascending Lord. The call to morality becomes a summons to believe, to the faith that this Jesus, in his life, death, and resurrection, reveals the activity of God himself. Paul in Phil 2:6ff., therefore, calls not simply for a moral strategy of mutual respect and humility, the content of the life to which believers are called. He calls also for faith in the source of that life, supremely revealed in Jesus, in God himself, as the one from whom comes the power that makes mutual respect and humility possible. And so, the call to participate in the dying and rising Christ and to walk in his way demands the faith that in him we encounter the redeeming, forgiving, redirecting work of the God who is beyond us but has drawn near. We are called to participate in the joy that wells from this experience. Joy and gratitude as a mark of the Christian liberation is a constant note in Paul (1 Cor 15:57; 2 Cor 2:14; Rom 5:2, 3).[34]

THE WAY OF FAITH: DISCIPLINE
IN LIBERATION

And thus we are led to the third part of our subject: the way in which the experience of Paul is to be recaptured or appropriated by believers; the call to faith—in Christ as the person through whom our liberation is made possible and by incorporation with whom believers are taken up into the redemptive purpose of God. In Paul the nature of faith, because of the centrality which it has assumed in his interpretation, cannot easily be stated. Because in his epistles Paul has discussed faith in Christ over against works done in obedience to the law and opposed justification by faith to that by works; and because the doctrine of justification by faith apparently dominates his controversy with his Jewish Christian and Jewish opponents, that doctrine, thus conceived, has been regarded as the cornerstone of Paul's thought, his central message.[35] In this view, the central message of Paul's gospel is the free, unmerited acceptance of the guilty by God through faith in Jesus Christ, whereby the pangs of conscience are relieved. Faith becomes an almost passive acceptance of the forgiveness offered through Christ, particularly through his death. C. H. Dodd's definition of faith has been deservedly quoted.[36] Though sophisticated, it is determined by this point of view. He wrote: "For Paul, faith is that attitude in which, acknowledging our complete insufficiency for any of the high ends of life, we rely utterly on the sufficiency of God. It is to cease from all assertion of the self, even by way of effort after righteousness, and to make room for the divine initiative."

This definition is valid only provided its full implications are spelled out. Faith in Christ is not simply the acceptance of his mercy toward the sinner, although it *always* includes this. Rather, faith is that act by which not only justification, but all the other benefits of Christ's work—redemption, adoption, liberty, new creation, peace, expiation—are all taken up into a person's own life and made real to him or her.[37] It is not primarily with the pangs of conscience of the individual sinner that Paul was concerned in proclaiming justification by faith, but with the lost condition of humankind and the creation of a people of God, a new humanity.[38] In other words, he was primarily concerned with the question: who can belong to Israel, the people of God?[39]

In Galatians and Romans his discussion of justification by faith precedes that of "Israel." Faith in Jesus Christ, taken in its full range, is the grateful acceptance of the fact that "in Christ" and him crucified, a new humanity has emerged in history, as an objective fact, into which we can now enter. From this point of view, Dodd's definition, moving and true as it is, may too much emphasize the passive dimension of faith in Christ, because that faith implies the recognition and appropriation of a new objective situation created by the life, death and resurrection of Christ. This faith is itself a gift from God in Christ, as is the justification which it brings: our very appropriation of the new situation is a gift.

There is to all this another aspect. We wrote above that "in Christ," as an objective fact, there has emerged in history a new humanity. Paul himself states in somewhat absolute terms, "If any man be in Christ, there is a new creation (*ktisis*): the old things have passed away" (2 Cor 5:17). Such language could easily be understood to indicate a life where effort and restraint would be unnecessary. So, too, Paul's emphasis on liberty of his people from the law could and did easily lead to antinomianism. In Thessalonica, Galatia, and Corinth, in Rome and elsewhere, Paul had to face enthusiasts who cherished a life already marked by the fullness of the age to come, beyond good and evil. He rejected all such

claims by insisting that, while the end, the age to come, had been inaugurated, it had not been completely realized: there is a future dimension
to the new humanity. In 1 Corinthians 15 Paul conservatively falls back
on the future expectations of the completion of the resurrection of which
Christ was the first fruit; in other epistles, Thessalonians, Galatians, 2
Corinthians as in 1 Corinthians also, and Romans, he insists on the ethical
dimension of the Christian life. True legalism, in the sense of reliance
upon our own efforts to achieve the new life, is ruled out, but the moral
obligations of that life are inescapable. To be "in Christ" is to have died
with him, to have been crucified with him, which means to have died to
ourselves as members of the old humanity under the dominion of sin; and
it is also to rise with him in newness of life into a new humanity which
has an inescapable moral concern. Paul, we repeat, rejects antinomianism
with vigor. The life in Christ is marked by *agapē,* described in 1 Corinthians 13, which reflects the *agapē* of the life of Christ himself. The battles
of Paul over the observance of the Law in Galatians and Romans especially have made it easy to think of him as the apostle of liberation from
all restraint. But, the battle over the Law was not directly over morality
but over the nature of the people of God. His epistles reveal a Paul who
was a catechist, concerned with the humdrum duties of daily life. His
new Exodus in Christ has its new Sinai in the demand for *agapē* and in
the working out of its meaning in the complexities of life. Nowhere is this
more clearly seen than in Rom 12:1ff. As a result of the acts of God in
the life, death, and resurrection of Jesus, believers are called upon to live
in a new way. The Christian's experience of the mercies of God, that is,
his or her gratitude for them, becomes a dynamic for the good life. The
motive for Christian living is not a dutiful obedience to any Law, but
gratitude for the mercies of God in Christ. In Romans 12 Paul appeals for
the Christian life, not from the pinnacle of his own moral purity and
achievement, not because it is reasonable or prudent or pleasurable, but
because of what God has wrought in Christ. Gratitude—the most ethical
of the emotions—for his mercies has become the dynamic of the new life.

But, that gratitude, of itself, is not enough. A discipline also is demanded. In Rom 12:1 Christians are called to present themselves a living
sacrifice, wholly acceptable unto God. Elsewhere Paul speaks of bringing
every thought captive to the obedience of Christ (2 Cor 10:5), or of beating
his body black and blue (1 Cor 9:26ff.), of a Law of Christ to be fulfilled
(Gal 6:2). For Paul, Christian living is born in spontaneous gratitude, but
it is never effortless: it has to be informed and controlled if it is not to
be stillborn. Paul was often made aware in his churches that birth into

Christ and gratitude to him can degenerate into a sentimental emotionalism, an ineffective religiosity, an irrelevant piety, and even a dangerous disorder unless it is harnessed to life and directed by knowledge. The new man still lives in the flesh and in the world, and so, the necessary corollary of his liberation is discipline: *apolutrōsis* implies *askesis*. To be "in Christ" is not to indulge in ecstatic irresponsibility but to be under the constraint of his *agapē*. Another way of saying the same thing is to claim that the possession of the Spirit could only be indicated by the fruit of the spirit. That fruit could express itself in various activities (1 Cor 12:4), but its most excellent expression was *agapē* (1 Corinthians 13). This meant that the Spirit was the source of unity, despite the multiplicity of its expressions: disunity among Christians was a mark of its absence (1 Cor 12:12–13). Because the Spirit could be so easily misunderstood in terms of intense ecstatic enthusiasm, Paul found it necessary to give guidance for its understanding. He insisted that the Spirit is not only rational in its content, but, above all, that it strengthens the bonds of the community in building up the common life of the Church (1 Cor 12:12–13). For example, because speaking with tongues does not do this, Paul listed it last in his description of the gifts of the Spirit. More important than any ecstasy are wisdom, knowledge, faith, and, above all, love (*agapē*)—that is, the unmerited, overflowing persistent goodwill of God toward people and of people toward people "in Christ" (1 Cor 13:4–7). Paul impresses upon the Corinthians that enthusiasm without understanding, ecstasy without knowledge, intensity of experience without *agapē*, are all of secondary worth. The true marks of life in the Spirit Paul expresses in the memorable words: "But the harvest of the Spirit is love, joy, peace, patience, kindness, goodness, fidelity, gentleness, and self-control" (Gal 5:22). But these were the marks of the character of Jesus himself, and this implies that, for Paul, fundamental to any interpretation of the Spirit is the recognition that what matters is the relation between the Spirit and Jesus. All "spiritual" phenomena are to be tested by their relationship to him (1 Cor 12:3). The Spirit is Jesus himself living in the community of those who love him and bear his fruit.

But again, this harvest is not "spontaneous." True, against the fruits of the Spirit there is no law (Gal 5:23). And yet, Paul places before his converts, as part of their very liberation, certain demands. In this he was again true to Jesus. The ministry of Jesus has been one of infinite grace and freedom. But, it had also opened up to people new vistas of obedience and placed before them such absolute standards as we read in the Sermon on the Mount. Life "in Christ" or "in the Spirit" is also a life under law—

the law of Christ, which is the law of *agapē*. Paul uses both the words of Jesus and certain Hellenistic and Jewish codes to bring home in the most practical and earthy way possible the moral aspect of the new life "in Christ." Liberation "in Christ" is a way, a halakah, in accordance with him, and it is an increasingly narrow way.[40]

So far we have emphasized the appropriation of the new humanity as born in faith and disciplined by the constraints of Christ's *agapē*. The liberation bears another mark, one which in Rom 5:1–5 is given special prominence in Paul's summary of the content of the life in Christ. It reads:

> Therefore, now that we have been justified through faith, let us continue at peace with God through our Lord Jesus Christ, through whom we have been allowed to enter the sphere of God's grace, where we now stand. Let us exult in the hope of the divine splendour that is to be ours. More than this: let us even exult in our present sufferings, because we know that suffering trains us to endure, and endurance brings proof that we have stood the test, and this proof is the ground of hope. Such a hope is no mockery, because God's love has flooded our inmost heart through the Holy Spirit he has given us.

Here Paul fixes upon the hope of sharing in the glory of God as one of the marks of the new life in Christ. He repeats the word "hope" three times, thereby indicating its centrality. Later in Rom 8:24, Paul even claims that Christians are saved by hope. In fact, what we have previously written implies the necessity of hope if Christians are not to despair. We pointed out the realism of Paul in demanding an unrelenting discipline (*askēsis*) and his insistence that the Christian liberation is only incipient, but not complete. If the Christian road, as Gabriel Rossetti put it, "winds uphill all the way/ yes, to the very end," and if "the journey takes the whole long day/ from morn till night," how can the believer sustain this pilgrim condition—often miserable—unless there be a hope to sustain him? In Rom 8:18, Paul refers to "the sufferings of this present time." Doubtless he included in these sufferings the constant (shall we say inevitable?) sufferings to which all flesh is heir: "the slings and arrows of outrageous fortune," and more particularly those which believers in a hostile world necessarily, though voluntarily, undertook for the sake of their Lord. But, there is a further dimension to this suffering. It is a fundamental suffering shared by all things—humankind, the believer, and the very creation itself. Can we define this? It is the suffering born of humanity's sense of the vanity or futility, the cruel absurdity of its existence and that of the created order. Humankind's suffering is part of the groaning of the whole of creation because it is subject to futility (*ma-*

taiotēti, Rom 8:20) and to the bondage of corruption (*tēs douleias tēs phthoras,* 8:21).[41] In this context so conducive to enervating anxiety and total despair, Paul urges that the believer is "saved by hope" (8:24). Since Christian liberation for Paul, objectively grounded in the life, death, and resurrection of Jesus as it is, is nevertheless not a status achieved but a continuous process; it must be sustained by hope.

Paul's emphasis on hope as a mark of our liberation must be examined in its context and content. As to its context, we have already referred to that of life in general and of the Christian life in particular. The historical context of Paul is also important. Especially under the belief in astrology and fate, hopelessness was a mark of Paul's age. To offer hope in the first century was to speak a particularly timely word.

But what of the content of Paul's hope? In Rom 5:2 he defines it as sharing in God's glory. But, how is this to be understood? The question, along with other factors, has created a major cleavage among the interpreters of Paul. Is this glory of which he speaks to be experienced within history, as the culmination of a long historical process? That is, did Paul think of history and of human destiny in linear terms? There are two alternatives to this. The first is to spiritualize the Christian's hope and transcendentalize it—that is, to remove it beyond any possible earthly, historical experience to the order which "eye hath not seen nor ear heard." True, there are anticipations of this supernatural glory in the believer's experience on earth—but they are only pale anticipations, a pledge of that which is to come. The other alternative is to concentrate hope in that moment of decision for Christ, here and now. Into the debate over this question we cannot enter here.[42] The ultimate content of hope must remain a mystery; the ultimate ground of it Paul himself makes clear in Rom 8:28–32. He points to the overarching activity of God in all things, in the very suffering of humanity and the groaning of creation, and the presence of God with humankind, demonstrated in the death of Christ, who makes it possible to believe that there is now no condemnation to those who are "in him," and demonstrated in the love of Christ. Paul asserts that all the human tyrannies at work in the believer's life—sin, suffering, persecution, and famine—and all the unseen demonic tyrannies and death, the last terrible enemy itself, cannot separate him from the love of God. The present and the future, whatever form they take, need not be feared. And so, hope turns into endurance or courage—another mark of the liberated life.

Finally, the reference to courage—a virtue which in Paul's life needs no documentation—as a mark of the liberated life brings us to the need to face the actualities which Christians encounter in every age, including our own. We have emphasized liberation as the abandonment of false gods, the pursuit of the good life and, above all, as participation, in obedience and forgiveness, in the death and resurrection of Christ, in the community of the Spirit with the discipline that this involves. The dimensions of the liberation to which we have pointed are determined by the context within which Paul worked. In the eyes of many in our time that context, though rich, is limited; in particular, it does not face those economic and political realities of the human condition which are now emphasized, for example, by Frederick Herzog and by Dorothee Soelle in her work, *Political Theology* (Philadelphia: Fortress Press, 1974). In conclusion here, let us ask how this emphasis on economic and political liberation appears in the light of Paul. The issue raised can, of course, only be touched upon. There are two major facts to be considered.

First, we must consider whether economic and political liberation were envisaged by Paul in any way. Certain general considerations militate against this. His conviction, shared by many Christians, that the end was at hand made it unlikely that he should have envisaged any long-term political and economic amelioration, even had he thought in such categories at all. Attempts to interpret his missionary strategy in imperial terms, as if he thought of furthering an "empire of Christ" over against the empire of Rome, have failed.[43] Nor can it be certainly held, as we saw before, that in his understanding of Christ as having vanquished the unseen demonic forces, the prince of the power of the air and his minions, Paul was thinking of the mastery of the unregenerate economic, political, and cultural structures of his time. When we turn to more specific considerations, the same negative conclusion emerges. Was Paul once a revolutionary—an anticipatory Zealot bent on destroying the oppressive Roman power? More probably, he had belonged to a quietistic apocalyptic Pharisaism which relegated political change to God's own direct intervention. There is nothing in Paul's epistles which explicitly indicates that liberation for him had a political content. He seems deliberately to have avoided the term "kingdom of God" because it might be understood politically.[44] In 1 Corinthians he presents an ethic of the status quo; 1 Cor 7:24 and his reference to slavery in Philemon are explicit on this. Philemon is to receive Onesimus as a brother beloved: he is not asked to free him. Later in Rom 13:1 Paul advocates submission to the powers that be. Even if he is there thinking of the ordinary officers for the collection of taxes and the maintenance of everyday order, which had nothing sacred about them, and not raising the fundamental questions of the nature of the state, his counsel is unequivocal.[45] The organs of public administration fulfill the purpose of God in the maintenance of justice: public power is of God. Again, 1 Thessalonians is instructive at this point. Messianism by its very nature had a revolutionary tendency and often engendered among early Christians a disregard for social order in the interests of unrestrained, enthusiastic brotherhood, which could engender anarchy as easily as charity. Against such anarchistic disorder Paul had to set his face from the beginning. He urged that Christians not disturb or unsettle the existing order but conduct themselves with propriety and dignity, so as not to bring the Christian community and movement into disrepute. The effect of the conduct of Christians on those without is emphasized. This attitude, as we say, is carried over later into Paul's deferences to slavery and the public life.

Further, Paul gives no positive directions about the duty of Christians in public life apart from urging obedience to civil, police, and political authorities. He does not even advocate cooperation with them. He urges Christians to solve their own civil problems without appeal to pagan tribunals (1 Cor 6:11), regarding it as beneath the dignity of Christians to do so. He is apparently governed solely by the necessity of avoiding the criticism of the world and the wisdom of avoiding entanglement with it in order to avoid hindering the cause of the gospel. Paul, the stormy petrel of early Christianity, had no small measure of worldly wisdom in maintaining this very distance from the world.[46]

But the matter does not end with this wholly negative note. At one point especially, Paul's treatment of marriage, a positive note enters. In this sphere the eschatological doctrine of the new creation logically demanded that a Christian's marriage, especially with a pagan partner, be regarded as terminated.[47] But Paul refuses to follow this logic. He recognizes the institution of marriage even between Christian and pagan as of continuing validity and introduces the note that through her conduct the Christian wife can "gain" the non-Christian partner for the faith. The latter stands, through his wife, in the ambience of the new humanity in Christ, just as the children, from birth on, belong to God. "In Christ" the natural ties of marriage can be influenced for good. Here a principle of immense importance is implied. Although Paul himself does not draw out this conclusion, can we not deduce that Christians in society can, when obedient to their Lord, help to bring it too into "holiness"—that is, help it to belong to God by a process of permeation? It is from such an awareness of the "contagious" effect of those "in Christ" that the notion of the Church as "the soul" of the world could emerge. Paul, despite his eschatological stance and his apparent unconcern for changing society's political and economic structures, does suggest one indirect way, at least, through which the life "in Christ" can impinge upon them.

But we cannot go farther than this. From Paul to the explicit concern of modern Christians for transforming society politically and economically, there is no direct passage.[48] The world of Paul has frequently been compared with ours. Some have condemned him for not having engaged in political and economic concerns which preoccupy us; others have sought to apply the answers he gave to his own problems directly to ours.[49] But, the temporal and cultural gulf between Paul and ourselves cannot be directly bridged. To find any *direct* practical relevance in Paul's theology for our world is anachronistic and fruitless. "Context defines content." The content of Paul's understanding of liberation was defined by his first-century milieu. In its political and economic stance, time has made this not only unacceptable but even barbarous. We can no longer tolerate slavery; we can no longer counsel women to be silent in the church. But, neither the context nor the political and economic content of Paul's theology should primarily concern us. Rather, we should concentrate on the ground on which it was founded—that is, on the reality of God revealed in Christ to redirect the world in his Spirit.

Nevertheless, at one point Paul had to spell out what this redirection meant in social terms: he faced the social cleavage that most immediately harassed him personally—that between Jew and Gentile. Doubtless this was the deepest social cleavage in Paul's world. The causes of that cleavage were religious, social, and political. Religiously the Hellenistic Age was syncretistic: it demanded a religious pluralism which Jews could not countenance. However far they could go out toward their Gentile neighbors, the commandments of the Torah made final assimilation impossible. For the Gentiles, freedom and universalism meant in the sphere of religion the right to worship any god one pleased; for the Jews, it could only mean the worship of the living God before whom there was no other. Paradoxically then, the Jews were atheists (*atheioi*). This fundamental religious stumbling block engendered social tensions. At its simplest, the inevitable refusal to share in pagan meals because of their pagan religious associations made Jews appear inhospitable. Their dietary practices appeared to be fanatical; the Sabbath observance, ridiculous. Philosophers joined the masses in condemning the irrational particularism of Israel. Moreover, politically Jews were Orientals in the eyes of Rome and shared by association in the Oriental plague of sects—mystery, magical, astrological, and philosophical—against which Rome took strong measures. (Economic factors, though operative especially in connection with the withdrawing of money from the Diaspora to Jerusalem through the Temple tax, were secondary in anti-Judaism.)

Paul, a Jew, open to the fascination of Gentile culture, knew the meaning of social tension between Jew and Gentile to a painful degree. The tyranny of social hatred—one of the great, tangible and intangible forces in the world—was another result of sin. It is not surprising that there are passages where despite his veneration for the Law, because it demanded the fence between Jew and Gentile and could therefore be regarded as a source of the cleavage to which we refer, Paul counts the very Law as among the evil elements of the world (*ta stoicheia tou kosmou,* Gal 4:4, 9). But, just as he mellowed in his understanding of the Law, he faced the cleavage with which we deal with a courage, an insight, and a tolerance which most twentieth-century Christians have not yet shown. That was where the Spirit of Christ led him. He declared that "in Christ" there was neither Jew nor Greek, bond nor free, male nor female. While the Spirit did not lead him to revolutionary activity against the state for the amelioration of desperate economic conditions, it did lead him to seek to overcome the barrier between Jew and Gentile by demanding of Jews the surrender of much that they had held to be the will of God for them, while demanding of Gentiles tolerance and largesse of spirit toward Israel after the flesh that did not come easily. He demanded of both Jew and Gentile the recognition that there is no distinction between them because all have sinned. To be "in Christ" was to be in a new humanity born of grace. We may well ask why Paul was so sensitive on the Jewish question, and, by modern standards, so blind to other economic and political enormities. Is not the answer that in his day, in his world, it was the Jewish-Gentile enmity that was the spearhead of divisiveness ("nationalism" in the modern sense had hardly been born), and therefore the point where the test of the new humanity came most crucially for him? That the test, to our shame, still comes to us at that same point, despite the large tolerance taught by Paul twenty centuries ago, should strip us of any sense of superiority over him, even while we now recognize his inevitable limitation in matters economic and political. The spearhead of challenge to the believer varies from age to age and even country to country. It is not for us, of necessity, either to follow Paul in his political quietism or to apply in the twentieth-century answers he gave to questions in the first. For us it is to confront, with our new sociological and other knowledge, issues especially threatening the new humanity in our day in the spirit in which Paul confronted the supreme Jewish-Gentile problem of his day—that is, in the Spirit of Christ who redirects the world.

There is being urged upon us at this time a political theology. Its emphasis—as I understand it—on our human solidarity and the need for a new sensitivity to the often horrendous economic and social realities of this technological age, which so often leave us depersonalized, fragmented and despairing, is not alien to Paul or to the rest of the New Testament, but indeed of its essence. The same is true of this theology's criticism of the "privatization" of the gospel. The confinement of the life in Christ to the "now" of decision in the individual life, or, again, primarily to a transcendent order, does not do justice to its communal dimensions. Professor Enslin has seen in this communal awareness of Paul a distinctive contribution which distinguishes it from that of the other religions and philosophies of the first century.[50]

But, in endorsing these political emphases in the name of Paul, we also issue certain caveats in his name.[51] Paul flew a magnificent kite—the kite of the new humanity "in Christ." But he also pricked the balloons of Christians when they indulged in flights of fancy about that new humanity, by recalling them to the rigorous demands of the Law of Christ, the law of *agapē*—that is, of openness to suffering in others and its acceptance for their sake. Because that demand of the gospel is usually too much even for the finest Christian hearts, he makes clear that the new humanity is not a merely human achievement. It can never simply be engineered, politically or otherwise. All such achievement stands under the judgment, and in the need, of the grace of God in Christ. To recognize this is to be on the way to that tolerance and forgiveness without which even our very efforts to save the world, like most revolutions, will bring forth monsters who devour their own children.

Section 3:
New Testament Miscellanea

12

Law in the
New Testament (NT)
[νόμος; תורה]

By "law," or "the law," the NT usually means the law of God revealed in the Old Testament (OT). Except, by implication, in Matt 17:24–27; Mark 12:13–17; Rom 13:1ff.; 1 Pet 2:13 ff., the civil and criminal laws of states are not dealt with. Even in 1 Tim 1:8 the reference is probably to the Mosaic law, and in Rom 2:12–16 the law written on the heart (see herein, chapter 13) is also probably to be understood as "what the [Mosaic] law requires" (v. 15). Our main concern, therefore, will be with the law of the OT in the NT.

THE LAW IN THE SYNOPTIC GOSPELS[2]

The term "law" (νόμος) does not occur in Mark at all; in Matthew and Luke it occurs eight and ten times respectively, always with the article, except in Luke 2:23, where also the reference is to the law of the OT. Usually the term denotes the Pentateuch (e.g., Matt 5:18–19). Probably the phrase "the law and the prophets" is used for the whole of the OT (Matt 5:17; 7:12; 11:13; 22:40; Luke 16:16; 24:44 [here the Psalms are distinguished]), as are also "the Scripture" (ἡ γραφή; e.g., Mark 15:28) and "the Scriptures" (ἁι γραφαί; e.g., Mark 14:49). The "oral law" (תורה שבעל פה) is not described as "law" (νόμος), but as the "tradition of the elders" (παράδοσις τῶν πρεσβυτέρων; Mark 7:5) or the "tradition of men" (παράδοσις τῶν ἀνθρώπων; Mark 7:8).

The meager incidence of the term itself is no measure of the deep significance of the problem of "the law" in the synoptics. But at the outset it must be said that it is beyond dispute—however much it may have been exaggerated by some scholars—that in the course of their transmission, the words and works of Jesus have been colored by the experience and needs of the churches that preserved them. To distinguish the attitude of Jesus himself toward the law from that of the early church, therefore, is exceedingly difficult. Here the synoptic evidence is presented without any attempt to establish how far it accurately represents the position of Jesus himself.

Criticism of the Law

According to the synoptics, the ministry of Jesus implied and possibly explicitly recognized that the law, as understood by Judaism, no longer regulated the ways of God with men and that Jesus himself had taken over the place previously held by the law. "The law and the prophets were until John; since then the good news of the kingdom of God is preached" (Luke 16:16; cf. Matt 11:11–13). The coming of Jesus has inaugurated a new order in which, in some sense, the law is superseded; the new wine of this new order cannot be put in old wineskins (Mark 2:22). This is most marked, not only in the parables, which illumine a crisis in which the kingdom of God is now in the process of realizing itself, but also in the relationship of Jesus with publicans and sinners, the "people of the land." A "friend of sinners," he ignored limitations placed on social intercourse by the law, and by implication he broke down barriers essential to the maintenance of the distinction between "clean and unclean" (Mark 2:13–17; Matt 11:19). An examination of his attitude toward the sabbath (Mark 2:23—3:6), toward things clean and unclean (Mark 7:1–24), and toward divorce (Mark 10:2ff.), reveals that: (a) Jesus rejected the oral tradition (in this sense he was, from one point of view, near the Sadducees); (b) he set one passage of Scripture over against another, not to harmonize them, but to invalidate the one by means of the other (Mark 2:23–28; 10:5–9); and (c) he elevated moral above ceremonial commandments (cf. Mark 12:28–33).

Moreover, Jesus appealed to men to judge of themselves that which was good (Luke 12:57), and himself claimed the right to reinterpret the will of God (Matt 5:17–48). Nurtured as he was in the law and the prophets, Jesus passed beyond his nurture to an intuitive awareness of the will of God. We cannot doubt that he followed the immediate deliverances of his own conscience, and the view is probable (though many would contest this) that his attitude toward the law implies his messianic awareness or consciousness. This may be implicit in his use of the messianic "I" in Matt 5:21ff. (in the phrase "but I say to you," though some take this to be merely a rabbinic formula of no such significance) and even more so in his appeal to creation. The messianic age was to inaugurate a new creation comparable with the first. It is in the light of this that we are to understand the teaching of Jesus on divorce in Mark 10:2ff., where he appeals to the order of creation as supplying a truer clue to the intention of God than the law, and much in the parables and other passages (Matt. 5:45ff.; 6:25–33). It is not surprising, therefore, that Mark sets Jesus in opposition to the scribes and Pharisees from the beginning (2:1—3:6), while Matthew places the ethical demands of Jesus in antithesis to those of the law (5:17ff.) and ascribes to Jesus a bitter attack on Pharisaic casuistry and hypocrisy (chapter 23), even while accepting the validity of the teaching of the Pharisees (23:1–2). Henceforth it is man's relationship to Jesus, not to the law, that is decisive (Matt 10:32—40; Mark 8:38). The inadequacy of even a strict adherence to the law, rather than humble readiness to receive God's grace, is clear in Luke 18:10–14.

Affirmation of the Law

On the other hand, the synoptics recognize that Jesus was not concerned (or, at least, not primarily) with annulling the law. While some of the alleged evidence for this may be due to Jesus' desire to comply with necessary civil laws (Mark 1:44), his personal conservatism in the observance of the law is noteworthy. He goes to the synagogue on the Sabbath (Mark 1:21; Luke 4:16; 13:10); he appears in Jerusalem at the festivals (Luke 2:41ff.; Mark 11:1ff.); he teaches in the synagogues and in the temple (Mark 1:29ff.; 14:49); he celebrates the Passover (Mark 14:12ff.; Luke 22:15–16); he does not speak disapprovingly of religious usages as such—fasting, almsgiving, prayer (Matt 5:23–24; 6:1–18); he wears the prescribed fringes on his garments (Mark 6:56; Luke 8:44). Even where he or his disciples do break the law, this is justified, not in any spirit of iconoclasm or unprincipled "liberalism." Either this breaking of the law happens in the interests of the emerging messianic community (as in Mark 2:23–28, where the "Son of man" may connote the "people of the saints of the Most High"—that is, Jesus and his disciples—and where no impatience with sabbatarianism is shown, but rather a desire to enlighten his opponents), or Jesus reacts to certain situations in immediate response to the will of God, thereby recognizing the supreme claims of that will without considering the effect of his action on the law (so Mark 3:1ff., where no mere antisabbatarianism governed Jesus' action). Similarly, Jesus' inability, even against himself, to resist the priority of human need or the claims of the rule of God governs his action in Luke 13:10–13 rather than frivolous antisabbatarianism. What the latter called forth from him we see in the Western text (D) at Luke 6:5.

Unless Mark 7:15 be so interpreted, there is no explicit assertion of the annulling of the law by Jesus, and many interpret Mark 7:15 not as a rejection of the distinction between things clean and unclean but an assertion of the priority of the moral over the ritual. The moral demand of Jesus is expressed, in part at least, in terms of the Law and the prophets

(Matt 22:34–40; Mark 12:28–34; Luke 10:25–28), and, in Matt 5:17ff., Jesus probably, as a second Moses (parallel to, and not only antithetical to, the first one), is sent not to annul the law but to fulfill it.

Explanations of Jesus' Dual Attitude

As the synoptics present him, then, Jesus had a twofold attitude toward the law: he seemed to annul it, at least by implication, and at the same time affirm it. This contradiction has been variously explained:

a) Possibly the attitude of Jesus toward the law changed during his ministry. As they now stand, our sources set Jesus in opposition to the Jewish religious leaders from the start; but there are indications that at some stage in his ministry, Jesus attempted to be friendly with Pharisees. He well understood how natural it was for them to suspect his position and sought to conciliate them (Matt 23:23; Mark 12:28–29; Luke 5:39, 13:31; 17:20). Nevertheless, although there may have been development in the mind of Jesus, the chronology of the ministry is so confused that it would be hazardous to trace this too confidently.

b) The conservatism of Jesus on the law, it has been claimed, is the result of Jewish Christian influences on the tradition which have "Judaized" Jesus. Thus Matt 5:17–18 has been declared unthinkable on the lips of the historical Jesus; and Matthew 23, by making him attack merely scribal and Pharisaic hypocritical misuse of it rather than the law itself, has falsified the position of Jesus. But the passage upholding the law in every iota and dot occurs, not only in the Jewish Christian source M, but in Q which is often connected with the Gentile church at Antioch. There is nothing in Matt 5:17–19 which cannot be connected with Jesus' ministry, with his encounter with the "people of the land," with discussions between Hillel and Shammai and others on knowing and doing the law and on heavy and light commandments. Since friend and foe could find sufficient cause in both the practice and the teaching of Jesus to stimulate the suspicion of iconoclasm, Matt 5:17ff. could have been called forth by conditions during the ministry itself in which Jesus disclaimed any intention to annul the law.

c) The contradiction under discussion may be due to the fact that Jesus attacked not the law itself, but the oral tradition. In his treatment of the Sabbath and divorce, Jesus always criticizes the law from within the law (Mark 2:23–26; 3:1–6; 10:2–3). At two points, however, the attempt to relate Jesus' conflict with the law exclusively to the "fence" around it—that is, the oral tradition—has been claimed to fail. In Mark 7:15, Jesus seems to annul the law itself (although even here he may still be attacking the ceremonial laws merely in order to emphasize the ethical), and in Matt 5:31, 38, the law itself is cited and particular provisions abrogated (although here, too, Jesus may merely be offering a new interpretation of the law. As we saw, scholars are divided as to the exact force of the phrase: "But I say to you"—some regard it as messianic in significance; others treat it as a customary rabbinic formula to denote that Jesus is merely presenting his understanding of the law).

d) Another possible explanation of Jesus' twofold attitude toward the law is that there was a distinction in Jesus' mind between the period before his death, which is the final culmination of the old order, and that which comes to birth through his death. In the former, the law is not annulled by him, although "signs" that it is passing are given. Only after his death has sealed the new covenant and fully inaugurated the new order does the law cease to govern relations between God and man. This may be the meaning of Matt 5:18, the phrase "until all is accomplished" (ἕως ἄν πάντα γένηται) possibly referring to the death of Christ. This view has been little discussed and is highly tentative; but it might explain why Paul connects the death of Christ so closely with the end of the law (Gal 2:19–21; 3:13; 5:11; Eph 2:13–14; Col 2:14) and why Jesus, who looked to a future incursion of Gentiles into the kingdom (Matt 8:10–11), nevertheless confined his ministry to the Jews.

e) The reference to the death of Jesus may supply us with a clue that we need. Jesus went to his death in obedience to the will of God (Mark 14:36); and thus fulfilled the law as the demand of God as he understood it (Luke 24:25–27). It may be impossible for us to disentangle the precise attitude of Jesus toward the ceremonial laws (he himself perhaps would not have made the rigid distinctions that we make at this point), but we can be sure that the moral demand of the law, as the expression of the will of God, Jesus never annulled. His very call to repentance implies this (Mark 1:15; Matt 4:17): the prodigal son is to return to obedience to his father (Luke 15:19); to know and to keep the two great commandments of love to God and neighbor is to be near the kingdom (Mark 12:28–34). Jesus has his own yoke to impose (Matt 11:25–30). The concept of "law" as the demand of God would not have repelled Jesus. Nevertheless, it was not in terms of the law of Judaism that he issued his call to repentance, but in terms of the kingdom of God (Mark 1:15). By setting the call to repentance in the context of the givenness and immediacy of the kingdom, Jesus freed it from mere moralism and utterly radicalized it. Thus, too, he came to understand the law in terms of the will of God, not the will of God in terms of the law. And the will of God for him was one of absolute love, so that God's demand was one for such love (Matt 5:17–48). And to know the demand of God as such—that is, for absolute love—is to recognize that one cannot "obey" it fully nor set up any claim to merit before God, that the "broken and the contrite heart" alone is possible for us. This was at the root of the criticism that Jesus made of the scribal and Pharisaic tradition: that it assumed the "achievability" of a right relation to God on grounds of obedience—whereas to stand under the will of God as love, as Jesus understood it, was to know that even when we have done all that is commanded, we are unworthy servants (Luke 17:10). But Jesus does not deliver us from all commandments. He gives us a commandment, that of love, and we must ask whether this means that he introduced a new law.

f) Matthew 5 possibly makes of Jesus a new Moses proclaiming new, radical commandments to be applied. It is, moreover, not unlikely that Jesus set himself in conscious parallelism to Moses. But we can only speak of the words of Jesus as a new law with extreme caution. The total obedience to the will of God, which is one of love, could not be reduced to a written code in a prescriptive sense. This obedience has to discover its own means of expression in any given situation, even though it be informed by the law, tradition, or even the words of Jesus himself. Precisely because the law could, and often did, hide the immediate demands of love in any particular situation, and could and often did lead to external observance without the true intent and to a concern for merit and reward and hence to hypocrisy, Jesus opposed scribes and Pharisees. And he himself spoke, not primarily at least as a lawgiver—though he commanded—but as one sent of God in the last hour to reveal the absolute will of God. His hyperbolic statements of the demand of God, though to be taken with the utmost seriousness, are therefore to be interpreted not as a "new law," but as pointers to the true nature of God's demand for love.

THE EARLIEST CHRISTIANS AND THE LAW

Radicalism: Stephen

The ambiguity which marked the attitude of Jesus toward the law, according to the synoptics, reappears in the attitude of the earliest Christians—that is, the claims of the law are recognized and, at the same time, rejected. In the very earliest days, to judge from Acts, Christians continued to "practice Judaism" and were occupied more with asserting that Jesus of Nazareth was the Messiah than with what their attitude should be toward the law (Acts 2—3). This is true, probably, despite the work of the firebrand Stephen, who was accused of talking against the Temple and the law (Acts 6:13ff.). Although in fact there is no attack on the law as such in Stephen but only on the Temple and on the history of the Jews, nevertheless his attitude implies a detachment from the tradition of Judaism, which could lead to a rejection of the law on which the service of the Temple was based. (Though Stephen was a Hellenist, it is not justifiable on this ground to ascribe his radicalism to liberal, Hellenistic influences, because Acts 6:9ff. makes it clear that the Hellenists opposed him; his attitude arose either from an antilegalistic and anticultic tradition in Judaism itself or under the influence of Jesus' example.) Stephen's wholesale dismissal of the Temple and, by implication, the law, and his condemnation of the people of Israel, were not embraced by the church, which found his attitude too radical and the problem of the relation between law and gospel too complex to be thus summarily solved. This problem emerged fully only later, when numbers of Gentile converts entered the church.

Compromise[4]

To judge from Galatians 2 and Acts 15, there was common agreement among the leaders of the church that salvation was by faith in Jesus Christ and not by works of the law. Difficulties arose when the actualities of a community including Jews and Gentiles had to be faced. Did the acceptance of the gospel imply that Jews should now forswear the observance of the law in order to make it possible for them to enjoy table fellowship, and especially the Eucharist, with Gentile Christians; or, conversely, for the sake of Jewish sensibilities, should Gentile Christians be circumcised and submit to the observance of the law? No problems arose as long as communities were exclusively Gentile or Jewish, and the church tactfully recognized a division in its missionary task. In Jewish Christian churches, while justification was proclaimed on the basis of faith, it was acknowledged that Jewish Christians might obey the law—the mission to the circumcision was assigned to Peter. In Gentile churches obedience to the law was not observed—the uncircumcision was the field of Paul (Gal 2:7–8). This approach to the law was virtually ratified in the Council of Jerusalem, and, either at this council or slightly after, the conditions on which there could be actual intermingling of Gentile and Jewish Christians were laid down (Acts 15:1–30). The exact significance of these conditions has been variously assessed, either as a minimal ethic to be observed by all (but the nature of the conditions and the Jewish attitude toward the law as a unity are against this), or as a safeguard against Gnostic influences (a vague phrase which does not take us very far), or, last, as the Noachian commandments which Judaism laid upon all men—the most probable interpretation. The church virtually followed Judaism at this point, because the presence of Gentiles in many synagogues had long involved the mother faith in the same problem, and it had dealt with it in terms of the Noachian commandments. Here the actualities of the situation which confronted the church have to be grasped:

a) While most Christians were aware that salvation was only in the name of Jesus, they also had to recognize that if there was to be any effective approach to Jewry, the law had to be honored. A movement that sat loose to the law would be condemned among Jews from the outset. Not only would it be difficult for Jews brought up in obedience to the law to reject it (even though they no longer placed their hope of salvation upon it), but Romans shows how naturally they feared moral laxity should the law be abandoned and justification by faith alone be offered (Romans 6). There were understandable reasons why the church was cautious on the question of law and took a *via media*.

b) In Galatians, however, Paul ascribes to certain champions of the law more dishonorable motives. They favored the law from fear of persecution, in order to make a good showing in the flesh (Gal 6:12–13). It was these, who are usually referred to as the Judaizers, who, centered in Jerusalem, invaded the Pauline churches to undo the work of Paul. While it is possible to overemphasize the significance of the Judaizing movement and to give to James, the brother of the Lord, and to Peter a Judaizing role which they never played, it is even more erroneous so to minimize the gulf between Paul and the primitive community as to deny the differences of emphasis between him and Peter and James, and, in particular, the reality of the Judaizing opposition which he faced. Two extreme positions are to be, therefore, avoided—the one which tends to equate the Christianity of the primitive church with that of later Jewish Christianity so as to make it legalistic, and the other which would obliterate any real distinction between the primitive church and Paul. The Judaizing elements eventually led to Jewish Christianity, which demanded the observance of the law from all Christians, and to the Nazoreans, who held fast to the law for Jewish Christians only. Attempts to ascribe to Jewish Christianity a major role in the struggle of the church against Marcion and incipient Gnosticism have not always been convincing.[5]

PAUL AND THE LAW[6]

Terminology

By the term "law" (νόμος) Paul usually means the law of God as contained in the OT, whether he uses "the law" or "law" without the article. This is so even when the law is not defined as the law of Moses

(1 Cor 9:9) or the law of God (Rom 7:22, 25; 8:7). Occasionally, perhaps, it refers to the Decalogue as such (Rom 2:20ff.; 7:7; 13:8–10), but there is no essential difference in Paul between the Decalogue and the rest of the law. Though he uses "the law and the prophets" for the whole of the OT (Rom 3:21), and although "law" may refer to the Pentateuch in isolation, this is not to be pressed, because in 1 Cor 14:21; Rom 3:19, the single term "law" stands for all the OT. The term is also used without reference to the OT. In Rom. 3:27 it seems to mean "dispensation" or "order," the order of faith over against the order of works (διὰ παίου νόμου; τῶν ἔργων; οὐχί, ἀλλὰ διὰ νόμου πίστεως). In Rom 7:21 "Law" is a kind of inexorable necessity. Followed by a genitive, it refers to what we may call a governing principle, either internal (Rom 7:21–25) or "external" (Rom 8:2; Gal 6:2), though this distinction is not to be pressed. In Rom 7:1–3, "law" refers simply to a legal enactment; in Rom 5:13, to a "commandment"; in Rom 2:14–15, to an interior law, written on the heart, but not to be identified with conscience;[7] in Rom 13:8 "the law" is summed up in the commandment to love the neighbor.

Paul never uses the plural "laws," probably because he regards all "law," in and outside Judaism, as a unified whole. In Judaism this takes the form of the law of the OT, and among Gentiles of a "law written on the heart" (Rom 2:15). In both cases "the law" is a living demand of God. This enables Paul almost to personify the law (Rom 3:19; 4:15, 7:1; 1 Cor 9:8); but this personification is found in Judaism also.[8]

Life under the Law and "in Christ"

As a Pharisee, Paul would have regarded the law as the perfect expression of God's will. But his "conversion" compelled him to reassess Judaism and particularly the law. Historical factors lay back of his concentration on the relation of the law to the gospel, rather than on other aspects of the relation between Judaism and Christianity—its cruciality in his previous life as a Jew, and the practical pressure of problems in the church on the relation between Jewish and Gentile Christians. But not only so. It was Paul's very zeal for the law of God that had blinded him to the Son of God and led him to persecute his church (Gal 1:13–14; 3:13; Phil 3:5–6)—the law had proved a veil to hide Christ (2 Cor 3:14–15). This fact governed his reexamination of the law. Its staggering character was reinforced by the difference which Paul found between his life under the law and "in Christ," which his antitheses set forth. The law was powerless; Christ was the power of God (Rom 3:20–21, 27–28; 4:14; 8:3–4; 9:31–32; Gal 2:16, 21; 3:2, 5, 11, 19; 5:4; Phil 3:9). The law condemned; Christ saved from the wrath and curse and death (Rom

3:21–25; 4:15; 5:1–11, 20–21; 6:22; 7:7–13; 8:1–14; 1 Cor 1:30; 3:7; 15:25–27; 2 Cor 5:17–19; Gal 1:3–4; 3:10, 13, 21–22). The yoke of the law was bondage (Gal 3:23; 4:1–7, 21–23; 5:1–3); the service of Christ was freedom (Rom 6:18–22; 8:2, 21). It is in the light of these antitheses, which arose out of his conversion—there being no evidence that before this Paul had found the law weak, condemnatory and tyrannical (Phil 3:6)—that his understanding of the law is to be comprehended. What, then, was Paul's analysis and interpretation of the function of the law?

To begin with, it expresses the will of God, and is holy, just, good, and spiritual (Rom 3:2; 7:12, 14); to be outside the law is to be at enmity with God (Rom 7:12; 8:7). That the law cannot give life does not mean that its demands are evil, but that no one can keep them; it is at the point of obedience, not of demand, that the law is to be judged; and it is an empirical fact that all have sinned and therefore cannot be justified under the law (Rom 3:20, 23). Why?

First, the law usually confronts us as prohibition, expressing the negative aspect of God's will (Rom 7:7). And while the prohibition makes humankind responsible by revealing sin to it, it leaves it powerless in its responsibility.

The law actually incites to sin. This is not merely because prohibition promotes desire but because by confronting humankind with God's demand, it excites what lies behind all sin—namely, the rejection of God's rightful claims, the refusal to recognize dependence on him. And the rebellious desire thus created by the prohibition becomes the base from which sin attacks man. Thus, the law, intrinsically good, subserves the ends of sin, which is intrinsically evil but which is, apart from the opportunity provided by law, impotent. What is good in itself, the law, thus becomes a power for evil. While sin is in a person before he or she encounters the law, it is the latter that brings it to life by presenting the possibility for transgression (Rom 4:15; 5:20; 7:13; Gal 3:19). The law even aims at transgression (Rom 5:20; Gal 3:19).

Nevertheless, the law condemns sin (Rom 2:12; 3:19; 8:1), works wrath (Rom 4:15) and death (1 Cor 15:56; Rom 7:9–10), and if never identified with sin, by Paul comes to be closely connected with it (1 Cor 15:56; Rom 3:20; 4:15; 6:14; 8:3).

But how is it that what was intrinsically good has been thus diverted to the service of sin? Paul would seem to give two answers:

a) The powerlessness of the law is due to its relation to the flesh (Rom 8:3); and part of the meaning of 2 Cor 3:6ff. is that this is due to the external character of the law, which works not from within, but approaches man from without.

b) More important, Paul regards the law as related to the "elemental spirits of the universe" (τὰ στοιχεῖα τοῦ κόσμου; Gal 4:3, 9; Col 2:8, 20). Whether Paul thought of the law as itself one of the demonic principalities and powers, whose might was canceled on the cross (Col 2:13–14), or as an instrument used by demonic-angelic powers (Gal 3:19; 4:1–11; 2 Cor 4:4), which had not only gained control of the law in Judaism but in the Gentile world reigned under the form of pagan gods, is difficult to determine. Under the influence of these powers, as we best understand it, the law had itself come to serve an evil purpose, so that its functions would seem (it has been claimed) to correspond to those of Satan (as prosecutor, executioner, and tempter; Rom 2:12; 3:19, 7:7–8; 2 Cor 3:6ff.).

Role of the Law in History

But if so, has the law any positive role in history? Yes, but only in a relative and transitory sense. Its role is relative because it came into being not of God's primordial purpose, but as a result of his reaction to human sinfulness. God's dealing with man reveals two stages: (*a*) a covenant based on a gracious promise to Abraham (Gal 3:1ff.; Rom 4:20); (*b*) a covenant which followed this based on the law (Gal 3:19, 22:25; Rom 5:20). Thus, the law slipped in between the promise and its fulfillment in Christ, which means that now its writ is at an end. It was allowed to slip in to increase trespass (Rom 3:20; 5:20; 7:7)—that is, to reveal sin as sin—because sin is only seen as sin when it becomes transgression and thus engenders guilt. And the recognition of sin as sin, through the advent of the law, was an advance preparing the way for Christ. In this way the law was a custodian (παιδαγωγός) unto Christ (Gal 3:24); it had quickened the recognition of the need for deliverance by deepening the sense of sin. The merely relative value of the law is apparent also to Paul in its ordination through angels (Gal 3:19)—that is, it was mediated from God indirectly, not directly, as was the promise to Abraham. From its very promulgation it was a phenomenon not capable of lasting (2 Cor 3:13).

Christ the End of the Law

Paul's criticism of the law culminates in the claim that with the coming of Christ the law's dispensation is at an end (Rom 6:14; Gal 3:13, 25; 4:5; 5:1). But it has ceased only for those who have died and risen with Christ (Gal 2:19; Rom 7:4, 6; Col 2:20)—this experience is symbolized in baptism (Gal 2:21; Rom 6). But that Christ is the end of the law (Rom 10:4) signifies, not that the law has come to an end, but that it has reached its final purpose in him; Christ was the goal to which the law was directed (cf. Rom 3:21); he has achieved its destiny. The cessation of the law was associated with the cross (Gal 2:19, 21; 3:13; 5:11; Eph 2:13–14; Col 2:14). But the cross is also the most complete obedience to God, which is precisely the demand of the law (Rom 8:34ff.). To share "in Christ" is to fulfill the law (Rom 3:31). The demand of the law, in its essence, is not violated by the Christian, because it can be gathered up in love (Gal 5:14; 6:2; Rom 8:4; 13:8, 10). Paul is thus no antinomian. And he reveals the same ambiguity on the law as do Jesus and the early church (Rom 3:31; 10:4).

This ambiguity is due not merely to fluidity in the use of the term "law," because it pervades Paul's personal conduct and missionary policy. Thus he allowed Jewish Christians to observe the law (Acts 21:21–26) and himself did so, certainly when necessary, possibly always (1 Cor 7:18; Acts 16:3, 21; 23:6). Certain practical considerations would incline Paul to this; any deviation from orthodoxy would inevitably close the doors of Judaism against him; and an increasingly ironic attitude toward the law emerges in his letters (cf. Gal 4:25; 5:1; Rom 7:12, 14, 8:3; 2 Cor 3:14–18).

It became clear to Paul early in his ministry that obedience to the law of Christ sometimes demanded obedience to the old law (1 Cor 9:19–20) In giving rules to churches Paul even drew upon the law (1 Cor 9:8, 13). Nevertheless, he did so parenthetically, and he finally appeals to a commandment of the Lord (1 Cor 9:14). Here, as elsewhere, the law is understood in the light of Christ.

This is why scholars have, on the whole, been loath to admit that Paul understood Christ in terms of the law but, only and always, the law in terms of Christ. But the possibility is not to be ruled out that much in Paul's understanding of his Lord as the preexistent agent of creation, for example (Col 1:15ff.), may be due to his ascription to Christ of attributes ascribed by Judaism to the law. It is certain that Christ, in his person and words, has taken the place of the law in Paul's life and thought and in this sense has become for him a new Torah. The influence of the Reformation, because of its emphasis on the gospel as justification by faith, makes it difficult for us to do justice to this aspect of Paul's thought. His criticisms of the Law belong chiefly to his polemic letters, Galatians and Romans; nor must they be minimized. Paul did come to believe that to accept life under the law as the means to salvation was to enter upon an impossible road marked either by despair at failure or by overweening, insensitive pride (ὕβρις, καύχημα) at achievement, but this was so only because the light of Christ had revealed the more excellent way to him.

His criticism of the law is a consequence of his faith in Christ, but not its center. Polemic and the historic circumstances attending the emergence of Christianity have somewhat hidden the fact, but the center of Paulinism lies not in the relation of gospel and law, but in Paul's awareness that with the coming of Christ the age to come was becoming present fact, the proof of which was the advent of the Spirit: it lies in those conceptions of standing under the judgment and mercy of a new Torah, Christ, of dying and rising with this same Christ, of undergoing a new exodus in him, and so being incorporated into a new Israel, the community of the Spirit.

THE LETTER TO THE HEBREWS

The term "law" refers here again to the law of the OT, even in Heb 7:16, where it may mean "order." The plural "laws" occurs only in quotations from the OT in 8:10; 10:16. Unlike Paul, who was concerned with the law as a system of prohibitions and commandments designed to make man righteous and with the moral problem thus created for a Pharisee, Hebrews was concerned with the problem of worship, of access to the presence of the Holy God, which the priesthood and sacrifices were designed to achieve. Hence the law is significant for Hebrews as it is related to the priesthood and sacrificial system (the reference to foods in 13:9 is secondary). This relation is twofold. The law was, on the one hand, the foundation on which the priesthood and sacrifices were built because it had ordained them (although 7:11 makes the law almost dependent on the priesthood, this must not be taken to mean that God was not the source of the law). On the other hand, because the law was broken the media for expiation, the priesthood and sacrifices, became necessary for continued life under the law (7:5, 11–12; 8:4; 10:8). How, then, does Hebrews regard the law?

First, like the rest of the OT, the law was the word of God. Although mediated by angels—this mediation implied its inferiority (as in Gal 3:19)—it was valid. There is nothing in Hebrews comparable with the radical dismissal of the Temple and, by implication, the law in Stephen (Acts 7:47–50); no suggestion that in the past the law should not have been obeyed. Moreover, the ordinances of the law had a positive value. They pointed upward to what was already eternally existent in the mind of God, and forward to a real fulfillment of that after which they grope in the future. The Temple, the priesthood, the sacrifices, the covenant, all are copies of the real (8:5) and foreshadowings of better things to come (10:1). Thus the old covenant, including the law, was not false but imperfect; was premonitory rather than satisfying. The force of this can be gauged only by reading the whole of Hebrews, but especially 7:1—11:1. Here the merging of Platonic and eschatological concepts is implied.

Nevertheless, the critical attitude of Hebrews toward the Law is noteworthy. The dispensation of the Law had been ineffective. Priest and sacrifice had failed in their aim of bringing men near to God by the cleansing of their consciences (7:15; 9:14; 10:4). This was so because: (*a*) the OT ordinances were only outward arrangements, which could not effectively deal with sin and guilt (9:9–10); (*b*) the priests, the human agents of reconciliation, were themselves mortal and sinful and could not, therefore, really be effective (5:3; 7:27); and (*c*) the very repetitive nature of the sacrificial system showed its inefficacy (10:1ff.). Moreover, that the OT itself looked forward to better things to come (Jeremiah 31) *ipso facto* implied and recognized its incompleteness (Heb 8:8–12).

Thus, though Paul and Hebrews are not concerned with the same aspects of the law, they agree in much of their understanding of it. The difference between them is clear. In Hebrews the law is especially connected with the priesthood (7:11). A change in priesthood meant a change in the law (7:12). Christ is a new kind of priest after the order of Melchizedek. This priesthood was announced to Abraham before the Levitical priesthood existed, and the latter has not abrogated it. Had the Levitical priesthood procured access to God, the rise of a priest after the order of Melchizedek, as was predicted in Ps 110:4, would have been unnecessary. But the antiquating of the cultus through the high priesthood of Christ carries with it the supersession of the law. The argument is very similar to that applied directly to the law by Paul in Gal 3:17–18, except that for Paul it is the abrogation of the law in Christ that implies the supersession of the cultus. For both Paul and Hebrews, moreover, the Christian dispensation is a higher order than that of Judaism; but the element of discontinuity between them may be more marked in Paul because he found in Christ what Judaism could not give, whereas Hebrews found in Judaism what pointed forward to Christ (but see Rom 3:21).

THE LETTER OF JAMES

This letter is concerned with the relation of faith and works (not faith and law, as is Paul; 2:14ff.), and the term "law," which occurs ten times, refers not primarily to the OT law as such. In 1:25 the "law," with which James is occupied, is defined as the "perfect law . . . of liberty," and the context makes it clear that this is a summary description of the Christian message—that is, the "Word" referred to in 1:21–23, the gospel itself. Does this mean that James understands the gospel in terms of law? This possibility, which is enforced by the explicit injunctions in 2:1ff.; 3:1ff.; and so forth, is offset by the emphasis on liberty or freedom in the phrase "perfect law of liberty." The "Word" demands obedience, but "in freedom."

The law of freedom is further defined in 2:8ff. as the "royal law," which in the light of 2:9 consists of the Golden Rule. This rule is to be obeyed in all its demands, but these are not expressed in specific directions for conduct. This is the implication of 4:11ff. This passage echoes Rom 14:4, which asserts that each person stands or falls before his or her own master—that is, is not subject to any fixed law which can be discerned by outsiders and which prescribes a set course of action. He or she is free to decide what should be done, under the constraint of love or of Christ; to judge another's action is to presume to know the meaning of that constraint for him or her, to judge the law of love itself; and this very judgment is itself a transgression of that law.

Thus James, too, despite his sane earthiness, takes seriously the principle of freedom from specific enactments and in this is like Paul, as he is also like Paul in his ethical seriousness (1:22ff.; 2:14ff.). Pauline controversies over the Jewish law as such are outside the purview of James, although the possibility is a real one that, especially in 2:14–26, he may be attacking certain misunderstandings of Paul which were current in his circles. The method of argument suggests this.

THE FOURTH GOSPEL

Here "law" (νόμος) is used in four ways: (a) a specific commandment (7:19, 23); (b) the system governing the administration of justice among Jews, though this was for them part of the law of God (7:51; 8:17; 18:31; 19:7); (c) the Pentateuch (1:45), the law of Moses (7:23), or the law given by Moses (7:19) or the law given by God through Moses (1:17), which was the authoritative basis for Jewish life; (d) the whole of the OT (10:34; 12:34; 15:25; and probably 7:49).

Though an intimate knowledge of rabbinic interpretation of the law appears, the evangelist looks at the law from the outside also. For instance, 8:17, where he uses a phrase ("In your law it is written") used by Gentiles in discussions with Jews; 1:17, where grace and truth, particularly as associated with the law in the OT (Pss 25:10; 85:11; 89:15), are claimed to be in Christ, not in the law; and 5:39, where the true quest for eternal life in Christ is contrasted with the misguided quest for him in the law, point to a major theme of the gospel—namely, the superiority of the revelation of God given in Christ over that given in the law.

It is this point of view that largely governs the symbolic forms under which Christ is presented. In 2:6–10 the water of the dispensation of the law, or again its inferior wine (2:10), is contrasted with the wine that Christ brings. Water, a symbol of the law in Judaism, is applied to Christ in 4:12–14; he is the living water; the evanescent manna, which probably here (through its association with bread, a regular symbol for it) stands for the law, is contrasted with the true bread, which Christ brings (chapter 6); similarly, Christ becomes the light (8:12; 9:5; 12:35), the way, the truth, and the life (14:6). Christ is the source of the true light (1:9); he is the true bread (6:32), the true judgment (8:16), the true vine (15:1)—that is, Christ introduces us to the world of realities. The law, it is implied, dealt only with shadows. Here the Fourth Gospel and Hebrews show an affinity. But most noteworthy is the ascription to Christ, as the Word, of attributes Judaism had reserved for the law. Preexistence (1:1–2), association with God (1:1), sonship (1:14), light and life (1:4), creative activity in the beginning (1:3)—all these are ascribed to Christ as the Word, just as they are ascribed to wisdom in the OT and Judaism[9] and to the law. The prologue, no less than the rest of the Gospel, thus proclaims the reality of the revelation in Christ as superseding that given in the law.

We have seen the parallelism between John and Hebrews. The concept of the law as a shadow is not explicit in John, however, although it is implicit. Does John ascribe a further positive value to the law? In 1:45 this would seem to be the case: the law has borne witness to Christ. To deny Christ is to deny the Scriptures (5:39 ff.); and the law is fulfilled in his ministry (8:17; 10:34; 12:34; 15:25). But this fulfillment, while it lends partial validity to the Law, also spells its end. For the Fourth Gospel, as for Paul—even though it is not concerned as was he with the law as a rule for life, as commandment—loyalty to Christ has replaced obedience to the law as the demand of God (5:19ff.; 7:17), and this means sharing in his love (13:34; 15:12–15).

CONCLUSION

The NT documents throughout reveal the same ambiguity in evaluation of the law that we found in Jesus. Just as they reveal a parallelism between Moses and Christ which is sometimes antithetic (John and Hebrews) and sometimes synthetic (Matthew and Paul, broadly speaking), so they find in the law both the passing shadow of the gospel to come and that which is completed or fulfilled "in Christ." They all affirm that the law, insofar as it is the expression of the holy will of God, remains valid, radicalized, and at the same time relativized by the absolute claim of love.[10]

13

Conscience and Its Use in the New Testament

Conscience is roughly, and mainly, a witness within man which condemns his Sin [ἡ συνείδησις, τὸ συνειδότος, ἡ συνέσις, τὸ συνειδός]. Other nuances in its meaning, such as "consciousness," will appear below.

BACKGROUND OF THE TERM[1]

Not derived from the OT

In the Septuagint (LXX) συνείδησις, "conscience," occurs once only (Eccl 10:20). The underlying Hebrew term is מדע rendered in the Revised Standard Version (*RSV*) by "thought" (elsewhere the Hebrew word occurs in 2 Chr 1:10–12; Dan 1:17, is translated by συνέσις, and simply means "knowledge"). Conscience, as the whole context shows, here merely means "the mind" or "the inner, secret place of thought." Codex Sinaiticus reads συνείδησιν instead of εἴδησιν at Eccl 42:18. But since we do not know the underlying Hebrew, the reading of Sinaiticus cannot safely be regarded as pertinent. Most significant is Wis 17:10. Here conscience emerges with a moral connotation, as a witness within man, which condemns his sin. This approximates to what we find later in the NT. At this point, it should be emphasized that the Wisdom of Solomon shows marked Hellenistic influences and that the emergence of the term "conscience," with a moral significance, points to the Hellenistic world as its source. This is not surprising. Hebrew thinking is theocentric, not introspective. It emphasizes God as king and man as his obedient servant. The obedience demanded by God has been revealed to man from a source outside him in the Law and the prophets. Not knowledge of the self (including the conscience) but the fear of the Lord was the beginning of wisdom (Prov 1:7; 9:10). Hence there was no urge to examine the inner motives of man's behavior or to concentrate on what might be called subjective psychological phenomena. In such a soil, the development of an examined theory of conscience was not to be expected. Similarly in rabbinic Judaism, where again the Law given on Sinai was the light of men, the absence of any term corresponding to "conscience" is natural. The concept of the "good impulse" (יצר הטרב) affords no real parallel to conscience; in any case, this was far less developed than that of the "evil impulse" (צר רע'). This is not to assert that the OT and Judaism were unaware of the phenomena which gave rise to the idea of "conscience," but that they lacked the theoretical interest to interpret them psychologically or anthropologically.[2]

Hellenistic Origin

The Hellenistic world, then, seems to be suggested as the background of the term "conscience" (συνείδησις); and it has been customary to connect it specifically with Stoicism. Does the evidence support the Stoic derivation of "conscience," which most NT exegetes seem to assume without question? Stobaeus, who noted down in the sixth century c.e., the most interesting passages that he had ever read, including those dealing with conscience (though the term he used was τὸ συνειδότος), refers to Periander (625–585 b.c.e.) and Bias (550 b.c.e.) as having used the term "conscience." But there is little doubt that he was mistaken in this. The term first occurs in a passage in Democritus (460–361 b.c.e.), whose philosophy was akin to that of Epicurus (342–270 b.c.e.) and whose works were praised by Cicero. The passage reads: "Some men, not knowing the dissolution of mortal nature, suffer wretchedly throughout their lifetime from distress and fear because of their consciousness of the evildoing in their lives, making false speculations about the time after death" (Democritus 297).[3] Here "conscience" (συνείδησις) has a moral connotation: it consists of the consciousness of wrongdoing, which causes man to spend his days in fears and anxieties, and leads him to form false ideas of the time after death, since man does not know that dissolution awaits him. The usage, however, is not precisely defined. The term next appears in Chrysippus, a celebrated Stoic philosopher born ca. 280 b.c.e. Words of his are cited by Diogenes Laërtius 200–250 (c.e.) 7.85: "It is suitable [or fitting] for every living thing to be *aware of* its own structure and of itself." "Conscience" is here predicated of all living creatures and not only of man: it seems merely to designate a creature's self-awareness and is without moral connotation. After Chrysippus we again note the appearance of "conscience" (συνείδησις) with moral significance in Wis 17:10 (see above), and in Philodemus (50 b.c.e.) *Rhetoric* 2.40, and in Dionysius of Halicarnassus (died 7 b.c.e.) *Ant.* 8.1.3, where conscience disturbs Coriolanus in his approach to the Volsci, whom he had often treated brutally in battle. In Diodorus Siculus (a contemporary of Julius

Caesar and Augustus) we find the term at 4.65.7, but here also it may mean "consciousness." In all these passages, with the exception of that by Chrysippus the Stoic συνείδησις has a moral reference.

Another Stoic, Epictetus (first century C.E.), is supposed to have employed the term in a famous passage which reads: "When we were children our parents handed us over to a nursery slave who should watch over us everywhere lest harm befall us. But when we were grown up, God hands us over to the conscience [συνειδήσει] implanted in us, to protect us. Let us not in any way despise its protection for should we do so we shall be both ill-pleasing to God and have our own conscience [συνείδοτι] as an enemy." This is the only passage in Epictetus as far as is known where συνείδησις occurs, and its ascription to him rests on the slenderest grounds; most scholars do not now regard the passage as authentic. But the ascription to Stoics of the term "conscience" has become very fashionable, as we saw. Stoics are said to have coined the term. Nevertheless, apart from its use by Chrysippus (and he used it without a moral connotation) there is no reason at all, to judge from the Greek sources, for regarding the term as peculiarly Stoic. Must we conclude that the Stoic origin of the term must be rejected? Not only do the Greek lexicographical data lead to this, but it is what we should expect. The term "conscience" (συνείδησις), as the passages cited already reveal and as subsequent treatment will confirm, has undertones of emotion, anxiety or concern, which little comport with the Stoic ideal of self-sufficiency (ἀπάθεια). Moreover, not only is "conscience" not a Stoic term, but also some claim that there is no evidence that it was significant in Greek philosophy outside Stoicism. Thus it does not occur in Aristotle's *Ethics*. Consequently, they turn to popular Hellenistic thought for the origin of the term.[4]

Usage in Latin Writers

The term is found in writers of Greek, such as Philo and Josephus, with a developed moral connotation, as in Paul, so that in Hellenistic circles it was in literary circulation in the time of the Apostle. Latin authors, however, use it far more frequently than do the Greeks. Cicero (106 B.C.E.), who used the term *conscientia* seventy-five times, and Seneca (born a few years before Christ) connect "conscience" with Epicureanism, which counseled the avoidance of wrongdoing for fear of the reproaches of conscience (Cicero *De Finibus* 1.45; 1.51;; 2.53–54; Seneca *Epistles* 43.5; 105.7–9), which had the role of accuser (Seneca *Epistles* 43.5; 28.9–10), and the cultivation of a "good conscience" (Seneca *On a Happy Life*

19.1; 20.5). Moreover, a connection has been traced between the idea of conscience in Epicurus and Euripides, on the one hand, and in Philo, on the other.[5] As in Epicureanism, so in Cynicism, the Latin authors find conscience emphasized. It, rather than fear of men or of gods, is the rule and motive for conduct (Cicero *On the Nature of the Gods* 3.85): it is not only punitive but also directive (Horace [65 B.C.E.]: *Epodes* 5.29; *Epistle* 1.61). It is his conscience that also gives to the Cynic his authority: he aims so to live that his conscience itself has become his public, he lives under his conscience always as in the public eye (Seneca *Epistle* 43.5; *On a Happy Life* 20.3–5; Epictetus 3.22.94 [τὸ συνειδός]).

When we ask whether the Latin writers reveal in Stoicism an emphasis on conscience, the answer is in the negative. Seneca shows that Athenodorus, a Stoic teacher of Augustus, used the term "a good conscience" (*On Tranquility of Mind* 3.4); he also ascribes the use of "conscience" to Musonius, the teacher of Epictetus the Stoic (*Epistle* 52.9). Seneca himself uses the term in *On Benefits* 4.34.3, where the necessity of arriving at a strong conscience is urged. This enables a person to overcome all timidity, so that he is no longer at the mercy of the opinions of others. But the use of "conscience" in Stoicism cannot have been central, and whenever the term does occur in Stoic connections, it undergoes modification. Thus the strong conscience, desired by Seneca, really signifies strong character. The Latin writers, therefore, lend no support to the view that conscience was a peculiarly Stoic doctrine, while they suggest that in its Latin form at least, conscience was a concept much employed in literary circles. Two explanations of this are possible: (*a*) that Latin writers were closer to popular usage than the Greek, and had borrowed a popular term; (*b*) that many Greek documents from the Hellenistic period have been lost to us, so that we should be prepared to find in Latin writers much that had already appeared in Greek sources no longer extant. These Latin writers reveal that the term "conscience" was known to Epicureanism, Cynicism, and—although not native or even congenial to it—Stoicism. The use of "conscience" by Stoic writers suggests that the needs of moral guidance overrode the niceties of philosophy. Thus Seneca, who deplored making the fear of conscience the motive for conduct, yet inconsistently in his instruction of Nero himself appealed to it (*De Clementiae* 1.1.1). Probably the term "conscience" was familiar in the teaching of popular moralists. While it was not in use in the technical language of the "schools" of philosophy, it was well established perhaps in more popular philosophic-moralistic teaching among Epicureans, Cynics, and even at times Stoics. This view, while it rests mainly on the assumption that Latin authors do reflect Greek usage, finds some support at least in the first century from Philo and Josephus, who can hardly be claimed to have been influenced by Paul (this although Philo prefers the term τὸ συνειδός to ἡ συνείδησις).

MEANING IN GENERAL USE

The term "conscience" (συνείδησις) is to be understood in conjunction with a number of similar words and phrases sometimes used interchangeably. These are τὸ συνειδότος, τὸ συνειδός, σύνεσις, αὐτῷ συνιστορεῖν τι, αὐτῷ συνειδέναι τι. All these stem from the verb σύνοιδα, which means "I know in common with." It usually implies knowledge about another person which can be used in witness for or against him. Hence σύνοιδα came to mean "I bear witness." Of particular importance is the phrase αὐτῷ συνειδέναι τι, which means "to share knowledge with oneself," "to know with oneself," to be a witness for or against oneself," because συνείδησις (like τὸ συνειδός and σύνεσις) is its substantival equivalent. The necessity for finding a single substantive to convey the meaning of a phrase would be natural. It is also easy to see why συνείδησις and συνειδός, because of their greater similarity in form and sound to αὐτῷ συνειδέναι τι, would be more likely to be chosen for this than σύνεσις. It is more difficult to understand why συνείδησις should have been preferred to συνειδός. Possibly συνείδησις is the wider term, including all senses of the verb σύνοιδα while συνειδός was restricted to ἐμαντῷ σύνοιδα. But this is uncertain. By the time of the NT, in any case, συνείδησις was the most popular term for expressing what was conveyed by the phrase αὐτῷ συνειδέναι τι.

An examination of the pertinent passages suggests the following connotations for the term:

a) Conscience is a faculty implanted in man as part of his very nature, so that it functions by necessity as an expression of his very constitution. Thus in Xenophon's account of the trial of Socrates, the latter believes that those induced to bear false witness against him will, *of necessity,* suffer the pangs of conscience ("It is necessary that they should be conscience striken about much impiety and wickedness" [*Apology* 24]).

b) This faculty is a necessary characteristic of every man. Thus Polybius (204 B.C.E.—), using the term σύνεσις, which is the equivalent of συνείδησις, claims that there is "no witness so fearful nor accuser so terrible as that conscience which dwells in the soul of every man" (18.43.13).

c) Often the implanting of conscience is, by implication if not explicitly, traced to God. Thus Xenophon (*Cyropaedia* 1.6.4) connects it with prayer: "Owing to that very regard do you not come to the gods with a better heart to pray, and do you not expect more confidently to obtain what you pray for, because you feel conscious of never having neglected them?" Democritus asserts that in the popular mind, conscience is connected with punishment, presumably at the hands of the gods after death. Euripides (480 B.C.E.), using the term συνέσις, gives to conscience the function of the Eumenides or Erinyes, the avenging deities of Greek mythology. (These were concerned with punishing the wicked both in this world and after death, those who had been disobedient to parents, disrespectful toward the aged, guilty of perjury, murder, etc. The Eumenides were consequently dreaded by gods and men.) Menelaus: "What aileth thee? What sickness ruineth thee?" Orestes: "Conscience [ἡ συνέσις]—to know I have wrought a fearful deed." (*Orestes* 395–96.) The equation of conscience with these figures is, therefore, highly significant. The same equation probably occurs in Diodorus Siculus (4.65.7), who uses the phrase "on account of conscience" (διὰ τὴν συνείδησιν). Menander (342–291 B.C.E.) called "conscience" a god, but we cannot gather from his words what he meant by the term: "To all mortals conscience is a god" (*Gnomai Monostichoi* 654). Philo does not make explicit the divine origin of conscience, but probably assumes it (*On the Decalogue* 37; see below).

d) As the above references reveal, conscience comes into activity in connection with a person's deeds, and particularly his bad ones (as in Xenophon *Apology* 24).

e) Primarily, if not exclusively, it is a person's own acts that concern the conscience. In agreement with the verbal form αὐτῷ συνειδέναι τι which it represents, conscience, immediately on the commission of a wrong, comes to know something with the person himself and bears witness against him. The operation of conscience is, so to speak, "automatic."

f) While it is conceivable that conscience could denote a constant state of criticism of a person's character (this is especially suggested perhaps by the identification of conscience with the Eumenides, although they, too, become avengers of particular acts of wrong); nevertheless, it is specific acts of wrongdoing, not so much a continued or habitual condition of character, that call forth conscience. And usually, since conscience has been "called forth," it follows naturally that it has reference most frequently to past acts.

g) Stirred into activity, of necessity, by wrongdoing, conscience emerges as a pain. Philo reveals this: "For every soul has for its birth-fellow and house-mate a monitor [ἔλεγχος] whose way is to admit nothing that calls for censure, whose nature is ever to hate evil and love virtue, who is its accuser [κατήγορος] and its judge in one. If he be once roused as accuser he censures, accuses and puts the soul to shame, and again as judge, he instructs, admonishes and exhorts it to change its ways. And if he has the strength to persuade, he rejoices and makes peace. But if he cannot, he makes war to the bitter end, never leaving it alone by day or night, but plying it with stabs and deadly wounds until he breaks the thread of its miserable and ill-starved life" (*On the Decalogue* 87).[6] The term used is ἔλεγχος, but it is to be identified here with συνείδησις. Here conscience (the convictor) appears as a pain. Similarly, Plutarch describes conscience (τὸ συνειδός = συνείδησις). He quotes first Euripides's *Orestes* 395–96: "My conscience [σύνεσις], since I know I've done a dreadful deed, like an ulcer in the flesh, leaves behind it in the soul regret which ever continues to wound and prick it. For the other pangs reason does away with, but regret is caused by reason itself, since the soul, together with its feeling of shame, is stung and chastised by itself. For as those who shiver with ague or burn with fevers are more distressed and pained than those who suffer the same discomforts through heat or cold from a source outside the body, so the pangs which Fortune brings, coming as it were, from a source without, are lighter to bear; but that lament, None is to blame for this but me myself, which is chanted over one's errors, coming as it does from within, makes the pain even heavier by reason of the disgrace one feels" (*On Tranquility of Mind* 476f-477a).[7] Xenophon asserted that no one who suffered the pangs of conscience could again be accounted happy (*Anabasis* 2.5.7).

h) The passage from Philo depicts conscience also as an agent of pain—that is, to inflict pain—as, by implication, do other sections by the same author (for instance, *Frg.* 11.p.652; *QDSI* I.128 (τὸ συνειδός); and possibly *QDPIS*.27). Plutarch refers to the chastising and gnawing of conscience in *Publicola* IV.99b. That it could be equated with the dread Eumenides speaks for itself.

i) Conscience is said to suffer pain (*The Orphic Hymn* 63.3–5 [τὸ συνειδός]; Dionysius of Halicarnassus in *On Thucydides* 8.4; μηδὲ μιαίνειν τὴν αὐτοῦ συνείδησιν—of Thucydides' care and conscientiousness as a historian; he refused to pollute his conscience). Perhaps the most widespread concept of conscience in the Hellenistic period can best be gleaned from the fragment wrongly attributed to Epictetus already cited above. There συνείδησις, conscience, implanted by God, is by implication compared with the nursery slave παιδαγωγός): its function was not so much to teach morals as to protest against immorality by inflicting pain designed to safeguard good conduct. We must assume that the writers of the NT, who had connections with the Hellenistic world, would be at least familiar with this concept. But before we turn to the NT we must notice certain issues not yet faced—namely, whether the activity of conscience is concerned with the acts of others as well as of its subject; whether it is a guide for the future as well as a judge of the past; and, finally, whether any positive connotation can be given to the concept of a "good conscience"—in fact, whether such a thing exists at all or whether the phrase merely signifies the absence of "conscience." Since we are dealing with a concept noted in popular Greco-Roman philosophy, not with that of the schools, no "scientific" or philosophical accuracy and refinement in the use of the term should be expected.[8]

IN THE NEW TESTAMENT

The NT usage further attests the Hellenistic derivation and affinities of συνείδησις. On the one hand, in the four Gospels, which are concerned with a tradition that however much under Hellenistic influences was primarily Hebraic or Palestinian, the term does not occur. But perhaps we are to see synonyms of it in the term "heart" in Mark 3:5, and, more doubtfully, in Mark 6:52; Matt 15:10–20 (here "heart" seems in accordance with much Semitic usage to be the equivalent of "mind" because it is the source of "thoughts," although in John 3:20–21 "heart" seems to be identical with "conscience"). Again, we may have circumlocutions for συνείδησις: in Matt 6:23, the "light within"; in Luke 12:57 the reference may be to "conscience," although the appeal here too may be to the rational faculty in man. On the other hand, συνείδησις appears thirty times in the rest of the NT, always in documents which were wide open to the influences of the Hellenistic world. There are fourteen occurrences in Paul, six in the pastorals, five in Hebrews, three in 1 Peter, two in Acts. Thus among NT writers Paul first used the term and most frequently; perhaps it was he who gave it prominence in Christian usage.[9]

Pauline Usage

The term occurs first in 1 Corinthians 8, a chapter dealing with the eating of food offered to idols. On the ground of their superior knowledge that idols to which the food had been dedicated were literally nonentities, so that the dedication of food to them was without significance, "strong"

Christians were tempted to ignore the scruples of their weaker brethren and override their objections. But Paul insists that for them to do so would submit the weak to pains of conscience and actually injure or wound that faculty in them. To avoid this pain and injury to the weak, the strong should forever avoid eating meat sacrificed to idols. But in 1 Corinthians 10, more cautious than in 1 Corinthians 8, Paul recognizes that the strong are not to be fettered in their freedom by the weak. As a general rule, a man should be guided by freedom; but he should pay respect, not to the weak brother's opinion, but to his pains of conscience. This means that, while the bludgeoning of the strong by the weak is not to be countenanced, because this would be tyranny, nevertheless, consideration for the pain of the weak becomes a principle of conduct.

1 Corinthians 8 and 10 reveal, first, that Paul recognizes a variety in conscience. The weak conscience may be due to lack of knowledge (1 Cor 8:7), force of habit (1 Cor 8:7), or lack of ability to withstand the example of others (1 Cor 8:10); it is not merely feeble and vulnerable but has a stronger connotation: the weak conscience does not have the force necessary to act according to knowledge. (The concept has been claimed to be original with Paul, but we meet the contrast between the strong and the weak in Latin authors. The sage is strong; in his strength he is tempted to become presumptuous, puffed up. And the origin of the Pauline contrast between the strong and the weak in Corinth has been found in Stoicism. Others prefer to find a parallel to the Pauline contrast in such passages as Matt 18:1ff.)

The discussion raises the question whether conscience, in these passages, has a future reference. At least at first glance, in 1 Cor 8:10; 10:25ff, "conscience" seems to be a regulative principle. The weak brother, contemplating the strong brother in 1 Cor 8:10, must have been cogitating over the problem of eating food offered to idols and is dissuaded from this by his "conscience"; so too in 1 Cor 10:28. The translation of 10:25 is difficult: how are we to understand the phrase $\delta\iota\grave{\alpha}$ $\tau\grave{\eta}\nu$ $\sigma\upsilon\nu\epsilon\acute{\iota}$-$\delta\eta\sigma\iota\nu$, "on the ground of conscience"? It is possible to take this verse to mean: Eat any food that is sold in the meat market without letting scruples of conscience induce you to ask questions about it—that is, avoid deliberating over the act beforehand in terms of your conscience. This implies that conscience has a future reference. But 1 Cor 10:25 may merely mean: Because of conscience avoid asking questions; because as long as you do not know the source of the meat, you can eat without suffering pangs of conscience afterward. Nevertheless, unless we are to draw a very rigid distinction between the scruples, at least discomforting if not painful, which a man has before doing wrong and the pain which follows his act, it is exceedingly difficult to exclude all future reference from conscience in both these sections. Rom 13:5 may be adduced in support of this: "Therefore one must be subject [to the state], not only to avoid God's wrath but also for the sake of conscience." Submission to the state, Paul has argued, is a necessity, not merely because the state has power to enforce its demands. This power is derived from God (Paul is not here dealing with evil governments as such), and therefore commands a rightful obedience. To obey the state, therefore, will not bring on the pangs of conscience. For the sake of conscience, therefore, it should be obeyed. But it is difficult not to understand that the conscience has been informed about the nature of the state before obedience to it can be "according to conscience" or "on the ground of conscience"; the future reference can hardly be ruled out completely. Conscience in Paul, therefore, is at least on the way to becoming a regulative principle.[8]

This raises the question of the relationship between "the conscience" and "the mind" or "reason." Perhaps the difficulty of deciding whether conscience in Paul has a future reference arises from his failure to clarify the distinction between these. That he does distinguish them appears from Rom 2:14–15. Here three things are distinguished: all people are presumed to have (a) a law written on the heart, a moral awareness (here Paul may be influenced by Stoic concepts, although he would not subscribe to the Stoic view that for those who recognized the "natural law" it was possible to fulfill it); (b) the conscience; (c) reason or thought. But in Rom 14:5 the "mind" ($\nu o \hat{\upsilon} \varsigma$) seems to have taken the place of what in 1 Cor 8:10 is the "conscience." And in 1 Corinthians, Paul has not been careful at all to distinguish between reason and conscience; hence the problems of exegesis. It cannot be sufficiently emphasized that "conscience" was not a fully examined concept in Paul's day, and that he did not introduce scientific consistency into his use of it, although he did refine it.

1 Corinthians 8 and 10 show the seriousness of ignoring the claims of conscience, be they regarded as prevenient scruples or as retrospective pain. The effect of the inconsiderate conduct of the strong is to defile the conscience of the weak (1 Cor 8:7), so that he or she is destroyed; that is, led to emulate the strong and to ignore his or her own awareness of what is right, the weak Christian is likely later to lose his faith and relapse into pagan ways. To ignore conscience—that is, to lay oneself open deliberately to its pains and not to escape from them as frequently as possible—is to develop a resistance to it; to wound the conscience so as to

blunt its attacks, to become "acclimatized" to conscience so that its impact becomes dulled—this is to be destroyed. This raises the question as to the exact meaning of the phrase "a good conscience." Is its significance merely negative—that is, does it simply denote absence of pain—or has it a positive sense?

In 1 Cor 10:28–29, the implication is that conscience passes judgment, not on the subject's own acts only but on those of others also. This is a meaning not to be ruled out in 2 Cor 4:2; 5:11, although here the term συνείδησις may merely signify "consciousness" or "awareness." In 2 Cor 4:2 every person, Jew and Gentile, is credited with a moral discernment which assesses the conduct of others "in the sight of God"— that is, the assessment is analogous to that of God himself. Thus there should be no criticism of Paul's exercise of his ministry. That the gospel does not find acceptance with some is due to the fact that their minds (τὰ νοήματα) have been blinded by the god of this world; these are the perishing (οἳ ἀπολλυμένοι). The same verb is used of what happens to the weak Christians in 1 Cor 8:11. The blinded minds of unbelievers (νοήματα τῶν ἀπίστων) might be a synonym for the "perished consciences," as if νοήματα and συνείδησις were equivalent: in this case συνείδησις in 2 Cor 4:2 should be rendered by something like "thoughts" (see above on the lack of precision in Paul's usage). The same applies to 2 Cor 5:11: here "conscience" is the subject of "knowledge" or "awareness." Nevertheless, it is possible that in 2 Cor 4:2 the reference is to conscience in all its forms, and that in 2 Cor 5:11 the reference is specifically to the individual consciences of people, not to their intellects (the plural "consciences" occurs only here).

The other places where Paul uses συνείδησις may be claimed to fall well within the Hellenistic usage traced on p. 244. But certain associations are noteworthy: (*a*) In Rom 2:14–15; 13:5, conscience is associated both with necessity (ἀνάγκη) and with "the wrath" (ἡ ὀργή). In Rom. 2:14–15 "conscience" is a property of man by nature or necessity, and its operation, in part at least, insofar as it is a pain following upon acts of wrongdoing, may be regarded as the inner counterpart of the process of "wrath" which Paul found at work in the natural order and society (Rom 1:18). (In 2 Cor 1:12 "conscience" is used absolutely and calls for no comment.) (*b*) In Rom 9:1 the witness of conscience is conjoined with that of the Holy Spirit and Christ. This is of the utmost importance for Paul's estimate of "conscience." There can be little doubt that Paul derived the term "conscience" from his opponents at Corinth. It was no favorite of his, and in Rom 14:15, when he is dealing with precisely the same problem as in 1 Cor 8:10, he avoids the term. In 1 Corinthians, following his policy of being all things to all men, he had used his opponents' term. But that he did not give to "conscience" the overriding significance in ethics that they did appears in 1 Cor 4:4. There, although he uses the verbal form (ἐμαυτῷ σύνοιδα), not the substantival (συνείδησις), he makes it clear that conscience is not his ultimate court of appeal. This is Christ himself. Open to corrupting influences, as it is, conscience is to be quickened by the Spirit and enlightened by Christ.

In Non-Pauline Letters

Outside the Pauline letters, "conscience" emerges in 1 Peter, the pastorals, Hebrews, all of which probably reflect late Hellenistic literary usage. In 1 Pet 2:19, συνείδησις probably simply means "consciousness"; the *RSV* is right (over against Selwyn) in rendering "mindful of God." So in 3:16, "conscience" refers to a consciousness of innocence of any misconduct which might justify the criticism of outsiders. The occurrence in 3:21 is difficult. The *RSV* (so also *Moffatt*), which takes baptism to signify on its human side the prayer for a clean conscience is probably to be rejected, the correct translation being that "baptism is the appeal made to God by a good conscience." The context does not allow us to define precisely what this means. Significant is the emergence here of the phrase "a good conscience." This is a mark of the pastorals and of the literature of the end of the first century and the beginning of the second (1 Tim 1:5, 19 ["good conscience"]; 3:9; 2 Tim 1:3 ["clear conscience"]; 1 Tim 4:2 and Tit 1:15 refer to the corruption or searing of conscience). See also, for example, Acts 23:1; 1 *Clem.* 41.1; Pol. 5.3; 2 *Clem.* 16.4.

Noteworthy in the pastorals are: (*a*) The close relationship between conscience and loyalty to the faith (1 Tim 1:5, 19; 3:9; 4:2; less clearly, 2 Tim 1:13). This association of conscience and loyalty to the gospel had already been prepared for by Paul (2 Cor 4:2). But here it is carried further. In 1 Tim 1:19–20, in particular, the conduct of the Christian life is dependent upon having faith and a good conscience. To cast away the latter is to make shipwreck of the faith (a quasi-technical term in the pastorals), which here means right belief. (*b*) The concept of conscience emerges over questions concerning foods (1 Tim 4:1ff; Tit 1:13ff). Those who make distinctions in this matter are "unbelieving" (Tit 1:15), their mind and conscience corrupted, whereas a sound faith demands a conscience undefiled. While in Paul a tolerant attitude toward "the weak" is advised on the ground of their conscience (Rom 14:14; 1 Cor 8:10; Col

2:20–23), in the pastorals the attitude of "the weak" is condemned out-right. It has become more of a menace and has to be openly opposed: under the influence of developing Gnosticism "the weak" have become diabolic and anti-Christian (1 Tim 4:1–5). As there are degrees of enlight-enment in conscience, so in the pastorals there are degrees in the toler-ation of the dictates of the same. In both 1 Tim 1:19–20; Tit 1:13ff, a "good conscience" implies a positive loyalty to the truth. The verb tenses are here significant. In 1 Tim 1:19–20 the act by which the "good con-science"—which is not merely the absence of pain following evil deeds, but a determination to "wage the good warfare" (1 Tim 1:18)—is re-jected, is in the aorist tense (that is, it consists of a single, decisive event [ἀπωσάμενοι; 1 Tim 1:19]), but the process whereby the conscience has been deadened is in other passages in the perfect tense (1 Tim 4:12; Tit 1:15). This last regards the corruption of the mind (νοῦς) and conscience (συνείδησις) as a process, and sharply distinguishes the two concepts. The Greek perhaps suggests that the corruption of the faculty of remorse for sin (συνείδησις) is a worse calamity than the corruption of the rational faculty which enables us to distinguish sin. This should not be pressed. But the clear distinction between mind and conscience at this point should warn us against overemphasizing what directive function conscience may have had.

c) It has been urged that in the pastorals the "conscience" has become domesticated in this world. Unlike Paul, who urged that our citizenship is in heaven, the pastorals are concerned with developing an ethic for citizenship on earth. For them the "good conscience" signifies the soft pillow of the man who has not disturbed his society: it is a mark of the static conception of Christianity found in the pastorals. But caution is necessary here. Also in the pastorals, the Christian life is a battle, and conscience is tied to the faith. But even more important is the usage of the phrase "a good conscience" and of conscience itself in the Letter to the Hebrews, associated here with the literature to which the pastorals belong. In Heb 10:2 "conscience" again merely means "consciousness" (so RSV); in Heb 9:14 it has an accusing function, where the dead works are not the works of the Law, but of sin, which are to be forgiven by God through the sacrifice of his Son. So in Heb 10:22 we have a wicked conscience—that is, an accusing conscience. From Heb 9:9 we gather that the old sacrificial system cannot deal with that where man confronts God's holiness—that is, his conscience. Throughout Hebrews conscience is directed toward God—it is not primarily a moralistic but a theological concept. Here Hebrews differs from Paul, where conscience is not primarily oriented toward God but toward humankind; and if in the pastorals conscience is domesticated, Hebrews differs from them also. In Hebrews the "clear conscience" occurs only once, in 13:18, and has reference to a concrete situation in a dynamic context. The author is sure that in the particular situation confronting him he is not at fault. But he is faced with the necessity to act honorably in all things, as befits a Christian—that is, in response to God's truth. There is no suggestion of a "soft pillow" in this world, no bourgeois complacency, but the desire for that purity which comes from doing God's will, which is possible only through the blood of the eternal covenant.

14

From Schweitzer to Scholem:
*Reflections on Sabbatai Svi**

The place of Albert Schweitzer in the history of the interpretation of the New Testament (NT) is secure. Although the predominance of the history of religions school often led to the neglect of his work, especially in Germany,[1] ultimately it could not be ignored; and that for one reason. Along with Johannes Weiss, Schweitzer established once and for all the eschatological dimensions of the NT. Necessary modifications of his work, compelled by C. H. Dodd and others, have not shaken the rightness of his main emphasis. The continuing insistence on eschatology by Schweitzer's fellow Alsatian, Oscar Cullmann, in many influential studies; the recent reiteration of apocalyptic as the matrix of Christian theology by Ernst Käsemann,[2] Ulrich Wilckens,[3] and others; the emerging concentration on the examination of the apocrypha and pseudepigrapha, especially in this country;[4] and the call by Klaus Koch to rediscover apocalyptic[5] all implicitly reinforce the significance of Schweitzer's contribution.

"Context defines content." This rediscovery of the significance of apocalyptic for the theological understanding of the NT has been stimulated by the temper of our disjointed times and by certain important discoveries. The Qumran documents (providing first-hand sources especially for the examination of a sect living in the tension of an eschatological situation) and the documents of Nag Hammadi have made possible a deeper understanding of apocalyptic and Gnostic attitudes. Here I want to point to still another sphere (not strictly a source) where we can find illumination for the understanding of the apocalyptic world within which the writers of the NT moved. The invitation to prepare this lecture arrived when I was rereading Gershom G. Scholem's great work *Sabbatai Svi: The Mystical Messiah, 1626–1676*.[6] Its relevance for the study of the NT struck me with renewed force, and I dared offer as a title, "From Schweitzer to Scholem." This theme turned out to be too broad, and I

* The Albert Schweitzer Memorial Lecture at the meeting of the Society of Biblical Literature and the American Academy of Religion, 1 November 1975, The Palmer House, Chicago, Illinois

257

can only deal with the preface to it. I shall offer reflections on the value
of Scholem's study for what could lead to a reassessment of Schweitzer's
work. These reflections, which have turned out to be more interrogatory
than affirmative, are based mainly on *Sabbatai Svi,* but also on Scholem's
other profound contributions to the study of messianism and mysticism.
I emphasize that it is impossible to do justice to their vast riches and deep
penetration here. I rely entirely upon Scholem's interpretation of the
sources for Sabbatianism (a fact which he would be the first to admit is
not without its dangers)[7] and shall consider the purpose of this lecture
fulfilled if only it helps to integrate Scholem's insight into the nature of
Judaism more closely into the study of Christian origins.

Sabbatai Svi was born in Smyrna in 1626. In 1648 he proclaimed himself
to be the Messiah, but was met with scorn. Three years later the Jewish
community outlawed him. But in 1665 Nathan of Gaza, a young rabbi
trained in the talmudic schools in Jerusalem, became convinced, through
a vision, that Sabbatai Svi was the Messiah. He persuaded a reluctant
Sabbatai of this destiny and proceeded to disseminate the astounding news
of his identity throughout the Diaspora. The movement spread to Jewish
communities in Yemen and Persia in the East and to those in the West
as far as England, Holland, Russia, and Poland. It was stirred by massive
repentance, expressed in fasts and mortifications and by extraordinary
enthusiasm, visions, and miracles. The date of the end of all things was
fixed for 1666 but was conveniently moved when necessary. The antinomian acts of Sabbatai Svi failed to dampen the enthusiasm of the believers, who through him were experiencing the emotional reality of redemption. Neither the astounding apostasy of Sabbatai Svi to Islam, his
attempts to persuade believers to apostatize, nor even his death destroyed
the movement. There still exist a few believers in Sabbatai Svi.[8]

Scholem has traced the history of this messiah and his movement. Can
a seventeenth-century messianic movement illumine early Christianity?
The dangers of parallelomania (especially when movements long separated in time are compared) are familiar, particularly since Samuel Sandmel's noted address on this theme.[9] But this being recognized, I welcome
one salutary outcome of Protestant–Roman Catholic interchange in our
time. Protestants have tended to think that movements are best understood in the light of their origins, Catholics, in terms of their developments.
We now see more clearly that both origins and developments help to
reveal the essence of movements. We can learn much about the nature
of apocalyptic in the first century from the ways in which it expressed
itself in the seventeenth. Scholem is right to draw attention to phenomena
in early Christianity which seem to be illumined by counterparts in Sab-

batianism. Was Sabbatianism directly influenced by Christianity? Scholem faced this question.[10] Sabbatai himself had a real interest in those who claimed to be messiahs before him, especially in Jesus. Some Gentile Christian chiliasts were well informed about Sabbatianism and perhaps indirectly influential in shaping it. But direct Christian influences cannot be proved, and Scholem prefers to regard Sabbatianism as an independent, indigenous phenomenon within Judaism.[11] In Sabbatianism, we can examine in depth a major Jewish messianic movement other than Christianity.

One point is of special note. If an early Christian Aramaic literature ever existed, it has not survived. The documents produced by early Christianity are few and written in Greek. There is a leanness about them. They demand infinite labor to give them flesh and blood, color and substance. The NT is a distillation. On the contrary, in Sabbatianism, thanks to the immeasurable labors of Scholem, the documentation is rich.[12] Through it one can feel and know the historical actuality of the movement more directly than is the case with early Christianity. We shall attempt to show what Scholem's work offers the student of the NT under three headings: first, the new light it sheds on the nature of Judaism; second, on messianism; and third, on early Christianity.

NEW LIGHT ON THE NATURE OF JUDAISM

To begin with, the Judaism that one encounters in Sabbatianism does not conform to the picture of it handed on to us even by Jewish scholars. Long ago Scholem emphasized two hitherto ignored facets of Judaism: the deep penetration of it by mystical currents and the domestication of apocalyptic within Pharisaism.[13] The picture of a predominantly halakic Judaism largely untouched by mystic experiences and apocalyptic visions has had to be abandoned. Scholem has now further unearthed and examined a world of mystical secrets, symbols, images, enthusiasms, and esoterica which rabbinic leaders and scholars had considered unworthy of serious attention and treated with contempt. In doing so he has further discredited the concept of a normative Pharisaic Judaism.[14] He has made such a concept untenable, not only by insisting on the two broad aspects hitherto denied Judaism to which I have referred, but also in a more detailed way. To illustrate, let us consider one phenomenon in Sabbatianism which has customarily been taken to be utterly non-Jewish.

Judaism has usually been described as insisting on the qualitative difference between God and man. The notion of the divinity of a human being was regarded as one of the marks of Hellenistic religion which sharply differentiated it from the Jewish.[15] The doctrine of the incarnation has always been regarded as the Rubicon between Christianity and Judaism. But the case of Sabbatai Svi is instructive. Divided and uncertain of himself as he was, at certain points he claimed to be divine and did not offer explanations for his claim. The evidence for all this is ambiguous but not to be ignored. He was regularly called by the term "Our Lord."[16] It can be objected that Sabbatai's mind was diseased and that it is illegitimate to deduce anything about Judaism from his case. Scholem has shown that he was a pathological figure suffering from a manic-depressive condition.[17] But this makes it all the more striking that his followers, including rabbis despite the criticisms of some rabbinic leaders, do not seem to have objected to his claim to divinity, nor found it in itself impossible. Moreover, the role ascribed to Sabbatai Svi by Nathan of Gaza was such as to demand that he possess divine power, because, through his activity and the faith in himself which he engendered among his followers, the whole cosmos was to be redeemed to achieve restoration. In previous studies Scholem had indicated that in the Merkabah mysticism of an earlier period in Jewish history,[18] the unbridgeable gulf between man and God remained. But in Sabbatianism this gulf seems to have been crossed. Within a messianic context a new dimension of union between God and man had opened.

But before Sabbatai Svi appeared, Judaism had known the long development of a mysticism in the medieval period in which the relationship between man and God had been constantly pondered under other than simply scriptural influences. This long development makes any direct comparison with Judaism in the period before the appearance of Jesus very precarious.[19] But we can at least say this. Schweitzer drew a sharp distinction between the mysticism of Paul, that of being "in Christ," and the mysticism of the Fourth Gospel, that of being "in God."[20] The former he considered Jewish and messianic, the latter Hellenistic. In the light of the history of Sabbatai Svi, such a distinction need not point outside Judaism. Sabbatai Svi's claims to divinity did not signify or imply any departure from it, nor involve the emergence of a new religion.[21] Given belief in the advent of the Messiah, the possibility for transcending the customary categories of Judaism as they had traditionally been understood, was immensely enhanced.

NEW LIGHT ON MESSIANISM

The reference to the Messiah brings us to the second sphere where Scholem's work is illuminating, our understanding of messianism.[22] In a remarkable way Sabbatianism shows that messianic movements are always likely to have presented certain constants. The same characteristics recur in such movements, although separated widely in space and time. Certain phenomena reemerge in Sabbatianism which had characterized early Christianity. There are so many that is tempting to find in Sabbatianism simply a late, distorted replica of Christianity (a temptation that, as we saw, Scholem has taught us to resist). It is impossible to enumerate completely the phenomena to which we refer. We shall divide them into two groups: first, what we shall call, without prejudice,[23] secondary characteristics; and second, primary or essential phenonema. The former are many; the latter can be reduced to two.

The secondary phenomena may be divided as follows. First, certain strictly religious emphases are common: for example, repentance, prayer, fasting, enthusiasm. Although Paul (in this, he was very unlike Nathan of Gaza) apparently never emphasized repentance directly,[24] early Christianity was preceded or accompanied by a movement of repentance which Jesus himself joined. The same phenomenon in an even more marked form emerged at the birth of Sabbatianism. Sabbatai Svi himself, but in particular his prophet, Nathan of Gaza, inaugurated a vast movement of repentance and mortification of the flesh, a mortification which Paul at times might have exemplified (1 Cor 9:27). The sources for Sabbatianism reveal the extremes to which such premessianic repentance was liable: some followers of Sabbatai Svi died fasting.[25] Doubtless, had we more sources, early Christianity would reveal the same. Similarly in the strictly religious dimension, the habits of prayer of Sabbatai Svi recall the immediacy of the prayer of the Jesus of the synoptics. The religious intensity of Sabbatai Svi, his experience of mystical absorption and ecstasy, and the almost bizarre unrealism of some of the Sabbatian believers recall the kind of enthusiasm which one detects both in and behind the synoptics.[26] Käsemann's brilliant detection of an early Christian enthusiasm has probably simply raised the lid of a caldron.[27] The enthusiasm, for example, which led to the so-called communism of Acts finds its parallel at the advent of Sabbatai Svi in the sale of their property by countless rich Jews in many quarters.[28]

Second, the miraculous is as marked in Sabbatianism as in early Christianity. For example, the manner of the birth of Sabbatai Svi was dwelled upon in a way reminiscent of the birth narratives in Matthew and Luke; and Sabbatai Svi urged a cult of his mother, comparable with later Christian mariolatry.[29] There was a tradition that between 1648 and 1650 Sabbatai Svi was miraculously saved from drowning: "He rose from the sea and was saved," as was Jesus when he walked on the sea.[30] Magical

elements which have been discovered in the synoptic tradition have their
parallels, in an enhanced form, in Sabbatianism. Sabbatai Svi seems at
times to have inaugurated a magical enterprise. There were attempts to
force the end by what has been called a "practical Qabbala," which
amounted to magic.[31] That Jesus' work could be and has been regarded
in a similar magical fashion the studies of A. Schweitzer himself show;
in the end the Jesus of Schweitzer is an apocalyptical magician who seeks
to "force" the end.[32]

Third, the nature and activity of Sabbatai Svi and Jesus as messiahs
are often similar: for example, that the Messiah could be in the world
unknown reappears in Sabbatianism,[33] he also is parallel with Moses and
Adam,[34] his coming inaugurates or is accompanied by the "birth pangs
of the Messiah."[35] Like Jesus, Sabbatai Svi chose twelve to represent
the Twelve Tribes of Israel.[36] Like Jesus also, Sabbatai Svi was a messiah
without armies.[37] In a strange way, but with a great difference in the
nature of their pains, both Jesus and Sabbatai were suffering messiahs.

Fourth, among these secondary phenomena—if such a term be permitted in this connection—both Sabbatai Svi and Jesus were conceived
to have overcome death, the former by occultation and the latter by resurrection. And both were expected to return again to earth to complete
their work.[38]

Fifth, we note the striking phenomenon that the roles of John the Baptist
and Paul in early Christianity and that of Nathan of Gaza in Sabbatianism
are parallel.[39] *Mutatis mutandis,* Nathan of Gaza in himself was to Sabbatai Svi what both John the Baptist and Paul were to Jesus. Until Nathan
convinced him, Sabbatai Svi was uncertain of his messianic identity.
Though more directly so (the synoptic and Johannine materials are here
so varied), Nathan was a witness to Sabbatai in a way parallel with that
of John the Baptist to Jesus. But it was Nathan also who later provided
the theological structure for the interpretation of Sabbatai Svi, and in this,
he played the role of Paul to Jesus. Like Paul, Nathan refused to be
impressed by or to demand "signs" that the Messiah had come.[40] But
this single parallel of Nathan with the Baptist and Paul must not be
pressed. It is altogether natural that the founder of any movement should
have significant interpreters.

Finally, much as many scholars urge that there was little interest in the
life of Jesus even on the part of Paul, Sabbatianism flourished apparently
without much active interest among the masses of believers in the history
and character of Sabbatai.[41] What mattered was *that* the Messiah had
appeared, not *who* had appeared as Messiah. The strange behavior of
Sabbatai Svi, a manic-depressive, caused consternation among the rabbis

and others who believed in him, as among those who did not. He changed
the calendar,[42] ignored the food laws,[43] pronounced the ineffable Name,[44]
and was sexually irregular.[45] His conduct was often, to use Scholem's
vivid phrase, "an Exodus from the Law."[46] The justification of Sabbatai's
behavior, his attitude toward and disobedience of the Law—culminating
in his monstrous apostasy to Islam—posed a problem for his followers,
comparable with that facing early Christians by the free attitude of Jesus
toward the Law and by his suffering and death. The theology of both
movements began with an initial disappointment which had to be explained. Both turned to the same exegetical methods to do so, and both
concentrated on the suffering servant of Isaiah 53 for illumination. Both
developed a doctrine of the Parousia; both demanded faith, unattested by
works or signs. Perhaps, in early Christianity a new element had entered
Judaism, that is, faith in a pure or neat form, not necessarily associated
with good works, became the mark of redemption, and that a faith in a
paradoxical messiah. Such a faith reemerged in Sabbatianism.[47] Both
movements produced a doctrine of incarnation. In both a deeply felt faith,
an immediate experience of being in a new eon, a "realized eschatology"
of incalculable emotional intensity, enthusiasm, and exultation led to a
radical criticism of Jewish tradition, a new standard of measurement being
applied to it. The experience of the freedom of the children of God led
to antinomian tendencies, especially and unrestrainedly in Sabbatianism
but also in early Christianity, which at times broke out into license.[48]

Taken together, the phenomena to which we have pointed—and many
more such could be noted—are extremely valuable. To read the history
of Sabbatai is to encounter the emotional intensity of a messianic movement at first hand, a temper or an atmosphere strikingly like the very
enthusiastic, ecstatic world of feeling which was the "new creation" of
early Christianity. This is not all. The history of Sabbatai suggests that
a messianic movement of any depth is most likely, almost inevitably, to
call forth certain phenomena—ecstasy, mortifications, visions, miracles,
enthusiasms and certain inescapable parallel responses. The reason for
this is simple. The messianic tradition had developed into a popular tradition, so that the advent of a messiah at any time stirred up among the
masses certain age-long, stereotyped expectations. Discouraged as they
might be to do so even by the messiah himself, the believing masses found
"signs" everywhere. Moved by the age-old concepts and symbols of messianism rooted in the Scriptures and enlarged upon in tradition, they were
eager to clothe their messiah, in every age, with the kind of characteristics
they thought proper to him.[49]

Probably in every messianic movement—certainly in Sabbatianism and early Christianity—a distinction should be clearly recognized between the understanding of it among the masses and among the more sophisticated leaders. Attempts to explain Sabbatianism and early Christianity in predominantly political or economic or sociological terms have generally failed to convince. Believers in Sabbatai Svi were drawn from the rich and the poor, the underprivileged and the established, from the ignorant ʿam hāʾ āreṣ and the rabbinic authorities.[50] Similarly, early Christianity was probably indifferent to barriers of wealth, class, and learning, although the evidence is not as clear as in Sabbatianism.[51] Nevertheless there were real differences of comprehension among the believers in both movements. Nathan of Gaza and Paul of Tarsus understood the respective messiahs in whom they believed in a far more theologically informed manner than most of their fellow believers.[52] One is tempted to find here a suggestive datum for the interpretation of the symbols of apocalyptic in both movements. Recently we have been urged to distinguish between "steno symbols" and "tensive symbols." This distinction should probably be related to differences between the masses and the more subtle believers in early Christianity as in Sabbatianism. Because in both movements most believers belonged to the masses, they both tended to take on, especially incipiently, the marks of the popular understanding of the messianic age to which we have drawn attention. But it would be very unwise to find the essence of any messianic movement in the kind of phenomena which such an understanding magnified. Bizarre miracles, the froth of enthusiasm and ecstasy must not be given equal weight with, or (perhaps better) must not be understood apart from the underlying formative factors in a messianic movement,[53] to which we now turn.

More important than the secondary phenomena, then, are certain fundamental similarities, accompanied by equally fundamental differences, between early Christianity and Sabbatianism. These we have called primary phenomena. They may be introduced under two rubrics.

First, in both movements there was a radical confrontation with the established order focused on the ultimate authority within Judaism, the Torah. In both, social, political, and religious loyalties and oppressions were challenged so that there emerged an inevitable concentration on the person of the messiah in whose name the challenge was issued. In both, faith in the messiah became the primary mark of the believer.[54]

Second, both movements within a very short period spread extensively. Sabbatianism and early Christianity are in one thing peculiar. Most of the many messianic movements in Judaism have been short-lived and concentrated in specific localities. But Sabbatianism and Christianity are alike in having had an ecumenical appeal.[55] Within two years, Sabbatianism spread throughout Europe and the Near East. Confined almost exclusively to Jews, it affected almost the whole of Jewry. Within a slightly longer period, Christianity spread from Palestine to Rome in the West and eastward as well, to some extent among Jews but also, and particularly, among Gentiles. This means that both Sabbatianism and Christianity were understood to satisfy the spiritual needs of Jews and especially, in the case of the latter, of Gentiles. Movements do not spread without reason: emotionally, at the least, both early Christianity and Sabbatianism conveyed the living experience of redemption.[56]

At first sight, these two rubrics seem to justify Scholem's claim that messianism is essentially constituted by two fundamental elements. First, there is the emergence of a messianic figure. He serves as a catalyst, negatively, for radical criticism of the existing order; positively, of dreams at long last come true, of barriers long standing being broken down, of a new creation—all this accompanied by an impulse to propagate the good news. And second, this messianic figure must meet a widespread need and be understood to satisfy that need in terms of an interpretive ideological structure of magnitude and depth. Infinitely complex as are all historical movements, Scholem claims that significant messianic movements are usually born of coincidence—that of the interpretation of this person within a large conceptual framework which can illumine his significance for that need. To put the matter concretely, a significant messianic movement demands the coincidence of a Jesus and a Paul or of a Sabbatai Svi and a Nathan of Gaza. The catalyst of a messianic movement is a messianic figure, but its spread and significance are necessarily determined by the scope and profundity of the conceptual framework or myth within which such a figure can be or is interpreted.

This dual aspect of messianic movements is especially clear in Sabbatianism. Owing to the absence of contemporary sources of sufficient richness, it is not so immediately clear in early Christianity. Does Scholem's analysis help to clarify early Christian history?

Scholem points out that among Jews in the seventeenth century, when Sabbatianism arose, there was one single, dominant theology, Lurianic Qabbala, which constituted a rich, comprehensive myth.[57] It varied in its forms but was profoundly united in essentials and almost universally accepted by Jews. It was the universal dominance of a single theology or myth that enabled Sabbatai Svi, through Nathan of Gaza, to initiate such a widespread messianic movement. The reason for the hold of Lurianic Qabbala on Jews everywhere was that it provided a key to the mystery of their suffering at the hands of the Gentile world and made that suffering tolerable. In medieval Europe, the one inescapable fact about Jews was that they were in exile, at the mercy of the whims of their Gentile rulers. In 1492 they had been expelled cruelly from Spain; in 1648–49 there were horrendous massacres in Poland. How could Jews continue to bear the burden of their exile? Lurianic Qabbala provided the answer in subtle, mystical terms which satisfied. At first the doctrine, absorbed in strictly theological concerns, had not been particularly concerned with the question of exile as such. But it had developed in such a way as to provide a sustaining explanation for the terrible experiences of Jews in exile: it spoke directly to their needs.[58] It did so by setting their exile in a cosmic, divine perspective: it connected the historical exile of Jews with a supramundane exile of man from God, and indeed, with a rupture in the very being of God himself. By enduring their exile, while remaining loyal to the disciplined, austere, ascetic tradition of the Torah and the knowledge of it supplied by the Qabbala of Luria, suffering, exiled Jews were assured that they were making possible a cosmic reintegration and with this the restoration of man to God and a reconciliation within God himself. The technical term for this process of restoration was *tiqqûn*. Lurianic Qabbala was not simply a mystical and intellectual structure of vast complexity and insight; it became the strength and stay of a despairing people, crushed in the ghetto. In their insignificance it gave Jews cosmic significance. It enabled them to believe not only that even *this* world, in which they knew exile, *could* be saved or undergo *tiqqûn,* but that through their obedience to the Torah it was they who were to be its saviors. When that obedience would have reached its fulfillment, the Messiah would appear. It was not the Messiah who would make the restoration possible; rather he would be a sign that it was near. He would usher in the end, made possible by the Jews' own obedience.

Within this context the impact of Sabbatai becomes understandable: without it, his name would probably by now be forgotten like that of many another messiah in Jewish history. As we already noted, his claim to be the Messiah was at first ridiculed. But when a recognized prophet interpreted that claim in the light of the all-pervasive Lurianic Qabbalistic expectations, a new movement was born: the interpretation was as crucial as the claimant, the myth as the fact. Jews became convinced that the ultimate *tiqqûn* or restoration had now begun. The end was at hand; deliverance was at the door. The results of this conviction were staggering. The one decisive factor was *that* the Messiah had appeared. Who he was, or what he was like, was for many unimportant. Interest in the personal character and conduct of Sabbatai was at best secondary and probably, among the majority of believers, nonexistent.[59] What made him significant was his role as the Messiah, proclaimed and authenticated by Nathan. In the Lurianic world, among Jewish hearts made sick by hope deferred, the magic word, Messiah, was enough to set the world on fire. That among certain of the Sabbatians, at least, the neglect of a radical assessment of the character of Sabbatai Svi was to bring its terrible nemesis will become clear as we turn now to our main concern: the light that Sabbatianism throws on early Christianity.

EARLY CHRISTIANITY AND SABBATIANISM

Before we deal with the most significant questions that Scholem's works have provoked, it is desirable first to recognize their contribution to our understanding of the apocalyptic terminology of the NT. I am acutely conscious of my incompetence in dealing with this. I am versed neither in linguistic analysis nor in literary criticism as it is currently practiced. I can simply point to certain facts. Sabbatianism used the terminology of apocalyptic as symbolic of a supernatural, unseen reality; this it did as heir to the Qabbala.[60] But equally certainly it took that terminology quite literally. For example, when Sabbatai's messiahship was accepted at Smyrna, he proceeded forthwith geographically to carve up the world, which he was soon to rule. He assigned to several of his followers different parts of the world as their dominions. Some of his wealthy followers sold their possessions, convinced that the end of the old order was literally at hand.[61] The Turkish authorities took very seriously the political implications of Sabbatai's activity.[62] On his side, he behaved like a monarch.[63] Much modern discussion of the meaning of apocalyptic language which overmuch spiritualizes it must be regarded as misguided. For example, to understand the term "kingdom of God" as used in early Christianity, as nonpolitical and nonterrestrial, is unjustifiable, if it be taken to have been so used universally.[64] Whatever their limitations, in their tenacious insistence on a literal understanding of the messianic prophecies chiliastic movements are doubtless true to much in Sabbatianism and early Christianity.[65] There was a literal dimension to apocalyptic language which must not be evaded, and it had a catastrophic political and social relevance. In particular, the political and sociological implications of early Christianity and their actual impact would be more adequately recognized if this literalism were taken more seriously. This would help us to comprehend that all messianism has a revolutionary, subversive potential.[66] This is not to underrate the symbolism of apocalyptic. A literary critic might do justice to our point by claiming that apocalyptic terminology is both conceptual and symbolic.

This applies especially to the understanding of early Christianity among the masses, which embraced apocalyptic literally and uncritically. To bear this in mind is to see both Jesus and Paul as corrective of a popular messianic political revolutionary enthusiasm and, therefore, despite the new wine which they dispensed, as in a certain sense conservative. In this light they both emerge as reductionists of a fecund apocalyptic enthusiasm that sometimes led to political theatrics and discovered in the new creation a legitimation of license.[67]

But even more important are the two factors, the coincidence of which, according to Scholem's analysis, is necessary for the emergence of a significant messianic movement. Do they apply to early Christianity? First, can we point with certainty, as we did in the case of Sabbatianism in the seventeenth century, to a dominant ideological or theological framework in the first-century Judaism into which Jesus of Nazareth was fitted as Messiah to give birth to early Christianity? Or, to put it in another way, does first-century Judaism present an ideological counterpart equivalent in depth and extent to the Lurianic Qabbala in seventeenth-century Judaism which made Sabbatianism possible?

The answers given to this question will be familiar. As representative, we refer to those of E. R. Goodenough and Wilhelm Bousset. Goodenough was concerned with explaining how a Palestinian movement so quickly penetrated and prevailed over the Greco-Roman world. His answer was that by the first century certain Jews in the Hellenistic world had opened their minds to pagan notions and made them "at home" in Judaism. When Hellenistic Jews became Christians, they carried over these notions into their understanding of their new faith. This rapidly enabled the gospel to penetrate the Hellenistic-Roman world. But did such a Hellenistic Judaism as Goodenough describes exist universally among first-century Jews as did Lurianic Qabbala among those of the seventeenth, and was it as theologically dominant and accepted? Goodenough's position has not won the assent of those best qualified to assess Judaism. His treatment of the extent and potency of rabbinic influence as over against the almost autonomous Hellenized Judaism which he delineates remains questionable.[68]

Bousset, whose work *Kyrios Christos* often seems to anticipate much in Goodenough, nevertheless points to another alternative. For him nascent Christianity employed ideas anticipated in the apocalyptic tradition in Judaism. For example, a christology of preexistence lay hidden in the idea of the Son of Man of Jewish apocalyptic.[69] In the first century an apocalyptic structure was ready into which Jesus, as Messiah, could be fitted, as Sabbatai Svi was fitted into Lurianic Qabbala in the seventeenth. Faith in Jesus had merely to clothe itself with apocalyptic. How others have followed Bousset in this view we need not trace. But here again the difference between the role of apocalyptic in the first-century Judaism and Lurianic Qabbala in that of the seventeenth is unmistakable. The relative importance of apocalyptic in the complex of first-century Judaism is much disputed. The older view that apocalyptic was as peripheral in first-century Judaism as, let us say, the chiliastic sects in modern Christianity is no longer tenable.[70] Apocalyptic belonged to the main streams of Judaism; but that Judaism was extremely variegated and certainly not dominated by a single apocalyptic ideology. In isolation, apocalyptic, although it has taken up Alexander the Great's notion of world empire, cannot provide a universal, dominant theological parallel to the Lurianic Qabbala of the seventeenth century.

The two clear answers do not satisfy, then, the question of whether there was a dominant theological counterpart to Lurianic Qabbala in first-century Judaism. Does a combination of them do so? This might be suggested by the very nature of Lurianic Qabbala itself. In it two things were fused: an eschatological ideology derived from Jewish apocalyptic, modified and reinterpreted in terms of the notion of the *tiqqûn*, and a form of Gnosticism tracing its lineage apparently back to the early Christian centuries. This fusion enabled Lurianic Qabbala to connect the terrestrial messianic hopes with an inward and supernal order and constituted its extraordinary dynamism. Scholem's work prompts the question whether in the first century, too—in an inchoate form at least—a comparable fusion of a modified apocalyptic and proto-Gnosticism had occurred to provide the framework for interpreting Jesus. Paul D. Hanson[71] has recently insisted on the prophetic connections of the origins of apocalyptic. But by the first century what Hellenistic and other influences, including possibly pre- or proto-Gnostic ones, had penetrated it? Unfortunately the NT is so laconic that it allows no certainty as to any one dominant framework, apart from the Scriptures, into which Jesus was fitted. Moreover, whereas Sabbatai Svi had one outstanding, almost unique interpreter in Nathan of Gaza, Jesus had various interpreters at least as different as Matthew, Mark, John, and Paul. And again sources outside the NT are either insufficiently examined or too confusing to allow for certainty. There are increasing, although disputed, indications of the fusion or interaction of apocalyptic with pre- and proto-Gnosticism, if not Gnosticism, in the first century, and that before 70 C.E.[72] But even allowing for such a fusion before that date, can we claim that it provided a dominant theological outlook for first-century Judaism as did Lurianic Qabbala for that of the seventeenth? It would be a bold person who would claim this. If a unified ideology was the mark of seventeenth-century Judaism, we have long been taught that diversity was that of the first. But is this the whole truth? In reaction to G. F. Moore have we overemphasized that diversity and overlooked a possible overarching unity provided by a rich fusion of Law, apocalyptic, and pre- or proto-Gnosticism? This question is made more and more pressing by Scholem's understanding of messianism.[73]

Perhaps the problem as to what theological framework most governed early Christianity can best be approached obliquely. The social and political structures favoring the spread of Christianity are clear—a ubiquitous synagogue, made accessible by Roman imperial roads and favored by Roman policy, provided a ready-made platform for Christian missionaries. We may ask what particular need had arisen among Jews in the first century. Sabbatianism met the needs of Jews in exile. Was there a dominant need that first-century Judaism had to face? *The* crucial question which it confronted was that posed by the Gentile world. In the first century, Jews, although occasionally living apart as in Alexandria, were not in a ghetto.[74] They were free to respond to the fascination of Gentile life. This constitutes a crucial difference between the larger context of Sabbatianism and that of early Christianity. At the time of Sabbatianism, Judaism was turned in upon itself, "cabined, cribbed, and confined." Sabbatianism arose within a suffering ghetto to meet its peculiar needs. By no means was the Gentile question central to it. By the seventeenth century that question had been closed; Gentiles had rejected Jews. Jews in turn had largely rejected Gentiles and had become introverted; the references to Gentiles in a thousand pages of Scholem's work are few.[75]

It was otherwise in the first century. Then the question of how to relate to the Gentile world pressed ubiquitously upon Jews. There was a vast missionary movement to the Gentile world.[76] Before 70 C.E. there were elements in apocalyptic which directly occupied themselves with the fate of Gentiles and with hope for them.[77] The relation of such elements to any pre- or proto-Gnosticism we cannot pursue. But these elements did speak with particular force to the need of first-century Jews to come to terms with Gentiles. That they were a marked aspect of first-century Judaism before 70 C.E., after which apocalyptic became more discredited, seems clear. Based on the Scriptures of Judaism,[78] they were also the outcome of three centuries of the exposure of Jews to Hellenism—an exposure that time and again created a crisis: the crisis constituted by the insidious attraction of Gentile life. It could be resolved either by greater and greater intensity to achieve a total obedience as at Qumran, or by reinterpretation and adaptation as in Pharisaism, or by a blind hatred as among Zealots; or, on the other extreme, by acceptance and assimilation and interpenetration.[79] Whatever the solution adopted, first-century Judaism faced at boiling point the fascinating impact of Hellenism. Within that context apocalyptic, in those elements of it to which we refer, provided a hope for the final redemption of Gentiles. Was it apocalyptic, characterized by this universalist hope, that provided the framework for presenting Jesus as the "Savior of the World"? And although it reflected a challenge produced by the attraction of the outside world, while Lurianic Qabbala was the product of an internal crisis produced by the rejection of Jews by the outside world, can we regard this apocalyptic, modified by Hellenistic influences, as a first-century counterpart to Lurianic Qabbala in the seventeenth?

There are two difficulties. First, there is that already mentioned with reference to Bousset's position. How significant in first-century Judaism was the kind of apocalyptic to which we refer, among other matters, concerned with the Gentiles and possibly infiltrated by a pre- or proto-Gnosticism? How pervasive was the hope for the Gentiles within it? That the hope existed is clear, but was it widespread, not to say dominant? The answer is not easy. The wide infiltration of apocalyptic ideology into the Greco-Roman world would seem to be likely. It began, according to Martin Hengel, before the third century B.C.E.[80] J. Daniélou insisted that up to the Council of Nicaea the substructure of Christian theology remained Semitic and largely apocalyptic in its terminology.[81] The bog of terminological inexactitude must be avoided, but if Gnostic thought was from the beginning related to apocalyptic, it is significant that R. M. Wilson writes of "something of an atmosphere in which the people of the early Christian centuries lived and moved."[82] The work of such scholars gives us pause. They justify the question which Scholem's work compels us to ask. Behind the variety of first-century Judaism did there perhaps exist a single, widely diffused, and popular eschatological frame of reference in both Palestinian and Hellenistic Judaism (to use a distinction now largely obsolete)? Sweeping generalizations are out of place. In the present state of our knowledge it is as difficult to give an affirmative answer as a negative one. For example, Robert M. Grant, who once urged that Gnosticism was born of the collapse of apocalyptic, now denies this outright.[83] Daniélou's evidence is more abundant than convincing. Unless or until new texts from Nag Hammadi, Qumran, and elsewhere enlighten us further, we must tentatively assert that the role of apocalyptic, however modified and reinterpreted under Hellenistic influences, cannot have been so important in the spread of Christianity as was Lurianic Qabbala in that of Sabbatianism. Such apocalyptic did not dominate the whole of Judaism, which was not in the first century a ghetto but spanned several cultures. We conclude that one element in the twofold coincidence to which Scholem points as necessary to significant messianism is not clear in early Christianity. Whereas in Sabbatianism there was a decisive conceptual framework or myth in the dominant Lurianic Qabbala, to judge from the sources we now have, the conceptual background in early Christianity appears to have been far more complex and varied.

We referred to the need of Jews to come to terms with Gentile life. The opposite must not be underestimated: the need that Gentiles often felt to embrace Judaism. The multiplicity of God-fearers and proselytes, which according to some largely accounts for the magnitude of the Diaspora,[84] indicates that the primordial and nuclear certainty of Jewish monotheism and the sustaining discipline of life under the yoke of the Torah exercised a deep attraction for Gentiles. Any simple conceptual framework which should—on Scholem's terms—dominantly sustain the interpretation of Jesus would have to embrace the Jewish and the Gentile worlds. Where is it to be found?[85]

This brings us to the second apparent difficulty in finding a dominant apocalyptic, one oriented toward the Gentiles, one of the two decisive factors in the spread of Christianity. It springs to mind. To judge from the Gospels the Gentile question, although recognized, was not central to Jesus of Nazareth.[86] This disturbing fact leads to the question, what role did the person of Jesus of Nazareth play in early Christianity? Was it as decisive as that of Sabbatai Svi in Sabbatianism? Despite the comparative infrequency of Jesus' engagement with Gentiles, we suggest that the answer to this question is in the affirmative because Jesus had his Paul and others to interpret him, as Sabbatai Svi had Nathan. Where was the heart of the matter for Paul? He found the significance of the emergence of Jesus as the Messiah particularly in the grace that he had shown to the ʿam hāʾāreṣ, and then, why not to Gentiles?[87] The Gentile mission was for Paul implicit in the ministry of Jesus. His call was to the Gentiles. This is fundamental information. There was little if any ground for a concern for Gentiles in the life of Sabbatai Svi. It is this ultimately that explains why Christianity became not only a Jewish but also a Gentile movement, whereas Sabbatianism remained Jewish.[88]

Here we enter disputed ground. Many believers probably existed in both Sabbatianism and early Christianity for whom the personalities of Sabbatai Svi and Jesus, respectively, were a matter of indifference and even unknown. But this must not mislead us. Ultimately it was the personality of each messiah that gave to the movements they inaugurated their peculiarity. One ventures to urge that in the end, what moved Sabbatians was *that* the Messiah had appeared, incidentally as Sabbatai Svi; whereas what astounded early Christians was that it was Jesus of Nazareth who had come as the Messiah. The difference between Sabbatai Svi and Jesus, draped as they both came to be in the traditional messianic mantles, is ultimately a difference, quite simply, of what we might call "character." Rabbinic leaders were so embarrassed by Sabbatai Svi's conduct that they sought to destroy the evidence for it.[89] In Sabbatai Svi, despite his appeal to the masses, there seems to be no real concern for them such as breaks through the Jesus of the Gospels. There is an insensitivity to the ostentatious and bizarre which is unthinkable in Jesus and, unless (paradoxically) antinomianism is its expression, an absence of sensitive moral concern. Sabbatai Svi was not a teacher of morality. The difference between the two messiahs comes to clearest expression in the apostasy of Sabbatai Svi and the death of Jesus on the cross. Scholem calls the apostasy the most execrable act possible in the Jewish mind.[90]

Two ways were open to Sabbatians after Sabbatai Svi's apostasy—either to follow his actions, to imitate him, or to see in his fate a call to ever greater rigor in obedience to the Law. Sabbatianism developed along both ways. Some believers followed the latter course and showed a zeal in piety and morality which outshone that of other Jews and, indeed, became a mark of their heretical faith. Such Sabbatians recognized that while Sabbatai lived on the brink of the new aeon, they themselves did not and could not follow his freedom from the Law.[91] Their attitude could be compared with that of early Jewish Christians who retained their zeal for the Torah even though believing in Jesus as the Messiah. In the course of time these nomistic Sabbatians declined and reverted to the mainstream of Judaism; historically they were not significant. Other Sabbatians took the former of the two possible courses noted. They took Sabbatai Svi as a paradigm and an example to be imitated. To do so they had to call evil good. They had to justify apostasy itself as messianic and redemptive. To do so in the end was to destroy all values dear to Judaism. It implied an ultimate cynicism and nihilism, born doubtless of a profound despair, in which the demand of God was mocked. It is no accident that the most distinctive doctrine of Sabbatianism came to be that of redemption through sin.[92] The infinitely complex and even pathological reasons for the conduct of Sabbatai Svi excite our pity. In the radical Sabbatian wing, its theological and practical consequences were disastrous. Despite the indifference of the masses of Sabbatians to the character of their Messiah, his passive surrender to the power of impurity and iniquity, even as he persisted in his messianic mission, stamped itself upon his radical followers. In loyalty to their apostatized redeemer, they too were led to strange acts. Like the Messiah himself, they too had to descend into impurity; for them too good had to become evil. The very weakness of Sabbatai Svi they took for strength. And it was the radical Sabbatians who persisted; it was they who became historically significant. As time went on, the figure of Sabbatai Svi, within Sabbatianism itself, became vague almost to the point of anonymity.[93] Perversely, his lack of integrity alone remained significant, and that diabolically.

Scholem has referred to the gulf that separates the character of Sabbatai from that of Jesus of Nazareth.[94] As we indicated, the interest of much of primitive Christianity in the history and personality of Jesus has been denied.[95] But while we recognize the force of the arguments of those who hold this view and the support it receives to a degree from developments in Sabbatianism, it is wiser to urge that, as the very emergence of the Gospels indicates, the character of Jesus at least, if not the inner recesses of his personality and the minute biographical details of his life in various degrees and dimensions, remained central for early Christianity. That *he* was the Messiah was significant for early Christianity in a way that Sabbatai Svi as a person was not for Sabbatianism. We consider it legitimate to speak of the personality of Jesus or his character and do not find easily dismissable the suggestion recently made by Dean S. W. Sykes of Cambridge, that the heart (I reject the word essence, as did R. W. Funk) of Christianity lies in the character of Jesus.[96] But because so many find difficulty in speaking of or in picturing the personality of Jesus, we shall seek to pinpoint the essential difference between Sabbatai Svi and Jesus, not in terms of their characters, but in terms of another dimension, the Law.

Judaism lived by a moment, that of revelation, and by a dimension, that of tradition, the latter being the explanation and application of the former. The meaning of the revelation at Sinai was variously interpreted. As the Temple Scroll at Qumran has illustrated with astonishing force, the extent to which the Law itself was examined and even questioned in first-century Judaism was far greater than we had often assumed.[97] Currents emerged in Judaism in which in the messianic age even a new *tôrâ* was anticipated. Whether these currents were as early as the emergence of Christianity is questioned; certainly they existed in the Judaism that Sabbatai Svi knew.[98] Messianic freedom, as Sabbatai understood it, allowed him to live beyond the Law. His position led to antinomian nihilism. If allowed to develop unchecked, the freedom of early Christianity could have had the same result. But whereas in Sabbatianism the messianic founder (who was, we repeat, not a teacher) could supply no check to antinomianism but only a stimulus, in early Christianity there could be found such a check in the ministry, character, and teaching of Jesus.[99] The attitudes of Jesus and Paul toward the Law cannot be discussed at the tail end of a long lecture. Perhaps the Fourth Gospel best sums up that attitude when it speaks of the new commandment of the gospel as constituted by *agapē*. The concentration on *agapē* as the quintessence of the Law is not a negative dismissal of the tradition of Judaism, but its radical reduction to one dominating dimension. The life of Jesus of Nazareth, as understood by his followers, was consonant with this dimension, an expression of *agapē*. It could, therefore, always provide a corrective to any antinomian messianic license that might emerge. This did not prevent antinomianism from emerging in early Christianity. Over against the concentration on the Law in Jewish Christianity stood the amorality and immorality of Gnostics and other Christians. The situation in both early Christianity and Sabbatianism was highly dialectical and complex. But at the root of the Christian tradition was a founder whose impact could provide a salutary control in a way that Sabbatai could not. The Lord with whom the Christian tradition was sometimes virtually identified was such that he could be a constant corrective, even though misinterpreted in both nomistic and antinomian terms.[100] As we have expressed it elsewhere, Jesus became the Torah of Christians.[101] Here lies the heart of the matter, not in the apocalyptic imagery and fantasies with which he, like Sabbatai Svi, came to be clothed.

We have sought to apply Scholem's categories to early Christianity. With regard to one of the two essential dimensions which he finds behind significant messianic movements, caution is necessary. It is easier to isolate Lurianic Qabbala as the one Sabbatian framework than to point to such a single conceptual framework, apart from the Scriptures, governing early Christianity. As for the role of the messianic figures, Jesus and Sabbatai, they were both significant in their respective movements, not only as catalysts or initiators but also as formative factors. The constructive constraint of Christ's ministry in early Christianity stands markedly over against the negative, distorting, and ultimately nihilistic influence of Sabbatai in Sabbatianism.

One final word. Lurianic Qabbala was far too complex and comprehensive a phenomenon to be simply labeled as apocalyptic. But it had absorbed apocalyptic elements.[102] So ingrained in our minds is the halakic conception of Judaism, especially after 70 C.E., that it requires an effort to grasp that apocalyptic, messianic expectations which had emerged before the common era persisted in strength throughout the medieval period and down to the seventeenth century so that Sabbatai Svi could easily draw upon their dramatic dynamism. Jewish engagement with apocalyptic did not cease with the fall of Jerusalem in 70 C.E.,[103] and so one cannot read the history of Sabbatai Svi, at least with Albert Schweitzer in mind, without being compelled to reflect upon the significance of apocalyptic. One might gather from Schweitzer that it is a dead end,[104] from others that it is a kind of collective megalomania.[105] But using the term in a broad sense at this point, apocalyptic presents both positive and negative aspects. To assess these would require a knowledge of the meaning of symbols which is beyond my competence. An examination of the nature of the symbolism of apocalyptic, such as has been begun by Amos Wilder[106] and others, is a crying need. On the positive side, apocalyptic, emerging and reemerging in times of extreme suffering and despair, is the expression, in the light of the divine purpose, of a legitimate critical response to the iniquities, corruptions, and distortions of this world, to which, alas, most of us are at least half-blind. It is the element of divine discontent, of the desire for something afar, of the aim which exceeds our grasp. Without this discontent, the dead hand of custom, stagnation, and insensitivity throttles life, and even ancient good becomes uncouth. From this point of view, apocalyptic is the leaven of history. Its societal and cosmic imagery, symbols and hopes, which turn human longings to vivid expectations, are always necessary as a spur to sensitivity and a corrective against a false, irresponsible, individualistic piety. Even more, these expectations themselves—unrealistic as they often are—have a creative impact and, against themselves, modify societies even when those same societies reject them. Such hopes open up new possibilities, new pathways to utopia, even if one never arrives there. A literature produced when humankind is at the end of its tether has its own stark, unblinded, and penetrating insight, even though its actual practical counsels, born of despair, are often dubious. The plea of Klaus Koch for the rediscovery of "apocalyptic" is understandable.[107]

But, on the negative side, it needs careful control. A good stimulant, does it constitute a good diet? The ivied walls of the academy in which we dwell at ease make the appreciation of apocalyptic difficult for most of us. But this being admitted—again to use the term in an undifferentiated sense—apocalyptic has an ugly face. To read Scholem's work is to stand amazed, overwhelmed, and—it must be said—alienated by the bizarre, unhealthy, and unsavory possibilities of apocalyptic, messianic, political, and other indulgence.[108] Despite its suffering and courage, its moral and intellectual striving and daring, the practical consequences of what we normally refer to without differentiation as apocalyptic are no less baffling and even terrifying than its often lurid imagery. The rabbinic reaction to such apocalyptic as a pernicious menace is understandable. In Sabbatianism, an unrestrained utopian apocalyptic mysticism worked itself out in antinomianism. Early Christianity knew the same temptation, but in its main developments, though not in all its expressions, it was often spared from the more undesirable tendencies by the constraint of its founding figure. Early Christianity was apocalyptic, but it was so under the constraint of the *agapē* (to risk distortion through brevity) of Christ. The sum of the matter is this: if we are to continue to describe early Christianity as apocalyptic, it seems to me that we can only do so by carefully differentiating what we mean. Paul D. Hanson has led the way by drawing a distinction between prophetic eschatology and apocalyptic eschatology, a distinction which is not without parallel with that drawn by Scholem for a later period between restorative and utopian messianism.[109] But this we cannot pursue here.

In his centennial lecture I have referred only very sparingly to the great Albert Schweitzer. But I have tried to recall you to the haunting question which he bequeathed us: how are we to preserve visionary intensity without an illusory fanaticism? It is because it offers a sobering warning against any uncritical concentration on and endorsement of an undifferentiated apocalyptic that I have reflected with you on Scholem's great work.

15
*The Moral Teaching of the Early Church**

My friend and colleague, Professor William F. Stinespring, is best known as a philologist, a teacher of Semitic languages and a translator of significant studies from modern Hebrew. But to those who share his daily life, he is also known for the warmth of his humanity. In particular, his colleagues have been made aware of his concern with the social and moral issues that have confronted this country. It is, therefore, not unfitting that in this volume there should be one essay dealing with the biblical grounds of that concern which has so much governed him. And it is a real pleasure for me to be able to offer in his honor not a technical study, but one in which I seek to set forth the broad outlines of the moral teaching of the early Church. My aim is to present, not so much a detailed analysis, as the way in which that teaching has impressed itself upon me after years of preoccupation with it.

The title of this essay—"The Moral Teaching of the Early Church"— is meant to suggest, rightly, that the term *ethics,* which connotes philosophic reflection upon human conduct, is inappropriate for a description of the *moral* teaching of the early Church; but it implies that in the early Church there was a clearly defined body of teaching on morality that can be neatly described. Let me begin by emphasizing that this was not so. In its moral teaching, as in other matters, the early Church presents a coat of many colors. The documents of the New Testament reveal varying emphases. Any neat presentation of early Christian teaching must immediately be suspect. But having said this, it is possible to point out certain themes which do convey the moral seriousness of much of the primitive church, and I shall now attempt to point out what these are.[1]

---

* This essay is one of the Haskell Lectures which, along with Dean Krister Stendahl, I delivered at Oberlin College, Oberlin, Ohio, in March 1968. Its companion lecture, "The Relevance of the Moral Teaching of the Early Church"—which presupposes the contents of this one—was published in *Neotestamentica et Semitica, Studies in Honour of Matthew Black,* ed. E. Earle Ellis and Max Wilcox (Edinburgh: T & T Clark, 1969), pp. 30–49. See below, chapter 16. Both lectures should be read together. It is felicitous in this indirect way to link together two such distinguished Semitic scholars to whom I owe so much.

I begin with a central fact: through the life, death and resurrection of Jesus of Nazareth, early Christians believed that they were living "in the end of the days," in the time of fulfillment.[2] This conviction is to be understood, as is made evident in all the New Testament, in the light of the expectations expressed in the Old Testament and in Judaism that at some future date, God would act for the salvation of his people.[3] The life, death and resurrection of Jesus of Nazareth were the fulfillment of these expectations. And this fulfillment did not ignore the moral content of those expectations. The ethical aspirations of the Old Testament and Judaism, the prophets and the Law, were not annulled in the Christian dispensation; they were fulfilled.[4] The early Church consciously accepted the moral concern of Israel as it was illumined and completed in the light of the life, death and resurrection of Jesus.

This acceptance emerges clearly in that in much of the New Testament the experience of the Church was understood as parallel to that of the Jewish people. The emergence of the church was, if not the emergence of a new Israel, at least the entrance of Israel onto a new stage of its history.[5] In the creation of the Church the exodus was repeated, as it were. And as a corollary to the experience of a new exodus, the church understood itself as standing under the new Sinai of a new Moses. This complex of ideas—exodus, Sinai, Moses[6]—largely governs Paul's references to the New Covenant,[7] Matthew's[8] presentation of the Sermon on the Mount, and Mark's[9] reference to a new teaching which John presents as a new commandment.[10] In its vital contents, the moral teaching of primitive Christianity must be understood in relationship to the teaching which Judaism traced back to Sinai: this relationship is variously expressed, sometimes in terms of reform, sometimes of antithesis, and sometimes of fulfillment. What is clear is that "Law" is bound up with the Christian gospel as it was with the message of the Old Testament and Judaism.[11] To put this in technical terms, the structure of primitive Christianity is, in some aspects at least, modeled upon or grows out of the structure of Judaism. This means that Law is integral to the gospel of the New Testament as it was to that of the Old.[12]

But in what sense can this be asserted? What Law is integral to the gospel? This brings us to the motif which most governs early Christian thought on morality. I have already asserted that the early church reinterpreted the moral tradition of the Old Testament and Judaism in the light of Christ; and it is the person of Christ that is normative for the understanding of morality, as of all other aspects of life, in the New Testament.[13] Just as early Christians reinterpreted the Temple,[14] Jerusalem,[15] the Sabbath,[16] and all the significant symbols of Jewish self-identity in terms of Christ, so they reinterpreted the Law. They found "in Christ" a new demand under which they stood, so that—although the precise phrase does not occur—Christ became their Law. I have argued elsewhere that for Paul Jesus took the place of Torah. The demand of Christianity is concentrated in the person of Christ.[17]

But what precisely does this mean? I think that it has three aspects which are exceedingly difficult to hold in proper balance. First, the moral life of Christians bears constant reference to, or is molded by, the actual life of Jesus of Nazareth, that is, his ministry of forgiveness, judgment, healing, and teaching.[18] Second, the moral teaching has its point of departure not only in the ministry of Jesus but also in his resurrection. The resurrection was the ground for the emergence of the primitive community, as a well-knit and self-conscious group. But the resurrection was also the immediate inspiration of its morality. The resurrection was not only a triumph of life over death, it was also a triumph of forgiveness over sin. The resurrection was an expression, perhaps *the* expression of God's grace in Christ, because the risen Christ came back to those who had forsaken him and fled, who had slept during his agony. He forgave their failure. The resurrection as forgiveness emerges clearly in Paul and elsewhere.[10] The resurrection, which reassembled the scattered disciples to form the church, was founded in the grace of Christ and of God in Christ. It was of a piece with the whole ministry of Jesus, and the morality of the community, like that of his ministry, was to be one governed by grace—that is, it was the morality of forgiven people who had known the risen Lord as a forgiving Lord, and who in gratitude (the most ethical of all the emotions) gave themselves to the good life in his name.[20]

But third, the model of the presence of this risen Lord in the community was that of "the Spirit." There have been attempts to maintain that the Spirit, in the earliest days of the Church, had no ethical significance, that it was merely a wonder-working power, mysterious and nonmoral. But these attempts are vain. It was the Spirit who had inspired the greatest teachers of morality, the prophets—who had discerned between the precious and the vile; it was the Spirit who would create a new heart in the new Israel of Ezekiel's vision and inspire the messianic times with counsel, wisdom, and righteousness. And above all else, the Spirit was the inspirer of the Scriptures. This in itself implied the ethicization of the Spirit, because it was through the Scriptures that Israel knew the demands made upon it. Through the resurrection, the Spirit was again experienced.

The coming of the Spirit in primitive Christianity should never be separated from the resurrection as grace. Like the resurrection itself, the coming of the Spirit is "an energy of forgiveness." Thus it became the source of morality, because gratitude for forgiveness is the ground of Christian being. Love, joy, peace, righteousness, and every victory "in the moral sphere" are the fruits of the Spirit. The enthusiasm of the Spirit, much as it was open to more superficial expressions, found its true fruit in love.[21]

When, therefore, we say that for the early Church the Law had been Christified, we recognize that the earthly ministry of Jesus, the risen Lord, and the Spirit—inextricably bound together as they are, so that often what was uttered in the Spirit could be ascribed to the earthly Jesus himself— all these together became the source of the demand under which the early Church lived. Christian morality, in short, always has as its point of reference the life, resurrection, and living Spirit of Jesus Christ. And it is this that determines its manifold dimensions. These can be conveniently gathered under two main headings: its vertical and horizontal dimensions.[22]

THE VERTICAL DIMENSIONS OF
CHRISTIAN MORALITY

As we have seen, then, the ground on which the early Church stood was the life, death, resurrection, and Spirit of Jesus Christ. To put the matter geometrically, it was their vertical relationship with the risen Lord, the participation of the early Christians in the experience of being forgiven by the risen Lord and the Spirit, that lent to Christians a common grace wherein they stood. They had been grasped by him and their response was primarily, through the promptings of this Spirit, to him. All Christian fellowship was rooted in a particular event—immediately in the resurrection and behind this in the life and death of Jesus, with which the resurrection, as we have seen, as an expression of grace was wholly congruous. The ethic of the community is linked to the understanding of an event—the life, death, and resurrection of Jesus. In this the Church saw the act of God himself in history.

Now in much of the New Testament, though not in all, morality is understood in terms of the appropriation of this event, the recapitulation of it in the life of the believer. To put it in other words, the moral life is a life "in Christ"; it is the living out in daily conduct what it means to have died and risen with Christ. This is true of Paul and, it is arguable, of Matthew also.[23] For Paul, morality is inseparable from the life, death, and resurrection of Jesus. He divided his own life clearly into two parts:

first, his life under the law when he was a Jew, and second, his life in Christ. The two parts were distinctly separated by his experience on the road to Damascus. The act by which a Christian acknowledged his or her faith and really began to live "in Christ" was baptism. This act symbolized a death to the old life under the Law and a rising to newness of life "in Christ" or "in the Spirit." By baptism[24] the Christian through faith had died, had risen, had been justified: he or she was a new creation. And what was now necessary for him or her was to become what he or she was. The moral life was now rooted in this new creation in Christ. Just as we call on each other to "act like a man," so Christians are called upon to "act like a Christian"—to be what they are. To use theological jargon—the imperative in Paul is rooted in the indicative. There is a vertical dimension to Christian living—an attachment to the fact of Christ, his life, death, and resurrection.[25]

And so, too, in the Fourth Gospel the life of the Christian person is to reenact the self-giving of God in sending Christ into the world. The "love" which exists between the Father and the Son is to be reproduced in the relationship of the disciples to one another. Here again there is a vertical relationship between the believer and Christ and God which determines his or her relationship with others.[26]

But this vertical dimension of morality in the early Church has another aspect which is easier to understand. Not only the imitation of God's act through dying and rising with Christ, but also the imitation of the Jesus of history (if we may so put it) played a real part in the moral development of the early Church. Early Christians looked up to Jesus of Nazareth— so a modern educator would put it—as their "identifying figure." Part of the reason for the preservation of stories about the life of Jesus such as we have in the Gospels was the desire to imitate Jesus in his acts.[27] During his ministry Jesus had demanded readiness to enter upon his way of suffering: his followers were literally to take up the cross (Mark 8:34ff.). In the life of the early Church, while persecution (walking the way of the cross literally) was always a possibility, more often Christians were called upon to imitate their Lord, in the witness of the common way less spectacular perhaps, than readiness to die, but no less arduous— with love, forbearance, patience, mercy—in messianic grace. Luke's change of Mark 8:34 in 9:23 is significant.[28] The degree to which the imitation of Jesus informed the lives of early Christians has been variously assessed. But it is difficult to deny its presence. Christ is an object of imitation to Paul as Paul expects to be such an object to his own followers (1 Cor 11:1). The apostle holds up certain qualities of the historic Jesus which were to be imitated: he points to Jesus who pleased not himself (Rom 15:3), to his meekness and gentleness (2 Cor 10:1), and Paul commands liberality through a reminder of him who was rich and became poor (2 Cor 8:8-9).[29] The description of love in 1 Corinthians 13 which is probably based upon the life of Jesus is, in short, a character sketch of him. There can be little question that for Paul every Christian is pledged to an attempted moral conformity to Christ. So also is it with the Fourth Gospel (John 13) and 1 Peter 2:2.[30] The life of Jesus is a paradigm of the Christian life.

So far we have noted two aspects of the vertical dimensions of Christian morality in the early Church: The Christian is raised up with Christ to newness of life and is to live out his resurrection daily; and he or she looks to Jesus as an object of imitation. There is a third aspect to this vertical dimension. The Christian is taken up into the purpose of God in Christ. To be a believer was to be directed to and by Jesus of Nazareth as the Messiah. That is, there is always an eschatological reference to Christian living: the Christian shares in the purpose of God in the salvation revealed in Jesus. This comes out most clearly in Paul's understanding of his call to be an apostle. This meant for him that he was taken up by God's grace to share in the redemptive activity of God now at work through Christ in the Church. True, the apostolic consciousness of Paul was more intense than that of most Christians and his calling as the apostle to the Gentiles, perhaps, unique. But the whole community also was called, that is, caught up into the large counsel of God. Christians were delivered from futility; they shared in the work of salvation (including their own) inaugurated by Jesus and to be completed in the future. In the light of the redemptive purpose revealed in Christ they made their decisions, they discerned the things that further and hinder this purpose, and they became fellow workers with God.[31] The life of early Christians was a life born of the grace of God in the resurrection and sustained by the hope of the end: Christian morality is rooted in a "lively hope"[32] even as it is informed by the earthly Jesus. It is governed by a memory and an anticipation.

THE HORIZONTAL DIMENSIONS OF CHRISTIAN MORALITY

So far in describing the moral life of early Christianity, I have emphasized what I have called its vertical dimension—its attachment to the Risen Christ who was one with the Jesus of history; its contemplation of him in imitation and its participation in the divine purpose in him. But

the early Christians were not exclusively oriented to these vertical realities, and early Christian morality contains a horizontal or, if I may put
it, a human, societal dimension: it is the morality of a community born
of the grace of the resurrection. The New Testament knows nothing of
solitary religion and it knows nothing of an individual morality: it points
to a community with a life to live. This community was not to luxuriate
in grace, absorbed in irrelevant, vertical privileges. As a community of
grace, it took practical steps to give expression to grace in its life. How
was this achieved? We may summarize the answer to this question under
two main headings.

The emphasis on the Christian community. First, there was a constant
concern among early Christians for the quality of their common life. This
it was that led to the experiment usually referred to as the "communism"
of the early chapters of Acts.[33] This experiment of having all things common was the natural, spontaneous expression of life in the Spirit with
which the neglect of the poor was incompatible. This appears from the
naiveté of the experiment. Owners sold their property and handed over
the proceeds to the apostles, who administered a common fund from
which the needs of the poor were met, presumably in the form of common
meals. The contributions to the common pool were voluntary (Acts 5:1–
11). The experiment failed, not to be repeated in this form; but it witnessed
to the societal or communal morality of the primitive community in its
realism and its impracticability. That experiment took place in the light
of an absolute demand for love informed by the intensity of the Church's
experience of forgiveness and therefore of grace.

The emphasis on the communal nature of the Christian way persists
throughout the New Testament. It is rooted in such an emphasis in the
ministry of Jesus himself, who gathered the twelve as the representatives
of the new community of Israel to follow him.[34] It is from this probably
that there developed Paul's "Christ Mysticism," which issued not in "a
flight of the alone to the Alone" but in the building up of the Church, the
new community.[35] Along with rationality[36] and the recognition of personal
integrity[37] Paul sets forth as the criterion of Christian action the building
up of the Church.[38] Similarly, in the Johannine literature one finds the
love of the brothers and sisters as the mark of the church. "If you love
not your brother whom you have seen, how can you love God whom you
have not seen?"[39]

But the same impulse which led to the experiment in communism, the
awareness of the horizontal significance of the life in grace, in part at
least, led to other developments:

The emphasis on specific moral teaching. At first, in the awareness of its resources in grace, the Church attempted to live in the light of the absolutes, in messianic license, as Stendahl has characterized this. The absolutes constitute the peculiarity, though not the totality, of the teaching of Jesus. For certain elements in the early Church, the commandments of Jesus in their absolute form were guides for conduct. But under inevitable pressures it became necessary for the Church to apply these absolutes to life. There began that process which tended to transform the absolutes into practical rules of conduct—Christian casuistry.[40] The classic example is the way in which the prohibition of divorce was made practical by the addition of the exceptive clause: "except on the ground of unchastity" (Matt 5:32ff.). Because it is Matthew that reveals this best, it has been claimed that the words of Jesus as such played a significant part in the moral development of the church only in Jewish Christian circles. But this is not so. The Pauline letters also appeal to the words of Jesus as authoritative. These words were at least one source for Paul's moral teaching. The extent to which the Pauline letters are reminiscent of the tradition as represented in the synoptics has been insufficiently recognized. The matter has been the subject of acute debate and continues to be so.

Two factors emerge clearly: first, Paul interweaves words of Jesus almost "unconsciously," as it were, into his exhortations, which suggests that these words were bone of his bone. The following parallels are clear:

Rom 12:14
Bless those who persecute you; bless and do not curse them.

Matt 5:43
You have heard that it was said, "You shall love your neighbor and hate your enemy."

Rom 12:17
Repay no one evil for evil, but take thought for what is noble in the sight of all.

Matt 5:39ff.
But I say to you, Do not resist one who is evil. But if any one strikes you on the right cheek, turn to him the other also.

Rom 13:7
Pay all of them their dues, taxes to whom taxes are due, revenue to whom revenue is due, respect to whom respect is due, honor to whom honor is due.

Matt 22:15–22
Render therefore to Caesar the things that are Caesar's, and to God the things that are God's (22:21b).

Rom 14:13
Then let us no more pass judgment on one another, but rather decide never to put a stumbling block or hindrance in the way of a brother.

Matthew 18:7
Woe to the world for temptations to sin! For it is necessary that temptations come, but woe to the man by whom the temptation comes!

Rom 14:14
I know and am persuaded in the
Lord Jesus that nothing is
unclean in itself; but it is unclean
for any one who thinks it
unclean.

Matthew 15:11
Not what goes into the mouth
defiles a man, but what comes
out of the mouth, this defiles a
man.

1 Thess 5:2
For you yourselves know well
that the day of the Lord will
come like a thief in the night.

Matt. 24:43–44
But know this, that if the
householder had known in what
part of the night the thief was
coming, he would have watched
and would not have let his house
be broken into. Therefore you
also must be ready; for the Son
of man is coming at an hour you
do not expect.

1 Thess 5:13
. . . and to esteem them very
highly in love because of their
work. Be at peace among
yourselves.

Mark 9:50
Salt is good; but if the salt has
lost its saltness, how will you
season it? Have salt in
yourselves, and be at peace with
one another.

1 Thess 5:15
See that none of you repays evil
for evil, but always seek to do
good to one another and to all.

Matt. 5:39–47
But I say to you, Love your
enemies and pray for those who
persecute you . . . (5:44).

In addition to these clear parallels there are many other possible or probable ones. The evidence for these is given elsewhere.[41]

Second, there is also clear evidence that there was a collection of sayings of the Lord to which Paul appealed (Acts 20:35; 1 Cor 7:10; 9:14; 11:23ff; 14:37; 1 Thess 4:15–16; see especially 1 Cor 7:25). Not only in matters of a legislative character does Paul find guidance in the words of Jesus, but also in more personal matters (Romans 7), where possibly his discovery of the supreme importance of motive goes back to Jesus. In 1 Cor 7:25 he refers to a word of Christ as a commandment; in two places, once explicitly and once implicitly, he uses the very words "the law of Christ"[42] where the reference is, in part at least, to the teaching of Jesus. This is no declension on Paul's part to a primitive legalism, but the recognition of the fact that his exalted Lord was never, in his mind, divorced from Jesus, the teacher, that the Spirit is never divorced from the historic teaching of Jesus. And although in the Fourth Gospel the moral teaching of Jesus as such plays little part, the function of the Spirit is to recall the words of Jesus.[43] The same emphasis appears in 1 John, where there is constant appeal to the commandments of the Lord and frequent echoes of them.[44]

Nevertheless, there is a difference of emphasis (but only of emphasis) in Matthew and Paul as over against the Johannine literature. The words of Jesus appear in the former two over their wide range. But even there they are summed up in one word, *agapē*. Thus the climax of the Sermon on the Mount at Matt 7:12 is the Golden Rule. And Paul and John, like the synoptics, emphasize the centrality of "love" (Rom 13:8–10; 1 Cor 8:1; 13; Col 3:14; John 13:34–35; 1 John 3:1; 2:7–10; 4:7–16). The meaning of *love* has again to be carefully noted. Partaking more of active good will than of emotion, it can be commanded as emotions cannot. In 1 John it is used in a down-to-earth manner as involving willingness to share one's goods (1 John 3:17). For Paul it is the fulfillment of the law and the principle of cohesion in the Christian community. The expression of love is multiple (1 Corinthians 13), but its essential nature is revealed in Christ's dying for humankind. It is this kind of act that is demanded of those who love.[45]

The necessity which led to the application of the absolutes of Jesus to life led the church to take over for its own use codal material whether from Hellenism or from Judaism or both. Most of the letters reveal a twofold structure: a first part, dealing with "doctrine," is followed by a second, dealing with "ethics." Romans is typical. Chapters 1–11 deal with doctrine, 12:1ff. deals with ethics, and it is casually connected with chapters 1–11. The ethical sections of the various letters reveal a common tradition of catechesis, which may have been used in the instruction of converts, especially at baptism (cf. Rom 12:1; Eph 4:20–6:19; Col 3:8—4:12; Heb 12:1–2; Jas 1:1—4:10; 1 Pet 1:1—4:11; 4:12—5:14).[46] This common tradition must not be regarded as having a fixed pattern, but the similarity in the order and contents of the material in the above sections is too marked to be accidental. The presence in them of the imperative participle (e.g., Rom 12:9–19), a form found but not common in Hellenistic Greek but familiar in Hebrew legal documents, suggests that Paul and other Christian writers drew upon codal material, such as is found in the Dead Sea Scrolls (*Manual of Discipline* [*Serek hayyaḥad*] 1:18ff. actually has the imperative participle), *m. Demai* and *Derek Ereṣ Rabba* and *Zuṭa*.[47] There are also parallels to the tradition in Hellenistic sources. The Church probably took over much pagan moral convention from the Jewish Diaspora. Whatever the exact source of the material, the church found it necessary to borrow from non-Christian sources. It not only domesticated the absolutes of Jesus, it took over domestic virtues from the world.[48]

This brings us to the last aspect of New Testament moral teaching with which we shall deal here. That the church was able to draw upon moral teaching from Judaism and Hellenism means that there was a continuity between the moral awareness of Christians and of the non-Christian world. Wherein did this continuity lie? It lay probably in the doctrine of creation which the early church held. It cannot be overemphasized that creation and redemption are congenial in the New Testament, as indeed in Judaism. The messianic age had cosmic dimensions for Judaism. So too in the New Testament the creator and the redeemer are one. It is this that explains the ease with which Jesus can discover redemptive, spiritual truth in the natural order as in Matt 5:43–48 and in his parables; it explains how Paul can find in Christ the wisdom—the creative agent—of God, and how John and Hebrews can find in him the Word by which all things were made. For the New Testament writers the good life is the truly natural life. Morality is rooted in creation.[49]

In the above I have sketched in very broad strokes the context, center of gravity, and dimensions of the moral teaching of the early Church; its context in primitive Christian eschatology; its center of gravity in the life, death, and resurrection of Jesus of Nazareth, the Christ; its dimensions both in its vertical concentration in Christ, the Risen Lord, and in its horizontal concern with the community and its cosmic affinities. We have not touched upon the relevance of this teaching to the life of the world outside the church. That theme is dealt with in the following chapter.

16

The Relevance of the
Moral Teaching of the
*Early Church**

In a study of "Ethics in the New Testament"[1] I traced the context, center of gravity, and dimensions of the moral teaching of the early Church: its context in primitive Christian eschatology; its center of gravity in the life, death, and resurrection of Jesus of Nazareth, the Christ; its dimensions both in its vertical concentration in Christ, the risen Lord, and in its horizontal concern with the community. It might appear from that study that the moral teaching of the early Church was somewhat ingrown, concerned with the Christian verities and experience and with the Christian community alone, unrelated to the larger world. Was the moral teaching of Christianity at first that of a ghetto, just as so much Protestant morality has historically been "ghetto morality"? As we shall see later, the answer to this question is exceedingly difficult. In this essay I shall address myself to the question whether the moral teaching of the early Church was pertinent to the larger world of the first century and whether it remains relevant to that of the twentieth. It is a question which, despite his immersion in the minutiae of technical biblical studies, has always concerned my friend, Matthew Black, and this treatment, inadequate as it is, may serve not only to indicate my debt and gratitude to him, but also to salute him, not so much as a scholar of a vast erudition—the other contributors will liberally do this—but as a concerned Christian and *pastor pastorum*.

But before I do so, it is well to recognize a familiar and not altogether irrelevant fact. In much of the New Testament and the practice of the early Church there is no clear indication of the relevance of the early Christian moral teaching to society and the world at large. It would be easy to gather from a reading of the New Testament that its moral teaching was primarily, if not entirely, designed to cultivate the garden of the Church. The fragrance of that garden was, indeed, to sweeten the wilderness of the surrounding world and to attract people into the redeemed

---

* This is one in the series of *Haskell Lectures* which, along with Dean Krister Stendahl, I delivered at Oberlin College, Oberlin, Ohio in March 1968. The first lecture, which it presupposes, was "The Moral Teaching of the Early Church," see above, chapter 15.

community, but only as an indirect consequence.[2] There is no suggestion in the New Testament that the Church should in any way instruct the world as to how to carry on its business. The secular magistrates and judges, the rulers of this world, are not directly addressed as if the Church had either any right to do so or any superior wisdom to offer. There was, generally, a deep awareness of the cleavage between the Church and the world, and even of an antagonism, a necessary antagonism, between the two.[3] It was not the primary concern of the Church to influence society and culture but to be itself in its moral life, as in other respects, the people of God, in the world but not of it.

Must we then, in the light of this, give up any attempt at finding early Christian moral teaching relevant to our world? If I understand it aright, this is the thrust of some protests against the profound secularization of the Christian faith which is now so prevalent. I may illustrate from a recent article by Paul Peachey entitled "New Ethical Possibility: The Task of Post-Christendom Ethics?"[4] According to him, the notion that Christians should make society as a whole Christian was the outcome or concomitant of a disastrous event in the history of the Church, the recognition of Christianity by Constantine as the established religion of the Empire. It was then that Christendom, as distinct from Christianity, was born. As Peachey puts it: "the ethical consequence of the Constantinian shift was the transfer of the framework of Christian ethical thought from the community of grace, the new people of God, to the larger domain of the natural performance which, paradoxically, she could not postulate for her own members . . . [the churches after Constantine] while failing in their internal ethical discourse, enlisting the legislature and police power of civil government to demand of the whole society levels of performance not yet implicit in their own life."[5] Peachey pleads that the Church should give up the idea that it can create a Christendom, that is, a Christian civilization, as generations of Christians have understood such a phrase, and concentrate on the cultivation of its own garden. History has disowned the idea that world society can be made more Christian: let us abandon it. The task of the Church is itself to be the Church before it seeks to direct the world. Before it can or should address the world let it be true to itself. Peachey quotes with approval the words of Walter Hobhouse:

> The Church of the future is destined more and more to a condition of things somewhat like that which prevailed in the Ante-Nicene Church: that is to say, that instead of pretending to be coextensive with the world, it will accept a position involving a more conscious antagonism with the world, and will, in return, regain to some measure its former coherence.[6]

Few who are familiar with certain pietistic and nonconformist traditions will find such a view strange. There have always been in the Church monasteries, convents, sects, groups. The most recent expression of this view in British life is that of T. S. Eliot in his well-known essay *The Idea of a Christian Society* (New York, 1940), in which he argues for what he calls a clerisy or Christian community. He writes: "We need therefore what I have called 'the Community of Christians,' by which I mean, not local groups and not the Church in any of its senses, unless we call it 'the Church within the Church' . . . These will be consciously and thoughtfully practicing Christians especially those of intellectual and spiritual superiority."[7] And yet before we accept this view, attractive as at first sight it might seem, and while, indeed, we might not only agree but insist that the first call upon the Church is to be the Church we must ask whether it does justice to what was implicit, if not made explicit, in the New Testament. Before we concede that the early Church was turned in upon itself and not directly concerned with the structures of this world, let us consider certain aspects of its thinking.

Two aspects of early Christian thought have been claimed to justify the view that the early Christian moral teaching had relevance to the world. They center on two points, first, eschatology, and second, creation.

First, it has been claimed that the eschatological ideas of the early Church have a direct bearing on the political realities of society as a whole. Two scholars in the Anglo-Saxon world have made this view familiar— the late G. H. C. Macgregor[8] and Amos N. Wilder. In a now famous article in the *Festschrift in Honour of C. H. Dodd,*[9] Wilder made the attempt to find a basis for what he called "a kerygmatic social ethic and an aggressive social action" in Paul's view of the conflict between God, Christ, the Church and the evil, unseen forces, the demonic principalities and powers, the rulers of this world, about which we read in his epistles, and also especially in Colossians and Ephesians. These demonic powers are not simply mythological beings. For the early Church they represented the structural elements of unregenerate society, the false authorities, or rather tyrannies, of culture and power. Early Christians spoke of principalities and powers just as Blacks today speak of the white-power structure, that is, as social and political realities to be opposed.

For the early Church, the might of these demonic powers had been confronted in a set encounter with Christ. During his ministry of exorcism, and especially in his death, he had overcome them. The demonic in the world and in society had been subdued. But it had not been completely subdued. The struggle between Christ and the demonic goes on until the

Parousia. In this struggle Christians are called to share. This justifies social action: here is the sanction for the social gospel, for Christian involvement in politics. To participate in the defeat of the demonic means to be pitted against all the evil structures, customs, and powers that exploit humanity.

This impressive attempt to find the relevance of the Christian way in its eschatology, that is, more particularly, in its understanding of the victory of Christ over the demonic, breaks down in the quagmire of what is called demythologization. We must ask whether the demythologization of the principalities and powers proposed by MacGregor and Wilder is justified. Did the early Church understand them to refer to political and social realities? It may be plausibly argued in the light of Jewish concepts of the relationship between angels and the states[10] that the principalities and powers and such entities in the Pauline epistles may be mythological expressions of social, political, and economic actualities. But it is exceedingly difficult to ascribe them this significance in the Gospels, which belong largely to the same milieu. In the Gospels the demons attack individuals, not society as a whole. The proposed justification of social action in terms of the vanquished demons of eschatology must be regarded as dubious.

But despite this, the appeal to the moral relevance of eschatology is not to be dismissed. It was the conviction of the early Church that it was taken up "in Christ" into the purpose of God in a cosmic drama of redemption. Part of this drama was the defeat—incipient as it might be—of the world powers by Christ. In this defeat, by participation in the redemptive activity of God in Christ, the Christian shares. It is his to *discern* the activity of the divine purpose in Christ, to prove it and to throw in his lot in decision for it. The moral activity of the Christian consists of discerning the times and the purpose of God in the times: it is his or hers to *decide* for that purpose, to recognize the things that are different.[11] In this sense the whole of the Christian moral life is eschatologically determined. Christian morality has a cosmic awareness. In this connection it is exceedingly important to read the New Testament, which otherwise can seem to be and has often been treated as a very parochial document, against its total background in the large world of the Old Testament and Jewish eschatology.

And, finally, the moral life of the early Church was even more strictly governed by eschatology. It was governed by a lively hope—the hope that at the end victory was assured, the kingdoms of this world were to become the kingdoms of our God and of his Christ. Christians were called to a hope which informed all their moral life. In this way the eschatological determined the ethical, and by its very nature the former gave to the latter a social and cosmic dimension.[12]

More directly convincing perhaps is the second factor in early Christian thought to which we now refer. It cannot be sufficiently emphasized that the moral teaching of the early Church was conceived of in intimate relationship to creation. The Church took over for its own purposes non-Christian ethical forms and norms. It borrowed from Judaism and Hellenism codes which it readily applied, without any sense of incongruity, to its own life. The paraenetic sections of the Pauline epistles bear eloquent testimony to this. The moral teaching of the early Church was not severely cut off from non-Christian moral traditions. On the contrary, it was open to and appreciative of such traditions: it used them without compunction.

There was, therefore, a point of contact of some kind between Christian teaching and morality and the non-Christian. There was not a complete break between the moral teaching of the Church and that of the Greco-Roman world: there was some affinity between them.[13] Where did this affinity lie? It lay in the relationship of the morality demanded by the New Testament to the created order which both Christians and non-Christians shared. This relationship first appears in the teaching of Jesus as it is presented in the Gospels. For Jesus there was an inward affinity between the natural and the moral, a kind of "natural law" in the "spiritual world." He found natural human relationships, at one level, a clue to the will of God. Matt 7:11 reads:

> If you then, who are evil, know how to give good gifts to your children, how much more will your Father who is in heaven give good things to those who ask him?

In Matt 5:43ff. the created order is clearly made a paradigm for the moral order:

> You have heard that it was said, "You shall love your neighbor and hate your enemy." But I say to you, Love your enemies and pray for those who persecute you, so that you may be sons of your Father who is in heaven; for he makes his sun to rise on the evil and on the good and sends rain on the just and on the unjust.
>
> For if you love those who love you, what reward have you? Do not even the tax collectors do the same? And if you salute only your brethren, what more are you doing than others? Do not even the Gentiles do the same?
>
> You, therefore, must be perfect, as your heavenly Father is perfect.

Quite as clearly the natural order is a paradigm for the moral in the parables of Jesus. C. H. Dodd's words deserve quotation:[14]

> There is a reason for this realism of the parables of Jesus. It arises from a conviction that there is not mere analogy, but an inward affinity, between the natural order and the spiritual order; or as we might put it in the language of the parables themselves, the Kingdom of God is intrinsically *like* the processes of nature and of the daily life of men. Jesus therefore did not feel the need of making up artificial illustrations for the truths He wanted to teach. He found them ready made by the Maker of man and nature. That human life, including the religious life, is a part of nature is distinctly stated in the well-known passage beginning "Consider the fowls of the air . . . (Matt 6:26–30; Luke 7:24–28). This sense of the divineness of the natural order is the major premise of all the parables. . . ."

The appeal to the created order is found not only in the strictly didactic portions of the Gospels, as in the Sermon on the Mount and the parables, but also in discussions between Jesus and his opponents on moral questions, as in Mark 10:2–9, where monogamy is grounded in the creation. "But from the beginning of creation, God made them male and female!" (10:6).

What we find in Jesus reemerges in Paul. In teaching that Christ was the agent of creation, Paul, too, we cannot doubt, was seeking to express that to live after Christ is the natural life. Paul was essentially a city dweller, and hardly ever does he turn in Wordsworthian fashion to nature's "old felicities" for parable or illustration,[15] but strange as it may seem his doctrine of the agency of Christ in creation really sets forth the truth, to which we have already referred, that Jesus always assumed in his parables—that there is an inward affinity between the natural order and the spiritual order. He can, therefore, refer to what nature itself teaches in order to derive a rule for worship, as in 1 Cor 11:13ff., which reads:

> Judge for yourselves; is it proper for a woman to pray to God with her head uncovered? Does not nature itself teach you (οὐδὲ ἡ φύσις αὐτὴ διδάσκει ὑμᾶς) that for a man to wear long hair is degrading to him, but if a woman has long hair it is her pride? For her hair is given to her for a covering.

Paul here appeals to "nature" in order to decide an issue of custom. In the same way he used the term—a Stoic one— "what is fitting" (τὰ καθήκοντα), as in Rom 1:28. By this he means what is truly natural or what nature itself teaches. There is a kind of conduct which is improper because it is unnatural. This appears particularly from Paul's references to sexual perversions. Again in Romans 1, 2 the Apostle makes appeal to a "law" written on the hearts of all men in virtue of their creation, a kind of natural law, if such a loose term be permitted. We read:

> When the Gentiles who have not the law do by nature what the law requires, they are a law to themselves, even though they do not have the law. They show that what the law requires is written on their hearts, while their conscience also bears witness and their conflicting thoughts accuse or perhaps excuse them (Rom 2:14–15).

The use of the term "conscience," although not an important concept in Paul's thought,[16] points in the same direction we have indicated. It is further possible to argue that the apostolic decree in Acts 15, in which it was agreed to write to the Gentiles that they should "abstain from the pollution of idols and from unchastity and from what is strangled and from blood"—that this decree rests on the Noachian commandments,[17] that is, laws which were considered as binding upon every living soul, which had been given to Noah, the father of mankind, before the revelation of Sinai.

But more important than all these details is what we first pointed out in Paul and was surely true for the early Church generally—that Christ, the redeemer and revealer of God's moral purpose, is also the agent of creation (see John 1:1ff.; Col 1:15ff.; Heb 1:1ff.). The redeemer is the creator. Thus the ethics of the New Testament, rooted as it is in the gospel, is not only of relevance to the Church but also to the world insofar as it affirms and confirms what is truly natural for all people in virtue of their creation. The created order and humankind as part of this order is of God. It is, therefore, to be expected that the ethical tradition of humankind should be of use to the Church and often be consonant with its moral teaching. Christ, creation, and the Church and the moral dimensions of that Church and of that creation are not in opposition. The Christian moral life is the "natural" life and the teaching of the Church does not annul the virtues of the natural person: rather it confirms them and even depends on them. In this sense the moral teaching of the Church is continuous with the morality of those outside even while it is a mirror of what that morality should be. That there are also elements of discontinuity or peculiar emphasis in the moral teaching of the Church is to be expected.

But, it will be noted, all the above does not take us very far. Granted that the moral teaching of the early Church is a mirror in which the world can judge itself, can we go further? Can we claim that the early Church provides an ethic directly relevant to our society? Has its moral teaching not merely a judgmental role in the world but a regulative one? Can it supply society with positive, direct guidance?

Before we attempt to answer this question, it is important to recognize two salient facts about the early Church. First, during the period of the New Testament the Church was an insignificant minority, numerically and otherwise, in the Greco-Roman world. Its position was such that it was unlikely to indulge in any notions that it might wield any political or social influence or power. And, second, although there was evident in the early Church a real Christianizing of personal relationships within the existing order, as for example in the life of Philemon, that order was expected to end at a not too distant future. Under the influence of this expectation it was natural that the Church, at first at least, was not concerned with changing social and political structures, evil as many of them were. For example, when Paul discovered that the term "Kingdom of God" had disturbing political implications, he was led to drop it from his vocabulary.[18] Stormy petrel though he was, Paul was anxious not to be a disturbance. It was not quite clear—though perhaps probable—that Paul would advise a slave who could do so to take advantage of a chance to be free.[19] Even in 1 Cor 6:1-11, where Paul deals with legal procedures, he gives no rules for institutional reform even in the Church but merely demands that at each step Christians should be aware of their role as the people of God who in the future but not now were to judge the world. This appears generally to be the case. Paul does not seem to be directly concerned with political panaceas of any kind. In Romans 12 he merely warns against being conformed to the world. But in Rom 13:1ff. he explicitly enjoins obedience to the worldly powers.[20] At first at least, the expectation of the end seems to have turned Christians in upon themselves despite their vast missionary activity.[21] And we may well ask again whether this means that the early Church was in any way concerned with sustaining a frontal attack on the evils of society. Was it not concentrated on its own communal life as it awaited the end despite its deep missionary urge?

The answer is both negative and positive. There was no direct road from the early Church to social action and what would now be called "relevance." And yet the early Church did speak to both the Jewish and Hellenistic worlds of its day by its very existence as the people of God with all the challenges that this set before the world. And it presents the same challenges *mutatis mutandis* to our world. These challenges may be conveniently presented as follows.

The early Church confronted the world with a body of moral teaching, a messianic law. Elements of this teaching were, although simple in their forms, stark in their demands, inescapable in their penetration, impossible of fulfillment. Other elements were prescriptive, catechetical, or paraenetical. Christians brought with them to any situation which they encountered a body of moral prescriptions and insights: they were not only open, as were all others, to the demands of the 'context' in which they moved, but they confronted that 'context' with demands under which they knew themselves to stand. The body of moral teaching which they cherished they thought of as directed primarily to themselves: the messianic law was for the messianic community. But inevitably, even when the Church was unworthy of it, this teaching of necessity challenged the world also. This is still so, even though it cannot be precisely delimited.

At this point the distinction between the absolute aspect—what Stendahl has called the messianic "license"—of the moral teaching of early Christianity and its prescriptive, catechetical directions must be emphasized. The New Testament presents both absolute and paraenetic demands.

Let us look at the latter first. The moral teaching of the early Church contains specific rules for conduct in and through which that Church considered that it could manifest its true life. These rules express for it the structure of *agapē;* they are the ways in which "love" has worked itself out in daily traffic.[22] These principles, prescriptions, laws—however we choose to call the New Testament directives—are part of the moral experience of the Church as it ordered its life beyond the resurrection and, after the Parousia had delayed, when it had to settle down to live in a cold world in the light of a common day. And as long as we are in the period before the Parousia, which is the period of the Church, he or she would be a bold person who would without much circumspection scrap the prescriptions for the ordering of its life which the Church preserved.[23] No one generation can lightly set itself above, condemn or reject the element of moral directive set forth by the early Church. Without these, a single generation might perchance live, but the generations would starve.

This, most emphatically, does not mean that every generation is called upon to accept the body of the moral directives of the early Church in the same way. The deposit of that tradition must remain: its interpretation must vary. As I have shown elsewhere, the early Church itself engaged in the application of the moral demands under which it lived in a casuistic manner.[24] And there must be a Christian casuistry today. So, too, just as the early Church borrowed from the surrounding culture in the formulation of its moral teaching, all the resources available to us from the contemporary world—psychological, sociological, philosophical— should be exploited for the same purpose. It is impossible not to recognize in the early Church a prescriptive, casuistic concern. And such a concern remains indispensable.

But once this is recognized, it has also to be noted that prescriptive casuistry was not very highly developed in the early Church: it remained comparatively uncomplicated. Contrast with the very simple casuistry of the New Testament the elaboration of casuistic materials in Judaism as exemplified in the Mishna. The peculiar genius of Christian moral life does not lie with these moral directives with which we are now dealing.[25]

And this leads me to the other kind of moral teaching in the early Church—the presentation of the absolutes of Jesus. Here is the peculiarity of Christian moral teaching: that it places us not in the presence of the normal moral virtues but under the judgment of absolute demands. These remain to stir up what Stendahl has called "the eschatological itch."[26]

All this means that the moral teaching of the Church in its two forms recognizes the necessity of two things which seem incompatible but must be kept in living tension. It recognizes the need for patient application of moral rules and duties to the ongoing life of the Church and the world in which the Parousia has not taken place, and also the need to stand always under the absolute demands of the New Sinai. In short, it allows for patience and impatience, the inevitability of gradualness and the inevitability of radical change.

So far I have dealt with the direct moral teaching of the early Church, but this is only part and not the chief part of the challenge of the Church to the world. There is another challenge to which we now turn, which is really inextricable from the first. In the New Testament, along with the Christian legal tradition, there is also, in some documents especially, a tendency to subsume all the moral requirements of the Gospel under the demand of *agapē*, "love," and to see in the cross of Jesus the supreme expression of *agapē*.[27] From the earliest days there has, therefore, been a concern to let *agapē* rule in all moral activity, or, to put the same thing in other words, to make the self-giving exemplified in the cross normative for all behavior. All the demands of the new law of the gospel are placed under the sign of *agapē* or of the cross.[28] However seriously they are taken, all response to the demands of the gospel, expressed in prescriptions, is to be informed by *agapē,* translatable as openness to suffering and moral sensitivity. The prescriptions are not annulled but understood in the context of grace; they are themselves to become the expression of grace. This can best be illustrated from the Sermon on the Mount itself, where the demands of the Messiah are placed after the Beatitudes, which are an expression of grace.

It follows that along with a tradition of both paraenetic and absolute moral prescriptions, the early Church presented to the world the challenge of a way of life governed by the cross, the sign of *agapē,* the ultimate demand of God. Under this cross all human activity is finally to be judged. That this is relevant in the twentieth century I need not argue.

But we have remained in the realm of moral generalities. Apart from the challenge of the moral tradition of the early Church and of the cross, can we go farther to assert that that tradition offers positive guidance for the directions in which society should move? I think it can. But we can best see the relevance of the Christian "way" today by looking at its relevance to the world of the first century.

At this point I must reiterate that this treatment is inextricably connected with the essay on "The Moral Teaching of the Early Church," in its theological dimensions, as its sequence. Our concentration on "relevance" in this the present essay endangers this connection because it isolates the moral teaching from its context in the total life of the Church and therefore distorts its character. Suffice it as a corrective here to recall that the morality of the early Church was a communal morality, that of a community under the authority of a living Lord and the guidance of the Spirit, sustained by a great hope. Within the total life of that community the paraenesis and absolute demands to which we have referred above played their part, as we have seen. But more important was the Spirit that dwelled in the community and the quality of life which it was designed to embody and which was both informed by and "interpreted" those demands. Our question, then, as to what positive guidance is provided by the moral tradition of the early church can best be answered by looking at the relevance of the "way" of the Christian community in the first century and thereby discovering, perhaps, its relevance for today.

First, let us consider how "the way" of the Church infringed upon society in the realm of allegiance to the state. The attitude of Jesus himself and of the early church was ambiguous. Sometimes, as in Rom 3:1, submission to "the powers that be" was enjoined; at others, as in Revelation, an abortive hatred that could only lead not to their redemption but to their destruction. Care is expressed to recognize the state as in 1 Peter.[29] We may sum up the matter by claiming that while the due rights of the state are acknowledged so that whenever possible obedience to it is enjoined, in early Christianity, as in Judaism, any overweening rights claimed by the state are denied.[30] Early Christians, like Jews, could not worship the emperor. But neither could they support the Zealots.[31] Jewish Christians, in what numbers we do not know, refused to enlist in the war against Rome. The New Testament forbids us to give to the state rights that do not belong to it. I know of few things more relevant to our present situation than the demand urged upon us in the New Testament to honor the state but not to make it divine or absolutize it. Nationalism, often defined as man's other religion, finds its proper evaluation in the Christian moral tradition.

The second way in which I find the "way" of the early Church particularly relevant is in what I may call the realm of culture. Here I have to be brief to the point of distortion. The Christian community came to be understood as one in which there was to be neither Jew nor Greek, bond nor free, male nor female.[32] It was to transcend cultural, economic, and sexual differences. On the cultural side it aimed at the reconciliation of Jew and Greek, between whom there was probably the deepest social, cultural, and religious cleavage of the first century.[33] But the Church, as the community of the Messiah, conceived its very purpose to be to inaugurate the eschatological unity of which the initial unity of creation is the prototype, that is, to recreate the unity broken between person and person as well as between humankind and God.

The most impressive expression of this is found in the Epistle to the Ephesians, where Paul, or at least one of his followers, sets forth the purpose of the Church. C. H. Dodd[34] has summarized this as follows:

> In Ephesians the Church is regarded as the society which embodies in history the eternal purpose of God revealed in Christ. This purpose is the ultimate unity of all being in him. While in the universe at large there are still unreconciled powers affronting the sovereignty of God, the ultimate issue is certain. God has determined to "sum up all things in Christ." That might be pure speculation, but for the fact that history and experience witness to the reconciling power of Christ in the creation of that supernatural society in which warring sections of the human race are perfectly reconciled into a whole of harmoniously functioning parts—the Church. That Jews and Gentiles should have found their place in the unity of the Church seems to the writer the most signal manifestation of reconciling grace. The enmity of Jew and Gentile was one of the fiercest in the ancient world: and the unity of Jewish and Gentile Christians in the one church *a mystery and a miracle*. He saw that the reconciliation was not accomplished by any kind of compromise between the diverse parties, but by a divine act creating out of both one new humanity. This new humanity is mediated by Christ. He sums up in Himself the whole meaning of God, and communicates Himself to men so that humanity may come to realize and express that meaning. The Church is "in Christ", it is His body, and its members have "put on"

the new humanity which is Christ in them (2:11–22). . . . In the great universe, too, there is a movement toward unity and completeness: Christ's work will not be done till the whole universe is one in Him, to the Glory of God. The living and growing unity of the Church is, so to speak, a sacrament of the ultimate unity of all things.

But not only in Ephesians does this become clear. The Pauline doctrine of Christ as the second Adam is pertinent here. Paul accepted the traditional rabbinic doctrine of the unity of humankind in Adam. That doctrine implied that the very constitution of the physical body of Adam and the method of its formation was symbolic of the real oneness of humankind. In the one body of Adam, east and west, north and south were brought together, male and female. Paul, when he thought of the new humanity being incorporated "in Christ," conceived of it as the "body" of the second Adam, where there was neither Jew nor Greek, male nor female, bond nor free. The difference between the body of the first Adam and that of the second Adam was for Paul that whereas the former was animated by the principle of natural life, was *nephesh*, the latter was animated by the Spirit; and the purpose of God in Christ is "in dispensation of the fullness of times" to "gather together in one all things in Christ" (Eph 1:10), that is, the reconstitution of the essential oneness of humankind in Christ as a "spiritual" community, as it was one in Adam in a physical sense. Finally, we refer to the farewell discourses in the Fourth Gospel where the meaning of the Christian *ecclēsia* comes to full expression again. Christ prays not only for the Twelve but for Christians yet unborn. "Neither pray I for these alone, but for them also which shall believe on me through their word; that they all may be one; as thou, Father, art in me and I in thee, that they also may be one in us: that the world may believe that thou hast sent me" (John 17:20–21).

This goal of the Christian community to achieve a truly universal society remains urgently relevant at a time when the division between East and West, rich and poor threatens the stability of the nations, and the tension between black and white is rending the most powerful of them all.

The third area where the "way" of the early Church is relevant is that of sex, where, although much in the New Testament seems to remain legislatively cold, a new spirit, that of *agapē*, was shed abroad. The demand for radical *agapē*, which in the tradition of the early Church is the true interpretation of God's will, indicates the quality and direction at which the life of sex as the life of all spheres is to aim. This, it must be emphasized, does not do away with casuistry in this realm but rather demands it.[35]

And in the fourth place, the Pauline verse cited from Gal 3:28 indicates the quality at which economic relationships should aim. Economic distinctions are not fundamental and whenever they become a hindrance to the true equality of people "in Christ" they are to be combated. It requires no profound subtlety to recognize that the *agapē* under which those "in Christ" stand demands a realistic, earthly recognition of the economic rights of all at which all social legislation and political action should aim.[36] The "social gospel," after all, in this sense, requires no other justification.

I have pointed out some areas where, it seems to me, the moral tradition of the early Church provides us with what President John Bennett would, I think, call "middle axioms,"[37] although he would not derive them as directly as is here done from the New Testament—deference but not subservience to the state, racial equality, sexual responsibility, and economic justice. They are derived, albeit indirectly, from the Christian "way" in the early Church. They provide broad guidelines in their respective areas for moral action. That they cannot and must not always be directly implemented in terms of the New Testament suggests that in other, newer realms of moral perplexity about which early Christians could know nothing but which now confront mankind it is the creative way and the Spirit of the early Church that will guide us rather than rigid adherence to its prescriptions, however valuable these still are.

In conclusion, two things remain to be noted. The implementation of all the axioms, "crucifix" patterns, the *agapē*, and prescriptions about which we have written depends on the convictions which gave them birth: they are the implications of the Christian gospel and it is from it that they draw their vitality. This essay must, therefore, be read in conjunction with its predecessor, to which I have already referred.

And finally, it is not superfluous to point out the relevance of all the above to the current ethical debate.[38] Those who favor a prescriptive ethic[39] are impatient with the contextualists who emphasize the free response of *agapē* in the "*Koinōnia*."[40] In between these extremes are those who favor "middle axioms." To a student of the New Testament—who may, probably, always be guilty of simplifying matters—the debate seems unreal or to use a term borrowed from Professor James M. Gustafson—"misplaced."[41] Each "school" can find support for its position in parts of the New Testament. But what is more important, they all can find themselves reconciled there in the rich totality of the New Testament Church, where prescriptive morality, *agapē* and *koinōnia* morality and, we might suggest, middle axioms, all coexist in mutual interaction. The relevance of the genius of the moral tradition of the early Church is that it holds all these approaches in living tension, if not reconciliation.[42]

Notes

LAW IN FIRST-CENTURY JUDAISM

1. In addition to the works cited in the following text and footnotes, see W. Bacher, *Die exegetische Terminologie der jüdischen Traditionsliteratur* (Leipzig, 1905); R. Marcus, *Law in the Apocrypha* (New York: Columbia University Press, 1927); C. H. Dodd, *The Bible and the Greeks* (London: Hodder & Stoughton, 1935; 2d ed., Naperville, Ill.: Alec R. Allenson, 1954); J. Z. Lauterbach, *Rabbinic Essays* (Cincinnati, 1957); E. P. Sanders, *Paul and Palestinian Judaism* (Philadelphia: Fortress Press, 1977); "The Covenant as a Soteriological Category and the Nature of Salvation in Palestinian and Hellenistic Judaism," in *Jews, Greeks, and Christians: Studies in Honor of W. D. Davies,* ed. R. Hamerton-Kelly and R. Scroggs (Leiden: E. J. Brill, 1976), pp. 11–44; "On the Question of Fulfilling the Law in Paul and Rabbinic Judaism," in *Donum Gentilicium: New Testaments Studies in Honour of David Daube,* ed. E. Bammel, C. K. Barrett, and W. D. Davies (Oxford: At the Clarendon Press, 1977), pp. 103–26; L. Finkelstein, *Pharisaism in the Making* (New York: Ktav, 1972); A. Jaubert, *La notion d'alliance dans le judaïsme* (Paris, 1963); G. F. Moore, "Christian Writers on Judaism," *HTR* 15 (1922), pp. 41–61; A. Marmorstein, *The Doctrine of Merits in Old Rabbinical Literature* (New York: Bloch, 1920); W. O. E. Oesterley, *Judaism and Christianity* (New York: Ktav, 1969); A. Büchler, *Studies in Sin and Atonement in the Rabbinic Literature of the First Century* (New York: Ktav, 1967); and J. Neusner, *Development of a Legend: Studies on the Traditions Concerning Yohanan ben Zakkai* (Leiden: E. J. Brill, 1970); idem, *Eliezer ben Hyrcanus: The Tradition and the Man,* 2 vols. (Leiden, E. J. Brill, 1973); idem, *A History of the Jews in Babylonia,* 5 parts (Leiden: E. J. Brill, 1966–70); idem, *A History of the Mishnaic Law of Purities,* 22 vols. (Leiden: E. J. Brill, 1974–77); idem, *A Life of Yohanan ben Zakkai* (Leiden: E. J. Brill, 1970); idem, *The Rabbinic Traditions about the Pharisees before 70,* 3 vols. (Leiden: E. J. Brill, 1971); idem, ed., *The Formation of the Babylonian Talmud* (Leiden: E. J. Brill, 1970); idem, ed., *The Modern Study of the Mishnah* (Leiden: E. J. Brill, 1973); idem, ed., *Understanding Rabbinic Judaism* (New York: Humanities Press, 1974); H. L. Strack and G. Stemberger, *Einleitung in Talmud und Midrash* (Munich: Beck, 1982); E. Rivkin, *The Hidden Revolution* (Nashville: Abingdon Press, 1978).

2. Law: in Hebrew תורה; Aramaic אורייתא, אוריפא; in Greek νόμος.

3. It must be emphasized that this essay was written before the author could have read Neusner, *Rabbinic Traditions.* Neusner's pioneering work puts the complexity of the theme in a new light, although I venture to think that the substance of this essay remains intact, modified as it may have to be at points—for example, on the role of Hillel.

4. The high evaluation of prophecy as a gift of the Spirit was to suffer eclipse. Whether under the influence of Christian emphasis on the prophets or of the divisive tendencies that had led to so much sectarianism and created the need to close ranks against innovators, prophecy came to be little regarded by the sages, if not suspect. The doctrine of the cessation of prophecy with the last of the prophets has been connected with the needs of canonization at Jamnia, but there was "prophetic" activity of various kinds after Malachi. See my *Gospel and the Land* (Berkeley and Los Angeles: University of California Press, 1974), p. 49; *Paul and Rabbinic Judaism: Some Rabbinic Elements in Pauline Theology*, 4th ed. (Philadelphia: Fortress Press, 1980), p. 363, n. on p. 212. I avoid the term "man" and prefer the term "people" in referring to the demands made by the Law. There were some differences in the demands made upon men and women, but they cannot be pursued here. See especially Raphael Loewe, *The Position of Women in Judaism* (London: SPCK, 1966).

5. G. F. Moore, *Judaism in the First Centuries of the Christian Era, the Age of the Tannaim*, 3 vols. (Cambridge, Mass.: Harvard University Press, 1927–30), 3, p. 64.

6. See Moore, *Judaism*, 1:235–80. See further my *Setting of the Sermon on the Mount* (New York and Cambridge: Cambridge University Press, 1964), pp. 273–75; K. G. Kuhn, "Giljonim und sifer minim" in *Judentum, Urchristentum, Kirche: Festschrift für Joachim Jeremias*, ed. W. Eltester, *BZNW* 26 (1960): 24–61. For the necessary caution in writing of Jamnia, see J. Lewis, "What Do We Mean by Jamnia?" *JBR* 32 (1964): 254–61; L. G. Stemberger, *Kairos* 19 (1977), pp. 14–21; Peter Schäfer, "Die sogenannte Synode von Jabne zur Trennung von Christen in 1./2. Jh. n. Chr." *Studien zur Geschichte und Theologie des rabbinischen, Judentums* (Leiden, 1978), pp. 45–64.

7. For the meaning of "defile the hands," see Neusner, *Yohanan ben Zakkai*, p. 76. On the necessity to distinguish between "sacred" books and canonical ones, see my forthcoming essay, "Reflections About the Use of the Old Testament and the New."

8. The evolution of *Targumim*—roughly, translations or paraphrases in another language from that of the sacred text—was governed by two factors: linguistic needs and those of making the text contemporary to the actual.

9. J. A. Sanders, *Torah and Canon* (Philadelphia: Fortress Press, 1972) has made much of the elevation of the Pentateuch, rather than the Hexateuch, to preeminence in Judaism; to him it indicates the demotion of emphasis on the conquest of the land in favor of the Mosaic tradition. But this underestimates the importance of Joshua. That the Hexateuch as a unit could be a reality for the sages appears from *b. Nedarim* 22*b*. On the Hexateuch, see my *Gospel and the Land*, pp. 23–24, and D. N. Freedman, *JBL* 95 (1976): 503–6.

10. The precise way in which Moses received the Law from God was much discussed. Heschel, in his work *Torah min Ha-Shamaim*, 2 vols. (New York, 1962–65), distinguished two dominant views on this question—that of Akiba, that the Law was mysteriously given, in an ineffable way, from heaven (מן השמים תורה) and that of R. Ishmael, that it was given by a "rational" process, not a supernatural one, at Sinai. Heschel's views have not been examined seriously. It is argued that he has schematized the material too much and distinguished two

watertight compartments, when in fact the sources reveal much interpenetration.

The whole problem of the nature of revelation much occupied Judaism. The so-called Temple Scroll (llQTemple) reveals an "author" prepared to write not only haggadah but halakah as if he himself were God: he not only enlarged or corrected the Pentateuch but dared compose a "new Pentateuch." Such a development not only helps explain why the sages placed an interdiction against the writing of the oral Law, but also shows how radically the Mosaic tradition could be questioned. Again in 4 Ezra 14, Ezra fulfills a role parallel to that of Moses. An old age is dead and Ezra is given a *new* revelation, as was Moses.

> And it came to pass after the third day, while I sat under the oak, lo! there came a voice out of a bush over against me: and it said, Ezra, Ezra! And I said: Here am I lord. And I rose upon my feet. Then said he unto me: I did manifestly reveal myself in the bush, and talked with Moses when my people were in bondage in Egypt: and I sent him, and led my people out of Egypt, and brought them to Mount Sinai; and I held him by me for many days.
>
> I told him many wondrous things,
>   showed him the secrets of the times,
>   declared to him the end of the seasons;
>   Then I commanded him saying:
> These words shalt thou publish openly, but these keep secret.
>   And now I do say to thee:
>   The signs which I have shewed thee,
>   *The dreams which thou hast seen.*
>   *And the interpretations which thou hast heard—*
>   lay them up in thy heart! For thou shalt be
> taken up from (among) men, and henceforth thou shalt remain with my Son,
> and with such as are like thee, until the times be ended.
>   For the world has lost its youth,
>   The times begin to wax old. (4 Ezra 14:1-10)

The Mosaic law "was burnt" (presumably in the fall of Jerusalem in 587 c.e.), 4 Ezra 14:21, but Ezra, in retreat for 40 days, like Moses, is inspired directly by the Holy Spirit to renew the Law: he "drinks" inspiration directly from God.

> So I took the five men as he had commanded me, and we went forth [into the field] and remained there.
>   And it came to pass on the morrow that, lo! a voice called me, saying:
>   Ezra, open thy mouth
>   and drink what I give thee to drink!
> Then I opened my mouth, and lo! there was reached unto me a full cup, which was full as it were with water, but the colour of it was like fire.
>   And I took it and drank; and when I had drunk
>   My heart poured forth understanding,
>   wisdom grew in my breast,
>   and my spirit retained its memory:
> and my mouth opened, and was no more shut.
> (4 Ezra 14:37-41)

Compare this understanding of revelation as ecstatic with that of Philo *Quis rerum divinarum heres sit*, 51-52.

Contrast with it, however, the understanding of revelation through study of the Law found at Qumran. There the Teacher of Righteousness reveals by his *inter-*

pretation things in Habakkuk that the prophet himself had been unaware of. The Temple Scroll especially makes the kind of claim made by the Matthean Jesus in Matt. 5 : 17ff. less "peculiar" than might previously have been thought, as indeed does *Jubilees*, where there is a rewriting of the Pentateuch to serve the author's ends, and 1 Enoch 82 : 1ff., which lays claim to a new wisdom. In all these documents there is no suggestion that Moses is being replaced in principle: even the Temple Scroll is a rewriting of *his* work. But in practice it is difficult not to recognize the supersession of it by various newer revelations. First-century Judaism was even more divided than we had conceived possible. There is no doubt that a certain number of books were regarded as authoritative; see Josephus, *Ag.Ap.* 1.8, and 4 Ezra 14 : 4ff., which recognize 22 and 24 such books respectively, both referring to the Hebrew Bible (the number 22 probably was reached by combining Ruth with Judges and Lamentations with Jeremiah). However, in view of the astounding claims to revelation to which we have referred, it is doubtful whether before 70 c.e. at least (as we indicated above) it is at all justified to speak of "canonical" books. As noted previously, the term "canon" is more of a Christian provenance than Jewish even after 70 c.e. Notice further that just as in Pharisaic Judaism, Moses was credited with having given both a public and a more esoteric revelation in other currents of Judaism, as is clear from 4 Ezra 14 and 1 Enoch.

11. The superiority of the Torah over the Prophets and the Writings can be illustrated from targumic usage. In targumic practice, in order not to dishonor it, skipping a passage from the Torah was forbidden, although this was allowed in the case of the prophets. Similarly the *meturgeman* (translator) gave his Targum after each verse of the Torah, but after *three* verses of the Prophets; *m. Megilla* 4. This is difficult to date: see especially 4 : 4. Compare this also with the demand to close the synagogue readings with the Law. (Unfortunately, the passages making this clear elude me at this writing.)

12. See Mark 7 : 3, 5, 8, Matt 15 : 3, 6.

13. Note that according to the Jerusalem Talmud, *Meg.* 4.1,74*d* (with which compare *b. Giṭṭin* 66*b*; *Tem.* 14*b*), "That which has been expressed orally [must be transmitted orally] and that which has been expressed in writing [must be transmitted] in writing." See on this S. Lieberman, *Hellenism in Jewish Palestine* (New York: Jewish Theological Seminary, 1962), p. 87. The Talmud contains no reference to a written Mishna. But that the interdiction of the writing down of the oral tradition cannot be pressed for the rabbinic period has been argued by R. Meyer, *TWNT* 9. 34–35: it was, in his view, legendary. Note that the interdiction covered both *halakah* and haggadah. On the distrust of the written word among Jews and Greeks, see C. H. Roberts, "Books in the Graeco-Roman World and in the New Testament" in *The Cambridge History of the Bible*, ed. P. R. Ackroyd and C. F. Evans (Cambridge: At the University Press, 1970), 1 : 49.

14. In general, any law, although unchangeable in theory, has in practice to be adaptable. Indeed, among the sages, in certain circumstances it came to be recognized that the Law *had* to be changed. Rabbi Johanan asserted that it is better to do away with a law than to bring the name of God to public disgrace. (*b. Yebam.* 79*a*). At the end of the *m. Berakot*, we have the idea expressed that it might be necessary under certain conditions to act for God by breaking his law.

See *The Mishnah*, trans. H. Danby (New York: Oxford University Press, 1933), *Ber.* 9:5 with his note:

> And it is written, *It is time to work for the Lord: they have made void thy Law* (Ps 119:126). R. Nathan says: They have made void thy Law because it was a time to work for the Lord. [See Moore, *Judaism*, p. 259. In times of emergency it may be right to set aside or amend the commandments of God enjoined in his Law: the Law may best be served by breaking it.]

To the sages, while the Law was a gift from God, the interpretation and application of it to life and the labor of study that this involved were also regarded as part of the revelation. The patient, rational activity of the sages in applying the Law made them partners in the revelatory process. Their activity became part of Torah. It is this that accounts not only for their fecund freedom within what might at first be regarded as literalism toward the Torah, but also for the high evaluation of the study of the Torah and—along with other factors—for the suspicion of prophetic, visionary, mystical, and historico-philosophical concerns. Rabbinic scholars are divided in their understanding of the process of interpretation: did the sages conceive of it as an exercise in reasonableness only, or was there for them an element of inspiration present in the very act of interpretation? Passages later than our period could be cited in support of both positions.

15. Particularly illuminating for this period is E. J. Bickerman, *From Ezra to the Last of the Maccabees: Foundations of Post-Biblical Judaism* (New York: Schocken Books, 1962). Ellis Rivkin, *A Hidden Revelation* (Nashville: Abingdon, 1978) sees in the Pharisaic insistence on the oral law a revolution. He underestimates the continuity with previous adaptations of the Law. (See, e.g., J. Weingreen, *From Bible to Mishnah: The Continuity of Tradition* [Manchester, 1976].) But his treatment of the oral Law and the Scribes and the Pharisees deserves more serious consideration than it has received, although we find his method, stimulating as it is, excessively reductionist.

16. The work of Neusner (*Rabbinic Traditions*) makes it extremely difficult to write with confidence about early Pharisees, including Hillel. The "class" interpretation of Pharisaism is associated especially with L. Finkelstein, *The Pharisees*. For a popular treatment see my *Introduction to Pharisaism* (Philadelphia: Fortress Facet Books, 1967).

17. See J. Neusner, "The Meaning of Oral Torah: With Special Reference to Kelim and Ohalot," in *Early Rabbinic Judaism* (Leiden: E. J. Brill, 1975), pp. 3–33; and Ellis Rivkin, *Hidden Revelation*, pp. 223–51. For the latter, "By any measure the Mishnah is incongruent with the Pentateuch" (p. 223). See also J. Goldin in *The Cambridge History of Judaism*, vol. 3 (forthcoming).

18. Here it is impossible to enter into the question of the style, structure, characteristics and nature of the Mishna. See the chapter by D. Zlotnik in *The Cambridge History of Judaism*, vol. 4 (forthcoming), "The Mishnaic Method of Transmitting the Oral Tradition," and J. Neusner, *Midrash in Context* (Philadelphia: Fortress Press, 1983).

19. See J. Neusner, ed., *The Modern Study of the Mishnah*, and the older work of J. Z. Lauterbach, *Rabbinic Essays* in note 1.

20. H. Strack, *Introduction to the Talmud and Midrash* (Philadelphia: Jewish

Publication Society of America, 1959), pp. 12ff. The German original has now been revised in a seventh edition by G. Stemberger as *Einleitung in Talmud und Midrasch* (Munich: Beck, 1982) with excellent bibliographies.

21. See note 16 above.

22. See further my *Setting of the Sermon on the Mount*, pp. 256–315; S. Lieberman, *Hellenism in Jewish Palestine* (New York: Jewish Theological Seminary, 1962), pp. 83–99 on "The Publication of the Mishnah."

23. D. Daube, "Alexandrian Methods of Interpretation and the Rabbis," *HUCA* 22 (1949): 239ff.

24. See J. Bonsirven, *Le Judaïsme Palestinien*, 2 vols. (Paris, 1934–35), 1: 247ff.; *Exégèse Rabbinique et Exégèse Paulinienne* (Paris, 1939).

25. See my essay on "Law in the New Testament," chapter 12, herein.

26. See Morton Smith, "Palestinian Judaism of the First Century," in *Israel: Its Role in Civilization*, ed. M. Davis (New York: Harper & Brothers, 1956), pp. 67–81. D. Daube, orally, has urged that the traditional view of the Pharisees as "liberal" and the Sadducees as "conservative," insisting on strict adherence to the letter of the Law, must be abandoned. It is because the Sadducees wanted to preserve the liberty of every Jew to follow his or her understanding of the Law that they resisted the encrustation of the oral Law. It is curious that the specific term "Pharisee" only occurs six times in the Mishna, at *Sota* 3:4; *Toharot* 4:12; *Yad.* 4:6–8. In all places except *Tohar.* 4:12 the Pharisees are under attack. See Rivkin, *Hidden Revelation*, pp. 176–79, for the evidence of the Mishna on the Pharisees. It cannot be examined here in detail.

27. I have here changed the title, "The Law as the Agent of Salvation," used in *IDB*, 3: 93d, to preserve an emphasis that the brevity of the original article made difficult to express. See further, E. P. Sanders, *Paul and Palestinian Judaism*. This great study came to hand after I had written this work; it confirms the position indicated with a richness of data unequalled elsewhere.

28. In all legal activity God himself was deemed to be present. Compare Ps 82:1 and *b. Sanh.* 6*b*; the judge is God's partner (*b. Sabb.* 10*a*).

29. There is a fascinating, highly pertinent discussion in D. Daube, *Ancient Jewish Law* (Leiden: E. J. Brill, 1981) on "Error and Ignorance as Excuses in Crime," pp. 49–69.

30. David Hartmann, in an unpublished lecture, goes so far as to claim that the sages were not concerned with ultimate, absolute truth—in any "Platonic" sense—but with what they deemed to be reasonable. Rational *behavior*, not rational *truth*, was their concern. It agrees with this that theology, in the sense of conceptual concentration on and interpretation of their faith, did not generally occupy them (see my *Gospel and the Land*, pp. 390ff.). Another way of claiming the same is to urge that the givenness of the Torah was not subjected to radical doubt. It would be untrue to say that what Tillich called "the Protestant principle," which allows for uncertainty, was known to the sages, but they allowed for it in the determination of *halakah*. (An example of this from a much later period is found in Aḥad Ha-ʿAm, who was rebuked by his teacher for reading philosophical literature. Among the Ḥasidim, among whom Aḥad Ha-ʿAm grew up, it was a tradition that one should not read those portions of Maimonides' *Guide to the Perplexed* which treat of doubt with regard to the existence of God,

lest one might stop before reaching the answers to the doubts and as a result go through life without faith and belief in God.) See H. Gottschalk, "Aḥad Ha-Am, The Bible and the Bible Tradition," (Los Angeles: University of Southern California, 1965): 98.

31. For the view criticized here, see Strack and Billerbeck, *Kommentar*, 1: 3–6, and E. P. Sanders, *Paul and Palestinian Judaism*.

32. Moore, *Judaism*, 1: 507–19, 520–34; S. Schechter, *Some Aspects of Rabbinic Theology* (1909), pp. 313–44.

33. Str-B, 1: 13–15.

34. For the doctrine of repentance in later Judaism, see Ze'ev Falk, "On Repentance" in *Niv Hamidrashia, A Journal Devoted to Halacha, Jewish Thought, Education and Literature* (Jerusalem, 1972): 29.

35. See my *Gospel and the Land*, pp. 396ff.

36. Michael Stone, orally, suggested that the need to emphasize the eternal immutability of the Law was born largely of the divisive tendencies to which we have previously referred. But if we follow V. Aptowitzer, political necessities contributed to the ascription to the Law of those cosmic characteristics to which we have referred above. See his *Parteipolitik der Hasmonaërzeit* (Vienna: Kohut Foundation, 1927), pp. 116 ff.

37. On the notion of preexistence, see R. G. Hamerton-Kelly, *Pre-existence, Wisdom and the Son of Man*, SNTSMS (New York and Cambridge: Cambridge University Press, 1973).

38. See now E. E. Urbach, *The Sages* (Jerusalem: Magnes, 1975), pp. 257ff. His indispensable treatment endorses our rejection of Schoeps's rigid distinction between the Hellenistic and Palestinian understanding of covenant. Urbach supplies the bibliographical references.

39. See my *Torah in the Messianic Age and/or the Age to Come* (Lancaster, Pa.: Society of Biblical Literature, 1952); *Sermon on the Mount*, pp. 109–90, 446–50; P. Schäfer, "Die Torah der messianischen Zeit," in *Studien zur Geschichte und Theologie des Rabbinischen Judentums* (Leiden: E. J. Brill, 1978), pp. 198–213; H. Schürmann, "Das Gesetz Christi (Gal 6:2): Jesus Veschalten und Wort als Letztgültige Sittliche Norm nach Paulus, Neues Testament und Kirche," *Pastorale Aufsätze*, Band 6 (Leipzig, 1974), pp. 95–102. See further the literature cited by Schäfer.

40. See E. E. Urbach, *The Sages*, pp. 263ff. Unfortunately, we have been unable to deal with issues raised by J. A. Sanders in his excellent work in the Supplementary Volume of the *IDB* on the theme of this chapter.

REFLECTIONS ON TRADITION:
THE ʾABOT REVISITED

1. R. T. Herford, *Pirke Aboth; The Ethics of the Talmud: Sayings of the Fathers* (New York: Schocken Books, 1962) pp. 9ff.

2. However, the objection that it would be more natural, if its aim were such as Herford asserts, for ʾAbot to be the prologue to the Mishna is a Western one. Professor Heschel pointed out to me that the haggadic materials often close tractates in the Mishna (see, for example, the end of *m. Soṭa*); he finds in the inclusion

of the ʾ*Abot* in the Mishna the recognition by Judah the Prince that Haggadah was as significant as *halakah*. Herford refuses to regard ʾAbot as haggadic: *Ethics of the Talmud*.

3. For a recent approach to the ʾ*Abot*, see B. Viviano, *Study as Worship: Aboth and the New Testament* (Leiden: E. J. Brill, 1978). Strikingly enough, the ʾ*Abot* never mentions God directly, although it uses the circumlocution "heaven." But we cannot speak of any *Toraholatry* in the ʾ*Abot* because the Torah is God's gift any more than we can speak of a Christolatry in the New Testament because it was God who was "in Christ."

4. See, for example, H. J. Cadbury, "New Testament Scholarship: Fifty Years in Retrospect" in *JBR* 28 (1960): 144ff.

5. The late W. L. Knox once wrote to me about disreputable pro-Semitism in New Testament scholarship.

6. R. H. Charles, *Religious Development between the Old and the New Testaments* (New York: Holt, 1914), p. 14, n. 1. Again recall the words of B. H. Streeter: "Christianity began as a de-ossification, so to speak, of the emphatically monotheistic legalism of Pharisaic Judaism. It was as though the Lord, who spake of old by Amos and Isaiah, had awaked as one out of sleep, and like a giant refreshed with wine . . . John the Baptist . . . summons to righteousness against the background of that hope of a catastrophic world-redemption which had been generated by two centures of Jewish apocalyptic . . ." (*CAH*, 11:264.)

7. Translations from the Mishna are from Danby unless otherwise stated.

8. W. Bacher, *Tradition und Tradenten* (Leipzig: Durr'sche Buchhandlung, 1914), pp. 35ff.

9. See G. Östborn, *Tora in the Old Testament* (Lund, Sweden: Hakan Ohlssons Boktryckeri, 1945), *ad rem*.

10. This holds whatever view be taken of him. It is generally assumed that Simeon is either Simeon I, the high priest from *c.* 300–270 B.C., who is called "the just" in Josephus, *Ant.* 12.2.5, or Simeon II, probably a grandson of the former, the high priest around 220–200 B.C. The majority of scholars favors the identification with Simeon II, who also seems to be the high priest, Simeon, praised by the author of Sirach at the end of his praise for his forefathers (50:1–24).

11. *M. Ḥag.* 2:7. He is mentioned with Jose b. Johanan of Jerusalem in *Soṭa* 9:9. In *Gen. Rab.* 65:22, Jakum of Zeroroth was a nephew of R. Jose b. Joezer of Zeredah. (Note that here Jose is a rabbi.) Since Jakum is usually identified with Alcimus, the high priest at the time of the Maccabean revolt, we *may* draw the inference that since Alcimus is a priest, his uncle is also. My pupil, T. J. Kitchen, pointed this out to me. See *Jewish Encyclopedia* (New York: Funk & Wagnalls, 1925) 7:242. But this cannot be certain.

12. On the nature of Pharisaism, see L. Finkelstein, *The Pharisees: The Sociological Background of Their Faith* (Philadelphia: Jewish Publication Society of America, 1940); also now the numerous, important works of Jacob Neusner and Ellis Rivkin, *A Hidden Revolution* (Nashville: Abingdon Press, 1978).

13. See my *Paul and Rabbinic Judaism: Some Rabbinic Elements in Pauline Theology,* 4th ed. (Philadelphia: Fortress Press, 1980), pp. 210ff.

14. It should be noted that Moses is both the mediator of the Torah and "the

prophet"; see Deut 18:15. In himself he breaks down the distinction between Law and prophecy. Professor Heschel referred me to *Exod. Rab.* 42:8, where Rabbi Joshua b. Levi (A.D. 219–79) says: "Each one was fully occupied with his own prophecy, save Moses who delivered all the prophecies of others with his own, with the result that all who prophesied later were inspired by the prophecy of Moses. . . ." See A. J. Heschel, *Torah min ha-Shamain* (New York and London, 1962, 1965): 2: 262.

15. In *m. Pe'a* 4:2 the pairs of *'Abot* 1:1 receive the tradition directly from the prophets. The prophets are interpreters of the Law in 1QS 8:14–16; and in Josephus *J. W.* 2. 10. 12 there are prophets among the Essenes; part of their task is to read sacred books. Halakic activity is ascribed to prophets in *m. Yad.* 3:4. G. F. Moore, *Judaism in the First Centuries of the Christian Era, the Age of the Tannaim*, 3 vols. (Cambridge, Mass.: Harvard University Press, 1927–30), 1:6 points out that Ezra was a student of the Law in Babylon under Baruch, the son of Neriah, the disciple and amanuensis of Jeremiah. Ezra 9:11f. puts the prohibition of intermarriage into the mouth of the prophets.

16. For the various theories on this, see G. F. Moore, *Judaism*, 3:7–11. Note also Gershom Scholem, *The Messianic Idea in Judaism* (New York: Schocken Books, 1971), p. 288.

17. The editor of the passage in the Soncino translation takes these three prophets to be Haggai, Zechariah, and Malachi. The reason they could sacrifice even though there was no Temple was that the sanctity of the Temple had hallowed the spot for all time (Soncino translation, editor, p. 305, nn. 4, 5).

18. In this connection C. H. Dodd pointedly remarked that the prophets to whom the *'Abot* does refer are very minor ones and probably the least "prophetic." This was in criticism of the position taken here.

19. In *Num. Rab.* 11:16–17 (Soncino translation, p. 660), the elders are identified by R. Tanḥuma (A.D. 427–68) with teachers.

20. Notice that although Shammai rested the *halakah* on the prophet Haggai, he also gave reasons based on the text for his position (See Soncino translation, p. 215).

21. See Soncino translation on *b. Sukka* 44a, p. 203.

22. *Ma'amad*: literally "place of standing," is "the name given to a group of representatives from outlying districts, corresponding to the four "courses of priests." Part of them went up to the Temple as witnesses of the offering of the sacrifices (*Ta'an.* 4:2), and part came together in their own town, where they held prayers at fixed times during the day coinciding with the fixed times of sacrifice in the Temple. According to some, this is the origin of the synagogue system, in which the various daily offices were called by the names made familiar in the routine of the Temple" (Danby, *The Mishnah* [New York: Oxford University Press, 1933], p. 794). Others prefer to find its origin in the "meeting at the gates." See F. Huttenmeister on "The Synagogue" in *The Cambridge History of Judaism*, vol. 3 (forthcoming).

23. *B. Yoma* 9b; *b. Soṭa* 48b; *b. Sanh.* 111a.

24. *The Cultic Prophet in Ancient Israel* (Cardiff, Wales: Univ. of Wales Press Board, 1942).

25. *Das Gesetz und die Propheten: zum Verständnis des Alten Testaments* (Göt-

tingen: Vandenhoeck & Ruprecht, 1963). But see also R. E. Clements, *Prophecy and Covenant* (London: SCM Press, 1965), especially chapter 4, "The Law in the Pre-Exilic Prophets." He emphasized the criticism of the cultus by the canonical prophets: for him Amos was never a cultic prophet.

26. J. Lindblom, *Prophecy in Ancient Israel* (Philadelphia: Fortress Press, 1962), pp. 183, 209.

27. In view of the position taken by R. H. Charles, mentioned above, it is also important to note here that the rigid separation of apocalyptic and Pharisaism is no longer possible; see my *Christian Origins and Judaism* (Philadelphia: Westminster Press, 1962), pp. 19–30, on "Apocalyptic and Pharisaism." To note only one point not mentioned there, the *Shemoneh Esreh* in all its members shows the influence of apocalyptic ideas. Notice further that on the Day of Atonement itself portions of the book of Daniel were read to the high priest; see *m. Yoma* 1:6. To some extent all minds in Israel were colored by apocalyptic. And, finally, as Professor Heschel again reminded me, the mere fact that both the Law and the Prophets (the *Haphtaroth*) were already being read regularly in synagogue services in the first century meant that prophecy and Law were not conceived of as opposed to one another. But see D. Rössler, *Gesetz und Geschichte, Untersuchungen zur Theologie der jüdischen Apokalyptik und der pharisäischen Orthodoxie* (Neukirchen: Kr. Moers, 1960), for a different approach.

28. See my article "Paul and Judaism" in *The Bible in Modern Scholarship*, ed. J. Philip Hyatt (Nashville: Abingdon Press, 1965), pp. 178–83, for bibliographical details. Add to the details there supplied the following: A. Schlatter, *Markus, Der Evangelist für die Griechen* (Stuttgart, 1935); *Der Evangelist Matthaeus, seine Sprache, sein Ziel, seine Selbständigkeit* (Stuttgart, 1948), ad rem.; B. Lifschitz, on "L'hellenisation des Juifs de Palestine," in *RB* 4 (1965): 520–38; M. Hengel, *Judaism and Hellenism: Studies in Their Encounter in Palestine During the Early Hellenistic Period*, 2 vols. (Philadelphia: Fortress Press, 1975); M. Hengel, *Jews, Greeks, Barbarians: Aspects of the Hellenization of Judaism in the Pre-Christian Period* (Philadelphia: Fortress Press, 1980); M. Smith, *Palestinian Parties and Politics That Shared the Old Testament* (New York: Columbia University Press, 1971), esp. pp. 27–81; Henry A. Fischel, ed., *Essays in Greco-Roman and Related Talmudic-Mishnaic Literature* (New York: Ktav, 1977). Following S. Lieberman, Lifschitz rejects the view propounded by G. Alon (who wrote in Hebrew) that only the maritime areas had been Hellenized. "La langue grecque et la culture hellénique ont penetré dans toutes les communautés juives de l'Orient Grec" (p. 538). I have garnered in recent reading the following items to confirm this:

(a) *On the educational side*, there was a considerable influence from Hellenism on the Jewish schools that evolved in the first century. See B. Gerhardsson, *Memory and Manuscript* (Uppsala, 1961). pp. 27, 56, 68, 88f.; V. A. Tcherikover, *Hellenistic Civilization*, trans. S. Applebaum (Philadelphia: Jewish Publication Society of America, 1959), ad rem.

(b) *On the literary side*, note that the *Wisdom of Solomon* is regarded by J. Reider and J. Fichtner as a Palestinian work. See J. Reider, *The Book of Wisdom* (New York, 1957), p. 18 n. 81; J. Fichtner, *Weisheit Salomos*, HAT 6: 7–8, who recognized Greek influence but holds that the work remains essentially Jewish.

On the Servant Songs as a drama or tragedy patterned directly after Greek tragedy, with a distinct succession of speakers including a chorus and with easily recognizable dramatic progression of time and action, see Julian Morgenstern, "The Suffering Servant—A New Solution," in *VT* 2 (1961): 292–320, 406–31; 13 (1963): 321–32. The Servant Songs—it is suggested—were written by a Galilean in touch with an Athenian garrison at Dor in South Galilee in 460–450 B.C., especially under the influence of Aeschylus. This view is merely mentioned here; I have not examined it. Again Philo has been claimed to know more about Palestinian Judaism than did Josephus; so S. Belkin, *Philo and the Oral Law* (Cambridge, Mass.: Harvard University Press, 1940). See also T. F. Glasson, *Greek Influence in Jewish Eschatology* (London: SPCK, 1961).

(c) *On the philosophical side,* one indirect cause of Aher's (Elisha b. Abuyha) apostasy was apparently his interest in Greek philosophy and literature. According to *b. Hag.* 15 b, Aher did not stop singing Greek songs and when he would get up in the academy, many unworthy Greek books would drop from his lap. Doubtless there is legendary elaboration, but the passage is no less significant for that.

For the view that Hillel betrays a Sophistic element, see I. Sonne, *Louis Ginsberg Jubilee Volume* (New York: American Association for Jewish Research, 1945), on "The Schools of Shammai and Hillel Seen from Within." On Platonism in the Old Testament, see E. Burrows, "Some Cosmological Patterns in Babylonian Religion," in *The Labyrinth,* ed. S. H. Hooke (London: Macmillan & Co., 1935), pp. 59ff. I discovered a Platonic note in connection with the Torah in *Gen. Rab.* 17:5, which reads: "The incomplete form of the heavenly wisdom is the Torah" (Soncino translation, p. 136, of *nōbeleth hocmāh shel maʿlak tōrāh*). The whole passage is pertinent: "R. Ḥanina [or, Ḥinena] b. Issac said: There are three incomplete phenomena: the incomplete form of prophecy is the dream; the incomplete form of the next world is the Sabbath. R. Abin added another two: the incomplete form of the heavenly light is the orb of the sun; the incomplete form of the heavenly wisdom is the Torah." The limitation of the incomplete forms to five is alien to anything Platonic.

For a priest and ruler of a Synagogue before A.D. 70 bearing a Greek name, Theodotus, see A. Deissman, *Light from the Ancient East: The New Testament Illustrated by Recently Discovered Texts of the Graeco-Roman World,* rev. ed., Eng. trans. L. R. M. Strachan (Garden City, N. Y.: Doubleday, Doran & Co.; London: Hodder & Stoughton, 1927), app. 15, p. 440.

(d) *On the archaeological side,* G. E. Wright and L. E. Toombs, *BA* 2 (1957): 19ff. and 92ff. respectively, report Hellenistic influences in Shechem. W. F. Albright, *The Archaeology of Palestine* (Harmondsworth, England, 1949), shows that the names of the deceased were written on ossuaries in Hebrew, Aramaic and Greek. In an excavation conducted in 1945 by E. L. Sukenik a tomb was discovered in the suburbs of Jerusalem containing two casques bearing Greek inscriptions, see *AJA* 51 (1947): 351ff.; A. Parrot, *Golgotha and the Church of the Holy Sepulchre,* trans. E. Hudson (London: SCM Press, 1957), pp. 113ff. The buildings of Herod the Great were in the Hellenistic tradition; see Josephus, *Bell.* 1.21.4. Samaria was renamed Sebaste by Herod in honor of Caesar; see G. E. Wright, *Biblical Archaeology* (Philadelphia: Westminster Press, 1957), pp. 218ff., for the magnificient temple dedicated to Caesar; G. A. Reisner, C. S. Fisher, and D. G. Lyon, *Harvard Excavations at Samaria 1908–1910* (1924): 1: 48ff.; J. W. Crowfoot, K. M. Kenyon and E. L. Sukenik, *The Buildings at Samaria* (London, 1942), pp. 123f. Caesarea also shows Hellenistic influences: Antonia in Jerusalem was built in honor of Mark Antony, Josephus, *Bell.* 5.4.4; 5.5.8. On a pavement near Antonia there is a representation of a play board by Roman soldiers, see *RB* 59 (1952): 413ff. At Nazareth a slab of marble was found in 1878 containing a Greek inscription possibly from the time of Claudius (A.D. 41–54); for the text and bibliography on this see R. K. Harrison, *The Archaeology of the New Testament* (New York: Association Press, 1964), pp. 32 and 107, n. 66.

Goodenough has recently been criticized by E. E. Urbach in *IEJ* 9 (1959): 150ff., in an article entitled "The Rabbinical Laws of Idolatry in the Second and Third Centuries in the Light of Archaeological and Historical Facts." Goodenough has been defended against Urbach by J. Neusner in *JR* 43 (1963): 4: 285–94, on "Jewish Use of Pagan Symbols after 70 C.E." See also *Judaism* 15 (1966): 2: 231ff. on "Judaism in Late Antiquity."

29. *RB* 59 (1952): 44–54.

30. A. D. Nock in the *CAH* 11:471, lists as the marks of the Augustan age the wish for revival and restoration in religion, the value set on tradition and legend.

31. See P. Boyance, *Le Culte des Muses chez les philosophes Grecs* (Paris, 1937), pp. 261–67, 299–327.

32. For references, see E. Bickerman, *From Ezra to the Last of the Maccabees: Foundations of Post-Biblical Judaism* (New York: Schocken Books, 1962). The date of Suidas, the lexicographer, is about A.D. 970, but his lexicon contains valuable early materials. For all these figures, see *PW* (1927). Sotion's chief work was entitled *The Succession of the Philosophers*.

33. It should be recalled that the use of genealogies is familiar in the Old Testament and in Judaism. For a discussion of the purpose of genealogies, see M. D. Johnson, *The Purpose of the Biblical Genealogies* (New York and Cambridge: Cambridge University Press, 1969). The chain of tradition gives a "professorial" genealogy, as it were, and cannot be wholly subsumed under the categories of the biblical genealogies. The Hellenistic parallels drawn by Bickerman seem to be more pertinent for the chain's understanding.

34. Incredulity that a Greek name could have been introduced as early as this would imply persuaded Krochmal that the Simeon the Righteous of *Abot* 1:3 could not be Simeon b. Onias I (around 300 B.C.); he had to be Simeon b. Onias II (219–199 B.C.). On the former view a Greek word would have entered the chain of tradition shortly after Alexander the Great. See the Hebrew commentary on the *Abot* by Krochmal. Professor Weiss of the Jewish Theological Seminary pointed this out to me. According to *m. Ḥag.* 4:11, a Ben Antigonus brought up firstlings from Babylon. But some manuscripts here read "Antinos." One of the disciples of the School of Shammai probably bore a Greek name—Dositheus of Kefar Yatmah; see *m. 'Orla* 2:5. On Antigonus, see G. F. Moore, *Judaism*, pp. 3, 14. Note that the name of the chief power in Palestine after the death of Alexander (323 B.C.), from 315–306 B.C., was Antigonus Monophthalmos.

35. Even the term "pairs," *zgwt,* has been given a Hellenistic derivation from the Greek ζεῦγος, but this is not necessary. The verbal form *zwg* lies behind the form *zgwt*. Moore, *Judaism*, 3 vols., reprint (New York, 1971), 3: 14.

36. *'btlywn* = Πτυλίων; *'ntygns* = Ἀντιγένης (*'ntygnws* = Antigonos); *dwsty* = Δοσίθεος; *hwrknws* = Ὑρκανός; *trpwn* = Τρύφων; *lwyts* = Λευίτης; *sndlr* = σανδαλάριος; *trdywn* = θηραδίων(?). The following terms have been suggested as transliterations of or borrowed Greek words: 3:19 *gymtry'* = γεωμετρία; 4:16 *trqlyn* = τρικλίνον; 6:2 *krz* = κῆρυξ; 6:9 *mrglyt* = μαργαρίτης; 4:11 *sndlr* = σανδαλάριος; 5:15 *spwg* = σπόγγος; 3:17 *pnqs* = πίναξ; 4:16 *przdwd* = προστάς; 1:3 *prs* = φόρος; 3:18 *prprt* = περιφορά; 4:11 *prglyt* = παράκλητος; 4:11 *qtyqwr* = κατήγορος. But not all these items are acceptable. Bickerman, *Ezra,* does not take *peras* to be derived from φόρος. How risky the connecting of Hebrew with Greek words is appears from the fact that W. Bacher refused to connect *gymtry'* with γεωμετρία and does so instead with γράμμα and γραμμστεία (see W. Bacher, *Die älteste Terminologie der jüdischen Schriftauslegung* [Leipzig, 1899], p. 127, under *Notarikon*).

37. E. Bickerman in *HTR* 44 (1951): 153–65, on "The Maxim of Antigonus of Soko."

38. Translation from Danby, *The Mishnah,* p. 307.

39. *Traditio (Studies in Ancient and Medieval History, Thought and Religion)* 21 (New York: Fordham University Press, 1965).

40. See *Lamentations Rabbah* 12; *b. Ḥag.* 14*b*.

41. H. Danby, *The Mishnah,* p. 397, n. 4.

42. There are untrustworthy instances of it in other places; see C. Y. Kasovsky, *Thesaurus Mishnae* (Hebrew) (Jerusalem, 1956) 1:261.

43. *Traditio, ad rem.*

44. Goldin prints the whole passage but it is too long to do so here.

45. The presence of Gnostic or proto-Gnostic currents in first-century or even earlier Judaism has now emerged clearly into scholarly discussion. For Gnostic infiltrations into Judaism, see especially A. Altmann, "Gnostic Themes in Rabbinic Cosmology," in *Essays in Honour of J. H. Hertz* (London, 1942), pp. 19ff: "The early stages of Tannaitic thought are already under the spell of Gnostic ideas" (p. 20). See also H. J. Schoeps, *Urgemeinde, Judenchristentum, Gnosis* (Tubingen, 1956); J. Daniélou, *Théologie du Judéo-Christianisme* (Tournai, 1958) 1:82ff; G. C. Scholem, *Jewish Gnosticism, Merkabah Mysticism and Talmudic Tradition* (New York: Jewish Theological Seminary, 1960), passim. Scholem's work is accepted by G. Quispel; see his essay on "Gnosticism in the New Testament" in *The Bible in Modern Scholarship,* pp. 259ff. He writes on p. 269: " . . . [T]he Gnostics have been influenced by a very specific current within Judaism, namely the esoteric traditions of Palestinian Pharisees. This should stop once and for all the idle talk of dogmatic minds about Gnosticism having nothing in common with Judaism proper." R. McLachlan Wilson remains cautious on the Jewish origins of Gnosticism; see his essay in *Modern Scholarship,* on "Gnosticism and the New Testament," p. 277. Writing on the same theme in the same volume, pp. 279–93, Hans Jonas, while admitting that Gnostics made liberal use of Jewish material, points to an anti-Jewish *animus* in Gnosticism. He states three hypotheses: (1) Gnosticism, *as an evolving state of mind, reacted against Judaism* when and where it encountered it. (2) Gnosticism *originated* out of a reaction (that is, *as* a reaction) to Judaism). (3) *It was so originated by Jews.* The first hypothesis is accepted by Jonas without question; the second is, in his view, possible but perhaps too narrow; the third remains very questionable because we

know of no Hebrew Gnostic writings, and the only Jewish name among the Samaritans is that of Simon Magus the Samaritan—a simple fact which Jonas considers very significant. U. Bianchi in *Numen* 12 (1965): 161–78, writing on "Le problème des origines du gnosticisme" recognizes the role of Judaism in its emergence, pp. 176ff. R. M. Grant, in *Gnosticism and Early Christianity* (New York: Columbia University Press, 1964), traces the origin of Gnosticism to Jewish sources. (Since this was written Grant has retracted this view in a lecture to the Society of Biblical Literature in Chicago, 1975). See the review of this work by J. Neusner, *Judaism*. The debate continues and has been intensified since the publication of the Nag Hammadi documents under the editorship of James M. Robinson, *The Nag Hammadi Library* (New York: Harper & Row, 1978). For a recent treatment of the problem, see Birger A. Pearson, "Jewish Elements in Gnosticism and the Development of Gnostic Self-Definition," in *Jewish and Christian Self-Definition,* ed. E. P. Sanders (Philadelphia: Fortress Press, 1980), 1: 151–60.

46. On "Cadre de la mystique Hellénistique," in *Aux Sources de la Tradition Chrétienne: Mélanges offerts à M. Maurice Goguel* (Paris, 1950), p. 78.

47. See J. G. Weiss in *JJS* 10 (1959): 169–71, "On the formula melekh ha-ʿolam as anti-Gnostic protest" and E. J. Weisenberg, *JJS* 15 (1964): 1–56, on "The Liturgical Term Melekh Ha-ʿOlam," and J. Heinemann, 15 (1964): 149–54, on "Once again Melekh Ha-ʿOlam."

48. Stromateis 1:20. See C. Taylor, *The Sayings of the Jewish Fathers*[2] (Cambridge: At the University Press, 1897), *ad rem.*

49. *HUCA* 22 (1949): 239ff.; also in *Festschrift Hans Lewald* (Basel, 1953), pp. 27ff.

50. Cited by J. Israelstam, Soncino translation of the Talmud (1935), 8:1. But we have seen that there is considerable uncertainty about the precise reference in the words of the Great Synagogue.

51. *The Setting of the Sermon on the Mount* (New York and Cambridge: Cambridge University Press, 1964), p. 303, where I refer to the work of L. Finkelstein, *Mabo le Massekot Abot ve Abot al Rabbi Nathan* (New York: Jewish Theological Seminary, 1950), *ad rem.*

52. See the reference to Friedlander in J. Israelstam, The Soncino translation of the Talmud, pp. 8, 34, *ad rem.*

53. J. Israelstam, Soncino Talmud.

54. Acts 24:5f.; 25:8. It should be noted that R. Eleazar of Modiʿim was aware of the Christian movement because he was a contemporary of Johanan b. Zakkai and was at Jamnia when the *Birkath ha-Minim* was introduced into the Eighteen Benedictions; see K. Marti and G. Beer, ʾAboth (Giessen, 1927), p. 76. Almost certainly among those whom R. Eleazer had in mind were Jews who had become Christians—that is, Jewish Christians whose good works he could not deny.

55. For textual details, see Taylor, *Sayings, ad rem.* Herford, *Ethics of the Talmud,* p. 89, attempts to reconcile the two texts by affirming that the first form refers to the works of man, the judgment of the individual. The other, the negative form of the text he takes to deal with the judgment of the world as a whole, the human race in general. But this is subtle to a degree.

56. *Sayings,* p. 59.

57. On this, see *Rabbinic*, p. 13.

58. *JBL* 59 (1940): 463, on "The Maxim of the Anshe Keneset ha-Gedolah." For change in rabbinic tradition, see B. Gerhardsson, *Memory and Manuscript*, p. 98.

59. The different forms which the various traditions took in different texts also bear witness to this pliability: an example of this has already been dealt with above in ʾAbot 3 : 16. On the other hand, unlike Finkelstein, other Jewish scholars with whom I have discussed this matter find it exceedingly difficult, if not impossible, to believe that Judah the Prince would have *deliberately* changed a given maxim. Is it not better to consider that he had a variant tradition which had developed unconsciously, that is, not by deliberate change, but by slow adaptation (so Heschel and Weiss in private conversation)? On the other hand, the ʾAbot de Rabbi Nathan does show how the maxim of Simeon the Righteous ("On three things the world stands—on the Torah, on the Temple Service, and on acts of loving kindness") came to be deliberately reinterpreted under the impact of the fall of Jerusalem. See especially J. Goldin in *PAAJR* 27 (1958): 52ff. The theme of the "adaptation" or "change" of tradition would demand the lifetime study of many. I have here sought to do justice to both continuity and adaptation or change. See further J. Goldin on "The End of Ecclesiastes: Literal Exegesis and its Transformation" in *Studies and Texts,* 3, *Biblical Motifs,* ed. A. Altmann (Cambridge, Mass.: Harvard University Press, 1966), pp. 135–38. Compare with p. 158 remarks by E. Käsemann, *Exegetische Versuche und Besinnungen* (Göttingen, 1964) 2 : 95, in an essay entitled, "Die Anfänge christliche Theologie."

60. ʾAbot 2 : 8 ". . . Eliezer b. Hyrcanus is 'a plastered cistern which loses not a drop. . . . If all the Sages of Israel were in one scale of the balance and Eliezer b. Hyrcanus in the other, he would outweigh them all'."

61. See R. N. Flew, *Jesus and His Church* (Nashville: Abingdon-Cokesbury, 1938), pp. 185f., for a convenient statement of Karl Holl's views and a critique of them. A. N. Wilder has emphasized recently the role of prophecy and charismatic authority in early Christian tradition in "Form-History and the Oldest Tradition" in *Neotestamentica et Patristica, Freundesgabe O. Cullmann,* ed. W. C. van Unnik (Leiden: E. J. Brill, 1962). But for a corrective see D. Hill, "On the Evidence for the Creative Role of Christian Prophets," *New Testament Studies* 18 (1972), pp. 401–18.

62. *Constitution and the Law of the Church in the First Two Centuries,* Eng. trans. (London, 1919).

63. See a discussion of this by E. P. Sanders, *The Tendencies of the Synoptic Tradition* (New York and Cambridge: Cambridge University Press, 1969), pp. 190–231. The pertinent literature is cited there.

64. I have underlined the regulative condition for all the above paragraph. How legitimate it is to pass from rabbinic methods of the transmission of tradition to that of Christian tradition is now a matter of acute debate spurred particularly by Birger Gerhardsson in his book *Memory and Manuscript,* and his later reply to his critics in *Tradition and Transmission in Early Christianity* (Lund: C. W. K. Gleerup, 1964). The matter is succinctly dealt with by Ed P. Sanders, *The Synoptic Tradition,* pp. 35ff. Sanders points out: (1) the necessity to study the early Christian tradition in its own right; and (2) the many factors which differentiate the

Christian tradition from the rabbinic—its belief in the living Lord, fostering a greater creativity; the brevity of its period of growth as compared with Old Testament and rabbinic tradition; its passage from one language to another, introducing increased possibilities of change; its transmission by untrained people. For our assessment of Gerhardsson we refer to *The Setting of the Sermon on the Mount*, Appendix 15, pp. 464–80. The necessity of studying the early Christian tradition in its own right is reinforced by our study of the ʾAbot, which is concerned with Pharisaism in its own right—the polemic elements in it, such as they are, being secondary. Both Pharisaic and Christian tradition are best understood, first of all, in their own light. But there is one aspect of Gerhardsson's treatment which should not be passed by easily and with which I find myself in agreement: it is that "All historical probability is in favor of Jesus' disciples, and the whole of early Christianity, having accorded the sayings of one whom they believed to be the Messiah at least the same degree of respect as the pupils of a rabbi accorded to the words of *their* master" (*Memory and Manuscript*, p. 258). Given this, the force of what we have written in the body of the text above remains. See further P. H. Davids, "The Gospels and Jewish Tradition: Twenty Years After Gerhardsson," in *Gospel Perspectives: Studies of History and Tradition in the Four Gospels*, ed. R. T. France and D. Wenham (Sheffield, 1980), 1: 75–99. A new turn has been given to the discussion. Both the approaches of Bultmann and Gerhardsson to oral tradition have been radically questioned by Werner H. Kelber in *The Oral and the Written Gospel* (Philadelphia: Fortress Press, 1983), who emphasizes "orality" in a much freer sense. See also D. Rhoads and D. Michie, *Mark as Story* (Philadelphia: Fortress Press, 1982).

65. Studies of Jesus have sometimes concentrated on his words (Bornkamm) or on his deeds (Fuchs). Truly to divine the tradition is to hold words and deeds together.

REFLECTIONS ON THE TERRITORIAL DIMENSION
OF JUDAISM

1. Compare R. J. Zwi Werblowsky, "Israel et Eretz Israel," in *Les Temps Modernes*, Directeur Jean-Paul Sartre, 253 B 15 (1967): 371–93. On p. 375 Werblowsky writes of the connection with The Land as an "élement essentiel." See also Martin Buber, *Israel and Palestine: The History of an Idea* (New York: East & West Library, 1952) and *Israel and the World* (New York: Schocken Books, 1963); the very rich chapter by G. Cohen in *Zion in Jewish Literature*, ed. A. S. Halkin (New York: Herzl Press, 1961), pp. 38–64; "Rabbinic Theology and Ethics," a forthcoming chapter by Louis Finkelstein for *The Cambridge History of Judaism*, volume 4; Arthur Hertzberg, *The Zionist Idea* (New York, 1968); Edmund Jacob, *Israel dans la perspective biblique* (Strasbourg, 1968), and "Les Trois Racines d'une Theologie de la 'Terre' dans l'A. T." in *Revue d'Histoire et de Philosophie Religieuses* 4 (1975): 469–80; *Jüdisches Volkgelobtes Land*, ed. W. P. Eckert, N. P. Levinson, and M. Stohr (Munich, 1970); Max Kadushin, "Aspects of the Rabbinic Concept of Israel," in *HUCA* 19 (1945–46): 57–96; F. W. Marquardt, *Die Juden und ihr Land*, (Hamburg, 1975); A. Neher, "Israel, terre mystique de l'Absolu," *L'Existence Juive* (Paris, 1962). The numerous

works of J. W. Parkes are important. A recent, very stimulating treatment is by W. Brueggemann, *The Land* (Philadelphia: Fortress Press, 1977). This deserves more attention than space allows here, as does R. Rendtorff, "Israel und seine Land" in *Theologische Existenz Heute* 188 (Munich, 1978). In "Réflexions sur la pensée nationale juive moderne," *Jerusalem Quarterly* 7 (1978): 3–9, Rotenstreich emphasizes the newness of Zionism or modern Jewish nationalism. It is, for him, discontinuous with traditional Jewish religious thought: "It attempts to create a new Jewish unity with living institutions rooted in the present rather than surviving to the present" (p. 5). He connects Zionism, therefore, with the collapse of the foundations of traditional Jewish life which succumbed to the attack of the Enlightenment on the traditional authorities grounded in a suprahistorical authority (pp. 3–4). One can hardly agree that Zionism is so utterly newborn. As will be clear from our presentation, for us Zionism is "twice-born" in the sense that it was preceded by a long tradition of concentration on The Land. On its religious dimension, see Rolf Rendtorff, "Die Religiosen und geistigen Wurzeln des Zionismus," in *Aus Politik und Zeit Geschichte* B. 49/76 (4 December, 1976): 3–49. This does not mean that the precise forerunners of Zionism can be easily categorized; see Jacob Katz on "The Forerunners of Zionism," *Jerusalem Quarterly* 7 (1978): 10–21.

2. For the emergence and function of the Pentateuch, see J. A. Sanders, *Torah and Canon* (Philadelphia: Fortress Press, 1972; French translation with additional response to criticisms, 1975); also "Adaptable for Life: The Nature and Function of Canon," *Magnalia Dei: Festschrift for G. Ernest Wright*, ed. F. M. Gross and others (New York: Doubleday & Co., 1976), pp. 531–60. Illuminating also is J. van Goudover, "Tora und Galut," in *Judisches Volkgelobtes Land*, pp. 197–202. As far as I am aware, the implications of Sanders's study for the question of The Land have not been adequately examined: its provocativeness can only be mentioned here. See also Truman Research Institute publication, 1970, of papers in a *Colloquium on Religion, People, Nation and Land*, Jerusalem.

3. See my *The Gospel and the Land: Early Christianity and Jewish Territorial Doctrine* (Berkeley and Los Angeles: University of California Press, 1974) for the supporting evidence.

4. See G. Cohen in *Zion*, p. 39.

5. See my *Setting of the Sermon on the Mount* (New York and Cambridge: Cambridge University Press, 1964), pp. 295f., and literature cited there; also G. Cohen, *Zion*, p. 45f.

6. On all the above, see for further details *The Gospel and the Land*, pp. 1–158.

7. G. Cohen in *Zion*, p. 41.

8. F. W. Marquardt, *Die Juden*, p. 28.

9. *Sabbatai Svi: The Mystical Messiah, 1626–1676* (Princeton: Princeton University Press, 1973); see my reflections on this: "From Schweitzer to Scholem: Reflections of Sabbatai Svi," herein, chapter 14.

10. The lateness of the emergence of the division of history to B.C. and A.D. is not often realized: it is not followed by the Jews.

11. See F. W. Marquardt, *Die Juden*, pp. 107ff.

12. M. Noth, *History of Israel* (New York: Harper & Brothers, 1958), pp. 448,

453. See further G. Klein, *Anti-Judaism in Christian Theology* (Philadelphia: Fortress Press, 1975), pp. 15–38.

13. F. W. Marquardt, *Die Juden,* p. 107.

14. R. J. Zwi Werblowsky, "Eretz Israel," pp. 374–75, puts the matter in a nutshell: "On considéra comme acquis . . . que le peuple juif a eu conscience de former un peuple à presque toutes les époques de son existence historique. Une conscience de soi spécifique, c'est à dire une connaissance de son destin est un fait constant de la culture juive." We deal here with the *religious* consciousness of Jews, but ultimately it is not separable from the historical. Werblowsky, above, and in a paper privately circulated on "Israel: The People and the Land" assumes this, with much good reason and brilliance. The impact of the figure of the wandering Jew—an individual, although he could and did serve as a symbol of the Jewish people as a whole—may have helped to blur the reality of the continuance of the Jewish community as a unity.

15. The Christian practice of pilgrimages to holy places, which formed the long devotional background of the Crusades, and Jewish practice were probably mutually stimulating throughout the Middle Ages. For many centuries after the Mohammedan capture of Jerusalem in 637, pilgrimages by Christians to that city continued and it is probable that the church never gave up the hope for the recovery of the holy places from Mohammedan control. From the eighth century on, the church's practice of imposing a pilgrimage instead of a public penance added to the number of pilgrims. Jewish pilgrimage to The Land increased especially after Justinian (483–565). Here we can only point to the main expressions of the devotion to The Land in Judaism. The reader is referred to the standard histories of the themes.

16. *Selected Poems Jehudah Halevi,* trans. by Nina Salaman, ed. H. Brody (Philadelphia: Jewish Publication Society of America, 1944), p. 2. Professor Diez Macho pointed out to me that Halevi was not an isolated figure but part of a well-defined tendency if not a movement. The father of Israel Zangwill provides one example of individual devotion to The Land. At an advanced age, he left his house and family to go there to die. See J. Leftwich, *Israel Zangwill* (Toronto: Smithers & Bonellie, 1957), p. 163. There are countless examples of such devotion. See further T. Dreyfus, "The Commentary of Franz Rosenzweig to the Poems of R. Judah Halevi," in *Tarbiz,* vol. 47, 1–2 (March–October 1978): 91ff.

17. F. W. Marquardt, *Die Juden,* p. 131.

18. See G. Scholem, *Sabbatai Svi.*

19. David Vital, *The Origins of Zionism* (Oxford: At the Clarendon Press, 1975), p. 7. Marquardt, *Die Juden*, pp. 131ff.

20. This remains true although the concentration on The Land among religious Jews who revered and even went to *Eretz Israel* has to be distinguished from the purely historical and geographic and archaeological interest in it of many of the Zionists. See especially D. Vital, ibid., pp. 6ff. In this article we deal with Judaism and The Land, not with Jews and The Land. But the impression must not be given that these two themes can or should be effectively separated. Werblowsky illuminates the problem. He points out that in the nineteenth century assimilationist Jews were fascinated and blinded by the Enlightenment. In this enthusiasm for

assimilation they shed both their religious and national identity. But they soon discovered the falsity of their hopes for being fully integrated and "normalized" in Western society. In their disillusioned reaction to the society that had previously been so seductively attractive to them, they turned again to the tradition that they had shed. But for "enlightened" and "assimilationist" Jews to *rediscover and to return all at once to both their religious and national identity* was hardly possible: the rediscovery of *one* element of their tradition at a time was traumatic; to discover *both* at the same time would have been overwhelming. So it was that the "enlightened" Jews who saw the futility of assimilation under the influence of the climate of the nineteenth century turned first to "nationalism," socialism, romanticism, to their strictly "national" tradition: they rediscovered themselves as belonging to the people of Israel, not necessarily to the religion of Israel which they still found it easy to regard as a fossilized survivor. (Even Werblowsky himself seems able to think of the liturgical practice somewhat in these terms. Of the belief in the relationship between Israel and The Land he writes, in "Eretz Israel," p. 377: "Très souvent, il était à la fois vivant et 'gélé,' comme dans une chambre froide, par les prières chaque jour répétées, les formules liturgiques et le rappel des promesses prophetiques.") All this helps to explain the insensitivity of some of the leaders both before and in the Zionist movement itself to the strictly religious dimension of relation to The Land. See Werblowsky "Eretz Israel," in *Les Temps Modernes,* p. 388; see also the citation in n. 14. Of Zionist leaders, he writes, "beaucoup d'entre eux ne pouvaient faire qu'une seule découverte à la fois." This concentration on the tradition among religious Jews who revered and even went to *Eretz Israel* has to be distinguished from the purely historical and geographical interest which secular Jews, who in the nineteenth century, for reasons we shall touch upon later, showed in The Land. For such the religious devotion to The Land symbolized all that was particularistic, "scandalous," nonassimilable in Judaism, even when they themselves ultimately become Zionists. On Rabbi Nachman of Bratzlov, see Arthur Green, "Rabbi Nachman Bratslaver, Journey to the Land of Israel," in *Mystics, Philosophers, and Politicians: Essays in Jewish Intellectual History in Honor of Alexander Altmann,* ed. Y. Reinharz, D. Swetschienski, K. Bland (Durham, N.C.: Duke Monographs in Medieval and Renaissance Studies #5, 1982), pp. 181–212.

21. "Eretz Israel," in *Les Temps Modernes,* p. 377.

22. The recognition of the variety of pre-Jamnian Judaism has now become a commonplace of scholarship. It is doubtful whether Judaism has any "dogmas," that is, doctrines as such which are regarded as necessary for salvation, as does Christianity. See my article "Torah and Dogma: A Comment," *HTR* 61 (1968): 87–105, reprinted in *Papers from the Colloquium on Judaism and Christianity held at Harvard Divinity School, 17–20 October, 1966* (Cambridge, Mass.: Harvard University Press, 1968); also *The Gospel and the Land,* pp. 390–404, especially pp. 399ff.

23. Naḥmanides was a Talmudist who was compelled to leave Spain and spent his last years in Palestine. According to the *Encyclopedia of the Jewish Religion,* (1965), s. v. "Naḥmanides," he was the first outstanding rabbi to pronounce the resettlement of The Land of Israel to be a biblical precept (*mitzwah*). It is very

surprising that such a pronouncement came so late, only in the twelfth to the thirteenth centuries. Doubtless it was assumed by many before the time of Nahmanides that there was such a *mitzwah*. Nahmanides found in Lev 26:22 a proof of this faith. Since the loss of The Land by Israel no other power had been able to colonize it successfully. The Land had refused to accept any other than the people of Israel: see his commentary on the Pentateuch. The rabbis saw a correspondence between the history of The Land and that of the people; see Werblowsky, private paper cited in n. 14, and Lev 26:42. Compare J. W. Parkes, *End of an Exile* (New York: Library Publications, Inc.; London: Vallentine, Mitchell & Co., 1954), pp. 12–13. For Maimonides's view that the messianic era would witness the return of Israel to The Land, see A. Cohen, *The Teachings of Maimonides* (New York: Ktav, 1968), pp. 225f. and the whole section on eschatology, pp. 220–40. The contents of *The Guide to the Perplexed* could be taken to prove that Maimonides's interests lay mainly elsewhere. But the purpose of *The Guide* must be borne in mind: it was natural for Maimonides not to deal with The Land there. We are not competent to enter into the debate about the Great Eagle. But note the view of Leibovitz: "Le précepte de resider en Israel a été amplement commenté par Rambam, mais, bien qu'il soit abondamment attesté dans le Midrash et la Haggadah, *il appartient au folklore religieux.*" According to Leibovitz, "On pourrait souligner, à cet egard, que la réalité concrète du Judaïsme, que au cours de l'histoire s'est manifestée dans l'accomplisement de la Loi, n'a jamais accordé à la Terre d'Israel une place centrale ni au plan de la pensée, ni au plan des mobiles d'action." See *Le Monde* 8–9 April, 1979, p. 2. One could wish for a more qualified statement of the case.

24. D. Vital, *Origins of Zionism*, p. 207.

25. H. Cohen, *Religion der Vernunft aus den Quellen des Judentums* (Frankfurt, 1929), English translation by Simon Kaplan, 1972, pp. 311–12. Before we can answer this question of the relation between The Land and the State, certain clarifications are required. The words quoted from Cohen make clear that it is easy to move from the idea of a State of Israel to that of The Land of Israel or the reverse. This easy transition invites confusion. The doctrines of a State of Israel and of "The Land of Israel" are to be distinguished. That Judaism regards a "state" to be essential to its existence may legitimately be argued. To begin with, it is erroneous to think that the people of Israel in the Old Testament is to be understood as a community bound to a land and governed by a law, as a modern national state might be. One thing has emerged clearly from studies on Law in the Hebrew Scriptures. The laws were not related primarily to the political organization of a state, but rather to a community of men and women in which a common allegiance to Yahweh was the constitutive element. The context or setting in life in which Israel had received the Law was the covenant, a sacral act, and the communication of the Law was connected with the celebration of the covenant which bound Israel to its God. To maintain the validity of this covenant—of which the proclamation of the Law was an essential part—Israel celebrated or commemorated it in regular feasts. The foundation of Israel lay in this religious act. "The Israelite nation had its true existence apart from and prior to the erection of [its] political, social and economic order in Canaan" (R. B. Y. Scott, *The Relevance of the Prophets* [New York: Macmillan Co., 1968], p. 189).

The community is to be understood as a corollary of the covenant entered into at Sinai.

After 587 B.C.E., when Jerusalem fell, the idea of a state declined. The Jews became again primarily a religious community: in time priests came to rule them under God. Israel is the people of Yahweh alone. In Ezra and Nehmiah the primary, if not the only, concern is that the people should obey the Law. If we follow the traditional view of the origin of the Pharisees, it was loyalty to the Law alone that governed them, and initially it was this that moved the Maccabees also. After the Exile, the Jews became a people of the Torah: the whole history of Pharisaism is necessarily concentrated on the Torah more than on the political control of The Land.

The messianic ideas of Judaism, which have persisted from biblical to modern times—for example in Sabbatianism—have retained a political dimension, and one aspect, the Davidic state, has remained central to them. But those ideas have often been spiritualized and transcendentalized and made symbolic. Without further elaboration we shall assume here that the doctrine of the inseverability of The Land from Yahweh and his people is not to be easily equated with the eternal connection of any state with the people and with Yahweh.

And yet despite the data to which we have referred in *The Gospel and the Land* and Scholem's apparent distinction, caution is necessary. There is the question which forcibly came to the surface, not to be reinterred, in 1948. Can a people be a people without political self-expression or the right to self-determination (two concepts not usually distinguished)—that is, without being allowed to be a nation? Is the distinction between a people living in The Land of Israel and the nation of Israel ultimately a false one? Does not the full life in The Land demand that people control their own land?

And there is the exact interpretation of the Jewish evidence. The best guide to the inner life and meaning of a religious community is its liturgy. If so, in the most familiar and central prayer of Judaism, the *Shemoneh Esreh,* the distinction between life in The Land and "national" control of The Land is not usually recognized. In the Fourteenth Benediction, which is usually dated in the Maccabean period, the reference to the kingdom of the House of David (*malkûth bêth David*) is unambiguous. For religious Jews, we must conclude, ultimately The Land is inseparable from the State of Israel, however much the actualities of history have demanded their distinction.

In this essay we are concerned not with the role of a Jewish state, but with that of The Land as such, that is, the Promised Land. But we must issue the caveat that such a distinction, although often necessarily recognized in Jewish life and thought, and therefore unavoidable in this discussion, is in the final analysis alien to the Jewish faith. To religious Jews the separation of The Land and The State is the abortive child of Jewish history, not of the Jewish religious consciousness and intent. In any case, despite the vicissitudes of Jewish history, the sacred documents on which religious Jews have rested—the Tanak, the Mishna, the Midrashim, and the Talmud—the liturgies they have constantly celebrated, and the observances which they have kept across the centuries all point to "The Land" as an essential aspect of Judaism.

26. D. Vital, *Origins of Zionism*, p. 156; on Aḥad Ha-ʿAm, pp. 188–201. One

may detect echoes of Aḥad Ha-ʿAm in Buber; see for example, *Israel and the World* (New York: Schocken Books, 1965), p. 229, although there is no mistaking Buber's insistence on the need for the soil of *Eretz Israel* for his people.

27. See "With Gershom Scholem: An Interview," in *Jews and Judaism in Crisis* (New York, 1976), pp. 1–48.

28. There was a struggle among the precursors of the movement over what came to be called "territorialism"—that is, the view that the specific place to which the suffering Jews of Russia and other countries should go was not important, provided they could settle in a place of their own. This territorialism was especially connected with Yehuda Leib Pinsker (1821–1891), a Russian physician from Odessa, the author of a most significant pamphlet *Auto-emancipation, Mahnruf an seine Stammesgenossen von einem russichen Juden,* 1892. For him, at first, it was not the Holy Land that the Jews needed but *a* land. It was having their own territory, not its being located in *Eretz Israel*, that was crucial. Ultimately few Jews were to follow Pinsker in this view. The thesis that in *Eretz Israel* alone would Jews cease to be "foreigners" prevailed. See on all this, Vital, *Origins of Zionism*, pp. 109–32, especially p. 131; Werblowsky, in *Les Temps Modernes*, pp. 338–89.

29. *Jews and Judaism,* p. 44. But see above p. 71 on the impossibility of separating the religious from the national and the socialistic in Zionism.

30. *Jews and Judaism,* p. 375.

31. See Vital, *Origins of Zionism*, p. 375. Vital concludes his excellent treatment with the claim that what kept the Zionists together and their institutions intact was that the terrible "social reality was always stronger than the disputes about it." The misery of the Jews' conditions of the Pale of Settlement, in Galicia and Rumania could not wait for relief: it outweighed "both the force of inertia and of religious teaching." To this was added anti-Semitism in the West. With Vital's emphasis one can agree, but when he sets the force of "religious teaching" against the need for relief, one hesitates to concur. His conclusion at this point ignores his opening chapter, which had pointed to the pervasive religious substructure of all Jewish thinking on The Land. The misery of Jews in itself would not have been creatively dynamic had it not been sustained by hope, however differently and variously expressed. Misery alone only breeds despair. Did not the endemic hope for The Land, even when denied its religious character, provide the light at the end of the tunnel which helped to sustain Jews? The history of movements of social reform and of revolutions sufficiently indicates that total misery in itself merely leads to inertia. Those movements have usually been born out of an element other than the misery itself.

32. See *The Gospel and the Land,* pp. 90–104.

33. Isa 44:28; Ezra 1:1f., the Chronicler; Jos. *Ant.* 12. 3.3, 138; 13. 13.5, 372f.; 17. 11.1, 299f.; Diodorus, *Bibliotheca Historica* 40. 2; cf. M. Stern, *Greek and Latin Authors on Jews and Judaism* (Jerusalem, 1974), pp. 185–86.

34. See above, pp. 64–65.

35. See on all this G. Scholem, *Sabbatai Svi.*

36. G. Scholem, ibid.

37. This phrase, "the portable land," I learned from Louis Finkelstein. (The Talmud is sometimes called a "portable state.")

38. On the essential quietism of apocalypticism, see David Daube, *Civil Disobedience in Antiquity* (Edinburgh, 1972), pp. 85–86.

39. The debate on all this continues. To some Jews, such as Richard J. Rubenstein, the tradition of submission historically advocated by rabbinic Judaism has become an impossible policy or stance since the Holocaust. See, for example, his *After Auschwitz* (New York: Charles Scribner's Sons, 1974), and his *Power Struggle* (Indianapolis: Bobbs-Merrill, 1974), pp. 171–79, on "Rabbi Yochanan's bargain." Rubenstein speaks of the "impotence" of the Jews. But to Jacob Neusner, not the abandonment of that tradition is necessary, but its more emphatic reappropriation and comprehension by the Jews. For him, "Studying the Torah is [we might write here "remains"] a mode of attaining transcendence through learning, not merely because God, too, studies Torah. Study of Torah is the way to the apprehension of God, the attainment of the sacred" (in a paper on "Transcendence and Worship through Learning: The Religious View of the Mishnah," *CCAR Journal* [Spring 1978]: 28). See also Neusner's "Toward a Jewish Renewal," in *Moment* 3, (May 1978): 11–16. The question is how far the development of Pharisaism after 70 C.E.—which led to the elevation of Torah and Torah study into the way of holiness—was such that holiness became radically separated from a single place, the Temple, and by that very fact from The Land. Baruch M. Bokser in a review of *The Gospel and the Land* even says that rabbinic Judaism was more radically divorced from The Land than was early Christianity (*Conservative Judaism* 30 [Fall 1975]: 73–74):

> Torah, as the rabbis say it, contains the key to the world and to the nature of existence. Of course, some rabbinic circles provided means to *remember* the Temple. But holiness was now divorced from a single place. The way of Torah enabled each individual to bring holiness into daily life, no longer by means of the Temple. The new set of metaphors reflects a conscious discontinuity, in contrast to the Christian concept which merely contined the old motif of holiness of Temple in a new way. The holiness of a single person, Jesus, replaces that of a single place; in faith, the Christian community represents the true Temple. In contrast, Torah, in the emerging rabbinic movement, was not just a comfort to Jews without a Temple, but was the basis for a new piety, one quite different from that of Christianity and of the Second Temple.

On this theme see B. Viviano, *Study as Worship* (Leiden: E. J. Brill, 1978); and, by implication, G. Cohen, *Zion*, pp. 45–48.

40. *From Ezra to the Last of the Maccabees,* Foundations of Post-Biblical Judaism, Part II, trans. M. Hadas (New York: Schocken Books, 1962), pp. 3f.

41. An interesting comment on all this comes from Israel itself. Israelis have recently found it necessary to make a conscious effort to counteract what is described as attitudes toward the Diaspora within Israel itself which range from indifference to negation. To this end a museum has been opened in Tel Aviv designed to depict twenty-five hundred years of Jewish life and to show that the Diaspora was not "a continuous story of persecution and suffering, with the Jews always in the passive role of the victim" (*New York Times* [21 May 1978]: 6). Indifference and negation generally characterize the attitude of those in a homeland to those who have left to live outside it. This attitude was probably at work

in the dispute between the "Hellenists" and the "Hebraists" in the first century. It operates at the present time to downgrade the significance of the exile in Judaism. See *Le Monde* (18–19 March 1979): 2, where Nahum Goldmann refers to a "slogan des quelques sionistes que souhaitaient abolir la diaspora."

42. G. Cohen, *Zion*, p. 52. From this point of view, without the experience of "exile" the dispersed Jews would not have retained The Land in their consciousness. Exile was thus ultimately as time unrolled necessary for the preservation of The Land.

43. This is well brought out by D. Vital, *Origins of Zionism*, pp. 1–20, to whom I am much indebted. André Nehier also emphasizes the point in his very moving, almost lyrical essay in *L'Existence Juive* (Paris, 1962), pp. 166–76, on "Israel, terre mystique de l'Absolu," See especially p. 169:

> On aurait pu croire que les urgences de l'Exil altèrent dans la pensée juive, la précellence d'Eréts et lui enlèvent certaines de ses vertus au profit des terres de la diaspora. Or il n'en est rien. Dès les premiers moments de la diaspora, tout au contraire, et à un rhythme que ira sans cesse grandissant, la pensée juive, talmudique d'abord, puis philosophique et mystique et, enfin, politique, saisait le thème biblique d'Eréts non pour l'edulcorer, mais pour lui conférer plus de poids encore, plus de gravité absolue.

In the light of the preceding pages, one might venture to question the undeviating nature of the development to which Nehier points, but of the continued reality of devotion to The Land there can be little question. Gershom Cohen finds the fundamental reason for this continuity in one fact. This was that the Diaspora never abandoned the understanding of its existence as a *galuth,* exile. *"That is to say, by the time Palestine ceased to be the central Jewish community, its centrality had been so impressed upon the Jewish mind that it could not be uprooted";* *Zion*, p. 52, our italics. There is another glaring reason which may possibly have been of even greater significance—that is, the fact of anti-Semitism. The hostility of the Gentile world would time and again stir up the hope for The Land embedded in the tradition (see Weblowsky in *Les Temps Modernes*, pp. 381–82).

44. See *The Gospel and the Land,* pp. 75–158.

45. See G. Cohen, *Zion*, p. 48.

46. Edmund Jacob, *Israël dans la perspective biblique*, p. 22.

47. See E. E. Urbach, *The Sages* (Jerusalem, 1975), "On Redemption," 649–92, especially p. 679: "'The End at its due time' is something different from liberation from the servitude of the kingdoms and cannot be attained by rebellions."

48. See G. Scholem, *Sabbatai Svi,* pp. 15–22. See my article on Sabbatai Svi (also cited above in n. 9), chapter 14, herein.

49. See S. W. Sykes, on "The Essence of Christianity," *RelS* 7 (1971), pp. 291–306.

50. Ibid., passim.

51. A. Lacocque, "Une Terre qui decoule de Lait et de Miel," *Revue du Dialogue* 2 (1966): 28–36. The thesis that The Land flowing with milk and honey gives a maternal quality to The Land as mother seems to us a *tour de force,* especially in its grammatical and lexicographical details.

52. To this concept belongs the Pauline notions of "building," "planting," and "watering" in 1 Cor 3:6–15. See the fascinating discussion by M. A. Chevallier, *Esprit de Dieu, Paroles d'Hommes* (Neuchatel, 1966), p. 26f. If we are correct to call the emergence in Christianity of the concept of being "in Christ" an equivalent of being in The Land, the notion of a "return" in Christianity is thus made redundant except in the sense of a "return to Christ." But Paul probably never wholly escaped the territorial understanding of Jerusalem and The Land as the *centrum mundi*. John certainly reveals a displacement of these centers. We find Chevallier's suggestion that the same was true of 1 Peter an excellent one; see *Paganïsme, Judaïsme, Christianïsme: Influences et affrontements dans le monde antique. Mélanges offerts à Marcel Simon* (Paris: Boccard, 1978), pp. 117–30: "Israël et l'Église selon la première Épître de Pierre." Chevallier shows how the notion of exile and Diaspora is taken up by "Peter" and reinterpreted. It is significant that he has no occasion to deal with the motif of "return." He writes (on p. 122):

> Pas plus que le peuple des croyants en Jesus Christ n'a de consistent ethnique il n'a de réalité géographique. Jesus Christ n'est pas localisé comme l'était Jerusalem et partout où des hommes 's'approche de lui,' le temple spirituel se construit (2:5) de sorte que le peuple de Dieu est *tout entier diaspora* (1:1), fait 'd'étrangers' et de 'residents' au milieu des nations païennes (2:11).

53. Quoted by G. F. Moore in *Judaism in the First Centuries of the Christian Era: The Age of the Tannaim*, 3 vols. (Cambridge, Mass.: Harvard University Press, 1927–30), 1:234.

54. Werblowsky, *Les Temps Modernes*, p. 376.

55. See further my work, *The Territorial Dimension of Judaism* (Berkeley and Los Angeles: University of California Press, 1982). It is not possible to discuss in this essay what happens when the Jewish understanding of The Land comes into conflict with other inhabitants of it.

REFLECTIONS ON THE SPIRIT IN THE MEKILTA: A SUGGESTION

1. *The Setting of the Sermon on the Mount* (Cambridge: At the University Press, 1966), app.

2. 3 vols. (Philadelphia: Jewish Publication Society of America, 1949).

3. His thesis that the schools of R. Ishmael and R. Akiba represented two different streams of Tannaitic theology—the rationalistic and the mystical—he set forth in *Torah min Ha-Shamaim*, 2 vols. (New York, 1965; London, 1962). It has not been examined or discussed adequately. The two volumes need to be translated.

4. *Paul and Rabbinic Judaism*, new rev. ed. (Philadelphia: Fortress Press, 1980) pp. 178ff., especially pp. 183ff.

5. See my work *The Gospel and the Land: Early Christianity and Jewish Territorial Doctrine* (Berkeley and Los Angeles: University of California Press, 1973).

6. "The infinitive absolute היה in this passage is considered as having the force of a pluperfect" (Lauterbach, *Mekilta of Rabbi Ishmael*, p. 6 n. 6).

7. "By contrast with the Ninevites, who would readily listen to the prophet and repent, Israel could stand condemned for not so readily listening to the prophets" (Lauterbach, *Mekilta*, p. 7 n. 7).

8. *Paul and Rabbinic Judaism,* pp. 208ff.

9. L. Finkelstein, *New Light from the Prophets* (London, 1967), p. 26.

10. Lauterbach, *Mekilta*, vol. 1., p. 5 n. 5.

11. Lauterbach, *Mekilta*, pp. 7f.

12. *Torah min ha-Shamaim,* vol. 1., *ad rem.,* where the notion of Yahweh's exile with His people is emphasized. The passage on Exod 15:1 is interesting for another reason. The Israelites are insisted to have sung at the Exodus not because of the miracles wrought for them but because of the faith of Abraham— so say R. Nehemiah and R. Simeon b. Abba. We know that Judaism reacted negatively to the emphasis on miracles in early Christianity—a parallel to its reaction to that on the Spirit. See A. Guttmann, *HUCA* 20 (1947): 363ff.; but see also the criticism of him by J. Neusner, *The Rabbinic Traditions About the Pharisees Before 70,* Part 3 (Leiden: E. J. Brill, 1971), pp. 347ff.

13. Lauterbach, *Mekilta*, vol. 1, p. 210.

14. For the larger context of the comparison of the Spirit in Pharisaic Judaism and early Christianity, see *Rabbinic Judaism,* pp. 200–201. The suggestion made above, that reaction to the wide spread of early Christian experience of the Spirit may have influenced the discussion of the geographic provenance of the Spirit among the rabbis, is not intended to ignore the fact that there were influences within Judaism itself tending to the geographic limitation of the Spirit. Oddly enough, however, the declaration that lands outside *Eretz Israel* were unclean, which is variously dated, came late, for economic as well as other reasons. See Neusner, *Rabbinic Traditions,* 1:69, 72. Neusner's work makes it unmistakably clear how much needs to be done on the form and redaction criticism of the sources.

15. An earlier version of this essay appeared in the "*Festschrift* for Theodor H. Gaster," in *JANESCU* 5 (1973): 95–105.

A NOTE ON JOSEPHUS, ANTIQUITIES 15.136

1. *SBL* Monographs 7 (Philadelphia, 1952).

2. Str-B vol. 3 (Munich, 1928).

3. Ed. G. Kittel and G. Friedrich (Stuttgart, 1933).

4. 4th ed. (1952).

5. *The Works of Flavius Josephus* (London, 1906), p. 41.

6. For the evidence see Str-B, 3: 554ff.

7. See, for example, T. H. Robinson, *Prophecy and the Prophets* (London, 1923), p. 45.

8. *Josephus and the Jews* (New York: Harper & Brothers, 1930), pp. 59ff.

9. *Ag.Ap.* 1.37§3.

10. *The Works of Josephus* (London: LCL, 1926) 177–8.

11. *TWNT*, ibid.

12. *J.W.* 2.142. Here again the *onomata angelôn* may be ambiguous; do they refer to the messengers or agents by which the books mentioned previously were

transmitted? More probably in view of Essene angelology, they refer to the names of angels. See *TWNT*, 1:74f.

13. *TWNT*, 1: 80.

14. The ambiguity of the meaning of *angelos* emerges in the translation of Gal 4:14 and 1 Tim 3:16 (see E. DeWitt Burton, ICC, *Galatians* [1920], 242–43, and C. Spicq, *Les Épitres Pastorales* [Paris, 1947], p. 107), though in both cases most scholars prefer to render it "by angels." Moulton and Milligan point out that the meaning "angel" is the older signification of the term in Homer. See *Vocabulary of the Greek New Testament* (London, 1930). H. D. Betz, *Galatians*, Hermeneia: A Critical and Historical Commentary on the Bible (Philadelphia: Fortress Press, 1979) takes the meaning to be "angels."

15. *TWNT*, p. 82.

16. Cf F. F. Bruce, *The Acts of the Apostles* (London: Tyndale Press, 1952), p. 177.

17. See Foakes–Jackson, *Josephus and the Jews*, pp. 85, 90.

18. *Moses* 11:44. F. H. Colson's translation in LCL.

19. Some passages suggest that after the close of the New Testament period efforts were made in some quarters to belittle the role of angels on Mt. Sinai. In *Deut. Rab.* 7:9, Yahweh refused to give the Torah to the ministering angels though they coveted it. In *Deut. Rab.* 8:2 the ministering angels eagerly desired the Torah, it is claimed, but it was too abstruse for them. According to other passages, Moses had, metaphorically, to wrestle with the angels of Mt. Sinai: they pleaded that humankind was unworthy of the Torah and wanted it for 'themselves (see *Exod. Rab.* 21:1; *Šabbat* 88b). In *Cant. Rab.* 1:2, R. Johanan's view that angels mediated between Yahweh and the Israelites at Sinai is expressly set against that of the rabbis who insisted that it was each commandment itself which went in turn to each of the Israelites, not an angel mediating a commandment. It will be recalled that in a passage near the first two cited above—that is, *Deut. Rab.* 8:6— there is probably anti-Christian polemic (see my *Torah in the Messianic Age,* pp. 87f.). It is possible that a similar polemic emerges in the tendency revealed in the passages cited to make it clear that the angels did not receive the Law from Yahweh. Judaism would be anxious to counteract the Christian notion that the Law, because it was mediated by angels, was an inferior revelation. Perhaps it is not wholly irrelevant to point out further that all the prophets and all the sages could be conceived as having received their messages, whether in the form of phophecy or wisdom, directly from God at Sinai (See *Exod. Rab.* 28:6).

PAUL AND THE LAW: REFLECTIONS ON PITFALLS IN INTERPRETATION

1. H. Berman, *The Interaction of Law and Religion* (Nashville: Abingdon Press, 1974).

2. H. von Campenhausen, *The Formation of the Christian Bible*, Eng. trans. J. A. Baker (Philadelphia: Fortress Press, 1972).

3. That *ha-Torah* is to be sharply distinguished, as the Pentateuch, from the totality of the Torah is disputed. My article in the text does not always convey this meaning. See W. Bacher, *Die Exegetische Terminologie der jüdischen Trad-*

itionsliteratur (Leipzig, 1899–1905) 1; J. Bonsirven, *Le Judaisme Palestinien* (Paris, 1934), pp. 247–302; G. F. Moore, *Judaism* (Cambridge, Mass.: Harvard University Press, 1971), 1: 235–50; E. Urbach, *The Sages*, trans. I. Abrahams (Jerusalem: The Magnes Press, 1975), pp. 286–399.

4. See S. Lauterbach, *Rabbinic Essays* (Cincinnati: Hebrew Union College, 1951).

5. The most convenient translation is H. Danby, *The Mishna* (Oxford: At the Clarendon Press, 1933).

6. This aspect of the question has recently been powerfully emphasized in E. P. Sanders, *Paul and Palestinian Judaism* (Philadelphia: Fortress Press, 1977).

7. For a bibliography, see my *Paul and Rabbinic Judaism* (Philadelphia: Fortress Press, 1981), pp. 147–77.

8. The struggle in Paul's breast between the two cultures of Jerusalem and Athens expressed itself in his engagement with the Torah. I have discussed his deliberate and conscious concern with this struggle in a study of the allegory of the two olives in Rom. 11 : 17–24 in the *Festschrift for Marcel Simon*. See herein, chapter 8.

9. See the brilliant and massive contribution of Sanders, *Palestinian Judaism*, pp. 33–59. The true assessment of this work will necessarily be long in coming. One of its contentions, indicated in our text, certainly cannot be ignored. Sanders's work is the first deliberately systematic confrontation with the classical Protestant interpretation of Paul, especially as expressed in German scholarship. The question is whether Luther, with whom Sanders does not deal directly, understood Paul at a deeper level than Sanders allows. Luther recognized that to any sound Christian theology, Law is fundamental as the implicate of grace; he realized, as my teacher J. S. Whale writes, "that grace presupposed the sacred moral law by transcending it in forgiveness." (Letter from J. S. Whale to W. D. Davies, January 31, 1978). A discussion of the age-long tension between justice and mercy, judgment and forgiveness, or of the traditional Protestant understanding of Luther's and Paul's concern with this tension, is beyond the scope of this article. See J. S. Whale, *The Protestant Tradition* (Philadelphia: Westminster Press, 1955), pp. 3–103. It is important to recognize the distinction between Luther and his *epigoni*, who produced "Lutheranism," a distinction not without a parallel in that between Paul and "Paulinism." The literature on Paul and the Law is immense. The best treatment to provide guidance for recent discussion is that of E. P. Sanders, *Paul, the Law, and the Jewish People* (Philadelphia: Fortress Press, 1983). He enters into dialogue with Hubner, *Das Gesetz bei Paulus* (Göttingen: Vandenhoeck & Ruprecht, 1980), and others. See also G. Lüdemann, *Paulus und Das Judentum*, (Munich: Chr. Kaiser, 1983).

10. See, for example, F. Leenhardt, *Two Biblical Faiths: Protestant and Catholic*, trans. Harold Knight (Cambridge: At the University Press; 1964), 2.

11. The view referred to is associated especially with K. Stendahl, *Paul Among Jews and Gentiles* (Philadelphia: Fortress Press, 1976). See my "Paul and the People of Israel," herein, chapter 7.

12. Gal 4 : 4.

13. Isa 10 : 22, 35 : 4, 43 : 3, 45 : 17–22, 60 : 16. See Hempel, "Eschatology of the Old Testament," ed. G. A. Buttrick, in *IDB* (1962), E–J: 153. For apocalyptic

and ethics, see H. H. Rowley, *The Relevance of Apocalyptic* (London: Lutterworth Press, 1944); D. S. Russell, *The Method and Message of Jewish Apocalyptic 200 b.c.–a.d. 100* (Philadelphia: Westminster Press, 1964).

14. Matt 4:4, 6–7, 5:17–18; Mark 12:28–37.

15. See P. Richardson, *Israel in the Apostolic Church* (Cambridge: At the University Press, 1969). According to Richardson, the designation of the church as "the true Israel" did not occur until the mid-second century in the works of Justin Martyr. Use of the phrase in referring to the church is not found in the NT.

16. See D. Daube, *The Exodus Pattern in the Bible* (London: Faber & Faber, 1963); Davies, *The Setting of the Sermon on the Mount* (Cambridge: At the University Press, 1966); P. Démann, *Moïse dans la pensée de Saint Paul*, pp. 189–241; A. Déschamps, "Moïse dans les Évangiles et dans la tradition Apostolique," pp. 171–80, in *Moïse, L'Homme de L'Alliance: Cahiers Sioniens* (Paris, 1954) 2, 3, 4; T. F. Glasson, *Moses in the Fourth Gospel* (London: SCM Press, 1963); J. L. Martyn, *History and Theology in the Fourth Gospel* (New York: Harper & Row, 1968), pp. 88, 91; W. A. Meeks, *The Prophet King: Moses Traditions and the Johannine Christology*, NovTSup 14 (1967); H. J. Schoeps, *Theologie und Geschichte des Judenchristentums* (Tübingen: J. C. B. Mohr [Paul Siebeck], 1949) H. M. Temple, *The Mosaic Eschatological Prophet*, SBL Monograph series (1957); J. Jeremias, "Moses," *TDNT* (1967): 4: 848–73; H. Sahlin, "The New Exodus of Salvation According to Saint Paul," in *The Root of the Vine*, ed. A. Fridrichsen (London: A & C Black, 1953), p. 81; M. Smith, "Exodus Typology in the Fourth Gospel," *JBL* 81 (1962): 329–42. But see J. Dupont, "L'arrière-fond biblique du récit des tentations de Jésus," *NTS* 3 (1956–57): 287–304; Thompson, "Called—Proved—Obedient: A Study in the Baptism and Temptation Narratives of Matthew and Luke," *JTS* 11 (1960): 1–12.

17. See *Sermon*, pp. 1–108.

18. Mark 1:27. The emphasis on "teaching" in Mark emerges from R. Morgenthaler, *Statistik des neutestamentlichen Wortschatzes* (Frankfurt am Main: Gotthelf, 1959); Morgenthaler's data are reproduced in *Sermon*, p. 97 n. 1. See E. Schweizer, "Anmerkungen zur Theologie des Markus," in *Neotestamentica et Patristica: Freundesgabe Oscar Cullman* (Leiden, 1962), p. 37.

19. John 13:34. The context of this commandment within the Last Supper, which at least has Passover undertones, is important.

20. See Davies, "Torah and Dogma," *HTR* 61 (1968): 87–105.

21. See W. van Unnik, "La conception paulinienne de la nouvelle alliance," in *Littérature et Theologie Pauliniennes: Recherches Biblique* (Louvain, 1960), pp. 109–26, 224; van Unnik, "Η ΚΑΙΝΕ ΔΙΑΘΗΚΗ: A Problem in the Early History of the Canon," in *4 Studia Patristica*, reprinted in *79 Texte und Untersuchungen zur Geschichte der altcchrislichen Literatur*, ed. F. L. Cross (Berlin, 1961). Van Unnik notes the neglect of this theme in Pauline studies. Emphasis on the notion of the new covenant was so strong in early Christianity that both Joseph Bonsirven and H. J. Schoeps claim that it led to a neglect or muting of that theme in rabbinic Judaism. See J. Bonsirven, *Le Judaïsme palestinien au temps de Jesus Christ* (Paris: G. Beauchesne et ses fils, 1950), 1:79; H. J. Schoeps, *Theologie und Geschichte des Judenchristentums* (Tübingen: J. C. B. Mohr [Paul Siebeck], 1949), p. 90; G. Quell, "Diatithemi," in *TDNT* 2 (1964): 106–34. See also R. A. Har-

risville, *The Concept of Newness in the New Testament* (Minneapolis: Augsburg Publishing House, 1946). For a discussion of the covenant in Judaism, see the exhaustive study by A. Jaubert, *La Notion d'Alliance dans le Judaïsme aux abords de l'ère Chrétienne* (Paris; Edition du Seuil, 1963). On the presence of Law in the early Church as in the Old Testament, see G. von Rad, *Old Testament Theology,* trans. D. M. G. Stalker (New York: Harper & Row, 1962) 2: 391: "The saving event whereby Israel became Yahweh's is undissolubly bound up with the obligation to obey certain norms which clearly mark out the chosen people's sphere, particularly at its circumference. The same thing, however, occurs in the early Christian community. From the very beginning it too was conscious of being bound to certain legal norms and it put them into practice unreservedly. . . ." See 1 Cor. 5:5, 16:22; cf. Acts 8:20; 2 Tim 2:19. Important sources on this topic are G. Bornkamm, "Das Anathema in der urchristliche Abendmahls Theologie," in *Das Ende des Gesetzes: Paulus Studïen* (1952), p. 123; Käsemann, "Sätze Heiligen Rechts in Neuen Testament," *New Testament Studies* (Manchester, Eng.: Manchester University Press, (1955): 1:248. On the difficulty which Protestants have in doing justice to the Mosaic element in the New Testament, see the brilliant work of F. J. Leenhardt, *Two Biblical Faiths: Protestant and Catholic,* trans. H. Knight (1964): "Protestants have the greatest difficulty in not underestimating the value of the Mosaic tradition in the corpus of revelation. . . . [T]he Pauline polemic against the threat of Judaism and Judaic Christianity often remains, in the mentality of Protestant readers of the apostle, the sole key to the understanding of the Gospel. What is argued by St. Paul against the Judaic and Judaizing interpretation of the Law is applied by them in the most massive way to the whole structure of the Mosaic faith." On "Law" in Paul, see the suggestive essay by W. R. Schodel, "Pauline Thought: Some Basic Issues," in *Transitions in Biblical Scholarship,* ed. J. C. Rylaarsdam (Chicago: University of Chicago Press, 1968), p. 263.

22. One of the most illuminating developments in Old Testament studies has been the rehabilitation of the Law. Through the work of Alt, Von Rad, Martin Noth, Buber, Zimmerli, Clements, and others, the influence of the covenant tradition with its Law on the prophets has become clear. And just as the prophets have been connected with the Law that preceded them, so Finkelstein, in a brilliant study, has connected them with the Law that followed them in Judaism. The old antithesis of Law and Prophet has been challenged. The prophets are emerging as "teachers." This has an important bearing on our understanding of Jesus. To place him among the prophets is not to displace him from the role of teacher. See A. Alt, *Die Ursprünge des Israelitischen Rechts* (Leipzig: S. Hirzel, 1934); M. Noth, *Die Gesetze im Pentateuch* (1958), pp. 9–141; G. von Rad, *Das Formgeschichtliche Problem des Hexateuch* (1938), reprinted in *Gesammelte Studien zum A. T.* (Munich: Chr. Kaiser Verlag, 1958), pp. 9–86. Walter Zimmerli, in a series of lectures, gives a fascinating account of the theme in scholarship. See *The Law and the Prophets: A Study of the Meaning of the Old Testament* (Oxford: Basil Blackwell & Mott, 1965); on the same topic, see R. E. Clements, *Prophecy and Covenant* (London: SCM Press, 1965). On the prophets in Judaism, see my "Reflections on Tradition: The 'Abot Revisited," chapter 2, herein. Martin Buber puts great emphasis on the influence of the Sinai tradition on the prophets. See M. Buber, *The Prophetic Faith* (New York: Harper Torchbooks, 1960).

23. E. Käsemann, *New Testament Questions of Today* (Philadelphia: Fortress Press, 1969), p. 24.

24. See Richardson, *Apostolic Church* pp. 1–32 *et passim;* E. Trocmé, "Le Christianisme primitif, un myth historique?" in *49 Études Theologiques et religieuses* (Montpelier, 1974) 1: 19. S. Sandmel approaches Paul from a Hellenistic point of view, but agrees that to speak of the "Christianity" of Paul is anachronistic. See Sandmel, *The Genius of Paul: A Study in History* (New York: Schocken Books, 1970), p. 21. Cf. K. W. Clark, "Israel of God," in *Studies in the New Testament and Early Christian Literature,* ed. D. E. Aune (1972), pp. 161–69.

25. Moreover, the precise translation of the word " 'Ioudaismos" is not clear. It is not so much a reference to Judaism as a religion as to the Jewish way of life. The term is not found in the LXX, the Apocrypha or the Pseudepigrapha, except at 2 Macc 2:21, 8—14:38, and 4 Macc 4:26 in the context of loyalty to the Jewish religion as it confronts Hellenistic pressures. Hengel defines it as referring to "both political and genetic association with the Jewish nation and exclusive belief in the one God of Israel, together with observance of the Torah given by him." M. Hengel, *Judaism and Hellenism: Studies in Their Encounter in Palestine during the Early Hellenistic Period,* trans. J. Bowden (Philadelphia: Fortress Press, 1974). The term occurs only in Gal 1:14 in the New Testament. The view of A. Oepke that the term there indicates contempt for a Judaism clearly separated from Christianity must be treated very cautiously. See A. Oepke, *Der Brief des Paulus an die Galater* (1957), p. 30; cf D. Guthrie, "Galatians," in *NCB* (1969), p. 67.

26. See Davies, "From Schweitzer to Scholem: Reflections on Sabbatai Svi," chapter 14, herein. D. Moody Smith has suggested that first-century Judaism may have had its "divine men." But recently the whole notion of a divine man has been subjected to much criticism. See D. M. Smith, "The Milieu of the Johannine Miracle Source," in *Jews, Greeks and Christians,* ed. R. Hamerton-Kelly and R. Scroggs (Leiden: E. J. Brill, 1976), pp. 169–80.

27. D. Daube, *Civil Disobedience in Antiquity* (Edinburgh: Edinburgh University Press, 1972), pp. 115–16.

28. D. R. A. Hare, *The Theme of Jewish Persecution of Christians in the Gospel According to Saint Matthew,* SNTSMS 6 (New York: Cambridge University Press, 1968), pp. 1–18.

29. See my *Sermon,* pp. 256–315, and literature cited therein. The importance of the negative reaction of Jamnian Judaism to the gospel cannot be overemphasized as a factor contributing to radical separation. The separation is best understood probably less as a break-off by Christians from Jews than as one by Jews from Christians. Both parties bore responsibility. For example, the favorable presentation of the Samaritans in the New Testament is not unrelated to their disfavor among Jews. For caution regarding Jamnia, see J. P. Lewis, *JBR* 32 (1964): 125–32; G. Stemberger, *Kairos.*

30. 2 Pet 3:15–16. See also J. A. Sanders, "The Ethic of Election in Luke's Great Banquet Parable," in *Essays in Old Testament Ethics,* ed. J. L. Crenshaw and J. T. Willis (New York: Ktav, 1974), pp. 247–71.

31. Cf. Richardson, *Apostolic Church,* p. 1. For example, 1 *Clem.* has been described by some as a document of Judaism despite its Christian elements.

32. The best-known example possibly is R. Akiba's acceptance of Bar Kokba as the Messiah and remaining within the Jewish community.

33. Cf. N. A. Dahl, *The Crucified Messiah and Other Essays* (Minneapolis: Augsburg, 1974); A. T. Hanson, *Studies in Paul's Technique and Theology* (Grand Rapids: Wm. B. Eerdmans, 1974). But cf. Sanders, *Palestinian Judaism*, p. 495.

34. See my *Sermon*, pp. 109–90; J. Jervell, "Die offenbarte und die verborgene Tora: Zur Vorstellung über die neue Tora im Rabbinismus," in *ST* 25 (1971): 90–108; P. Schäfer, "Die Torah der messianischen Zeit," in *ZNW* 65: 27–42. H. Schürmann, "Das Gesetz Christi (Gal. 6:2): Jesus Verhalten und Wort als Letzgültigue sittliche Norm nach Paulus," *Neues Testament und Kirche*, Pastoral Aufsätze 6 (1974): 95–102; C. H. Dodd, "Έννομος Χριστοῦ," *More New Testament Studies* (Grand Rapids: Wm. B. Eerdmans, 1968), pp. 134–48.

35. Cf. Yadin, "The Temple Scroll," in *New Directions in Biblical Archeology*, ed. D. N. Freedman and J. C. Greenfield (New York: Doubleday & Co., 1969), pp. 139–48.

36. *T. Soṭa* 14, p. 9.

37. See B. Reicke, "The Law and the World According to Paul," *JBL* 70 (1951): 259–76; G. Delling in *TDNT* 7: 672; G. A. Deismann, *Encyclopedia Biblica*, vol. 2, ed. T. K. Cheyne and J. S. Black, p. 1258.

38. See note 34.

39. Cf. my *Sermon*, p. 353.

40. Cf. P. Vielhauer, "Paulus und die Kephaspartei in Korinth," *NTS* 21 (1974–75): 341–52.

41. C. K. Barrett, *A Commentary on the Second Epistle to the Corinthians* (New York: Harper & Row, 1974), p. 7 n. 81.

42. The translation is that of Barrett. The *NEB*, less forcefully, renders: "What matters is to keep God's commandments."

43. See J. A. Sanders, "Torah and Christ," *Int* 29 (1975): 382, and "Torah and Paul," *Festschrift for N. A. Dahl* (Philadelphia: Fortress Press, 1978).

44. Cf. J. Jervell, "Der Brief nach Jerusalem: Über Veranlassung und Addresse des Römerbriefs," *ST* 25 (1971): 61–73; U. Wilckens, *Über Abfassunszweck und Aufbau des Römerbriefes, Rechfertigung als Freiheit: Paulus-Studien* (1974). On the other hand, K. P. Donfried thinks Romans was written by Paul to deal with a concrete situation in Rome. See Donfried, "False Presuppositions in the Study of Romans," *CBQ* 36 (1974): 332–55; Cf. P. Minear, *The Obedience of Faith* (London: SCM Press, 1971).

45. See my *Rabbinic Judaism;* O. Cullmann, "Paradosis et Kyrios: Le problème de la tradition dans le paulinisme," *RHPR* 1 (1950): 12. For a discussion of the "new Torah" in later Judaism, see M. Simon, *Verus Israel* (Paris: Boccard, 1948), p. 100. The best critique of the position advocated in *Rabbinic Judaism* is P. Démann, *Möise at la Loi*, p. 239. It should be recalled that some scholars have found ideas connected with the Torah applied to Christ in the prologue of the Fourth Gospel. See, for example, C. H. Dodd, *The Interpretation of the Fourth Gospel* (Cambridge: At the University Press, 1953), p. 270.

46. Apart from some such assumption, the preservation of the tradition about the works and deeds of Jesus in the Gospels is difficult to understand. Even granted that much of that tradition is a creation of the primitive community, its

attachment to the figure of Jesus is itself significant. Cf. G. Bornkamm, *Jesus of Nazareth*, 3d ed., trans. I. and F. McLuskey and J. M. Robinson (New York: Harper & Row, 1960). See also herein, ch. 15.

47. To connect the resurrection with morality is not usual. But this is implicit in 1 Cor 15:7. It is significant that in 1 Cor 15:5, the risen Lord is said to have appeared first to Cephas, who had betrayed Jesus three times, and then to the twelve, who had all forsaken him and fled. We must assume that Paul knew the tradition about those betrayals. In the fourth Gospel, Jesus first appears to Mary Magdalene, whose sins were well known. It is no accident that in the Sermon on the Mount, the Beatitudes, which are the expression of God's grace, precede the statement of the demands of Jesus, which are thus deliberately set in a context of grace.

48. See *IDB*, E–J, p. 168; J. Knox, *The Ethic of Jesus in the Teaching of the Church* (Nashville: Abingdon Press, 1961; London: Epworth Press, 1962), p. 73.

49. See *Rabbinic Judaism*, p. 215, and references to literature therein. In the Fourth Gospel the Spirit, which is "Holy," is to teach and to recall what Jesus had taught. See John 14:25; Gal 5:22; 1 Cor 13; John 14:15–17, 15:9–10, 16:8–11.

50. Rom 6:3; 1 Cor 12:13; Gal 3:27. But baptism was not universal. See Acts 1:14–15, 19:1–7.

51. 2 Cor. 8:9, 12:1; Phil 2:5–8; Rom. 8:11 and especially 6:1–7:6. On the history of the emphasis on what is generally referred to as the "indicative-imperative" motif in Paul, see the excellent appendix entitled "A Survey of Nineteenth- and Twentieth-Century Interpretations of Pauline Ethics" in V. P. Furnish, *Theology and Ethics in Paul* (Nashville: Abingdon Press, 1968), p. 242. Like Furnish, I find the work of Maurice Goguel especially original and provocative. See M. Goguel, *The Primitive Church*, trans. H. C. Snape (New York: Macmillan Co., 1964).

Stendahl has objected to connecting the motif of "dying and rising with Christ" with morality on the grounds that while the tense of the verbs referring to dying with Christ is in the past, that of verbs referring to rising with Christ is in the future. The matter is discussed in Furnish, *Theology and Ethics*, p. 171. The future tenses in Rom 6:5, 8 are important: "We *shall* be united in his resurrection" and "we *shall* also live with him." But as Furnish also makes clear, the newness of life is associated with the resurrection. Rom 6:4 reads: "We were buried therefore with him by baptism into death, so that as Christ was raised from the dead by the glory of the Father, we too might walk in the newness of life." The power of the future life is already at work in the present. The Christian is to walk in the power of that life here and now. Rom 8:4–5; 2 Cor 10:2–3; 1 Cor 3:3; Rom 13:13; Phil 3:18. See Furnish, p. 214; W. R. Schoedel, "Pauline Thought: Some Basic Issues," in *Transitions in Biblical Scholarship*, p. 279 n. 34. On the understanding of the "indicative-imperative" relation as not only an individual one I wholeheartedly agree with Ernest Käsemann. See E. Käsemann, "The Righteousness of God in Paul," in *New Testament Questions of Today*, trans. W. S. Montague and W. F. Bunge (Philadelphia: Fortress Press, 1969), pp. 175–76. Cf. *Rabbinic Judaism* at xii.

52. This is brought out in C. H. Dodd, *The Interpretation of the Fourth Gospel*,

p. 418, in his treatment of the Prayer of Christ in John 17: "We have now to enquire in what precise way this prayer is related to the discourses which preceded it. If we look back on these discourses, we see that they turn upon one central theme—what it means to be united with Christ (with Christ crucified and risen). This theme is treated in a kaleidoscopic variety of aspects. Let us briefly recapitulate a few of them. Jesus washes His disciples' feet that they may 'have part with Him' (*meros echeis met emou*, 12:8). They are to be bound together with the *agapē* which is a reflection, or reproduction, of His (*agapē*) (8:34). Such *agapē* is capable of transcending the separation made by death between Christ and His own: His 'return' to them is a realization of *agapē* (9:19–24). After He has passed through death they will be united with Him as branches of the true Vine (15:1–9), and the fruit which the branches yield is once again *agapē* proceeding from the *agapē* of God revealed in Christ (15:8–10)."

53. It has been pointed out that Paul and Peter and other figures in the early church were regarded as "models" to be imitated. See J. Wagenmann, *Die Stelling des Apostels Paulus neben den Zwölf* (1926), pp. 52–76. The Paul of the Pastorals, who finished his course, was a "model." John 13:5 makes clear that specific acts in the life of Jesus were "models"; Moody Smith referred me also to John 14:12, where "imitation" of some kind seems to be involved.

54. Stendahl has orally raised the question whether the cross, as such, was made the ground of an appeal for the moral life in the New Testament. If we exclude all moral considerations from discipleship, such a question might be answered in the negative. If we do not, as is surely more likely, then as Harald Riesenfeld has pointed out, it is significant that discipleship is closely related to the cross not only in the synoptics but in the Fourth Gospel. Compare Matt 16:21–27 with John 12:31. See H. Riesenfeld, *Gospel Tradition,* trans. E. M. Rowley and R. A. Kraft (Philadelphia: Fortress Press, 1979). The obedience of Christ in death, Rom 5:19, cf. Phil 2:8, is an "act of righteousness," Rom 5:18, and preminently an expression of God's love, Gal 2:19, 5:6. Christ crucified becomes "wisdom, righteousness, sanctification, and redemption for us," 1 Cor 1:30–31. God's love revealed in the cross forgives, renews, and sustains, 2 Cor 5:14. See Furnish, *Theology and Ethics,* p. 168. It is difficult to divorce the appeal to the cross from an appeal to the good life. Furnish, rightly in my judgment, thinks that Paul's use of the hymn in Phil 2:5 is at least partly hortatory. However, some have denied that the cross has moral implications, even in Phil 2:5. See R. P. Martin, *Carmen Christi* (Cambridge: At the University Press, 1967), pp. 68, 84.

55. See W. P. de Boer, *The Imitation of Paul: An Exegetical Study* (Leiden, 1962); M. Hengel, *Nachfolge und Charisma: Eine Exegetisch-Religionsgeschichtliche Studie de Matt. 8:21f und Jesu Ruf in die Nachfolge* (1968), p. 1 n. 2; E. Larsson, *Christus als Vorbild* (1962), pp. 29–47; E. Löhse, "Nachfolge Christi," in *4 Die Religion in Geschichte un Gegenwart,* 3d ed., col. 1286; A. Schulz, *Nachfolgen und Nachahmen* (Uppsala, 1962), p. 270; E. J. Tinsley, *The Imitation of God in Christ* (Philadelphia: Westminster Press, 1960); J. Weiss, *Die Nachfolge, Christi und die Predigt der Gegenwart* (1895); D. M. Stanley, " 'Become Imitators of Me': The Pauline Conception of Apostolic Tradition," *Biblica* 40 (1959): 859; D. Williams, "Imitation and Tradition in Paul" (dissertation, New York: Union

Theological Seminary). Furnish discusses the matter acutely and with a wealth of bibliographical detail. See *Theology and Ethics,* p. 217. He speaks of Christ's obedience as "paradigmatic for the believer's new life in Christ," also at p. 218, but rejects any inference that it should be emulated. Similarly at p. 223. He endorses Dibelius's view that "when Paul speaks of following Christ, he is not thinking first of all of the historical person Jesus of Nazareth, but of the Son of God who emptied himself and lived and died for others." Similarly at p. 224. This very sharp dichotomy is difficult to accept: it was precisely in Jesus of Nazareth that early Christians saw the son of God and it was the actuality of his life that lay behind their Christological and mythological assertions about him. To separate the historical person, Jesus of Nazareth, so sharply from the Son of God or the *Kurios* is to make the myth govern the history rather than the history the ground of the myth. On the relation of "Jesus" to the "Lord" in Paul, see *Sermon,* p. 341. Furnish writes: "W. D. Davies goes so far as to contend that the preservation of Jesus' sayings and stories about him was due largely to the importance his followers attached to imitating his example," Furnish, *Theology and Ethics,* p. 219. This seems not so very different from what is now a common assumption of most New Testament scholars that the needs of the Church are reflected in the tradition—except that for some form critics the Church, to serve those needs, created a tradition and a history. I prefer to think of a history fashioned by the Church and then transmitted by the tradition—that is, given in the ministry of Jesus. I agree with what Furnish affirms but not with what he denies. Perhaps we differ over what we consider historically probable. For a discussion of H. D. Betz, *Nachfolge und Nachahmung Christi im Neuen Testament* (Tübingen: J. C. B. Mohr [Paul Siebeck], 1967), see Hengel, *Nachfolge und Charisma* (Berlin: A. Töpelmann, 1968), p. 94. The pertinent texts on "imitation" are discussed in Furnish, *Theology and Ethics* (Nashville: Abingdon Press, 1968), p. 220.

56. See E. G. Selwyn, *The First Epistle of St. Peter* (Toronto: Macmillan & Co., 1947), p. 20. On "The Imitation of Christ and the Atonement," see 1 Pet 2:20b: "But if when you do right and suffer for it you take it patiently, you have God's approval. For to this you have been called, because Christ also suffered for you, leaving you an example, that you should follow in his steps. He committed no sin; no guile was found in his lips. When he was reviled, he did not revile in return, when he suffered he did not threaten. . . ." See also Pet 4:1.

57. See O. Cullmann, *Christ and Time* (Philadelphia: Westminster Press, 1962); O. Cullmann, *Salvation as History,* trans. G. S. Sowers (New York: Harper & Row, 1967); Furnish rightly emphasizes that all Christian discernment is informed by *agapē.*

58. This is explicitly expressed in 1 Pet 1:1, but implied throughout the New Testament.

59. See Dodd, "Communism in the New Testament," *IDB* 18.

60. I find no reason to reject the historicity of the twelve. See J. Wagenmann, *Die Stellung des Apostels Paulus neben den Zwölf.*

61. This is one of the important insights of Albert Schweitzer. See A. Schweitzer, *The Mysticism of Paul the Apostle,* trans. W. Montgomery (London: A. & C. Black, 1931), p. 105. But caution is necessary in accepting Schweitzer. See *Rabbinic Judaism,* p. 98.

62. Thus knowledge is placed by Paul as the second of the gifts of the Spirit, after wisdom, 1 Cor 12:8. The importance of rationality is made clear in 1 Cor 14. The necessity of the renewal of the mind is recognized in Rom 12:2. In John emphasis on the truth of the witness to Christ is frequent. See, for example, John 10:41, 19:35, 21:24. Rationality is included in this truth, although it does not exhaust it. Compare 1 Pet 3:15 with 2 Tim 1:27.

63. Cf. Philemon 15, 16.

64. For Paul, the criterion of love among the brethren is normative. Rom 14:21; 1 Cor 12—14. See also Eph 4: 1–16; H. A. A. Kennedy, *The Theology of the Epistles* (New York: Charles Scribner's Sons, 1920), p. 145.

65. 1 John 4:20; John 17 and passim.

66. I have dealt with Matthew at length in *Sermon*, pp. 366–93, where I refer to the crisis character of material from Q and the *gemaric* character of much in Matthew.

67. See my *Rabbinic Judaism*.

68. For a recent treatment of this problem see the study of my student, Dale C. Allison, Jr., "The Pauline Epistles and the Synoptic Gospels: The Pattern of the Parallels," *NTS* (January 1981).

69. See C. F. D. Moule, *The Birth of the New Testament* (New York: Harper & Row, 1962), p. 212; "Important Moral Issues," *Expository Times* 74 (1963): 370–73.

70. The words appear explicitly in Gal 6:2 and implicitly in Rom 8:2. 1 Cor 9:20–22 reads: "To the Jews I became as a Jew, in order to win Jews; to those under the law I became as one under the law—though not being myself under the law—that I might win those under the law. To those outside the law I became as one outside the law—not being without law toward God but under the law of Christ—that I might win those outside the law. To the weak I became weak, that I might win the weak. I have become all things to all men, that I might by all means save some." Furnish points out that there is only one certain rabbinic reference to "the Law of the Messiah," that from *Midr. Qoh.* 11:8 (52a). But it is surely implied in other passages. See *Sermon*, p. 172. And, in the recently discovered *Targum Yerušalmi to the Pentateuch* of the *Codex Neofiti I* of the Vatican Library, the contents of which have been traced by Diez Macho to the second century A.D. at least, Isa 11:3 reads, "Behold, the Messiah who is to come shall be one who teaches the Law and will judge in the fear of the Lord."

On the *Codex Neofiti*, see A. D. Macho, "The Recently Discovered Palestinian Targum: Its Antiquity," in *VT*Sup 7 (1960). In Diez Macho's view, *Codex Neofiti* shows that the Palestinian Targum is of pre-Christian origin. There is no new Torah in the *Dead Sea Scrolls*. See my small work, *The Sermon on the Mount* (Cambridge, 1966), p. 63. But see N. Perrin, *The Kingdom of God in the Teaching of Jesus* (Philadelphia: Westminster Press, 1963), p. 76.

71. See *Sermon*, p. 401 concerning James and the Johannine sources. C. Spicq, *Agape dans le Nouveau Testament: Analyses des Textes* (1958–59).

72. See Selwyn, *The First Epistle of St. Peter*.

73. See *Rabbinic Judaism*, p. 329; S. Winning, *Die Tugend und Lasterkataloge im Neuen Testament* (1959), p. 237. The 1QS 1:18 actually has the imperative participle.

74. See M. Dibelius, *The Pastoral Epistles*, trans. Philip Bottolphan, Adela

Yarbro, ed. Helmut Koester (Philadelphia: Fortress Press, 1972); B. S. Easton, *The Pastoral Epistles 98* (New York: Charles Scribner's Sons; London: SCM Press, 1948). On conscience in the New Testament, see the article herein, chapter 13.

75. See W. D. Davies, "The Relevance of the Moral Teaching of the Early Church," chapter 16, herein.

76. J. Noonan, Jr., *Persons and Masks of the Law* (New York: Farrar, Straus & Giroux, 1976), especially his brilliant chapter, "The Alliance of Law and History," pp. 152–67.

77. D. Daube, *Studies in Biblical Law* (New York: Ktav, 1969), p. 1.

78. This is peculiarly true with respect to Paul because obedience to the Torah was for him as a Jew not only the guide to and source of the good life for society but the sign of being in the covenant and of justification before God, though not its ground. On the dangers of confusing morality and Law, see Holmes, "The Path of the Law," *Harvard Law Review* 10 (1896–97): 457–58.

79. See K. Stendahl, *Paul Among Jews and Gentiles* (Philadelphia: Fortress Press, 1976).

80. See *People of Israel*.

81. Rom 13:1.

82. D. Daube, *Studies in Biblical Law* 1–3; D. Daube, "The Duty of Procreation," Presidential address to the Classical Association (1977).

83. Rom 13:1–6; cf. *m. Pirqe ʾAbot* 3:2: "[Rabbi] Hanna the Prefect of the Priests said: Pray for the peace of the ruling power, since but for the fear of it men would have swallowed up each other alive."

84. H. J. Berman, *The Interaction of Law and Religion* (Nashville: Abingdon Press, 1974).

85. See, for example, Berman, "Comparison of Soviet and American Law," *Harvard Law Journal* (1961): 96.

86. The Torah was given not to the worthy but to the unworthy. See, for example, Deut 7:7; 9:4, 6–29. On the criticism of the Law in Paul, see *People of Israel; IDB* 2: 167–76; 3: 89.

87. See D. Daube, "Pauline Contributions to a Pluralistic Culture: Re-Creation and Beyond, Jesus and Man's Hope," in *Jesus and Man's Hope,* ed. D. G. Miller and D. Y. Hadidian (1971), 2: 223–45.

88. On this motif in rabbinic Law, see D. Daube, "Concessions to Sinfulness in Jewish Law," *JJS* 10 (1959): 1.

89. On this phrase in 1 Cor 9:20, see D. Daube, *The New Testament and Rabbinic Judaism* (New York: John DeGraff, Inc.; London: University of London, Athlone Press, 1956), pp. 336–41; H. Chadwick, "All Things to All Men," *NTS* 4 (1954–55): 201.

90. G. C. Christie, *On Laws, Norms and Authority* (forthcoming); Noonan, *Masks of the Law,* pp. 6–14, It is clear that Paul would not have endorsed what has come to be called "situation ethics." He confronted the world with a moral teaching simple in its form but stark and penetrating in its demands. It was not merely the context which informed his response to any moral question. But at the same time the genius of Paul was not in legislation. See Davies, "The Relevance of the Moral Teaching of the Early Church," chapter 16, herein.

91. J. Noonan, *Masks of the Law,* p. 153. He questions the view of Holmes

that the "history [of law] is the history of the moral development of our race."
Noonan discusses the notion of "development." On the fallibility and corrupti-
bility of the law revealed in much modern political and sociological discussion,
see L. Woolf, *An Autobiography of the Years 1880–1904* (London, 1972), pp. 99–
100; Review of *The Politics of the Judiciary* by J. Griffith, in *Times Literary
Supplement,* 9 January, 1978, p. 11.

92. H. Berman, "Comparison of Soviet and American Law," p. 9. For a brief
bibliography, see B. Konstantinovsky, *Soviet Law in Action* (Cambridge, Mass.:
Harvard University Press; Oxford: At the Clarendon Press, 1953).

93. H. Berman, "Comparison of Soviet and American Law, p. 24.

94. The phrase "exodus from the Law" I learned from G. Scholem's treatment
of Sabbatai Svi. Whether Paul, in the very first flush of his call, indulged in such
a concept cannot be established or denied. If he did, he soon abandoned it. The
question of change and development in Paul is extremely complex.

95. See, for example, Rom 13:11, 12.

96. One brought up under the British legal system would have to confess—
despite its perhaps rightly vaunted comparative excellence—that in contemplating
many of its laws and many of its victims he would have to echo the famous words
of George Borrow, in *Lavengro,* on the reading of the Newgate Lives and Trials:
"As I read over the lives of these robbers and pickpockets, strange doubts began
to arise in my mind about virtue and crime."

97. Lawyers are sometimes likely to react with impatience to a plea for simplification or a critical stance toward tradition. The legal mind is rightly fearful
of plunging into chaos if it leaves the trodden path. And it can understandably
be asked how the complexities involved in the settling of disputes of all kinds
can be dealt with except through the intricate procedures and safeguards of precedent. Yet the need for simplification is often recognized in what appear to be
spontaneous, self-generated corrective steps in the history of law itself. One example, pointed out to me by K. Pye, Chancellor of Duke University, Durham,
N.C., is the development of equity in England. Arising out of the attempt to seek
relief from unreasonable penalties where the remedy at law was inadequate, equity
appealed to the conscience of the chancellor. "By and large equity never became
as rigid a system as did the common law, and it retained throughout a substantial
place for the exercise of judicial discretion in the light of 'reason and conscience,'" F. James, Jr., *Civil Procedure* (Boston: Little, Brown & Co., 1965),
p. 13. A. Larson referred me to three other examples of the same kind: the development of the concept of "no-fault" insurance in workers' compensation and
more recently in the field of automobile insurance and medical malpractice, and
the increasing accountability by businesses for the character of their products.
But in each of these examples the tendency has been for the simplification itself
(for example, in "no-fault" cases) to become increasingly complex. Simplification
seems to be a constant necessity even in those areas where it has already been
at work. On the inadequacy of simply relying on traditional law, recall the words
of Holmes: "It is revolting to have no better reason for a rule of law than that it
was laid down in the time of Henry IV. It is still more revolting if the grounds
on which it was laid down have long since vanished," "The Path of the Law."

98. See *Rabbinic Judaism,* pp. 147–76. Criticisms of the concept of the new

Torah in Paul have centered on the date and authorship of Colossians and on the paucity of references to the words of Jesus in Paul. But the concept is tied up, not only with the words of Jesus used by Paul, but also with the totality of his person; the wisdom Christology of Colossians has its antecedant in 1 Corinthians. For the notion of Christ as himself constituting the living tradition of the early Church, see the seminal study of O. Cullmann, "Kyrios as Designation for the Oral Tradition concerning Jesus," *SJT* 3 (1950): 180–97.

99. J. Noonan, *Masks of the Law*, p. xii.

100. M. Grant, *Saint Paul* (New York: Charles Scribner's Sons, 1976), pp. 197–98 (emphasis in original).

101. It is only with trepidation that I have ventured to write on tradition and precedent in Law in this concluding section. The work of Karl N. Llewellyn enlarged my awareness. See, for example, K. Llewellyn, *The Common Law Tradition: Deciding Appeals* (Boston: Little, Brown & Co., 1960), pp. 62–76. I am particularly grateful to my colleague, Professor G. C. Christie, for his stimulating conversations and guidance. Any errors in my understanding are not due to him but to my ignorance. My debt to Professor David Daube I cannot adequately express.

PAUL AND THE PEOPLE OF ISRAEL

1. P. H. Menoud, "Revelation and Tradition: The Influence of Paul's Conversion on his Theology," *Int* 7 (1953): 131–41.

2. J. Dupont, "La conversion de Paul et son influence sur sa conception du salut par la foi," *Analecta Biblica* 42 (1970): 67–88; discussion on pp. 88–100. An English version appeared in *Apostolic History and the Gospel: Biblical and Historical Essays Presented to F. F. Bruce on his 60th Birthday*, ed. W. W. Gasque and R. P. Martin (Grand Rapids: Wm. B. Eerdmans, 1970), pp. 176–94; see also Morton Smith, "The Reason for the Persecution of Paul and the Obscurity of Acts," *Studies in Mysticism and Religion Presented to Gershom G. Scholem* (Jerusalem, 1967), pp. 261–68. G. Bornkamm, *Paul*, trans. D. M. Stalker (New York: Harper & Row, 1969), pp. 13–25, finds the meaning of the "conversion" in Phil. 3:7–9 (pp. 16ff). Although he recognizes that it concerned the discovery of "who Jesus really was" (p. 23), he does not deal strictly with the messiahship of Jesus. On the impropriety of using the term "conversion" rather than the "call" of Paul, see K. Stendahl, *Paul Among Jews and Gentiles* (Philadelphia: Fortress Press, 1976), pp. 7–23. For the reasons for the Jews' rejection of the Christian movement, see D. R. A. Hare, *The Theme of Jewish Persecution of Christians in the Gospel According to St. Matthew*, SNTSMS 6 (Cambridge: At the University Press, 1967), pp. 1–18. The obvious example of Jewish tolerance is Akiba's accepting Bar Kokba's messiahship and yet remaining within Judaism, although this has now been questioned.

3. Nils A. Dahl, "Die Messianität Jesu bei Paulus," *Studia Paulina in honorem Johannis de Zwaan* (Haarlem, 1953), pp. 83–95; English translation in *The Crucified Messiah and Other Essays* (Minneapolis: Augsburg, 1974), pp. 37–47.

4. See my "From Schweitzer to Scholem: Reflections on Sabbatai Svi," chapter 14, herein.

5. This helps explain the comparative paucity of passages dealing directly with God in the New Testament. See N. A. Dahl, "The Neglected Factor in New Testament Theology," *Reflection* (November 1975), sections 5–8; and now A. C. Wire, *Pauline Theology as an Understanding of God: The Explicit and the Implicit* (Ph.D dissertation, University of Michigan, 1974) H. Moxnes, *Theology in Conflict: Studies in Paul's Understanding of God in Romans*, NovTSup 53 (Leiden: Brill, 1980).

6. See Martin Dibelius, *Paul*, trans. F. Clarke (Philadelphia: Westminster Press, 1953), pp. 51–52, and my *Invitation to the New Testament* (New York: Doubleday & Co., 1965), pp. 260–62.

7. The question of the genuineness of 2 Thessalonians is still open. B. Rigaux, *Les Epitres aux Thessaloniciens* (Paris, 1965), and E. Best, *A Commentary on the First and Second Epistles to the Thessalonians* (New York: Harper & Row, 1972) accept it. W. Trilling, *Untersuchungen zum Zweiten Thessalonicherbrief* (Leipzig, 1972), takes it to be Deutero-Pauline.

8. See especially B. Rigaux, *Les Epitres aux Thessaloniciens*, p. 453, and E. Best, *The First and Second Epistles to the Thessalonians*, p. 121; the former favors the translation "pour la fin" (the eschatological end) and the latter "finally."

9. B. A. Pearson, "1 Thessalonians 2:13–16: A Deutero-Pauline Interpolation," *HTR* 64 (1971): 79–94. On the literary structure of 1 Thessalonians as pointing to 1 Thess. 2:13–16 as an interpolation, Hendrikus Boers, "The Form Critical Study of Paul's Letters: 1 Thessalonians as 'a Case Study,'" *NTS* 22 (1976): 140–58; Daryl Schmidt, "1 Thess 2:13–16: Linguistic Evidence for an Interpolation," *JBL* (forthcoming) (1983). J. Moffatt, *An Introduction to the Literature of the New Testament* (New York: Charles Scribner's Sons, 1911), p. 73, rejecting the view that all of verses 14–16 were interpolated (his bibliographical details are valuable here), suggested that 16c was a marginal gloss, provoked by the horrors of the fall of Jerusalem. Rigaux, *Les Épîtres aux Thessaloniciens*, p. 456, rightly rejects this.

10. So most rightly Rigaux, Best, and J. Coppens, "Miscellanées bibliques 80: Une diatribe anti-juive dans 1 Thess 11:13–16," *Ephemerides Theologicae Lovanienses*, (May, 1976), pp. 90–95.

11. O. Michel, *Antijudaismus im Neuen Testament*, hrsg. von W. P. Eckert, N. P. Levinson, M. Stöhr (Munich, 1967), p. 58, rightly says that our passage reflects certain experiences Paul had when a missionary to the Jewish Diaspora.

12. But contrast M. Hengel, "Das Gleichnis von den Weingärtnern Mc 12:1–12 im Lichte des Zenopapyri und der rabbinischen Gleichnisse," *ZNW* 59 (1968): 1–39.

13. Compare O. H. Steck, *Israel und das gewaltsame Geschick der Propheten: Untersuchungen zu Spätjudentum und Urchristentum*, WMANT 56, 23 (Neukirchen-Vluyn, 1967), pp. 267f.

14. E. Bammel, "Judenverfolgung und Naherwartung," *ZTK* (1959): 294–315.

15. See above, n. 7.

16. On these terms see K. L. Schmidt, *Die Judenfrage im Lichte der Kapitel 9–11 Römerbriefs*. Theologische Studien, hrsg. von Karl Barth, Heft 13 (Zurich, 1947), pp. 3–25; D. Georgi, *Die Gegner des Paulus im 2. Korintherbrief*, WMANT 11 (Neukirchen-Vluyn, 1964), pp. 51–63; C. K. Barrett, *The Second Epistle to*

the Corinthians (New York: Harper & Row, 1973), pp. 293–95. Georgi and Barrett understand "the Hebrews" and "the Israelites" in a broadly similar way. The point is that Paul in 1 Thess 2:13–16 does not use the term "Hebrews" with the ethnic or familial connotation of a people of Palestinian origin, culture, tradition, and religion nor the term "Israelites" with the connotation of a people of the Jewish faith particularly, but the more generalized term "Jews." Where he seeks to emphasize the specifically ethnic and religious dimensions of "the Jews" he speaks of the Hebrews and the Israelites and again of the "seed of Abraham." On the significance of this phrase which occurs in Gal 3:29, 2 Cor 11:22, and Rom 9:7; 11:1, Georgi and Barrett differ, the latter most probably to be followed.

17. Rom 9:1–6. Compare the excellent study by E. Trocmé, "Le Christianisme primitif, un mythe historique?" in *Etudes théologiques et religieuses,* Revue Trimestrielle (Montpelier, 1974): 1:19.

18. Paul's dependence in 1 Thess. on "Christian vocabulary" is shown by B. Rigaux, "Vocabulaire chrétien antérieur à la première épître aux Thessaloniciens," in *Sacra Pagina, Miscellanea Biblica* (Bibliotheca Ephemeridum Theologicarum Lovaniensium, vols. 12–13; ed. J. Coppens, A. Descamps, E. Massaux [Gembloux, 1959]), 2: 380–89. Rigaux's observations do not necessarily exclude our proposal.

19. K. Stendahl, "Judaism and Christianity: Then and Now," in *New Theology No. 2.,* ed. M. E. Marty and Dean G. Pearman (New York: Macmillan Co., no date), p. 161. See especially his "The Apostle Paul and the Introspective Conscience of the West," *HTR* 56 (1963): 199–215. On the emphasis on the cross in Galatians, see Beverly Gaventa (M. Div. thesis, Union Theological Seminary, New York 1971); G. S. Duncan, *The Epistle of Paul to the Galatians* (New York: Harper & Brothers; London: Hodder & Stoughton, 1934), pp. xli–xliii.

20. See especially P. Richardson, *Israel in the Apostolic Age,* SNTSMS 10 (New York and Cambridge: Cambridge University Press, 1969), p. 79. He thinks that "Israel of God" in Gal 6:16 refers to "an Israel [of God] within [all] Israel" (p. 82). The most recent commentator, F. Mussner, *Der Galaterbrief* (Freiburg, 1974), ad rem., questions this limitation (of Israel of God) to a part of Israel and identifies "Israel of God" with πᾶς Ἰσραήλ of Rom 11:26 (p. 417 n. 61). But since Paul's use of Israel in Rom 9–11 is not uniform (contrast Rom 9:6 with 11:26 and with 11:5ff.) the decision cannot be made with certainty. Note also that E. de Witt Burton (*A Critical and Exegetical Commentary on the Epistle to the Galatians,* ICC [New York: Charles Scribner's Sons, 1920]), when dealing with Gal 6:16 (like Mussner) could also refer to Romans 9–11, that is 11:5, so as to get another interpretation of "Israel of God" in Gal 6:16 ("not . . . the whole Jewish nation, but . . . the pious Israel . . . including even those who had not seen the truth as Paul saw it," p. 358); cf. Richardson.

On the other hand the interpretation of Gal 6:16 as referring to the church of Jews *and* Gentiles has recently been advocated by U. Luz, *Das Geschichtsverständnis bei Paulus* (Munich, 1968), p. 269; cf. my *The Gospel and the Land: Early Christianity and Jewish Territorial Doctrine* (Berkeley and Los Angeles: University of California Press, 1974), p. 171 n. 18. As Luz rightly says, Gal 6:16 is the *only* passage in the Pauline letters which could have the meaning "Israel of God" = church of Jews and Gentiles. If this proposal were correct, one would have expected to find support for it in Romans 9–11 where Paul extensively deals with "Israel."

21. See D. Georgi, *Die Gegner des Paulus im 2. Korintherbrief,* p. 8 n. 2.

22. See W. D. Davies, *The Setting of the Sermon on the Mount* (Cambridge: Cambridge University Press, 1964), p. 179 n. 1.

23. C. K. Barrett, *From First Adam to Last: A Study in Pauline Theology* (New York: Charles Scribner's Sons; London: A. & C. Black, 1962), p. 52 n. 1; *A Commentary on the Second Epistle to the Corinthians* (New York: Harper & Row, 1974), pp. 110–26.

24. See W. C. van Unnik, "La conception paulinienne de la nouvelle alliance," in *Littéraire et Théologie Pauliniennes,* RB 5 (Bruges, 1960): 109–26, 224f.; see also his "Η Καινὴ Διαθήκη: A problem in the early history of the Canon," in *Studia Patristica* 4, ed. F. L. Cross, *Texte und Untersuchungen zur Geschichte der altchristlichen Literatur* 79 (Berlin, 1961). He notes the neglect of this theme in Pauline studies. Compare van Unnik with C. E. B. Cranfield, "St. Paul and the Law," *SJT* 17 (1964): 43–68. But contrast J. A. Fitzmyer, "Saint Paul and the Law," *The Jurist* 27 (January 1967), p. 22 n. 11. Emphasis on the notion of the new covenant was so strong in early Christianity that both Joseph Bonsirven, *Le Judaïsme Palestinien* (Paris, 1934–35), pp. 1, 79f. and H. J. Schoeps, *Theologie und Geschichte des Judenchristentums* (Tübingen, 1949), p. 90, claim that it led to a neglect or muting of that theme in rabbinic Judaism. Compare also Gottfried Quell, "διατίθηνι, διαθήκη," *TDNT* 2, ed. R. Kittel and G. Friedrich, trans. G. Bromiley (Grand Rapids, 1964), pp. 106–34. See also Roy A. Harrisville, *The Concept of Newness in the New Testament* (Minneapolis: Augsburg, 1960), pp. 46ff. For the covenant in Judaism see the exhaustive study by Annie Jaubert, *La Notion d'Alliance dans le Judaïsme aux abords de l'ère Chrétienne* (Paris, 1963). J. W. Drane, *Paul, Libertine or Legalist? A Study in the Theology of the Major Pauline Epistles* (London: SPCK, 1976), pp. 72–74, cites P. E. Hughes, ed., *Paul's Second Epistle to the Corinthians* (Grand Rapids: Wm. B. Eerdmans, 1962), p. 100, to support his view that Paul is concerned in 2 Cor 3, in his distinction between *gramma* and *pneuma,* to assert that here it is "the difference between the Law as externally written at Sinai on tablets of stone and the *same* law as written internally in the heart of the Christian believer" that is intended. We might substitute *covenant* for *Law* in this sentence.

25. C. K. Barrett, "Pauline Controversies in the Post-Pauline Period," *NTS* 20 (1974): 230.

26. Rom 10:18–21. Contrast J. Munck, *Christ and Israel,* (Philadelphia: Fortress Press, 1967), p. 9.

27. Rom 13:11–14.

28. For the cosmic and human rather than simply "Jewish" scope of Paul's thought in Romans, see D. Georgi in a forthcoming chapter on Paul from the Greek point of view in *The Cambridge History of Judaism,* vol. 2. For the interpretation of Romans 9–11, see below, chapter 8.

29. The most convenient discussion is still that of J. Munck, *Christ and Israel;* see also U. Luz, *Das Geschichtsverständnis.* For further discussion of the problem of the election of Israel see P. Benoit, "Conclusion par mode de Synthèse," in *Die Israelfrage nach Rom 9–11,* ed. Lorenzo di Lorenzi (Rome: Abtei von St. Paul von den Mauern, 1977), pp. 217–36.

30. It is not necessary here to enter into the literary history of various parts of the epistle (see especially R. Scroggs, "Paul as Rhetorician: Two Homilies in Romans 9–11" in *Jews, Greeks and Christians, Religious Cultures in Late Antiquity* [vol. 21 of *Studies in Judaism in Late Antiquity* ed. J. Neusner], ed. R. Hamerton-Kelly and R. Scroggs [Leiden: E. J. Brill, 1976], pp. 270–98).

31. For reasons for this rejection, see Benoit, in *Die Israelfrage*, pp. 225f.

32. The precise relation of the sections 9—11 and 1—8 must be carefully considered because of the significance given to it recently by K. Stendahl. This relationship is highly problematic. The interpretations proposed for it—not here exhaustively canvassed—divide roughly as follows.

(1) There is a break between the two sections. Paul has not made this break as clear as that in 3:1, because of his extreme sensitivity in dealing with the Jewish question (see J. Munck, *Christ and Israel*, p. 28, and especially Sanday and Headlam, *Romans*, p. 226). Originally 9—11 constituted a separate entity, possibly an independent sermon or homily which the apostle frequently used and gradually refined in his churches before he composed his epistle. He has here inserted it after the massive presentation of his understanding of the gospel in 1—8; 8:39 is more naturally followed by 12:1 than by 9:1. Possibly Paul had it in mind to use his old "sermon" as he was composing the epistle. True, 9—11 is not merely alien interpolation, but the section can be understood in isolation. It is essentially an appendix on the Jewish question to the more central themes of 1—8. See especially C. H. Dodd, *Romans*, pp. 148–50.

(2) Chapters 9—11 are a commentary on Paul's fundamental concern, justification by faith, expounded in 1—8. This doctrine is applied to the special case of the Jewish people in 9—11. This view relates the latter more closely to 1—8 than does the first interpretation and yet subordinates the Jewish question to the more central one of justification by faith. See G. Bornkamm, *Paul*, English translation, p. 149, and especially E. Käsemann, *An die Römer*, pp. 241–44. Käsemann entitles 9—11 as "The Righteousness of God and the Problem of Israel," thus fully integrating it with 1—8, which deals with the righteousness of God in other connections. The issue which supplies continuity between 1—8 and 9—11 is the faithfulness of God. Compare C. K. Barrett, *Romans*, p. 175: he writes ". . . chapters 9—11 are not at all concerned with Paul's patriotic sentiments, but with the character and deeds of God who elected the Jews and now calls the Gentiles." Is not this too unqualified? F. J. Leenhardt, *Two Biblical Faiths*, p. 242, does justice to both the faithfulness of God to his promise and to "the bonds of blood" in 9—11. Sanday and Headlam, *Romans*, pp. 225–26, also find the concentration in 9—11 on the rejection of the Jews as does O. Michael, *Der Brief an die Römer* (Göttingen, 1955), p. 190.

(3) Käsemann, *An die Römer*, 3d ed. (Tübingen, 1974), p. 242, points out that the emphasis on the relation between 9—11 and 1—8 in terms of justification by faith understood eschatologically, which has reemerged with force especially in recent German studies by Stuhlmacher and others, was sidetracked as early as F. C. Baur, who, placing 9—11 in the context of the struggle between universalism and particularism in early Christianity, opened the way for the separation of 9—11 from the doctrine of justification, and thus to Schweitzer's insistence on that doctrine as a secondary crater in Paulinism. This approach has been carried farther by K. Stendahl (see *Paul Among Jews and Gentiles*). Assuming the national ap-

proach to 9—11 as did Sanday and Headlam, *Romans*, pp. 226, 341, and others—
that is, that Paul was there concerned, not with a multitude of individual Jews,
but with the Jewish people as a totality—and dismissing what he regards as an
excessive concentration on the pangs of individual conscience in Western Christianity in its understanding of justification by faith, Stendahl insists that Rom
9—11 is not an appendix to chapters 1—8 but the climax of the latter. There are
of course other approaches to 9—11, such as that by P. Minear, *The Obedience
of Faith*, SBT 2119 (London, 1949), and by Robin Scroggs. The brief but illuminating treatment of the relation between 1—8 and 9—11 by F. F. Bruce, *The
Epistle of Paul to the Romans* (London: Tyndale Press, 1963), pp. 181–84, is
especially valuable because it takes into account with admirable clarity many of
the considerations which emerge in the various views indicated.

Our treatment does not directly depend on the acceptance of any one of the
enumerated views. We have noted these here in order to show how uncertain
must be any reconstruction of Paulinism. Stendahl has dramatically reopened the
discussion. It is not necessary to deny to Paul the pangs of conscience which, in
whatever terms expressed, are surely human and not merely Western Christian.
But Stendahl is justified in refusing to find in the justification of the individual
by faith the core of Paulinism. He is also right to insist that Paul was intensely
concerned with Israel as a totality, the Jewish people as such, and not with a
multitude of individual Jews. But is he right in finding the *essential* focus of
Paulinism in that concern and in the concern to justify "the status of Gentile
Christians as honorary Jews" (*Paul Among Jews and Gentiles*, p. 5)? Paul's engagement with the rejection of the gospel by his own people and their ultimate
destiny was a very important part of his immediate concern throughout his "Christian" career. That engagement has, therefore, an inescapable prominence in his
epistles, especially the polemical ones. Stendahl has enlightened us at this point.
He is right in what he asserts. But polemic—including Stendahl's own—usually
distorts. The center of gravity for Paul was the messiahship of Jesus and its implications. It was this fact which ultimately gave rise to the very question of the
relation between Jews and Gentiles in the church: the messiahship—enlarged as his
understanding of Christ came to be, so that it was not merely messianic—must
be regarded as the central *focus* of his ultimate concern; his other concerns were
secondary derivatives. Neither Paul's undeniable emphasis on justification by
faith (whether understood in individual or other terms) nor on the question of
Israel must be allowed to shift the center of gravity for him from the act of God
in Christ to redeem the totality of humankind and of nature (2 Cor 5:19; Rom
8:18–39). Is Stendahl in danger of failing to do justice both to a necessary, individual, personal dimension in Paul, and (although he refers to God's plan for
the world, p. 27) to an altogether cosmic one because of his too isolated concentration on the Jewish-Gentile question, important as this was? That other aspects of Stendahl's immensely stimulating work need careful consideration before
receiving endorsement will appear above. Stendahl warns us that he is merely
being playful (p. viii). If so, one can hardly think that he is not serious in his play,
and he must be judged accordingly.

In all this I have been much helped by correspondence with Professor John
Knox, although he should not be held responsible for any views here expressed.

His understanding of Romans is set forth in the moving work *Life in Christ Jesus: Reflections on Romans 5—8* (New York: Seabury Press; Toronto: Oxford University Press, 1961). He finds the heart of the epistle in those chapters. See also his commentary on Romans in the *IDB*.

The adjective πιστος does not occur of God in Romans, but his faithfulness is conveyed by the insistence that his promise is firm or valid (9:16, 21; see especially 11:29) and that God is ἀληθής (3:4, 7). It is impossible that God's word should prove false (9:6). The appeal to the patriarchs in 11:28 looks back to chapter 4: the calling of God is irrevocable: the coming of Christ as a servant to the Jewish people is Βεβαιῶσαι τὰς ἐπαγγελίας τῶν πατέρων (15:8).

33. O. Cullmann, "Le caractère eschatologique du devoir missionaire et de la conscience apostolique de Saint Paul," *RHPR* 16 (1936): 210–45, followed by J. Munck, *Paulus und die Heilsgeschichte*, Acta Jutlandica, Publications of the University of Aarhus, 36:1, Teologisk Serie 6 (Copenhagen, 1954).

34. The meaning of "all Israel" has been much discussed. With most, we take it to refer to the whole people of the Jews, including the remnant, but not necessarily to every individual Jew. See J. Munck, *Christ and Israel*, p. 136. Paul is throughout sensitive to the existence and significance of those Jews who have already become Christians. This explains his careful insertion of ἀπὸ μέρους in 11:25. (But it is important to note that the remnant exists for the whole.) See also 4:16, 15:7.

35. See my *Paul and Rabbinic Judaism*, new rev. ed. (Philadelphia: Fortress Press, 1980), pp. 293–95.

36. C. K. Barrett, *A Commentary on the Epistle to the Romans* (New York: Harper & Brothers, 1957), p. 257. The exact translation of οὕτως in Rom 11:26 is disputed. Is it to be understood temporally as the context seems especially to suggest? (Bauer—Arndt—Gingrich, *A Greek Lexicon to the New Testament* [Cambridge: At the University Press, 1952].) There are parallels for such a temporal use; see John 4:6. οὕτως would then be the equivalent of τότε. So Käsemann and many others. U. Luz, *Das Geschichtsverständnis des Paulus*, p. 294, rejects this. The οὕτως according to him refers to the manner of Israel's salvation (that is, it will be under the conditions indicated by Paul) not to its chronology: Israel will be saved in an unexpected and paradoxical manner. Compare H. Ridderbos, *Paulus* (Wuppertal, 1970), p. 253. But even so, the reconciliation of Israel does come after the incoming of the Gentiles. This together with the express reference to time in 11:25 lends probability to a temporal meaning for οὕτως. This does not exclude the force of what Luz urges, but is compatible with it. Compare P. Stuhlmacher, "Zur Interpretation von Römer 11:25–32," in *Problems biblischer Theologie, Gerhard von Rad zum 70. Geburtstag*, hrsg. von. H. W. Wolff (Munich, 1971), pp. 560–61.

37. Rosemary Reuther, *Faith and Fratricide: The Theological Roots of Anti-Semitism* (New York: Seabury Press, 1974), pp. 95–107, especially p. 104.

38. Paul's claim to be ἐκ γένους Ἰσραήλ cannot be greatly pressed: it is parallel to φυλῆς βενιαμίν and, referring to a people or a nation, has no "racial" connotation. So Bauer-Arndt-Gingrich, *A Greek Lexicon*, p. 155. The precise nature of the hatred of Jews in the first century is highly complex. Sevenster uses the term anti-Semitism for it (*The Roots of Pagan Antisemitism in the Ancient*

World [Leiden: E. J. Brill, 1975]). Even so, there is a qualitative difference between its expression in the twentieth and previous centuries. See Maurice Samuel, *The Great Hatred* (New York: Alfred A. Knopf, 1940). For bibliography on pagan antisemitism, see. J. G. Gager, *Moses in Greco-Roman Paganism*, SBLMS 16 (Nashville: Abingdon Press, 1972), p. 16 n. 4.

39. E. Käsemann, *New Testament Questions of Today*, Eng. trans. W. J. Montague (Philadelphia: Fortress Press, 1969), pp. 132–37.

40. See my forthcoming "Paul from the Semitic Point of View," for *The Cambridge History of Judaism*, vol. 3. Compare J. W. Drane, *Paul, Libertine or Legalist*, pp. 132–33.

41. W. D. Davies, *The Gospel and the Land*, pp. 185–220.

42. P. Richardson, *Israel in the Apostolic Age*, pp. 1–32 *et passim*.

43. E. Trocmé, "Le Christianisme primitif, un mythe historique?"; S. Sandmel, *The Genius of Paul: A Study in History* (New York: Schocken Books, 1970) approaches Paul from a Hellenistic point of view, but agrees that to speak of the "Christianity" of Paul is anachronistic (p. 21). Compare K. W. Clark, "Israel of God," in *Studies in the New Testament and Early Christian Literature*, ed. D. E. Aune (Leiden: E. J. Brill, 1972), pp. 161–69.

44. Moreover, the precise translation of this word is not clear. It is not so much a reference to Judaism as a religion over against Christianity as to the Jewish way of life. The term is not found in the LXX, the Apocrypha, or Pseudepigrapha, except at 2 Macc 2:21, 8—14:38 and 4 Macc 4:26 in the context of loyalty to the Jewish religion as it confronts Hellenistic pressures. Hengel defines it as referring to "both political and genetic association with the Jewish nation and exclusive belief in the one God of Israel, together with observance of the Torah given by him." See *Judaism and Hellenism: Studies in their Encounter in Palestine during the Early Hellenistic Period*, trans. J. Bowden (Philadelphia: Fortress Press, 1974), 1: 1–2. The term occurs only in Gal. 1:13 in the New Testament. The view of A. Oepke, *Der Brief des Paulus an die Galater* (Berlin, 1957), p. 30, and D. Guthrie, *Galatians* in NCB, p. 67, that the term there indicates contempt for a Judaism clearly separated from Christianity must be treated very cautiously. A. M. Rabello, in the forthcoming *Cambridge History of Judaism*, vol. 4, ed. W. D. Davies and L. Finkelstein, writes that "Judaism [in Roman law] was considered as the sum total of the Jewish people's national rules, customs and usage." Note that the Roman Empire emphasized the *national* character of Judaism and this emphasis was hardly directed at halting the phenomenon of Jewish proselytism.

45. See "From Schweitzer to Scholem: Reflections on Sabbatai Svi," chapter 14, herein. D. Moody Smith has suggested that first-century Judaism may have had its "divine men." "The milieu of the Johannine Miracle Source," in *Jews, Greeks and Barbarians*, ed. R. Hamerton-Kelly and R. Scroggs (Leiden: E. J. Brill, 1976), pp. 169–80.

46. D. Daube, *Civil Disobedience in Antiquity* (Edinburgh: Edinburgh University Press, 1972), pp. 115–16.

47. Hare, *Jewish Persecution*, pp. 77–79.

48. See my *Setting of the Sermon on the Mount*, pp. 256–315 and literature cited there. The importance of the negative reaction of Jamnian Judaism to the

gospel cannot be overemphasized as a factor contributing to radical separation. The separation is best understood probably less as a break-off by Christians from Jews than as one by Jews from Christians. Both parties bore responsibility for the separation. For example, the favorable presentation of the Samaritans in the New Testament is not unrelated to their disfavor among Jews. For caution regarding Jamnia, see J. P. Lewis, *JBR* 32 (1964): 125–32; G. Stemberger, "Die sogennante 'Synode von Jabne' und das frühe Christentum," *Kairos*, 19 (1977), pp. 14–21.

49. 2 Peter 3:15, 16. On all this see J. A. Sanders, "The Ethic of Election in Luke's Great Banquet Parable," in *Essays in Old Testament Ethics* (J. P. Hyatt: In Memoriam) (New York: Ktav, 1974), pp. 247–71.

50. See H. J. Cadbury in *The Joy of Study*, ed. S. E. Johnson (New York: Macmillan Co., 1951), pp. 43ff.; J. Munck, *Paulus und die Heilsgeschichte*, pp. 87–134.

51. Compare P. Richardson, *Israel in the Apostolic Age*, pp. 1ff. For example, 1 *Clement* has been described by some as a document of Judaism despite its Christian elements.

52. See pp. 29f. Richardson, *Israel in the Apostolic Age*, p. 10, writes of Justin that the corollary to his opposition to Judaism was "an unparalleled emphasis on the Gentiles as the heirs of the promises . . . whose 'otherness' is so stressed that *a Gentile exclusiveness almost replaces the former Jewish exclusiveness.* Along with this, he implies that to accept Christianity means the abandonment of one's Jewishness" (*Dialogue with Trypho* 64.5) (our italics).

53. See H. A. Wolfson, *Philo* 2 (Cambridge, Mass.: Harvard University Press, 1947), p. 418.

54. This is recognized (unless we misinterpret them) by Sanday and Headlam, *Romans*, ICC (1911), p. 339, even though they read τοὺς πάντας.

55. P. Benoit in a response to Professor Flusser's review of my work *The Gospel and the Land* admirably points out the significance of this point: "[Le Professeur Flusser] reproche aux Chrétiens de réclamer des Juifs qu'ils cessent d'être des Juifs, et deviennent des Gentils dans le Christ. Je réponds à ce grief par une distinction. Le dilemme de Flusser est ambigu: il parle du Juif devenant chrétien 'sans abolir le caractère et le mode qui lui sont propres, et sans renoncer aux promesses spéciales qu'il a reçues de Dieu,' ou au contraire 'en abandonnant le caractère spécial et les prétentions spéciales du Juif.' L'alternative est mal proposée dans la mesure où elle ne distingue pas entre l'aspect ethnico-politique qui est en effet propre au peuple particulier d'Israël, et l'aspect proprement religieux qui devait selon le plan de Dieu s'étendre en s'élargissant à toute la communauté humaine." For the review by Flusser to which Prof. Benoit responds, see *Christian News from Israel* 25 (1975), 3: 136–39: see *RB* 84 (1977): 147–50.

56. This is the implication of K. Stendahl, *Paul Among Jews and Gentiles*, pp. 3–4. We have here attempted to carry through this implication as much as possible.

57. A. D. Nock, *Conversion* (New York: Oxford University Press, 1933), pp. 1–16, especially p. 14.

58. In 1 Thess 1:9 this term is used of Gentiles turning to the Christian faith. It can be used of Jews returning to their own tradition as in *T*. Dan 6:4. In Gal

9:9 it refers not strictly to the conversion of Gentiles but to their reverting to "the mean and beggarly spirits of the elements"; and in 2 Cor 3:16 to Moses turning to the Lord (in a quotation from Exod 34:34). Paul never uses μετα-βάλλεῖν, or στρέφε.ν. Usually the dominant meaning of σώζω is deliverance from some binding, oppressive force or forces. Contrast E. P. Sanders, *Paul, the Law, and the Jewish People* (Philadelphia: Fortress Press, 1983).

59. In Mark 4:11-12 and parallels those who refuse the gospel do *not* understand and are therefore not culpable as are the Jews in Rom 10:19. Paul does not excuse the unbelief of Israel. But contrast Rom 10:8 and 10:18-21 with 2 Cor 4:4, where it is the God of this world who has blinded those who do not believe. See C. K. Barrett, *Second Epistle to the Corinthians*, pp. 130f., and especially J. Munck, *Christ and Israel*, pp. 100-103.

60. To J. A. Sanders "the hardening" was for Paul "but a symbol of God's use of disobedience and human frailty to work out his plans. . . ." In a letter of 1977. See his "Enemy" in *IDB*.

61. K. Stendahl, *Paul Among Jews and Gentiles*, p. 4, writes: "Paul does not say that when the time of God's kingdom, the consummation comes, Israel will accept Jesus as the Messiah! He says only that the time will come when 'all Israel will be saved' (Rom 11:26)."

62. The Old Testament usage does not lend support to a messianic reference for ὁ ῥυόμενος: this form is not frequent even in Deutero-Isaiah, where the past participial form ῥυσάμενος is more used. The *NEB* translates Isa 59:20 as "come as the ransomer of Zion," without capitalizing ransomer. The reference in the MT is to the "glory of God"—a circumlocution for God himself? Stendahl, *Paul Among Jews and Gentiles*, finds it stunning "that Paul writes this whole section of Rom 10:17—11:36 without using the name of Jesus Christ." Unfortunately he does not discuss the meaning of ὁ ῥυόμενος. But this is to avoid the point at issue. See below p. 27. Scroggs draws no theological conclusions from the emphasis on God in Rom 1—4; 9—11; see below p. 26 n. 2.

63. Contrast with that of the *NEB* ("And this if the covenant *I will grant them*, when I take away their sins") the translation of Sanday and Headlam (*Romans*, p. 337): "and whensoever I forgive their sins, then shall my side of the covenant *I have made* will them be fulfilled" (our italics).

64. So most commentators, for instance, C. H. Dodd, *The Epistle of Paul to the Romans*, MNTC (New York: Harper & Brothers; London: Hodder & Stoughton, 1932), p. 182; E. Käsemann, *An die Römer*, HNT, 8a (Tübingen, 1974), p. 30; M. Black, "Romans," NCB (London, 1973); F. F. Bruce, *The Epistle of Paul to the Romans* (Grand Rapids: Wm. B. Eerdmans, 1975), p. 220. Dodd does recognize that the new covenant is with the church as a whole and the covenant of Rom 11:27 with Jews only. O. Michel (*Der Brief an die Römer* [Göttingen, 1955], p. 251) is ambiguous. Does he think of a new covenant with Jews beyond that already established? He writes: "Die σωτηρία Israels besteht also in der Ankunft des Messias und einen neuen Gottesbund."

65. Compare P. Richardson, *Israel in the Apostolic Age*, p. 128 n. 8.

66. On this interpretation it is understandable that the view of the two covenants urged by Rosenzweig has been compared with that of Paul. (See K. Stendahl, *Paul Among Jews and Gentiles*, p. 128 n. 8.) Sanday and Headlam, *Romans*,

strangely do not discuss the covenant noted in 11:27 at all. C. K. Barrett, *Second Corinthians*, p. 224, simply refers to a "new covenant of salvation in which Israel's sins will be done away." He loosely refers to Jer 31:33 but does not discuss the possibility of there being two distinct covenants in view here. In our judgment, the text is not clear enough to allow us to assert the similarity of Rosenzweig's views. What is to be recognized is that in Rom 9—11 it *is* God's activity and purpose that Paul emphasizes. In 11:29–35 (we refer to the doxology later) he provides what is an explanatory commentary on what has preceded. To take these verses seriously is to see that for the apostle, through God's mercy, there is a solidarity between Christians and Jews (11:32). See K. L. Schmidt, *Die Judenfrage*, p. 35 n. 15. Robin Scroggs has pointed to "the sparseness of explicit Christian language and content throughout chapters 1—4, 9—11. It is God who is emphasized in these chapters, one might even say the 'Jewish God'" (in "Paul as Rhetorician," p. 138).

67. P. Benoit, *Exégèse et Théologie* 11 (1961): 339, in a review of K. L. Schmidt, *Die Judenfrage*; Schmidt thinks of the fulfillment of salvation for the Jews as resting on an intervention by God to accomplish what the Church had been able to achieve: "Doch das alles wird Gott selbst am Ende der Tage ordnen," p. 34 (compare K. Stendahl, p. 25, as cited above in n. 2). Christoph Plag, whose work I was unable to consult, has argued against the unity of 11:25–32 and regards 25–27 as a late interpolation, 11:28 following directly on 11:24. The criticism of Plag's position by P. Stuhlmacher, "Zur Interpretation von Römer 11:25–32," p. 562, is convincing. Stuhlmacher deals with the German discussion illuminatingly, but in his excellent conclusion, pp. 567–70, he does not sufficiently point to the significance of the passage for the problem with which we are concerned.

68. See Krister Stendahl, *Paul Among Jews and Gentiles*, p. 132. An objection to the view expressed in the text that Paul no longer regards it as a direct task to challenge Israel must here be met. Would he ever, it is asked, have given up trying to present the claims of Christ wherever he encountered a Jew? The answer is surely in the negative. But a distinction must be drawn between a possible personal approach to individual Jews, whom he almost certainly encountered, and a deliberate presentation of the gospel to the Jewish people as a whole.

69. Behind 11:25–27 stands the hope for the incursion of the Gentiles at the end. For the details, see especially Sanday and Headlam, *Romans*, pp. 336–37; J. Munck, *Christ and Israel*, pp. 136–37. On the basis of parallels in 2 Thess 2 and Matt 24:10–12, Munck draws up a picture of the second coming according to Paul. The words of Luz, *Geschichtsverständnis bei Paulus* are important. He points out that when dealing with the end, Paul could use a kind of shorthand: he did not need to spell out every item in the sequence of events leading to the end in detail: his readers would know the full context of his laconic, even cryptic references. Verses 25–27 of chapter 11 must therefore be read over against and informed by the full richness of the Jewish eschatology which Paul inherited. From this point of view the alleged silence in 11:25–27 about the Messiah, for example is purely accidental. His presence at the end could be assumed and the reference to him in ὁ ῥυόμενος would be clear.

70. *The Gospel and the Land*, pp. 195–97. The change of the MT ל to the ἐκ of Paul in 11:26 may be very significant. In Deutero-Isaiah, God, who has shared

the exile of his people, in redeeming his people comes *to* Zion (Isa 49:56, 52:8, 63:75). When Paul thinks of the redeemer coming *from* Zion, is the implication that the eschatological procession to Zion has already taken place? God needs no longer to come *to* Zion but comes *from* Zion.

71. *Romans*, p. 334; see also Käsemann, *An die Römer*, p. 301.

72. So K. Stendahl, *Paul Among Jews and Gentiles*, p. 132.

73. See above, pp. 140–41.

74. Sanday and Headlam, *Romans*, p. 336; their presentation of this view remains classic. R. Batey, "So all Israel will be saved: An interpretation of Romans 11:25–32," *Int* 20 (1966) 2:225, quotes the strange thought of Luther in *Der Römerbrief*, p. 183: "Christus ist also noch nicht zu den Juden gekommen, aber er wird kommen, nämlich in der letzten Zeit, wie die oben angeführten Schriftstellen zeugen [11:26]."

75. Compare Käsemann, *An die Römer*, p. 296.

76. M. Black, *NCB*, p. 146, questions the view that the Gentile Christians at Rome were anti-Semitic. We agree; but they *were* in need of correction about their attitude toward Jews.

77. Note P. Richardson's point, *Israel in the Apostolic Age*, p. 131, that: "The obvious feature of the olive tree figure, sometimes overlooked, is that a pruned Israel retains its place in God's activity . . ." His treatment on pp. 126–47 is invaluable.

78. See further Hans-Werner Bartsch, *Antijudaismus im Neuen Testament* (1967), pp. 27–43 on "Die antisemitischen Gegner des Paulus in Römerbrief." But it is unjustifiable to subsume the whole of Romans under the struggle over the so-called anti-Semitism of the Roman Gentile Christians as does Bartsch.

79. G. Dalman, *Arbeit und Sitte,* in P-J 4 (1935): 153–54. Oddly this point is not mentioned by J. Munck, *Christ and Israel*, pp. 128–30, excursus 3: "The True Olive Tree and the Wild Olive Tree," nor by any commentators consulted except T. W. Manson in the new *PCB* (London, 1962), p. 949 (although his reference to Dalman is in error). C. K. Barrett, *First Adam*, p. 217, claims that "it is the root and branch metaphor which suggests to Paul the allegory of the olive tree." But the latter is very deliberately employed and stands out as having a special significance of its own. It does not simply grow out of the previous metaphors.

80. I develop this in an essay in a *Festschrift* for Marcel Simon. See herein, chapter 8.

81. E. Jacob, *Israel dans la prespective biblique* (Strasbourg, 1968), p. 32.

82. A Harnack, *Neue Untersuchungen zur Apostelgeschichte* (Beiträge zur Einleitung in das Neue Testament, Heft 4 [Leipzig, 1911], p. 44 n. 2. See further Miles Bourke, *A Study of the Metaphor of the Olive Tree in Romans 11* (diss., Washington, D.C.: Catholic University of America Press, 1947), pp. 80–111.

83. *Romans*, pp. 74–188; Contrast C. E. B. Cranfield (see p. 353 n. 87), pp. 150, 177.

84. *Olive Tree*, p. 82.

85. *An die Römer, passim.*

86. By privilege, I mean a favor gratuitously conferred (here by God); by advantage, a benefit which is not conferred but which emerges inevitably under certain circumstances. This is not a mere play on words, a distinction without a difference, as J. S. Whale urged, see p. 353 n. 99.

87. E. Käsemann, *An die Römer*, pp. 20–21: "Paulus hat um der Kontinituät des Heilsplans willen dem Judentum eine Prävalenz eingeräumt . . . Gottes Selbstbekundung bestimmt die gesamte Geschichte . . . Die Theologie des Apostels involviert eine bestimmte heilgeschichtliche Betrachtungsweise." But he adds, "Anders als im Jundentum wird freilich der Vorrang Israels nicht exklusiv verstanden." Compare the excellent comments of C. E. B. Cranfield, *The Epistle to the Romans*, pp. 90, 176ff. In Rom 1:16 most commentators do not do justice to the significance of πρῶτον and of τε. The latter serves to point to the equality of Jew and Gentile, the former to the priority of the Jews.

88. See George Steiner, *In Bluebeard's Castle: Some Notes towards the Redefinition of Culture* (New Haven, Conn.: Yale University Press, 1971), pp. 36–39; C. E. B. Cranfield, *Romans*, in ICC, p. 179.

89. J. W. Drane, *Paul, Libertine or Legalist*, pp. 118–19. He connects the Gentile reaction to the apostolic decree with the appearance of "Gnostic ideas" in the Gentile churches. This must be considered speculative.

90. See Richard Rubenstein, "The Death Camps and the Decision of Faith," in *The Contemporary Explosion of Theology*, ed. M. D. Ryan (Metuchen, N.J.: Scarecrow Press, 1975), pp. 140–41; K. Stendahl, *Paul Among Jews and Gentiles*, p. 131. Both Käsemann's suspicion of "theologies of history" (*Perspectives on Paul* [Philadelphia: Fortress Press, 1971], p. 64) and Stendahl's condemnation of the ill effects of the interpretation of the gospel solely in terms of justification by faith are justifiable. But Stendahl's criticism of Käsemann at this point is itself an example of polemics creating unnecessary oppositions. One might remind both scholars that the misuse of any philosophy or doctrine is no criterion of its validity.

91. This mellowness can be maintained despite Rom 16:17–20 and Phil 3:2ff., which are best understood as generalized warnings probably against judaizers (possibly against Jews in Phil 3:2). A. F. J. Klijn, "Paul's opponents in Philippians 3," *NT* 7 (1964): 278–84. See also J. W. Drane, *Paul, Libertine or Legalist*, pp. 132–36 n. 80, on development in Paul.

92. Compare E. Käsemann, *Perspectives on Paul* (London, 1969), pp. 102–21.

93. Jacques Maritain has most emphasized this in "The Mystery of Israel," *Ransoming the Time* (New York: Charles Scribner's Sons, 1941), p. 169, and *passim*.

94. *The Epistle to the Romans*, pp. 174, 182.

95. E. Dinkler, "Prädestination bei Paulus," in *Festschrift für Günther Dehn zum 75. Geburtstag* (ed. E. Scheemelcher [Neukirchen, 1957], pp. 81–102) (= *Signum Crucis. Aufsätze zum Neuen Testament und zur christlichen Archäologie* (Tübingen, 1967), pp. 241–66; especially pp. 260 and 266–69.

96. D. Daube, in *Jesus the Hope of the World*, ed. D. G. Miller and D. Y. Hadidian (Pittsburgh: Pickwick Press, 1971), pp. 223–45.

97. For bibliography on this, see *The Gospel and the Land*, pp. 203–8.

98. In a private communication.

99. Thomas Chubb, cited by R. S. Franks, *A History of the Doctrine of the Work of Christ* (London, 1918), 2 part 4, p. 174. I owe this reference to J. S. Whale in a letter of 1976.

100. F. F. Bruce, *Romans*, p. 10, warns generally against the peril of modernizing Paul, and U. Luz, *Das Geschichtsverständnis*, pp. 294f. particularly against taking over Paul's approach to Jews in Romans 11 and applying it directly

to our twentieth-century situation. Dennis Nineham rightly rejests any overconfidence at this point. See his *The Use and Abuse of the Bible: A Study of the Bible in an Age of Rapid Culture Change* (New York: Barnes & Noble, 1976), pp. 27–34 *et passim*. On Paul see especially pp. 28–29. With their warning we agree. There is also, however, the peril of "archaizing" Paul so completely that his letters have no continuing significance and become an irrelevance—unthinkable as that is.

101. The most illuminating recent work on the relation between early Christianity and the Law is that of J. A. Sanders in "Torah and Christ," *Int* 29 (October 1975): 4: 372–90; and a forthcoming chapter on "Torah and Paul" in the *Festschrift* for Nils A. Dahl. In these essays Sanders, carrying further his understanding of the Old Testament as expressed in his *Torah and Canon* (Philadelphia: Fortress Press, 1974), applies to the New Testament the distinction he makes between the two elements which he distinguishes within Torah; *mythos* (gospel—story—identity—*haggadah*) and *ethos* (law—ethics—life style—*halachah*), see *Int*, p. 373. For Sanders, as for us, the early Church up to 70 C.E. was a daughter of Judaism: only after that date did it leave its nest. After 70 C.E. "Rabbinic Judaism, following the emphasis of Pharisaism, stressed the *ethos* or *halachah* aspect of Torah, while Christianity emphasized the *mythos* or *haggadah* aspect." (Compare my article in *HTR* 61 [1968]: 87–105, "Torah and Dogma: A Comment," reprinted in *Papers from the Colloquium on Judaism and Christianity held at Harvard Divinity School, Oct. 17–20, 1966* [Cambridge, Mass.: Harvard University Press]; and see *The Gospel and the Land*, p. 390 n. 1, and p. 398, a paragraph where I owe much to Professor David Daube.) Sanders writes, "Paul's conversion may be seen . . . as a move on his part from emphasis on the *ethos* aspect of Torah to the *mythos* aspect" (in "Torah and Christ," p. 375); and again, "It was Paul's conviction that if one read the Torah story, emphasizing it as a story of *God's* works of salvation and righteousness for ancient Israel, one could not escape seeing that God had wrought another salvation and committed another righteousness, in Christ, just like the ones of old but an even greater one!" (p. 380). For Paul the Torah remains authoritative and canonical, but the interpretation of it differs in Pharisaism and in Paul because the latter has elevated the "story" of Jesus to be the norm of understanding it. Sanders notes this position as similar to that proposed in my *Rabbinic Judaism*, pp. 147–76, where I urged that Christ became Torah for Paul, but Sanders has modified, refined, and enriched that claim by placing it firmly and directly in the interpretative activity of first-century Judaism. He argues, in a private communication (1 April 1977), that "Paul . . . was no more anti-Semitic than Amos, Micah, Hosea . . . etc. had been."

We are not competent to assess the cogency of Sander's elevation of the "canonical principle," consisting of the response to the need for stability and adaptability in the life of "Israel," to a central place in the interpretation of the whole of the *Tanak*. The post-exilic documents—Proverbs, Song of Songs, Esther, Ruth, Job—can be understood, as Morton Smith has brilliantly argued, as responses, not to the need to preserve, to stabilize, and to adapt "Israel" to its own needs, but to the impingement upon it (not always unwelcome) of the Gentile world: not Israel's identity as such but its openness was at stake in these documents of the Persian period. The principle of *ethos* and *mythos* does not seem to be applicable to all the documents of the *Tanak*. Sanders himself recognizes that there were additions to what he conceives of as the essential canon in the *Tanak*.

An attempt to apply his very persuasive distinction and "canonical principle" in the Pauline epistles provokes certain reflections. The distinction between *ethos* and *mythos*, however probable and important, is almost certainly more clear to us, looking back on the struggles of early Christianity over the Law, than it was to Paul as he was pursuing his tortuous discussions with his opponents. He was probably fumbling his way towards Sanders's clear principle, not consciously or directly applying it. Paul was constantly in a maelstrom of controversy over points of detail in the interpretation of the Torah, so that his thought was probably less tidy at this point than that of his American interpreter, who has the advantage of seeing the outcome of the Apostle's struggles. However, Sanders is convincing in his insistence that "Each generation reads its authoritative tradition in the light of its own place in life, its own questions, its own necessary hermeneutics" (*Adaptable for Life: The Nature and Function of Canon: Festschrift for E. W. Wright*, p. 34). The same was true of Paul: he read the *Tanak* "from his own place in life" and that place he understood as a messianic one. He looked at Christ in the light of the *Tanak* and at the *Tanak* in the light of Christ. In doing so, Sanders holds that he operated on the principle of the separation of *mythos* and *ethos* in the Torah, elevating the former and depressing the latter. To examine Paul's letters from this point of view is not possible here. However, a rereading of 2 Corinthians 3 with the "canonical principle" of Sanders in mind is illuminating. In our treatment of 2 Corinthians 3 on p. 129 we underlined the word *narrative*; we could have there written *story* or *mythos*. Again in Romans 9—11 Paul scans the story of God's dealings with his people and rejects the understanding of those dealings in terms of *ethos* (to use Sanders's term) in favor of the *mythos* or *story* of God's past selective activity in history. In Rom 11:25ff, he continues this past *story* into the future, now making the selective activity of God inclusive, not exclusive. In this Sanders underlines what we wrote on p. 132: "Paul's Gospel provides a particular way of understanding and interpreting the tradition" of his people.

But here a question arises. According to Sanders, the "canonical principle" was spurred into activity in a time of crisis for the identity of the people of Israel when they found themselves deprived of the traditional symbols of that identity. To put it otherwise, the canon within the canon emerged in the experience of exile: the nation was seeking that whereby it could live. Clearly we cannot speak of Paul being driven to a reinterpretation of the tradition in a quite similar situation. He was not in exile: his people were living in their own land. Nevertheless we do know that first-century Judaism was bitterly divided religiously over the Law, politically over the appropriate response to the Roman occupation, and socially between rich and poor. (See on this a forthcoming paper by my colleague, F. W. Young.) There is evidence that the preaching of Christ crucified further opened up powerful revolutionary possibilities and divisions. Although it was now in its own land, Israel's future was in the balance. It was the risen Christ that was the light in whom Paul reread the tradition of his people, so that we might superficially claim that the "canonical principle" as Sanders expounds it, that is, as arising out of a direct external challenge to the identity of the people, was not directly at work in his epistles but rather only the christological one. But, in fact, the "canonical principle" indicated and Paul's christological principle were not mutually exclusive. We saw above that Paul was concerned from first to last with the meaning of "Israel" precisely because Jesus of Nazareth had come as Messiah. The crisis that faced Judaism after the fall of Jerusalem in 70 C.E. and which led to what Sanders calls the "Jamnian mentality" was different in form from the crisis that was constituted for it by the coming of the crucified Christ; but ultimately, in substance, it was not dissimilar. The crisis precipitated for Paul by the crucified but also risen Christ led him to give an answer different from that given later by the sages of Jamnia. These reflections, preliminary and inadequate as they are, may serve to indicate the stimulation and importance of Sanders's works and point to the necessity for further examination of them.

See further F. Mussner, *Traktät über der Juden*, 1980 (Eng. trans. forthcoming from Fortress Press), and G. Lüdemann, *Paulus und das Judentum* (Munich: Chr. Kaiser, 1983) and E. P. Sanders, *Paul, the Law, and the Jewish People*. Unfortunately, his great work, *Paul and Palestinian Judaism* (Philadelphia: Fortress Press, 1977), had not been published when the chapter was written. I have tried to respond to it in *Paul and Rabbinic Judaism*, 1980, pp. xxix–xxxviii.

PAUL AND THE GENTILES: A SUGGESTION CONCERNING ROMANS 11:13–24

1. I have not felt it necessary to discuss the relationship among symbol, metaphor and allegory; the olives in Romans 11 have been variously categorized.

2. See especially A. R. Johnson, *The One and the Many in the Israelite Conception of God* (Cardiff: University of Wales, 1942).

3. See W. D. Davies, *Paul and Rabbinic Judaism: Some Rabbinic Elements in Pauline Theology*, rev. ed. (New York and Cambridge: Cambridge University Press, 1967), pp. 293–95.

4. J. Munck, *Christ and Israel: An Interpretation of Romans 9—11*, trans. Ingeborg Nixon (Philadelphia: Fortress Press, 1967), pp. 123–24.

5. "The root" has been variously interpreted as has the olive; see the standard commentaries. We present here what seems to be the most satisfactory view.

6. The Greek *en autois* (among them) must refer to the branches lopped off; as Ernst Käsemann rightly insists, *An die Römer*, HNT, 8a, 3d ed. (Tübingen, 1974), p. 296, it cannot mean "instead of." Paul is not dealing with the processes of nature, but with the astonishing activity of Divine Grace as he understands it. The attempts made to find horticultural parallels to the grafting here described do not convince! See J. Munck, n. 4 above, excursus 3 on "The True Olive Tree and the Wild Olive Tree." The most thorough discussion is still that of Myles M. Bourke, S.T.L., *A Study of the Metaphor of the Olive Tree in Romans XI* (Washington, D.C.: Catholic University of America Press, 1947), pp. 65–111.

7. See n. 26.

8. Arnoldo Momigliano, *Alien Wisdom: The Limits of Hellenization* (Cambridge: At the University Press, 1975), pp. 74–122. "In the first thirty or forty years after the destruction of the Persian Empire, Greek philosophers and his-

torians discovered the Jews. They depicted them—both in fact and in fiction—as priestly sages of the type the East was supposed to produce" (p. 86). The use of the term racism in reference to anti-Semitism in this period requires caution. Modern anti-Semitism (a term which surfaced in late nineteenth-century Europe) has a genetic connotation which can only be dubiously ascribed to anti-Jewish sentiments in the period with which we are concerned. But scholars do use it, for example, J. N. Sevenster, *The Roots of Pagan Anti-Semitism in the Ancient World* (Leiden: E. J. Brill, 1975).

9. For bibliography on anti-Semitism in our period, see J. G. Gager, *Moses in Greco-Roman Paganism*, SBLMS 16 (Nashville: Abingdon Press, 1972), p. 16 n. 4.

10. See, for example, R. M. Grant, *The Sword and the Cross* (New York: Macmillan Co., 1955), pp. 9–34.

11. The use of the term "philosophy of history" for Paul's thought may be questioned (see R. N. Cochrane, *Christianity and Classical Culture* [Oxford: At the Clarendon Press, 1940], p. 456). Buber found in Romans 9—11 a thoroughly Hellenistic approach to history—see M. Diamond, *Martin Buber, Jewish Existentialist* (New York: Oxford University Press, 1960), pp. 180ff.; but this is surely to ignore its Old Testament roots. Alexander the Great may have contributed to Jewish apocalyptic expectations but this would not have made them less "ridiculous" to the Greeks and Romans.

12. See F. W. Walbank, *A Historical Commentary on Polybius*, vol. 1 (New York and Toronto: Oxford University Press, 1957), p. 16.

13. P. Jean-Baptiste Frey, *CIJ* (Citta del Vaticano, 1936).

14. M. Black, *Romans: NCB* (London, 1973), p. 145.

15. Frey, *CIJ*: "Elle comprenait les Juifs originaires d'une ville ou d'une quartier de ville appelé Elea. On peut négliger tout autre essai d'explication." Frey refers to various possible places, p. 1xxviii.

16. For the bibliographical details on the several points, see Harry J. Leon, *The Jews of Ancient Rome* (Philadelphia: Jewish Publication Society of America, 1961), pp. 145–47.

17. *A Companion to Greek Studies*, ed. Leonard Whibley, vol. 4 (Cambridge: At the University Press, 1937), 605.

18. See E. Bickerman, "La Chaine de la Tradition Chrétienne," *RB* 59 (1962): 44–45; A. D. Nock, in *CAH* 10.

19. See W. Smith, *A Smaller Classical Dictionary*, rev., ed. E. H. Blakeney (1936), p. 85, under "Athena" and "Athenae." Consult Herodotus, 8.55 (ἐλαίη) Apollodorus, 3. 14. (ἐλαία), LCL trans. Sir J. G. Frazer (London: William Heinemann, 1921), p. 78. According to Frazer, "the [sacred] olive tree [at Athens] seems to have survived down to the second century of our era." He supplies references in proof of this. It is reasonable to think that the Athenian sacred olive would have been familiar to Paul and his Roman readers.

20. *Companion to Greek Studies*, p. 61. I have not been able to verify this form (μοιρίαι) in any text. Is the *Companion* in error here?

21. The Academy met in the northwest suburb of the city in the *Ceramicus* by the banks of the Ilissus. The course of the river Cephisus, which was not far,

was marked by a broad band of olive groves. The *Ceramicus* was situated between the olive groves and the town. The olive was the most important produce of the Athenian plain. See E. A. Gardner, *Ancient Athens* (New York: Macmillan Co., 1902), pp. 7, 135ff. Olive trees of Athens were regarded as sacred; the special olive tree of Athena grew in the *Pandroseum* to the west of the Erechtheum (ibid., pp. 170, 365). It is reasonable to infer that the groves of the Academy were olive groves.

22. Certain classes of vases had special purposes. The Panathenian prize amphorae were made to hold oil from the sacred olive trees of Athens. This sacred oil was given as a prize to victors in the Panathenain games (Gardner, *Ancient Athens*, p. 171). The leaves of the wild olive were used for wreaths for victors in the Olympic games; see Whibley, *Companion to Greek Studies*, p. 411. There the term ὁ, ἡ κότινος is used, not ἀγριέλαιος. κότινος is identified by Liddell-Scott-Jones with the *olea oleaster*. The suggestion has, in turn, been made that the ἀγριέλαιος of Romans 11 is the *olea oleaster* (see p. 160 n. 4).

23. 1 Kings 6:23. The Hebrew is עֲצֵי־שָׁמֶן (LXX omits it here, but elsewhere has ξύλων ἀρκευθίνων and ξύλων πευκίνων). It is rendered by the *KJV* as olive tree, but the *RSV* has olivewood, and the *NEB*, "wild olive." Here again there is a botanical problem which can hardly be resolved. Moreover, it is not legitimate to transfer the appreciation of the olive—cultivated or wild—in Palestine to Greece or alternatively.

24. The doors giving entry to the very sanctuary and to the nave were made of wild olive (*NEB*: overlaid with gold).

25. Certainly of Athens; see Gardner, *Ancient Athens*, p. 7, but also generally. Wine might be more delectable than olive oil, but less essential. See W. E. Shewell-Cooper, *Plants and Fruits of the Bible* (London: Darton, Longman & Todd, 1962), on the "Olive."

26. See Otto Warburg, *Die Pflanzenwelt* 3 (Leipzig, 1922), p. 125. Of the Olbaum he writes: "Er verwoldert häufig, und zwar in einer strauchigen, dornigen der Wilden Art ähnlichen kleinfrüchtigen"; G. Dalman, *Arbeit und Sitte in PJ*, vol. 4 (Gütersloh, 1935), 153–54. He points out that one searches in vain in the Old Testament and the rabbinic sources for any special significance given to the wild olive. This makes its emergence in Paul all the more striking. There are four hundred varieties of olive plants. To identify the ἐλαία and ἀγριέλαιος of Rom 11:17, 18, 24 with botanical precision is impossible. The suggestion has been made that the ἀγριέλαιος is the *olea oleaster* which produces four-angled thorny shoots and whose fruits are small and quite inedible (Shewell-Cooper, *Plants and Fruits of the Bible*, p. 33). Is this the plant from which the wreaths for the Olympic games were made or is it to be distinguished clearly from ὁ, ἡ, κότινος, the term usually employed for these wreaths? Clement of Alexandria *Stromateis*, 6.15.115 § 3, in a passage specifically referring to the Olympic games, seems a little confused on the point. He writes: "διὸ κἂν ἀγριέλαιος ὁ κότινος τυγχάνῃ ἄλλα τοὺς ὀλυμπονίκας στέφει . . ." as if there was some doubt in his mind that he could equate them. Liddell-Scott-Jones equate ὁ, ἡ, κότινος with the *olea oleaster*. On the fruitlessness of the wild olive, see further *The International Standard Bible Encyclopaedia*, James Orr general ed. (1957), 4:

2135; Zaharie Michael in *Encyclopaedia Biblica* (1954), 2: 913–14 (Hebrew). I owe this reference to M. Mor.

27. 1 Cor 9:18–22.

28. Rom 1:14.

29. This has recently become increasingly clear especially in studies of 1 Thessalonians and Galatians. See also especially H. D. Betz, *Der Apostel Paulus und die Sokratische Tradition: Eine exegetische Untersuchung zu seiner Apologie in 2 Korinther 10—13*, BHT (Tübingen, 1972), p. 45. D. Georgi, *Die Gegner des Paulus im 2 Korintherbrief: Studien zur religiösen Propaganda in der Spätantike*, WMANT (Neukirchen-Vluyn, 1964), p. 11; and a forthcoming study by D. Georgi for further details.

30. *The Works of Saint Cyril of Jerusalem*, ed. R. J. Deferrari (Washington, D.C.: Catholic University of America Press, 1968), p. 93:

Δ. "Οπλον λαμβάνεις οὐ φθαρτὸν, ἀλλὰ πνευματικόν. Καταφυτεύῃ λοιπὸν εἰς τὸν νοητὸν παράδεισον. Λαμβάνεις ὄνομα καινὸν, ὃ πρότερον οὐκ εἶχες. Πρὸ τούτου Κατηχούμενος ἦς, νῦν δὲ κληθήσῃ Πιστός. Μεταφυτεύῃ λοιπὸν εἰς τὰς ἐλαίας τὰς νοητὰς, ἐξ ἀγριελαίου εἰς καλλιέλαιον ἐγκεντριζόμενος · ἐξ ἁμαρτιῶν εἰς δικαιοσύνην, ἐκ μολυσμῶν εἰς καθαρότητα.

31. *Funeral Orations by Saint Gregory Nazianzen and Saint Ambrose*, ed. R. J. Deferrari (Washington, D.C.: Catholic University of America Press, 1953), pp. 6–7.

32. Cyril of Alexandria *De Trinitate* (Migne, *PG*) 1. 1149.

33. Clement of Alexandria *Stromata* 6. 15. 115, 3–119, 4 (Migne, *PG*, *The Ante-Nicene Fathers*, ed. A. Roberts and J. Donaldson [Grand Rapids: Wm. B. Eerdmans, 1951], 2: 507.

The Greek is:

Αὐτίκα ἡ ἀγριέλαιος ἐγκεντρίζεται εἰς τὴν πιότητα τῆς ἐλαίας καὶ δὴ καὶ φύεται ὁμοειδῶς ταῖς ἡμέροις ἐλαίαις · χρῆται γὰρ τὸ ἐμφυτευόμενον ἀντὶ γῆς τῷ δένδρῳ τῷ ἐν ᾧ φυτεύεται · πάντα δὲ ὁμοῦ τὰ φυτὰ ἐκ κελεύσματος θείου βεβλάστηκεν. διὸ κἂν ἀγριέλαιος ὁ κότινος τυγχάνῃ, ἀλλὰ τοὺς ὀλυμπιονίκας στέφει καὶ τὴν ἄμπελον ἡ πτελέα εἰς ὕψος ἀνάγουσα εὐκαρπεῖν διδάσκει. ὁρῶμεν δὲ ἤδη πλείονα τὴν τροφὴν ἐπισπώμενα τὰ ἄγρια τῶν δένδρων διὰ τὸ μὴ δύνασθαι πέττειν. τὰ οὖν ἄγρια τῶν ἡμέρων ἀπεπτότερα ὑπάρχει, καὶ τὸ αἴτιον τοῦ ἄγρια εἶναι αὐτὰ στέρησις δυνάμεως πεπτικῆς. λαμβάνει τοίνυν τροφὴν μὲν πλείονα ἡ ἐγκεντρισθεῖσα ἐλαία διὰ τὸ ἀγρίαν ἐμφύεσθαι · οἷον δὲ ἤδε πέττειν ἐθίζεται τὴν τροφὴν, συνεξομοιουμένη τῇ πιότητι τῆς ἡμέρου, ὡς δὲ καὶ ὁ φιλόσοφος, ἀγρίᾳ εἰκαζόμενος ἐλαίᾳ, πολὺ τὸ ἄπεπτον ἔχων, διὰ τὸ εἶναι ζητητικὸς καὶ εὐπαρακολούθητος καί ὀρεκτικὸς τῆς πιότητος της ἀληθείας, ἐὰν προσλάβῃ τὴν θείαν διὰ πίστεως δύναμιν, τῇ χρηστῇ καὶ ἡμέρῳ ‹ἔγ›καταφυτευθεὶς γνώσει, καθάπερ ἡ ἀγριέλαιος ἐγκεντρισθεῖσα τῷ ὄντως καλῷ καὶ ἐλεήμονι λόγῳ πέττει τε τὴν παραδιδομένην τροφὴν καὶ καλλιέλαιος γίνεται. ὁ γάρ τοι ἐγκεντρισμὸς τὰς ἀχρείους εὐγενεῖς ποιεῖ καὶ τὰς ἀφόρους φορίμους γίνεσθαι βιάζεται τέχνῃ τῇ γεωργικῇ καὶ ἐπιστήμῃ τῇ γνωστικῇ.

34. Ibid. Here Clement thinks of "philosophy" in terms of "dogmas," but it was also a way of life. See A. D. Nock, *Conversion* (Oxford: At the Clarendon Press, 1933), pp. 164–86. On Gnostic interpretation of Romans, preceding that of Clement, see Elaine H. Pagels, *The Gnostic Paul* (Philadelphia: Fortress Press, 1975), pp. 13–52.

PAUL AND JEWISH CHRISTIANITY ACCORDING TO CARDINAL DANIÉLOU: A SUGGESTION

1. *The Theology of Jewish Christianity*, trans. J. A. Baker (Philadelphia: Westminster Press; London: Darton, Longman & Todd, 1977), p. 7. Italics mine.
2. Ibid., p. 8.
3. Ibid., p. 9.
4. Ibid.
5. Ibid.
6. J. Munck, *Paul and the Salvation of Mankind* (London: SCM Press, 1959). The important chapter is the one on "The Judaizing Gentile Christians," pp. 87–134.
7. Munck, *Salvation*, gives two reasons for the emergence of the Judaizing movement, in his view on extra-Palestinian soil; first, Paul himself had given such a sympathetic picture to Gentile Christians of the primitive Palestinian churches that some of his Gentile converts desired to imitate them, and, second, the LXX, which the Gentile Christians in the Pauline churches used, was easily understood to affirm that Israel after the flesh was the object of God's special favor, and, therefore, the desire to be like Israel after the flesh became natural. For a criticism of Munck's work see my review in *NTS* 2 (1955): 1: 196.
8. See H. J. Cadbury, "A Reconversion in Paul's Churches," in *The Joy of Study: Papers on New Testament and Related Subjects Presented to Honor Frederick Clifton Grant*, ed. S. E. Johnson (New York: Macmillan Co., 1951), p. 43.
9. There is here—it is to be emphasized—no attempt to summarize Daniélou's position in detail, but merely to indicate the main thrust of his argument in *The Theology of Jewish Christianity*.
10. This emphasis has a long history and is recently most forcefully expressed by R. Bultmann, in *The Theology of the New Testament*, vol. 1 (New York: Charles Scribner's Sons, 1951). But it is becoming increasingly evident that distinctions such as "Hellenistic" and "Jewish," as applied to the life of the primitive church, have to be very carefully scrutinized. For example, O. Cullmann, "The Significance of the Qumran Texts for Research into the Beginnings of Christianity," *JBL* 74(1955), 4: 213–26, found it possible to connect the Hellenists of Acts with the Sectarians of Qumran. I once thought such a connection exceedingly unlikely, because it seemed too paradoxical to connect the "universalist" element in primitive Christianity in any way with a particularistic group such as the Sectarians. But recent work, especially a brilliant article by A. Jaubert, in *RB* 65 (1958): 214–48 on "Le Pays de Damas," has caused me to be more open to Cullmann's suggestion in the light of the cross-currents in pre-Christian Judaism. A. Jaubert's article is not without importance indirectly also for Daniélou's thesis:

it shows how very widespread were the geographic interests of the Sectarians and, therefore, of their ideas.

11. Many have felt that his third definition is so loose as to be meaningless, but M. Simon, *Recherches d'Histoire Judéo-Chrétienne* (Paris, 1962), p. 7, seems to accept it.

12. *Salvation*, chapter 5: "The Church Without Factions." According to Munck, in 1 Corinthians not the parties in the Church but the whole Church was the object of Paul's attack: there were no parties and no Judaizers. Compare H. Koester, *HTR* 58 (1965): 311 n. 95.

13. Compare H. J. Schoeps, *Die Theologie des Apostels in Lichte der jüdischen Religionsgeschichte* (Philadelphia: Fortress Press, 1961; Tübingen, 1959), pp. 61 f.

14. Reitzenstein, Loisy, Lake come to mind. But Bousset ascribes to Paul in relation to Hellenistic religion the same function *mutatis mutandis* as we suggest might be ascribed to him in relation to Jewish Christianity. Bousset sees Paul "not so much as the Hellenizer of Christianity as the cleansing filter through which the waters of the Christian faith which have been muddied by Hellenism pass" (A. Schweitzer, *The Mysticism of Paul the Apostle* [New York, 1968], p. 30; cited by Schoeps, *Paulus*, p. 19).

15. Contrast, for example, Cerfaux on 1 Cor 15:28 (*Le chrétien dans la theologie Paulininne* [Paris, 1962], p. 30), which he regards as the final Hellenization of Paul's thought. On our view it might be regarded as the final stage in a simplification of such eschatological thinking.

16. J. Christiaan Beker (*Paul the Apostle: The Triumph of God in Life and Thought* [Philadelphia: Fortress Press, 1980]) has recently argued that apocalyptic constitutes the heart of Paul's gospel, and he sets himself against those who have attempted to diminish in any way the impact of apocalyptic on Pauline theology. But Beker fails to treat the apocalyptic tradition within which Paul stood: significant reference to the major Jewish apocalypses is, for example, lacking. (The same general charge could be levelled against much of Ernst Käsemann's work.) The result is a distorted picture. If one directs proper attention to the relevant sources, and then makes a comparison with Paul, the apostle emerges as one who reduced or simplified the apocalyptic tradition of Judaism. For although the Pauline *corpus* shares much with apocalyptic texts, it is also true that much in the apocalyptic tradition found no place in Paul's thought.

GALATIANS: A COMMENTARY ON PAUL'S LETTER TO THE CHURCHES IN GALATIA

1. One of my students, Dr. Dale Allison, expresses surprise, which others may perhaps share, that I am not more critical of H. D. B.'s structural analysis of Galatians. He writes: "Betz's proposed outline, so finely balanced and neatly arranged, strikes me as inconsistent with the tone of the letter . . . written in the heat of anger, in some apparent haste. . . . How does an angry, urgent, upset Paul manage to compose such an intricately structured epistle?" The question ignores two things—the physical process of writing involved, which was not as easy and casual as in our world, and also the fact that channeled, controlled, deliberate, cold anger is more effective than uncontrolled. Paul's anger was more

felt *through* the disciplined structure of the epistle than it would have been had it been allowed to vent itself without form. It is reported that in the 1980 U.S. presidential election, the more uncontrolled and undisciplined Mr. Carter's polemic, the more ineffective it became. Form is not the enemy of sincerity but its handmaid.

2. See my *Paul and Rabbinic Judaism*, new rev. ed. (Philadelphia: Fortress Press, 1980), 1–16.

3. H. J. Schoeps, *Paul: The Theory of the Apostle in the Light of Jewish Religious History* (Philadelphia: Westminster Press, 1961), pp. 178–80.

4. M. Simon, "A propos de l'école comparatiste," in *Jews, Greeks and Christians: Religious Cultures in Late Antiquity: Essays in Honor of William David Davies*, ed. R. Hamerton-Kelly and R. Scroggs (Leiden: E. J. Brill, 1976), pp. 261–70.

5. See my "Paul and Jewish Christianity According to Cardinal Daniélou: A Suggestion," chapter 9, herein.

6. H. J. Schoeps, *Geschichte des Judenchristentums* (Tübingen: J. C. B. Mohr [Paul Siebeck], 1949).

7. A. Suhl, *Paulus und seine Briefe: Ein Beitrag zur paulinischen Chronologie* (Gütersloh: Gerd Mohn, 1975). See also A. J. M. Wedderburn, "Some Recent Pauline Chronologies," *SJT* (forthcoming).

8. R. Jewett, "The Agitators in the Galatian Congregation," *NTS* 17 (1971): 198–212.

9. C. F. D. Moule, *An Idiom Book of New Testament Greek* (New York and Cambridge: Cambridge University Press, 1953), p. 106 n. 1.

10. See my "Paul and the Gentiles: A Suggestion Concerning Romans 11:13–24" from *Paganïsme, Judaïsme, Christianïsme: Influences et affrontement dans le monde antique. Mélanges offerts à Marcel Simon* (Paris: Boccard, 1978), pp. 131–44, and chapter 8 herein.

11. See p. 49, *tarassō,* political language (cf. p. 267); p. 55, *peithō*: "Persuading men by pleasing them" (*areskein*) is "of course one of the notorious strategies of political rhetoric and demagoguery"; p. 67 n. 112, *portheō*: "common as a description of political expression"; p. 90, *pareiserchesthai* "describes a military or political conspiracy"; p. 91 n. 310, *katadouloō*: "to enslave us," again an originally political term; p. 108, *hupostellō*, "from the arsenal of miltary and political language"; p. 109, *sunupekrithēsan auto*: "The background is most likely the political sphere."

12. See now C. K. Barrett, "Shaliaḥ and Apostle," in *Donum Gentilicium*, ed. E. Bammel, C. K. Barrett, and W. D. Davies (Oxford: At the Clarendon Press, 1979), pp. 82–102.

13. J. A. Sanders, *Torah and Canon* (Philadelphia: Fortress Press, 1972).

14. E. P. Sanders, *Paul and Palestinian Judaism* (Philadelphia: Fortress Press, 1977).

15. Daniel Patte, *Paul's Faith and the Power of the Gospel* (Philadelphia: Fortress Press, 1983).

16. H. J. Schoeps, *Geschichte des Judenchristentums*.

17. K. Stendahl, *Paul Among Jews and Gentiles* (Philadelphia: Fortress Press, 1976).

18. See further the excellent reviews in *Religious Studies Review* 7 (1981).

FROM TYRANNY TO LIBERATION: THE PAULINE EXPERIENCE OF
ALIENATION AND RECONCILIATION

1. For a convenient summary, see *Man in God's Design According to the New Testament,* P. I. Bratsiotis, R. Bultmann, H. Clavier, C. H. Dodd (Newcastle-upon-Tyne, 1952). Also C. H. Dodd, *Ingersoll Lecture on the Immortality of Man* (Official Record, Harvard University, 1950).

2. J. N. Sevenster, *Paul and Seneca* (Leiden: E. J. Brill, 1961); Max Pohlenz, "Paulus und die Stoa," *ZNW* 42 (1949): 69–104, denies that Acts 17 is from Paul.

3. Philo was capable of calling Moses "god" (*theos*), but the precise meaning he gave to the term "god" in this connection we cannot pursue here. See *De Vita Mosis,* pp. 155–58, §8–10. See W. A. Meeks, "Moses as God and King," in *Religions in Antiquity,* ed. Jacob Neusner (Leiden: E. J. Brill, 1968), p. 355.

4. Reference has often been made to the chronic depression of the Emperor Marcus Aurelius. R. E. Taylor, writing of the Emperor's fears, asserts: "If Stoicism as a system is responsible for these fears, it is, I think, because the doctrine offers only a "God without' to whom one can call for grace against temptation." *JRS* 11 2: 233.

5. See R. K. Bultmann, *The Theology of the New Testament,* trans. Kendrick Grobel (New York: Charles Scribner's Sons, 1951), vol. 1, *ad rem.*

6. There are two main approaches to Pauline anthropology, that through Hellenistic and that through Jewish channels. For the latter see, for example, my *Paul and Rabbinic Judaism,* new rev. ed. (Philadelphia: Fortress Press, 1980). See the exhaustive and illuminating survey of discussion of the subject in recent research by R. Jewett, *Paul's Anthropological Terms: A Study of Their Use in Conflict Settings* (Leiden: E. J. Brill, 1971). The discovery of the Dead Sea Scrolls is important in this field, as is the increasing recognition of the interpenetration of Hellenism and Judaism in Paul's time, even in Palestine.

7. See my *Invitation to the New Testament* (Garden City, N.Y.: Doubleday & Co., 1966), pp. 42ff.

8. See, especially, Stig Hanson, *The Unity of the Church in the New Testament* (Stockholm: Almqvist & Wiksells Boktryckeri, 1946).

9. *The Five Stages of Greek Religion* (Boston: Beacon Press, 1952).

10. On the whole subject see the following: G. E. H. Aulén, *Christus Victor: An Historical Study of the Three Main Types of the Idea of Atonement,* trans. A. G. Hebert (New York: Macmillan Co., 1951); G. B. Caird, *Principalities and Powers* (Oxford: At the Clarendon Press, 1956); O. Cullmann, *The State in the New Testament* (New York: Charles Scribner's Sons, 1956); M. Dibelius, *Die Geisterweit im Glauben des Paulus* (1909); A. D. Galloway, *The Cosmic Christ* (New York: Harper & Brothers, 1951); G. H. C. Macgregor, "Principalities and Powers: The Cosmic Background of Paul's Thought," *NTS* 1 (1954):17–28; A. N. Wilder, "Kerygma, Eschatology and Social Ethics," in *The Background of the New Testament and its Eschatology: Studies in Honour of C. H. Dodd,* ed. W. D. Davies and D. Daube (Cambridge: At the University Press, 1956), pp. 509–36.

It is strange, if the unseen demonic forces have the political and cosmic significance referred to above, that in the synoptic Gospels, which emerged from a milieu not altogether removed from that of Paul, they attack individuals. A cursory glance at newspapers and bookstores makes evident the reality of astrology in the modern world. See T. S. Eliot, "Four Quartets: Dry Salvages, V":

> To communicate with Mars, converse with spirits,
> To report behaviour of the sea monster,
> Describe the horoscope, haruspicate or scry,
> Observe disease in signatures, evoke
> Biography from the wrinkles of the palm
> And tragedy from fingers; release omens
> By sortilege, or tea leaves, riddle the inevitable
> With playing cards, fiddle with pentagrams
> Or barbituric acids, or dissect
> The recurrent image into pre-conscious terrors—
> To explore the womb, or tomb, or dreams; all these are usual
> Pastimes and drugs, and features of the press:
> And always will be, some of them especially
> When there is distress of nations and perplexity
> Whether on the shores of Asia, or in the Edgware Road.

> *The Complete Poems and Plays, 1909–1950* (New York: Harcourt, Brace & Co, 1952), pp. 135–36.

11. See *Rabbinic Judaism,* pp. 17–35; and my essay "Paul and the Dead Sea Scrolls: The Flesh and the Spirit," in *The Scrolls and the New Testament,* ed. K. Stendahl (New York: Harper & Brothers, 1957), pp. 157–82, and the references there given.

12. On Adam, see Robin Scroggs, *The Last Adam: A Study in Pauline Anthropology* (Philadelphia: Fortress Press, 1966), in which he trenchantly criticizes E. Brandenburger, *Adam und Christus* (Neukirchen, 1962). For an illuminating treatment of representation, see D. Soelle, *Christ the Representative: An Essay in Theology After the Death of God,* trans. D. Lewis (Philadelphia: Fortress Press, 1967).

13. See *Rabbinic Judaism,* pp. 114ff., 325ff.

14. Ibid., p. 19; also see, "Paul and the Dead Sea Scrolls."

15. For recent research, see R. Jewett, *Anthropological Terms.*

16. Simone de Beauvoir expresses something like Paul's view. In *The Prime of Life,* trans. P. Green (Cleveland and New York: World Publishing Co., 1962), pp. 54–55, she writes: "The idea of any discrepancy between my physical emotions and my conscious will I found alarming in the extreme: and it was precisely this split that in fact took place. My body [flesh] has its own whims, and I was powerless to control them; their violence overrode all my defenses . . . my physical appetites were greater than I wanted them to be." For Paul the physical and moral aspects of flesh seem to be inseparable. C. H. Dodd's comments, *The Epistle of Paul to the Romans* in the Moffatt New Testament Commentary (New York: Harper & Brothers; Chicago: Henry Regnery Co.; London: SCM Press, 1932), pp. 112ff., are still rewarding; but see also J. A. T. Robinson, *The Body, A Study in Pauline Theology* (London: Hodder & Stoughton; Toronto: Musser Book Co., 1952), *ad rem.*

17. On Sin in Paul, see treatments of his theology by R. Bultmann, H. Conzelmann, H. Bornkamm, and D. E. H. Whiteley, *The Theology of St. Paul* (Philadelphia: Fortress Press, 1966).

18. See especially C. H. Dodd, *The Epistle of Paul to the Romans, ad rem.,*

who interprets the wrath as the process of cause and effect in the moral universe, and contrast C. K. Barrett in his commentary on the same epistle (New York: Harper & Brothers, 1957). Particularly illuminating are A. J. Heschel, *The Prophets* (New York: Harper & Row, 1963), pp. 33, 279ff.; and E. Bevan, *Symbolism and Belief* (New York: Macmillan Co.; London: George Allen & Unwin, 1938). Heschel distinguishes between the psychology of passions and the theology of *pathos*. Is this the distinction preserved in the Book of Common Prayer when it is not content with one word, but speaks of "the Wrath and indignation of God"?

19. I have followed a commonly expressed view in the text on p. 199. But Dr. Dale C. Allison in conversation has reminded me of the innumerable books now being published on the themes of death and life after death, and of the increasing concern with death under the possibility of a nuclear holocaust.

20. Paul is certainly thinking of physical death. He does use "death" in other ways. See further the moving words of John Knox, *Life in Christ Jesus: Reflections on Romans 5–8* (Greenwich, Conn.: Seabury Press; Toronto: Oxford University Press, 1951), pp. 124–28; and J. S. Whale, *Christian Doctrine* (Toronto: Macmillan & Co., 1941), pp. 171–87.

21. The debate to which I refer is best clarified in two articles, one by J. Dupont, "The Conversion of Paul, and Its Influence on His Understanding of Salvation by Faith," trans. in *Apostolic History and the Gospel: Biblical and Historical Essays Presented to F. F. Bruce,* ed. W. W. Gasque and R. P. Martin (Grand Rapids: Wm. B. Eerdmans, 1970), pp. 176ff.; and the other by P. H. Menoud, "Revelation and Tradition, the Influence of Paul's Conversion on His Theology," *Int* 7 (1953): 2: 131–41. I deal with this question in my article on Paul in the forthcoming *Cambridge History of Judaism,* vol. 3, ed. W. D. Davies and L. Finkelstein. On the titles for Jesus in Paul, see W. R. Kramer, *Christ, Lord, Son of God,* trans. B. Hardy (Naperville, Ill.: Alec R. Allenson, 1966). See also Beverly Gaventa, "Paul's Conversion: A Sifting of the Epistolary Evidence," (Ph.D. dissertation, Duke University, 1978).

22. See especially the works by R. Bultmann and G. Bornkamm.

23. Here the work of O. Cullmann is fundamental. Beginning with his work, *Christ and Time, the Primitive Christian Conception of Time and History,* rev. ed., trans. F. V. Filson (Philadelphia: Westminster Press, 1964), he set forth, as over against Bultmann, a linear interpretation of Paul's eschatology. He meets the criticisms levelled against his position in *Salvation in History,* trans. S. G. Sowers (New York: Harper & Row; London: SCM Press, 1967). See also my work *The Gospel and the Land: Early Christianity and Jewish Territorial Doctrine* (Berkeley and Los Angeles: University of California Press, 1974), pp. 201ff,; J. A. Fitzmyer, *Pauline Theology: A Brief Sketch* (Englewood Cliffs, N.J.: Prentice-Hall, 1967), pp. 23ff, especially 30ff. On apocalyptic as the matrix of Paulinism, see J. C. Beker, *Paul the Apostle: The Triumph of God in Life and Thought* (Philadelphia: Fortress Press, 1980).

24. It is impossible within the space available to document what follows. Readers are referred to the works already cited for bibliographical guidance.

25. This is forcefully insisted upon by M. S. Enslin, *Reapproaching Paul* (Philadelphia: Westminster Press, 1972), pp. 132ff. See *Rabbinic Judaism,* pp. 136–46.

26. On Paul and the historical Jesus, a question which, according to many (in

our judgment erroneously), we should have dismissed long ago as unimportant, see V. Furnish, "The Jesus-Paul Debate: From Baur to Bultmann," *BJRL* 47 (1965): 2: 342–81, and now Dale C. Allison, "The Synoptic Gospels and Pauline Epistles: The Pattern of the Parallels," in *NTS* (January 1982): 1–32. A new turn is being given to the discussion by W. H. Kelber in *The Oral and the Written Gospel* (Philadelphia: Fortress Press, 1983); this still further complicates, this time linguistically, any attempt at the recovery of the historical Jesus.

27. See *Rabbinic Judaism,* pp. 147–76.

28. See A. Schweitzer, *The Mysticism of Paul the Apostle,* trans. W. Montgomery (New York: Henry Holt; London: A. & C. Black, 1931), *ad rem.;* George Johnston, *The Doctrine of the Church in the New Testament* (Cambridge: At the University Press, 1943); also on this still useful is R. N. Flew, *Jesus and His Church* (Nashville: Abingdon-Cokesbury, 1938).

29. On all this see *Rabbinic Judaism,* and literature there cited. Important is L. Cerfaux, *The Church in the Theology of St. Paul,* trans. G. Webb and A. Walker (New York: Thomas Nelson & Sons; Breisgau, Germany: Herder & Co., 1959). On the objectivity of the new humanity, see J. Knox, *Life in Christ Jesus.*

30. See *Rabbinic Judaism* and *The Gospel and the Land,* p. 193. In the light of the work of P. Stühlmacher, I am now more prepared to see in Paul's use of *hilastêrion* in 3:21–26 the actual replacement of the *kapporeth.* For the reasons for this, see *Jesus und Paulus: Für Werner Kümmel,* ed. E. E. Ellis and R. Grässer (Göttingen, 1975).

31. Here I have not the space to indicate how Paul's gospel involved a radical criticism and rejection of much in the tradition within which he had been nourished. The Sabbath, the festivals, the dietary regulations—how did he deal with these? C. K. Barrett has dealt with the problem of continuity and discontinuity in Paul. See "Conversion and Conformity: The Freedom of the Spirit and the Institutional Church," in *Christ and Spirit in the New Testament: Studies in Honour of C. F. D. Moule,* ed. Barnabus Lindars and S. S. Smalley (New York and Cambridge: Cambridge University Press, 1973), pp. 359–81. I would stress more than he the continuity, especially as I consider that the covenantal structure of Judaism is retained by Paul: his God is the God of Abraham and Isaac and Jacob, and His demands remain in the Law of Christ. From this point of view, Paul, as it were, works within "the system" to change it, not against it to destroy it. See my essay, "The Moral Teaching of the Early Church," chapter 15, herein. Enslin (*Paul,* p. 137), while he recognizes the personal element in Paul's moral seriousness, rightly derives his moral outlook from Judaism. Enslin does not connect this, as I should, with the covenantal structure of the Gospel as of Judaism.

32. Most conveniently dealt with in English by R. P. Martin, *Carmen Christi, Philippians 2:5–11 in Recent Interpretation and in the Setting of Early Christian Worship* (New York and Cambridge: Cambridge University Press, 1967), pp. 84ff.

33. On all this, see my popular treatment, *Invitation to the New Testament,* pp. 345ff.

34. This has been well expressed by John Knox, *Life in Christ Jesus,* p. 124, where he also emphasizes warnings about misunderstanding Christian "joy" that we have already sounded.

35. See, for example, J. Jeremias on Paul in *The Central Message of the New Testament* (New York: Charles Scribner's Sons; London: SCM Press; Don Mills,

Ontario: Saunders of Toronto, 1965), But this position permeates much Protestant scholarship, especially in Germany.

36. *Epistle of Paul to the Romans,* p. 41.

37. Compare J. Knox, *Life of Christ Jesus,* p. 12. We agree with Knox but should be inclined to emphasize more directly being brought into relation with Christ than with the community. But whether a clear distinction can ever be made at this point is difficult to assess. What is important is that Knox rightly does recognize the communal dimension in Paul even at the point usually taken to be the most personal and private: justification.

38. I shall deal with this in a forthcoming work.

39. See especially the noted article by K. Stendahl, on "The Apostle Paul and the Introspective Conscience of the West," *HTR* 56 (1963): 3: 199–215; also, *Paul Among Jews and Gentiles* (Philadelphia: Fortress Press, 1976). The discussion is carried further by Käsemann, Stuhlmacher, and others but cannot be pursued here. The question is bound up with the strange absence in Paul of the theme of repentance, the actuality of which, however, in Christian liberation cannot be doubted.

40. See *Rabbinic Judaism* and my essay, "Moral Teaching of the Early Church," cited above. Enslin acclaims Paul's realism over against the moral absolutism of Jesus, which he very daringly designates "fanatic," *Reapproaching Paul,* pp. 146ff. I have elsewhere suggested that the marks of the sage appear in Jesus also. See my *Setting of the Sermon on the Mount* (New York and Cambridge: Cambridge University Press, 1964). Did Jesus lay his absolutes on all or only on a *corps élite?* But that Enslin has recalled us again to a cardinal note in Paul, that of a *halakah,* must be gratefully recognized. Particularly moving is his emphasis on 2 Cor 5:14 ("For the love of Christ constraineth us") as the central note of Paul, *Reapproaching Paul,* p. 147. This is another way of pointing to the meaning of "in Christ." On the moral dimensions of the Spirit, still useful is H. A. A. Kennedy, *The Theology of the Epistles* (New York: Charles Scribner's Sons, 1920), pp. 142ff.

41. See John Knox, *Life in Christ,* pp. 111–18, on "God's Sovereign Goodness." Sarah Freedman referred me to a moving passage on the same theme in Graham Greene, *The Honorary Consul* (New York: Simon & Schuster Pocketbooks, 1973), pp. 259ff., where his character speaks of "the horror" that is in life: "We belong to Him [God] and He belongs to us. But now at least we can be sure where evolution will end one day—it will end in a goodness like Christ's. It is a terrible process all the same and the God I believe in suffers as we suffer." (p. 262).

42. It is difficult to escape a futurism in Paul. For him the believer was taken up "in Christ" into the purpose of God in a cosmic drama of redemption. It is for him to discern the activity of the divine purpose in Christ, to prove it, and to throw in his lot in decision for it. It is *agapē* that governs his discerning. As I wrote elsewhere: "The moral activity of the Christian consists in discerning the times and the purposes of God in the times: it is his to *decide* for that purpose, to recognize the things that are different. In this sense the whole of Christian moral life is eschatologically determined," herein, chap. 15. Especially important is O. Cullman on "Salvation History and Ethics," (*Salvation in History,* p. 328). On "hope," see John Knox, *Life in Christ,* and C. F. D. Moule, *The Meaning*

of Hope: A Biblical Exposition (Philadelphia: Fortress Press, 1963). J. C. Beker, *Paul the Apostle*, has stressed this.

43. See my article, "The Apostolic Age and the Life of Paul," especially p. 877c, in *PCB,* ed. M. Black and H. H. Rowley (London and New York, 1962); also G. Bornkamm, *Paul,* trans. D. M. G. Stalker (New York: Harper & Row, 1971), p. 55.

44. See *Rabbinic Judaism,* p. 295.

45. Hans von Campenhausen, *Tradition and Life in the Church,* trans. A. V. Littledale (Philadelphia: Fortress Press, 1968), p. 146.

46. Compare Campenhausen, ibid.

47. See David Daube, "Pauline Contribution to a Pluralist Culture: Re-creation and Beyond," in *Jesus and Man's Hope,* ed. D. G. Miller and D. Y. Hadidian, Pittsburgh Theological Seminary vol. 2 (Pittsburgh: Pittsburgh Theological Seminary Festival on the Gospels, 1970–71), pp. 223–45.

48. I have tried to deal with this problem in the article already cited herein, chapter 16.

49. For example, the role of women in the Church. On this, see K. Stendahl, *The Bible and the Role of Women: A Case Study in Hermeneutics,* trans. E. T. Sander (Philadelphia: Fortress Press, 1966).

50. *Reapproaching Paul,* p. 138. For political or liberation theology, see, for example, the works of F. Herzog and D. Soelle.

51. One who has kept watch over the growth of Christian Socialism in Britain constantly overhears in the discussion of political or liberation theology, among much that is new, echoes of things heard before, and is warned (see, for example, *Charles Raven,* by F. W. Dillistone [Grand Rapids: Wm. B. Eerdmans, 1975]) against the assumption that Christians *can* have the sociological, economic, and political awareness demanded by that theology. What has emerged with terrible force is the vast complexity of the human scene. This must not be allowed to stimulate a false quietism, but it must inform any enthusiasm, to sober it. See the review of Fernand Brandel, *The Mediterranean,* 2 vols., trans. Sian Reynolds (New York: Harper & Row, 1975), in the *New York Times* Book Review, May 18, 1975, especially p. 45.

The struggle between restoration and utopianism is as old as the fifth century B.C.E., at least. But this cannot be pursued here. See the salutary work of Paul D. Hanson, *The Dawn of Apocalyptic* (Philadelphia: Fortress Press, 1975) which is very pertinent to current discussion of political theology.

LAW IN THE NEW TESTAMENT (NT)

1. R. Schnackenburg, *The Moral Teaching of the New Testament,* trans. J. Holland-Smith and W. J. O'Hara (New York: Herder & Herder, 1965), supplies helpful bibliographical information.

2. See in addition to what follows B. H. Branscomb, *Jesus and the Law of Moses* (London: Hodder & Stoughton, 1930); W. G. Kümmel, "Jesus und der jüdische Traditionsgedanke," *ZNW* 33 (1934): 105–30; H. J. Schoeps, *Aus frühch-ristlicher Zeit* (Tübingen, 1950), pp. 212–20; E. Schweizer, "Anmerkungen zum Gesetzesverständnis des Mätthaus," *TLZ* 77 (1952): 479–84; W. D. Davies, *The*

Setting of the Sermon on the Mount (New York and Cambridge: Cambridge University Press, 1964); idem, "Matthew 5 : 17, 18," in *Christian Origins and Judaism* (Philadelphia: Westminster Press, 1962), pp. 31–66; H. Hübner, *Das Gesetz in der synoptischen Tradition* (Witten, 1973); idem, "Mark 7 : 1–23 und das 'judisch-hellenistische' Gesetzverständnis," *NTS* 27 (1975–76): 319–45; K. Berger, *Die Gesetzauslegung Jesu. Teil I: Markus und Parallelen* (Neukirchen, 1972); M. Hengel, "Jesus und die Tora," *Theologische Beiträge* 9 (1978): 152–72; G. Barth, "Matthew's Understanding of the Law," in *Tradition and Interpretation in Matthew,* by G. Bornkamm, G. Barth, and H. J. Held, trans. P. Scott (London: SCM Press, 1963); J. Lambrecht, "Jesus and the Law," *ETL* 53 (1977): 24–82; H. Braun, *Jesus of Nazareth: The Man and His Time,* trans. Everett R. Kalin (Philadelphia: Fortress Press, 1979), pp. 53–72; Schnackenburg, *Moral Teaching,* pp. 56–65; Joachim Jeremias, *New Testament Theology,* trans. John Bowden (New York: Charles Scribner's Sons, 1971), pp. 203–18; E. Schweizer, *Jesus,* trans. David E. Green (Atlanta: John Knox Press, 1971), pp. 30–39; and Rudolf Pesch, *Das Markusevangelium. 1. Teil, Einleitung und Kommentar zu Kap. 1, 1–8, 26,* HTKNT 2 (Freiburg: Herder, 1977): 1: 170–97, 367–84. Pesch supplies an extensive bibliography for the Markan texts.

3. On the Hellenists, see especially M. Hengel, "Zwischen Jesus und Paulus. Die 'Hellenisten,' die 'Sieben' und Stephanus (Apg. 6, 1–15; 7, 54—8, 3)," *ZTK* 72 (1975): 151–206; idem, *Acts and the History of Earliest Christianity,* trans. John Bowden (Philadelphia: Fortress Press, 1979), pp. 71—80; M. Simon, *St. Stephen and the Hellenists* (New York: Longmans, Green & Co., 1958); Robin Scroggs, "The Earliest Hellenistic Christianity," in *Religions in Antiquity,* ed. J. Neusner (Leiden: E. J. Brill, 1968), pp. 176–206.

4. On the so-called apostolic council, see Hengel, *Acts,* pp. 111–26; G. Klein, "Galater 2:6–9 und die Geschichte der Jerusalemer Urgemeinde," in *Rekonstruktion und Interpretation* (Munich, 1969), pp. 99–128; B. Reicke, "Der Geschichtliche Hintergrund des Apostelkonzils," in *Studia Paulina,* ed. J. N. Sevenster and W. C. van Unnik (Haarlem, 1953), pp. 172–87; P. Gaechter, "Geschichtliches zum Apostelkonzil," *ZKT* 85 (1963): 339–54; M. Dibelius, "The Apostolic Council," in *Studies in the Acts of the Apostles,* trans. M. Ling (London: SCM Press, 1956), pp. 93–101; W. Schmithals, *Paul and James,* SBT 46 (London: SCM Press, 1965); G. Bornkamm, *Paul,* trans. D. M. G. Stalker (New York: Harper & Row, 1971), pp. 31–42; and Ernst Haenchen, *The Acts of the Apostles: A Commentary,* trans. B. Noble et al. (Oxford: At the Clarendon Press, 1971), pp. 440–72.

5. Concerning the role played by Jewish Christianity in the Church's struggle against Marcion and incipient Gnosticism, see H. J. Schoeps, *Theologie und Geschichte des Judenchristentums* (Tübingen, 1949).

6. H. J. Schoeps, *Paul,* trans. Harold Knight (Philadelphia: Westminster Press; London: Lutterworth Press, 1961), pp. 168–218; W. D. Davies, *Paul and Rabbinic Judaism,* new rev. ed. (Philadelphia: Fortress Press, 1980), especially pp. 147–76; idem, "Paul and the Law," herein, chapter 6. C. H. Dodd, 'Ἔννομος Χριστοῦ,' in *More New Testament Studies* (Grand Rapids: Wm. B. Eerdmans, 1968), pp. 134–48: H. Hübner, *Das Gesetz bei Paulus* (Göttingen, 1978); R. N. Longnecker, *Paul: Apostle of Liberty* (Grand Rapids: Wm. B. Eerdmans, 1964); H. Schürmann, "'Das Gesetz des Christus' (Gal. 6, 2)," *Neues Testament und*

Kirche, ed. J. Gnilka (Freiburg, 1974), pp. 282–300; C. E. B. Cranfield, "St. Paul and the Law," *SJT* 17 (1964): 43–68; P. Stuhlmacher, "Das End des Gesetzes," *ZTK* 67 (1970): 14–39; E. P. Sanders, "Torah and Paul," in *God's Christ and His People,* ed. J. Jervell and W. A. Meeks (Oslo, 1978); P. Démann, "Moïse et la Loi dans la pensée de Saint Paul," *Cahiers Sioniens,* 2–4 (1954): 171ff.; R. Bultmann, *Theology of the New Testament,* trans. K. Grobel (New York: Charles Scribner's Sons, 1951; London: SCM Press, 1952), 1: 259ff.; F. Lange, "Gesetz und Bund bei Paulus," in *Rechfertigung, Festschrift für Ernst Käsemann,* ed. J. Friedrich, W. Pöhlmann, and P. Stuhlmacher (Tübingen/Göttingen, 1976), pp. 305–20; J. W. Drane, *Paul, Libertine or Legalist?: A Study in the Theology of the Major Pauline Epistles* (London: SPCK, 1976); H. Räisänen, "Paul's Theological Difficulties with the Law," in *Studia Biblica 1978: 3. Papers on Paul and Other New Testament Authors,* ed. E. A. Livingstone (Sheffield: JSOT Press, 1980), pp. 301–20; and W. S. Campell, "Christ the End of the Law: Romans 10:4," in *Studia Biblica 1978,* pp. 73–81.

7. On conscience see my essay herein, chapter 13.

8. See my essay on law in first-century Judaism, chapter 1.

9. See my essay on law in first-century Judaism, chapter 1.

10. For further discussion see C. H. Dodd, *Gospel and Law* (Cambridge: At the University Press, 1951), and W. Neisel, "Gospel and Law," in *Reformed Symbolics* (London: Oliver & Boyd, 1962), pp. 211–24. The great work of E. P. Sanders, *Paul and Palestinian Judaism* (Philadelphia: Fortress Press, 1977) has reopened the question of Paul and the law very radically. See reflections on it in my *Paul and Rabbinic Judaism* (1980), and also G. Lüdemann, *Paulus und das Judentum* (Munich: Chr. Kaiser Verlag, 1983). Sanders' *Paul, the Law, and the Jewish People* (Philadelphia: Fortress Press, 1983) is also of great importance.

CONSCIENCE AND ITS USE IN THE NEW TESTAMENT

1. A. Meineke, *Fragmenta Poetarum Comoediae Novae* (Berlin, 1981); J. H. Moulton and G. Milligan, *The Vocabulary of the Greek Testament* (New York: Harper & Brothers; London: Hodder & Stoughton, 1930) (on συνείδησις in Epictetus, see index); E. Schwarz, *Ethik der Griechen* (Stuttgart, 1931), especially pp. 90–91 and 237 n. 31; E. Bréhier, *Les idées philosophiques et religieuses de Philon d'Alexandrie* (Paris, 1925), pp. 259–300 (on the connection between the idea of conscience in Epicurus and Euripides and in Philo); and C. Maurer, "σύνοιδα, συνείδησις," *TDNT,* ed. G. Kittel and G. Friedrich, trans. G. Bromiley (Grand Rapids: Wm. B. Eerdmans, 1971), 7: 899–913; F. Zucker, *Syneidesis-Conscientia* (Jenaer Akadentische Reden, Heft 6, 1928).

2. Professor Daube has now illumined this question for me. In a recent excursus, *Ancient Jewish Law* (Leiden: E. J. Brill, 1981), pp. 123–29, with characteristic penetration, he urges that the absence of a term does not necessarily imply the absence of the thing or idea it connotes. The biblical "sources contain no word for nuclear power: it was not invented" (p. 122). Moreover, not seldom "the late birth or adoption of a word is due to the previous self-understanding of what it expresses." For example, in current English, "while we do have 'vegetarian' we are without a settled label for the less gentle feeder—not because

he does not exist but, on the contrary, because he is taken for granted." Words are "coined to designate the striking not the ordinary" (p. 124). Both in English and French, the words "'bigamy' and 'polygamy' considerably antedate 'monogamy'" (p. 125). As for the fact of conscience in the OT, Daube refers to 2 Sam 9:1; 2 Sam 19:21; 2 Kings 2:44; Gen 42:21, where it is assumed or implied. The absence of a term for conscience in the Old Testament merely indicates that it was so assumed as to need no designation. Daube connects the development through which self-evaluation comes to be tied up with self-awareness (*sunoida*) with the philosophical climate of the fifth century B.C.E. in Greece, when that tie became fashionable: "That period is eminently philosophical. But, more specifically, the key to virtue is widely supposed to lie in information, successful schooling, learning taken in properly. It is quite likely this theory which chiefly leads to the identification of self-judgment with the sharing of knowledge with oneself" (p. 128). E. R. Dodds, *The Greeks and the Irrational* (Berkeley and Los Angeles: University of California Press, 1957), pp. 45–50, in dealing with the emphasis on guilt in that period points to the breakdown of the family and follows F. Zucker in placing "the internalization of conscience" uncertainly late in the Hellenic world: "it does not become common until long after secular law had begun to recognize the importance of motive" (p. 37). See F. Zucker, *Syneidesis-Conscientia, Jenaer Akademische Reden,* Heft 6, 1928.

3. In H. Diels, *Fragmente der Vorsokratiker,* 7th ed., ed. with additions by W. Kranz (Berlin, 1952), 2: 206–7.

4. For example, Schwarz, *Ethik der Griechen,* pp. 90–91, 237 n. 31.

5. E. Bréhier, *Les idée philosophiques,* pp. 259–300. He suggests perhaps a continuous literary and philosophical tradition.

6. Reprinted by permission of the publishers and of Loeb Classical Library from LCL vol. Philo, *Decalogue.*

7. Reprinted by permission of the publishers and of Loeb Classical Library from LCL vol. Philo, *On Tranquility of Mind.*

8. C. H. Dodd, "Conscience in the New Testament," *Mansfield College Magazine* 66 (1916): 150–54; M. Dibelius and Hans Conzelmann, *The Pastoral Epistles,* Hermeneia Series, vol. 2, trans. Philip Buttolph and Adela Yarbro (Philadelphia: Fortress Press, 1972), pp. 18–20; R. Bultmann, *Theology of the New Testament,* trans. K. Grobel (New York: Charles Scribner's Sons, 1951), 1: 216–20; Max Pohlenz, "Paulus und die Stoa," *ZNW* 42 (1949): 77ff.; C. A. Pierce, *Conscience in the New Testament* (London: SCM Press, 1955); Maurer, "σύνοιδα, συνείδησις," pp. 914–19; Johannes Stelzenberger, *Syneidesis im Neuen Testament* (Paderborn, 1961); Jacques Dupont, "Syneidesis aux origines de la notion chrétienne de conscience morale," *Studia Hellenistica* 5 (1948): 119–53; C. Spicq, "La conscience dans le Nouveau Testament," *RB* 47 (1938): 50–80; idem, *Saint Paul: Les Epitres Pastorales,* 4th ed. (Paris, 1969), pp. 29–38; M. Thrall, "The Pauline Use of συνείδησις," *NTS* 14 (1967–68): 118–25; B. Reicke, "Syneidesis in Röm. 11, 15," *TZ* 12 (1956): 157–61; K. Stendahl, "The Apostle Paul and the Introspective Conscience of the West," *HTR* 56 (1963): 199–215; Paul K. Jewett, *Paul's Anthropological Terms,* AGJU 10 (Leiden: E. J. Brill, 1971), pp. 402–46; and Rudolf Schnackenburg, *The Moral Teaching of the New Testament,* trans. J. Holland-Smith and W. J. O'Hara (New York: Herder & Herder, 1965), pp. 287–96.

9. For a review of the discussion of συνείδησις in Paul see Jewett, *Anthropological Terms,* pp. 402–21.

10. On συνείδησις and the future in Paul, see further Thrall, "The Pauline Use of συνείδησις," pp. 118–23.

FROM SCHWEITZER TO SCHOLEM: REFLECTIONS ON SABBATAI SVI

1. See K. Koch, *The Rediscovery of Apocalyptic* (London: SCM Press, 1972), pp. 57–59; W. G. Kümmel, *The New Testament: The History of the Investigation of Its Problems* (Nashville: Abingdon Press, 1972), pp. 243–80.

2. "The Beginnings of Christian Theology," *New Testament Questions of Today* (Philadelphia: Fortress Press, 1969), p. 82; "On the Subject of Primitive Christian Apocalyptic," ibid., p. 108.

3. "Die Bekehrung des Paulus als religionsgeschichtliches Problem," *ZTK* 56 (1959): 273–93.

4. Especially under the direction of Robert A. Kraft for the SBL and of James H. Charlesworth at Duke University. In Britain the work proceeds under H. F. D. Sparks at Oxford University.

5. K. Koch, *Rediscovery of Apocalyptic* (see n. 1); this work provides a convenient summary of the recent discussion. See also J. M. Schmidt, *Die jüdische Apokalyptik* (Neukirchen-Vluyn: Neukirchener Verlag, 1969); W. G. Rollins, "The New Testament and Apocalyptic," *NTS* 17 (1970–71): 454–76. Now see further J. C. Beker, *Paul the Apostle: The Triumph of God in Life and Thought* (Philadelphia: Fortress Press, 1980).

6. *Šbty Ṣby whtnwʿh hšbtʾyt bymy ḥyyw* (Tel Aviv: Am Oved, 1957); now excellently translated into English by R. J. Zwi Werblowsky (Princeton: Princeton University Press, 1973).

7. The chief pertinent works are: *Major Trends in Jewish Mysticism,* Eng. trans. (New York: Schocken Books, 1961); *The Messianic Idea in Judaism and Other Essays on Jewish Spirituality* (New York: Schocken Books, 1971); *Jewish Gnosticism, Merkabah Mysticism and Talmudic Tradition* (New York: Jewish Theological Society of America, 1960). Other works by Scholem are listed in the *Festschrift* for him: *Studies in Mysticism and Religion: Presented to Gershom G. Scholem,* ed. E. E. Urbach, R. J. Zwi Werblowsky, and C. Wirszubski (Jerusalem: Magnes, 1967), p. 368. For the caution necessary, compare Scholem, *Major Trends,* p. 3. He quotes Byron's query: "Who will then explain the explanation?"

8. For all this see G. G. Scholem, *Sabbatai Svi;* and *Major Trends,* pp. 286–324.

9. *JBL* 81 (1962): 1–13.

10. *Sabbatai Svi,* pp. 153–54, 166.

11. Ibid., pp. 284–86.

12. Scholem draws upon contemporary documents. He lists the Hebrew sources in *Sabbatai Svi,* pp. 933–47; secondary sources on Sabbatai Svi and his movement, ibid., pp. 947–55; cf. other studies, ibid., pp. 955–56.

13. See *Major Trends,* pp. 40–79. The thesis of D. Rössler (*Gesetz und Geschichte,* WMANT 2 [Neukirchen-Vluyn: Neukirchener Verlag, 1960]), distin-

guishing sharply between rabbinic and apocalyptic Judaism, although very influential in German circles (for example in the work of U. Wilckens—see K. Koch, *Rediscovery of Apocalyptic,* p. 40), is untenable. See, among others, A. Nissen, "Tora and Geschichte im Spätjudentum," *NovT* 9 (1967): 241–77. I urged the interpenetration of Pharisaism and apocalyptic in *ET* 49 (1948): 233–37. Cf. O. Cullmann, *Salvation in History* (Philadelphia: Fortress Press, 1967), p. 60. This interpenetration, with varying emphases, is not generally conceded. See Joshua Bloch, *On the Apocalyptic,* JQRMS 2 (Philadelphia: Dropsie College, 1952); and Scholem's works.

14. Made familiar by G. F. Moore but increasingly abandoned. The works of E. Bickerman, D. Daube, S. Lieberman, and M. Smith have abundantly established the interpenetration between Hellenism and Judaism by the first century, so that Pharisaism itself can be regarded as a hybrid. See my *Paul and Rabbinic Judaism* new rev. ed. (Philadelphia: Fortress Press, 1980), pp. 1–16; my "Reflections on Tradition: The ʾAbot Revisited," herein, chapter 2; and now, above all, the monumental study by Martin Hengel, *Judaism and Hellenism,* 2 vols. (Philadelphia: Fortress Press, 1974). For important reviews of the latter, see M. Stern, *Kirjath Sepher* 46 (1970–71): 94–99; and A. Momigliano, *JTS* 21 (1970): 149–53. For a summary statement, see H. A. Fischel, "Greek and Latin Languages, Rabbinical Knowledge of," *EncJud,* 16 vols. (New York: Colliers-Macmillan, 1972), pp. 884–87. For a summary statement of the variety of first-century pharisaic Judaism, see M. Stone, "Judaism at the Time of Christ," *Scientific American* 115 (1973): 79–87. But the historically significant stratum of first-century Judaism proved to be the pharisaic, so that whatever its comparative numerical strength and social or political influence, it unmistakably possessed a more enduring vitality than other strata. See my article on "Contemporary Jewish Religion" in *PCB,* ed. M. Black and H. H. Rowley (1962), pp. 705–11. For a criticism of Hengel, see the review by L. H. Feldman, *JBL* 96 (1977), 371–82.

15. For a convenient statement, see C. H. Dodd, with P. I. Bratsiotis, R. Bultmann, H. Clavier, *Man in God's Design according to the New Testament* (Newcastle-upon-Tyne: Studiorum Novi Testamenti Societas, 1952). But it should be noted that Philo was capable of calling Moses "God" (*theos*); see *De vita Mosis* 1.28 §155–58; *De sac. Abel, et Caini* 2 §8–10. See also W. A. Meeks, "Moses as God and King," in *Religions in Antiquity,* ed. J. Neusner (Leiden: E. J. Brill, 1968), p. 355.

16. *Sabbatai Svi,* pp. 835–36, 871. Scholem writes of a tendency that Sabbatai Svi had of "toying—though never explicitly—with the idea of his divinity." At one point he signed his name *Turco,* which, among other things, could mean "the mountain of God." Scholem asks, "Did he mean to imply that the Deity was resting upon Mount Sinai? A liturgical practice developed among believers of saying: "Every morning and every evening we say: he and no other is our God" (p. 835). At one stage in his life Sabbati Svi wore symbolic rings. One of his rings was engraved with the name *Shadday* (234); he discovered that the numerical value of the two Hebrew words for "God moved" (*ʾelōhîm měraḥepet*) [sic!] in Gen 1:2 was equal to that of his name, and that *běrêšît,* "in the beginning" (Gen 1:1) contained the letters of his own name, "Sabbatai." Scholem compares the utterances ascribed to Jesus in the Gospels as pointing to a peculiar intimacy with

God (p. 235). The "divinity" of Sabbatai Svi became a subject of acute debate. The name by which Sabbatai Svi was known to his followers was *ʾAmirah,* which is made of the initials of the Hebrew words for "Our Lord and King, his majesty be exalted" (pp. 263, 314, 329).

17. See especially *Sabbatai Svi,* pp. 125–38. In Jerusalem opposition to Sabbatai Svi reached the highest point, however, when he claimed "I am the Lord your God, Sabbatai Svi" (pp. 361, 389); on p. 607 there is a reference to a rabbi ascribing divinity to Sabbatai Svi.

18. "The fact is that the true and spontaneous feeling of the Merkabah mystic knows nothing of the divine immanence; the infinite gulf between the soul and God the King on His throne is not even bridged at the climax of mystical ecstasy" (*Sabbatai Svi,* p. 55). Note that in emphasizing the role of the messiah as the agent of the *tiqqûn,* Nathan was departing from Lurianic qabbalists, for whom obedience to the law was the instrument of the *tiqqûn.*

19. See *Major Trends,* pp. 80–286. Professor Kalman Bland of Duke University emphasized this (orally) to me: it is, indeed, a major consideration. On the other hand, medieval Jewish mysticism was accompanied by a continuing tradition of apocalyptic, going back before the first century. G. W. Buchanan, in *Revelation and Redemption* (Dillsboro: Western North Carolina Press, 1978), has gathered rich evidence for this. This continuity makes the assessment of first-century apocalyptic in the light of that of the seventeenth more realistic than might at first appear.

20. The propriety and precise meaning of the term "mysticism" as used by Schweitzer we need not here discuss. See the criticism of it, going back to the work of Nathan Soderblom, in Gustaf Aulén, *Dag Hammarskjöld's White Book: The Meaning of Markings* (Philadelphia: Fortress Press, 1969), p. 38.

21. Scholem notes this of Sabbatianism. It was also true probably of early Christianity, at least up to 70 C.E. See P. Richardson, *Israel in the Apostolic Church,* SNTS 10 (New York and London: Cambridge University Press, 1969).

23. Scholem's work *The Messianic Idea in Judaism* is the most important study of messianism known to me. It should be compared and contrasted with that of Joseph Klausner, *The Messianic Idea in Israel from Its Beginnings to the Completion of the Mishnah* (New York: Macmillan Co., 1955). The former raises our understanding of its theme to a new dimension and compels a reassessment of early Christianity as a messianic movement. This simply opens up an area for further exploration.

23. It is necessary to insert "without prejudice" because included among them are parallels in the crucial "moments" in early Christianity, for instance, the resurrection and the parousia. The term "secondary" is applied to such moments here within the context of Scholem's study.

24. See John Knox, *The Ethic of Jesus in the Teaching of the Church* (Nashville: Abingdon Press, 1961), p. 86; H. J. Schoeps, *Paul* (Philadelphia: Westminister Press, 1961), p. 188. But contrast C. F. D. Moule, "On Obligation in the Ethic of Paul," *Christian History and Interpretation: Studies Presented to John Knox,* ed. W. R. Farmer, C. F. D. Moule, R. R. Niebuhr (New York and London: Cambridge University Press, 1967), p. 398.

25. *Sabbatai Svi,* pp. 260, 291, and esp. 472. Nathan emphasized repentance

paradoxically as he did the nearness of the end which would change all things. Joy and penitence coexisted (p. 262). On fasts and enthusiasm, see also pp. 328, 356. For examples of the extremism, see pp. 358, 364, 434. Nathan and one hundred Jews immersed themselves naked in snow at Hebron.

26. Ibid., pp. 112–13, 123, 146, 185. Particularly striking are the references to :he face of Sabbatai Svi as "shining" (pp. 132, 142, 188–90). These naturally recall the accounts of the transfiguration of Jesus, but that moment must not be too easily interpreted in their light. The prayer life of Sabbatai Svi recalls Matthew 6 (pp. 118, 185). On this see the extremely important work of H. D. Betz, "Eine judenchristliche Kult-Didache in Matt 6:1–18," *Jesus Christus in Historie und Theologie: Festschrift für Hans Conzelmann,* ed. G. Strecker (Tübingen: J. C. B. Mohr [Paul Siebeck], 1975), pp. 445–57; his struggle with demons recalls those of Jesus in the Synoptics (see *Sabbatai Svi,* pp. 174–75).

27. See n. 2 above, and also "Sentences of Holy Law in the New Testament," *New Testament Questions of Today,* pp. 66–81. Even if Käsemann's reconstruction of the oldest interpretation of the gospel in terms of apocalyptic does not always convince from lack of evidence (for example, it has been pointed out that the Son of man and the parousia are absent from our earliest kerygmatic formula, 1 Cor 15:3–5), that the earliest Christians were "enthusiasts" need not be questioned. It is impossible to ignore this. See, for example, *Sabbatai Svi,* p. 257, for a description of enthusiasm at Aleppo. In Gaza, Hebron, and Safed, very early after Nathan began his preaching, "the people slept in the streets and bazaars because the houses and courtyards could not contain" the multitudes. "No business is transacted and all—boys and old men, young men and virgins, pregnant women and such as have just given birth—are fasting from Sunday to Friday without suffering any harm" (*Sabbatai Svi,* p. 261 n. 176). See further pp. 367, 423–25, 634, 652. The penitence called for by Nathan brought normal business to an end. Compare 1 and 2 Thessalonians. For mass hysteria and ecstasy and prophecy, see p. 417–24, 435–40.

28. The desire to return to Palestine was widespread. Routes to be followed were discussed. There was sale of landed property (ibid., pp. 287, 358, 474, but also pp. 477 n. 20, 637, 647, 652–53). By 1669, according to some, not a single Jew would remain behind "on the impure soil outside Palestine" (p. 652). Nathan of Gaza at one period wanted the Chief Rabbi of Jerusalem to stop the sending of funds to the city, on the grounds that soon, in the messianic time, there would be enough money there (see pp. 364, 435–47).

29. Ibid., 109–10. "The merit of visiting her grave," he wrote to the Jews of Smyrna, "and of placing one's hand on it was equal to a pilgrimage to the Temple of Jerusalem." He initiated the worship of his mother (pp. 613–14).

30. Ibid., pp. 145–46; he stilled the sea (p. 446 n. 209).

31. Ibid., pp. 149, 171, 191, 198; Sabbatai Svi had studied "practical Qabbala" (that is, the process of using holy names and Qabbalistic magical formulas to force the end), and he had learned the magical use of divine names (p. 75). For Nathan and practical Qabbala, see pp. 209–13.

32. See also Morton Smith, *The Secret Gospel: The Discovery and Interpretation of the Secret Gospel according to Mark* (New York: Harper & Row, 1973); *Jesus the Magician* (New York: Harper & Row, 1979); and M. Smith, *Clement*

of Alexandria and a Secret Gospel of Mark (Cambridge, Mass.: Harvard University Press, 1973). On magic in Judaism, E. E. Urbach, *The Sages: Their Concepts and Beliefs* (Jerusalem: Magnes, 1975), beginning p. 97. He recognizes the belief in miracles as a *necessary* aspect of Judaism as of all religions (p. 102) and that "without doubt miracles played a great role in the propagation of Christianity in the ancient world" (p. 115). The sages no less than the masses believed in miracles. The NT reveals how easily the magical can be appropriated by and absorbed into the eschatological. See, for instance, Mark 3:19ff. For discussion see Davies, *Rabbinic Judaism,* p. 363, additional notes to p. 212, and G. Vermès, *Jesus and Jew* (New York: Macmillan Co., 1973) pp. 78–82.

33. See *Sabbatai Svi,* pp. 199–207, on the way in which Nathan of Gaza *found* the Messiah in Sabbatai Svi (also pp. 251–52). The fact that there was no well-defined dominant "image" of the Messiah had its nemesis. There could be many claimants.

34. Ibid., pp. 304, 306, etc.

35. The suffering of Sabbatai Svi was explained in these terms.

36. Ibid., p. 222.

37. Ibid., p. 287.

38. On the occultation of the Messiah, see ibid., p. 314.

39. Ibid., pp. 204, 207.

40. Ibid., pp. 221, 267. This was connected with the emphasis on faith as the peculiar merit of the believer (p. 222). But such an attitude was inevitably challenged. Later in the movement the absence of the signs traditionally associated with the messianic age was emphasized by some rabbis.

41. For example, ibid., pp. 25, 290. The evaluation of Sabbatai Svi by the rabbis depended on their evaluation of Nathan the Prophet (pp. 245–46). The absence of Sabbatai Svi from Jerusalem helped the movement which was, in a sense, not related to him (pp. 252–53). Cf. p. 162, *et passim.*

42. He abolished the Feast of Tammuz in 1665; there are numerous examples of his tampering with the calendar (ibid., p. 237). He visited the Temple as a symbol of its rebuilding; he wanted to ride through Jerusalem on a horse (pp. 241–42). He changed the prayers (p. 277).

43. He allowed the eating of kidney fat (ibid., p. 242); he urged others to break the Law (p. 243). In the earliest stages of his messiahship all this was not accompanied by moral debauchery (pp. 245–46). This was to come later.

44. Ibid., pp. 160–61.

45. The attitude of Sabbatai Svi toward women was extremely complex (p. 403). That he married a prostitute has been taken to indicate his desire to liberate women, to free them from the curse of Eve. The subject cannot be dealt with here. That the liberation of women played a real part on Sabbatianism is clear. Sabbatai Svi distributed kingdoms to women (as to priests and Levites) p. 397.

46. After 1655 Sabbatai Svi regarded himself as no longer under the authority of the Law that he had studied in his youth, nor under rabbinic authority; he was subject to a higher Law, ibid., pp. 163–66.

47. See especially the very important pp. 282–84.

48. It is impossible to document these sentences adequately. All points indicated are dealt with by Scholem himself in an extremely illuminating manner (particularly on pp. 795–800).

49. Thus Nathan of Gaza had to counteract the popular expectations of the masses (ibid., pp. 287–88).

50. Scholem discusses the economic, social, and political causes proposed for the emergence and development of Sabbatianism starting on the first page. The evidence that not only the depressed but the wealthy and the established rabbinic leaders accepted the messiahship of Sabbatai Svi and were involved in his movement is abundant (for example, p. 392). The participation of many rabbis and wealthy men was too marked to be simply another example of the familiar phenomenon that sect leaders tend to come from a higher class than those whom they lead. The best brief treatment known to me of early Christianity as a "sect" exhibiting typical sectarian characteristics is the very illuminating study by R. Scroggs, "The Earliest Christian Communities as a Sectarian Movement," *Christianity, Judaism and Other Greco-Roman Cults: Studies for Morton Smith at Sixty*, SJLA 12 (Leiden: E. J. Brill, 1975), 2: 1–23. Scroggs cites Werner Stark, *The Sociology of Religion, 11: Sectarian Religion* (London: Routledge & Kegan Paul, 1967), p. 46, on the generally superior social status of the leadership of sects. There is much in Sabbatianism both to support Scroggs's thesis and to modify it.

51. See, for example, H. von Campenhausen, "The Christian and the Social Life according to the New Testament," *Tradition and Life in the Early Church* (Philadelphia: Fortress Press, 1968), pp. 141–59. The several recent studies of Gerd Theissen are also important in this regard. The appeal of early Christianity and Sabbatianism to the underprivileged, however, while not the explanation of their growth, was real. For example, a certain wealthy Raphael Joseph in Egypt served as a Maecenas to believers there. "He would provide food to all the people in Gaza that were with Nathan, and everyone that came from afar would leave his moneybag with him and then proceed to Gaza," *Sabbatai Svi*, p. 269. There is some indication that the rabbis feared to oppose Sabbatai Svi because of the masses (pp. 361–63). A bodyguard of the poor followed Sabbatai Svi (pp. 391–92). At Smyrna Sabbatai Svi gave alms very liberally to the poor (p. 384). At that city when public homage was rendered to him as king, he was offered money to be used for charitable purposes and to buy the freedom of Jewish prisoners who had been sentenced to the galleys (p. 412).

52. David Daube drew a distinction between the popular teaching of Jesus and that to his inner following, "Public Report and Private Explanation," *The New Testament and Rabbinic Judaism* (University of London: Athlone Press, 1956), p. 14. Morton Smith has introduced the distinction in the teaching of Jesus himself between that for ordinary Jews and that for the masses and, in addition, between that for both of these groups and for his intimate initiates; see "The Reason for the Persecution of Paul and the Obscurity of Acts," *Studies in Mysticism and Religion Presented to G. G. Scholem* (Jerusalem: Magnes, 1968), pp. 261–68.

53. There was much mass hysteria and ecstasy and megalomania in Sabbatianism; see, for instance, *Sabbatai Svi*, pp. 417–19, 435, 468–70.

54. Ibid., pp. 210–12, 282–84, 390. This explains a problem dealt with by N. Dahl ("The Neglected Factor in New Testament Theology," *Reflection* 73 [1975]): that is, the relative paucity of materials dealing directly with the doctrine of God in the NT.

55. *Sabbatai Svi*, p. 2. This distinguishes early Christianity and Sabbatianism

from other messianic movements, for example, in modern Africa and Asia. These often reveal the twofold structure proposed by Scholem, but are localized. See Bryan Wilson, *The Noble Savages: The Primitive Origins of Charisma and Its Contemporary Survival* (Berkeley and Los Angeles: University of California Press, 1975) 37–92.

56. Scholem emphasises particularly the very wide extension of Sabbatianism, as of Christianity, in space and time, as calling for an explanation other than that required for more localized and evanescent movements (*Sabbatai Svi*, p. 2). In Sabbatianism what provided ecumenicity (a word which we use in its strict sense) was Lurianic Qabbala which (despite the counter influence of the Great Eagle, Maimonides) had developed within it. "Wherever Lurianism came, it produced Messianic tension" (ibid., p. 67). "Lurianic teaching functioned as a means to draw down the Messiah" (ibid., p. 70). To this Nathan of Gaza could appeal in interpreting Sabbatai Svi.

57. The first chapter of *Sabbatai Svi* is especially illuminating for all this.

58. *Sabbatai Svi*, pp. 15–22, esp. p. 20. On p. 42 Scholem writes: "The exile of the 'lower' terrestrial Congregation of Israel in the world of history is thus merely a reflection of the exile of the supernal Israel, that is, the Shekhinah. Israel's state is symbolic of the state of creation as a whole. It is the Jew who holds in his hands the key to the *tiqqûn* of the world, consisting of the progressive separation of good from evil by the performance of the commandments of the Torah. *Tiqqûn* is thus an essentially spiritual activity directed at the inner side of the cosmos. But once it will have achieved its end, then this hidden, spiritual perfection will also become manifest outwardly, since outward reality is always symbolic of inner reality. In exile, spiritual activity and mystical concentration (*qawwānāh*) affect the inner strata of the cosmos only, 'but the [outer] worlds in general are not elevated until the advent of the messiah, when they will all rise by themselves. At present the only exaltation of the worlds is in their inner aspect. . . . In the present period of exile we can raise—even on the Sabbath—the inner side of the worlds only, but not their outside. For if the outer reality were elevated too, then we could behold with our eyes the exaltation of all the worlds on the Sabbath' " (Hayyim Vital, "Sha'ar ha-Tefillah," chap. 6 *Peri 'Es Hayyim:* Dubrovna, 1804, fol. 7c). Once the last trace of holiness is extracted from the *qelippah* so that no divine sparks are left in it, the world of *tiqqûn* will become manifest. This is the meaning of redemption."

59. See, for instance p. 118 (". . . clearly the course of the movement was determined by the public climate more than by the personality or the inner life of the young qabbalist . . .") pp. 207–8, 252, 289–90, and n. 41. Indeed, within Lurianic Qabbala itself with its characteristic eschatological tension what is most surprising "is the feebleness of its image of the Messiah." In the process of *tiqqûn* "the Messiah himself plays a pale and insignificant role. Except for the highly developed and firmly established tradition of the Messiah, perhaps the Qabbalists would have dispensed with him altogether. . . . By transferring to Israel, the historic nation, much of the task formerly considered as the Messiah's, many of his distinctive personal traits, as drawn in Apocalyptic literature were now obliterated" (ibid., p. 52).

60. Scholem writes as follows: "The character of Lurianic symbolism presents

a special problem. The accusation of anthropomorphism directed against the qab-balists is an old one. Their manner of speaking in a material fashion about things spiritual was often held to fall little short of actual blasphemy, yet it merely ex-emplified the essential paradox of all symbolism. Symbols express in human speech that which is properly inexpressible. Hence they are always material and anthropomorphic, even though the mystic may regard them as mere crutches to aid his frail human understanding. The qabbalists, whose mystical thinking strained after expression in symbolic forms, endeavored to evade responsibility for their symbols by the frequent use of qualifying phrases such as 'so to speak,' 'as if,' 'as it were,' and the like. These reservations were supposed to minimize the real significance of the symbols employed. The qabbalists used the most out-rageous material and even physical and sexual imagery but immediately qualified their statements by adding the solemn warning, 'Cursed be the man that makes any graven or molten image,' that is, who attributes reality to symbolic expres-sions. *From their higher theological vantage point the qabbalists might argue that the material interpretation of their symbols was a misunderstanding, yet it was precisely this creative misunderstanding that determined the public significance of qabbalistic symbolism.* He was a bold man indeed who undertook to draw the line between understanding and misunderstanding in such matters. The inescap-able dialectic of symbolism is central to a proper appreciation of the historical and social function of qabbalism, even as it underlies most of the discussions between qabbalists and their opponents.

"Lurianism is mythological in the precise meaning of the term. It tells the story of divine acts and events, and it accounts for the mystery of the world by an inner, mystical process which, taking place within the Godhead, ultimately pro-duced also the 'outer,' material creation. According to the qabbalists everything external is merely a symbol or intimation of an inner reality that actually deter-mines the external reality which we perceive. The main concepts of Lurianism all refer to the mystery of the Godhead, but on each and every level they also point to a corresponding aspect in the manifest cosmos" (*Sabbatai Svi*, pp. 26–27 [italics mine]). One of our most urgent needs is to reexamine apocalyptic sym-bolism. Amos Wilder, in his poetry and elsewhere, has pioneered the way. See now G. B. Caird, *The Language and Imagery of the Bible* (Philadelphia: West-minster Press, 1980).

61. Ibid., pp. 397–403, 426–32, 468. Believers were given royal titles; the names of their future dominions were assigned. The brothers of Sabbatai Svi were to constitute a kind of caliphate (p. 430). Sabbatai believed that a supernatural act was to bring all this about. How unimportant financial matters became appears from Nathan's opposition to the sending of money to Jerusalem, his attack on money changers and on alms from abroad (pp. 365–67). Charitable funds had to be set up (pp. 497–99). The opposition of some wealthy Jews to the movement was probably spurred by its antifinancial and anticommercial aspects. Calcula-tions of profit and loss, when it came to the demand to sell all to go to Palestine, would, of course, often reinforce their orthodoxy and rational inhibitions. Con-nected with this literalism is the widespread and recurring contemporary Christian (millenarian) emphasis outside Sabbatianism and Judaism on the reappearance of the Lost Ten Tribes of Israel (pp. 332–54). And again, although Nathan did not

think of Sabbatai Svi as a warlike messiah, the popular messianism in Sabbatianism counteracted this emphasis (p. 363).

62. See, for instance, ibid., pp. 369, 383, 432, 450, 674–77.

63. Ibid., pp. 384, 386, and esp. 412–17.

64. Especially important in this connection is the much neglected study by B. Reicke, *Diakonie, Festfreude und Zelos* (Uppsala: Lundequistaka, 1951), pp. 242–47. He refers to "materialisierung der Eschatologie" (p. 243) and to "anarchische Einstellung" (p. 244) in early Christianity.

65. See *Sabbatai Svi*, pp. 93–102, esp. 98.

66. On the catastrophic aspect of messianism which is related to its utopian dimension, which in turn is related to apocalyptic, see G. G. Scholem, *The Messianic Idea in Judaism*, pp. 4–12, esp. 7. The whole volume is indispensible for a comprehension of the dynamism of messianism.

67. See my article "Paul and Jewish Christianity According to Cardinal Daniélou," herein, chapter 9. E. Käsemann has illuminated Paul from a different point of view (*New Testament Questions of Today*, p. 132). For him "Paul is the classical witness for a struggle against enthusiasm under the banner of primitive Christian apocalyptic . . ." (n. 24). But he also recognizes that it is only "relics of apocalyptic theology which are to be found everywhere in the Pauline epistles" (p. 131).

68. *Jewish Symbols in the Graeco-Roman World*, 13 vols. (New York: Pantheon, 1953–68). See M. Smith, "The Image of God," *BJRL* 41 (1958): 473–512; and reviews by S. S. Kayser, *RR* 21 (1956): 54–60; A. D. Nock, *Gnomon* 17 (1955): 558–72; 21 (1957): 525–33; C. Roth, *Judaism* 3 (1954): 129–35, 179–82; E. E. Urbach, "The Rabbinical Laws of Idolatry in the Second and Third Centuries in the Light of Archaeological and Historical Facts," *IEJ* 9 (1959): 149–245.

69. W. Bousset, *Die jüdische Apokalyptik: Ihre religionsgeschichtliche Herkunft und ihre Bedeutung für das Neue Testament* (Berlin: Reuther & Reichard, 1903). The relevant passages are translated in W. G. Kümmel, *The New Testament: The History of the Interpretation of Its Problems* (Nashville: Abingdon Press, 1972), pp. 260–62. The discussion of the "History of Religions School of New Testament Interpretation" (pp. 206–324) is particularly relevant in this context.

70. See n. 14 above.

71. *The Dawn of Apocalyptic: The Historical and Sociological Roots of Jewish Apocalyptic*, 2d ed. (Philadelphia: Fortress Press, 1979). This rich work carries further that of F. M. Cross, "New Directions in the Study of Apocalyptic," *Apocalypticism*, JTC 6, ed. R. W. Funk (1969): 157–65. H. H. Rowley and D. S. Russell, among others, had earlier pointed in the same direction. Contrast H. D. Betz in the same volume. For bibliographical detail, see my *Gospel and the Land: Early Christianity and Jewish Territorial Doctrine* (Berkeley and Los Angeles: University of California Press, 1974), p. 156 n. 166.

72. For these distinctions, see R. McL. Wilson, *Gnosis and the New Testament* (Philadelphia: Fortress Press, 1968). pp. 1–30, esp. 17.

73. See S. Sandmel, *The First Christian Century: Certainties and Uncertainties* (New York and London: Oxford University Press, 1969), pp. 63–66.

74. See V. Tcherikover, *Hellenistic Civilization and the Jews* (Philadelphia: Jewish Publication Society of America, 1959).

75. In *Sabbatai Svi* there are references to Gentiles and to the "mission" of exiled Jews in the world, but it is significant that in the most excellent and comprehensive index to the volume there is no separate entry under "Gentiles," nor to the attitude of Sabbatai Svi himself or of the Sabbatian movement to them.

76. See, for instance, J. Jeremias, *Jesus' Promise to the Nations* (London: SCM Press, 1958; Philadelphia: Fortress Press, 1982), pp. 11–19.

77. The relevant documents are: Tobit (200–170 B.C.E., Palestine); *Sibylline Oracles*, Book 3 (second/first century B.C.E., Egypt); *1 Enoch* (mostly from second/first century B.C.E., Palestine [Milik, for example, takes chs. 37–71, The Similitudes as Christian]); *2 Baruch* (end of first century C.E., Palestine), and the *Testaments of the Twelve Patriarchs* (the stages of composition and the date are much disputed; R. H. Charles, 109–107 B.C.E. with additions in first century B.C.E. and later Christian additions; but J. T. Milik and M. de Jonge argue for a first/third century C.E. Christian expansion of two earlier Jewish testaments from Palestine).

Some of the relevant texts are Tob 13:11; 4:6–7; *Pss. Sol.*17:32–38; *Sib. Or.* 3:710–31; 772–76; *1 Enoch* 10:21; 48:4; 50:2–5; 90:30, 33, 35; 91:14; *2 Bar.* 68:5; 72:4–6; and, in the *Testaments of the Twelve Patriarchs, T. Sim.* 7:2; *T. Levi* 2:11; 4:4; 5:7; 8:14; 18:9; *T. Judah* 22:2; 24:6; *T. Zeb.* 9:8; *T. Dan* 6:7; *T. Naph.* 8:3–4; *T. Asher* 7:3; *T. Jos.* 19:11; and *T. Benj.* 3::8; 9:2, 4; 10:5, 10; 11:2–3.

Some of the leading ideas are that some or all of the Gentiles will be saved, and that the Gentiles will glorify Jerusalem. On this see P. Volz, *Die Eschatologie der jüdischen Gemeinde im neutestamentlichen Zeitalter* (Tübingen: J. C. B. Mohr [Paul Siebeck], 1934), pp. 356–59; and D. S. Russell, *The Method and Message of Jewish Apocalyptic* (Philadelphia: Westminster Press, 1964), pp. 298–303.

78. Some of the relevant texts are: Gen 12:3; 17:3–8; 1 Kings 8:41–43; Ps 47:9; 67; 68; 72:17; 86:9; 87; 99:9; 113; 117; 148:11–12; Isa 2:1–3; 19:24–25; 25:6–9; 42:1–4, 7; 44:1–5; 45:22–25; 49:9, 12–20; 51:4–5; 53:10; 55:5; 56:7; 60:1–11; 61:1; 66:18–21; Jer 4:2; Dan 2:35; Jonah; Mic 4:1–5; 7:12; Zeph 3:9; Zech 2:11; 8:13, 20–23; 9:9–10; 14:16.

For notes 77 and 78 see further R. H. Charles, *APOT*; M.-J. Lagrange, *Le judaïsme avant Jésus-Christ* (Paris: Gabalda, 1931); A. Causse, "Le mythe de la nouvelle Jérusalem du Déutero-Esaïe a la IIIe Sibylle," *RHPR* 18 (1938): 377–414; and E. J. Hamlin, "Nations," *IDB* 3: 515–23. (I am grateful to Mr. Joseph Trafton for help in the garnering of these references.)

79. Another alternative came to be Christianity.

80. In *The Cambridge History of Judaism*, ed. W. D. Davies and L. Finkelstein (forthcoming).

81. *Théologie du judéo-christianisme: Histoire des doctrines chrétiennes avant Nicée* (Paris: Desclée, 1958), 1: 1: "La théologie chrétienne utilisera à partir des Apologistes les instruments intellectuels de la philosophie grecque. Mais auparavant il-y-a eu une première théologie de structure sémitique."

82. *Gnosis and the New Testament* (Philadelphia: Fortress Press, 1968), p. 16.

83. In a lecture at the AAR/SBL Annual Meeting, Chicago, 1975.

84. See M. Stern, "The Jewish Diaspora," *The Jewish People in the First Century: Historical Geography, Political History, Social, Cultural and Religious Life and Institutions*, Compendia rerum iudaicarum ad Novum Testamentum, 1 (Philadelphia: Fortress Press, 1974), pp. 117–83. He calls proselytism a "major source of [Jewish] population increase."

85. Here we have only asked the question whether *Judaism* provided a unified ideological structure for the interpretation of Jesus. The answer was largely negative. M. Smith and K. Stendahl have reminded me that in the Greco-Roman world of the first century there were very numerous religious categories into which Jesus could be placed to ensure him a spiritual significance in the eyes of Gentiles, for example, those of "the divine man," "the magician," "the mystagogue." J. S. Whale has further recalled to me that A. Toynbee emphasized parallels with the figure of Jesus in the Hellenistic world at length (*A Study of History* [London: Oxford University Press, 1939], 6: 376–539) in a highly detailed discussion of the astonishing correspondence between the gospel story and stories of certain Hellenic saviors. See esp. pp. 418 onward. Here such categories and parallels are not strictly our concern, which it was with the nature of Jewish messianism, as understood by Scholem, and as it possibly illuminates early Christianity. One thing, however, we may propose. The diversity of Hellenistically derived categories (which were in varying degrees used to interpret Jesus and which doubtless helped the spread of early Christianity in countless ways) does not explain the dynamism of the new movement. The very religious diversity of the Greco-Roman world makes it, in fact, all the more difficult to understand that persistent vitality. S. Sandmel (*The First Christian Century in Judaism and Christianity*, p. 164) finds such parallels with Hellenistic mysteries as are indicated finally unimportant; he emphasizes the content of the Christian kerygma as that which "enabled Christianity to triumph." The dividing fertility of available Hellenistic categories helps to illuminate the struggle which Christianity had to face to reach "orthodoxy" (see especially W. Bauer, *Orthodoxy and Heresy in Earliest Christianity* [Philadelphia: Fortress Press, 1971]), but it does not finally explain the reality of its life. The problem raised is a real one, but is outside the scope of this essay, even though Judaism also was not exempt from its magicians, and possibly its divine men and mystagogues. See M. Smith, "Prolegomena to a Discussion of Aretalogies, Divine Men, the Gospels and Jesus," *JBL* 90 (1971): 181–84; P. J. Achtemeier, "Gospel Miracle and the Divine Man," *Int* 26 (1972): 174–97; and now C. H. Talbert, "The Concept of Immortals in Mediterranean Antiquity," *JBL* 94 (1975): 419–36. However, C. R. Holladay, *Theios Anēr in Hellenistic Judaism: A Critique of the Use of This Category in New Testament Christology* (Missoula, Mont.: Scholars Press, 1979), induces great caution concerning the "divine man."

86. See J. Jeremias, *Jesus' Promise to the Nations*.

87. For a brief statement, see my *Invitation to the New Testament* (New York: Doubleday & Co., 1966), pp. 260–62.

88. In another context, I should have sought to deal with this question in more detail, but that of the Schweitzer centennial demanded a concentration on the roles of Sabbatai Svi and Jesus in the respective movements. The difference between Sabbatianism and early Christianity on the Gentile question can be illustrated by a significant detail. Sabbatai Svi was not a teacher; his attempts at

theology were stumbling (*Sabbatai Svi*, p. 207). But he did claim one peculiar doctrine of his own. Scholem deals with it as "the mystery of the Godhead" as understood by Sabbatai Svi. The main concepts of Lurianism, in fact, all refer to "the mystery of the Godhead." Qabbalists were aware of their very material way of expressing spiritual truth and were disturbed by this (ibid., p. 27). It was part of their tradition that four persons—Abraham, Hezekiah, Job, and Messiah— were capable of arriving at the knowledge of God by themselves. It would be expected that Sabbatai Svi as Messiah would know the Godhead in a special way. He himself claimed that he attained his special doctrine of the mystery of the Godhead because he prayed with great concentration (*qawwānāh*) and always meditated on the plain meaning of his words like one praying before his king (ibid., p. 115); the doctrine developed over the years (ibid., pp. 119, 142–46). But what was the "mystery" which he knew? It developed in a gnostic direction. Scholem writes of the matter as follows: "The Hidden Mystery of the Godhead was the realization that the God, who revealed Himself to Israel in His Torah, was not the inaccessible and utterly transcendent *En-Sof*, but that particular aspect of His power which is manifest in *Tif'ereth*. The first formulations of the 'mystery' which were quoted later by Sabbatai's disciples in Smyrna, do not say very much more than this; and as this symbolism was a commonplace among qabbalists, one may rightly wonder what Sabbatai's original contribution to it was. . . . The fact that the later formulations are much more profound suggests that Cardozo's assumption may be correct and that Sabbatai's thought developed as time went on. But we must not exclude the possibility that there was a more profound layer in his teaching from the very beginning.

"This, at least, is certain: Those who received the Mystery of the Godhead from Sabbatai in later years heard it with a shift of accent which, however slight, made all the difference. Sabbatai revealed to them that 'the Tetragrammaton is our God and that He is superior to the whole emanation; He is also signified by the letter W of the Tetragrammaton YHWH and is called the husband of the Shekinah' (*Rasa᾽ de-Razin*, MS. Jewish Theological Seminary of America, Deinard 153, fol. 3a). Similar extant formulations of the 'Mystery' no doubt express Sabbatai's thinking as it had crystallized beginning in 1666. But again it is not impossible that even in his first period he had already arrived at the idea that it was not the *sefirah* (that is, the emanation) itself that was called the 'God of Israel' but something superior to the emanation that merely manifested and clothed itself in the particular *sefirah* from which it borrowed its names and symbols.

"The decisive feature of this conception of the 'Mystery' is the distinction between the *En-Sof*, or unmanifested Root of Roots, and the divine Self called YHWH, which is *above* the sefirotic emanations, though it manifests itself *in* one of them. The latent implication of this paradox came to light only in later years and is not explicitly referred to in the testimonies regarding the early period. It amounts to transferring the supervision of providence from the hidden substance (*En-Sof* or whatever we choose to call it) to the 'God of Israel.' We cannot decide, in the light of our present knowledge, whether at this early stage Sabbatai intended this doctrine, to which there is no analogy in traditional Jewish thought—including that of the qabbalists—but which became notorious in the Sabbatian movement a generation or two later. What we know for certain is that Sabbatai's mystical thinking developed in a definitely gnostic direction. The symbol YHWH no longer signified one *sefirah* among others, but a substance that derives from the highest and utterly hidden Root, and that, together with the Shekhinah, remains above the whole structure of *sefiroth*. There is good reason for dating this development to a period when Sabbatai had come into contact with Lurianic qabbalism. He could have found support for its conception that there were substances distinct from *En-Sof* and yet above the *sefiroth* and attributes in the Lurianic doctrine of *parssufim*, or 'configurations,' which similarly places an entity called the 'most primordial man of all,' or simply the 'Primordial Man' (*Adam Qadmon*), above the world of emanation (of *sefiroth*). Although Sabbatai never accepted the propositions of Lurianism as they are formulated in the qabbalistic writings of the school, it is quite possible that they stimulated him to a more novel and daring formulation of his own Mystery of the Godhead'' (ibid., pp. 120–22). This lengthy quotation reveals the world of speculation or myth within which Sabbatai Svi moved. Contrast with the mystery with which he was concerned that which occupied Paul and the Ephesian epistle: that concerning Israel and the Gentiles. There are hints of mysteries not shared by all in the NT, but generally there is a simplicity about its teaching (see, for example, Matt 11:25–30) which is far removed from the involved speculation of Sabbatianism and of Sabbatai Svi himself (see BAG, 532a). Particularly for Paul and his circles it was the Jewish-Gentile question which set the terms for discussing the mystery of God. And Paul found the significance of the emergence of Jesus as Messiah particularly in the grace that he had shown to sinners, including Gentiles. Paul's activity modified the sequence of events as anticipated in Jewish apocalyptic. Gentiles symbolically entered Jerusalem *before* Israel had all been saved. But, for our purpose here, this is less important than to recognize the apocalyptic framework presupposed by Paul and others. This did enable early Christianity to interpret Jesus as the Savior of Gentiles as well as of Jews.

89. See, for example, *Sabbatai Svi*, pp. 750, 760–67, esp. 763. Scholem writes: ''Penitential exercises and extreme mortifications having been a characteristic feature of the movement, the rabbis of Venice demanded their cessation. The believers, on the other hand, wished to continue them. The Venetian rabbis also wrote to all the communities, commanding them to destroy all documents relating to the movement of 1666 and to obliterate all testimony to this shameful episode. This attempt at censorship is mentioned by R. Samual Aboab in a responsum written about eight years after the event. Aboab states that after the apostasy all the congregations in the Holy Land, Turkey, Germany, Holland, Poland, and Russia admitted that opponents of the movement had been right, and recognizing their error they ''burned all the records and writings in which his name was mentioned, in order that it should not be remembered. . . . And that which we heard from the far-away cities we beheld ourselves in the cities of Italy. . . . They are repented [of their belief in Sabbatai] . . . and confessed, 'Woe unto us, for we have sinned.' Also the rabbis of Constantinople . . . sent orders to the communities near and far . . . [to do away] with everything that had been written about that deceitful affair, . . . that it should be forgotten and mentioned no more'' (*Debar Shemu'el*, fol. 97a).

The large-scale suppression of records and documents relating to the movement was no doubt successful, much to the detriment of historical research.

90. Particularly illuminating is *The Messianic Idea*, pp. 6, 78–82. Scholem describes the apostasy as a "final step of holy sinfulness, in fact, its apotheosis," in the chapter "Redemption Through Sin."

91. Even Nathan of Gaza did not believe that he himself was free from the law; there was a qualitative difference between himself and Sabbatai Svi. Nathan remained a pious, observant Jew. He interpreted the actions of the Messiah but did not imitate them (see *Sabbatai Svi*, p. 229). There developed two opposing factions in Sabbatianism, one moderate and piously inclined and the other radical, antinomian, and ultimately nihilistic. The former did not consider that it had to imitate Sabbatai Svi. See Scholem, *The Messianic Idea*, pp. 100–108.

92. Ibid., p. 78.

93. See, for example, *Sabbatai Svi*, pp. 252, 254, 290, 371.

94. *The Messianic Idea*, p. 62.

95. See most recently H. Conzelmann, "Das Selbstbewusstsein Jesu," *Theologie als Schriftauslegung: Aufsätze zum Neuen Testament* (Munich: Kaiser, 1974), pp. 30–41.

96. "The Essence of Christianity," *RelS* 7 (1971): 298. Drawing upon D. Knowles, Sykes understands character as "the final and most precious thing in a man, his goodness of will, achieved by conscious and tenacious choice" (*The Historian and Character* [Cambridge: At the University Press, 1963], p. 11). Precisely this kind of steeled will was absent in Sabbatai Svi. He was incapable of consistency in his conduct, probably for psychological reasons. Outside his periods of "illumination," as they were called, he was a pious, observing Jew. This is stressed by Scholem (*The Messianic Idea and Sabbatai Svi*, p. 11).

97. See Y. Yadin, "The Temple Scroll," *New Directions in Biblical Archaeology*, ed. D. N. Freedman and J. C. Greenfield (Garden City: Doubleday & Co., 1969) 139–48, esp. 141.

98. See my *The Setting of the Sermon on the Mount* (Cambridge: At the University Press, 1964), pp. 109–90.

99. See my chapter on "The Moral Teaching of the Early Church," herein, chapter 15. It is not only the motif of the "imitation of Christ" that points to this.

100. See O. Cullmann, "Paradosis et Kyrios: Le problème de la tradition dans le paulinisme," *RHPR* 17 (1937): 424. The same oscillation between moral earnestness and immorality emerges in certain Gnostic sects as among the Sabbatians; see Wilson, *Gnosis and the New Testament*, p. 11.

101. See my *Rabbinic Judaism*, 2d ed. (London: SPCK, 1958), p. 147. The theme is developed by J. A. Sanders, "Torah and Christ," *Int* 29 (1975): 372–90.

102. See *Sabbatai Svi*, pp. 8, 15, 52–77. Apocalyptic elements emerged in Sabbatianism. Scholem connects them especially with the masses. He offers as one of the reasons for the success of the message of Nathan of Gaza that it "contained a curious combination of traditional popular apocalyptic and of hints at its reinterpretation in the light of Lurianic qabbalism" (ibid., p. 465). He holds that "it has been one of the strangest errors of modern *Wissenschaft des Judentums* to deny the continuity of Jewish apocalypticism" (ibid., p. 9).

103. C. K. Barrett proposes that the last decade of the first century, with few exceptions, saw "the end of Jewish apocalyptic, *for this expression of Jewish faith had fulfilled its purposes*" (the words that I here italicize could be qualified

by some such phrase as "for the time being, perhaps"). That Jewish apocalyptic did not come to an end at the date suggested is now beyond dispute, and not only "with few exceptions." See *The Gospel of John and Judaism* (Philadelphia: Fortress Press, 1975), p. 58.

104. It is not easy to grasp Schweitzer's meaning in his dismissal of the historical Jesus and the quest for him. In his second edition of *The Quest of the Historical Jesus*, which has not been translated into English, his words are shattering. In the translation of the relevant portion offered by Henry Clark (*The Ethical Mysticism of Albert Schweitzer* [Boston: Beacon Press, 1962], p. 198), Schweitzer wrote that moderns "continually tried to make of this 'fanatic' a contemporary man and a theologian. . . ." It is possible that Schweitzer did not see Jesus as a "fanatic," but that smug scholars saw him as such and tried to "tame" him to their small hearts. The precise examination of Schweitzer's thought is not possible here. For a brief presentation, see D. L. Dungan, "Reconsidering Albert Schweitzer," *The Christian Century* (October 8, 1975): 874.

105. This phrase, borrowed from N. Cohn, *The Pursuit of the Millenium* (London: Secker & Warburg, 1957), I owe to H. Anderson, who allowed me to see an unpublished lecture on "A Future for Apocalyptic?" now published in *Biblical Studies: Essays in Honor of William Barclay*, ed. J. R. McKay and J. F. Miller (Philadelphia: Westminster Press, 1976), pp. 56–71. Anderson recognizes that apocalyptic has a future because "the untamed and, perhaps, untameable" element of man's spirit will always demand and issue in fantasy. He also allows that apocalyptic has served to overcome the frequent isolation of Christian theology from cosmology. But he too has seen an aspect of its ugly face. To him it is not the fruit of a living hope, but of a world-weariness and pessimism which issues in an ultimately apathetic waiting for the divine intervention rather than in any active transformation of present ills. In this he has much to support him in the sources. His distrust of apocalyptic leads him to urge the simple use of the term "eschatology" to express the hope of Jesus. His lecture reinforces the need for the kind of terminological exactitude which we desiderate. On this, see also J. Carmignac, "Les dangers de l'eschatologie," *NTS* 17 (1970–71): 365–90, who even pleads for the dropping of the term "eschatology." But, as Anderson notes, "we cannot solve a problem by getting rid of the words associated with it." We can only attempt to use them precisely.

106. See "The Rhetoric of Ancient and Modern Apocalyptic," *Int* 25 (1971): 436–53.

107. *The Rediscovery of Apocalyptic*, pp. 25–28, 405.

108. This makes understandable the reluctance of many Christian scholars to classify Jesus among the apocalypticists. This reluctance antedates the work of Schweitzer, but the latter provoked the reaction of C. H. Dodd who, although he does not state this and seldom if ever refers to Schweitzer's work, had the latter in mind. Cf. W. G. Kümmel, *The New Testament: The History of the Investigation of Its Problems* (Nashville: Abingdon Press, 1972), p. 260; K. Koch, "The Agonised Attempts to Save Jesus from Apocalyptic: Continental New Testament Scholarship," *Rediscovery of Apocalyptic*, pp. 57–97. History makes one suspicious of what Stendahl has called "the eschatological itch." But it may be well to recall also that "if hopes were dupes" (and they have often been such in messianism), yet fears may be liars."

109. See *The Messianic Idea*, passim. T. W. Manson's work ("Some Reflections on Apocalyptic," *Aux sources de la tradition chrétienne: Mélanges offerts à M. Maurice Goguel* [Neuchâtel: Delachaux et Niestlé, 1950], pp. 139-45) still deserve pondering. He finds that "apocalyptic is an attempt to rationalize and systematize the predictive side of Prophecy as one side of the providential ordering of the Universe. The other side of the systematizing process of the scribal treatment of the Law leads to the codification of the Mishnah" (p. 142). He expresses no condemnation of either development, but rather implies that apocalyptic supplied evidence for the intensity with which the belief in providence was held in Judaism. He refers especially to Josephus's treatment of Daniel (*Ant.* 10.11.7 §266-81). (One is reminded here of the position of Santayana referred to by Amos N. Wilder, *Modern Poetry and the Christian Tradition* [New York: Charles Scribner's Sons, 1952], p. 3 n. 1) that "poetry and religion are identical in essence, though they relate themselves differently to practical life: *poetry by a dramatic presentation of values and religion by precepts and codes* [italics mine].) Is "apocalyptic" the poetry of religion? If so, it is romantic poetry, accompanied by the dangers of the romantic. These are well expressed by Wallace Fowlie, in dealing with Rimbaud (*The Age of Surrealism* [Bloomington: Indiana University Press, 1972]). Pointing to classicism as involving order, control, considered choice, synthesis, rules, Fowlie refers to the romantics and to romanticism as always associated with revolution and liberation (p. 14). He emphasizes the perilous aspect of romanticism in Rimbaud (p. 58), "It exacts so much destruction, of order and conventionality, of familiar patterns, and rules which had seemed indispensable disciplines, that it makes the poet a despiser of order, an anarchist in temperament and technique. . . . I call this way perilous, because it opens the gates to all kinds of charlatans, of undisciplined writers, of false visionaries." It is easy to connect apocalyptic with this kind of romanticism, but the connection cannot be examined here. D. Daube urges again that apocalyptists despite their violent writings are quietists and that this should modify the criticisms I express above. See his *Civil Disobedience in Antiquity* (Edinburgh: Edinburgh University Press, 1972), pp. 85-86. J. C. Beker does not share the unease about "apocalyptic" expressed here; see his highly stimulating and provocative work, *Paul the Apostle* (Philadelphia: Fortress Press, 1980). Before reading this I had attempted to come to terms with "apocalyptic" in addressing students. See *The Duke Divinity School Bulletin,* Fall 1981, Vol. 46, No. 1, on "For such a time as this," pp. 13-26.

THE MORAL TEACHING OF THE EARLY CHURCH

1. The moral teaching of the NT in recent years has not been given the attention it deserves: "theological" or "kerygmatic" interests have led to its neglect. See J. M. Gustafson, "Christian Ethics" in *Religion,* ed. Paul Ramsey (Englewood Cliffs, N.J.: Prentice-Hall, 1965), p. 337f.; and my *Setting of the Sermon on the Mount* (Cambridge: At the University Press, 1966), p. 436ff. (henceforth *Setting*). V. P. Furnish, *Theology and Ethics in Paul* (Nashville: Abingdon Press, 1968), by far the most stimulating volume in this field in recent years, on p. 7 quotes Thomas C. Oden, who suggests that "the simple task of honest and clear exegesis may be the undiscovered beginning point for contemporary Protestant ethics";

see Oden, *Radical Obedience: The Ethics of Rudolf Bultmann* (Philadelphia: Westminster Press, 1964), pp. 18, 21. For the works which have been found most useful, apart, of course, from the standard works on NT theology and ethics, see W. D. Davies, "Ethics in the New Testament," *IDB* E–J: 167–76. Furnish supplies a most helpful bibliography, pp. 280–94.

   2. Gal 4:4.

   3. Isa 10:22; 35:4; 43:3; 45:17–22; 60:16; 1 Cor 10:11. See J. Hempel, "Eschatology of the Old Testament," *IDB* E–J: 153ff. For apocalyptic and ethics, see H. H. Rowley, *The Revelance of Apocalyptic* (London: Lutterworth Press, 1944); D. S. Russell, *The Method and Message of Jewish Apocalyptic, 200 B.C.–A.D. 100* (Philadelphia: Westminster Press, 1964).

   4. Matt 4:4, 6–7; 5:17–18; Mark 12:28–37; etc.

   5. On this see Peter Richardson, *Israel in the Apostolic Church,* SNTSMS 10 (Cambridge: At the University Press, 1969). According to him, the designation of the church as "the true Israel" does not occur until the mid–second century in the works of Justin Martyr. The phrase "the New Israel" used of the church is not found in the NT.

   6. On this see the following: "Moïse, L'Homme de L'Alliance," *Cahiers Sioniens: Revue Trimestrielle 8e année,* nos. 2–3–4 (Paris, 1954), especially §3 by Albert Déscamps, "Moïse dans les Evangeles et dans la tradition Apostolique," pp. 171–80, and Paul Démann, "Moïse dans la Pensée de Saint Paul," pp. 189–241; Harold Sahlin, "The New Exodus of Salvation According to St. Paul," in *The Root of the Vine,* ed. Anton Fridrichsen (London: Dacre Press, 1953), pp. 81ff.; my *Setting,* pp. 25–93; H. M. Teeple, *The Mosaic Eschatological Prophet* (Philadelphia: SBL, 1957); and for the Fourth Gospel, R. H. Smith, "Exodus Typology in the Fourth Gospel," *JBL* 81 (1962): 329–42; J. L. Martyn, *History and Theology in the Fourth Gospel* (New York: Harper & Row, 1968), pp. 88, 91ff.; T. F. Glasson, *Moses in the Fourth Gospel* (London: SCM Press, 1963); W. A. Meeks, *The Prophet-King: Moses Traditions and the Johannine Christology,* NovTSup 14 (Leiden: E. J. Brill, 1967); H. J. Schoeps, *Theologie und Geschichte des Judenchristentums* (Tübingen, 1949); David Daube, *The Exodus Pattern in the Bible* (London: Faber & Faber, 1963); Joachim Jeremias, "Μωυσῆς," *TDNT* 4: 848–74. On the "wilderness" motif, see Ulrich W. Mauser, *Christ in the Wilderness: The Wilderness Theme in the Second Gospel and its Basis in the Biblical Tradition* (Naperville, Ill.: Alec R. Allenson; London: SCM Press, 1963); contrast Ernest Edwin Best, *The Temptation and the Passion* (Cambridge: At the University Press, 1965), pp. 25ff. But see also Jacques Dupont, "L'arrière-fond biblique du récit des tentations de Jésus," *NTS* 3 (1956–57): 287–304; G. H. P. Thompson, "Called-Proved-Obedient: A Study in the Baptism and Temptation Narratives of Matthew and Luke," *JTS* 11 (1960): 1–12. On "Law" in Paul, see also the suggestive essay by W. R. Schoedel, "Pauline Thought: Some Basic Issues," in *Transitions in Biblical Scholarship,* ed. J. C. Rylaarsdam (Chicago: University of Chicago Press, 1968), pp. 263ff.

   7. See W. C. Van Unnik, "La conception paulinienne de la nouvelle alliance," in *Litterature et Theologie Pauliniennes, RechBib* 5 (Bruges, 1960), pp. 109–26, 224f.; see also his Ἡ καινὴ Διαθήκη: A Problem in the Early History of the Canon," in *Studia Patristica* 4; and in F. L. Cross, ed., *Texte und Untersuchungen*

zur Geschichte der altchristlichen Literatur, vol. 79 (Berlin, 1961). He notes the neglect of this theme in Pauline studies. Emphasis on the notion of the New Covenant was so strong in early Christianity that both Joseph Bonsirven, *Le Judaïsme Palestinien* (Paris, 1934–35), 1: 79f., and H. J. Schoeps, *op. cit.,* p. 90, claim that it led to a neglect or muting of that theme in rabbinic Judaism. Compare also Gottfried Quell, "Διαθήκη," *TDNT* 2: 104–35. See also Roy A. Harrisville, *The Concept of Newness in the New Testament* (Minneapolis: Augsburg Publishing House, 1960), pp. 46ff. For the covenant in Judaism see the exhaustive study by Annie Jaubert, *La Notion d'Alliance dans le Judaïsme aux abords de l'ère Chrétienne* (Paris, 1963). On the presence of law in the early church as in the OT, see Gerhard Von Rad, *Old Testament Theology,* trans. D. M. G. Stalker (New York: Harper & Row; London: Oliver & Boyd, 1962), 2: 391ff. "The saving event whereby Israel became Yahweh's is indissolubly bound up with the obligation to obey certain norms which clearly mark out the chosen people's sphere, particularly at its circumference. The same thing, however, occurs in the early Christian community. From the very beginning it too was conscious of being bound to certain legal norms and it put them into practice unreservedly. . . ." See 1 Cor 5:5; 16:22; cf. Acts 8:20; 2 Tim 2:19. Important are Günther Bornkamm, "Das Anathema in der urchristliche Abendmahls Theologie" in *Das Ende des Gesetzes: Paulus Studien* (Munich, 1952), pp. 123ff.; E. Käsemann, "Satze Heiligen Rechts in Neuen Testament," *NTS* 1 (1955): 248ff. On the difficulty which Protestants have in doing justice to the Mosaic element in the NT, see the brilliant work of F. J. Leenhardt, *Two Biblical Faiths: Protestant and Catholic,* trans. Harold Knight (Philadelphia: Westminster Press, 1964), pp. 42f. "Protestants have the greatest difficulty in not underestimating the value of the Mosaic tradition in the corpus of revelation . . . the Pauline polemic against the threat of Judaism and Judaic Christianity often remains, in the mentality of Protestant readers of the apostle, the sole key to the understanding of the Gospel. What is argued by St. Paul against the Judaic and Judaizing interpretation of the Law is applied by them in the most massive way to the whole structure of the Mosaic faith."

8. See Davies, *Setting.*

9. Mark 1:27ff. The emphasis on "teaching" in Mark emerges from R. Morgenthaler, *Statistik des neutestamentlichen Wortschatzes* (Zurich, 1959); his data are given in p. 97 n. 1 of *Setting.* See Eduard Schweizer, "Anmerkungen zur Theologie des Markus" in *Neotestamentica et Patristica, Freundesgabe Oscar Cullmann* (Leiden: E. J. Brill, 1962), pp. 37f. See also R. T. France, "Mark and the Teaching of Jesus," in *Gospel Perspectives: Studies of History and Tradition in the Four Gospels,* ed. R. T. France and David Wenham (Sheffield: JSOT Press, 1980), pp. 101–36.

10. John 13:34; the context of this new commandment within the last supper, which at least has Passover undertones, is important.

11. See my article "Torah and Dogma," *HTR* 61 (1968): 700ff., reprinted in *The Gospel and the Land: Early Christianity and Jewish Territorial Doctrine* (Berkeley and Los Angeles: University of California Press, 1974), pp. 390–404.

12. One of the most illuminating developments in OT studies has been the rehabilitation of the law. Through the work of Alt, Von Rad, Noth, Buber, Zim-

merli, Clements, and others, the influence of the covenant tradition, with its law, on the prophets has become clear. And just as the prophets have been connected with the law that preceded them, so Finkelstein in a brilliant study (*New Light on the Prophets* [London: Vallentine, Mitchell, 1969]) has connected them with the law that followed them in Judaism. The old antithesis of law and prophet has been challenged. The prophets are emerging as "teachers." This has an important bearing on our understanding of Jesus. To place him among the prophets is not to displace him from the role of teacher. On the above, see Albrecht Alt, *Die Ursprünge des Israelitischen Rechts* (Leipzig, 1934); Gerhard Von Rad, *Das Formgeschichtliche Problem des Hexateuch* (Stuttgart, 1938), reprinted in *Gesammelte Studien zum A. T.* (Munich, 1958), pp. 9–86, and his *Old Testament Theology* (2 vols.); Martin Noth, *Die Gesetze im Pentateuch* (Munich, 1958), pp. 9–141. Walther Zimmerli in a series of lectures *The Law and the Prophets: A Study of the Meaning of the Old Testament* (Oxford: Basil Blackwell & Mott, 1965) gives a fascinating account of the theme in scholarship; see also R. E. Clements, *Prophecy and Covenant* (Naperville, Ill.: Alec R. Allenson; London: SCM Press, 1965). On the prophets in Judaism, see my article, "Reflections on Tradition: The 'Abot Revisited," herein, chapter 2. Martin Buber in his work *The Prophetic Faith* (New York: Harper & Row, 1960), pp. 24ff., puts great emphasis on the influence of the Sinai tradition on the prophets.

13. This essay was completed before V. P. Furnish's work *Theology and Ethics in Paul* (Nashville: Abingdon Press, 1968) reached me. On p. 114, he writes: "In the discussion of Paul's preaching which follows, the traditional 'chronological-dogmatic' approach has been abandoned altogether. Instead, it is suggested at least as a working hypothesis that the heuristic key to Pauline theology as a whole [and therefore to Pauline ethics (my addition)], the point in which his major themes are rooted and to which they are ultimately oriented, is the apostle's eschatological perspective. Eschatology, therefore, is properly the *first,* not the last, section in an exposition of Paul's theology." Furnish refers in support of his position to H. D. Wendland, "Ethik und Eschatologie in der Theologie des Paulus," *NKZ* 10 (1930): 757ff., 793ff.; and Henry M. Shires, *The Eschatology of Paul in the Light of Modern Scholarship* (Philadelphia: Westminster Press, 1966). It will be noticed that I, too, have begun to discuss the moral teaching of the NT with its eschatology, and particularly with an aspect of that eschatology— that of the new Exodus, a motif to which Furnish pays little attention. So far the emphasis of Furnish is to be accepted. But I immediately went on to assert that the central fact in the moral teaching of the NT is the person of Jesus Christ. This means that even the eschatology of the NT and, therefore, its ethic, is subordinate to its Christology. Here I find myself in much sympathy with the position urged by Joseph A. Fitzmyer in a review of his work, published in *PSTJ* (spring 1969): 113ff. which Dr. Furnish himself kindly sent me. Fitzmyer writes: "To my way of thinking, such labels as 'the heuristic key to Pauline theology' or 'the fundamental perspective (Furnish, *Theology and Ethics*, p. 214)' should be applied to what Paul himself says: 'we proclaim a Christ who has been crucified' (see 1 Cor 1:21–25; cf. Rom 1:16; 2 Cor 4:4). In other words, the starting point is the preaching of the Christ event, a redemptive christology" (p. 114b). Such an emphasis on the centrality of Christ himself is not new; and it is more likely that his

person, rather than any perspective, should govern our understanding of NT theology and ethics. Furnish does allow the importance of the christological motif in the Pauline ethic (p. 216), but not, in our view, its primacy. This has results in the understanding of that ethic as it is related to Jesus' own teaching.

14. See Alan Cole, *The New Temple* (London, 1950); R. J. McKelvey, *The New Temple: The Church in the New Testament* (Oxford: At the Clarendon Press, 1969), with excellent bibliographies. See John 1:14; 2:21f.; 4:21ff.; 7:37–38; 10:16; 11:52; etc. See especially John C. Meagher, "John 1:14 and the New Temple," *JBL* 88 (1969): 57. For him the community is the locus of the Word, that is, the new Temple, in John 1:14; contrast McKelvey, pp. 60ff.; 2 Cor 6:14—7:1; 1 Cor 3:16–17; Eph 2:19–22; 1 Pet 2:4–10; Heb 12:22–24 and passim; and Revelation, passim. See also Bertil Gärtner, *The Temple and the Community in Qumran and the New Testament* (Cambridge: At the University Press, 1965).

15. Gal 4:25, 26; Heb 12:22; Rev 3:12; 21:10. Possibly also Matt 5:14.

16. Heb 4:9.

17. See *Rabbinic Judaism*. Oscar Cullmann, "Paradosis et Kyrios: Le problème de la tradition dans le paulisme," *Revue d'histoire et de philosophie religieuses* (1950), 1: 12ff.; for the "new torah" in later Judaism, see M. Simon, *Verus Israel* (Paris: Boccard, 1948), pp. 100ff. The best critique of the position advocated in *Rabbinic Judaism* is by P. Démann, "Moïse et la Loi dans la pensée de Saint Paul," *Cahiers Sioniens* (1954): 239ff. It should be recalled that some have found ideas connected with the Torah applied to Christ in the prologue of the Fourth Gospel also—see, for example, C. H. Dodd, *The Interpretation of the Fourth Gospel* (Cambridge: At the University Press, 1953), pp. 270ff.

18. Apart from some such assumption the preservation of the tradition about the works and deeds of Jesus in the Gospels is difficult to understand. Even granted that much of that tradition is a creation of the primitive community, its attachment to the figure of Jesus is itself insignificant. Cf. Günther Bornkamm, *Jesus of Nazareth,* trans. Irene McLuskey, Fraser McLuskey, and James M. Robinson from 3d. ed. (German) (New York: Harper & Row, 1960).

19. To connect the resurrection with morality is not usual. But this is implicit in 1 Cor 15:7ff. It is significant that in 1 Cor 15:5 the Risen Lord is said to have appeared first to Cephas who had betrayed Jesus three times, and then to the twelve who had all forsaken him and fled. We must assume that Paul knew the tradition about the betrayals. In the Fourth Gospel Jesus first appears to Mary Magdalene whose sins were well known. It is no accident that in the Sermon on the Mount, the Beatitudes, which are the expression of God's grace, precede the statement of the demands of Jesus, which are thus deliberately set in a context of grace.

20. On this see further Davies, "Ethics in the New Testament," *IDB*, E–J: 168; John Knox, *The Jesus in the Teaching of the Church* (Nashville: Abingdon Press, 1961), pp. 73ff.

21. On all this see Davies, *Rabbinic Judaism,* pp. 215ff. and references to literature there given. In the Fourth Gospel the Spirit, which is "holy," is to teach and to recall what Jesus had taught: see John 14:25ff. See also Gal 5:22; 1 Corinthians 13; John 4:15–17; 15:9–10; 16:8–11.

22. This division of the material, although adopted for the sake of convenience,

is not accidental. To some degree at least it corresponds to the distinction which Furnish, *Theology and Ethics,* p. 279, has rightly emphasized—that between the concrete moral teaching of Paul in ethical warnings, prohibitions, exhortations, etc., and his preaching as a whole, especially his theological presuppositions and convictions—as constituting the essential problem of the Pauline ethic, although this cannot be pressed.

23. See Davies, *Setting,* pp. 341ff.

24. Rom 6:3; 1 Cor 12:13; Gal 3:27. But baptism was not universal, Acts 1:14–15; 19:1–7.

25. 2 Cor 8:9; 12:1; Phil 2:5–8; Rom 8:11; and especially Rom 6:1—7:6. On the history of the emphasis on what is generally referred to as the "indicative-imperative" motif in Paul, see the excellent appendix by Furnish, *Theology and Ethics,* pp. 242ff.: "A Survey of Nineteenth- and Twentieth-Century Interpretations of the Pauline Ethic." Like him, I found the work of Maurice Goguel in *The Primitive Church,* trans. H. C. Snape (New York: Macmillan Co.; London: George Allen & Unwin, 1964), especially original and provocative. In the discussion at Oberlin, Stendahl objected to connecting the motif of "dying and rising with Christ" with morality, on the grounds that while the verbs referring to dying with Christ are in the aorist tense, that of those referring to rising with Christ are in the future. The matter is discussed by Furnish, *Theology and Ethics,* pp. 171ff. The future tenses in Rom 6:5, 8 are important: "We *shall be* united in his resurrection"; "we *shall* also live with him." But, as Furnish also makes clear, the newness of life *is* associated with the resurrection. Rom 6:4 reads: "We were buried therefore with him by baptism unto death, so that as Christ was raised from the dead by the glory of the Father, we too might walk in the newness of life." The power of the future life is already at work in the present. The Christian is to walk in the power of that life here and now. Rom 8:4–5; 2 Cor 10:2–3; 1 Cor 3:3; Rom 13:13; Phil 3:18; etc. See Furnish, *Theology and Ethics,* pp. 214ff.; and especially W. R. Schoedel, "Pauline Thought: Some Basic Issues," in *Transitions in Biblical Scholarship,* ed. J. C. Rylaarsdam (Chicago: University of Chicago Press, 1968), p. 279 n. 34. On the understanding of the "indicative-imperative" relation as not only an individual one, I wholeheartedly agree with Ernest Käsemann, who writes in his essay on "'The Righteousness of God' in Paul," trans. by W. S. Montague and W. F. Bunge in *New Testament Questions of Today* (Philadelphia: Fortress Press, 1969) as follows:

> In many quarters today we hear the relationship between indicative and imperative in Paul described in terms of the formula "Become what you are"; while this is certainly not wrong, it is yet, in view of the origin of the formula in idealism, not without its dangers. Paul was not primarily concerned with the Christian in some purely notional individual capacity, much less with the Christian personality. To say that a man only believes as an individual is simply to say that here, as in the case of ministry in the world, he cannot shrug off responsibility. But I find myself totally unable to assent to the view that Paul's theology and his philosophy of history are orientated towards the individual. To understand the righteousness of God exclusively in terms of gift is to ask for trouble: the inevitable result is that the Pauline anthropology is sucked under by the pull of an individualistic outlook. The sense of the parenetic imperative as the logical implication and the verifi-

cation of the indicative is much better described in terms of the formula "Abide by the Lord who has been given to you and by his lordship," which constitutes the core of the conception of "abiding" in the Johannine farewell discourses. This is the way in which the Christian really does become what he is. For Paul sees our existence as determined at any given time by the Lord whom we are serving. If a transformation of our existence is really effected in baptism and if God's Word does posit a new creation, this cannot help but mean a change of lordship. The new Lord cuts us off from what we were before and never allows us to remain what we are at any given time, for otherwise he might be the First Cause but he would not be our Lord in the true sense. In this particular theological context, man is never seen as free in the sense of autonomous. But he does receive—eschatologically—the possibility of choosing between the kingdom of Christ and the kingdom of Satan, and the ordeal of temptation, like the call sounded in preaching, is forever demanding that the Christian should make this choice anew; thus the Christian life may rightly be seen as a perpetual return to baptism (pp. 175–76).

Compare my introduction to *Rabbinic Judaism,* pp. xiif.

26. This is brought out in C. H. Dodd, *The Fourth Gospel,* p. 418, in his treatment of the Prayer of Christ in John 17:

We have now to enquire in what precise way this prayer is related to the discourses which preceded it. If we look back on these discourses, we see that they turn upon one central theme—what it means to be united in Christ (with Christ crucified and risen). This theme is treated in a kaleidoscopic variety of aspects. Let us briefly recapitulate a few of them. Jesus washes His disciples' feet that they may "have part with Him" (μέρος ἔχεις μετ' ἐμοῦ, 8:8). They are to be bound together with the ἀγάπη which is a reflection, or reproduction, of His ἀγάπη (8:34). Such ἀγάπη is capable of transcending the separation made by death between Christ and His own: His "return" to them is a realization of ἀγάπη (14:19–24). After He has passed through death they will be united with Him as branches of the true Vine (15:1–9), and the fruit which the branches yield is once again ἀγάπη proceeding from the ἀγάπη of God revealed in Christ (15:8–10).

27. It has been pointed out that Paul and Peter and other figures in the early church were regarded as "models" to be imitated; see Julius Wagenmann, *Die Stellung des Apostels Paulus neben den Zwölf* (Giessen, 1926), pp. 52–76. The Paul of the Pastorals—who finished his course—was a "model." John 13 makes clear that specific acts in the life of Jesus were "models"; 13:15 reads "For I have given you an example, that you should do as I have done to you." Moody Smith referred me also to John 14:12 where "imitation" of some kind seems to be involved.

28. Again in the discussion at Oberlin, Stendahl raised the question whether the cross, as such, was made the ground of an appeal for the moral life in the NT. If we exclude all moral considerations from discipleship, such a question might be answered in the negative. If we do not, as is surely more likely, then as Harald Riensenfeld has pointed out, it is significant that discipleship is closely related to the cross not only in the synoptics, but in the Fourth Gospel. (Cf. Matt 16:21–27 and parallels; John 12:31ff.). See his *Gospel Tradition,* trans. E. Margaret Rowley and R. A. Kraft (Philadelphia: Fortress Press, 1970). The obedience

of Christ in death (Rom 5:19; cf. Phil 2:8) is an "act of righteousness" (Rom 5:18) and preeminently an expression of God's love (Gal 2:19ff.; 5:6ff.). Christ crucified becomes "wisdom, righteousness, sanctification, and redemption for us" (1 Cor 1:30–31). God's love revealed in the cross forgives, renews, and sustains (2 Cor 5:14). See further Furnish, *Theology and Ethics*, p. 168. It is difficult to divorce the appeal to the cross from an appeal to the good life. Furnish, rightly in my judgment, thinks that Paul's use of the hymn in Phil 2:5ff. is at least partly used in a hortatory sense; some have denied that the cross has moral implications even in Phil 2:5ff.; see, for the literature, R. P. Martin, *Carmen Christi* (New York and Cambridge: Cambridge University Press, 1967), pp. 68ff., 84ff.

29. On this question, see Johannes Weiss, *Die Nachfolge Christi und die Predigt der Gegenwart* (1895); Edvin Larsson, *Christus als Vorbild* (1962), pp. 29–47; Anselm Schulz, *Nachfolgen und Nachahmen* (Munich, 1962), pp. 270ff.; W. P. deBoer, *The Imitation of Paul: An Exegetical Study* (Kampen, 1962); Eduard Lohse, "Nachfolge Christi," in *RGG*, 3d ed., 4, cols. 1286ff.; D. M. Stanley, "'Become Imitators of Me': The Pauline Conception of Apostolic Tradition," *Biblica* 40 (1959): 859ff.; E. J. Tinsley, *The Imitation of God in Christ* (London: SCM Press, 1960). For further details, see Martin Hengel, *Nachfolge und Charisma: Eine exegetisch-religionsgeschichtliche Studie zu MT 8:21f und Jesu Ruf in die Nachfolge* (Berlin, 1968), p. 1 n. 2. Furnish discusses the matter acutely and with a wealth of bibliographical detail, *Theology and Ethics*, pp. 217ff. He speaks of Christ's obedience as "paradigmatic for the believer's new life in Christ" (p. 218), but rejects any reference in this paradigm to "any particular qualities of the earthly Jesus with the insistence that they be emulated" (p. 223). He endorses Dibelius's view that "when Paul speaks of following Christ, he is not thinking first of all of the historical person Jesus of Nazareth, but of the Son of God who emptied himself and lived and died for others (*RGG*, 2d ed., 4, cols. 395–96)," p. 224 n. It is this so sharp dichotomy which is difficult to accept: it was precisely in Jesus of Nazareth that early Christians saw the Son of God: it was the actuality of his life that lay behind their christological and mythological assertions about him. To separate the historical person, Jesus of Nazareth, so sharply from the Son of God or the Kurios is to make the myth govern the history rather than the history the ground of the myth. On the relation of "Jesus" to the "Lord" in Paul, see Davies, *Setting*, pp. 341ff. Furnish writes: "W. D. Davies goes so far as to contend that the preservation of Jesus' sayings and stories about him was due largely to the importance his followers attached to imitating his example" (p. 219). But is this so very different from what is now a common assumption of most NT scholars that the needs of the church are reflected in the tradition, except that for some form critics the church, to serve those needs, "created" a tradition and a history while I prefer to think of a "history"—fashioned, indeed, by the church—transmitted by the tradition, that is, given in the ministry of Jesus? I agree with what Furnish affirms, but not with what he denies. Perhaps we differ over what we consider to be historically probable. For a discussion of H. D. Betz, *Nachfolge und Nachahmung Christi im Neuen Testament* (1967) see Hengel, pp. 94ff. The pertinent texts on "imitation" are discussed by Furnish, *Theology and Ethics*, pp. 220ff.

30. See E. G. Selwyn, *The First Epistle of St. Peter,* 2d ed. (Toronto: Macmillan Co., 1947), pp. 90ff., on "The Imitation of Christ and the Atonement," especially 1 Pet 2:20b f.: "But if when you do right and suffer for it you take it patiently, you have God's approval. For to this you have been called, because Christ also suffered for you, leaving you an example, that you should follow in his steps. He committed no sin; no guile was found in his lips. When he was reviled, he did not revile in turn, when he suffered he did not threaten. . . ." See also 1 Pet 4:1ff.

31. See especially on all this, Oscar Cullmann, *Christ and Time* (Philadelphia: Westminster Press, 1964; London: SCM Press, 1962); idem, *Salvation in History,* trans. G. S. Sowers et al. (New York: Harper & Row; London: SCM Press, 1967). Furnish, *Theology and Ethics,* p. 235, rightly emphasizes that all Christian "discerning" is informed by *agapē.*

32. Explicitly expressed in 1 Pet 1:1, but implied throughout the NT.

33. See C. H. Dodd, "Communism in the New Testament," *Int* 18 (1921).

34. I find no reason to reject the historicity of the twelve; see C. K. Barrett, *The Signs of an Apostle* (Philadelphia, 1975), pp. 23–24.

35. This is one of the important insights of Albert Schweitzer, *The Mysticism of Paul the Apostle,* trans. W. Montgomery (London, 1931), pp. 105ff. But for the caution necessary in accepting Schweitzer, see *Rabbinic Judaism,* pp. 98ff.

36. Thus knowledge is placed by Paul as the second of the gifts of the Spirit, after wisdom (1 Cor 12:8). In 1 Cor 14:13ff. the importance of "rationality" is clear as in 1 Corinthians 14. The necessity of the renewal of the mind is recognized, Rom 12:2. In the Fourth Gospel emphasis on "the truth" of the witness to Christ is frequent, 10:41; 19:35; 21:24, etc. Rationality is included in this truth although it does not exhaust it. Cf. 1 Pet 3:15; 2 Tim 1:27.

37. Cf. Philemon 15, 16.

38. For Paul the criterion of love among the brethren is normative; Rom 14:21; 1 Corinthians 12—14. See also Eph 4:1–16. H. A. A. Kennedy, *The Theology of the Epistles* (New York: Charles Scribner's Sons, 1920), p. 145.

39. 1 John 4:20; John 17, and passim.

40. I have dealt with this at length in *Setting,* pp. 366–93, where I refer to crisis character of material from Q and the *gemaric* character of much in Matthew.

41. See my *Rabbinic Judaism.* See also now Dale C. Allison, Jr., "The Synoptic Gospels and the Pauline Epistles: The Pattern of the Parallels," in *NTS* (January 1982) 1:1–32.

42. Explicitly in Gal 6:2 and implicitly in Rom 8:2. 1 Cor 9:20–22 reads:

> To the Jews I became as a Jew, in order to win Jews; to those under the law I became as one under the law—though not being myself under the law—that I might win those under the law. To those outside the law, I becames as one outside the law—not being without law toward God but under the law of Christ—that I might win those outside the law. To the weak I became weak, that I might win the weak. I have become all things to all men, that I might by all means save some.

Furnish points out that there is only one certain rabbinic reference to "the Law of the Messiah," that from *Midr. Qoh.* 11:8 (52a). But it is surely implied in other passages. See *Setting,* pp. 172ff. And, in the recently discovered *Targum Yeru-*

šalmi to the Pentateuch of the *Codex Neofiti I* of the Vatican Library, the contents of which have been traced by Diez Macho to the second century A.D. at least, Isa 11:3 reads:

> Behold, the Messiah who is to come
> shall be one who teaches the Law
> and will judge in the fear of the Lord.

On the *Codex Neofiti,* see A. Diez Macho, "The Recently Discovered Palestinian Targum: its Antiquity . . .", *VTSup* 7 (1960). In Diez Macho's view *Codex Neofiti* shows that the Palestinian Targum is of pre-Christian origin. There is no new torah in the DSS; see my *Sermon on the Mount,* p. 63. Contrast Norman Perrin, *The Kingdom of God in the Teaching of Jesus* (Philadelphia: Westminster Press, 1963), pp. 76f.

43. John 14:25–26.

44. On this see C. H. Dodd, *The Johannine Epistles,* MNTC (New York: Harper & Brothers; London: Hodder & Stoughton, 1946), p. xxxviii. The whole problem is dealt with by Furnish, *Theology and Ethics,* pp. 51ff., and by F. W. Beare, "Sayings of the Risen Jesus in the Gospel Tradition: An Inquiry into their Origin and Significance," in *Christian History and Interpretation: Studies Presented to John Knox,* ed. W. R. Farmer, C. F. D. Moule, R. R. Niebuhr (Cambridge: At the University Press, 1967), pp. 161–82; see also his article, "Concerning Jesus of Nazareth," *JBL* 87 (1968): 125ff. Furnish finds only eight convincing parallels to the materials in the synoptic Gospels in the whole of Paul (he regards Colossians, Ephesians, 2 Thessalonians, the Pastorals as deutero-Pauline: he does not consider his omission of these as significant; *Theology and Ethics,* pp. 11–12). The other "allusions" usually cited he does not find persuasive. He dismisses the work of Alfred Resch, *Der Paulinismus und die Logia Jesus in ihrem gegenseitigen Verhaltnis untersucht in Texte und Untersuchungen zur Geschichte der altchristlichen Literatur* (1904), vol. 27, as "imaginary" (p. 59), as he criticizes C. H. Dodd's treatment of the phrase *Ennomos Christou* in *More New Testament Studies* (Grand Rapids: Wm. B. Eerdmans, 1968), pp. 134–48. Furnish's treatment is salutary; but it does not convince me that the words of Jesus were not highly significant for Paul if not "his primary" source for moral teaching. Does Furnish deal justly with the richness of the oral tradition which prevailed in the early Church and which finally coalesced, in part, in the Gospels? Here the method employed by H. Riesenfeld, in his articles, "Parabolic Language in the Pauline Epistles," "Paul's 'Grain of Wheat' Analogy and the Argument of 1 Corinthians 15," and "The Parables in the Synoptic and in the Johannine Traditions," in *The Gospel Tradition* (Philadelphia: Fortress Press, 1970), is more appropriate and sensitive in dealing with tradition. The detection and dismissal of allusions are not as simple as Furnish suggests, particularly in a milieu where the reception and transmission of tradition were so living. The work of A. M. Hunter, *Paul amd His Predecessors,* new rev. ed. (Philadelphia: Westminster Press; London: SCM Press, 1961), and P. Carrington, *The Primitive Christian Catechism* (Cambridge: At the University Press, 1940), Furnish refers to only in bare footnotes. See pp. 38 n., 261 n. A very useful and balanced discussion is that by David L. Dungan, *The Sayings of Jesus in the Churches of Paul* (Philadelphia:

Fortress Press, 1971). As for the imperative participle, the evidence of the Scrolls demands more attention than is given to it, see p. 39 n. 33. The role of Jesus as moral teacher is less difficult to understand in the light of the recent brilliant work of L. Finkelstein, *New Light from the Prophets* (London: Vallentine, Mitchell & Co., 1969). Dr. Finkelstein writes that "to the magnificence of the poetry of the Prophets and the inspiration of their rhetoric, must now be added the greatness of their academic teaching which raised disciples who became teachers of succeeding generations of teachers" (p. 1). They are the precursors of the sages of Israel (ibid.). His work should warn us against thinking that the prophetic, charismatic, eschatological aspects of Jesus' ministry precluded his role as patient teacher. See *Setting*, pp. 415ff. Rudolf Bultmann recognized Jesus as rabbi, in *Jesus and the Word* (New York: Charles Scribner's Sons; London: Ivor Nicholson & Watson, 1934). This is questioned by M. Hengel in his fascinating study, already cited, n. 30, pp. 41ff. But he does recognize a continuity between the teaching of Jesus and that of the early church. He writes:

> Die Diagnose 'Gemeinde-bildung' musste so im Munde des Forschers nicht unbedingt immer nur im Sinne eines grossen Abstandes zum historischen Jesu verstanden werden. Die darin sichtbar werdende, vom prophetischen Geist geleitete, Freiheit der Gemeinde könnte auch ein Ausdruck dafür sein, dass diese sich selbst in ihrer missionarischen Verkündigung ihrem Ausgangspunkt, dem Handeln des historischen Jesus, besonders nahe wusste. Diese Linie liesse sich bis zu Paulus ausziehen. Wenn dieser 1 Cor 3:9 von sich und Apollos sagt: θεοῦ γάρ ἐσμεν συνεργοί oder auch pointerter 2 Cor 5:20: ὑπὲρ Χριστοῦ οὖν πρεσβεύομεν ὡς τοῦ θεοῦ παρακαλοῦντος δἰ ἡμῶν so steht er bewusst oder unbewusst—direkt in der Linie jenes Geschehens, das Jesus durch seinen Ruf in die Nachfolge und seine Jüngeraussendung cingeleitet hatte [p. 93].

See further C. H. Dodd, "Some Johannine 'Herrenworte' with parallels in the Synoptic Gospels," *NTS* 11 (November 1955) 2:75ff., and A. Schlatter, *Die Parallelen in den Worten Jesu by Johannes and Matthaus* (Gütersloh, 1898). See *Sermon*, appendix xiv, pp. 463f. The whole matter is bound up with the question of the relation between Jesus and Paul which is surveyed by Furnish in *BJRL* 47 (March 1965), 2:342ff., in "The Jesus-Paul Debate: From Baur to Bultmann." I remain unconvinced that Paul was not interested in the historical Jesus; it does not seem to me that the interpretation of 2 Cor 5:16 and Gal 1:11f. and the argument from silence appealed to, demand such a conclusion. See now C. F. D. Moule, "Jesus in New Testament Kerygma," in *Verborum Veritas*, ed. O. Böcher and K. Haaker (Wuppertal, 1970), pp. 15–26.

45. On all this see *Setting*, pp. 401ff., where James and the Johannine sources are considered. See the monumental study of C. Spicq, *Agape dans le Nouveau Testament: Analyse des Textes*, 3 vols. (Paris, 1958–1959).

46. See Carrington, *Catechism*, and Selwyn, *1 Peter*.

47. See *Rabbinic Judaism*, pp. 329, 130f.; S. Wibbing, *Die Tugend und Lasterkataloge im Neuen Testament* (Berlin, 1959).

48. See B. S. Easton, *The Pastoral Epistles* (New York: Charles Scribner's Sons; London: SCM Press, 1948), p. 98; Martin Dibelius, *Die Pastoralbriefe* (1931). On conscience in the NT, see my article herein, chapter 13.

49. I have dealt very briefly with this theme in the companion lecture, "The Relevance of the Moral Teaching of the Early Church," herein, chapter 16. Here it can only be touched upon; see the especially rich contribution of N. A. Dahl, "Christ, Creation, and the Church," in *The Background of the New Testament and Its Eschatology: Studies in Honour of C. H. Dodd,* ed. W. D. Davies and D. Daube (Cambridge: At the University Press, 1956), pp. 422ff., and the bibliography on p. 423 n. 1. See also W. R. Schoedel in *Transitions,* pp. 272–75, especially p. 274 n. 22. That the Christian life can be regarded as the truly natural life may not sound as strange as it once did to judge from much in modern biology. These are the words of a recent writer, Robert Ardrey, in *The Territorial Imperative* (New York: Atheneum Press, 1966): "The portrait of life being painted by the new biology bears small resemblance to that natural world of anarchistic instinct and relentless self-interest which depressed a Tennyson, inspired a Freud, perturbed a Darwin, and confused a century. It is a world of order and ordained self-sacrifice to greater and longer goods. . . ." But Ardrey has another emphasis which seems to contradict this. In *African Genesis* (New York: Atheneum Press; Don Mills, Ont.: William Collins Sons, 1961), p. 316, he claims that "man is a predator whose natural instinct is to kill with a weapon." Humankind like the animal has an innate compulsion to gain and defend his property—this is the major motif of his work, *Territorial Imperative.* For this emphasis he has been severely criticized by M. F. Ashley Montagu in "The New Litany of 'Innate Depravity' or Original Sin Revisited" in *Man and Aggression,* ed. M. F. Ashley Montagu (New York: Oxford University Press, 1968), pp. 3–16. Montagu takes an even more sanguine view of humanity than is implied in the first quotation given above from Ardrey: "It is not man's nature, but his nurture, in such a world (overcrowded, highly competitive, threatening) that requires our attention" (p. 16). See also P. H. Klopfer, "The Evolution of Aggression" in *The Biology of Aggression,* eds. P. F. Brain and D. Benton (The Netherlands: Sythoff and Noordhoff International Publishers, 1981), pp. 3–15, and *Territories* (New York, 1969). See further H. Loewe, *A Rabbinic Anthology,* selected by C. J. G. Montefiore and H. M. J. Loewe (New York: Schocken Books, 1974), p. lxix: "What is true in nature is true in religion: what is false in science cannot be true in religion. Truth is one and indivisible. God is bound by His own laws. . . . It is indeed ironical to note that the unity of the nineteenth Psalm has been impugned by some people for the very reason that it asserts, first, God's supremacy alike in the natural and in the religious spheres and secondly, the congruence of those spheres. The sun, in going forth on its daily round, is fulfilling Torah as much as is a human being who worships God, as much as is a Jew when he peforms the commandments, which are 'pure and enlightening to the eyes.' Ps. 19.8." He refers to *Siphre Deut.* on 32:1 §306; see *Rabbinic Anthology,* p. 208. I recognize that there is in the NT something of an antinomy; there is on the one hand the belief that through the fall, creation itself has been affected, and on the other, the belief that in creation is visible "the eternal power of God." Cf. J. Weiss, *The History of Primitive Christianity,* trans. four friends and ed. F. C. Grant (New York: Macmillan Co.; Elmira, N.Y.: Wilson-Erickson, 1937), 2:597. Both views are native to Judaism. Stendahl reminded me that there is a certain "unnaturalness" in the operations of grace in the parables of Jesus, as when the seed in the parable of

the Sower increases a hundredfold. But, in fact, this is not so much "unnatural" as "the natural enhanced, or intensified." I suggest in my companion essay that it is the understanding of creation that provides a bridge between the moral teaching of the church and the world. See herein, chap. 16. The work of Teilhard de Chardin and, before him, C. E. Raven, who have both emphasized the cosmic continuities in Christian theology may be connected with this. The danger in the position of both is a possible neglect of the sense of the transcendent and of the antinomy to which I have referred above. See Christopher F. Mooney, *Teilhard de Chardin and the Mystery of Christ* (New York: Harper & Row; Don Mills, Ont.: William Collins Sons, 1966), p. 207, who notes that while the *concept* of the transcendent is never absent in Chardin's work, the *sense* of it gets lost; and my critique of Raven in *Rabbinic Judaism,* p. 190, and the reply to it in Raven's Gifford Lectures. The rich words of Donald M. Mackinnon, *Borderlands of Theology and Other Essays,* ed. G. W. Roberts and D. E. Smucker (New York: Cambridge University Press, 1968), pp. 44ff., on the significance of Raven and Chardin, deserve serious consideration. On law and nature in Plato and Hellenistic Judaism, see H. A. Wolfson, *Philo: Foundations of Religious Philosophy in Judaism, Christianity, and Islam,* 2 vols. (Cambridge, Mass.: Harvard University Press: London: Oxford University Press, 1947), 2:170f.; for Philo the law of nature and the Mosaic law, being derived from the same source—God—are in harmony. (192). This is why God put the creation of the world as preface to his laws in Genesis. Note that in Philo πρόνοια ("Providence") and νόμος της φύσεως are interchangeable. Philo's sense of the law and order of nature is keen (*Mos.* 2:48). He commands living according to nature: πρὸς τὸ βούλημα τῆς φύσεως (*Op. Mundi.* 3). For the Stoic root of these ideas, see Diogenes Leartius 7:87 in *Stoicorum Veterum Fragmenta,* ed.H. F. A. von Arnim (Leipzig, 1903–24), 1: 262. On eschatology and creation as illuminating the meaning of the law in Matthew, see Bornkamm, "Enderwartung und Kirche im Mattäusevangelium," in *The Background of the New Testament and Its Eschatology*, eds. W. D. Davies and D. Daube (Cambridge: At the University Press, 1956).

THE RELEVANCE OF THE MORAL TEACHING OF THE EARLY CHURCH

1. See *IDB*, E–J: 167–76.
2. John 17:20ff.
3. John 14:17; 15:18; Rom 12:2; 1 Cor 4:9ff; 1 John 2:15ff.; 2 Pet 1:4. But this antagonism did not prevent Christians from participating fully in the world's work. Paul urges the Thessalonian Christians to carry on with their work (2 Thess 3:11ff., etc.). Erastus was the city treasurer (Rom 16:23). Similarly, and very significantly, the emperor can be called God's *diakonos* and the officers of the state are *leitourgoi theou* (Rom 13:4, 6).
4. See *New Theology No. 3,* edited by M. E. Marty and Dean G. Peerman (New York: Macmillan Co., 1966). The secularization is best illustrated in Harvey Cox, *The Secular City,* rev. ed. (New York: Macmillan Co.; London: SCM Press, 1966).

5. See pp. 112–13.

6. P. iii. The quotation is from Walter Hobhouse, *The Church and the World in Idea and History* (London, 1910), pp. ix f.

7. *Christian Society*, pp. 34, 43. Has Eliot merely substituted intellectual pride for the pietistic self-righteousness of so many sects?

8. See G. H. C. Macgregor, "The Concept of the Wrath of God in the New Testament" *NTS* 7 (1961): 103ff.

9. The article has been reprinted in the Biblical Series of Facet Books (Philadelphia: Fortress Press, 1966) as "Kerygma, Eschatology and Social Ethics."

10. See, for example. G. B. Caird, *Principalities and Powers* (Oxford: At the Clarendon Press, 1956); C. D. Morrison, *The Powers That Be* (London: SCM Press, 1960); also D. S. Russell, *The Method and Message of Jewish Apocalyptic* (Philadelphia: Westminster Press, 1964), pp. 244ff.

11. It is Oscar Cullmann who has most made this clear. See his works, *Christ and Time* (Philadelphia: Westminster Press; London: SCM Press, 1951, 1964), and *Salvation as History* (New York: Harper & Row, 1967), the section in the latter on "Salvation History and Ethics," pp. 328ff., is particularly relevant: "The 'conscience' finds its function in the δοκιμάζειν performed in the context of salvation history" (p. 333). But it is important to know that it is *agapē* that governs this 'discerning.'" Here I agree with V. P. Furnish, *Theology and Ethics in Paul* (Nashville: Abingdon Press, 1968), p. 235.

12. It is the great service of Jürgen Moltmann in his excellent and seminal study *Theology of Hope* (New York: Harper & Row, 1967) to have brought this home to us. His words on pp. 334f. deserve quotation:
" 'Creative discipleship' cannot consist in adaptation to, or preservation of, the existing social and judicial orders, still less can it supply religious backgrounds for a given or manufactured situation. It must consist in the theoretical and practical recognition of the structure of historic process and development inherent in the situation required to be ordered, and thus of the potentialities and the future of that situation. Luther, too, could claim this creative freedom for Christian faith: *'Habito enim Christo facile condemus leges, et omnia recte judicabimus, imo novos Decalogos faciemus, sicut Paulus facit per omnes Epistolas, et Petrus maxime Christus in Evangelio.'* ('For when we have Christ we shall easily issue laws, and judge all things aright, and even make new decalogues, as Paul does in all his epistles, and Peter, and above all Christ in the Gospel.') 'Creative discipleship' of this kind in a love which institutes community, sets things right and puts them in order, becomes eschatologically possible through the Christian hope's prospects of the future of God's kingdoms and of man. It alone constitutes here in our openended history the appropriate counterpart to that which is promised and is to come. 'Presentative eschatology' means nothing else but simply 'creative expectation,' hope which sets about criticizing and transforming the present because it is open towards the universal future of the kingdom." It should not be overlooked, however, that in 2 Pet 3:5ff. there is revealed an eschatology which seems to be unrelieved pessimism; the world is to be destroyed not redeemed.

13. See C. H. Dodd, *Gospel and Law* (New York: Columbia University Press; Cambridge: At the University Press, 1951), pp. 22ff. I deeply regret that G. W. H. Lampe's illuminating study, "Secularization in the New Testament and the

Early Church," *Theology*, 71 (April 1968), 574: 163–75, came into my hands too late for use in the above. He rightly emphasizes the continuity between the "New Creation" in Christ and the old creation. But I ascribe more significance than does he to eschatology and its moral connotations.

14. *The Parables of the Kingdom* (Milwaukee and Chicago: Bruce Publishing Co., 1935), pp. 21f.

15. But W. Sanday and A. C. Headlam, *Critical and Exegetical Commentary on the Epistle to the Romans,* ICC (New York: Charles Scribner's Sons, 1923), p. 212, find that in Rom 8:21ff. Paul is Franciscan in his sensitivity to nature. "He is one of those (like St. Francis of Assisi) to whom it is given to read as it were the thoughts of plants and animals." But this is going too far. Can we think of Paul among the Romantics?

16. On conscience see above, chapter 13.

17. See my *Paul and Rabbinic Judaism*, new rev. ed. (Philadelphia: Fortress Press, 1980), pp. 114ff. But see also C. K. Barrett, *The Epistle to the Romans* (New York: Harper & Brothers, 1957), pp. 52, 99, 111; he finds no use of the concept of the Noachian commandments in Paul.

18. See *Rabbinic Judaism, ad rem.*

19. See "Χράομαι" on 1 Cor 7:21 in *A Greek-English Lexicon of the New Testament,* ed. W. Bauer, W. F. Arndt, F. W. Gingrich, new rev. ed. (Chicago: University of Chicago Press, 1979).

20. On this see Barrett, *Romans,* pp. 244ff.

21. It will be clear that I cannot follow the thesis of S. G. F. Brandon, *Jesus and the Zealots: A Study of the Political Factor in Primitive Christianity* (New York: Charles Scribner's Sons, 1968; Manchester: Manchester University Press, 1967), who finds Jewish Christianity "politically" oriented. I cannot give the reasons for my rejection of his brilliant but—in my judgment—misleading study here. For criticism see the review by Martin Hengel, *JSS* 14 (1969): 231–40.

22. See Paul Ramsey, "Faith Effective through In-principled Love," *Christianity and Crisis* (New York) 30 May, 1960.

23. It should be borne in mind that the prescriptions of the NT are not presented neatly. They are "Christified" by the addition of the phrase "in Christ." See *Rabbinic Judaism,* p. 136, where I refer to A. M. Hunter, *Paul and His Predecessors* (London: SCM Press, 1940), p. 64, and to M. Dibelius, *From Tradition to Gospel* (New York: Charles Scribner's Sons, 1935; London: Ivor Nicholson & Watson, 1934), p. 241. Paul Lehmann in his various works has been critical of any prescriptive element in Christian Ethics. For him ethics is an art. In this connection I am reminded of words in E. H. Gombrich, *The Story of Art* (London: Phaidon Press, 1952). He writes: "What an artist worries about as he plans his picture, makes his sketches, or wonders whether he has completed his canvas, is something much more difficult to put into words. Perhaps he would say he worries about whether he has got it 'right.' Now it is only when we understand what he means by that modest word 'right' that we begin to understand what artists are really after. . . . Anybody who has ever tried to arrange a bunch of flowers, to shuffle and shift the colours, to add a little here and take away there, has experienced the strange sensation of balancing forms and colours without being able to tell exactly what kind of harmony it is he is trying to achieve. . .

and suddenly [it] may seem to come 'right' . . . '' (p. 14). Doubtless the center of gravity of the moral teaching of the Early Church is grace and *agapē*. But the writers of the NT clearly thought that the 'art' of Christian living would not be quite right without a prescriptive element. The element, indeed, might be secondary, but to ignore it would have been to throw the picture of the moral life out of focus.'' (For Lehmann's work, see n. 40 below.)

24. See *Setting*, pp. 387ff.

25. Here I find myself in agreement with C. F. D. Moule in *The Birth of the New Testament* (New York: Harper & Row, 1962), p. 212, a page enlarged upon in his article ''Important Moral Issues: Prolegomena: The New Testament and Moral Decisions,'' *ET* 74 (1963): 370–73. I should, however, insist that, although, to quote Moule, ''The genius of the New Testament is not legislation [p. 371],'' nevertheless the Holy Spirit is informed by the moral, prescriptive teaching ascribed by the Gospels to Jesus, and that any ''ethical translation of the Gospel'' must likewise be informed. The Spirit is not autonomous but governed by the revelation in Christ. See *Rabbinic Judaism*, p. 196. For a criticism of my emphasis see Furnish, *Theology and Ethics,* pp. 51–65.

26. See R. Niebuhr, *An Interpretation of Christian Ethics* (New York: Harper & Brothers, 1935; London: SCM Press; Toronto: Musson Book Co., 1936) and John Knox, *The Ethic of Jesus in the Teaching of the Church* (Nashville: Abingdon Press, 1961; London: Epworth Press, 1962).

27. For the evidence, see *Setting*, pp. 401ff. The pertinent references are Matt 7:12; Mark 12:28; John 15:9–13; 1 John 3:16f.; Rom 13:9; Gal 5:14; Col 3:14; Jas 1:25; 2:8; 1 John 4:7–12; 4:21.

28. The effort to understand the ''crucifix'' form of all Christian living has been best exemplified by Joseph Sittler, *The Structure of Christian Ethics* (Baton Rouge: Louisiana State University Press, 1958). Christian ethics is for him ''a reenactment from below on the part of man of the shape of the revelatory drama of God's holy will in Jesus Christ. . . . Suffering, death, burial, resurrection, a new life—these are actualities that plot out the arc of God's self-giving deed in Christ's descent and death and ascension; and precisely *this shape of grace* in its recapitulation within the life of the believer and the faithful community, is the nuclear matrix which grounds and unfolds as the Christian life'' (p. 36). It is possible to urge that seldom, if ever, in the NT is the cross directly referred to as a ground for moral action. Even in Phil 2:5ff. it has been denied that the cross has ethical implications; see the discussion in R. P. Martin, *Carmen Christi,* (New York and Cambridge: Cambridge University Press, 1967), pp. 68ff., 84ff. But it is difficult not to see in the cross—the supreme act of obedience—an event which did have such implications.

29. 1 Pet 2:13ff.; cf. 1 Tim 2:1ff.

30. I have here followed O. Cullmann, *The State in the New Testament* (New York: Charles Scribner's Sons; Don Mills, Ont.: S. J. R. Saunders, 1965). He writes: ''Jesus' attitude is to be sought beyond any uncritical absolutizing of the Roman State, and at the same time beyond any thoroughgoing political resistance to it'' (p. 23). This might well be applied to the Early Church also.

31. It will again be clear that I cannot accept S. G. F. Brandon's reconstruction of early church history in his books *The Fall of Jerusalem* (New York: Macmillan

Co.; London, SPCK, 1951) and *Jesus and the Zealots*. For a critique of the former work—in part—see *Setting* pp. 317ff. Note also my work on *The Gospel and the Land: Early Christianity and Jewish Territorial Doctrine* (Berkeley and Los Angeles: University of California Press, 1974), pp. 336–44.

32. See Gal 3:28.

33. See my article on "The Jewish State in the Hellenistic World" in *PCB*, ed. M. Black and H. H. Rowley (1962), pp. 686ff.

34. "Ephesians," *The Abingdon Bible Commentary* (1929), pp. 1222f. See also Stig Hanson, *The Unity of the Church in the New Testament* (Uppsala, 1946).

35. The absolute principle not to divorce is enumerated by Jesus, but Paul found it necessary, in dealing with a specific problem of married life, to give his own judgment. He accepted the absolute principle; but nevertheless, engaged in his own casuistry. See on this C. H. Dodd, "'ΕΝΝΟΜΣ ΧΡΙΣΤΟΥ" *Studie Paulina, in hon. J. de Zwaan*, ed. J. N. Sevenster and W. C. van Unnik, (Haarlem, 1953), pp. 96ff., and contrast C. F. D. Moule, "Important Moral Issues," *ET* 74 (1963): 371.

36. I know of no more penetrating insistence on the "concreteness, almost crudity, in stating the moral requirements of religion [which] belongs to the genius of NT Christianity in general" than that presented by C. H. Dodd in his comment on 1 John 3:16–18. See *The Johannine Epistles*, MNTC (1946), p. 86.

37. J. C. Bennett, *Christian Ethics and Social Policy* (New York: Charles Scribner's Sons, 1946); "Principles and the Context," *Storm over Ethics* (Toronto: Ryerson Press, 1967).

38. The most convenient survey of this was pointed out to me by my colleague, Professor Waldo Beach. It is by James M. Gustafson, entitled "Christian Ethics" in *Religion*, ed. Paul Ramsey (Englewood Cliffs, N.J.: Prentice-Hall, 1965), pp. 287ff. The whole field is covered in its historical perspective in *A Survey of Christian Ethics* by E. LeRoy Long (New York: Oxford University Press, 1967).

39. Represented most forcefully and convincingly by Paul Ramsey in various publications, for example, "In-principled Love"; *Deeds and Rules in Christian Ethics*, enlarged edition (New York: Harper & Row, 1967; Edinburgh: Oliver & Boyd, 1965); *War and the Christian Conscience* (Durham, N.C.: Duke University Press, 1961); Ramsey's position has changed since the publication of his first book, *Basic Christian Ethics* (New York: Charles Scribner's Sons; 1950).

40. Best represented by Paul Lehmann, "The Foundation and Pattern of Christian Behaviour," *Christian Faith and Social Action*, ed. John A. Hutchinson (New York: Charles Scribner's Sons, 1953), pp. 93–116; *Ethics in a Christian Context* (New York: Harper & Row, 1963). R. Bultmann is usually included among contextualists. For a critique of his ethical interpretation, see C. W. Kegley, ed., *The Theology of Rudolf Bultmann* (New York: Harper & Row; London: SCM Press, 1966) *ad rem*.

41. See his excellent study, "Context versus Principles: A Misplaced Debate in Christian Ethics," *New Theology No. 3*, ed. Marty and Pearman, pp. 69ff. There is a plentiful bibliographical guide in the footnotes on pp. 99ff. In his recent book, already referred to in n. 11 above, Furnish writes as follows: "a survey of the various attempts to interpret Paul's ethic exposes as the central and decisive problem *the relation of concrete ethical materials to the apostle's preaching as*

a whole, especially to his basic theological presuppositions and convictions" (p. 279, his italics). I should understand that relationship more in terms of the "new covenant" than does Furnish as is apparent from chapter 15 and from *Rabbinic Judaism*, but his recognition of the "heart of the matter" is refreshing.

42. Compare E. LeRoy Long in *Int* 19 (1965): 149ff., in an article on "The Use of the Bible in Christian Ethics."

Indexes

OLD TESTAMENT

NEW TESTAMENT

APOCRYPHA AND PSEUDEPIGRAPHA

TARGUMIM

RABBINICAL LITERATURE

CLASSICAL AND HELLENISTIC AUTHORS
AND EXTRA-CANONICAL CHRISTIAN WRITINGS

NAMES

SUBJECTS

God, doctrine of, in early
  Christianity, 342, 345–47,
  377

Hebrews, epistle of, 239–40,
  255–56
Hellenism and early
  Christianity, 47, 115–16,
  132, 360–61, 382
Hellenism and Judaism, 13,
  15–16, 25, 34–43, 268, 270–
  72, 312–14, 373; and Paul,
  153–63, 170–88
Holy Spirit. *See* Spirit
hope, Christian, 283, 400; in
  Paul, 218–19

idolatry, in Paul, 204, 250–51
image of God, 191–92, 203
imitation of Christ, 110–11,
  213, 282–84, 337, 394
"in Christ," 205–12
incarnation, 259–60
indicative and imperative, in
  Paul, 110, 282, 335, 392–93
inspiration of Scripture, 3–4;
  degrees of, 6–7
Israel, the people of, in 1
  Thessalonians, 124–27; in
  Galatians, 127–29; in Paul,
  123–52, 153–62, 343; in
  Romans, 130–52; in 2
  Corinthians, 129–30

James, epistle of, 240–41
Jamnia, 4, 15, 33, 65, 98–99,
  137, 304, 333, 348–49
Jesus, in early Christianity,
  272–75, 317–18, 334–35;
  character of, 108–12, 274–
  75, 281–83; and the Law,
  227–32, 279–81; in Paul,
  108–15, 123–24, 205–6,
  281–88; and Sabbatai Svi,
  257–77; as teacher, 397
Jewish Christianity, 164–71,
  181–82, 234, 401
John, Gospel of, 37, 241–42,
  282
Judaizers, in Paul, 128, 181–
  84, 360
justification by faith, 94, 128–
  29, 185–87, 214–16, 233

Land, The, in Judaism, 49–
  71, 72–83
Law, in Judaism, 28–34, 304–
  7; as agent of creation, 23–
  25; as demand of covenant,
  17–23; in first-century
  Judaism, 3–26; in the
  future, 25–26, 87–88, 101–
  2, 338; meditation of, 84–
  88; in the Old Testament,
  34, 332; and Sabbatai Svi,
  262–63, 376. *See also* oral
  law; written law
Law in the New Testament,
  and early Christianity, 227–
  42, 354–56; in Hebrews,
  239–40; in James, 240–41;
  in John, 241–42; in Paul,
  234–39, *and see* next entry;

in pre-Pauline Christianity,
  232–34; in the synoptics,
  227–32
Law in Paul, 91–122, 216–18,
  234–39, 354–56; Christ as
  end of, 237–39; as
  commandment, 93–100;
  development of, 103–8; and
  grace, 117–18; and
  messianism, 100–103, 123–
  24; as moral demand, 108–
  16; and secular law, 116–17
liberation, in Paul, 199–224
Lord, Jesus as, in Paul, 206
love. *See* agapē

magic in Judaism and
  Christianity, 261–62, 376
Mekilta, 72–83
merit in Judaism, 21–22
Messiah, Jesus as, in Paul,
  100–101, 123–24, 178
messianism, 56–58, 257–77,
  323, 374, 378, 380; in Paul,
  100–103, 123–24, 178
midrash, 10–14
Mishnah, the, 3, 10–15, 27,
  92; and The Land, 51
moral teaching of the early
  church, 278–88; relevance
  of, 289–320. *See also*
  ethics, Christian
mysticism, Jewish, 259–60,
  374

nationalism, in Paul, 143–52
nature in the New Testament,
  288, 293–95
Noachian commandments, 7–
  8, 186, 233–34, 295

olive, 144–45, 153–63, 357–58
oral law, authority of, 10–14;
  codification of, 14–15;
  exegesis of, 15–17; rise of,
  8–10; in synoptics, 227–32
overconversion, 137

pastoral epistles, 254–56
parenesis in Galatians, 180
Paul, 35. *See also* alienation;
  anthropology; apocalyptic;
  commandment(s);
  conscience; cross, the;
  death; development;
  discipline; ethics; faith;
  flesh; freedom; Gentiles;
  Hellenism and Judaism;
  hope; idolatry; indicative
  and imperative; Israel;
  Jesus; Judaizers;
  justification by faith; Law;
  liberation; Lord; Messiah;
  messianism; nationalism;
  peace; philosophy of
  history; sin; tradition;
  wrath of God
peace, in Paul, 211–12
Pharisees and Pharisaism, 3,
  5, 9, 15–17, 19, 23, 27–28,
  31, 34, 46, 51, 63, 97–98,
  135–37, 229–32, 312, 323,
  373

philosophical schools, 35–36
philosophy of history, in
  Paul, 132–33, 157–58, 201–
  3, 237
pilgrimages to Israel, 56–58,
  320
Platonism, 189–90
priest(s) and priesthood,
  Jewish, 29, 34
principalities and powers,
  192–94, 237, 291–93, 363–
  64
prophet(s) and prophecy, 28–
  34, 52, 304, 311, 391–92;
  and The Land, 74–83; and
  Law in the Old Testament,
  389–90; in the New
  Testament, 47
proselytism in Judaism, 272,
  382

Qabbalah, 265–67, 269, 271,
  276, 378–79, 383–84
Qumran, 97, 101, 129, 135,
  166–69, 274–75, 305–6
repentance, 23
resurrection, 52; of Jesus as
  forgiveness, 108–10, 280–
  81; and morality, 335, 390,
  392
revelation, process of, 304–5
Roman Christians and epistle
  to the Romans, 105–8, 130–
  52, 153–63, 345–47
rules of exegesis, Jewish, 15–
  17

Sabbatai Svi and
  Sabbatianism, 56–57, 64,
  97–98, 124, 136, 257–77,
  373–79, 382–84
Sadducees, 5, 9, 15–17
salvation in Judaism, 17–23
Sanhedrin, 9, 46
scribes, 9, 14
sect, early Christianity as,
  135, 377
sin, in Paul, 106–7, 194–99,
  236; and the rabbis, 23
Spirit, Holy, 4–5, 31, 52, 72–
  83, 102, 109–10, 217, 280–
  81, 328, 335; in Galatians,
  179–80
Stoicism, 40–42, 190, 244–46
symbolism in apocalyptic,
  264, 276–77; in the
  Qabbalah, 378–79
synagogue(s), 159, 177, 311,
  313

Talmud, 56–57
Targum(s), 6, 338, 395–96
tradition, in Judaism, 7–17,
  27–48; in early Christianity,
  47–48, 317–18, 336–37,
  396–97; in Paul, 113–15

wrath of God, in Paul, 198
written law, 3–8

Zealots, 183–84
Zionist movement, 61–66, 68,
  319